OIL AND GAS LAW
CURRENT PRACTICE AND EMERGING TRENDS

OIL AND GAS LAW
CURRENT PRACTICE AND EMERGING TRENDS

2nd edition

Editors

Greg Gordon, LL.B., Dip. L.P., LL.M.,
Senior Lecturer in Law, University of Aberdeen

John Paterson, LL.B., Dip. L.P., LL.M., Ph.D.
Professor of Law, University of Aberdeen

Emre Üşenmez, B.Sc., B.A., LL.M.
Lecturer in Law, University of Aberdeen

DUNDEE UNIVERSITY PRESS
2011

First edition published in Great Britain in 2007 by
Dundee University Press
University of Dundee
Dundee DD1 4HN

www.dundee.ac.uk/dup

Second edition published 2011

Reprinted 2012, 2013, 2014(Twice)

ISBN 978-1-84586-101-8

No natural forests were destroyed to make this product; only farmed timber was used and replanted.

British Library Cataloguing-in-Publication Data
A catalogue for this book is available on request from the British Library.

Typeset by Fakenham Prepress Solutions, Fakenham, Norfolk NR21 8NN
Printed and bound by Bell & Bain Ltd, Glasgow

CONTENTS

FOREWORD TO THE FIRST EDITION

I write this Foreword at a time when crude oil prices have jumped to a record high of over US $80 a barrel (West Texas Intermediate). At the same time, there is a world credit crunch, and it remains to be seen what impact this will have upon the oil and gas sector.

At a recent major conference of the Association for the Study of Peak Oil, Lord Oxburgh (the former chairman of Shell) gave a stark warning that the price of oil could hit US $150 per barrel and that oil production could peak within the next 20 years. The rapid increase in the price of oil seems inevitable as demand continues to outstrip supply. However, it is also going to become very expensive indeed to extract oil from the ground. We already see that in our maturing province in the UKCS, with a considerable increase in costs for operating and developing oil and gas fields. This is an industry in a state of flux, and there is a great responsibility on industry lawyers and commercial negotiators to come up with innovative business models and flexible, streamlined legal agreements and processes to facilitate the maximum recovery of remaining reserves in the UKCS. This we must do by working closely with our technical colleagues who are charged with developing increasingly innovative and cost-effective technical solutions to reserves recovery. It is also the responsibility of lawyers, along with our commercial, tax and finance colleagues, to be effective advocates for appropriate changes to UK oil and gas legislation to ensure a successful future for the UKCS. To meet this responsibility, the industry needs dynamic and competent advice at a time when we are experiencing an extreme shortage of experienced oil and gas lawyers. It is all the more important, then, that lawyers coming into our industry have access to reliable and up-to-date reference books on oil and gas law. If we are to meet the challenges ahead, we must pass on the knowledge we already have to a new generation of lawyers; this book helps enormously in that task.

Often our oil and gas industry leaders decry lawyers as those who simply "paper" the deals and arrangements put in place by technical and commercial people. This book goes a long way towards dispelling that myth. It shows the complexity and sophistication of oil and gas law, and its breadth. UK oil and gas law is formed by a layering of statute, commercial agreements, EU and UK competition and procurement law, industry voluntary codes (such as CCOP and ICOP) and DBERR Guidance. Oil and gas law is a very important field of law and yet there are very few reference sources. This volume is long overdue and very welcome. It describes, in depth, most of the recent developments in this very broad and diverse field. Most importantly, it captures with great clarity the many joint industry and government initiatives since 2000 which impact the legal and commercial arrangements in our sector, for instance those on fallow acreage, stewardship, CCOP and ICOP. It is also the first time the legal basis for these initiatives has been analysed in detail.

There is an enormous challenge ahead. In a time of high oil prices, owners of infrastructure inevitably wish to protect their own production and fair allocation of risk remains difficult to achieve. The "mutual hold harmless" principle is being pushed to its limits, with creeping practices of uncapped liability and indemnity clauses on third-party infrastructure users.

As an industry lawyer for the past 15 years, I have been passionate about improving the way the industry conducts its business to take duplication and waste out of legal processes. This began in 1995 when I worked on the setting up of First Point Assessment Ltd ("FPAL") and the development of the Memorandum and Articles for the new entity. It is with pride that I note that FPAL celebrated its 10th anniversary at Offshore Europe this month.

It has been an enormous privilege for me to have played a part in many of the industry legal working groups which have brought about streamlined agreements (IMHH, Standard Contracts, ICOP, DSA, SPA and Master Deed). We can be proud of what has been achieved and the contribution made by industry and private practice lawyers alike to such progress. This book is an excellent consolidated source on all of these important initiatives and is testimony to the considerable progress made. May it foster even greater academic enquiry and innovation among oil and gas lawyers.

In summary, never has oil and gas law been more complex, never have the expectations of government and industry leaders on lawyers and commercial advisers been higher – and all this at a time of uncertainty as to how the oil and gas market will play out. The industry requires highly competent future lawyers, great clarity of legal thinking and drafting and – above all else – swift close-out of transactions. This excellent book stands us in good stead for meeting the exciting challenges ahead.

Jacquelynn F Craw
Legal Manager, Director and Company Secretary
Talisman Energy (UK) Ltd
September 2007

PREFACE TO THE FIRST EDITION

This book arose as a result of several inter-related stimuli. In developing the LL.M. in Oil and Gas Law, upon which course the editors and several of the book's contributors teach, it became increasingly apparent that while there has been a constant throughput of primary materials in the form of statutes, statutory instruments, guidance and codes, surprisingly little in the way of secondary comment has been published in the area of UK oil and gas law over the years. Moreover, although much of the work published is of a very high standard, there are some noticeable gaps in coverage – and some of the works which are available, and which continue to be of great value, are beginning now to show their age as the UKCS develops and new issues become increasingly relevant.[1] In addition, many of the materials which are available assume a considerable degree of industry knowledge and experience. It can be difficult for a student, or indeed a qualified lawyer making his or her way into the industry, to find a book which will provide a clear but concise account. Finally, many of the books which are available are so highly priced that they are prohibitively expensive to students, and indeed many libraries. The decision to write this book was taken by the editors over coffee while discussing these matters. Much coffee has been drunk by the editors since.

The editors have many people to thank. Our most obvious debt is to the contributors. The book could not have been produced within a reasonable timescale if the editors had had to write it all themselves, and some of the chapters here could not have been written at all. In addition to writing chapters within the book, Margaret Ross, Roderick Paisley, Norman Wisely, Judith Aldersey-Williams and Uisdean Vass read and offered useful comments upon other chapters. Valuable comments have also been received from Lorna Hingston of CMS Cameron McKenna, Bob Ruddiman of McGrigors and Angus Campbell of the University of Aberdeen. The editors are very grateful to all of them for taking the time and trouble to assist. The editors are also very grateful to Carole Dalgleish for commissioning

---

[1] This observation does not apply to Daintith, Willoughby and Hill's excellent and regularly updated *UK Oil and Gas Law*.

the work, and to her and all involved at Dundee University Press for their unfailing commitment and encouragement.

This book is not intended to supplant existing materials, but to supplement them, and hopefully to bring them to the attention of a wider readership. Nor is it intended to be a comprehensive exposition of all legal issues facing the oil and gas industry in the UKCS. There is more that could usefully be said in relation to many of the areas which have been covered, and many other topics could have been selected were it not for the constraints of space and time.[2] Finally, it is hoped that this book will go some way towards stimulating more writing about, and more debate in, what is a fascinating and important area of (or perhaps more properly, *context for*) the law. Towards that end, the editors invoke the spirit of Sir John Skene's dedication to the reader:

> "Quhatever I have done, I did it nocht to offend thee or to displease anie man, bot to provoke uthers to doe better."[3]

Greg Gordon
John Paterson
August 2007

---

[2] Environmental law, for instance, is dealt with at several points, but considerations of environmental law as relative to the oil and gas industry could very easily form the subject of a large book on their own.

[3] Sir John Skene, *De Verborum Significatione* (1597).

PREFACE TO THE SECOND EDITION

It is very gratifying to see the book go into a second edition. The editors' aim in producing the first edition of this work was to provide a clear, reasonably concise and affordable account of contemporary oil and gas practice in the UKCS. That aim is unchanged. The book attempts to describe the law as it stood in January 2011, but it has been possible to incorporate at proof stage passing reference to some later developments.

As before, the editors have many people to thank. First, the new contributors (Martin Ewan, Luke Havemann and Emre Üşenmez) who have allowed us to expand the scope of the book by authoring chapters on technology in the oilfield, environmental regulation, energy security and taxation. The inclusion of these topics is of great benefit to the book. Second, we must thank all of the original contributors who kindly agreed to update their chapters. Law and practice have certainly not stood still in the 4 years since the first edition of this book was published and in many cases this has involved a significant amount of work. Thanks are also due to David Roper for his preparatory work in the chapter on technology in the oilfield. The editors are also grateful to Christine Gane for allowing us to use her index for the first edition as the basis for the second and to Karen Howatson at Dundee University Press for updating the index. We would also like to thank Carole Dalgleish and all involved at Dundee University Press for their ongoing commitment and support.

Finally, the original editors are delighted to welcome Emre Üşenmez to both the editorial team of this work and the lecturing staff at the University of Aberdeen. Emre has undertaken a significant amount of the editing work for the new edition as well as contributing two new chapters to the book. He also makes a mean cup of coffee. This is not something we say lightly; readers of the preface to the first edition will know the importance which that beverage has played since the very inception of this book. But we should also emphasise that Emre was recruited on the basis of his legal and analytical skills alone.

Greg Gordon
John Paterson
Emre Üşenmez
April 2011

LIST OF CONTRIBUTORS

Judith Aldersey-Williams, B.A., LL.M., Solicitor
Partner, CMS Cameron McKenna LLP

Martin Ewan, LL.B., Dip.L.P., LL.M., M.A., B.Sc., M.Sc., Solicitor
Partner, McGrigors LLP

Greg Gordon, LL.B., Dip.L.P., LL.M.
Senior Lecturer in Law, University of Aberdeen

Luke Havemann, B.A., LL.B., Ph.D., Attorney-at-Law
Director, Havemann Inc, Specialist Energy Attorneys

Professor Alexander Kemp, O.B.E., F.R.S.E.
Schlumberger Professor of Petroleum Economics, Business School,
University of Aberdeen

Nicola Macleod, LL.B., Dip.L.P., LL.M., Solicitor
Director: Legal, Maersk Oil North Sea UK Ltd

Professor Roderick Paisley, LL.B., Dip.L.P., Ph.D., Solicitor
Professor of Commercial Property Law, University of Aberdeen

John Paterson, LL.B., Dip.L.P., LL.M., Ph.D.
Professor of Law, University of Aberdeen

Professor Margaret Ross, LL.B., Solicitor
Professor of Law, University of Aberdeen

Scott Styles, M.A., LL.B., Dip.L.P.
Senior Lecturer in Law, University of Aberdeen

Uisdean Vass, LL.B., LL.M., Solicitor
Partner, Head of Oil and Gas Unit, Maclay, Murray and Spens LLP

Emre Üşenmez, B.Sc., B.A., LL.M.
Lecturer in Law, University of Aberdeen

Norman Wisely, LL.B., Dip.L.P., Solicitor
Partner, CMS Cameron McKenna LLP

LIST OF ABBREVIATIONS AND ACRONYMS

AA	appropriate assessment
AAA/ICDR	American Arbitration Association/ International Court of Dispute Resolution
AAPL	American Association of Professional Landmen
ADR	alternative dispute resolution
AFE	authorisation for expenditure
AIPN	Association of International Petroleum Negotiators
ALARP	as low as reasonably practicable
AMI	Area of Mutual Interest Agreement
API	American Petroleum Institute
ARN	automatic referral notice
ASCOBANS	Agreement on Small Cetaceans of the Baltic and North Seas
BAT	Best Available Technique
BATNA	best alternative to a negotiated agreement
BEP	Best Environmental Practice
BNOC	British National Oil Corporation
boe	barrels of oil equivalent
BPEO	best practicable environmental option
CAEM	Center for the Advancement of Energy Markets
CAR	Construction All Risk
CCS	carbon capture and storage
CCW	Countryside Council for Wales
CEDR	Centre for Effective Dispute Resolution
CEFAS	Centre for Environment, Fisheries and Aquaculture Science
CERM	Co-ordinated Emergency Response Measures
CGT	Capital Gains Tax
CIMAH	Control of Industrial Major Accident Hazard Regulations (1984)
CMR	Convention on the Contract for the International Carriage of Goods by Road
COMAH	Control of Major Accident Hazard Regulations (1999)

CPA 1949	Coast Protection Act 1949
CPC	central product classification
CPR	Civil Procedure Rules (1998)
CRINE	Cost Reduction Initiative for the New Era
CSIS	Center for Strategic & International Studies
CT	Corporation Tax
CTA 2010	Corporation Tax Act 2010
DBERR	Department for Business, Enterprise and Regulatory Reform
DEAL	Digital Energy Atlas and Library
DECC	Department of Energy and Climate Change
DEFRA	Department of Environment, Food and Rural Affairs
DEn	Department of Energy
DNV	Det Norske Veritas
DOPWTS	Dispersed Oil in Produced Water Trading Scheme
DSA	decommissioning security agreement
DTI	Department of Trade and Industry
EA	environmental assessment
EAT	Employment Appeal Tribunal
EC	European Community
ECJ	European Court of Justice
ECT	Energy Charter Treaty
EEA	European Economic Area
EIA	environmental impact assessment
EMT	Environmental Management Team
EMV	expected monetary value
EPC Regulations	Offshore Installations (Emergency Pollution Control) Regulations 2002
ERA	Employment Rights Act 1996
ES	environmental statement
EU	European Union
FEPA 1985	Food and Environment Protection Act 1985
FPAL	First Point Assessment Ltd
FPSO	floating production, storage and offloading
FRS	Fisheries Research Services
FSA	Formal Safety Assessment
FY	financial year
GAAP	generally accepted accounting practice
GATT	General Agreement on Tariffs and Trade

GDP	gross domestic product
GFU	Norwegian Gas Negotiation Committee
GLA	General Lighthouse Authority
H₂S	hydrogen sulphide
HMRC	Her Majesty's Revenue and Customs
HP/HT	high pressure/high temperature
HSC	Health and Safety Commission
HSE	Health and Safety Executive
HSWA 1974	Health and Safety at Work, etc Act 1974
IAPP Certificate	International Air Pollution Prevention Certificate
IATA	International Air Transport Association
ICC	International Chamber of Commerce
ICOP	Infrastructure Code of Practice
ICSID	International Centre for Settlement of Investment Disputes
IEA	International Energy Agency
IEP Agreement	Agreement on an International Energy Program
IGIP	initial gas in place
IMCA	International Maritime Contractors Association
IMHH	Industry Mutual Hold Harmless Deed (strictly, the Mutual Indemnity and Hold Harmless Deed)
IMO	International Maritime Organization
IP	intellectual property
IRR	internal rate of return
IT	Income Tax
ITF	Industry Technology Facilitator
IUK	Interconnector UK Ltd
JBA	joint bidding agreement
JNCC	Joint Nature Conservancy Council
JOA	joint operating agreement
JOAUOA	joint operating and unit operating agreement
JOC	Joint Operating Committee
JV	joint venture
KP3	Key Programme 3
LCIA	London Court of International Arbitration
LCP	large combustion plant
LCPD	Large Combustion Plants Directive

LNG	liquefied natural gas
LOC	letter of credit
LOGIC	Leading Oil and Gas Industry Competitiveness
MC	Model Clause
MCA	Maritime and Coastguard Agency
Merchant Shipping (OPRC) Regulations	Merchant Shipping (Oil Pollution Preparedness, Response and Co-operation Convention) Regulations 1998
mmb/d	million barrels of oil per day
MOOIP	moveable oil originally in place
NARUC	National Association of Regulatory Utility Commissioners
NEC Regulations	National Emission Ceilings Regulations 2002
NERC	Natural Environment Research Council
NH_3	ammonia
NO_x	nitrogen oxide
NPV	net present value
NPV/I	net present value to investment ratio
NSRI	National Subsea Research Institute
NTS	National Transmission System or non-technical summary (in ES)
OC Regulations	Offshore Chemical Regulations 2002
OCA	Offshore Contractors Association
OECD	Organization for Economic Co-operation and Development
OED	Offshore Environment and Decommissioning Unit
OFT	Office of Fair Trading
OGIA	Oil and Gas Independents' Association
OGITF	Oil and Gas Industry Task Force
ONS	Office for National Statistics
OPA Regulations	Offshore Petroleum Activities (Oil Pollution Prevention and Control) Regulations 2005
Opcom	Joint Operating Committee
OPEC	Organization of the Petroleum Exporting Countries
OPOL	Offshore Pollution Liability Agreement
OSPAR	Convention for the Protection of the Marine Environment of the North-East Atlantic 1992
OSPRAG	Offshore Spill Prevention and Response Advisory Group

OTA 1975	Oil Taxation Act 1975
OTA 1983	Oil Taxation Act 1983
PAPS Regulations	Merchant Shipping (Prevention of Air Pollution from Ships) Regulations 2008
PCG	parent company guarantee
PED	Petroleum Engineering Division (of the Department of Energy)
PEDL	petroleum exploration and development licence
PILOT	successor to the Oil and Gas Industry Task Force
PON	Petroleum Operation Notice
PPSGS Regulations	Merchant Shipping (Prevention of Pollution by Sewage and Garbage from Ships) Regulations 2008
PPWG	Progressing Partnership Work Group
PRT	Petroleum Revenue Tax
PSPA	Petroleum and Submarine Pipelines Act 1975
PTW	permit to work
QCI	qualifying combustion installation
QRA	Quantified Risk Assessment
RFCT	Ring Fence Corporation Tax
ROV	remotely operated vehicle
RPGA	Rules and Procedures Governing Access to Offshore Infrastructure
SAC	Special Area of Conservation
SC	Supplementary Charge
SEA	strategic environmental assessment
SEAM	Senior Executive Appraisal Mediation
SECA	SO_x emission control area
SEPA	Scottish Environment Protection Agency
SGERAD	Scottish Government Environment and Rural Affairs Department
SMS	Safety Management System
SNH	Scottish Natural Heritage
SO_2	sulphur dioxide
SOAEFD	Scottish Office Agriculture, Environment and Fisheries Department
SPA	Special Protection Area
STOOIP	stock tank oil originally in place

t	tonnes (metric)
TDM	Transnational Dispute Management
TFEU	Treaty on the Functioning of the European Union
toe	ton oil equivalent
TPA	transport and processing agreement
TWJA 1878	Territorial Waters Jurisdiction Act 1878
UCTA	Unfair Contract Terms Act (1977)
UK LIFT	United Kingdom Licence Information for Trading
UKAPP Certificate	United Kingdom Air Pollution Prevention Certificate
UKCS	United Kingdom Continental Shelf
UKOOA	United Kingdom Offshore Operators Association (now Oil & Gas UK Ltd)
UNCITRAL	United Nations Commission on International Trade Law
UNCLOS	United Nations Convention on the Law of the Sea
UOA	unit operating agreement
UUOA	unitisation and unit operating agreement
VOC	volatile organic compound
WSCA	Well Services Contractors Association
WTO	World Trade Organization

TABLE OF CASES

TABLE OF STATUTES

TABLE OF STATUTORY INSTRUMENTS

TABLE OF EUROPEAN LEGISLATION

Decisions

TABLE OF INTERNATIONAL INSTRUMENTS

CHAPTER 1

OIL AND GAS LAW ON THE UNITED KINGDOM CONTINENTAL SHELF: CURRENT PRACTICE AND EMERGING TRENDS

Greg Gordon, John Paterson and Emre Üşenmez

If there is one word that best describes the United Kingdom   1.1
Continental Shelf (UKCS) at the beginning of the second decade
of the 21st century, it is "mature". The UKCS is no longer a new
frontier of oil and gas exploration, with the steep climb up the
production profile ahead of it and the principal question being how
high that profile will rise. Rather, it is an established hydrocarbon
province on the downward slope of the production profile, with the
main question being how steep that decline will be.

Presenting the current situation in those terms may appear to   1.2
raise the question not only of why a new book on the subject of the
law affecting oil and gas operations on the UKCS was required in
2007, but perhaps even more one of why a second edition is already
required: in so far as the UKCS appears to be in the endgame, is not
the legal picture already fairly clear? To the contrary, however, it is
the very fact that the UKCS is now a mature province that provided
the rationale for the first edition of this book and explains the need
for this expanded update: maturity can present existing problems
and challenges in a new light and has the potential continually to
throw up new problems and challenges. Accordingly, each of the
contributors to this book responds to the issue of maturity to a
greater or lesser extent, depending on the precise subject they are
treating.

Maturity, of course, also has a much more positive aspect: the   1.3
accumulation of years also means the accumulation of experience.
The industry and the Government (and their respective lawyers)
have learned a great deal in the almost 50 years of hydrocarbon

operations on the UKCS. Mistakes have been made along the way
and lessons have sometimes been learned the hard way. But the legal
and regulatory framework that is now in place on the UKCS can
justifiably claim to be one of the most advanced anywhere in the
world. Maturity therefore brings challenges, but that same maturity
leaves the UKCS well placed to respond to them.

1.4   An insight into the geological roots of maturity and a comprehensive overview of the economic implications are provided by Alex
Kemp in the second introductory chapter to this book. Put at its
most simple, a mature province is one in which the likelihood is that
all of the major fields have been discovered and that new discoveries will be relatively small scale. Beyond that, a mature province
is one in which the focus of industry and of the government is on
the steepness of the decline of the production profile: where is the
balance to be struck between the Government's desire to extend self-
sufficiency (or at least the contribution of domestic production to
the balance of payments and to energy security) and the industry's
desire to invest in projects (wherever in the world those happen to
be) where it can maximise its return? These basic characteristics of
the mature province ramify in a variety of different and sometimes
unexpected ways. Kemp goes on to review the economic dimension
of a number of issues that are treated in more detail from the legal
perspective by other contributors to this book. Thus, he considers
the way in which the Government has adapted the licensing regime
to encourage new entrants as well as the exploration and development of frontier areas. As regards existing fields, Kemp notes the
range of initiatives entered into jointly by government and industry
to respond to the challenges of maturity (including those relating to
fallow blocks/discoveries, access to infrastructure and Stewardship)
and reviews the current debate surrounding taxation. At the other
end of the lifespan of a field, he considers the way in which uncertainty surrounding decommissioning liabilities has an impact on
investment decisions as regards both new and existing developments and notes the deleterious effect which the Government's
ultra-cautious approach may have on the national interest. On the
fiscal side, he notes and welcomes the Government's recent attempt
to encourage high-cost development through the provision of field
allowances against Supplementary Charge and notes the inherent
instability in the UK's system of taxing oil and gas revenues, and the
barrier to investment which that represents. He concludes, however,
on a positive note, with a summary of the results of recent economic
modelling which show that – as long as the oil price does not dip –
the UKCS "still has a bright long-term future".

1.5   The third introductory chapter, written by Emre Üşenmez, who
joins the book in this second edition as both a contributing author

and co-editor, deals with the issue of energy security in the UK. Although energy security is commonly viewed from the perspective of consumers, Üşenmez distinguishes the dual identities of the UK as an energy producer and a consumer state and highlights the policies aimed at ensuring energy security from both perspectives. Within this context the definition of "energy security" is not confined to the security of energy supplies and of the associated infrastructures but also includes the demand security and market access. Following a brief discussion setting out the UK's energy context, Üşenmez first discusses the international dimensions of the UK's energy security, particularly the development of consumer nations' responses to certain energy crises. The discussions focus on the International Energy Agency's (IEA's) Co-ordinated Emergency Response Measures (CERM), and on the Energy Charter Treaty (ECT) within the contexts of supply disruption response mechanisms, energy supplier diversification and access to markets. Üşenmez then introduces the European Union dimensions of the UK's energy security. He argues that although the majority of EU policies – some developing in parallel with the IEA measures – have a very positive impact, some of the climate change policies may have an adverse impact on the UK's energy security. With the EU's Third Energy Package, homogenous liberalisation of the internal gas market would go a long way towards alleviating potential artificial arbitrage issues. On the other hand, the Large Combustion Plants Directive (LCPD), for example, which aims to reduce emissions of acidifying pollutants, will bring forward the closure of certain power plants without there being the capacity to fill the resulting power deficit from renewable sources but rather only from newly constructed gas-fired power stations. This in turn will increase the UK's import dependency. When viewed from the UK's producer state identity, therefore, the policies aimed at increasing indigenous production are equally important. As Kemp notes in the previous chapter, fiscal incentives, particularly the field allowances against Supplementary Charge (which are further discussed in Chapter 6), are welcomed policies despite further contributing to fiscal instability. Üşenmez also identifies certain non-fiscal incentives, specifically the variations in the offshore licences (discussed in detail in Chapter 4), as welcome developments, while drawing attention to two of the main investment difficulties for the industry: access to equity and credit, and access to infrastructure. The latter issue is discussed in detail by Uisdean Vass in Chapter 7. Üşenmez concludes that the policies implemented since the 1960s have made a significant contribution to the multi-dimensional challenges to the UK's energy security. However, as the UKCS progressively matures, changing the nature of the challenges, it will be difficult to assess the adequacy of the existing energy security structure.

1.6   Thereafter the book is divided into two parts. The first deals with licensing and regulatory matters and includes chapters on licensing, mature province initiatives, the UKCS fiscal regime, access to infrastructure, health and safety, environmental law and regulation, decommissioning and competition law. Two of these chapters, those addressing the fiscal regime and environmental law, are new additions to the book for the second edition. However, two of the chapters initially included in this section of the book do not appear in the second edition. The chapter on public procurement has fallen victim to the EU Commission's decision[1] to exempt the exploration for, and development and production of, oil and natural gas within Great Britain[2] from the operation of Directive 2004/17/EC (the "Utilities Directive"). The chapter on employment law issues has also been withdrawn, but on this occasion for purely instrumental reasons: the editors were unable to find a new contributor who was in a position to update this chapter within a timescale that would not delay publication of the book. It is hoped that this chapter will return to a future edition. The second part of the book deals with contracting and commercial issues and contains chapters dealing with joint operating agreements, unitisation, risk allocation, intellectual property issues (in another new chapter for the second edition, "Law and Technology in the Oilfield"), acquisitions and disposals, land law and dispute resolution. The chapters have been contributed by a wide range of authors from the worlds of academia and practice. In each case, and to the extent appropriate, they provide not only a thorough review of the law, practice and policy as they stand but also an indication of the way in which these are developing or are likely to develop in the context of a mature province.

LICENSING AND REGULATION

1.7 The first legal question that presents itself in the exploitation of natural resources is that of ownership. Where an industry entity wishes to explore for and produce hydrocarbons, it needs to know to whom it should address itself in order to seek the requisite permission. As Greg Gordon indicates in his Chapter 4 on licensing, while it is clear in international law that the relevant body on the UKCS is the UK Government, the precise nature of its rights in those

---

[1] Decision of 29 March 2010, *Official Journal* of 31 March 2010, L 181/53.

[2] It should be noted that the exemption does not apply to Northern Ireland. This development was by no means unexpected; the Commission had previously granted an application to exempt the Dutch exploration and production sector from the Utilities Directive's requirements: Decision of 8 July 2009, *Official Journal* of 14 July 2009, L 181/53.

reserves is a matter that has never actually been resolved. While some commentators opine that the Government is quite simply the *owner* of those reserves, others are less sure. Gordon himself suggests that the reserves are in fact *ownerless*. Be that as it may, international law assuredly vests *sovereign rights* in those reserves in the UK Government and the question then becomes one of knowing how it asserts its interests in them vis-à-vis the industry. In the case of the UK, this is via a licensing regime and Gordon goes on to consider its key features. He notes the hybrid nature of the licence – between contract and regulation – as well as the extent of the discretion enjoyed by the Secretary of State charged with the administration of the licensing system. Thereafter, he considers the basic technical details upon which the system is built, including the grid system and licensing rounds, as well as the extent to which this is increasingly impacted by environmental law. The second half of Gordon's chapter consists of a commentary on current forms of UK oil and gas licences, during which he criticises the Government's decision to revert to one single set of Model Clauses (as opposed to the multiple sets which existed at the time of the first edition) as signally failing to promote transparency and clarity, the Government's stated aims in changing the system. In keeping with the theme of the book, as much attention is given to frontier and promote licences (both of which are manifestations of the Government's desire to maximise interest in the mature province) as to the standard production licence.

This last point is taken up in Chapter 5 by Greg Gordon and John Paterson on mature province initiatives. Developing some of the themes introduced by Alex Kemp in his introductory chapter, Gordon and Paterson consider both the Fallow Areas Initiative and Stewardship. What is striking about each of these initiatives is the extent to which they are products of joint government and industry partnerships (the current manifestation of which is PILOT). The first initiative (which is composed of two components: Fallow Blocks and Fallow Discoveries) essentially aims to ensure that where acreage has been allocated under a licence, the licensee actually makes the best use of it – and where this is not the case the acreage must be handed back so that it can become available to others. The second initiative, Stewardship, appears to be even more intrusive. Here the concern is to ensure that existing fields are being operated to their full potential and where this is not the case to ensure that steps are taken to remedy the situation. Notwithstanding the state's undoubted interest in the exploitation of the natural resources in which it has sovereign rights, the scope in both of these cases for conflict over what the industry might regard as its operational decisions is clear. The chances of conflict might appear all the greater when it is appreciated that these initiatives depend almost entirely upon the discretionary powers of

1.8

the Secretary of State. And yet, as has been noted, they both emerged from joint industry–government discussions. While Gordon and Paterson's chapter accordingly reveals the full extent of the potential intrusion by the regulator into the activities of the industry, it also discloses the interest of the industry as a whole in ensuring that its less efficient or more recalcitrant members can be disciplined effectively in the context of a mature province where there is simply less margin for sub-optimal behaviour.

1.9   Also picking up some themes introduced by Alex Kemp, Emre Üşenmez in Chapter 6 considers the fiscal regime applying to operations on the UKCS, with a particular focus on those elements of taxation that are specific to the oil and gas industry. As a consequence, he discusses especially Petroleum Revenue Tax, Ring Fence Corporation Tax and the Supplementary Charge. Üşenmez concludes by speculating on the future direction of taxation offshore: given the extent of fiscal instability that has characterised the history of the UKCS as a hydrocarbon province and given the economic position of the country at present and for the foreseeable future, how will the Government strike the balance between regarding the industry as a cash cow to be milked when times are tough and the need to encourage continuing investment in the mature province to ensure maximum economic recovery?

1.10   A further aspect of the maturity of the UKCS is discussed by Uisdean Vass in Chapter 7 on access to infrastructure. As noted by Alex Kemp, the likelihood is that new discoveries on the UKCS will be relatively small. Their prospects for development (as well as those of many existing small discoveries, including those relevant to the discussion in the preceding chapter by Gordon and Paterson) will frequently depend upon their ability to be linked up with the existing pipeline infrastructure so that it is possible to transport the produced hydrocarbons. As Vass points out, the UKCS displays both positive and negative aspects in this regard. On the plus side, the existing infrastructure is so extensive that, at least within the established parts of the province, the chances are good that new discoveries will be within economic range. On the minus side, however, is the fact that while newer discoveries are likely to be developed by smaller companies (and, indeed, potentially new entrants), the infrastructure in the main belongs to the established majors. Furthermore, important elements of that infrastructure are approaching the end of their design lives and may thus be of use to these new discoveries for only a limited period. It is accordingly clearly in the interests of the state as well as of the companies keen to develop smaller discoveries for there to be access to the infrastructure in a timely manner and on reasonable terms and conditions. Vass goes on to consider how this matter is dealt with in practice and notes once again that this depends not only on the intervention of the Government but also upon the willingness of the industry itself to develop an approach which is in its overall interests. He accordingly reviews the three pillars upon which access to infrastructure stands: s 17F of the Petroleum Act 1998, together with the relevant provisions of the Energy Act 2008, which allows a third party in the event of a failure to negotiate access to petition the Secretary of State to serve a notice determining that party's access rights; the Industry Code of Practice on Access to Upstream Oil and Gas Infrastructure on the UKCS, which sets out principles covering such matters as the provision of information to prospective users and non-discriminatory access; and the Guidance on Disputes over Third Party Access issued by DECC, which supports the Code and sets out the principles the Secretary of State will apply in any case where an application is made for a notice under s 17F. In case there could be any doubt, this last document makes clear that the Government's main objective is to ensure that all economic oil and gas reserves are recovered.

Chapter 8 considers health and safety at work offshore. Here, John Paterson considers the evolution of the legislative and regulatory approach to this issue from the earliest days of the UKCS as a hydrocarbon province through to the current permissioning regime. Treating the subject in this way allows a consideration of the particular circumstances that attended the adoption of the three distinct approaches to the regulation of occupational health and safety that have now been tried on the UKCS. It thus provides a clear picture of the challenge that the issue has presented to regulators. It also allows the particularity of the current permissioning regime to be understood properly. Finally, and significantly, it allows an appraisal of the ability of the current regime to deal with the challenges thrown up by the fact that the UKCS is now a mature province: the major operators have long experience of the UKCS and have lived through the transitions from one legal approach to another, understanding well why they have occurred as well as the legislator's intention in each case, but questions arise in this regard about the new entrants who are figuring more prominently in the province precisely as much of the infrastructure is ageing. The picture is further complicated by the occurrence of two major accidents in offshore operations elsewhere in the world in the recent past: the Montaro oil spill in the Australian sector of the Timor Sea in August 2009 and the even more significant accident affecting the Deepwater Horizon drilling rig in the Gulf of Mexico in April 2010 which resulted in both loss of life and very significant pollution. The net effect of these events is that there is renewed focus on the orientation of offshore safety regulation globally. In the case of the UK, as Paterson notes, the European Parliament and the European

1.11

Commission have both expressed concern that action may need to be taken to enhance safety legislation within the EU. There is no guarantee that what the UK itself regards as fit for purpose will receive a similar stamp of approval from the European institutions. The long and convoluted history of safety regulation on the UKCS may be far from over.

1.12   The same offshore accidents in Australian and US waters that have turned a renewed spotlight on offshore safety regulation have also highlighted the importance of environmental law and regulation on the UKCS. This topic is the subject of another new addition to the book in the shape of the contribution from Luke Havemann. Chapter 9 offers an overview of the key legislative and regulatory instruments concerned with the environmental impact of the industry's offshore exploration, development and production activities. Having considered first of all the environmental aspects of petroleum licences generally and the regulations affecting licensing, the chapter is then divided into two broad sections. The first of these examines the environmental regulations that impact upon activities carried out under an exploration licence, while the second considers those that relate to activities carried out under a production licence. Noting the recurring theme of maturity that runs through the book, Havemann concludes that in such circumstances there is the potential for tension between environmental protection and, on one hand, the looming decommissioning point (which may encourage a reduction in expenditure and thus an increased risk of environmental damage) and, on the other, the desire to extend the life of infrastructure as far as possible to maximise economic recovery.

1.13   The issue of the ageing of the infrastructure is at the heart of the tenth chapter, which considers the question of the decommissioning of offshore installations. Barely considered amid the early excitement attending the development of the North Sea, the question of how to dispose of installations and pipelines once they have served their purpose and, perhaps more importantly, the question of who will pay for the process are among the issues at the top of the agenda in discussions between industry and government. In this chapter, John Paterson traces the evolution of both international and UK law in relation to decommissioning from the 1958 Convention on the Continental Shelf through to the present day, noting in the process the impact of the Brent Spar case in the mid-1990s. A striking feature of the legal treatment of this issue is the fact that, while the Secretary of State was granted power to regulate decommissioning under the Petroleum Act 1998, this power has never actually been used, the Secretary of State preferring to proceed by way of guidance. Paterson accordingly devotes coverage to the terms both of the 1998 Act as amended by the Energy Act 2008 and of the Guidance

Notes in an effort to elucidate the Government's likely approach, not least in cases where an operator seeks to derogate from the general obligations set out under international law. Picking up on some of the issues highlighted by Alex Kemp and Emre Üşenmez in earlier chapters, Paterson also considers some of the areas of uncertainty that have caused concern for the industry, notably residual liability and taxation, as well as discussing the issue of financial security. This last matter has taken on particular significance in the mature province as the Government has become concerned that new entrants, who are, generally speaking, smaller and often newer companies, present a higher risk of insolvency and thus of being unable to meet decommissioning liabilities.

The first part of the book concludes with Judith Aldersey-   1.14
Williams' Chapter 11 on competition law and the upstream oil and gas business. No one can nowadays doubt the vigour with which the competition authorities at both the UK and the EU levels pursue those whom they suspect of cartel activity. Aldersey-Williams notes in her introduction both the serious consequences that flow from infringement and the difficulty of actually complying with the rules. Her chapter is accordingly essential reading for those who need to know when it is time to call for specialist advice in this regard. She proceeds by outlining first of all what it is that competition law prohibits in the form of anti-competitive agreements and abuse of a dominant position, before considering how one decides whether one needs to take account of only UK law or to look also at European law. Aldersey-Williams then examines the issue of defining the relevant market that will require analysis in terms of competition law as well as the difference between vertical and horizontal agreements before moving on in the second half of her chapter to look at common competition issues that arise in upstream oil and gas business.

CONTRACTING AND COMMERCIAL MATTERS

Maturity is a factor that impacts not just upon the state's interact-   1.15
ions with the industry, but also upon the commercial contracts which industry players enter into between themselves. The reducing size of new discoveries and the corresponding increase in unit costs means that economies must be found where possible if developments are to continue to be profitable. This is an environment where waste and over-elaboration are to be avoided. Legal costs are among those which the industry has targeted as ones which may be cut without having a deleterious effect upon safety. This factor, together with the desire to accelerate the pace of the negotiation process (which desire is driven at least in part by the need to develop reserves

before the obsolescence of critical infrastructure) has led to the increasingly widespread use of standardised contracts (discussed in both Chapter 12, "Joint Operating Agreements", and Chapter 14, "Risk Allocation") and the launch of initiatives such as the Industry Mutual Hold Harmless scheme (also discussed in Chapter 14) and the Master Deed initiative (discussed in Chapter 16) designed to foster a uniformity in approach and promote economically efficient practices.

1.16   The part of the book devoted to contracting and commercial issues opens with Scott Styles' chapter on joint operating agreements. These agreements are fundamental to the way in which offshore oil and gas operations are undertaken in the UKCS. Styles' account explains the factors which drive the industry towards joint operations and describes and critically comments upon the key features of such agreements.

1.17   Chapter 13 by Nicola Macleod deals with the issue of unitisation – in other words, the legal response to the facts, first, that oil and gas fields may not lie wholly within one block of licensed acreage but may lie partly within another contiguous block which is allocated to a different licensee and, secondly, that oil and gas migrate once a well is drilled into a reservoir. These facts mean that in the absence of any provision to the contrary, the rule of capture in property law might lead to competitive drilling which would be detrimental to the reservoir as a whole. Unitisation is the means by which affected licensees agree to treat the reservoir as one unit, to develop it as such and to share the production equitably irrespective of which part of the reservoir it has come from. Unitisation has always been a live issue on the UKCS, but has become increasingly important as the province has matured because the area of the blocks being licensed is now considerably less than was previously the case, making it more likely that any discoveries, even of the small size now more usually encountered, will underlie more than one block. Having examined the concept of unitisation, Macleod goes on to look at the way in which it operates within the UK. This depends in particular on powers vested in the Secretary of State in this regard under the licence, which enable him in the ultimate to serve a notice compelling the preparation of a unitised development scheme. The mere existence of this power appears to have been sufficient to ensure that affected licensees actually do discuss and produce agreed development programmes for the approval of the Secretary of State. Macleod goes on to examine the unitisation and unit operating agreement that is required in such circumstances, as well as the sorts of issues that commonly arise, before concluding with a consideration of unitisation across international borders.

1.18   If the chapter on unitisation indicates how practice in the oil and gas industry departs from standard legal concepts in property law, the succeeding chapter by Greg Gordon indicates how it can also depart, even quite radically, from common-law presumptions with respect to risk allocation. The reasons for this are related, first, to the fact that oil and gas operations are subject to multiple risks and, secondly, to the prevalence of contractors and subcontractors in the industry. There is accordingly the potential for significant losses and a tendency towards complex contractual arrangements. Leaving the allocation of risk to the general law is, therefore, likely to lead to problems – particularly economic inefficiencies – which could hamper the development of the industry, and the industry has accordingly responded by evolving alternative methods of allocating risk, which Gordon discusses under three main headings: indemnity and "hold harmless" provisions; liability for consequential losses; and overall caps on liability. In each case he examines law and practice via a step-by-step approach, using diagrams where appropriate, to elucidate what is frequently regarded, with some justification, as a complex and difficult area. Significantly, given the recurring theme of this book, Gordon notes that the existing practice of the industry with regard to risk allocation may change as the relative strengths of the companies involved change: it is one thing for an operator to be prepared to offer indemnities when it is a major company and the other party is a small service company, but the assessment may very well have to change where the operator is itself a small company. In this second edition Gordon considers the likely impact of the recent decision of *Farstad* v *Enviroco*, the first UK Supreme Court decision on the legal nature of the "indemnity and hold harmless" clause, and also notes a softening in the previously unyielding rules of contractual construction as applied to this area.

The inter-relationship between factors such as, on the one hand, **1.19** the fact of maturity and the high cost of operations in the UKCS and, on the other, the law of intellectual property may not be immediately apparent. However, as Martin Ewan notes in Chapter 15, "Law and Technology in the Oilfield", the connection between these factors is clear. The days of elephantine finds are probably over – in the developed part of the UKCS, at least. To get oil, the industry must be more creative than ever before. It must develop new means of finding oil and new techniques of recovering higher proportions of each find. And it must develop new ways of carrying out exploration, development and production activity at reduced cost. There is, therefore, great commercial value in innovation: value which is lost if innovators are not scrupulously careful to protect their own interests. But in a co-operative industry, where contractors work side by side with each other and where the operator will have overall control of operations, it is practically impossible to keep new tools and processes wholly "under wraps". Ewan's chapter discusses the problems faced by the innovating contractor in greater detail, and sets out the main rights and remedies available to such a contractor through the law of intellectual property and the delict of breach of confidence.

1.20   The changing face of the UKCS is also the backdrop for Chapter 16 on acquisitions and disposals of upstream oil and gas interests. Here, Norman Wisely notes that such transfers of licence interests have increased significantly in recent years. In his chapter he focuses in particular upon asset sales for a cash consideration and examines in turn acquisition structures; the due diligence process; approvals and consents; pre-emption and restrictions on assignment and consents and approvals; acquisition agreements; and completion. This chapter accordingly offers a valuable insight into an area of legal practice about which it is not otherwise easy to gain information.

1.21   Vass's chapter mentioned previously touches upon the transport of oil and gas by pipelines on the UKCS, with particular reference to the issue of third-party access to that infrastructure. In so far as those pipelines lie outside the UK and territorial waters, no issues of property law arise. The same may not be true once they cross into territorial waters and is certainly not the case once they are onshore. In Chapter 17 on aspects of land law relative to the trans-portation of oil and gas in Scotland, Roderick Paisley focuses on the transport of oil and gas by pipelines passing through land in private ownership, which, as he notes, may well arise once they cross into territorial waters. His chapter is accordingly concerned with real rights, that is, ownership, leasehold and servitudes. Of these three, the most significant (and perhaps the least widely understood) is servitude. The bulk of the chapter is accordingly devoted to a consideration of how this right can be used to allow a pipeline to be laid across private land and oil and gas to be transported through it for commercial purposes – including the question of what happens when it is proposed to transport a different gas and in the opposite direction from originally envisaged, as might be contemplated in the
1.22   case of a carbon capture and storage scheme.

In the final chapter of the book, Chapter 18, Margaret Ross considers dispute management and resolution and notes that the nature and culture of the oil and gas industry have produced particular solutions in this regard. For example, the fact that delays are often extremely expensive means that dispute resolution processes must be fast and efficient, while the fact that parties to disputes are usually "repeat players" rather than "one shotters" means that there is frequently a reluctance to litigate and a preference for private and flexible alternatives. Ross considers the spectrum of responses to disputes under four headings: unilateral action; collaboration and negotiation; assisted consensual non-binding processes; and adjudication and beyond. She notes that while, historically, the industry has been in the vanguard as regards its willingness to explore alternative methods of dispute resolution, there is now a risk that it may be unduly tied to tried and tested approaches while the range of options has actually increased. Equally, the traditional reluctance to litigate may be being tempered as the UKCS matures and new players worry less about long-term relationships and more about enforceable remedies. Here, as elsewhere, maturity continues both to throw up new challenges and to encourage the evolution of new solutions.

CHAPTER 2

EVOLVING ECONOMIC ISSUES IN THE MATURING UKCS

Alex Kemp

The UK Continental Shelf (UKCS) is widely described as a mature 2.1
petroleum province. This phrase may be interpreted in different
ways but is generally taken to include several characteristics such as
declining production, declining average new field size and prospectivity and, along with these, rising unit operating costs and probably
development costs as well. The decommissioning problem also
looms large on the horizon.

All the above characteristics are present in the UKCS. Oil 2.2
production peaked in 1999 at around 2.85 million barrels of oil per
day (mmb/d) and has been falling steadily to just over 1.43 mmb/d
in 2009. Natural gas production peaked at 1.81 mmboe/d (oil
equivalent) in 2000 and has declined to around 1.02 mmboe/d in
2009. These are relatively steep rates of decrease. They reflect several
factors. Thus, the first generation of giant fields (such as Forties,
Brent, Ninian, Leman and Indefatigable) are now very mature, with
only modest levels of production. The newer generation of fields is
much smaller, with the average reserves being around 20 million boe,
compared with over 500 mmboe in the mid-1970s. The most likely
size is also less than 20 million boe, reflecting the log-normal distribution of field sizes. The further consequence is that a substantial
number of new developments are required regularly, to replace the
greatly reduced production from the older generation of large fields.
This is by no means easy to achieve on a recurring basis. Smaller
fields generally require a substantial managerial effort in relation
to the potential rewards. If the field is located in close proximity to
existing infrastructure which can be utilised, the development costs
may be substantially reduced (though the aggregate operating costs

(including tariffs) will be increased). Sometimes, however, appropriate infrastructure may not be available within easy proximity, and small gas fields in particular may be economically as well as geographically described as "stranded". This has held back developments in the West of Shetland region. In the North Sea, a major looming issue is the diminishing remaining economic longevity of the infrastructure of pipelines, terminals and processing platforms. Many of the facilities were developed a long time ago, to facilitate the development of fields which are now substantially depleted. The looming problem is compounded by the likely need to spend considerable sums to maintain the integrity of this infrastructure. In these circumstances it is important that the window of opportunity is seized to develop new projects which cannot only minimise the resource costs of these developments, but can extend the economic life of the infrastructure and justify the spending of funds on enhancing its integrity.

2.3   The implications of the above are that the current priorities should be to ensure that new project developments are not held up, and policies should be geared to the removal of any bottlenecks or impediments to investment and production. In practice this refers both to new field developments and to incremental projects in mature fields.

LICENSING POLICY ISSUES AND INITIATIVES

2.4   Several policy issues are involved in the facilitation of new developments. These refer particularly to licensing, broadly defined, and taxation. The licensing arrangements are very clearly designed to enhance the pace of exploration and development.[1] Thus, the recent conventional licences have an initial period of 4 years after which 50 per cent of the acreage has to be relinquished, and after another 4 years the remainder has to be relinquished unless a development is taking place. All this means that the licensee has to proceed expeditiously with his exploration programme. These current rules are significantly tighter than those employed in earlier licence rounds. Licence rounds now occur every year, and very large numbers of blocks (typically exceeding 1,000) are put on offer on each occasion.

2.5   Since 2003, a new form of licence termed the promote licence, has been introduced. This is designed to encourage small companies with exploration ideas to acquire data and undertake studies which could subsequently result in more substantial work programmes

---

[1] For a clear description, see P Carter, "The Regulator's Dilemma – How to Regulate yet Promote Investment in the same Asset Base: the UKCS Experience" (2007) 3/4 *International Energy Law and Taxation Review*.

being undertaken. For the initial 2-year period the licence fees are discounted by 90 per cent to encourage very small companies to proceed expeditiously with their work. A third form of licence is the frontier licence where tranches of blocks can be awarded on terms which provide for a 6-year initial term, with a reduction in the licence fees for the first 2 years of the duration of the licence.[2]

Another initiative designed to accelerate activity relates to fallow **2.6** blocks/discoveries. In essence the rules encourage current licensees to explore the acreage to a satisfactory extent or to develop a discovery within a stipulated time period, after which any unworked blocks would have to be traded or relinquished.[3] This scheme has already led to significant enhancement in the utilisation of fallow acreage.[4]

A more recent initiative relates to mature fields and has been **2.7** termed the Stewardship Initiative. Essentially, the Government desires to ensure that licensees are taking all reasonable steps to maximise economic recovery from the fields in question. The procedure is that the Department of Energy and Climate Change (DECC) examines the operators' plans for further development of and/or production from the fields and, if necessary, can make proposals for specified work to be undertaken. If this is not forthcoming within a specified time period the licensee may be asked to trade the asset in question.[5]

There can be no doubt that these initiatives are appropriate **2.8** and praiseworthy, and due credit should be given to the DECC and PILOT, the joint Government/industry consultative body. The Fallow, Stewardship, and Infrastructure Code of Practice Initiatives were all agreed within PILOT and did not require new legislation. The evidence on the effectiveness of the Fallow Initiative is encouraging. With the Stewardship Initiative judgement is required on what incremental investments should be deemed necessary to maximise economic recovery. While there may be some obvious cases, such as the need for well repairs, new compressors, infill drilling, or even water/gas injection schemes, the extent to which enhanced oil recovery schemes (including tertiary recovery) should be considered desirable elements of the initiative is open to debate. The appropriate investments for maximising economic recovery from a field could be viewed differently by two parties, who might have not only different technical solutions but also different economic cut-off

[2] For more detail on the legal treatment of licensing, see Chapter 4.
[3] For a detailed statistical analysis of this problem, see A G Kemp and A S Kasim, "A Longitudinal Study of Fallow Dynamics in the UK Continental Shelf (UKCS)" (2007) 35 *Energy Policy*. For further details on the Fallow Blocks/Discoveries Initiatives on the UKCS, see Chapter 5.
[4] For details see P Carter, above n 1.
[5] For further details on the Stewardship Initiative on the UKCS, see Chapter 5.

criteria and attitudes to risk. At least some of these problems could be solved by the encouragement of trading of mature assets, as the prospective buyer with more ambitious plans for the further development of a field should be willing to pay more than the field is worth to the current owner. The success of the Stewardship scheme may thus depend in part on how efficiently assets can be traded. It will also depend on how effectively the DECC operates the scheme in practice, which requires both technical and economic judgements on what incremental investments should reasonably be expected.

2.9   A further initiative relates to the Infrastructure Code of Practice. Currently, many new field developments and incremental projects utilise the existing infrastructure, and this is clearly in the national interest. Historically, however, third-party tariffing agreements have frequently involved protracted negotiations. In the 1990s a voluntary code was developed to try to expedite agreements, and involved the publication of indicative tariffs. But, while this had some beneficial effects, the result was still not satisfactory to all parties, and in August 2004 a more comprehensive Code of Practice was agreed between the United Kingdom Offshore Operators Association (UKOOA) and the Department of Trade and Industry (DTI). Key economic elements to the Code are that the asset owner and the prospective user agree to negotiate in good faith for up to 6 months on the terms of a third-party agreement. Agreed terms would be published. If no agreement were reached the DECC could be asked to intervene and set terms. The principle involved would be that the tariffs should reflect those which would pertain in a competitive market, taking into account the costs and risks involved.

2.10   Other principles of the Code include a commitment by infrastructure owners to provide transparent and non-discriminatory access and the provision of tariffs and terms for unbundled services where requested. In anticipation of a request[6] to make a determination, the DECC has published Guidance Notes indicating its approach to making a determination.[7] Several cases are distinguished. The first is where the infrastructure has been built as part of an integrated field development project. In such a case where the spare capacity is offered after the relevant capital costs have been recovered, it was anticipated that the terms would reflect the incremental cost and risks imposed on the asset owner. It was also acknowledged that, where the field originally associated with the infrastructure was nearing the end of its life, the tariff for third-party access would need to provide for levels above incremental cost

---

[6] Such a request was made by Endeavour International in May 2010.

[7] DECC, *Guidance on Disputes over Third Party Access to Upstream Oil and Gas Infrastructure* (April 2009).

to ensure that the infrastructure continued to be available. In the language of the economist this is essentially the distinction between marginal and average cost pricing. There is a considerable literature on this subject.[8] To put the debate in context, where the infrastructure owner has local monopoly power and can levy discriminatory tariffs to different infrastructure users according to their willingness to pay, this can lead to an optimal solution in the sense that all fields which are economic in the opinion of the relevant investors will be developed. This should also lead to the optimal provision and utilisation of the infrastructure in question. But if discrimination is not permitted, as is indicated by the Infrastructure Code of Practice, this solution would not be possible. The DECC Guidance Notes state that a cost-related tariff will form the basis of any determination it is asked to make. Pricing according to marginal (or incremental) cost in circumstances where adequate ullage is available would mean that the user was paying for the costs attributable only to his use of the facilities.

In practice, where the initial infrastructure investment cost has **2.11** been recovered, but the asset owner still has substantial production from the related field, these incremental costs would be very small because most of the costs of operating the infrastructure would be fixed in nature. Marginal cost would be much lower than average cost. While this might be tolerable when the asset owner has considerable production of his own, it would not produce a satisfactory longer-term solution. If marginal cost pricing became common (perhaps as a direct and indirect consequence of a determination by the DECC) the infrastructure activity would operate at a loss and its economic life would be terminated. This would occur when the production from the owner's own field became relatively low and unimportant. In these circumstances, in order to incentivise the asset owner to maintain and possibly enhance his infrastructure, tariffs based on average costs become more appropriate. Premature closure of the infrastructure could also have a negative effect on further exploration within its vicinity. Of course, the explorer would prefer the availability of the infrastructure to be on a marginal cost basis, but the non-availability of the facility would be a worse prospect compared with the payment of a tariff based on average cost.

Currently, tariff incomes are generally subject to Corporation Tax **2.12** at 30 per cent and Supplementary Charge at 20 per cent. PRT has also been payable on tariff incomes, but from January 2004 new tariff contracts have been exempt. Yet another tax arrangement applies to

---

[8] For a summary view of the issues, see A G Kemp and E Phimister, "Economic Principles and Determination of Infrastructure Third Party Tariffs in the UK Continental Shelf (UKCS)" (2010) *North Sea Study Occasional Paper No 116* (University of Aberdeen).

a purely transportation operation distinct from production activities in the UKCS. The North Sea tax system does not apply to such an operation which is subject to Corporation Tax at 28 per cent, with relief for the main items of investment expenditure being on a 20 per cent declining balance basis (compared with 100 per cent first year for North Sea activities). In the 2010 Budget it was announced that the rate of non-North Sea Corporation Tax would gradually be reduced to 24 per cent, with the relief for main items of capital expenditure falling to 18 per cent declining balance.

2.13 The question of the appropriate tax treatment of tariff incomes has been subject to debate over many years. Originally, PRT did not apply to tariff incomes but in the 1983 Budget this was introduced on the ground that asset owners were using their local monopoly powers to levy rates above cost-related levels. The removal of PRT from new tariff agreements in 2004 was to encourage a reduction in rates to enable the UKCS to become more competitive.

Following the logic of the above, it is arguable that, where cost-related determination of tariffs through Government intervention is introduced, it would be inappropriate to levy the Supplementary Charge on the tariff incomes. While this is justifiable when the profitability of the activity is substantial, it is not obviously appropriate with cost-related tariffs. Tariff determination by DECC is on an individual case basis. But it is expected that the principles employed will be widely examined by investors, and could be employed in negotiations relating to other fields. Thus, cost-related tariffs could become more common.[9]

DECOMMISSIONING LIABILITY ISSUES

2.14 Mention has been made above of the perceived need to ensure that mature assets are in the hands of those best equipped to maximise the remaining potential from them. There are now companies which specialise in operating mature fields and there is also evidence that there are willing sellers as well. While the Government is keen to see transactions which offer the prospect of extra economic recovery, a current problem relates to the decommissioning obligation and the related financial liability problem. Since 1987, joint and several liability has been imposed on licensees and, while this has protected the Government's position, it has caused problems for investors who have to consider not only their ability to meet their own obligations but the risks relating to their partners' obligations as well.[10]

---

[9] For further details on access to infrastructure on the UKCS, see Chapter 7.

[10] For further details on decommissioning, see Chapter 10.

In aggregate, the decommissioning costs will be very substantial, **2.15**
perhaps around £25–£30 billion to 2040 in real terms for the fields
and infield pipelines alone (ie excluding removal of trunk pipelines,
terminals and drill cuttings).[11] By definition, the costs are incurred after
the income from the field in question has ceased, and the possibility of
default has thus to be considered by all parties. While the Government
protected itself by imposing joint and several liability under the
Petroleum Act 1987, even this has not been foolproof, as is illustrated
by the case of the Ardmore field where the partners in the licence were
unable to meet their decommissioning obligations. In this particular
case the costs involved were not very large, but the experience has
made the Government even more risk-averse in its approach to the
problem. In June 2007 a Consultation Document was issued[12] which
indicated that an acceptable decommissioning security agreement could
be required not only in the later stages of field life (such as when the
remaining net present value (NPV) from the field started to fall below
a specified percentage of the estimated decommissioning costs (say 150
per cent)), but at the beginning of the life of a field where the flow
rates had not yet been established. This is to deal with the problem
of early reservoir failure (which happened with the Ardmore field).
The proposals also contemplated that security agreements might be
required from a variety of stakeholders, extending beyond the field
licensees, to include, for example, a company which had leased a
floating production, storage and offloading (FPSO) unit to the licensees
to enable production to take place.

While it is understandable that the Government should wish **2.16**
to take a risk-averse attitude on this matter, a calculation of the
national interest requires that consideration also be given to the
consequences of the proposals. Some of them may be unfortunate.
Thus, as discussed above, it is recognised that the maximisation of
economic recovery is best achieved when the assets in question are
in the hands of those best able to utilise them. Specialist mature
field operators certainly exist, but the problem of decommissioning
liability can hold back asset transactions which are in the national
interest. The risk aversion of the Government currently extends to
the right to retain the liability on the selling company licensees,
unless the DECC is satisfied that the buying company has the ability
to meet the obligation. If transactions are stopped as a consequence,
so may be the maximisation of economic recovery.

---

[11] For details, see A G Kemp and L Stephen, "Financial Liability for Decommissioning
in the UKCS: the Comparative Effects of LOCs, Surety Bonds and Trust Funds" (2006)
North Sea Study Occasional Paper No 103, (University of Aberdeen).
[12] DTI, *Decommissioning Offshore Energy Installations: a Consultation Document*
(2007).

2.17   But there are other unintended consequences of the present and prospective arrangements. Financial security can be procured in several ways, including (1) parent company guarantee; (2) third-party guarantee; (3) decommissioning trust fund; (4) Government grant; (5) mutual guarantee fund; (6) decommissioning levy; and (7) insurance scheme. All these have positive and negative features both from licensee and Government perspectives. In the UK, bank guarantees (letters of credit (LOCs)), trust funds and, to a lesser extent, surety bonds have been given serious consideration. To date, LOCs have been employed when the Government felt that a guarantee was required. This device can have undesirable consequences. The payments are quite substantial and give an incentive to accelerate the decommissioning date of a field to avoid ongoing operating losses in the late stages of the field's life. In cases where a whole new field development is quite marginal, the presence of an LOC obligation could also tip the balance from a viable to a non-viable project.[13] Further, the presence of an LOC has to be noted in a company's accounts, and it reduces the licensee's debt capacity. The device *adds* to the *total* decommissioning cost facing a licensee. The direct payments to the bank are tax deductible, and so the Government does share in the costs involved not only in this way but through the tax relief given when the decommissioning expenditures are actually made.

2.18   In the Gulf of Mexico, surety bonds are commonly employed. It is possible that the total costs of these are less than those of LOCs, but they still add to the total decommissioning costs and render a marginal field sub-marginal.[14] Economic recovery could also be curtailed.

2.19   Decommissioning trust funds (or escrow account arrangements) have become increasingly common in petroleum legislation/contracts around the world. For example, they exist in all the contracts in Angola; the primary legislation in Namibia; the large contracts in Azerbaijan and Sakhalin; and in the Joint Development Zone between Nigeria and São Tomé. No doubt they exist in other jurisdictions as well. This device has the key advantage of providing financial security for all parties involved, namely the Government vis-à-vis the licensees collectively and individually and each licensee vis-à-vis his partners. The fund works such that the contributions are alienated and accrue to become available to meet the decommissioning costs at the appropriate time.

2.20   Rules for such a fund have to be designed to enable it to function efficiently. Thus, contributions should start at a time during the

---

[13] For a quantification of this effect, see A G Kemp and L Stephen, above n 11.
[14] See A G Kemp and L Stephen, above n 11.

life of the field such that they, plus any income received from their investment, accrue to meet the decommissioning costs. The contributions come from the field cash flows and in practice rules have been designed which result in the required funds being available when required. Thus, in the Angolan contracts, alienated contributions commence after 70 per cent of the initial field reserves has been produced. Such a rule is an ad hoc one and may not result in the correct sum being available at the appropriate time because of the uncertainties of the likely size of the decommissioning costs, and other factors such as the behaviour of production and oil prices. But in typical situations a rule can be designed which works efficiently in practice. Provision can readily be made for annual adjustments to be made to the size of the contributions in the light of new knowledge regarding decommissioning costs and other relevant factors. In the event that there is some underprovision, the licensees would, of course, have the obligation to meet any shortfall.

The tax position relating to both the contributions to the fund and any income earned in it are important elements in its efficient operation. If the contributions were not tax deductible there could be an incentive to decommission the field prematurely because the increase in the operating costs in later field life would produce operating losses. Further, a very marginal field development could be rendered sub-marginal because of the acceleration in the payments relating to decommissioning. If the contributions were tax deductible these effects would be much less strong, and it is arguable that there would be little or no incentive to accelerate the decommissioning date. There is no increase in the aggregate decommissioning costs to the licensee from a trust fund scheme, unlike the case with LOCs and surety bonds. It should also be noted that the Government will receive tax revenues on the income earned from the monies in the fund. With a discretionary trust the tax rate on this income is 40 per cent. The income earned in the fund also contributes to the financing of the decommissioning costs. **2.21**

Despite these manifest advantages of a fund, the British Government has historically not favoured a scheme with tax-deductible contributions. Thus there was concern about allowing relief relating to an expenditure before it had been undertaken, and the possibility that investors would react by overproviding to take advantage of the tax reliefs. Concern was also expressed about what would happen to the monies in the fund and how these would be policed.[15] These objections are not conclusive. Tax-deductible provisions for future **2.22**

---

[15] See House of Commons Select Committee on Energy, *Decommissioning of Oil and Gas Fields*, Fourth Report (1990–91), evidence of Inland Revenue.

events occur for other activities (eg pensions) and tax deductions or cost-recovery provisions are now common in petroleum legislation around the world. Whether overprovision would be sought by licensees is extremely debateable, as the common reaction is that such alienated funds would earn a lower return than if reinvested in further exploration and development. In any case the Government can ensure that any overprovisions are fully subject to tax. This is what happens in the Netherlands, where annual provisions are allowed as deductions for both Income Tax and state profit share purposes. The rules in the Netherlands also provide for independent assessment of the likely decommissioning costs, with subsequent re-calculation of the annual provisions if necessary. A practical issue which would occur in the UK on some mature fields is that the remaining cash flows would be inadequate to ensure that the contributions would accrue to the required sum. The normal tax relief rules would then apply to the element of the costs which were not covered by the accrued contributions.

2.23   If the Treasury's opposition to providing tax relief on alienated contributions persists, along with the very risk-averse attitude of the DECC to the financial liability issue, there is a danger of a sub-optimal outcome from a national perspective. Thus the requirement for LOCs in practice may be reinforced and extended as a consequence of the present consultation. The DECC is not specifically requesting the use of this instrument, but it is the most widely known in the UK. It is also the instrument which produces the greatest extra aggregate costs (including the indirect costs from reduction in debt capacity), and the greatest distortion to maximum economic recovery (premature decommissioning). Alienated trust funds which allow tax relief for contributions were found to be the least distorting in terms of maximisation of economic recovery, and the least expensive in national economic terms with no extra costs and some tax revenues from the income of the fund.[16] To limit the (early) cost to the Exchequer, the need to contribute to a fund could be limited to cases where the DECC is concerned that licensees may be unable to meet their obligations.

TAXATION AND NEW DEVELOPMENTS/EXPLORATION

2.24   The current tax system applied to exploration and new developments is essentially a cash-flow tax for licensees who have appropriate tax cover. For Corporation Tax and Supplementary Charge the allow-

---

[16] See A G Kemp and L Stephen, above n 11.

ances for all costs are available on a 100 per cent first-year basis. Loan interest is not deductible against the Supplementary Charge.

From the viewpoint of encouraging investment (which is arguably 2.25 the key priority in the present phase of the life of the UKCS) a cash-flow tax has clear advantages. Thus *all* the investment risks are effectively shared with the Government on a 100 per cent first-year basis at the tax rate in question. The Government shares all the exploration, development and production risks to the extent of 50 per cent. Further, the post-tax internal rate of return (IRR) equals the pre-tax rate irrespective of the tax rate. Any positive pre-tax NPV remains positive after tax. Historically, in the literature on taxation economics it was often stated that no Government would introduce such a tax because the resulting extent of risk-sharing was too great.

Why, then, have tax incentives been required to foster the pace 2.26 of development at a time of relatively high oil (though not gas) prices? The answer lies in the combination of relatively small and very high cost fields plus the effects of the tremendous cost inflation which has occurred over the last few years. The latter has been due to the worldwide boom in activity since 2003 perhaps along with inadequate investment in earlier years. In turn this was due to the low level of oil prices in the 1990s and its repercussions. Currently many new fields and projects offer relatively low NPVs, especially at the cautious prices employed by investors for assessing long-term investments.

Even smaller oil companies now examine opportunities around 2.27 the world and make their capital allocations accordingly. On a world comparison the UKCS is likely to be categorised as (1) offering modest materiality in relation to other provinces; and (2) being relatively high cost on a per barrel basis.

In these circumstances licensees will not decide whether or not 2.28 to proceed with an investment project simply on the basis of the expected rate of return. The materiality required to compensate for the risks involved could be reflected in a minimum size of NPV or profit : investment ratio at the appropriate cost of capital. Ranking of projects in the industry is typically done on the basis of the (NPV/I) ratio, where NPV is post-tax and I is pre-tax, even though tax relief is given for the expenditure involved. It is likely that every investor will have his own screening criteria, such as the size of the minimum NPV; the discount rate (cost of capital) to calculate the NPV; and the threshold size of the (NPV/I) ratio. The Treasury and HM Revenue and Customs cannot be sure of the criteria employed by the different licensees and their attitude to risk. These behavioural issues can make tax discussions between the industry and the Government fraught and inconclusive: the two parties may not be using the same criteria to define what constitutes a "reasonable" Government share.

2.29   Understanding and agreement have not been enhanced in the past by Government Ministers quoting with approval from the calculations published by the Office for National Statistics (ONS) in its bulletin *Profitability of UK Companies*[17] when discussing the taxable capacity of the UKCS. These calculations show the accounting rate of return year by year. This is not a sensible measure of taxable capacity, which is better reflected by the NPV over the lifetime of the project. Year-by-year calculations of the accounting rate of return cannot give a reasonable measure of taxable capacity because they do not properly reflect the incidence of capital expenditure. Further, the ONS calculation refers to aggregate activity in the UKCS which means a very large number of fields at different stages in their lifecycles, with some being very mature and others at their early or development stage. The aggregate is not very meaningful. The ONS recognises this and states that the measure employed is not a good measure of performance for UKCS companies because of the nature of the fixed assets, which produces distortions in the average capital employed. Given this, it is surprising that the measure continues to be highlighted.

2.30   The specific procedure employed by the ONS is to calculate the ratio of net operating surplus to capital employed. Net operating surplus is found by calculating gross operating surplus (broadly, gross revenues minus operating costs) and deducting capital consumption. This is depreciation calculated according to the "perpetual inventory method" which in practice is apparently straight-line depreciation over a period averaging 11 years. All exploration costs are apparently capitalised. The denominator in the ratio is net capital employed. This incorporates the depreciation provision defined above, and the net capital employed reflects the written-down replacement cost of the fixed assets employed. The result of the calculation highlights the effects of oil price variations. Given the long-term nature of this very capital-intensive activity, emphasis on the accounting rate of return for any one year (or quarter) is misleading. The calculated return is not a sensible measure of the taxable capacity of the industry, which is best achieved with the use of NPVs at the field development stage and expected monetary values (EMVs) at the exploration stage. The discount rate should reflect the cost of capital. This can vary across licensees, with very large, integrated companies having much lower costs of capital than smaller ones, reflecting the diversity of their portfolio of assets. Currently the corporate weighted average cost of capital for a very large company could be under 10 per cent, while that for a small one will be considerably higher. Small companies

---

[17] Available online at http://www.statistics.gov.uk.

attempting to raise funds for exploration purposes may face very high costs of capital. Equity providers for this activity will typically seek IRRs on their investment in the 20–30 per cent range. The cost of debt capital to small companies, even when they have discoveries among their assets, will also be higher than for very large companies, with the result that the weighted average cost of capital could be in the 12.5–17.5 per cent range, depending on the perceived risks and collateral available.

In recognition of the need to incentivise high-cost developments   2.31 while preserving tax revenues, the Government has recently introduced a complex set of field allowances against the Supplementary Charge. There are four categories of relief, namely for (1) small fields; (2) ultra heavy oilfields; (3) ultra high pressure/high temperature (HP/HT) fields; and (4) deep water gas fields. The qualifying criteria for the relief depend on detailed specified physical characteristics of the fields. For small fields the total allowance is £75 million (spread over 5 years) for fields with reserves of 2.75 million tonnes of oil equivalent or less, reducing on a straight line basis to zero for fields with reserves of more than 3.5 million tonnes. The total allowance for ultra heavy oilfields is £800 million (again spread over 5 years). The qualifying characteristics are an American Petroleum Institute (API) gravity below 18° and a viscosity exceeding 50 centipoise at reservoir temperature and pressure. For ultra HP/HT the allowance is available for fields with a temperature exceeding 166°C and pressure exceeding 862 bar in the reservoir. The total allowance increases from £500 million at 166°C to £800 million at 176.67°C. For deep water gas fields there are three qualifying criteria, all of which have to be met. Thus: (1) more than 75 per cent of the field's reserves have to comprise gas; (2) the field has to be located in a water depth exceeding 300 metres; and (3) the planned route for the primary pipeline to the relevant infrastructure (such as a major existing pipeline) has to exceed 60 kilometres. The total amount of the allowance is tapered to the distance of the pipeline from the new field. It is £800 million where the distance exceeds 120 kilometres and this amount reduces to zero at 60 kilometres.

The complexity of these measures reflects the recognition by the   2.32 Government of the types of fields which the industry has highlighted as being particularly difficult from the viewpoint of economic viability. The use of physical characteristics as qualifying criteria should be seen as a proxy for the high (unit) costs of developing the fields. But equally high costs could pertain on other fields with non-qualifying physical characteristics. It is arguable that a scheme based on costs would be more appropriate. Thus the payment of Supplementary Charge could be related to the achieved rate of return on the field. A threshold rate of return would be specified and liability would be triggered only when the return achieved exceeds this.

TAXATION AND NEW PLAYERS

2.33 For some years the DECC has been encouraging the entry of new players into the UKCS, and this effort has paid off in the sense that the companies concerned have often substantially enhanced production from the mature fields they bought. The provision of rollover relief for Capital Gains Tax purposes has made a contribution to the execution of the transactions concerned. By purchasing producing assets the new player is able to obtain tax cover for any new investment. But some new players are interested in the exploration prospects, and do not have tax cover. Such companies are substantially disadvantaged compared with tax-paying investors, given the current tax rate of 50 per cent and the availability of 100 per cent first-year allowances. The new player cannot immediately use these valuable allowances, and can only carry them forward for use if and when a discovery is made and income from production subsequently obtained.

2.34 For an explorer such future income is, of course, not guaranteed. The Government has recognised the problem and the licensee is able to carry forward unutilised allowances for exploration, appraisal and development with compound interest. This procedure is conceptually sound and is consistent with the resource rent tax concept specifically designed to deal with the collection of economic rents from natural resources such as petroleum. The interest rate provided for in the legislation is currently 6 per cent (3.5 per cent real plus 2.5 per cent inflation). This is a riskless rate which is below the cost of capital of new players, and so they are not fully compensated for the disadvantage of being unable to claim their allowances when they become due. Unlike the investor with tax cover, they also have to continue to bear the full exploration risk. If no discovery is made there would be no relief. The scheme may be compared with that introduced in Norway for new players. There, the Government fully shares in the exploration risk by directly contributing to the costs involved to the extent of the tax rate. In current circumstances this is 78 per cent. This scheme puts the new player on an equal tax footing with an investor enjoying tax cover. It is known that without this tax concession some smaller new players in Norway would have been unable to enter the sector.

WIDER TAX REVIEW

2.35 The Government initiated a longer-term tax review of the UKCS, and in March 2007 the Treasury issued a discussion paper on the subject.[18] A main feature of the discussion paper was the idea that there were advantages in abolishing Petroleum Revenue Tax (PRT). This is now paid on comparatively few fields, although at current oil prices it still collects significant revenues to the state. Its abolition is not a straightforward issue and has several dimensions. On PRT-paying fields the overall rate of tax is 75 per cent and the removal of PRT would reduce this to 50 per cent. This should have a positive effect on investment in incremental projects in the fields in question. But there are other effects which have to be considered. Thus, straight PRT abolition would also result in the abolition of the PRT relief for decommissioning. On large, mature fields where the costs will be very great, this relief is very valuable. In some cases it could well be that the decommissioning relief is more valuable to the licensee than the PRT payments made on the remaining field production.

This is recognised by the Government, as is the need to take this into account in any scheme of abolition. One solution which was mooted was the idea that the licensee should "buy out" his remaining PRT obligations (including relief for decommissioning). In practice this would mean that, for any field, estimates of the remaining PRT payments and reliefs would be agreed with the Government, and a schedule of payments then also agreed. There are, of course, many uncertainties regarding these prospective payments, as they depend on the interaction of production, oil and gas prices, and investment, operating and decommissioning costs. There is thus plenty of scope for different views being taken of the size of the payments. Once a scheme had been agreed it would be fixed for the remaining life of the field, irrespective of what happened to oil prices, decommissioning costs or other variables affecting the tax position. The whole procedure would be fairly unique in British tax legislation. One consequence would be that, after an agreement had been reached, an incremental project which had not been subject to the PRT agreement, but which was subsequently designed and executed by a licensee, would be free of PRT. The provision of incentives for such projects on PRT-paying fields to maximise economic recovery from the UKCS constitutes the main case for removal of PRT. If that does not happen, the case for PRT allowances for incremental projects is worthy of consideration. **2.36**

Any review with the future of PRT as a central element means that the prospective tax relief for decommissioning on the relevant fields is unclear, as PRT abolition is not guaranteed. If it is not abolished, the allowances and tax rate could be changed from their present **2.37**

---

[18] HM Treasury, *The North Sea Fiscal Regime: a Discussion Paper* (March 2007).

levels, with obvious consequences for the effective rate of decommissioning relief. All this adds to the uncertainties surrounding the values of mature fields which are or may be the subject of sales, thus making valuation more difficult. At the time of writing the issue of the future of PRT has apparently been "parked" but it will almost certainly re-emerge as large-scale decommissioning looms closer.

2.38   The discussion paper made it clear that if PRT was removed the Government would not automatically seek to increase the supplementary charge to compensate for any loss in revenues. A change could, of course, be made for other reasons. On this subject the discussion paper states that the system should not be changed for short-term purposes but be credible for the medium and longer term. Historically, this has been a major issue in the UK, with many changes being made over the years. It should be noted that, while some of the changes were made by the Government entirely on its own initiative, others were the result of pressure from the companies. The field allowances are the obvious examples.

2.39   It is difficult to foresee a stable long-term system, given its present structure. The current system for new fields has several positive features from the perspective of encouraging investment, but there is only one rate and, given the range of field profitability under the oil and gas prices experienced over the past years, one fixed rate is most unlikely to be felt appropriate by either the industry or the Government. The industry did not favour redesigning the system such that the rate of tax would automatically vary with oil and gas prices, and the Government has dropped this idea from further serious consideration. The debate will continue, and the outcome remains uncertain. The situation is akin to one of permanent negotiation.

THE LONG-TERM PROSPECTS

2.40   Summary results of the economic modelling of the long-term prospects for the UKCS in terms of production are shown in Figures 2.1 and 2.2 under two price scenarios, namely $60/50 pence and $80/70 pence. The investment criterion employed is minimum (NPV/I) + 1 of 1.3. It is seen that the price sensitivity of long-term production is very high, with the numbers of viable fields in the categories of technical reserves and future discoveries being much greater under the high price. On this scenario, the UKCS still has a bright long-term future.[19]

---

[19] For full details, see A G Kemp and L Stephen, "The Prospects for Activity in the UKCS to 2040: the 2009 Perspective" (2009) *North Sea Study Occasional Paper No 114* (University of Aberdeen).

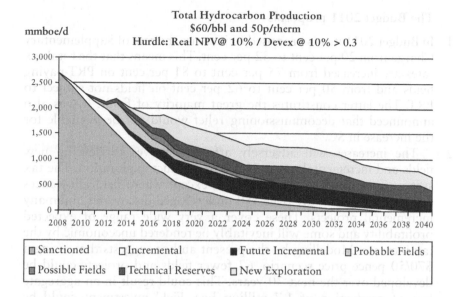

Figure 2.1: *Total hydrocarbon production $60/bbl and 50p/therm*

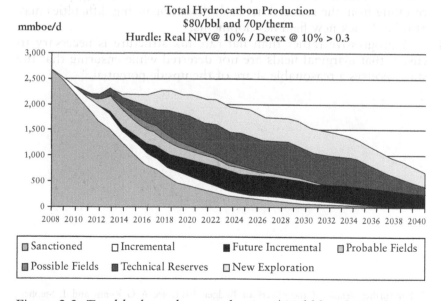

Figure 2.2: *Total hydrocarbon production $80/bbl and 70p/therm*

POSTSCRIPT

The Budget 2011 proposals

2.41   In Budget 2011 it was proposed to increase the rate of Supplementary Charge from 20 per cent to 32 per cent. This means that the total tax rates are increased from 75 per cent to 81 per cent on PRT-paying fields and from 50 per cent to 62 per cent on fields not subject to PRT. The latter constitutes the great majority of fields. It was also announced that decommissioning relief would not be available for the increase in SC.

2.42   The increases will adversely affect incentives to develop new fields and incremental projects and to conduct exploration. The tax system is essentially a flat-rate one, except where field allowances are available. There are over 350 undeveloped discoveries and many incremental projects. These cover a very wide range of expected profitability and some will inevitably be rendered uneconomic by the tax increase. Modelling by the present author suggests that, using a $70/50 pence price scenario, 62 fewer fields and projects could be developed over the next 30 years. This could result in an aggregate loss of production of 1.7 million boe. Field investment could be reduced by £12.8 billion over the period and total field expenditures reduced by £33.2 billion.

2.43   There will be further effects. The exploration effort will be reduced because of lower expected returns and financing problems resulting from the reduced net cash flows. Financing difficulties may also hold back new field developments.

2.44   A progressive rather than flat-rate tax structure is necessary to ensure that marginal fields are not deterred while ensuring that the state receives a reasonable share of the upside potential.[20]

---

[20] For further details of the effects of Budget 2011, see A G Kemp and L Stephen, *The Effects of Budget 2011 on Activity in the UK Continental Shelf, North Sea Study Occasional Paper No 120* (April 2011) (University of Aberdeen Department of Economics): http://www.abdn.ac.uk/~pec144/acreef/.

CHAPTER 3

THE UK'S ENERGY SECURITY

Emre Üşenmez

On 16 October 2008 as the Secretary of State for the Department 3.1
of Energy and Climate Change (DECC), Ed Miliband MP gave
his first statement to the House of Commons on the then newly
created Department. He identified energy security as one of the
three long-term challenges to be addressed by the DECC.[1] On 15
July 2009 the DECC published the *UK Low Carbon Transition
Plan*[2] which, among other things, emphasised the benefits of carbon
emission reductions to energy supply security. It also warned
that the "pathway to delivering low carbon energy supplies is a
necessary one but will need careful design to manage the energy
security risks".[3] Less than a month later, building on the strategies
laid out in that document, Malcolm Wicks MP[4] released a report
analysing how these strategies together with the developments in the
international energy arena impact the UK's future energy security.[5]
Commenting on the Wicks Report, Prime Minister Gordon Brown

---

[1] Ed Miliband identified the challenge as "ensuring that [Britain has] energy that is
affordable, secure, and sustainable". The other two challenges are "bringing about
the transition to a low-carbon Britain; and achieving an international agreement on
climate change at Copenhagen in December 2009": *Hansard* HC, col 939 (16 October
2008).
[2] DECC, *UK Low Carbon Transition Plan: National strategy for climate and energy*
(15 July 2009; amended 20 July 2009) (hereinafter "*UK Low Carbon Transition Plan*").
[3] DECC, *UK Low Carbon Transition Plan*, p 28.
[4] Malcolm Wicks is the MP for Croydon North. Between 2005/6 and 2007/8 he was
Minister of State for Energy in the UK Government, serving as a Science Minister in
the interim. In October 2008 he was appointed by the Prime Minister as his Special
Representative on International Energy.
[5] Malcolm Wicks MP, DECC, *Energy Security: A national challenge in a changing world*
(5 August 2009) (hereinafter "Wicks, *Energy Security*").

said: "The ability to maximize domestic energy reserves and establish home grown energy sources is vital alongside the UK's ability to pull on every lever internationally in support of energy security."[6]

3.2   The importance of energy security for the UK was also highlighted in the most recent National Security Strategy:[7]

> "Barring revolutionary developments in alternative energy, the competition for energy supplies will also increase. On present projections, global energy demand will be more than 50% higher in 2030 than today, at the same time as the supply of oil and gas becomes increasingly concentrated, much of it in regions with potential for political instability ... The premium attached to energy security, and the rising risk of energy shortages, will increase the potential for disputes and conflict.
>
> Like climate change, competition for energy is a global challenge, but also one with potentially serious security implications ... it is one of the biggest potential drivers of the breakdown of the rules-based international system and the re-emergence of major inter-state conflict, as well as increasing regional tensions and instability."[8]

3.3   It is evident that the issues surrounding environmental concerns and energy security are intertwined and, as priority areas for policy-makers, they are being discussed at the highest levels of the UK Government; but what, exactly, is meant by "energy security"?

3.4   The definitions of energy security vary depending on which aspect of[9] or which perspective[10] on it is being discussed. Towards the broader end of the spectrum it is defined as "a condition in which a nation and all, or most, of its citizens and businesses have access to sufficient energy resources at reasonable prices for the foreseeable future free from serious risk of major disruption of service".[11] This is an ideal definition from the perspective of a consumer state. However, viewed from the perspective of the UK as a producer country, the definition is incomplete. The description in the Wicks Report, on the other hand, is just broad enough to include both perspectives. The

---

[6] DECC, "Energy security analysis welcomed", Press Release, 5 August 2009: http://www.decc.gov.uk/en/content/cms/news/pn090/pn090.aspx (accessed 4 May 2010).

[7] Cabinet Office, *The National Security Strategy of the United Kingdom: Security in an interdependent world* (March 2008).

[8] *Ibid*, paras 3.38 and 3.39.

[9] For example, trade and investment issues, political issues, consumption/transmission/production efficiency issues, environmental issues, etc.

[10] Ie perspectives of an energy producer nation or a consumer nation.

[11] B Barton, C Redgwell, A Rønne and D N Zillman, "Introduction" in B Barton, C Redgwell, A Rønne and D N Zillman (eds), *Energy Security: Managing Risk in a Dynamic Legal and Regulatory Environment* (2004), p 5.

report regards energy security as a tripartite concept: a balance of "physical", "price" and "geopolitical" security which energy policies "must aim at achieving".[12] Under these definitions an energy policy must, respectively, avoid "involuntary interruptions of supply"; provide "energy at reasonable prices to consumers"; and ensure "the UK retains independence in its foreign policy through avoiding dependence on particular nations".[13]

Towards the more specific end of the spectrum, the approach 3.5 to defining energy security becomes more systematic. The Energy Charter Secretariat interprets it "as a triad consisting of security of supplies, security of infrastructure and security of demand, including thereafter, the issues of access to resources, infrastructure and markets".[14] The Center for Strategic & International Studies (CSIS)[15] has a similarly systematic approach to the concept. In a recent study, the CSIS identified "eleven factors closely associated with energy security: diversity of energy supplies; diversity of suppliers; import levels; security of trade flows; geopolitics and economics; reliability; risk of nuclear proliferation; market/price volatility; affordability; energy intensity (energy used per unit of gross domestic product); and feasibility".[16]

Although all of the above-mentioned definitions are valid, this 3.6 chapter aligns itself with the interpretation of the Energy Charter Secretariat as it is comprehensive enough to take all the perspectives into consideration and broad enough to include all the major aspects of energy security. The rest of the chapter is divided into five sections. The first will set out the UK energy context. The second and third sections will look at the European Union (EU) and the international dimensions of the UK's energy security. These will be followed by sections discussing the energy security issue from the viewpoints of the UK both as a producing country and as a consumer nation. Finally, the chapter will end with a brief discussion on the current and proposed steps towards alleviating the UK's energy insecurity.

---

[12] Wicks, *Energy Security*, p 8.
[13] *Ibid.*
[14] A Konoplyanik, "Energy Security: The role of business, governments, international organizations and international legal framework" [2007] IELTR 6 at 85–93.
[15] A bipartisan, non-profit organisation headquartered in Washington, DC, CSIS conducts research and analysis and provides policy solutions to decision makers in government, international institutions, the private sector and civil society.
[16] B Childs Staley, S Ladislaw, K Zyla and J Goodward, *Evaluating the Energy Security Implications of a Carbon-Constrained U.S. Economy* (January 2009, CSIS Issue Brief: Energy Security and Climate Change) at p 1. For full definitions of each of the factors, see Annex II of the Issue Brief.

ENERGY IN THE UK

3.7   The first important hydrocarbon discovery on the UKCS was in 1965 but it was not until the end of the 1970s that production reached significant levels. In 1965, the total crude oil production was at around 83,000 tonnes of oil equivalent (toe), which increased to about 410,000 toe in 1974; and then to a sizeable 77.8 million toe in 1979.[17] This increase was the result of the surge in exploration activity following the Fourth Licensing Round[18] in 1971, and the Organization of the Petroleum Exporting Countries (OPEC) oil embargo 2 years later. With these events, and the quadrupling of oil prices in 1973 as a result of the embargo, "[s]uddenly, the possibility of economic development in water depths of 400–500 ft was realised, and this initiated what was to become one of the great technological achievements in oil exploration and production".[19]

3.8   However, it was not until 1981, at the production level of 89.5 million toe, that the UK became a net exporter of crude oil.[20] That same year the UK also became a net exporter of overall energy[21] with an export surplus of 12.6 million toe of fuel.[22] The UK remained a net exporter of energy until the end of 2003 except for "the period between 1989 and 1992 when North Sea oil production dipped in the aftermath of the Piper Alpha disaster".[23] Both crude oil production and net exports of energy peaked in 1999 at approximately 137 million toe[24] and 51.5 million toe[25] respectively. They have been in decline since; and from 2004 onwards the UK became, once again, a net importer of energy (see Figure 3.1).

3.9   To say that the UK was a net exporter of energy does not mean that it was energy independent. Since the 1920s, at no point had the

---

[17] DECC Statistics, *Crude oil and petroleum products: production, imports and exports 1890 to 2008*. One tonne of oil equivalent is approximately 7.4 barrels of oil equivalent.
[18] For discussion on the Licensing Rounds, see Chapter 4.
[19] J M Bowen, "25 Years of UK North Sea Exploration", Geological Society, London, Memoirs 1991, v 14, pp 1–7 (doi: 10.1144/GSL.MEM.1991.014.01.01): http://mem. lyellcollection.org/cgi/reprint/14/1/1.pdf (accessed 3 October 2009).
[20] DECC, *Digest of United Kingdom Energy Statistics* (2009) (hereinafter "DECC, *DUKES*"), Table 3.1.1: Crude oil and petroleum products: production, imports and exports 1970 to 2008.
[21] In addition to the crude oil, it includes coal, natural gas and primary electricity. See DECC, *DUKES*, Table 1.1.2: Availability of consumption of primary fuels and equivalents (energy supplied basis) 1970 to 2008.
[22] DECC, *DUKES*, Table 1.1.3: Comparison of net imports of fuel with total consumption of primary fuels and equivalents, 1970 to 2008.
[23] Wicks, *Energy Security*, para 1.9. For discussion of the Piper Alpha disaster, see Chapter 8.
[24] DECC, *DUKES*, Table 3.1.1.
[25] *Ibid*, Table 1.1.3.

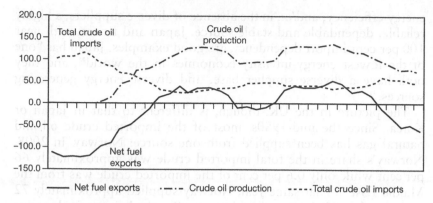

Figure 3.1 UK Net Energy Export and Crude Oil Production Levels 1970–2008

*Negative figures represent net energy imports.

Source: *DECC Statistics.*

UK reached energy self-sufficiency.[26] "It relied on imports to meet some of its coal needs and imported uranium to fuel its nuclear power stations, while the oil it consumed was traded and priced in an international market."[27] Even when it was exporting crude oil, the UK was simultaneously importing it (see Figure 3.1). This was due to the "demand by different refiners for different types of oil to North Sea crude, and to take advantage of pipeline infrastructure shared with some Norwegian fields".[28]

Nevertheless, since 2004 the share of the net fuel imports in the UK's energy consumption levels has been increasing rapidly. The UK's import dependency[29] rose from 4.5 per cent in that year to more than 26 per cent in 2008.[30] These figures, though, do not necessarily signal energy insecurity. A country can be completely reliant on imports and still not suffer from a lack of energy security. This is dependent on several things: diverse sources of energy supply; high

3.10

---

[26] Presumably this is true for the period before 1920 also, but the data is available only from 1920 onwards. See DECC Statistics, *Crude oil and petroleum products: imports by product 1920–2008.* It is important to note that "energy self-sufficiency" does not mean energy security; nor is it one of the goals of energy security.

[27] Wicks, *Energy Security,* para 1.9.

[28] *Ibid,* para 3.6. For discussion of the shared infrastructure with Norwegian fields, see Chapter 6.

[29] Calculated as the percentage ratio of net imports of fuel over gross inland consumption of primary fuels (inclusive of marine bunkers).

[30] DECC, *DUKES,* Table 1.1.3.

energy efficiency; and/or, in the absence of diverse suppliers, a highly reliable, dependable and stable source. Japan and Korea, with near 100 per cent import dependency, are good examples. Japan has "one of the lowest energy-intensity economies in the world", and they both have a diverse supplier base, and diverse energy generating sources.[31]

3.11   The picture in the UK, though, is different to that in Japan or Korea. Since the mid-1980s, most of the imported crude oil and natural gas has been supplied from one source: Norway. In 2008, Norway's share in the total imported crude was approximately 66 per cent while only 0.6 per cent of the imported crude was from the Middle East.[32] That same year, Norway supplied approximately 72 per cent of the UK's natural gas imports. Despite being a single major source for crude oil and natural gas imports, Norway is not an energy security concern. It is a reliable, dependable and stable supplier; and in addition to the geographical proximity, both countries enjoy an active bilateral relationship. Recently, the Secretary of State for the DECC and his counterpart in Norway released a Joint Ministerial Statement, agreeing to "intensify their co-operation" in carbon capture and storage (CCS);[33] in energy issues including improvements in the ultimate levels of oil recovery and further development of the "relationship between Norway as a gas supplier and the United Kingdom as an important gas consumer"; and in renewable energy.[34]

3.12   However, it should be noted that although Norway as a primary source does not in and of itself pose a threat to the UK's energy security, the concentration in the infrastructure conveying natural gas from Norway into the UK may. There are three entry points of

---

[31] For a very brief look into Japan's and Korea's energy security questions, see Wicks, *Energy Security*, Box 10: Japan, p 65; and Box 5: Republic of Korea, p 35.

[32] DECC Statistics, *Crude oil: Imports by country of origin 1938–2008*. In 2008, the remaining shares of crude oil imports were: Western Hemisphere (The Americas) 2.5%; Africa 14.7%; and Other (Rest of Europe, Far East, Russia ...) 15.8%. Until 1984, the majority of crude oil imports were from the Middle East.

[33] In simple terms CCS, as a climate change mitigation process, entails capturing carbon dioxide emissions from industry and other sources and permanently storing them in sub-seabed geological formations. In 2005, the UK's Energy Minister and Norway's Minister of Petroleum and Energy jointly established the North Sea Basin Task Force with the aims to "develop broad common principles that could form the basis for regulating the storage of CO_2 in the North Sea and to provide a consistent basis for managing this activity". For further information on the Task Force, see http://www.nsbtf.org (accessed 4 May 2010).

[34] Norwegian Ministry of Petroleum and Energy and DECC, *One North Sea: Joint Ministerial Statement on Climate Change and Energy Security* (Bergen, Norway, 28 May 2009).

Norwegian gas: the Vesterlad pipeline, the Tampen Link pipeline[35] – both of which deliver gas to St Fergus in Scotland – and the Langeled pipeline received at Easington in England.[36] Any prolonged disruptions to these three pipelines, or to the two receiving terminals, could potentially cause a considerable natural gas shortage.[37]

The UK has also been improving its energy efficiency. Its energy intensity is approximately 43 per cent that of the 1970 level. In 1970, the UK was consuming 389.5 toe per £1 million of gross domestic product (GDP). That number was successfully reduced to 169.1 toe by 2008.[38]   **3.13**

In terms of energy exports, the UK is heavily reliant on EU-based customers. In 2008, approximately 73 per cent of the total crude oil exports were destined for EU consumers. Within the EU the distribution of crude oil exports was not homogenous. With approximately 40 per cent, the Netherlands and, with approximately 38 per cent, Germany received the biggest share of the crude oil exported from the UK into the EU. The remaining non-EU crude oil exports were predominantly exported to the USA.[39] Similarly, in 2008, the UK's natural gas exports were almost exclusively to the EU.[40] Again, the EU being the sole customer in itself does not constitute an energy security concern. The EU, especially the Netherlands, Germany and the Republic of Ireland, have been, and still are, reliable, dependable and stable customers.   **3.14**

---

[35] Tampen Link ties into the UK's FLAGS system.

[36] The entire gas transport system within, and from, the Norwegian sector of the Continental Shelf has been under the operatorship of Gassco since 2002. Established in mid-2001, Gassco is a wholly state owned company: http://.gassco.no/wps/wcm/connect/Gassco-EN/gassco/Home (accessed 4 May 2010).

[37] This is not beyond the realm of possibility either. In February 2010, there was a serious risk of a strike at Milford Haven Port Authority which was eventually called off in mid-March: http://www.mhpa.co.uk/content.asp?article_id=2248 (accessed 4 May 2010). As the home to two brand new LNG terminals, and as a supplier of 25% of the UK's refined petroleum products, it was widely believed that a strike at Milford Haven could disrupt oil and gas supply to the UK. See J Guthrie, "Port strike risks oil and gas disruption", *Financial Times*, 16 February 2010. Similar action at either St Fergus or Easington could also have serious disruptive effects.

[38] DECC, *DUKES*, Table 1.1.4: Primary energy consumption, gross domestic product and the energy ratio 1970 to 2008.

[39] *Ibid*, Table G.4: Imports and exports of crude oil by country.

[40] 49% Republic of Ireland; 41% through the Bacton–Zeebrugge Interconnector, Belgium; 9.4% Netherlands; and the remaining exported to Norway for injection into the Ula reservoir (DECC, *DUKES*, Table G.6: Physical imports and exports of gas, 1997 to 2008).

THE INTERNATIONAL DIMENSION OF THE UK'S ENERGY SECURITY

International Energy Agency

3.15   The impact of international law on the UK's energy security was first felt in the aftermath of the oil embargo imposed by the Arab members of OPEC on states supporting Israel in the Fourth Arab–Israeli War in 1973. The energy crisis provoked by this embargo prompted collective action on the part of consumer countries. The industrialised nations in Europe, North America and the Far East were already joined together under the umbrella of the Organization for Economic Co-operation and Development (OECD). Established in December 1960,[41] the OECD provided a platform for the industrialised nations[42] to compare and co-ordinate policies predominantly on economic and development issues.[43] It was, however, deemed to be "wholly inadequate for the management of the risks of more troublesome hardships in the future",[44] including oil supply disruptions. On the other hand, it proved to have an adequate structure for establishing a permanent international body within the Organization that could manage risks sufficiently. On 18 November 1974, therefore, the member countries signed an international treaty, the Agreement on an International Energy Program (IEP Agreement), establishing the International Energy Agency (IEA).[45] The Agency

---

[41] Convention on the Organization for Economic Co-operation and Development, Paris, 14 December 1960.

[42] The initial signatories on 14 December 1960 were Austria, Belgium, Canada, Denmark, France, Germany, Greece, Iceland, Ireland, Italy, Luxembourg, Netherlands, Norway, Portugal, Spain, Sweden, Switzerland, Turkey, the UK and the US. Since then the following ten countries have joined the organization: Australia, Czech Republic, Finland, Hungary, Japan, Korea, Mexico, New Zealand, Poland, and Slovak Republic.

[43] OECD, *About OECD: Our Mission*, http://www.oecd.org/pages/0,3417, en_36734052 _36734103_1_1_1_1_1,00.html (accessed 4 May 2010).

[44] R Scott, *The History of the International Energy Agency Volume 1: Origins and Structure* (1994, OECD), http://www.iea.org/textbase/nppdf/free/1990/1-ieahistory.pdf, pp 29–30 (accessed 4 May 2010) (hereinafter "Scott, *History of the IEA(1)*"). For the OECD's response to the 1973–4 oil crisis, see pp 33–38 of the same volume.

[45] Scott, *History of the IEA (1)*, p 20. "Although the Program could have been adopted with binding effect in the Council Decision, the treaty form was thought to provide advantages flowing from parliamentary commitment, and from the treaty's formality, visibility and fully independent legal standing.": *ibid*, p 55. For the establishment of the IEA, see Agreement on an International Energy Program (as amended 25 September 2008) (hereinafter "IEP Agreement"), Art 1, read together with Chapter IX. Initially, only the 16 members of the OECD signed the IEP Agreement. These were Austria, Belgium, Canada, Denmark, Germany, Ireland, Italy, Japan, Luxembourg, Netherlands, Spain, Sweden, Switzerland, Turkey, the UK and the US. Currently, all the OECD Member States with the exception of Iceland and Mexico are members of the International Energy Agency.

was established under the OECD because it was "regarded as being fully in harmony with the OECD Convention and traditions".

> "There was an expectation that the Agency would also contribute a dynamic element to the Organisation and that the other bodies of the OECD would gain from close association with the work of the Agency, which in turn would benefit from its close association with the OECD. The establishment of the IEA would reduce neither the general co-operative efforts within the OECD nor the work of its various bodies on energy policies and related questions."[46]

3.16 The IEP Agreement obliged the members to hold emergency reserves equivalent to, first, 60 days of oil consumption levels,[47] then, from 1975 onwards, 90 days of consumption levels.[48] Despite this stock holding requirement, however, during the 1973–74 crisis the Participating Countries' stock levels were "standing only at about a seventy day supply".[49] This crisis clearly demonstrated the inadequate preparation for a serious supply disruption. "Their failure to co-ordinate the use of their stocks during the course of the crisis was a further failure of organization which weakened their response."[50] This organisational failure was probably why the IEP Agreement also established further response measures based on the co-operation of the Participating Countries.[51]

3.17 Under these additional response measures, the emergency "demand restraint" provisions[52] obliged the Participating Countries to have individual contingency plans to reduce consumption. When, as a group, the Participating Countries could "sustain" a reduction of certain levels "in the daily rate of its oil supplies", the IEP Agreement provided that they should each implement these contingency measures to reduce their "final consumption". If that sustainable reduction level in oil supplies reached 7 per cent of the "average daily rate of [the group's] final consumption" then each Country had to reduce its own final consumption by 7 per cent.[53] However, if a 12 per cent reduction level could be sustainable, each

---

[46] Scott, *History of the IEA (1)*, p 52.
[47] IEP Agreement, Art 2(1).
[48] *Ibid*, Art 2(2).
[49] Scott, *History of the IEA (1)*, p 37.
[50] *Ibid*.
[51] Participating Countries are defined as "States to which [the IEP Agreement] applies provisionally and States for which the Agreement has entered into and remains in force" (IEP Agreement, Art 1).
[52] IEP Agreement, Art 5.
[53] *Ibid*, Art 13.

Participating Country had to reduce its own final consumption by 10 per cent only. These limited levels of final consumption were referred to as "permissible consumption".[54]

3.18   Together with the emergency demand restraint measures, the IEP Agreement also provided allocation measures for available oil.[55] While these allocation measures used the same trigger levels as the demand restraint measures, ie 7 per cent and 12 per cent, the Agreement additionally provided that if the reduction in any Participating Country's final consumption levels were more than 7 per cent, then the available oil had to be allocated to that Country.[56] A Participating Country consequently had an "allocation obligation" if, during an emergency, its total available oil reserves[57] were more than its supply right.[58] Similarly, a Participating Country had an "allocation right" if its total available oil reserves were less than its supply right.[59] In simple terms, therefore, the group's aggregate available oil supply was allocated among Participating Countries based on a specific calculation mechanism aiming for an equitable distribution.

3.19   These emergency response measures were tested during the 1979–81 oil crisis that began with the political turmoil in Iran.[60] Even though this crisis "caused severe economic damage to the IEA countries",[61] "at no point had the supply loss approached 7 per cent for the IEA group as a whole";[62] thus, it failed to trigger the emergency response mechanism. The crisis demonstrated clearly that supply disruptions below the 7 per cent benchmark could also have serious consequences. The IEA, therefore, introduced

---

[54] IEP Agreement, Art 7(4).

[55] *Ibid*, Chap III.

[56] *Ibid*, Art 17(1), read together with Art 8.

[57] Defined as the sum of normal domestic production and actual net imports available.

[58] IEP Agreement, Art 7(3). "Supply right" is defined as the remaining level of permissible consumption after the emergency reserve drawdown obligation is subtracted. The emergency reserve drawdown is calculated by dividing the emergency reserve commitment (90-day consumption level) by the total emergency reserve level of the group and then multiplying it by the group supply shortfall.

[59] IEP Agreement, Art 7(2).

[60] The events surrounding the Iranian revolution and the Iran–Iraq War are beyond the scope of this chapter. For further information on the IEA's response to the oil crisis, see R Scott, *The History of the International Energy Agency Volume 2: Major Policies and Actions* (1994, OECD), http://www.iea.org/Textbase/publications/free_new_Desc.asp?PUBS_ID=1185, pp 114–32 (hereinafter "Scott, *History of the IEA (2)*") (accessed 4 May 2010).

[61] Scott, *History of the IEA (2)*, p 114.

[62] *Ibid*, p 119. Although the 7% limit was reached temporarily for some of the Participating Countries, it was never the case for the group as a whole.

in 1984[63] an additional set of measures called the Co-ordinated Emergency Response Measures (CERM) to complement the existing mechanism. While the allocation regime "was designed to ensure activation by virtue of an *administrative* rather than a prior *political* decision", the CERM required a "political decision".[64] The CERM were employed only once, during the 1990–91 Gulf Crisis. As a response to the invasion of Kuwait by Iraq, the United Nations embargoed all the oil exports from those two countries, resulting in a loss of 4.3 million barrels per day to the global market.[65] With the additional expected disruption to the oil supply due to a military campaign and the uncertainty surrounding the reaction of Arab oil producers, the IEA issued a formal notice on 17 January 1991 for the Member States "to activate the Co-ordinated Energy Emergency Response Contingency Plan to make available to the market 2.5 million additional barrels of oil per day within 15 days' time".[66]

Initially the CERM were being implemented for disruptions below the 7 per cent threshold. From 1995 onwards, however, the IEA Governing Board decided that CERM could be implemented even for the supply disruptions above that benchmark.[67] Today, the CERM are considered together with other emergency measures.[68]   3.20

Energy Charter Treaty

The emergency response measures were not the only method developed by the industrialised consumer nations in coping with   3.21

---

[63] IEA, *Decision on Stocks and Supply Disruptions*, 11 July 1984, IEA/GB(84)27, Item 2(a)(ii), Annex 1 and Appendices.

[64] Scott, *History of the IEA (2)*, p 128.

[65] *Ibid*, pp 133–134. Note that approximately "two-thirds of that loss directly affected IEA countries".

[66] *Ibid*, p 134. "Two million barrels were to come from participants' oil stocks, 400,000 barrels from demand restraint measures designed to reduce oil consumption, and 100,000 barrels from fuel switching out of oil and the use of spare capacity."

[67] IEA, *About IEA: Directorate of Energy Markets and Security (EMS): Emergency Policy Division*, http://www.iea.org/about/ems.htm (accessed 4 May 2010):

> "CERM measures were effectively used at the time of the first Gulf War (1991) when the IEA implemented a 2.5 million barrels a day contingency plan, most of which was stock draw. In September 2005, the IEA implemented a collective action, which made available to the market 60 million barrels of crude oil and oil products, in response to concerns about interruptions to oil supply as a result of the severe hurricane damage caused by Hurricanes Katrina and Rita in the US Gulf of Mexico. Most recently, IEA officials consulted closely with US Department of Energy officials in managing their response to Hurricanes Gustav and Ike in August/September 2008."

[68] Including drawdown of oil stocks, demand restraint, fuel-switching, surge oil production and the allocation of available supplies.

energy supply problems. Had it been possible during the oil crises of 1973–74 and 1979–81, diversification of the suppliers would also have reduced the impact of supply disruptions. Unfortunately, the opportunity for the OECD to diversify did not come until much later – with the collapse of the Soviet Union in 1990. In June of that year, at the meeting of the European Council in Dublin, the Prime Minister of the Netherlands suggested that "co-operation in the energy sector with the eastern European and former Soviet Union countries" would be mutually beneficial where these countries would benefit from faster economic growth and recovery while the EU would benefit from the strengthening of its energy supply security.[69] After a series of negotiations, in December 1994, the Energy Charter Treaty (ECT) and the Energy Charter Protocol on Energy Efficiency and Related Environmental Aspects were signed.[70] The Treaty was "designed to promote East–West industrial co-operation by providing legal safeguards in areas such as investment, transit and trade".[71] The purpose of the Treaty was to establish a "legal framework in order to promote a long-term co-operation in the energy field, based on complementarities and mutual benefits, in accordance with the objectives and principles of the Charter".[72] The ECT was unique in that it provided a multilateral legal framework for investment, trade and other related issues for a single sector – energy. Although "many of the Treaty's rights and obligations [were] of a 'hard law' nature, enforceable in legally binding arbitration or through GATT-type dispute resolution process",[73] there were also some soft law provisions that were not legally binding but rather left to the individual member's political will.[74]

---

[69] Europa, *Summaries of EU legislation: European Energy Charter*, under Background, 30.01.2007, http://europa.eu/legislation_summaries/energy/external_dimension_enlargement/l27028_en.htm (accessed 16 October 2009).

[70] Energy Charter Treaty (Annex 1 to the Final Act of the European Energy Charter Conference). Currently, there are 53 members to the Treaty. There are 51 countries that have either signed or acceded to the Treaty along with the European Community and Euratom.

[71] The Energy Charter Treaty and Related Documents: A Legal Framework for International Energy Cooperation, *Final Act of the European Energy Charter Conference*, II. Background.

[72] Energy Charter Treaty (Annex 1 to the Final Act of the European Energy Charter Conference), Art 2.

[73] C Bamberger, Legal Counsel of the IEA, *The Energy Charter Treaty: a description of its provisions* (January 1995), http://www.iea.org/textbase/nppdf/free/1990/charter94.pdf (accessed 4 May 2010), p 8.

[74] For example, Energy Charter Treaty, Art 19: Environmental Aspects. Article 19(2) provides that "At the request of one or more Contracting Parties, disputes concerning the application or interpretation of provisions of this Article shall, to the extent that

As the largest hydrocarbon producer in the region, the attitude 3.22
of Russia to the ECT has been crucial to its success or failure.
While the country applied the Treaty provisionally, long-standing
disagreements with the EU over a number of issues including transit
meant that it failed to ratify it. Finally, on 20 August 2009, Russia
announced that it was not going to become a party to the Treaty.
From 19 October onwards, Russia ceased to apply the Treaty provisionally.[75] Given that very little Russian gas is consumed in the UK,
this did not pose a direct, nor a significant, energy security problem
for the UK. However, the UK's "interconnection with the continent
and the geopolitical impacts of [potential] energy supply disruptions" meant that "this [was nevertheless] a UK concern too".[76] The
impact of Russia's decision on the viability of the ECT in its current
form as the most ambitious international legal instrument concerned
with energy security is very much an open question.

The UK's biggest oil and natural gas supplier, Norway, still has 3.23
not ratified the Treaty and is currently applying it provisionally.
However, because of the bilateral agreements and the traditionally
strong ties enjoyed between the two countries it is, again, of little
concern for the UK.

THE EU DIMENSION OF THE UK'S ENERGY SECURITY

While the international community at large had not taken collective 3.24
action in respect of energy security until 1973, the EEC (as it then
was) had become concerned about this issue some years earlier
following the Arab oil embargo against states supporting Israel at the
time of the Third Arab–Israeli War in 1967.[77] Directive 68/414/EEC[78]
underlined the significance of imported crude oil and petroleum
products for Europe and how "any difficulty, even temporary, having
the effect of reducing supplies of such products imported from third
States could cause serious disturbances in the economic activity of

---

arrangements for the consideration of such disputes do not exist in other appropriate
international fora, be reviewed by the Charter Conference aiming at a solution."

[75] Energy Charter Secretariat, *Russia*, http://www.encharter.org/index.php?id=414#c1338
(accessed 4 May 2010).

[76] Wicks, *Energy Security*, para 1.9. Hypothetically, in the event that Russia completely
cuts off the gas supplies to Europe, the natural gas supplies to the UK may be indirectly
disrupted as the demand in the EU for gas surges.

[77] The events surrounding the Six Day War and the oil embargo are beyond the scope of
this work. For an excellent and concise account, see D Yergin, *The Prize: The Epic Quest
For Oil, Money and Power* (1991), Chap 27.

[78] Council Directive 68/414/EEC of 20 December 1968 imposing an obligation on
Member States of the EEC to maintain minimum stocks of crude oil and/or petroleum
products [1968] OJ L308, 23.12.1968, pp 14–16.

the Community".[79] It, therefore, obliged Member States to hold stocks of "at least 65 days' average daily internal consumption".[80] This obligation was reduced by a maximum of 15 per cent for the States that had indigenous production.[81] The Governments could also individually agree among themselves – save for the Commission commenting on the drafts of those bilateral agreements prior to an agreement being reached – to hold stocks within its territory for the other, as long as the former would not restrict access to the owner of the stocks.[82] Unless there was a "particular urgency" or a need to "meet minor local needs" the only time a Member State could draw from the stocks was when "difficulties" arose, but only after a consultation with the Member States.[83] However, neither "urgency", "local needs" nor "difficulties" were defined.

3.25   The stock holding requirement was increased to 90 days with a Council Directive in 1972, "owing to changes in the pattern of oil supplies in Western Europe during [the then] recent years".[84]

3.26   The UK acceded to the EEC on 1 January 1973. On 24 July 1973 the Council issued a new Directive that introduced another set of mitigation strategies against supply disruptions.[85] In addition to the stock holding requirements it provided for restricting energy consumption. It obliged Member States to set up an authority within their jurisdictions that would not only act on these reserves in the event of a disruption, but also "impose specific or broad restrictions on consumption; … give priority to supplies of petroleum products to certain groups of users"; and "regulate prices in order to prevent abnormal price rises".[86] Additionally, the Directive provided for a group of delegates that would be working under the Commission to be consulted "in order to ensure co-ordination" of these measures.[87] These were to be in force, by way of law, regulation or adminis-

---

[79] Directive 68/414/EEC.

[80] *Ibid*, Art 1. For an excellent and concise account of stock holding obligations under the EU and the International Energy Agency, see Sanam S Haghighi, "Obligation to Hold Stocks of Crude Oil and/or Petroleum Products: The European Community and the International Energy Agency Compared", November 2007, OGEL Vol. 5, Issue 4.

[81] Directive 68/414/EEC, Art 1.

[82] *Ibid*, Art 6.

[83] *Ibid*, Art 7.

[84] Council Directive 72/425/EEC of 19 December 1972 amending the Council Directive of 20 December 1968 imposing an obligation on Member States of the EEC to maintain minimum stocks of crude oil and/or petroleum products [1972] OJ L291/154.

[85] Council Directive 73/238/EEC of 24 July 1973 on measures to mitigate the effects of difficulties in the supply of crude oil and petroleum products [1973] OJ L228/1.

[86] *Ibid*, Art 1.

[87] *Ibid*, Art 3.

trative action, within about 11 months' time – by 30 June 1974.[88]
This deadline proved to be too long as the then ongoing crisis in the
Middle East developed in October 1973 into the second Arab oil
embargo.[89]

A Council Decision in 1977 added a target-based approach to   3.27
the consumption reduction requirement.[90] Under this approach, the
Commission, after consulting the group of delegates, could impose
up to a 10 per cent reduction in the entire Community's energy
consumption for up to 2 months.[91] This approach was deemed to be
necessary "in order to safeguard the unity of the [common] market
and to ensure that all users of energy within the Community [bore]
a fair share of the difficulties arising from [a supply disruption]".[92]

By the late 1990s the European Union was actively pursuing the   3.28
goal of sourcing at least some of its energy from renewables not
only to respond to climate change concerns but also as a means of
reducing import dependency thus contributing to the security of
supply. In its White Paper[93] in 1997, the EU identified the need for
a "clear and comprehensive strategy [for renewables] accompanied
by legislative measures",[94] and set an "indicative objective" that
by 2010 12 per cent of the EU's electricity consumption had to be
from renewables.[95] These recommendations were duly accepted, and
were endorsed in Directive 2001/77/EC.[96] This Directive obliged
Member States to establish 10-year "indicative targets" which
were to be set every 5 years. These targets had to be "consistent
with the global indicative target of 12% of gross national energy
consumption by 2010 and in particular with the 22.1% indicative

---

[88] Council Directive 73/238/EEC, Art 5.

[89] It is likely that the drafters of the Directive were well aware of the developments in
the Middle East at the time. This is beyond the scope of the present chapter, but for an
excellent and concise account of the events leading up to the oil embargo of 1973 and the
aftermath, see Yergin, *Prize*, Chaps 29 and 30.

[90] Council Decision 77/706/EEC of 7 November 1977 on the setting of a Community
target for a reduction in the consumption of primary sources of energy in the event of
difficulties in the supply of crude oil and petroleum products [1977] OJ L292/9.

[91] *Ibid*, Art 1.

[92] *Ibid*, Preamble.

[93] Communication from the European Commission, *Energy for the Future: Renewable
Sources of Energy, White Paper for a Community Strategy and Action Plan*, COM(97)599
final, 26 November 1997.

[94] European Commission, *White Paper for a Community Strategy and Action Plan*, p 6.

[95] *Ibid*, s 1.3.1.

[96] Directive 2001/77/EC of the European Parliament and of the Council of 27 September
2001 on the promotion of electricity produced from renewable energy sources in the
internal electricity market [2001] OJ L283/33.

share of electricity produced from renewable energy sources in total Community electricity consumption by 2010".[97]

3.29   In 1998, the initial legislation, Directive 68/414/EEC, was amended for the second time.[98] While reiterating the minimum 90-day consumption level requirement for the stock holding obligation, the new Directive increased the percentage of reduction in this obligation for the indigenous producers to 25 per cent.[99] It also defined "difficulty" to include significant price hikes.[100] It introduced a more structured approach to the statistical calculation of the stocks[101] and to stock holding and maintenance.[102] Directive 98/93/EC also provided that the Member States would have to "ensure that fair and non-discriminatory conditions apply in [the] stockholding arrangements"; and when Member States hold stocks together they would be "jointly responsible for the obligations deriving from this Directive".[103] Consequently, in this last regard, where two or more Member States decided to hold the stocks jointly, the Directive provided for the option "to have recourse to a joint stockholding body or entity".[104] This possibility of recourse was available "in order to organise the maintenance of stocks"[105] which would ensure both that the stocks would be available and that the consumers could access them.[106] It was envisaged that within these organisational arrangements "the balance" of stocks would be "maintained by refiners and other market operators"[107] and, therefore, "partnership between the government and the industry [would be] essential to operate an efficient and reliable stock-holding mechanism".[108] The final version of this Directive was codified in 2006 as Council Directive 2006/67/EC, which is still in place.[109]

---

[97] Directive 2001/77/EC, Art 3. Note that the Directive also obliges Member States to provide every 2 years an "analysis of success in meeting the national indicative targets".

[98] Council Directive 98/93/EC of 14 December 1998 amending Directive 68/414/EEC imposing an obligation on Member States of the EEC to maintain minimum stocks of crude oil and/or petroleum products [1998] OJ L358/100.

[99] *Ibid*, Art 1(1).

[100] *Ibid*, Preamble, para 2.

[101] *Ibid*, Art 1(6) and (7).

[102] *Ibid*, Art 1(4).

[103] *Ibid*, Art 1(4)(3).

[104] *Ibid*.

[105] *Ibid*, Preamble, para 11.

[106] *Ibid*, Preamble, para 9.

[107] *Ibid*, Preamble, para 11.

[108] *Ibid*.

[109] Council Directive 2006/67/EC of 24 July 2006 imposing an obligation on Member States to maintain stocks of crude oil and/or petroleum products (Codified version) [2006] OJ L217/8.

As a member of the EU and a founding member of the IEA, the **3.30** UK has obligations under both Directive 2006/67/EC and the IEP Agreement. Even though both documents have similar provisions there are certain differences including the type and calculation of the stocks.[110] The UK implemented these obligations with the Energy Act of 1976.[111] Under this Act, the Secretary of State[112] has the authority to oblige any company that "produces, supplies or uses" crude oil or petroleum products to hold oil stocks.[113] This Act, however, does not deal with the differences in the provisions of the IEP Agreement and Directive 68/414/EEC other than providing for the Secretary of State to "prescribe" the type and the method of calculation of the stocks.[114] It should be noted that in the event of a crisis, however, the UK only employs the "full stock drawing" and not the other measures.[115]

The EU Commission, "with strong encouragement from the UK", **3.31** has also been looking into improving the openness and competitiveness of European energy markets.[116] As a result, the Council adopted the Third Internal Energy Package on 25 June 2009.[117] The package is intended to promote competition by separating transmission activities from production of gas, generation of electricity and energy supply activities.[118] With this package it is envisaged that the consumers would be protected and would enjoy the "lowest possible energy prices" by ensuring the smooth operation

---

[110] The discussion of the differences between the two documents is beyond the scope of this chapter, which only highlights the obligations for the UK. For an analysis of similarities and differences between the two documents, see Haghighi, "Obligation to Hold Stocks of Crude Oil and/or Petroleum Products", pp 11–25.

[111] Energy Act 1976 (c 76).

[112] Currently the Secretary of State for Energy and Climate Change.

[113] Energy Act 1976, s 6.

[114] *Ibid*, s 6(6).

[115] Together with the US and Japan, the UK does not restrain its demand (consumption reduction) nor employ fuel switching in the event of a crisis. Haghighi, "Obligation to Hold Stocks of Crude Oil and/or Petroleum Products", p 11.

[116] Wicks, *Energy Security*, para 5.20.

[117] Council of the European Union, "Council adopts internal energy market package", 11271/09 (Presse 191), 25 June 2009, http://consilium.europa.eu/uedocs/cms_data/docs/pressdata/en/misc/108740.pdf (accessed 18 October 2009):

"The texts of these legislative acts are set out in the following documents: the directive concerning common rules for the internal market in electricity 3648/09, 10814/09 ADD1 REV 3, the regulation on conditions for access to the network for cross-border exchanges in electricity 3651/09, 10817/09 ADD1 REV2, the regulation establishing an Agency for the Cooperation of Energy Regulators 3650/09, 10816/09 ADD1 REV1, the directive concerning common rules for the internal market in natural gas 3649/09, 10815/09 ADD1 REV1 and the regulation on conditions for access to the natural gas transmission networks 3652/09."

[118] Council of the European Union, "Council adopts internal energy market package", p 2.

of the internal market, and by enabling "the EU to achieve a more secure, competitive and sustainable energy supply".[119] It also aims to establish the Agency for the Cooperation of Energy Regulators that would "assist national regulatory authorities in exercising ... the regulatory tasks performed in the member states and, where necessary, [would] coordinate their action".[120] By providing "in great detail the objectives, duties and powers of regulatory authorities" this Agency would seek to increase consistency within the internal market. The Third Energy Package is not yet applicable, however. It will only come into force 18 months after being published in the *Official Journal* of the EU.[121]

THE DOMESTIC DIMENSION OF THE UK'S ENERGY SECURITY

3.32   While EU law in relation to the holding of oil stocks has had a significant positive impact on the energy security of Member States, it is arguably the case that a more important negative effect has been caused by EU law directed at climate change. On 23 October 2001 the European Parliament and the Council of the European Union adopted the Directive on the limitation of emissions of certain pollutants into the air from large combustion plants (Large Combustion Plants Directive – LCPD).[122] The aim was to tackle the acidification of air by reducing the emissions of acidifying pollutants, particularly sulphur dioxide (SO_2) and nitrogen oxides (NO_x).[123] In the UK, this Directive was implemented in late 2007 as the Large Combustion Plants Regulations.[124] It introduced annual emissions allowances and the procedures for the transfer of these allowances between the participating large combustion plants

---

[119] Council of the European Union, "Council adopts internal energy market package", p 2.

[120] *Ibid*, p 3.

[121] *Ibid*. Note that in July 2009 the Agency for the Cooperation of Energy Regulators was established under Regulation (EC) No 713/2009 of the European Parliament and of the Council of 13 July 2009 establishing an Agency for the Co-operation of Energy Regulators [2009] OJ L211/1. However, Arts 5–11 (ie the provisions on the various tasks of the Agency, consultation, transparency, monitoring and reporting) are not in force until after 2 March 2011. See Regulation 713/2009, Art 35(2).

[122] Directive 2001/80/EC of the European Parliament and of the Council of 23 October 2001 on the limitation of emissions of certain pollutants into the air from large combustion plants [2001] OJ L309.

[123] *Ibid*, p 1.

[124] Large Combustion Plants (National Emission Reduction Plan) Regulations 2007 (SI 2007/2325).

(LCPs).[125] Ninety-four existing[126] and operational LCPs "opted for the [National Emissions Reduction Plan]".[127]

However, ultimately the emission reductions meant plant closures. **3.33** Nine coal or oil fired plants with a combined electricity generating capacity of 12GW have already opted out of the LCPD and their operation will have to cease before 2016.[128] "More plant closure decisions may have to be taken as a result of the Industrial Emissions Directive currently under negotiation within the European Union."[129] Additionally, there are 10 nuclear plants with a total capacity of 10.3GW whose operating lives are expected to expire between 2010 and 2035.[130] The concerns over energy security relevant to the implementation of the LCPD and the associated plant closures were raised in the 2009 Economic Report of Oil & Gas UK:

> "As far as security of supply is concerned, the biggest concern is power generation. There are so many coal (plus the few remaining oil) fired and nuclear power stations to be closed in the next 15 years, on account of both age and more stringent emissions' limits (NO_x and SO_x) [due to the LCPD], that it has been estimated that replacement of this generating capacity with a mixture of coal and gas fired nuclear power stations will require some £30 billion of investment by mid-2020s. Taking account of the target for renewable energy supplies in 2020, however, will raise this already very large sum to of the order of £100 billion."[131]

Due to the Large Combustion Plants Directive there will be many **3.34** plant closures in the near future. In 2003, the Director of the

---

[125] Large Combustion Plants (National Emission Reduction Plan) Regulations 2007, reg 8.

[126] Defined as "any combustion plant for which the original construction licence or, in the absence of such a procedure, the original operating licence was granted before 1 July 1987": Directive 2001/80/EC, Art 2(10).

[127] The Environment Agency, *National Emissions Reduction Plan (NERP)*, 2 October 2009, http://www.environment-agency.gov.uk/business/topics/pollution/32230.aspx (accessed 4 May 2010). For more information on the individual plants and emission limits, see Annex A, Combined approach under the common stack: http://www.environment-agency.gov.uk/static/documents/Business/lcpd_1913495.pdf (accessed 4 May 2010).

[128] Directive 2001/80/EC, Art 4, para 4(a) gives the option for the plants to exclude themselves from complying with the Directive's obligations if they agree to shut down either after 20,000 hours of operation or by 31 December 2015. Consequently these nine plants will have to either close by that date or "after 20,000 hours of operation (of part or all of the plant) from 1 January 2008, whichever is sooner". See DECC, *Electricity Generating Plant Closures*, available at http://www.berr.gov.uk/files/file49437.pdf (accessed 4 May 2010).

[129] DECC, *Electricity Generating Plant Closures*.

[130] In 2008, the 0.47GW capacity Oldbury NPP was expected to shut down, but is still operational at the time of writing.

[131] Oil & Gas UK, *2009 Economic Report* (July 2009), Chap 4, "Security of Energy Supplies", p 15.

Institution of Civil Engineers revealed that the energy deficiency created by these closures will not be mitigated by renewable energy; instead "the outstanding balance will have to be replaced by gas-fired power stations, importing 90 per cent of their fuel".[132] In 2009, the Wicks Report reiterated this, stating that as "the cheapest and quickest technology", gas-fired power stations will "replace" these closing coal and nuclear powered plants, which would mean the UK "would potentially be locking-in import-dependence at an uncomfortable level."[133]

The UK as an energy producer

3.35 To reduce this import-dependency, therefore, the UK needs to maximise its indigenous production. In order to maximise the production, the Government needs to provide incentives necessary to attract enough investment.

3.36 One of the main incentive mechanisms the Government employs is the fiscal arrangements. On 21 July 2009, the Finance Act 2009 introduced certain fiscal incentives, including a "field allowance", targeting the "smaller oil and gas fields" that are "comprised of heavy oil and high pressure/high temperature fields" which are "facing the greatest challenges within the UKCS".[134] However, it has been argued that the allowance is too limited in its scope[135] and that the new fiscal arrangement ought to be "supplemented by further changes to the tax regime supporting exploration and production to maximize investment and production levels".[136] With these criticisms in mind, the Budget in March 2010 extended the field allowance "to support the development of remote deep water gas fields as found in the

[132] Institution of Civil Engineers, "Short-sighted energy planning threatens bleak future", Press Release, 1 July 2003: http://www.ice.org.uk/knowledge/newsdetail_ice.asp?PressID =238&NewsType=Press&FacultyID=3 (accessed 4 May 2010).

[133] Wicks, Energy Security, para 6.32.

[134] HM Treasury, Finance Bill 2009: Explanatory Note: Clause 89, Schedule 44: Supplementary Charge: Reduction for Certain New Oil Fields, under "Background Note", para 19. Discussion of the Finance Act 2009 is beyond the scope of this work. For further discussion on the fiscal incentives under this Act, see Emre Üsenmez, The Stability of the UK Tax Regime for Offshore Oil and Gas: Positive Developments and Potential Threats, [2010] 1(21) ICCLR.

[135] Energy and Climate Change Committee, UK Offshore Oil and Gas, First Report of Session 2008–09, Vol II: Oral and Written Evidence (17 June 2009), Ev 55, para 9.

[136] Wicks, Energy Security, para 6.34.

West of Shetland area".[137] This extension of field allowance was largely welcomed by the industry.[138]

The UK has also been seeking ways to encourage exploration and production activities in those areas lying to the West of the Shetlands and Hebrides. Potentially 3–4 billion boe, and "some 10 to 15% of remaining UK gas reserves" are estimated to be located there.[139] In recognition of this potential, in 2004 a new set of licences, "frontier licences", were created specifically for these areas with a set of incentives including a 90 per cent reduction in area rental charges.[140] However, the lack of infrastructure[141] has been the main deterrent to large investment, and almost all of "the discoveries made to date [have not been] of a scale to justify the necessary infrastructure on their own".[142] In order to assess and suggest solutions to this problem the Government established the West of Shetlands Task Force in 2006 as a joint Government–industry initiative.[143] The Task Force has been aiming to "find a technical and economic solution which will allow for infrastructure (pipelines) to be put in place that could allow the development and exploration of this area".[144] This was a very encouraging development and it has been argued that the Government should continue to strengthen its dialogue with the industry and further support the work of the Task Force. Development of this area is deemed vital in realising the full potential of the UKCS. The Government has been called to "stand ready to play a catalytic role in bringing together the interests necessary for

3.37

---

[137] HM Treasury, *Budget 2010: Securing the recovery* (24 March 2010), Chap 4: "Supporting Business and Growth", para 4.53.
[138] Oil & Gas UK, "Extension of New Field Allowance to Frontier Area will promote Investment, says Oil & Gas UK" (27 January 2010), available at: http://www.oilandgasuk. co.uk/news/news.cfm/newsid/474 (accessed 4 May 2010).
[139] Energy and Climate Change Committee, *UK Offshore Oil and Gas*, First Report of Session 2008–09, Vol II: Oral and Written Evidence (17 June 2009), Ev 69, para 25.
[140] Initially the model clauses for the Frontier Licences were in the Petroleum Licensing (Exploration and Production) (Seaward and Landward Areas) Regulations 2004 (SI 2004/352), Sch 2. However, for the licences issued after 6 April 2008, these model clauses are no longer applicable. Instead the new model clauses are to be found in the Petroleum Licensing (Production) (Seaward Areas) Regulations 2008 (SI 2008/225). For further discussion of frontier licences and licences in general, see Chapter 4.
[141] The area is around 400 km from the nearest gas terminal.
[142] Energy and Climate Change Committee, *UK Offshore Oil and Gas*, First Report of Session 2008–09, Vol I: Report, together with formal minutes (17 June 2009), para 83.
[143] *Ibid*, para 84.
[144] Department of Energy and Climate Change, *Oil and Gas: West of Shetlands Task Force*, https://www.og.decc.gov.uk/UKpromote/wos_task.htm (accessed 4 May 2010). See also, Dong Energy, *West of Shetlands Task Force*, http://www.dongenergy.co.uk/e_and_p/ development/pages/task_force.aspx (accessed 4 May 2010).

its further development, including an adequate gas transportation capacity".[145]

3.38   These calls, however, seem to have been heard. Some recent developments in West of Shetlands attest to the positive synergy between Government and the industry. First, HM Treasury's extension of the field allowance to the gas developments in this region is found to be "most encouraging".[146] Then recently, Total E&P UK Limited announced the go-ahead for the development of its West of Shetland fields, Laggan and Tormore.[147] As part of the project Total will construct "almost immediately" the associated infrastructure that includes some 140 km of gas pipeline to the Shetland Islands, a gas processing plant at Sullom Voe on Shetland and a 230-km export pipeline from Shetland that will be tied into the existing Frigg UK line.[148]

3.39   On 19 March 2010, when the DECC gave its consent for the development of this project, Lord Hunt, the Energy Minister, emphasised the importance of this infrastructure "for the wider development of the West of Shetland area" and for maintaining "secure energy supplies"; while Lord Mandelson, the Business Secretary, pointed to the impact of the recent fiscal incentives: "[t]he recent initiative by the Treasury in extending Field Allowance to such fields [that is, Laggan and Tormore] has been particularly important."[149] The industry representative, Oil & Gas UK, shared the sentiment:

"[this project] will stimulate exploration as it will enhance the viability of future discoveries in this frontier area. This can only lead to greater recovery of the UK's oil and gas resource. This move further underlines the importance of domestic oil and gas in [the UK's] energy supply. It's a positive example of what can be achieved by industry and Government working together to deliver the maximum recovery of the nation's oil and gas reserves."[150]

---

[145] Wicks, *Energy Security*, Recommendations: point 2, p 112.
[146] D Odling, "Storage is not the whole answer", *Wireline*, Issue 12, Oil & Gas UK, March 2010, p 5.
[147] Total News Release, "United Kingdom: Total launches the development of the Laggan and Tormore gas fields", 17 March 2010, available at: http://www.laggan-tormore.com/pdf/LagganTormore.pdf (accessed 4 May 2010).
[148] Total News Release, "United Kingdom: Total launches the development of the Laggan and Tormore gas fields". For the map of the planned associated infrastructure, see Total, *Laggan Tormore Pipelines Overview*, available at: http://www.uk.total.com/activities/images/pipelines.jpg (accessed 4 May 2010).
[149] DECC, "Go-ahead given for gas development West of Shetland", Press Release, 19 March 2010, available at: http://www.decc.gov.uk/en/content/cms/news/pn10_046/pn10_046.aspx (accessed 4 May 2010).
[150] Oil & Gas UK, "Government Approval for Gas Development West of Shetland will Help Secure UK Energy Supply, says Oil & Gas UK", Press Release, 19 March 2010:

Thanks to the steady rise in the oil price and to declining costs, it is 3.40
forecast that in 2010 the activity levels in the UKCS will increase,[151]
but the "investment will remain at levels similar to 2009, at about
£205 billion, down from a five-year peak of £234 billion in 2008".[152]
One of the main investment difficulties for the oil and gas companies
is the access to equity and credit. This difficulty is compounded by
the recent crisis in the banking sector. There is only a single UK
bank, the newly merged Lloyds/HBOS, which is still lending in
the North Sea.[153] Even in this "monopoly of lending", the Oil and
Gas Independents' Association (OGIA)[154] says, the "door would be
closed" for the new players in need of borrowing.[155] Those who can
borrow, however, are also facing increased borrowing costs, despite
the falling interest rates, due to the increase in the banks' up-front
fees.[156]

One other area the oil and gas companies, particularly the smaller 3.41
independents, are having difficulty in is access to infrastructure.[157]
For a field that is economical enough to produce but not large
enough to justify its own infrastructure, access to existing infrastructure is fundamental. The OGIA argues that the infrastructure
owners can have "disproportionate" demands "by creating delay or
offering inappropriate tariffs and liabilities in relation to the risks
they take"; and that the existing remedial arrangements are failing

---

available at http://www.oilandgasuk.co.uk/news/news.cfm/newsid/487 (accessed 4 May
2010).
[151] Martin Kelly interview, available at Wood Mackenzie, *Highlights: A Return to
Investment in the UK in 2010*, 2009, Wood Mackenzie http://www.woodmacresearch.
com/cgi-bin/wmprod/portal/energy/highlightsDetail.jsp?oid=1600266 (accessed 18
October 2009).
[152] D Telfer, "Oil investment warning to UK government: Woodmac says attractive fiscal
climate needed to make most of reserves", *The Press and Journal Energy Supplement*, 16
October 2009: http://energy.pressandjournal.co.uk/Article.aspx/1441693/ (accessed 18
October 2009).
[153] RBS withdrew from financing projects in the North Sea. See Energy and Climate
Change Committee, *UK Offshore Oil and Gas*, First Report of Session 2008–09, Vol II:
Oral and Written Evidence (17 June 2009), Ev 103, para 4.1.
[154] The OGIA is a self-help group of 34 oil companies active in the UKCS. For further
information, see http://www.ogia.co.uk/ (accessed 4 May 2010).
[155] Energy and Climate Change Committee, *UK Offshore Oil and Gas*, First Report of
Session 2008–09, Vol II: Oral and Written Evidence (17 June 2009), Oral Evidence: Taken
before the Energy and Climate Change Committee on Wednesday 11 March 2009, Q32–
Q33. Please note that in addition to Lloyds/HBOS "there may be few French banks" that
also lend in the North Sea.
[156] Energy and Climate Change Committee, *UK Offshore Oil and Gas*, First Report of
Session 2008–09, Vol II: Oral and Written Evidence (17 June 2009), Oral Evidence: Taken
before the Energy and Climate Change Committee on Wednesday 11 March 2009, Q34.
[157] Discussion on access to infrastructure is beyond the scope of this chapter: see
Chapter 7.

to make "any significant differences and many bad behaviours and practices still remain" in the North Sea.[158]

The UK as an energy consumer

3.42   It is evident that the only short-term viable option for replacing the energy loss that will come about from the planned plant closures is the building of replacement gas-fired plants. The UK, however, is import-dependent in terms of gas, supplied predominantly by Norway. The UK, therefore, first and foremost needs to maintain its good bilateral relationship with Norway to preserve its "attractive customer" status. In addition to the mature infrastructure between the two countries, the UK's liberal and transparent market and the "ease with which gas could be exported from the UK to continental Europe" are the main reasons why Norway finds the UK attractive.[159] There have accordingly been calls for the UK to continue to preserve the liberal structure of its gas market, and ensure that its regulatory system is "stable to enable partners to make strategic commitments to the UK market".[160]

3.43   This is also why the proper implementation of the EU's Third Energy Package is very important for the UK. If the gas markets are not homogenously liberalised throughout the EU, there is the risk of the UK having access to the gas markets of some of the other EU member states on less favourable terms than those the UK provides. This might result in gas flowing "out of the UK to states with less open markets than [the UK's] in the event of a crisis or a supply shortage".[161]

3.44   Despite the relative security of Norway as a natural gas supplier, the limited number of receiving terminals increases the potential for disruptions. The increase in the UK's liquefied natural gas (LNG)

---

[158] Energy and Climate Change Committee, *UK Offshore Oil and Gas*, First Report of Session 2008–09, Vol II: Oral and Written Evidence (17 June 2009), Ev 102, para 1.3.2. These difficulties faced by the small independents and the potential remedies in place are discussed in Chapter 7.

[159] Wicks, *Energy Security*, para 5.40.

[160] *Ibid.*

[161] Wicks, *Energy Security*, para 5.20. In fact this happened in early January 2009 following the payment dispute over gas imports between Russia and Ukraine, or the "Russian gas crisis" as it was called at the time, when traders diverted natural gas to cover the gas shortage in continental Europe. "[T]raders switched from importing to exporting gas through an interconnector pipeline [from the UK] to continental Europe as a growing row between Russia and Ukraine left many countries short of supplies." Terry Macalister, "Russian gas crisis to keep bills high as firms divert UK stocks", *The Guardian*, 8 January 2009.

infrastructure is therefore a welcome step in diversifying its natural gas suppliers.[162] "For geographic reasons, the UK draws most of its gas from the Atlantic Basin and from the Middle East."[163] It has imported at one time, or still imports, LNG from Algeria, Egypt, Qatar and Trinidad & Tobago.[164] Strengthening the ties with these countries would therefore be beneficial. The UK is already enjoying a strong relationship with Qatar, the largest supplier of LNG in the world.[165] Qatargas is rapidly expanding its fleet and its production to meet the rising global LNG demand.[166] "Yet, with their geographical position enabling Qatar to supply both Asia and Europe with gas, the UK will face increasing competition for Qatari supplies." There exists for the UK an opportunity to build on its good relationship and strengthen its political and commercial ties in order to get the "Qataris to commit to supply to the UK".[167]

On the other hand, because of an increased competition for Qatari LNG supply on the horizon, there would also be an opportunity to tap into other markets as well. There are new and significant developments in West Africa, particularly in Sierra Leone, Liberia, Côte d'Ivoire, São Tomé and Príncipe and Ghana, but also in more established producers like Nigeria, Angola and Gabon.[168] By entering into a bilateral or regional dialogue with these West African states the parties would assess the ways in which the commercial supply of natural gas can be mutually beneficial. In this regard, the UK–Nigeria Energy Working Group is a welcome development.[169] 3.45

---

[162] LNG constituted approximately 4.6% of total UK natural gas imports in 2007, which was only 0.6% of the global LNG trade in the same year. See, DECC, *DUKES*, Table 4.5, *Natural gas imports and exports*; as well as, National Grid, *Gas Transportation: Ten Year Statement 2008* (December 2008), para 4.5.1. Note that the share of LNG in total natural gas imports fluctuated from 0% in 2004 to 3.4% in 2005, 16% in 2006, 4.6% in 2007 and 2.2% in 2008 (DECC, *DUKES*, Table 4.5). However, note that even the developments in LNG should be cautiously welcomed. The potential impact of industrial action, discussed above at n 37 and associated text, needs to be considered.

[163] Wicks, *Energy Security*, para 5.46.

[164] The UK imported from Egypt and Qatar in 2006 and 2007 only: DECC, *DUKES*, Table G.6, *Physical imports and exports of gas, 1997 to 2008*.

[165] Wicks, *Energy Security*, paras 5.43–5.44.

[166] It had already commissioned eight new ships that are 80% larger than the existing fleet. It also commissioned and started the construction of four new mega LNG trains. Qatargas expects its production to increase to "42 million tonnes per annum by the end of the decade". See http://www.qatargas.com (accessed 4 May 2010).

[167] Wicks, *Energy Security*, paras 5.43–5.44.

[168] "What the latest Ghanaian discovery and Sierra Leone wildcat demonstrate is that hydrocarbon resources in the region are far richer than many ... had assumed." Press and Journal Energy Supplement, ("Hydrocarbons hunt heating up: Eyes turn to little-explored part of the West Africa sector", October 2009, p 10.)

[169] Wicks, *Energy Security*, para 5.46.

3.46   A third method that may possibly be employed in preparing for
a supply shortage is gas storage. The Energy Act 2008 provides for
a licensing regime for gas and LNG storage.[170] By simplifying and
clarifying the regulatory framework for gas storage it seeks to attract
the private sector to invest in commercial gas storage ventures.[171]
The UK currently has an existing total gas storage capacity of
4.4 billion cubic metres in six sites.[172] "This volume of storage
enables the UK to cover around 30 per cent of its maximum peak
day gas demand."[173] There are four new projects currently being
developed with a combined capacity of 1.13 billion cubic metres.[174]
An additional 4.3 billion cubic metres gas storage capacity is
potentially available in projects that either have received planning
permission and are waiting for final investment decisions, or have
applied for planning permission and are waiting for the outcome.[175]

3.47   These figures do not explain the whole picture, though. The
majority – 3.3 billion cubic metres – of the existing storage capacity
is in the Rough facility located in the Southern North Sea.[176] On
16 February 2006, there was an accidental fire on the Rough platform
which resulted in the operator Centrica declaring a *force majeure*
that lasted for about 9 months, until 20 November 2006.[177] Had
there been a disruption in the natural gas supplies to the UK during
this period, it would have left the country in a difficult position.
The additional projects that are currently under development are,
therefore, a welcome step in alleviating this vulnerability.

3.48   However, even after factoring in the future storage projects
under construction, the total capacity is still significantly lower
than comparable markets in Europe. The existing storage capacities
of Germany, Italy and France are 19.1, 12.9 and 10.8 billion

---

[170] Energy Act 2008, Chap 1: Gas Importation and Storage Zones.

[171] *Ibid*, Chap 2: Importation and Storage of Combustible Gas, read together with
Explanatory Notes, Energy Act 2008, para 17.

[172] National Grid, *Gas Transportation: Ten Year Statement 2008*, Table 4.6C, Existing
UK storage.

[173] Wicks, *Energy Security*, Box 12: UK gas storage. Note that the "maximum amount of
gas that can be delivered daily from storage stands at 130 million cubic meters".

[174] As of December 2008: National Grid, *Gas Transportation: Ten Year Statement 2008*,
Table 4.6D, Storage under development.

[175] As of December 2008: National Grid, *Gas Transportation: Ten Year Statement 2008*,
Table 4.6E, Storage with planning permission, and Table 4.6F, Storage awaiting planning
permission.

[176] As of December 2008: National Grid, *Gas Transportation: Ten Year Statement 2008*,
Table 4.6C, Existing UK storage.

[177] For all the news and press releases of Centrica on the event, see Centrica Storage,
News Releases, http://www.centrica-sl.co.uk/index.asp?pageid=22&year=2006 (accessed
4 May 2010).

cubic metres, respectively.[178] It has been suggested that one way of increasing the storage capacity "would be for the Government to contract for Strategic Storage", in a similar method to the emergency oil stock system of the IEA.[179] However, the feasibility of this proposal is debatable. The cost of storing gas is about 5 to 7 times that of "a comparable energy content of oil",[180] making it hardly an attractive proposition.

As a fourth method, the UK simultaneously needs to focus 3.49 on increasing energy efficiency in order to lower energy demand without seriously affecting consumption patterns. This was one of the priorities in the Government's plan[181] to switch to a low-carbon economy. *The UK Low Carbon Transition Plan* (the "Transition Plan") itself was the product of the Climate Change Act, which was enacted about 8 months earlier, in November 2008.[182] The Climate Change Act was a defining moment in that it set statutory targets for carbon reduction.[183] It obliged the Secretary of State not only to "ensure that the net UK" greenhouse gas emissions "for the year 2050 [were] at least 80% lower than the 1990" levels;[184] but also set emission targets, or "carbon budgets" for the UK, for 5-year "budgetary periods" from the period 2008–12 and onwards,[185] with a restriction that the "carbon budget" for the 2018–22 period must be "at least 26% lower than the 1990 baseline".[186] It also established a Committee on Climate Change to provide advice to the Secretary of State.[187]

By setting out the "UK's first ever comprehensive low carbon 3.50 transition plan to 2020",[188] the DECC's Transition Plan introduced

---

[178] As of December 2008: National Grid, *Gas Transportation: Ten Year Statement 2008*, Table 4.6H, Comparison of European Storage.

[179] Wicks, *Energy Security*, paras 6.55.

[180] *Ibid*, paras 6.56.

[181] DECC, *The UK Low Carbon Transition Plan*.

[182] Climate Change Act 2008, ss 12–14.

[183] As opposed to the indicative targets of policies.

[184] Climate Change Act 2008, s 1.

[185] *Ibid*, s 4.

[186] *Ibid*, s 5.

[187] *Ibid*, Pt 2. Section 33(3) of the Climate Change Act obliges the Climate Change Committee to publish an advisory report before 31 December 2008. This report was published as Committee on Climate Change, *Building a low-carbon economy: The UK's contribution to tackling climate change: The First Report of the Committee on Climate Change* (December 2008). The Climate Change Act 2008, s 36(1) also obliges the Committee to report on progress. This second report was published as Committee on Climate Change, *Meeting Carbon Budgets – the need for a step change: Progress report to Parliament, Committee on Climate Change* (12 October 2009). Both of these documents, however, are beyond the scope of this chapter. Environmental Law issues are discussed in Chapter 9.

[188] DECC, *The UK Low Carbon Transition Plan*, Executive Summary, p 4.

some very encouraging measures. The Plan identified that 13 per cent of all the UK's greenhouse gas emissions came from heating homes and household water,[189] 12 per cent from the energy used in workplaces,[190] 20 per cent from the transport sector,[191] and another 7 per cent from "farming and changes in land use".[192] Through the energy efficiency measures proposed,[193] by 2020 these emissions could fall by 29,[194] 13, [195] 14[196] and 13[197] per cent respectively from the 2008 levels. It provided that if all its proposals were to be implemented, the UK's gas demand could be reduced by 29 per cent in 2020.[198]

3.51   The obligation of an 80 per cent emission reduction in 1990 levels by 2050 also has a direct impact on the power sector. Coal and gas powered plants currently supply about three-quarters of the electricity consumed in the UK.[199] The Transition Plan envisages a 22 per cent cut in 2008 emission levels by 2020.[200] To achieve this, the Government intends to generate about 40 per cent of the electricity from low-carbon technologies.[201] The fifth method, perhaps more

---

[189] DECC, *The UK Low Carbon Transition Plan*, p 80.

[190] *Ibid*, p 112.

[191] *Ibid*, p 134.

[192] *Ibid*, p 152.

[193] Energy efficiency measures combined with other proposed measures. For all the measures proposed for households see DECC, *The UK Low Carbon Transition Plan*, Chap 4; the measures for workplaces are provided in DECC, *The UK Low Carbon Transition Plan*, Chap 5; the measures for the transport sector are provided in DECC, *The UK Low Carbon Transition Plan*, Chap 6; the measures for the agriculture sector and land use in general are provided in DECC, *The UK Low Carbon Transition Plan*, Chap 7.

[194] DECC, *The UK Low Carbon Transition Plan*, p 82. There has also been a recent consultation on heat and energy saving measures for the long term. See DECC, *Heat and Energy Saving Strategy Consultation*, 12 February 2009–8 May 2009: http://hes.decc.gov.uk (accessed 23 October 2009).

[195] DECC, *The UK Low Carbon Transition Plan*, p 116.

[196] *Ibid*, p 136.

[197] *Ibid*, p 155.

[198] *Ibid*, p 103.

[199] *Ibid*, p 54.

[200] *Ibid*, p 55.

[201] These technologies include "renewables, nuclear and fossil fuel fired generation fitted with carbon capture and storage technology". There is also a need for a "bigger, smarter electricity grid that is able to manage a more complex system of electricity supply and demand": DECC, *The UK Low Carbon Transition Plan*, p 54. This chapter, however, will only focus on renewables. For more information, see the following Government consultations: DECC, *Delivering secure low carbon electricity: A call for evidence* (5 August 2009–28 October 2009), http://www.decc.gov.uk/en/content/cms/consultations/electricsecure/electricsecure.aspx (accessed 4 May 2010); DECC, *Consultation on improving Grid Access* (25 August 2009–17 November 2009), http://www.decc.gov.uk/en/content/cms/consultations/improving_grid/improving_grid.aspx (accessed 4 May 2010); DECC, *Guidance on Carbon Capture Readiness and Applications under Section 36 of Electricity Act 1989: a consultation* (23 April 2009–22 June 2009), http://

as a medium- to long-term plan, therefore needs to focus on the consumption of less fossil fuel energy and more low-carbon sources.

The UK has been active in policies for diversifying its energy mix 3.52 for some time. In 2002, the Renewables Obligation Order[202] implemented Directive 2001/77/EC and set varying percentage targets for the amount of electricity to be supplied from renewables.[203] The 2002 Order has been modified, amended and revoked and re-enacted with modifications several times.[204] The most recent of them, the Renewables Obligation Order 2009,[205] set the UK's renewables obligation level for the 2009–10 period at 9.7 per cent with an increasing scale to 15.4 per cent by 2015–16.[206]

CONCLUSION

As North Sea production declines, the UK finds itself increasingly 3.53 dependent on energy imports. Since 2004, the UK has again become a net importer of energy. Today, it imports more than a quarter of its fuel consumption, predominantly from Norway. This in itself, however, does not constitute energy insecurity. Norway is a stable and a reliable supplier and there is an active bilateral relationship between the two countries further strengthened by the recent Joint Ministerial Statement. However, a strike or other disruption at one

www.dccc.gov.uk/en/content/cms/consultations/ccr_consultati/ccr_consultati.aspx (accessed 4 May 2010); DECC, *Towards a Nuclear National Policy Statement: Consultation on the Strategic Siting Assessment Process and Siting Criteria for New Nuclear Power Stations in the UK* (22 July 2008–11 November 2008), http://www.berr.gov.uk/consultations/page47143. html (accessed 4 May 2010). Also see DECC, *Nuclear white paper 2008: 'meeting the energy challenge'* (January 2008), http://www.decc.gov.uk/en/content/cms/what_we_do/uk_supply/energy_mix/nuclear/white_paper_08/white_paper_08.aspx (accessed 4 May 2010).

[202] Renewables Obligation Order 2002 (SI 2002/914).

[203] For the target levels and the time periods, see the Renewables Obligation Order 2002, Sch 1, read together with arts 3 and 6.

[204] It was modified by the Renewables Obligation Order 2004 (SI 2004/924), then revoked and re-enacted with modifications by the Renewables Obligation Order 2005 (SI 2005/926) which itself was revoked and re-enacted with modifications by the Renewables Obligation Order 2006 (SI 2006/1004), which was amended by the Renewables Obligation Order 2006 (Amendment) Order 2007 (SI 2007/1078), and which was finally revoked and re-enacted with modifications by the Renewables Obligation Order 2009 (SI 2009/785).

[205] It implements the changes provided in the Energy Act 2008, Pt 2: Electricity from Renewable Sources. (Note that this Order applies to England and Wales only.) There are complementary Orders for Scotland and Northern Ireland: the Renewables Obligation (Scotland) Order 2009 (SSI 2009/140) and the Renewables Obligation Order (Northern Ireland) 2009 (SSI 2009/154), respectively. The UK Renewables Obligation is the combination of the three.

[206] Renewables Obligation Order 2009, Sch 1.

of the limited number of entry points for Norwegian gas would be a serious concern for the UK's short-term energy security.

3.54   Similarly, the UK does not export its oil and gas to a diverse range of consumers. Its biggest oil and gas customer is the European Union. Again, the EU being the main importer does not constitute an energy security concern because the EU members are reliable and stable customers.

3.55   Given that the UK is not in isolation, a discussion on its energy security must take into account the measures also adopted by the European Union and the Organization for Economic Co-operation and Development. In response to the disruptions to the supplies from the Middle East in the late 1960s and the 1970s, the EEC obliged its members first to hold stocks to be used in emergencies, and then also to restrict their energy consumption. From the late 1990s onwards, the EU started to pursue sourcing some of its energy from renewables to respond to climate change concerns, to further reduce its import dependency and to contribute to security of supply. Finally, the European Council recently adopted the third energy package that intends to improve the openness and competitiveness of European energy markets.

3.56   Due to the same problems in the Middle East, the OECD members signed a treaty, the Agreement on an International Energy Program, in late 1974, establishing the International Energy Agency. Similar to the EU measures, the IEA obliged the Participating Countries first to hold emergency stocks, and then also to restrict their consumption. The IEA additionally introduced a stock allocation mechanism and a further set of complementary measures called the Co-ordinated Emergency Response Measures. Today, CERM are being used together with the other emergency measures including drawdown of oil stocks, demand restraint, fuel-switching, surge oil production and the allocation of available supplies. These IEA obligations, together with the EU measures, were implemented in the UK in the Energy Act of 1976.

3.57   The effects of these supply disruptions could have been less severe had the EU imported its energy from a diverse range of producers. However, the opportunity to diversify the suppliers did not come until the collapse of the Soviet Union. In 1994, the Energy Charter Treaty was signed to bring the energy co-operation between the hydrocarbon-rich former Soviet Union countries and the EU within a legal framework. Russia's recent actions, however, raise serious questions about the future of the ECT.

3.58   The UK's energy security is further affected by the issues surrounding climate change and other environmental concerns.

In order to tackle the acidification of the air, for example, the EU enacted the Large Combustion Plants Directive, which means for the UK a serious level of plant closures before the end of the next decade. The only feasible short-term solution to fill the energy gap that will be created from these closures is the construction of new gas-fired plants. This, in turn, however would mean an increase in the demand for gas which will have to be either imported or sourced domestically. This is one of the many reasons why the UKCS production needs to be maximised. The necessity for fiscal or other incentives to keep the UKCS relatively attractive for the industry appears clear.

In the meantime, maintaining good bilateral relationships with Norway and in the medium-term building stronger relationships with the traditional LNG producers would also be beneficial. In this, direct engagement, either through bilateral/regional deals or EU-level initiatives, with West African producers would provide the opportunity to tap into these emerging markets as well. The UK has the necessary technical expertise to offer in seeking ways in which the commercial supply of natural gas from this region could be mutually beneficial. **3.59**

Although significantly more expensive, the UK can assess ways to increase and diversify the current gas storage capacity. The Energy Act 2008 provides for a licensing regime for gas and LNG storage. This is a welcome development that needs to be built upon. **3.60**

Simultaneously, the UK needs to increase its energy efficiency to lower the energy demand levels. Both the Climate Change Act 2008 and the UK Low Carbon Transition Plan are also significant and welcome developments in laying the framework for increasing the energy efficiency of the UK. **3.61**

A final but very important development is the Renewables Obligation Order. As a consequence of EU Directive 2001/77, the most recent Order obliges the UK to generate about 15 per cent of its electricity from renewable sources by 2015. According to the Transition Plan, the Government expects this number to increase to 40 per cent by 2020. The measures to decrease the use of hydrocarbons in the UK's energy mix in the medium to long term is a very crucial step in tackling the UK's long-term import dependency. **3.62**

It is evident that energy security issues will be a priority on British policymakers' agenda for some time. The UK is trying to balance its energy security policies on hydrocarbon production and consumption, with its climate and environmental concerns. As the National Security Strategy suggests, the UK has **3.63**

> "an integrated strategy designed to ensure secure and reliable energy supplies; to reduce [its] vulnerability to security shocks elsewhere;

to reduce [its] contribution to tensions arising from competition for energy sources; and to tackle climate change."[207]

3.64 There is no doubt that both internationally and domestically, policies and laws have been adopted successively over the past few decades that have made a significant contribution to the multi-dimensional challenges of the UK's energy security. The unanswered question is whether the energy security architecture now in place will be sufficient for what looks to be an even more challenging future.

---

[207] UK Cabinet Office, *The National Security Strategy of the United Kingdom*, para 4.87.

CHAPTER 4

PETROLEUM LICENSING

Greg Gordon

The comparative study of petroleum laws discloses that, almost 4.1
universally,[1] a nation state will claim some manner of right to the oil
and gas deposits situated within its borders or located beneath the
Continental Shelf to the outer limit of its Exclusive Economic Zone.[2]
Such is the economic and strategic importance of oil and gas (or, more
properly, of energy-yielding minerals in general[3]) that this proposition holds true even in legal systems, such as those of Scotland and
of England and Wales, which ordinarily provide that subterranean
minerals are owned by the proprietor of the overlying land.[4] States
vary in the extent to which they become directly involved in the task
of exploiting these resources. Frequently, the state will be actively

---

[1] The major exception to this rule is the United States of America: see, eg, B Taverne,
Petroleum, Industry and Governments, (1999) (hereinafter "Taverne") at para 5.1.3.1.
In the USA, no over-arching state claim is made to oil and gas *in situ*. Licensing systems
exist, but apply only to offshore areas and onshore territory within public ownership. See
Taverne at paras 6.1.2–6.1.3.1.

[2] As determined formerly in accordance with the Convention on the Continental Shelf
done at Geneva on 29 April 158 (hereinafter the "Convention on the Continental Shelf"),
Art 1 and now by the United Nations Convention on the Law of the Sea done at Montego
Bay, Jamaica, 10 December 1982 (hereinafter "UNCLOS"), Art 57.

[3] Coal deposits are also commonly reserved to the state or at least to a public corporation:
in the UK, coal deposits in strata were vested in the Coal Corporation by the Coal Act
1938, s 3. By virtue of the Coal Industry Act 1994, s 1(1)(a) the Coal Authority is the
most recent statutory successor to the Corporation. The Atomic Energy Act 1946, ss 6 and
7 (as amended) empowers the state to search for and acquire rights to work radioactive
minerals: see Lord Mackay of Clashfern (General Editor), *Halsbury's Laws of England*,
(4th edn, 2003 Reissue) (hereinafter "*Halsbury*"), vol 19(2), paras 1192–1195.

[4] For the position in Scotland, see W Gordon and S Wortley, *Scottish Land Law*, (3rd edn,
2009) (hereinafter "Gordon and Wortley, *Scottish Land Law*"), para 5.02; for England,
see *Halsbury*, vol 31, para 363 *et seq*.

involved, commonly through the vehicle of a national oil company.[5] Sometimes, however, the state will effectively delegate this function to the private-sector oil and gas industry. Where the private sector is involved, the state needs to choose the vehicle through which its industry partners are to be involved. Some states favour a model based upon the grant of licences or concessions.[6] Others enter into contractual arrangements such as production sharing agreements or service contracts,[7] or hybrid models which involve elements of licence and contract. Whichever model is chosen, the state will expect to receive a return in the form of a share of produced hydro-carbon[8] and/or financial benefits, such as a cash premium paid in exchange for the grant of the licence,[9] rental payments in respect of the licensed area, cash royalties and/or revenue from taxation.[10] The private-sector oil industry player(s) involved will also expect to be rewarded for the work they have carried out and the risk they have undertaken.

---

[5] This approach is commonly utilised by Middle Eastern oil-producing states and in Latin America and West Africa but is not unknown in the West: see M Bunter, *The Promotion and Licensing of Petroleum Prospective Acreage* (2002) (hereinafter "Bunter, *Promotion and Licensing*") at 19–20. The UK experimented with this approach through the British National Oil Corporation which was created by s 1 of the Petroleum and Submarine Pipelines Act 1975 and which enjoyed a short period of active participation in the licensing rounds of 1976 and 1978. The election of a Conservative Government in 1979 led to a lack of political will for the enterprise: T Daintith, G Willoughby and A Hill, *United Kingdom Oil and Gas Law* (3rd edn, looseleaf, 2000–date), (hereinafter "Daintith, Willoughby and Hill") at paras 1-109 to 1-113. Norway's National Oil Company, Statoil, was founded in 1972 and although now part privatised, it continues to play an instrumental role in the development of the oil and gas industry in that province. For a detailed account, see M Thurber and B Tangen Istad, *Norway's Evolving Champion: Statoil and the Politics of State Enterprise*, Stanford University Program on Energy and Sustainable Development Working Paper 92, available online at http://iis-db.stanford.edu/pubs/22919/WP_92,_Thurber_and_Istad,_Statoil,_21May2010.pdf (accessed 25 January 2011).

[6] As we shall see throughout the remainder of this chapter, the UK is an example of such a state.

[7] A detailed treatment of such agreements is beyond the scope of this book. For an introductory account, see Taverne, Chapter 7.

[8] This is a classic feature of production sharing agreements but is not unknown in licensing regimes. For a time the UK Government inserted provisions in its petroleum licences which permitted the taking of royalty in kind: see, eg, Petroleum and Submarine Pipelines Act 1975, Sch 2, Pt II, Model Cl 11, "Delivery of petroleum instead of royalty".

[9] Cash premium bidding – which is to say, the letting of acreage to the highest bidder – is a feature of a number of licensing regimes, notably the USA: T Daintith, *Discretion in the Administration of Offshore Oil and Gas* (2006) (hereinafter "Daintith, *Discretion*") at paras 9109 and 9110. It has also been used, albeit infrequently, in the UK: see para 4.28.

[10] Various permutations of rental, royalties and sundry different forms of taxation have all been used at different times in the UKCS: see paras 4.28–4.30. For a detailed discussion of the current tax regime, see Chapter 6. For a comparative discussion on royalties and related financial payments see Daintith, *Discretion*, Chapter 9.

The UK, in common with the other Western democracies **4.2** possessing oil and gas reserves, has adopted a licensing model.[11] From rather primitive beginnings, the UK's licensing system has evolved into one of considerable complexity.[12] The main current regime[13] recognises a distinction between *seaward* and *landward* licences.[14] These categories are then subdivided: "landward" into the petroleum exploration and development licence and the supplementary seismic survey licence, and "seaward" into exploration and production licences. This latter subcategory is further subdivided into a range of variations: the traditional production licence, the frontier licence (of which there are now two variants named after the length of their initial terms – the 6-year and 9-year frontier licences), the promote licence, and the bespoke licence. We will discuss these various licences in turn after briefly introducing the legal concept of licensing and discussing the legal basis for the UK oil and gas licensing regime.

LICENSING AS A LEGAL CONCEPT

A licence is a permission that authorises an activity the conduct **4.3** of which would otherwise be unlawful. Licences take a number of forms. Many licences are best classified as "administratively granted

---

[11] The licensing approach has also been adopted by the USA, Canada and Australia. Each of these jurisdictions is discussed at length throughout Daintith, *Discretion*. Licensing systems have also been adopted by, eg, Norway (see Taverne, Chapter 6.4) and the Netherlands (see Taverne, Chapter 6.5).

[12] For an account of the evolution of the UK oil and gas licensing regime, see Daintith, Willoughby and Hill, Chapter 1; for an account of the development of the UK licensing regime prior to 1993, see also A Kemp, *Official History of North Sea Oil and Gas*, vol 1: The Growing Dominance of the State, and vol 2: Moderating the State's Role (Routledge, forthcoming).

[13] Separate licensing regimes are applied to onshore Northern Ireland (but not its territorial waters) and the Isle of Man and its territorial waters. Northern Ireland's licensing system derives from powers conveyed by the Petroleum (Production) Act (Northern Ireland) 1964 and is administered by the Devolved Executive's Department of Enterprise, Trade and Investment. Further information on the Northern Irish Licensing regime is available at http://www.detini.gov.uk/deti-energy-index/minerals-and-petroleum/petroleum_licensing_2.htm (accessed 29 January 2011). This chapter's focus is on the principal regime and although this chapter continues the general practice of referring to "United Kingdom" oil and gas licensing regime, it should be noted that no attempt will be made to describe Northern Irish or Manx law.

[14] The terms describe the areas' relative position to the low-water line, which is set by the Petroleum (Production) (Seaward Areas) Regulations 1988 (SI 1988/1213), reg 3(1), read together with Sch 1. An area lying to the seaward side of the line is a seaward area; an area lying towards the land, landward. Although commonly used throughout the industry, the terms "onshore" and "offshore" are not formally used in the licensing regime.

exemptions from legislative prohibitions".[15] Only the state, or a person to whom the state has delegated authority, can grant such licences. Most of the licences that a private individual encounters in day-to-day life,[16] as well as many commercial licences,[17] some of immense financial value,[18] fall into this category. The efficacy of such licensing systems depends upon the existence of a punitive sanction in the event that a licence is either not obtained or, if obtained, is not complied with.[19] Second, a legal entity – whether the state, a business organisation or a private individual – holding property rights may grant a licence permitting the licensee to make some kind of use of the licensor's property. The power to grant such licences stems from the legal status of ownership, not from the authority of the state. Licences to occupy land or premises are a feature of the land law of some jurisdictions.[20] Licences which stem from the licensee's status as a property owner are also commonly encountered in the context of intellectual property rights. It is not necessary, even when granted by an emanation of the state, for such licences to be fenced with a punitive sanction as the breach or non-observance of the licence's terms may result in its being terminated,[21] and a range of civil remedies ranging from damages to injunctive relief and actions of ejection will be available against any party who makes unauthorised use of the licensor's property. Landward petroleum licences are proprietary licences in the sense that they emanate from the Crown's ownership of hydrocarbon deposits *in strata*. The legal character of the seaward production licences is rather less clear: see the discussion at para 4.8.

4.4   Licences may also be *exclusive* or *non-exclusive*. It has been said that the holder of an exclusive licence has the comfort of knowing

---

[15] Daintith, Willoughby and Hill at para 1-302

[16] For instance, driving licences (Road Traffic Act 1988, s 87) and television licences (Communications Act 2003, s 363).

[17] For instance, a licence is required in order to carry on a consumer credit business: Consumer Credit Act 1974, s 21.

[18] In order to secure licences under the Wireless Telegraphy Acts to operate third-generation UK mobile telephone networks, the winning bidders in the auction process paid a combined total of more than £22 billion to the UK Government: K Binmore and P Klemperer, "The Biggest Auction Ever: the Sale of the British 3G Telecom Licences" (2002) 112 *Economic Journal*, C74.

[19] For example, operating a consumer credit business without a licence is a criminal offence (Consumer Credit Act 1974, s 39) which, if tried on indictment, may result in a guilty party being fined an unlimited sum and/or, imprisonment for up to 2 years (s 167 read with Sch 1).

[20] For the English position, see *Halsbury*, vol 27(1), paras 6–16; for the position in Scots law, see Gordon and Wortley, *Scottish Land Law* at para 18-17.

[21] It is however *possible* to do this: consider, for example, the various offences contained in Chapter 6 of the Copyright, Designs and Patents Act 1988.

that "so long as the licence is valid, no person other than the licensee itself is authorised to exercise the rights conferred".[22] However, as a matter of property law this is not strictly correct. As a licence confers no real right,[23] an exclusive licence confers on the licensee only a personal right to preclude the granter from issuing further licences in respect of the same geographic area. In so far as a petroleum production licence is contractual,[24] the Minister would be in breach of contract if he were to grant a second licence; however, that licence would be valid, albeit voidable. By contrast, a non-exclusive licence holder is merely one of a number of persons who may have received concurrent permissions from the licensor. As we shall see, production licences (whether landward or seaward) are exclusive in nature. Exploration licences are non-exclusive.

It is also worth noting here that while licences grant rights to   **4.5** licensees, they do not operate to take away the pre-existing rights of third parties. Given the legal status of the Continental Shelf, this is of little consequence outside the territorial sea. However, within territorial waters, rights of private property may very well exist. Thus, in addition to a statutory licence, grants of rights may also be needed from parties such as landowners or salmon fishers in coastal waters.[25]

THE LEGAL BASIS FOR THE UK OIL AND LICENSING REGIME

Domestic law

The law's evolution
Early UK oil and gas licences issued in accordance with the   **4.6** provisions of the Petroleum (Production) Act 1918 were of the administrative exemption type. The 1918 Act avoided the then-contentious question of who owned oil and gas deposits *in situ* by providing that only those holding a licence from His Majesty could "search or bore for or get" petroleum. Section 1(1) of the 1918 Act provided that anyone undertaking such works without authority would forfeit any petroleum so obtained and in addition pay a penalty of three times its value.

The Petroleum (Production) Act 1934 fundamentally altered the   **4.7** nature of the British petroleum licence.[26] Section 1(1) of the 1934

---

[22] Taverne at para 5.2.1

[23] For a discussion of what is meant by a "real right", see para 18.6.

[24] See further the discussion at paras 4.12–4.13.

[25] See para 18.1.

[26] The Act was introduced as the Government claimed that petroleum exploration activities had been unduly hampered by the deficiencies of the earlier legislation: Daintith, Willoughby and Hill, para 1-104. See also *Star Energy Weald Basin Ltd* v *Bocardo SA* [2010] UKSC 35, [2010] 3 WLR 654 at para 90 per Lord Brown.

Act expressly vested "property in petroleum, existing in its natural condition in strata in Great Britain"[27] in the Crown, and stated that the Crown held "the exclusive right of searching and boring for and getting such petroleum". The 1934 Act did not provide for penalties in the event of breach but, as the owner of petroleum *in situ*, the Crown would be in a position to take action to prevent any attempt at expropriation, or seek compensation therefor.[28]

4.8   The realisation in the late 1950s that geological formations associated with the Groningen gas field in the Netherlands might extend into the Continental Shelf underlying the North Sea[29] prompted the UK, in common with other North Sea coastal states, to promulgate a legal framework authorising the exploration for, and production of, petroleum.[30] The UK did this by exporting the existing but largely untested landward licensing regime into the seaward UKCS. Section 1(1) of the Continental Shelf Act 1964 vested in the Crown "any rights exercisable by the United Kingdom outside territorial waters with respect to the sea-bed and subsoil and their natural resources", except coal.[31] Section 1(3) of the 1964 Act applied most of the key licensing provisions[32] of the 1934 Act to the UKCS. However, s 1 of the 1934 Act (vesting of property in petroleum *in strata*) was not so applied as international law conveyed upon the state only a "sovereign right"[33] to exploit natural resources, not a right of full ownership.[34] The British approach is consistent with that taken by certain other coastal states.[35] However,

---

[27] Ie the land mass comprising England, Scotland Wales and the territorial seas appertaining thereto.

[28] See the discussion at para 4.3.

[29] Taverne: see the note appended to para 6.5.1 at the foot of p 238.

[30] For example, the Netherlands (on which see Taverne at para 6.5.2.1) and Norway (Taverne: see the note appended to para 6.4.1).

[31] Coal was reserved to the National Coal Board: s 1(2). The Coal Authority is its modern successor in title: see para 4.1.

[32] Ie, ss 2 (licences), 3 (compulsory acquisition of the right to enter land), 4 (power to supply natural gas), 5 (receipts and expenditure) and 6 (power to make regulations).

[33] Convention on the Continental Shelf, Art 2.1.

[34] P Cameron, *Property rights and sovereign rights: the case of North Sea oil* (1983) (hereinafter "Cameron, *Property rights and sovereign rights*") at 46–50.

[35] Eg Australia: see the Seas and Submerged Lands Act 1973, s 10A. Norway, by contrast, makes a straightforward proprietary claim: "The Norwegian State has the proprietary right to subsea petroleum deposits and the exclusive right to resource management." Act 29 November 1996 No 72 relating to petroleum activities (as amended), section 1-1, available for download from: http://www.npd.no/en/Regulations/Acts/Petroleum-activities-act/#Section%201-1 (accessed 25 January 2011). Danish law makes a similar claim: see Consolidated Act No 889 of 4 July 2007, *Consolidated Act on the Use of the Danish Subsoil*, ss 1 and 2. At first blush this may appear more straightforward than the UK approach, but this approach poses its own questions, most notably: if international law does provide a lesser right, on what basis can the state assert a right of full ownership?

the opacity of the nature of the right enjoyed by the state has led to debate over the legal character not just of the state's rights, but also of the rights enjoyed by the holder of a seaward production licence.[36] Taverne asserts that, within the UKCS as much as within Great Britain, full ownership of petroleum *in situ* is vested in the Crown.[37] However, given what has already been said above about the 1964 Act, the present author would respectfully suggest that this must be incorrect. At the opposite end of the spectrum of opinion, Marriage argues that oil and gas *in strata* within the UKCS is *res nullius*, which is to say, wholly ownerless.[38] Daintith and Hill adopt an intermediate position, namely that oil and gas deposits within the UKCS cannot properly be considered *res nullius* "as a determinate person, the Crown, has … the right to reduce them to possession and exclude others from so doing". Thus they argue that, although the Crown's right is not one of full ownership, it must still be essentially proprietorial in nature.[39] This, however, seems questionable. For example, an owner of land has the right, for so long as they are situated within his territory, to reduce wild birds and fish to possession and exclude others from so doing, but the mere fact that he is entitled to take this course of action conveys no ownership or cognate proprietary right in those things.

The matter has not been authoritatively settled, but the present **4.9** author inclines towards the view that Marriage's analysis is the correct one. Given the fundamental importance of the licence to the endeavour of obtaining oil and gas, and the very real practical implications which flow from the nature of the rights conveyed to the licensee, it may seem rather extraordinary that oil and gas exploration should have been proceeding in the UKCS for 45 years without this issue being resolved. In the previous edition of this book, it was noted that Oil & Gas UK was in the early stages of discussions with the industry and the Government concerning the possibility of moving to a Government-endorsed register of licences.[40] The author expressed the hope that this project might provide an ideal opportunity for the legal nature of the seaward licence and the rights flowing therefrom to be clarified by primary legislation. These discussions have not, however, borne fruit and so the legal nature of the seaward licence remains uncertain.

---

[36] The practical significance of these issues is highlighted by the series of questions posed by Daintith, Willoughby and Hill at para 1-344.

[37] Taverne at para 6.3.1.

[38] P Marriage, "North Sea Petroleum Financing in the United Kingdom" (1977) 5 *Int Bus Lawyer* 207 at 209.

[39] Daintith, Willoughby and Hill at paras 1-345 to 1-346.

[40] E-mail to the author dated 8 February 2007.

The current law

4.10   The licensing provisions of the 1934 Act were, together with a number of other statutory provisions bearing on oil and gas law,[41] consolidated and re-enacted in the Petroleum Act 1998. The 1998 Act leaves unchanged the essential features of the 1934 Act's licensing regime. All oil and gas licences to "search and bore for and get" petroleum within Great Britain, its territorial sea and the UKCS are now granted by the Crown under powers conferred by s 3(1) of the 1998 Act.

European Union law

4.11   As a Member State of the European Union, the UK is bound by EU law. The Hydrocarbons Licensing Directive[42] has had a considerable impact upon UK oil and gas licensing law. The main purpose of the Directive is to prevent the Minister from distorting competition by discriminating against persons from other members of the European Union.[43] The Directive and its implementing Regulations will be further considered below.[44]

KEY FEATURES OF THE UK OIL AND GAS LICENSING REGIME

A regulatory and contractual hybrid

4.12   A casual examination of a UK oil and gas licence might lead one to the conclusion that the licence is simply a commercial contract. The licence's opening narration states that it is "made between the Secretary of State ... on the one part and the companies listed ... on the other part".[45] It is executed by both parties.[46] It contains an arbitration clause,[47] a common feature of commercial agreements.

---

[41] But not the Continental Shelf Act 1964, which is not petroleum-specific but instead bears more generally on the state's right to regulate the use of and exploit the Continental Shelf.
[42] Directive 94/22/EC of the European Parliament and of the Council of 30 May 1994 on the conditions for granting and using authorizations for the prospection, exploration and production of hydrocarbons [1994] OJ L164/3 (the "Hydrocarbons Licensing Directive").
[43] See the recitals to the Hydrocarbons Licensing Directive: "Whereas steps must be taken to ensure the non-discriminatory access to and pursuit of activities relating to the prospection, exploration and production of hydrocarbons under conditions which encourage greater competition ... [and] it is necessary to set up common rules for ensuring that the procedures for granting authorizations for the prospection, exploration and production of hydro-carbons must be open to all entities possessing the necessary capabilities."
[44] See paras 4.16, 4.19, 4.20, 4.22 and 4.32.
[45] Copy sample licences provided to the author.
[46] *Ibid.*
[47] See Model Cl 43.

Model Cl 2 (Grant of Licence)[48] is careful to narrate that payments have been made, and will continue to be made, in exchange for the licence's grant, thus satisfying the requirements of the doctrine of consideration which forms part of English contract law.[49]

Daintith and Hill are therefore fully justified in describing the licence as "contractual in form".[50] However, the same authors are also surely correct to recognise that the licence also fulfils another function. A close examination of the licence makes it clear that it is as much a regulatory instrument as a document recording the terms of a commercial deal. Much of the licence is given over to imposing a set of controls and obligations upon the licensee,[51] the breach or non-observance of which may result in the licence being revoked.[52] By contrast, very few positive obligations are imposed upon the Minister. Moreover, by no means all disputes under the licence may be referred to arbitration: a large and important set of areas of potential disagreement is excluded from the scope of the arbitration clause.[53] In

4.13

---

[48] The focus of the discussion in this work is the current set of seaward production licence model clauses, which are to be found in the Schedule annexed to the Petroleum Licensing (Production) (Seaward Areas) Regulations 2008 (SI 2008/225), as amended by the Petroleum Licensing (Amendment) Regulations 2009 (SI 2009/3283) (the "2008 Regulations as amended"). Unless the context requires a contrary interpretation, any reference within this chapter to a numbered model clause is to this Schedule. However, earlier sets of model clauses continue to govern a large number of licences: see the discussion at para 4.17.

[49] The doctrine is unknown in Scots law: see, eg, W Gloag, *The Law of Contract* (2nd edn, 1929) at p 48.

[50] Daintith, Willoughby and Hill at para 1-323.

[51] For a short discussion of these controls, see paras 4.52–4.53. Two of the most significant controls, those relating to the licensee's obligation to submit work programmes (Model Cl 16) and production and development programmes (Model Cl 17), are discussed at length elsewhere in this chapter and in Chapter 5.

[52] The Minister's powers of revocation are set forth in Model Cl 41. For a discussion of the enforceability of the revocation provision, see Daintith, Willoughby and Hill, paras 1-342 to 1-343. A new power of partial revocation was introduced in 2008 and may be found in Model Cl 42. This power was in addition inserted into all existing licences with retroactive effect; see further the discussion at para 4.17.

[53] Model Cl 43(1) states that the arbitration provisions shall not apply to any matter or thing expressly said to be "determined, decided, directed, approved or consented to by the Minister". Some examples of ministerial determinations, decisions, directions, approvals or consents can be seen in Model Cll 4 (potential for discretionary decision as to term), 5 (potential for a ministerial direction that a frontier licence which would otherwise lapse should continue), 7 (power to determine that first or second licence term shall be extended), 14 (power to direct hat measuring devices be tested and, if found faulty, to determine how long the fault will be deemed to have subsisted) 17 (power to make directions relative to production and development plans), 21 (power to approve a programme of Completion Work), 23 (ministerial consent to potentially harmful modes of working), 24 (power to approve the appointment of operator) and 45 (power to determine that debris potentially dangerous to the fishing industry should be removed).

these circumstances it has been argued that in the event of a dispute
between state and licensee, the licensee will, in addition to any recourse
it may have in private law, be entitled to pursue a judicial review.[54]
The possibility also exists that the actions of the Minister and his
Department may in certain circumstances be susceptible to challenge
under the Human Rights Act 1998.[55]

An essentially discretionary system

4.14   The licensing provisions of the Petroleum Act 1998 do not set out
a code which stipulates in fine detail how the state is to administer
petroleum exploration or production activities.[56] Instead, the Act
provides the Minister with a number of broad enabling powers: the
Minister may grant licences to such persons as he thinks fit,[57] on such
terms and conditions as he thinks fit,[58] and for such consideration
as he, with the consent of the Treasury, may determine.[59] Thus the
system has been described as one of discretionary allocation, in
that no single criterion is determinative of the Minister's choice
of whether and to whom a licence is to be awarded.[60] But it is not
just in the allocation of licences that a high degree of ministerial
discretion is evident. Instead, discretion is a theme which recurs
throughout the whole administration of the licensing system.[61] As
we shall see throughout the next section of this chapter, however,
the Minister's powers, while still extensive, have over time come to
be limited in some significant respects by both the Hydrocarbons
Licensing Directive and domestic delegated legislation. Additionally,
the DECC has issued a significant quantity of guidance on the
practical operation of its procedures.

---

[54] S Dow, "Energy" in *The Laws of Scotland: Stair Memorial Encyclopaedia*, Reissue,
(2000) at para 19; T Daintith, "Contractual Discretion and Administrative Discretion: A
Unified Analysis" (2005) 68 MLR 554 at 592: "Courts in ... the United Kingdom will not
however accept even [unfettered] discretions ... as simply unreviewable."

[55] Daintith, *Discretion*, para 7304. There is no prospect of a challenge to ministerial *vires*
on the basis of the Scotland Act 1998 as oil and gas law is not a devolved matter.

[56] In this respect, the position in the UK can be distinguished from that in a number of
other jurisdictions, where the regime is more prescriptive and less discretionary in nature:
for instance, Australian petroleum law, discussed in some detail in Daintith, *Discretion*.
See also Bunter, *Promotion and Licensing*, at 19-25.

[57] Petroleum Act 1998, s 3(1).

[58] *Ibid*, s 3(3).

[59] *Ibid*.

[60] Daintith Willoughby and Hill, para 1-317.

[61] A fact demonstrated throughout Daintith, *Discretion*.

General remarks on the licence's terms and conditions

The discussion under this heading is restricted to selected points **4.15**
common to all UK petroleum licences. For a more detailed
commentary on some of the more significant traditional production
licence terms and conditions, see paras 4.38–4.53. For a discussion
of the terms and conditions of frontier and promote licences, see
paras 4.54–4.61 and 4.62–4.68 respectively.

Since the entry into force of the Hydrocarbons Licensing **4.16**
Directive Regulations,[62] which adopted the Hydrocarbons
Licensing Directive into domestic law, there has been a restriction
upon the types of terms that the Minister is entitled to include
in a licence. The only terms and conditions permissible are those
justified exclusively for the purpose of:

  (a) ensuring the proper performance of the activities permitted by
      the licence;
  (b) providing for the payment of consideration for the grant of
      the licence; and
  (c) for certain operational and other purposes set out in
      reg 4(2).[63]

Some of the most significant and commercially sensitive terms found **4.17**
in a licence have little or no statutory basis but are either simply
intimated in advance and imposed upon the licensee in accordance
with the DECC's usual practice[64] or are the subject of specific
agreement between the parties.[65] These terms are supplemented
by the model clauses which s 4(1)(e) of the Petroleum Act 1998
provides shall be prescribed by regulations and shall be incorporated
into petroleum licences, subject to the Minister's discretion to modify
them in particular circumstances.[66] The Act empowers the Minister
to prescribe different model clauses for different types of licence.[67]
The Minister has duly exercised this power: Regulations provide
one set of model clauses for exploration licences[68] and another for
seaward production licences.[69] Additionally, it is important to note

---

[62] Hydrocarbons Licensing Directive Regulations 1995 (SI 1995/1434) ("Hydrocarbons
Licensing Directive Regulations 1995").
[63] *Ibid*, reg 4(1).
[64] For instance, area rentals, discussed further at paras 4.40–4.41
[65] For instance, the exploration activities the licensee intends to carry out in its initial
work programme: see para 4.42.
[66] For a discussion on the occasions when the Minister has chosen to modify the model
clauses, see para 4.70.
[67] Petroleum Act 1998, s 4(2).
[68] Discussed further at para 4.35.
[69] Previously, more extensive use was made of this power. Immediately prior to the
current set of model clauses the practice was to provide a suite of different sets of model

that the licence does not incorporate the model clauses "as they are or may come to be"; it incorporates the relevant set of model clauses in force at the time of the licence's grant.[70] Thus, a large number of different sets of model clauses, each to a greater or lesser extent different in their terms, will be in force at any given time. Only the most recent licences will incorporate the most up-to-date iteration: licences of long standing will be governed by an elderly set of model clauses.[71] If these model clauses (or indeed any other terms within the licence) are subsequently thought to be undesirable, then they can be changed only by the agreement of the licensee or by the enactment of retroactive amending legislation.[72] This provides the licensee with a degree of protection against unilateral change. It should be remembered, however, that the licence does not comprise the totality of the licensee's relationship with the state. A whole host of significant fiscal and regulatory issues are governed not by the licence but by primary or secondary legislation, which may from time to time be amended so as to become more or less burdensome.[73]

---

clauses, one for each of the different types of production licences available: see Schs 1–7 of the Petroleum Licensing (Exploration and Production) (Seaward and Landward Areas) Regulations 2004 (SI 2004/352), as amended by the Petroleum Licensing (Exploration and Production) (Seaward and Landward Areas) (Amendment) Regulations 2006 (SI 2006/784). The move back to one set of model clauses for all seaward production licences has not been wholly unproblematic: see paras 4.49-4.51.

[70] Daintith, Willoughby and Hill, para 1-305.

[71] The 25th Round of licences was governed by the Petroleum Licensing (Exploration and Production) (Seaward and Landward Areas) Regulations 2004 (SI 2004/352), as amended by the Petroleum Licensing (Exploration and Production) (Seaward and Landward Areas) (Amendment) Regulations 2006 (SI 2006/784). The 24th Round was governed by the 2004 Regulations without amendment. The principal sets of preceding offshore model clauses may be found in the Petroleum (Current Model Clauses) Order 1999 (SI 1999/160), Schs 1–14.

[72] The Petroleum and Submarine Pipelines Act 1975, s 18, was a particularly contentious example of retroactive legislation in the oil and gas context: see further the discussion on the Fallow Areas Initiative and Stewardship in Chapter 5. More recently, s 77(2) of the Energy Act 2008 incorporated into all extant oil and gas licences with retrospective effect the changes contained in Sch 3 to that Act. However, these changes, which introduced the requirement to provide contact details to the Minister, a ministerial power of partial revocation of a licence, provisions intended to ensure that the Minister retains the right to revoke the licence even if the parties thereto have changed without the appropriate ministerial consent and enhanced ministerial powers relative to the plugging and abandonment of wells, had been the subject of advance consultation with the industry and this particular use of retroactivity did not prove to be contentious.

[73] For further information on the fiscal regime, see Chapter 6. For further information on the regulatory regime, see Chapters 8 (Health and Safety), 9 (Environmental Regulation) and 10 (Decommissioning).

SELECTED ISSUES IN ALLOCATION AND ADMINISTRATION OF LICENCES

Grid system

The petroleum law of some states contains provisions prescribing **4.18** the size of areas to be offered under licence.[74] By contrast, UK petroleum law views this matter as a purely administrative one within the discretion of the Minister: there is nothing compelling him to adopt a particular grid or block pattern.[75] In practice, standard UK blocks measure approximately 10 km by 25 km.[76] However, it would be a mistake to imagine that licensed interests in the UKCS are currently held in uniform 250 km² blocks. Relinquishments of parts of licensed areas[77] and the fact that the Government is now willing to consider granting requests for part blocks[78] mean that the block pattern has become increasingly disjointed. This can be seen graphically by examining a map relative to one of the UKCS longer-standing petroleum producing areas such as Quadrant 22.[79]

Public announcement of available acreage

It has long been the practice of the DECC to advertise publicly the **4.19** availability of acreage for exploration and development;[80] however, it was not until the entry into force of the Hydrocarbons Licensing Directive that it was formally bound to do so.[81]

---

[74] See, eg, Australia, where the Offshore Petroleum Act 2006, s 16 provides for a grid system consisting of blocks of 5 minutes latitude by 5 minutes longitude.

[75] Daintith, *Discretion*, para 2105.

[76] PILOT Progressing Partnership Work Group considered this a relatively large block area and considered this fact had at least contributed to certain problems with the UK licensing regime discussed further in Chapter 4: PILOT PPWG, *The Work of the Progressing Partnership Work Group* (2002), at para 3.2.1.1. While Australian blocks comprise an area of around a third of that size (Daintith, *Discretion*, para 2101), in reality the UK block size lies towards the lower end of the range that one tends to find: see Bunter, *Promotion and Licensing* at 167.

[77] Discussed further at paras 4.49–4.50.

[78] See DECC, *Applications for Production Licences: General Guidance* (DECC, *Applications Guidance*), available for download from https://www.og.decc.gov.uk/upstream/licensing/26_rnd/index.htm (accessed 29 January 2011) at para 28.

[79] DECC Overview map of quadrant 22 available for download from https://www.og.decc.gov.uk/information/bb_updates/maps/Q22.pdf (accessed 25 January 2011).

[80] See, eg, Department of Trade and Industry, *Notice Inviting Applications* under the Petroleum (Production) (Seaward Areas) Regulations 1988, *London Gazette*, 29 June 1990 at 11243 to 11245, available for download from http://www.gazettes-online.co.uk (accessed 29 January 2011).

[81] Hydrocarbons Licensing Directive, Art 3.

Licensing rounds

4.20 Petroleum production licences are generally issued within licensing rounds. Each round is presaged by the publication, at least 90 days before the closing date for applications, of a notice specifying which areas are to be made available and inviting bids from interested parties. Since the advent of the Hydrocarbons Licensing Directive, as part of the process of ensuring that enterprises located within other Member States of the EU receive an equal opportunity to apply for acreage, this notification must be placed in the *Official Journal* of the European Union.[82]

4.21   As at the time of writing, there have been 26 seaward licensing rounds since the UKCS was opened for oil and gas exploration.[83] Early licensing rounds were held at irregular intervals but, in 2004, the DECC stated that it was committed to a regular timetable of one seaward and one landward licensing round per year. This timetable – which was only ever an aspirational target and was not rigidly adhered to – is now expressed as an "aim" to hold a licensing round "every year or so".[84]

Out-of-rounds applications

4.22 The DECC may also grant licences outside the regular rounds-based process when presented with "compelling reasons"[85] to do so. The onus of establishing the existence of compelling reasons lies on the company approaching the Department seeking an out-of-round grant.[86] Even if the DECC is persuaded that there are compelling reasons for making an out-of-rounds award, there is no prospect of a private deal being done. In all but the case of neighbouring or "contiguous" blocks the Hydrocarbons Licensing Directive requires the Minister to advertise the area in the *Official Journal* on 90 days'

---

[82] Hydrocarbons Licensing Directive, Art 3(2)(a). See, eg, the announcement of the 26th Offshore Licensing Round in [2010] OJ C 12/32, available for download via http://eur-lex.europa.eu/JOIndex.do?ihmlang=en. Previously, the announcement was made in the *London Gazette*.

[83] For a discussion of landward rounds, see paras 4.71–4.73, below.

[84] DECC, *Licensing: Awards of Licences*, available for download at https://www.og.decc.gov.uk/upstream/licensing/licawards (accessed 25 January 2011).

[85] DECC, *Licensing: Awards of Licences*, which states "in the past we have accepted clear grounds of urgency (for example, temporary availability of a drilling rig). We will also consider cases where there is no prospect of competition anyway (generally because the acreage can only be of interest to a company whose existing licence covers adjoining acreage)". However the guidance states that neither "mere impatience" nor "expectations of oil price movements" would be acceptable justification for an out of rounds award.

[86] DECC, *Licensing: Awards of Licences*.

notice.[87] This is to prevent the use of out-of-rounds applications as a vehicle for a company having acreage let to it on a non-competitive footing.[88] Thus, out-of-rounds applications can come to resemble "a mini licensing round".[89]

In the case of contiguous blocks only, regulations[90] provide for the **4.23** possibility of a less formal allocation system: where the Minister is satisfied that it is justified for "geological or production reasons" he may choose not to advertise in the *Official Journal*, but only to write to the licensees of the contiguous blocks, inviting applications within a timescale of the Minister's choosing. Thus, even in this case there is the possibility of competition, albeit only within a limited category of persons.

Acreage selection: environmental issues

The decision as to which areas to invite applications for a particular **4.24** area in the UKCS is a matter for ministerial discretion, and ministerial practice has varied greatly.[91] However, the Minister's discretion is now subject to the limitations imposed by two significant EU environmental protection measures, namely: Council Directive 92/43/EEC of 21 May 1992 on the conservation of natural habitats and of wild fauna and flora (the "Habitats Directive") and Directive 2001/42/EC of the European Parliament and of the Council of 27 June 2001 on the assessment of the effects of certain plans and programmes on the environment (the "Strategic Environmental Assessment Directive").

Habitats Directive
Put broadly, the effect of the Habitats Directive is to prevent the **4.25** licensing of acreage where the activities that would be carried under the licence might have a significant impact upon a site of a type which the Directive protects.[92] The Government initially implemented the Habitats Directive by Regulations which applied it not

---

[87] Hydrocarbons Licensing Directive, Art 3(2)(b).

[88] That said, the company which makes the initial approach to the DECC may be in a stronger position than its rivals, if only because, as part of the process of demonstrating compelling reasons, it will generally have started to assess the area earlier than will have its competitors.

[89] Daintith, Willoughby and Hill, 1-316.

[90] Petroleum (Production) (Seaward Areas) Regulations 1988 (SI 1988/1213), reg 7(5), as amended by the Petroleum (Production) (Seaward Areas) (Amendment) Regulations 1995 (SI 1995/1435), reg 6.

[91] Daintith, *Discretion* at paras 2403 and 2407.

[92] *Ibid* at para 2403.

to the UKCS but only to the outer limits of the territorial sea.[93] However, this interpretation was successfully challenged in a judicial review mounted by the environmental pressure group Greenpeace, in which it was held that the Regulations had not adequately implemented the Habitats Directive and that this would now be applied throughout the UKCS under the doctrine of the direct effect of EU Directives.[94] New implementing regulations were promulgated following the judicial review.[95] The relevance of the Regulations for present purposes[96] is that they forbid the Minister from granting any petroleum licence "where he considers that anything that might be done or any activity which might be carried on pursuant to such a licence… is likely to have a significant effect on a relevant site"[97] without first making an appropriate assessment of the conservation implications for the site.[98] In making his assessment, the Minister is obliged to consult with the appropriate nature consultation body[99] and may, if he thinks it appropriate, in addition consult with the general public.[100] Subject to the exception described immediately below, the Minister may grant a licence only if he is satisfied that "nothing that might be done and no activity that might be carried out pursuant thereto" would have an adverse effect on the integrity of a relevant site.[101] The Minister is entitled to authorise the activity

---

[93] Conservation (Natural Habitats, etc) Regulations 1994 (SI 1994/2716).

[94] *R v Secretary of State for Trade and Industry, ex parte Greenpeace Ltd (No 2)* [2000] Env L R 221. The case was brought by Greenpeace as part of its attempt to prevent the development of the West of Shetland Atlantic margin: see S Tromans, *European Environmental Law Goes Offshore* (2000) IELTR 75. Greenpeace have not been wholly successful in securing this objective: subsequent licensing developments relating to this area are discussed at paras 4.54–4.61.

[95] Offshore Petroleum Activities (Conservation of Habitats) Regulations 2001 (SI 2001/1754) (as amended).

[96] The Directive and its associated Regulations are relevant not just at the time of the grant of licences, but also applies to *inter alia* consents granted pursuant to a UKCS licence: reg 5(1) read with reg 2. This aspect of the matter will be further considered at para 4.52–4.53 and in Chapter 9.

[97] Defined by reg 2 so as to include *inter alia* special areas of conservations and various sites listed under the Habitats or Wild Birds Directives or which, following consultation with the appropriate nature conservation body (discussed further below) is likely to be included in any forthcoming listing of such sites.

[98] Reg 5(1).

[99] In England and within English territorial waters, the Environment Agency; in Scotland and within Scottish territorial waters, the Scottish Environmental Protection Agency; for the remainder of the UKCS, the Joint Nature Conservancy Council (JNCC). For further information about the JNCC's activities in this regard, see http://www.jncc.gov.uk/page-1374 (accessed 25 January 2011).

[100] Reg 5(2).

[101] Reg 5(3).

only if, in his opinion, there is "no satisfactory alternative"[102] and if the Minister has certified that the project should be carried out for "imperative reasons of overriding public interest".[103] Where the reason of overriding public interest appertains to human health, public safety or to the "beneficial consequences of primary importance for the environment", the Minister is entitled to issue the certificate himself.[104] However, as an important check against the abuse of ministerial discretion, in all other cases he must obtain a consenting opinion from the European Commission.[105]

Environmental Impact Assessment Directive

An EU environmental impact regime which required relevant authorities to consider the environmental effects of "certain public and private projects"[106] has existed since 1985. That regime continues to be in force[107] and stipulates that certain projects "likely to have significant effects on the environment by virtue *inter alia*, of their nature, size or location" require to be the subject of an environmental impact assessment (EIA) before the relevant authority can consent to their being undertaken.[108] The extraction of petroleum is included among the activities listed in the annex to the Directive comprising projects which may require an assessment at the discretion of the Member State.[109] The EIA regime does not forbid development in the event of an unfavourable EIA being received, or even seek to define what an unfavourable EIA is; instead, it seeks to ensure that relevant authorities are provided with relevant environment information when exercising their decision-making function.[110]

4.26

---

[102] Reg 6(1)(a)

[103] Reg 6(1)(b)

[104] Reg 6(2)(a). Social and economic reasons are both expressly recognised as potentially valid.

[105] Reg 6(2)(b)

[106] Council Directive 85/337/EEC of 27 June 1985 on the assessment of the effects of certain public and private projects on the environment (the "Environmental Impact Assessment Directive"), Art 1.

[107] The original Directive of 1985 has been amended by Directives 97/11/EC, 2003/35/EC and 2009/31/EC all references are to the Regulations as so amended. The effect of the 2009 Regulations is to bring carbon capture, transportation and storage schemes under the ambit of the regime. For further information see European Commission, *Environmental Impact Assessment*, available at http://ec.europa.eu/environment/eia/eia-legalcontext.htm (accessed 25 January 2011).

[108] Art 2(1).

[109] Art 4(2), read with Annex 2, para 2(f) and (g).

[110] This aspect of the Directive is demonstrated by the provisions of Arts 5–7; See also C Reid, *Nature Conservation Law*, (2nd edn), 2002 (hereinafter Reid, "*Nature Conservation Law*") at para 8.3.13: EIA "regulates the process by which decisions are reached, not substantive outcomes."

Strategic Environmental Assessment Directive

4.27   One of the perceived weaknesses of the EIA system is that it applies
on a project-by-project basis. The decisions reached in this way
may lack the wider view of the policy made possible by taking
decisions at a more strategic level; thus there is the danger of a lack
of appropriate focus on environmental issues and of an incremental
erosion of environmental protection.[111] The Strategic Environmental
Assessment Directive,[112] which required to be implemented by all
Member States by the end of July 2004, attempts to address this
deficiency by providing that a strategic environmental assessment
(SEA)[113] shall be carried out for draft plans and programmes which
are likely to have significant environmental effects.[114] Certain plans
or programmes (including those pertaining to the extraction of
petroleum[115] and those determined to require an assessment under
the Habitats Directive[116]) are deemed, subject to a *de minimis*
provision,[117] to be likely to have significant environmental effects.
The SEA process, like EIA, is essentially concerned with gathering
information as an aid to informed decision-making.[118] The authority
is not bound by a SEA but must take it into account.[119] However,
this does not mean that the process is without effect: in the 24th
Offshore Licensing Round, 21 blocks which would otherwise have
been made available were withheld for environmental reasons, at
least "for the present".[120] Similarly, in the 26th Round, the process
led to a number of blocks which had previously been withheld
continuing to be made unavailable, as well as a range of other blocks

---

[111]   Reid, *Nature Conservation Law*, para 8.3.14.

[112]   Directive 2001/42/EC.

[113]   Defined in Art 2(b). The term "strategic environmental assessment" does not appear in
the Directive itself but has been adopted by commentators in order to differentiate these
assessments from those required under the EIA regime.

[114]   Art 3(1).

[115]   Specified by Art 3(2)(a) as being "those prepared for agriculture, forestry, fisheries,
energy, industry, transport, waste management, water management, telecommunications,
tourism, town and country planning or land use and which set the framework for future
development consent of projects listed in Annexes I and II to [the Environmental Impact
Directive]".

[116]   Art 3(2)(b).

[117]   For which see Art 3(3).

[118]   See, eg, Arts 5, 6 and 7.

[119]   Art 8.

[120]   DECC, *Strategic Environmental Assessment (SEA) – Post Adoption Procedures*,
available for download at http://www.og.DECC.gov.uk/upstream/licensing/24_rnd/24_
sea.htm (accessed 25 January 2011). DECC also maintains a dedicated SEA public
consultation site which, among other things, contains the SEA reports prepared to date:
http://www.offshore-sea.org.uk/site/index.php (accessed 25 January 2011).

in the south west, Cardigan Bay and the Moray Firth being held back, at least for the moment.[121]

Consideration

Section 3(3) of the Petroleum Act 1998 provides that licences shall be granted in exchange for "such consideration (whether by way of royalty or otherwise) as the Minister with the consent of the Treasury may determine". The discretion conveyed upon the Minister by this piece of legislation has not been fettered, either by statutory instrument or otherwise. The width with which this provision has been drafted is perhaps best demonstrated by noting that it has permitted the Minister occasionally to utilise cash premium bidding, not usually a feature of UK oil and gas law, without any requirement for primary, or even secondary, legislation.[122] **4.28**

In the early years of oil and gas production, royalty payments, consisting of a state claim to 12.5 per cent of the market value of produced oil and gas,[123] constituted a major element of the UK's revenue from oil and gas production.[124] However, amid concerns that royalty had an inhibiting effect upon exploration and development activity, a succession of provisions were enacted to exclude from the requirement to pay royalty the licensees of fields which received their development consent after 1 April 1982[125] before a declaration was issued "irrevocably revoking" royalty payments with effect from 1 January 2003.[126] Ministerial decree by press release is an unorthodox way of effecting a change to a legal instrument but the Government has declined to take measures to effect a more formal amendment of the relevant licences.[127] **4.29**

---

[121] DECC, *26th Seaward Licensing Round Strategic Environmental Assessment (SEA) – Post Adoption Procedures*, available online at https://www.og.decc.gov.uk/upstream/licensing/26_rnd/sea.htm (accessed 25 January 2011). However, these steps have not satisfied all in the environmental lobby, and on 12 November 2010 Greenpeace raised High Court proceedings against DECC in an attempt to stop the issue in the 26th Round of any licences relative to deep water areas. At the time of writing the case has yet to be heard.

[122] The UK experimented in the 4th, 8th and 9th Licensing Rounds with a two-tier system whereby cash premium bidding – effectively an auction – was utilised in relation to a relatively small number of fields alongside the usual discretionary arrangements. A variant upon this system was in addition utilised in the 7th Licensing Round. For a fuller account, see Daintith, Willoughby and Hill at paras 1-317 to 1-322.

[123] Daintith, *Discretion*, para 9213.

[124] See the statistics at HMRC, *Government revenues from UK oil and gas production*, published at http://www.hmrc.gov.uk/stats/corporate_tax/table11_11.pdf (accessed 25 January 2011)

[125] Daintith, *Discretion*, para 9107.

[126] Daintith, Willoughby and Hill, para 1-336/1.

[127] Daintith, *Discretion*, para 9213.

4.30   The UK Government's revenue from petroleum now consists solely of licence fees (comprising application fees and area rental) and various elements of taxation.[128] Application fees are set by delegated legislation.[129] Area rental fees are not set by regulation but are determined by the Minister, advertised in advance and included as an annexation to the licence.[130] Although area rental fees are sufficiently high to have been believed to act as a barrier both to certain types of development[131] and to development by certain types of company,[132] the state's revenue from this source is dwarfed by the sums raised through taxation. Tax revenues can be collected only when oil is produced and profits made. Thus, the structure of the UK's fiscal regime provides a powerful incentive for the Government to promote maximum recovery of the UK's oil and gas reserves.[133]

Assessing competing applications

4.31   The manner in which the DECC assesses applications has altered markedly over time. Two main factors can be identified for this change: the requirements of European law; and the industry's own desire for greater transparency. These will be discussed in turn.

EU law

4.32   In the event of competition between two or more interested parties, the Minister uses a variety of published criteria in order to determine to whom a petroleum licence should be granted. Many of the criteria that have been used by the Minister over the years are uncontroversial from the standpoint of EU anti-discrimination law and continue to be used today.[134] However, some of the factors have proven to be more problematic. In 1985, the UK Government was warned that the Minister's willingness to take into account the

---

[128] For further information on the tax regime within the UKCS, see Chapter 6, below.

[129] The principal application fees were updated by the Petroleum Licensing (Amendment) Regulations 2009 (SI 2009/3283). The current application fee is £2,100 for seaward production licences and £1,400 for (landward) petroleum exploration and development licences.

[130] DECC, *Applications Guidance* per Annexe 1 at 10–12. A Schedule (in current practice Sch 2) containing the rental charges is incorporated into the licence by Model Cl 12.

[131] This is one of a number of factors which led to the creation of frontier licences, discussed further at paras 4.54–4.61.

[132] This is one of a number of factors which led to the creation of the promote licence, on which see paras 4.62–4.68.

[133] For further discussion on this point, see the discussion on Stewardship in Chapter 5.

[134] For example, the technical and financial capability of the licensee has been used since the early days of the regime: see para 5(a) of the Notice pursuant to the Petroleum (Production) Regulations 1976 of 8 August 1978: 1978 *London Gazette*, issue 47612, at 9508. The *London Gazette* is available online: http://www.london-gazette.co.uk/.

prospective licensee's contribution to the UK economy, readiness to involve UK organisations to participate in research and development activities and readiness to offer a full and fair opportunity to UK firms to compete for orders for goods and services were potentially discriminatory.[135] The initial effect of this warning was not particularly salutary: the Government stopped publishing detailed information on how it would determine applications.[136] However, the adoption of the Hydrocarbons Licensing Directive changed this position. The implementing regulations provide that "every application" for a licence shall be determined on the basis of the following criteria:

    (a) the technical and financial capability of the applicant;
    (b) the way in which the applicant proposes to carry out the activities that would be permitted by the licence;
    (c) in a case where tenders are invited, the price the applicant is prepared to pay in order to obtain the licence; and
    (d) where the applicant holds, or has held, a licence of any description under the Petroleum (Production) Act 1934, any lack of efficiency and responsibility displayed by the applicant in operations under that licence.[137, 138]

The Minister is specifically empowered to refuse an application for a **4.33** licence, even where there is no competition.[139] In the event that two or more applications for a licence have equal merit when assessed according to the principal criteria, "other relevant criteria" may be applied.[140] Neither the principal criteria nor any such "tie-break" criteria may be applied in a discriminatory manner.[141] All criteria to be used in determining applications must be included by the Minister

---

[135] Daintith, Willoughby and Hill, para 1-317. See, eg, the Notice of 8 August 1978: 1978 *London Gazette*, issue 47612 at 9508, paras 5(e) and (h).

[136] Daintith, Willoughby and Hill, para 1-317. See, eg, the Notice of 25 July 1986: 1986 *London Gazette*, issue 50609 at 9837, para 7.

[137] A nice point, which does not yet seem to have been tested, is whether the "and" in reg 3(1)(d) requires to be interpreted adjunctively or disjunctively; in other words, whether a company can lose standing only as a result of exhibiting both "a lack of responsibility and efficiency" or whether a lack of either "responsibility" or "efficiency" will be sufficient. This may be material. It is not difficult to conceive of a set of circumstances which could allow one to hold a licensee inefficient, but not irresponsible.

[138] Hydrocarbons Licensing Directive Regulations 1995, reg 3(1). In practice the third criterion is usually omitted from notices as the UK does not generally operate a cash auction system. See, eg, the announcement of the 21st Offshore Licensing Round in [2003] OJ C27/03, para 9.

[139] Hydrocarbons Licensing Directive Regulations 1995, reg 3(1).

[140] *Ibid*, reg 3(2).

[141] *Ibid*, reg 3(4).

in the notice inviting applications.[142] The Minister retains the power to refuse to grant a licence on the basis of national security where the applicant is effectively controlled by a foreign state other than a Member State of the EU (or by nationals of such a state).[143]

Enhanced transparency

4.34   The Oil Industry Taskforce[144] published its report *A Template For Change* in 1999. Among other innovations directed towards reducing the cost of oil and gas activity in the UKCS and creating "a climate for the UKCS to retain its position as a pre-eminent active centre of oil and gas exploration, development and production",[145] the report identified the need to improve licence administration.[146] This recommendation led to further work by the Taskforce which in turn led to it recommending the introduction of a marking scheme for applications. This recommendation was duly adopted by the Government. The marking scheme against which applications will be measured is now published in advance of each licensing round.[147] The DECC bases its assessment upon the technical understanding demonstrated by the applicant at interview, the generation of valid prospectivity derived from evaluation of available data, the quality of the work that it has already done, and the proposed work programme.[148] Thereafter, the marks awarded to the successful applications in blocks in respect of which there was competition are published, as are short particulars of the work programme associated with the successful application.[149] No marks are awarded in respect of the

---

[142] Hydrocarbons Licensing Directive Regulations 1995, reg 5. In practice the Government has not always formally publicised "tie-break" criteria: see, eg, the Notice announcing the 21st Offshore Licensing Round at [2003] OJ C27/03 which does no more than re-cast the reg 3(1) criteria in slightly different language. The current practice is for the Notice in the *Official Journal* to be in relatively brief form and to refer the reader to the DECC's website for further information: see, eg, the Notice relating to the 26th Offshore Round at [2010] OJ C12/32.

[143] Hydrocarbons Licensing Directive Regulations 1995, reg 3(4).

[144] The Oil Industry Taskforce was a group consisting of Government Ministers, and civil servants, members of other oil industry groups and initiatives and senior oil executives. See Oil Industry Taskforce, *A Template for Change* (1999) (hereinafter "Oil Industry Taskforce, *Template*") Appendices 2 and 3. PILOT is the group's successor organisation.

[145] Oil Industry Taskforce, *Template*, Foreword by Rt Hon Stephen Byers, Secretary of State for Trade and Industry.

[146] *Ibid*, at 12

[147] DECC, *Applications Guidance*, para 43; DECC, *Technical Information*, available online at https://www.og.decc.gov.uk/upstream/licensing/26_rnd/guidance_technical.doc (accessed 20 January 2011).

[148] DECC, *Applications Guidance*, para 43. A summary of the marking scheme used in the 26th Round is available at DECC, *Technical Information*, Annexe 2.

[149] The winning marks for the 26th Seaward Round process may be seen in DECC, *Winning Marks By Block List*, available for download from https://www.og.decc.gov.uk/upstream/

reg 3(1)(a) criteria of technical and financial capability. These are threshold criteria which are either met or not: any deficiencies in these respects cannot be made up by exceptional strengths in other areas of the application. In practice, the Department's published guidance on the marks scheme focuses wholly upon the details of what activities the licensee proposes to carry out: in other words, the criterion set out in reg 3(1)(b). The present guidance says nothing about the extent to which the Department would attach weight to the reg 3(1)(d) criterion, ie any lack of efficiency and responsibility historically displayed by the applicant.

COMMENTARY ON CURRENT FORMS OF UK OIL AND GAS LICENCES

Seaward licences

Exploration licence

An exploration licence is a licence to search for petroleum "in any seaward area and in those parts of any landward area below the low water line"[150] – in other words, within the territorial sea and to the outer limit of UK's Exclusive Economic Zone. Areas in respect of which a production licence is extant are excluded from the territorial extent of the exploration licence unless the production licensee agrees to the proposed exploration activities.[151] Exploration licences are non-exclusive in nature[152] and now run for a period of 3 years, renewable for a further 3 years on the provision of 3 months' notice.[153] The rights granted under such a licence are tightly circumscribed. In practice such licences are used to enable the carrying out of seismic surveys and other methods of geological prospecting.[154] An exploration licence does not convey a right to "get" petroleum, to drill wells for the production of petroleum, or indeed to drill any well with a depth greater than 350 metres below the seabed.[155] Thus, despite the potentially confusing similarity in terminology,

4.35

---

licensing/26_rnd/26_marks.pdf (accessed 20 January 2011). Short particulars of the work obligations for the same round may be found in *DECC*, List of potential awards in the 26th Seaward Licensing Round by name of operator, available for download from https://www. og.decc.gov.uk/upstream/licensing/26_rnd/index.htm (accessed 20 January 2011).

[150] Petroleum Licensing (Exploration and Production) (Seaward and Landward Areas) Regulations 2004, Sch 1, Model Cl 2.

[151] Model Cl 2.

[152] The licence and liberty is granted "in common with all other persons to whom the like right may have been granted or may hereafter be granted". See Model Cl 2.

[153] Model Cl 4.

[154] For a discussion of the regulation of the environmental impact of exploration activity, see Chapter 8.

[155] Model Cl 3.

exploration licences carry insufficient rights to authorise meaningful exploration drilling.[156] A production licence is required for that activity.

4.36   Because of the limited nature of the rights conveyed by an exploration licence, many of the provisions found in other sets of model clauses are unnecessary and therefore omitted. That said, the model clauses still run to 23 paragraphs and, among other provisions, require the licensee to avoid harmful methods of working, keep records and samples, file regular returns with the DECC and provide advance notice of certain activities to the Ministry of Defence and representatives of the local fishing industry.[157] Note, however, that this obligation to consult would not denude other rights held by fishermen; for instance, if, within territorial waters, they owned a separate right of salmon fishing.

Production licence

4.37   The production licence is the classic licence to "search or bore for or get" petroleum situated on the seaward side of the low water line.[158] It is an exclusive licence.[159] Initially, only one type of production licence was offered. However, as time has gone by, the state has responded to the challenges associated with development in frontier areas and the need to attract new entrants to the sector given the UK's status as a maturing oil and gas province by providing the petroleum industry with a suite of licences to choose from. These will be discussed in turn.

4.38   **Traditional (or standard) production licence.** The great majority of the production licences presently at large are traditional production licences.[160] Although the traditional production licence has been

---

[156] Oil and gas is not generally encountered on the UKCS in meaningful quantities at such shallow depths. Most UKCS finds have been encountered at depths in excess of 1,000 metres.

[157] Model Cll 9, 11 and 13, 12, 22 and 23 respectively. For a fuller discussion of the extent of the environmental protections provided by this set of model clauses, see paras 9.3–9.9.

[158] Petroleum (Production) (Seaward Areas) Regulations 1988 (SI 1988/1213), reg 3(1) read together with Sch 1.

[159] Model Cl 2 states that the licensee has "exclusive licence and liberty during the continuance of this licence and subject to the provisions hereof to search and bore for, and get, Petroleum in the sea bed and subsoil" underneath the licensed area.

[160] When the alternative licensing models further described at paras 4.54–4.68 were first introduced, "standard" was the term used in statutory instrument to describe the pre-existing licence format to which the new forms provided an alternative: see the Petroleum Licensing (Exploration and Production) (Seaward and Landward Areas) Regulations 2004, Sch 4. However governmental guidance and and press releases (see, eg, DTI, *North Sea oil and gas applications, 35-year high continues*, dated 19 June 2006, commonly referred to such production licences as "traditional" ones. Despite its lack

complemented by the introduction of alternative licensing options, it continues to be a highly significant licensing vehicle. In the most recent (26th) Seaward Licensing Round, of the 144 licences initially awarded,[161] the overwhelming majority – 123 – were issued on traditional terms.[162] All other things being equal, the traditional production licence continues to be the DECC's favoured licensing option.[163]

The terms on which traditional production licences are offered **4.39** have evolved over time. Some of the developments shall be noted in passing, but this discussion will focus on the most recent set of model clauses.[164] However, as has already been noted,[165] the terms of UK petroleum licences are fixed at the point of the licence's grant; instances of express retroactive amendment apart, the issuing of a new set of model clauses has no bearing upon the terms of existing licences. Thus many traditional production licences continue on terms and conditions which are, to a greater or lesser extent, different from those which will be described below.

Area rental payments. Area rental payments[166] are not determined **4.40** either by primary or secondary legislation but are instead published in guidance, disclosed by the Minister in the notice inviting applications, and included in the licence itself (under present practice, by Model Cl 12 read together with Sch 2 to the licence). The area rental payments for the most recent traditional production licences commence at £150 per square kilometre. The area rental remains at this level throughout the licence's initial term before doubling to £300 per square kilometre in the first year of its second term. It then escalates by annual increments of £900 until it reaches £7,500

---

of statutory basis the term "traditional" appears to have taken root (see, eg, DECC, *Licensing: Licence Types*, available for download from https://www.og.decc.gov.uk/upstream/licensing/lictype.htm, accessed 22 January 2011) and so that term will be used throughout this chapter.

[161] The decision on whether to grant a further 45 potential awards of licences in an additional 99 blocks was deferred pending a more detailed assessment of the potential impact upon protected nature conservation areas. Thus it may be that ultimately more than 144 licences will be granted in the 26th Round.

[162] DECC *List of Potential Awards in the 26th Licensing Round by name of operator*, available for download from https://www.og.decc.gov.uk/upstream/licensing/26_rnd/26_potential_op.xls (accessed 22 January 2011),

[163] See para 4.66.

[164] Ie the model clauses incorporated into licences granted under the 26th Seaward Licensing Round: those to be found in Schedule to the Petroleum Licensing (Production) (Seaward Areas) Regulations 2008, as amended by the Petroleum Licensing (Amendment) Regulations 2009 (SI 2009/3283).

[165] See para 4.17.

[166] Area rentals are an aspect of consideration, which was discussed in more general terms at para 4.28.

per area factor, at which figure it is capped,[167] subject always to the possibility that it will increase through the accompanying indexation provisions.[168]

4.41   The strategy of starting rental acreages at a relatively low figure provides the licensee with some degree of comfort in the early years of the licence, where only exploration and development work will be taking place and no oil, and therefore no revenue stream, will yet be flowing. It also provides the licensee with some measure of incentive, first, to explore and develop quickly, and, second, to surrender increasingly expensive acreage which is not being utilised. However, the standard consideration regime has been found to be inadequate in itself to achieve any of those purposes. This is one of a number of factors which led both to the introduction of variant types of licence variants in 2003 and 2004[169] and to the Fallow Area and Stewardship initiatives.[170]

4.42   *Work programme.* The term "work programme" is slightly misleading. It refers not to the totality of the work that will be carried out during the life of the licence, but only to exploration activities.[171] Moreover, it is used in two distinct senses. The "initial work programme" narrates the exploration work that the licensee has agreed to undertake in exchange for the receiving the grant of licence. In addition, the licensee might be called upon by the Minister to prepare a further "appropriate work programme". These categories will be discussed in turn.

4.43   Initial work programmes are effectively agreed between the licensee and the Minister: when applying for a licence, the licensee states the exploration work it intends to carry out; by agreeing to offer a licence to the applicant, the Minister agrees that this work programme is acceptable.

4.44   Such work programmes are now somewhat more detailed than was formerly the case. Many elderly licences contain surprisingly vague work programmes (expressed, in accordance with the then current terminology, as "working obligations") obliging the licensee to carry out, without further definition or qualification, "seismic survey work" and/or "drill at least one exploration well".[172] Modern work programmes are expressed with a greater degree of

---

[167] DECC, *Applications Guidance*, Annexe 1, para 2.

[168] *Ibid*, Annexe 1, para 3.

[169] Discussed at paras 4.54–4.61 and 4.62–4.68.

[170] Discussed in Chapter 5.

[171] The work to be undertaken in later phases of the licences will be described not in a work programme but in a development and production programme. These are discussed in greater detail in Chapter 5.

[172] Sample licences provided to the author.

particularisation. For example, they are likely to specify a minimum quantity and type of seismic data which must be acquired and/ or to state the depth to which the licensee is expected to drill.[173] Moreover, modern work programmes now differentiate between differing degrees of commitment. A "firm" well drilling commitment is an unequivocal undertaking to drill, appropriate only where the licensee is certain that they intend to execute these works.[174] A "contingent" well commitment is in effect a firm commitment which the DECC may waive in the event that a specified study or evaluation establishes that drilling is likely to be a futile exercise.[175] "Drill or drop" is a looser commitment by which the licensee under-takes either to proceed with drilling or to surrender the licence. The principal benefit of drill or drop is that, contrary to the position with the other degrees of commitment, the licensee does not lose good standing with the DECC in the event that it decides not to carry out the works.[176] By contrast, a failure to carry out without good reason either a firm commitment or a contingent commitment where the condition precedent has been satisfied is a factor which can lead the DECC to conclude that there has been a lack of efficiency and responsibility on the part of the licensee.[177]

As was noted in the discussion at para 4.34, the materiality of   4.45 proposed work programmes is a factor which weighs heavily in the marking scheme used by the Minister to choose between competing applications. This provides a powerful incentive for the licensee to offer to carry out an extensive work programme, at least in respect of acreage where the applicant knows or anticipates it will face competition. However, when the licence is granted, the work programme will be incorporated into it,[178] and the continuance of the licence from its initial term into a second term is made contingent upon the work programme's successful completion, subject only to the Minister's discretion to waive or modify this requirement.[179] This, and the potential loss of good standing discussed above, should serve to discourage companies from illegitimately securing acreage by promising much exploration activity and then delivering little. However, there is at least some concern within the industry that

---

[173] Sample licences provided to the author. The level of detail contained within the licences is greater than in the abbreviated work obligations posted on the DECC website.
[174] DECC, *Technical Information*, para 9, read with Annexe 1, Definitions, at para 4.
[175] DECC, *Technical Information*, para 9, read with Annexe 1, Definitions, at para 5.
[176] DECC, *Technical Information*, para 9, read with Annexe 1, Definitions, at para 6.
[177] Hydrocarbons Licensing Directive Regulations 1995, reg 3(1)(d), discussed further at para 4.32.
[178] Under current practice, the work programme will be annexed to the licence as Sch 3.
[179] Model Cl 4(2)(b).

certain prospective licensees may be securing acreage by offering firm work commitments in circumstances where only a lesser degree of commitment is justified, then failing to carry their commitments through and attempting to justify their failings by making reference to supposedly unforeseen difficulties which were, in fact, perfectly predictable.[180]

4.46   In addition to this initial agreed work programme the model clauses state that the Minister is entitled, at any time before the end of the licence,[181] to demand the preparation and submission by the licensee of "an appropriate work programme".[182] A work programme is "appropriate" for these purposes if it is one which would be prepared by a licensee seeking to exploit its licence rights to the best commercial advantage, and who had the competence and resources necessary so to do, and if it is one which could reasonably be expected to be completed by such a licensee before the end of the life of the licence.[183] This is an exacting standard, and one which takes no account of the licensee's other commitments. If no programme is served the Minister may revoke the licence or part thereof.[184] If a programme is served, the Minister may reject it if he is not satisfied that it is "appropriate"; if the parties are in dispute on this point the matter may be referred to arbitration.[185] The Minister may revoke the licence in whole or in part in the event of repeated failures to submit an appropriate programme[186] or a failure to undertake the works set out in an approved programme.[187] This is an important and powerful provision which effectively means that the Minister is entitled to demand that the licensee carry out exploration activities well into the planning and production stages of the licence. This model clause is discussed further in the context of the Fallow Areas initiative in Chapter 5.

4.47   *Term and relinquishments.* In some states, separate licences are granted to regulate the distinct phases of the life of an oil and gas development. Under such regimes, a licensee will hold two or more licences in succession as the discovery progresses on from one phase

---

[180] Daintith, *Discretion*, para 3227.

[181] Model Cl 16(2). Where the licensee has carried out a programme during a part of the term of this licence, the Minister may serve notice in pursuance of Model Cl 16(2) in respect of another part of that term: Model Cl 16(7).

[182] Model Cl 16(2). This power was one of a number of provisions controversially introduced with retrospective effect by Petroleum and Submarine Pipelines Act 1975: s 18, read with Sch 2, Pt II, Model Cl 14.

[183] Model Cl 12(2).

[184] Model Cl 41(2)(b), read together with Model Cl 16(2) and (6).

[185] Model Cl 16(4)(a).

[186] Model Cl 41(2)(b), read together with Model Cl 16(3), (4) and (6).

[187] Model Cl 41(2)(b), read together with Model Cl 16(3), (5) and (6).

to the next.[188] The traditional production licence, by contrast, covers the various phases of work on the discovery. The licence is presently divided into three distinct terms: the initial term, which is focused on exploration; the second term, which may be viewed as a phase of appraisal and preparation which acts as a bridge between the exploration and production phases; and the production period.[189] The current format, which was devised by the PILOT Progressing Partnership Work Group (PILOT PPWG) following a review of UK licensing law and practice,[190] was introduced[191] in 2002 for the 20th Licensing Round and has been in use since. Previously, a variety of configurations of terms had been used,[192] none of which was found to be wholly satisfactory and some of which have been criticised for failing properly to secure the state's interests due to their lack of sophistication and excessive aggregate length.[193]

4.48 The general philosophy of the modern traditional production licence is that, by the time that any given term comes to an end, certain tasks or activities should have been carried out. If they have, and if the licensee notifies the Minister that it wishes the licence to continue and is willing to surrender a certain amount of acreage, then the licence will carry on. Otherwise, the licence become susceptible to being brought to an end as a result of the licensee's failure to comply with its obligations.[194]

4.49 Broadly speaking, the initial term is intended to permit the licensee to carry out the exploration work set out in the licence's work programme. Under the previous set of model clauses, the licensee was permitted a period of 4 years to carry out this work and was under a strict obligation, at the end of that period, to surrender

---

[188] See, for instance, Canada and Australia: see Daintith, *Discretion*, at para 4001. Until relatively recently this approach was also taken by the UK in relation to landward licences: see para 4.71.

[189] Model Cl 3.

[190] PILOT PPWG, *The Work of the Progressing Partnership Work Group* (2002), para 3.2.

[191] Rather irregularly: revised model clauses were not prepared in advance of the 20th or 21st Rounds; instead the notices inviting applications indicated that licences would be issued in accordance with the then-extant model clauses subject to the deletion of certain clauses and the incorporation of a number of bespoke provisions: see, for the 20th Offshore Round, United Kingdom Government notice concerning Directive 94/22/EC of the European Parliament and Council of 30 May 1994 on the conditions for granting and using authorisations for the prospection, exploration and production of hydrocarbons [2002] OJ C12/03 at paras 2 and 13–16; and for the 21st Round, and the like notice of 5 February 2003; [2003] OJ C27/03. In due course the changes were formally introduced into UK petroleum law by the Petroleum Licensing (Exploration and Production) (Seaward and Landward Areas) Regulations 2004.

[192] See Daintith, *Discretion*, para 3502.

[193] PILOT PPWG, *Work*, paras 3.1.2 and 3.2.1.1 and 3.2.1.2.

[194] Model Cl 3(2).

an area comprising at least half of the initial licensed area,[195] subject only to the proviso that the licensee shall be entitled to retain at least 30 sections.[196] In the 2008 iteration of the model clauses, however, the position has changed markedly. The initial term is no longer fixed by statutory instrument at 4 years,[197] but becomes one of the many matters which fall to be determined by DECC and included in Sch 5 to the licence.[198] The extent of the licensee's surrender obligation is made similarly unclear by the 2008 Model Clauses: the obligation is to surrender no less than the "Mandatory Surrender Area", but what is meant by that expression is a matter for the DECC to determine in Sch 5. The purpose of a surrender requirement is two-fold. First, it acts as an incentive to thorough and timely exploration.[199] The licensee will wish to be as certain as it can be that it is surrendering the least promising part of its territory, an assessment which can be safely made only after detailed exploration. Second, requiring a surrender within this relatively short period allows the area to be offered for licence again within a reasonable period of time. Rapid recycling of discarded acreage is considered to serve the state's interest in securing the swift and thorough exploitation of the UKCS's hydrocarbon reserves. An examination of DECC's own summary of its understanding of its licensing powers suggests that the 2008 amendments were not intended radically to change the position which existed under the 2004 regime: the expectation appears to be that the initial term will for traditional production licences usually be 4 years, and the mandatory surrender area usually 50 per cent.[200] It is, however, to be regretted that so important an issue has been rendered so opaque and open textured[201] by a change in practice the stated purpose of which was to make the position simpler, clearer[202]

---

[195] 2004 Regulations as amended, Sch 4, Model Cl 4(4).

[196] *Ibid*, Sch 4, Model Cl 4(5).

[197] Strictly, of course, these matters were never entirely "fixed" in that the Minister always enjoyed a power to modify or restrict the application of the model clauses in a particular case: Petroleum Act 1998, s 4(1)(e). Thus the system provided for a set of general norms subject to a ministerial over-ride which could be applied in special circumstances. That set of baseline norms has now disappeared from the UK's petroleum law.

[198] Model Cl 6(3) imposes the obligation to surrender no less than the Mandatory Surrender Area. Model Cl 1 provides that "Mandatory Surrender Area" means whatever it is said to mean by Sch 5 to the licence.

[199] PILOT PPWG, *Work*, para 3.2.1.1.

[200] DECC, *Licensing Overview*, available for download from https://www.og.decc.gov.uk/upstream/licensing/overview.htm (accessed 23 January 2011).

[201] And, indeed, potentially problematic for the Department itself; the absence of a statutory basis stipulating the duration of the terms must at the very least increase the prospect of negotiation and special pleading by prospective licensees.

[202] Explanatory Memorandum to the Petroleum Licensing (Production) (Seaward Areas) Regulations 2008, para 2.

and more transparent.[203] The 2008 Model Clauses also provide the Minister for the first time with a discretionary power to extend the initial term for a period and subject to such terms and conditions as he shall see fit.[204]

The second term is granted in order to provide the licensee with **4.50** time to appraise how to exploit petroleum from the discoveries made during the initial term. If the licensee wishes the licence to continue beyond the second term into the production period it must, no later than 3 months before the end of the second term, provide the Minister with written notice of this intention.[205] At the end of the second term, the licence will be permitted only to continue in respect of the "producing part".[206] In the ordinary course of events, the producing part will be an area in respect of which the licensee has submitted, and the Minister has accepted, a detailed development and production programme that contains the licensee's proposals for how it is to get and transport the hydrocarbon it has discovered.[207] In previous practice, the second term, like the first, was of a fixed duration of 4 years.[208] It appears that the DECC intends this to continue to be the case,[209] but the changes introduced by the 2008 Model Clauses have again had the effect, whether by accident or design, of making the duration of the second term a matter for Sch 5 to the licence.[210] Thus there is at least a theoretical possibility that the duration of the second term may become a matter of individual negotiation. In a continuation of previous practice,[211] the 2008 Model Clauses provide the Minister with a discretionary power to extend the second term. The new wording of this provision makes it clear that this shall be for such period and subject to such terms and conditions as the Minister shall see fit.[212]

The purpose of the production period (third term) is to permit **4.51** the licensee to carry out the function of getting and conveying away

---

[203] DBERR, *The Petroleum Licensing (Production) (Seaward Areas) Regulations 2008 (2008/225)*, available for download at https://www.og.decc.gov.uk/upstream/licensing/licmodclause.htm (accessed 23 January 2011).

[204] Model Cl 7.

[205] Model Cl 8(1).

[206] *Ibid*.

[207] Model Cl 8(3)(b). Alternatively, the Minister may grant a consent (Model Cl 8(3)(a)) or himself serve a production and development plan upon the licensee (Model Cl 8(3)(c), read with Model Cl 176)).

[208] 2004 Regulations, Sch 4, Model Cl 1: definition of "Second Term".

[209] The DECC states on its Oil and Gas microsite that "the Second Term lasts four years": DECC, *Licensing: Licence Types*: https://www.og.decc.gov.uk/upstream/licensing/lictype.htm (accessed 23 January 2011).

[210] See further the discussion at para 4.49.

[211] See, eg, 2004 Regulations, Sch 4, Model Cl 5(3)(d).

[212] Model Cl 7.

the hydrocarbons which were discovered, and in respect of which development and production programmes were created, in the earlier phases of the licence. In previous practice, the third term was of an initial duration of 18 years,[213] a period which represented a significant reduction on the production phases permitted by earlier licences.[214] Again, it appears that the DECC intends this to continue to be the case,[215] but the changes introduced by the 2008 Model Clauses make the duration of the third term a matter for Sch 5 to the licence.[216] In the event that the field is still producing as it approaches the end of the third term, the licensees may seek an extension to the production period. Such an extension must be sought by applying to the Minister in writing no less than 3 months before the end of the production period. The Minister has a discretion as to whether to grant such an extension and, if so, on which terms and conditions.[217]

4.52   *Provisions permitting intervention and operational control.* It is sometimes colloquially said that a certain oil company "owns" a given oil field. In some respects this view is understandable. Oil and gas companies are commonly associated with a given field for decades, and need to invest massively in order to develop their licensed interests, at no little financial risk. In other respects, however, such thinking is misleading. The state may have chosen to make use of the capital and expertise of the international oil and gas industry; however, the fact remains that it is the Crown that ultimately holds the right to exploit oil and gas deposits *in strata*.[218] As we have seen, the Crown has a range of legitimate interests in relation to oil and gas deposits.[219] It needs to ensure that these interests are properly protected; so too other interests not so less intimately associated with oil and gas policy but which may be impacted by oil and gas operations, such as the rights of other parties who make use of the sea. Thus, the state needs to exercise some degree of control over operational matters.

4.53   The licence contains a range of provisions whereby the Minister requires the provision of information and/or seeks to exercise a degree of control over operations. The Minister's power under

---

[213] 2004 Regulations, Sch 4, Model Cl 6.

[214] Earlier iterations of model clauses permitted production periods of up to 40 years: Daintith, *Discretion*, para 3502.

[215] The DECC states on its Oil and Gas microsite that "the Third Term lasts 18 years": DECC, *Licensing: Licence Types*: https://www.og.decc.gov.uk/upstream/licensing/lictype. htm (accessed 23 January 2011) .

[216] See further the discussion at para 4.50.

[217] Model Cl 9.

[218] See para 4.7–4.10.

[219] See Chapters 1–3.

Model Cl 16 to demand a secondary work programme has already been discussed.[220] The licensee's obligation to submit a production and development plan has been noted in passing and will be further referred to in Chapter 5. The Minister is also entitled to decline to approve the appointment of an operator, or to revoke a previously given approval, on the basis that the operator is incompetent to exercise that function.[221] Many other examples of ministerial involvement or control may be given. For instance, the licensee is required:

- to measure the petroleum it extracts from the licensed area (Model Cl 14), keep "full and correct" accounts (Model Cl 15), and retain sundry records (Model Cl 29) and samples (Model Cl 31);
- to furnish quarterly and annual returns detailing (*inter alia*) all geological work and the results thereof (Model Cl 30) ;
- to liaise with the Ministry of Defence (Model Cl 44) and local fishing organisations (Model Cl 45) before undertaking certain works;
- to obtain ministerial consent before drilling or abandoning wells, to comply with conditions imposed in any given consent, and, when abandoning wells, to plug them to the Minister's specification and in a good and workmanlike manner (Model Cl 19) and to observe further specific requirements in relation to development wells (Model Cl 21) [222]
- to avoid harmful methods of working by maintaining appliances, apparatus and wells in good repair and condition and by executing all operations in a proper and workmanlike manner in accordance with methods customarily used in good oilfield practice (Model Cl 23);[223]
- to refrain from drilling wells in close proximity to boundaries (Model Cl 20), to unitise when required (Model Cl 27) and to follow the Minister's directions concerning cross-border developments (Model Cl 24).[224]

---

[220] See paras 4.43–4.46.

[221] Model Cl 24.

[222] In assessing whether to grant such consent, the Minister must bear in mind the appropriate environmental requirements: see paras 4.24–4.27.

[223] Good oilfield practice is not defined by the Regulations. It is described in DECC, *Guidance Notes on procedures regulating offshore oil and gas developments*, available for download from https://www.og.decc.gov.uk/regulation/guidance/reg_offshore/reg_offshore_guide.doc (accessed 25 January 2011) at p 8 as relating "largely to technical matters within the disciplines of geology and reservoir, petroleum and facilities engineering and to the impact of the development on the environment".

[224] For a further discussion of these topics, see Chapter 13.

4.54 Frontier licence. Geological exploration in the UKCS has tended in the northern (principally oil-producing) part of the province to be focused around the North Sea Basin lying between Great Britain and Norway, and in the region lying between Great Britain and Denmark and the Netherlands in the southern (principally gas-producing) part of the province. Certain other areas of considerable potential – most notably, the Atlantic margin area to the west of Shetland – have remained comparatively underexplored.[225] There are several reasons for the lack of investment in these so-called "frontier" areas. First, investors have naturally sought to shorten the odds of discovering oil and gas by exploring in areas where discoveries have already been made. Second, a reasonably well-developed infrastructure has gradually been built up in the longer established parts of the province. This is lacking in the frontier areas. The capital cost of building new infrastructure and/or the increased unit cost of moving oil not by pipeline but by tanker acts as a barrier to development, and means that small discoveries that might have been viable in the established regions are likely to be unprofitable in frontier areas.[226] Third, while no offshore development is ever free from difficulty, developments in the established basins are generally not as technically challenging as those in the frontier areas, where licensees require to deal with deep water,[227] difficult geology[228] and a harsh physical environment.[229] Given these risks and difficulties, frontier exploration has thus far been the preserve of major oil and gas companies.[230]

---

[225] House of Commons Energy and Climate Change Committee, *UK Offshore Oil and Gas: First Report of Session 2008–09*, vol II: *Oral and Written Evidence* (17 June 2009) (hereinafter "Commons, *First Report*, vol 2") Ev 16, Q99 and Ev 23, Q133.

[226] Commons, *First Report*, vol 2, Ev 16, Q99. Note that Total E&P UK, in partnership with DONG Energy, is developing the Laggan-Tormore area, and constructing a new gas pipeline system and a gas plant on Shetland, in Sullom Voe. See House of Commons Energy and Climate Change Committee, *UK Deepwater Drilling – Implications of the Gulf of Mexico Oil Spill: Second Report of Session 2010–11*, vol 1: *Report, together with formal minutes, oral and written evidence*, (6 January 2011) (HC 450-I), (hereinafter "Commons, *Second Report*, vol 1"), para 13.

[227] Early developments in the North Sea were commonly in depths of water of 50–100 metres. Modern developments in the Atlantic margin commonly have to deal with water depths between 350 and 400 metres.

[228] Commons, *First Report*, vol 2, Ev 7, Q54.

[229] *Ibid*, Ev 58, para 2.1.1.

[230] The DECC's list of operators and equity partners in each licence in West of Shetlands Area (blocks 204, 205, 206 and 207 particularly) reveals that most of the frontier licences awarded to date have been granted to "major players". See DECC, *Offshore Licence Data – by Block* (14 January 2011), available at https://www.og.decc.gov.uk/dti-lift/DTI_licence_data_release/offshore_data_by_block/offshore_data_by_block.htm (accessed 14 January 2011).

Frontier areas are therefore comparatively underexplored and, **4.55** viewed from a commercial perspective, underexploited.[231] The criticality of these facts increases as the UKCS matures as an oil and gas province and production from its established fields begins to decline, and the average size of new-find fields within established basins decreases.[232]

As long ago as 1991, when a group of "frontier area licences"[233] **4.56** was awarded relative to certain parts of the Atlantic Margin, it was recognised that, in order to encourage the opening up of new parts of the province, licences might have to be granted on special terms. After a period of quiescence, this recognition led in 2004 to the creation of the modern frontier licence. This form of licence (now known as the "6-year frontier licence") continues to be utilised. In addition, a new variant (the "9-year frontier licence") was created in the 26th Licensing Round to encourage further exploration activity west of Scotland.

In most respects the frontier licence is very similar to the traditional **4.57** production licence. The principal differences between the licences lie in their respective terms, area rental costs and surrender provisions. When first introduced in 2004, the frontier licence had four terms, as opposed to the traditional licence's three: a 2-year initial term, a 4-year second term, a 6-year third term and a production period which, like that of the traditional production licence, lasted for 18 years. The structure of the licence changed for the 26th Licensing Round and, as with the other licensing variants, the model clauses no longer set out the duration of each of the terms; this instead becomes a matter for Sch 5 to the licence.[234] Moreover, the licence will now consist of three terms, not four; what was previously the initial term and the second term have been collapsed together into one. It appears, however, that notwithstanding these changes, the broad thrust of the licence remains the same. The DECC has indicated that the licence will comprise a 6-year initial term, a 6-year second term

---

[231] Many environmentalists would contend that they have already been *over*-exploited: see para 4.25. In the 22nd Licensing Round only approximately 7% (7 out of 97) of the licences awarded were frontier. For the 23rd and 24th Licensing Rounds this number was reduced to almost 4% (6 of the 152 and 150 licences awarded, respectively); and down to about 3.5% (6 out of 172 awarded) for the 25th Licensing Round. For the most recent, the 26th Licensing Round, this figure is, at present, a little over half a per cent as only one of the 144 licences awarded thus far was a frontier licence. This figure may increase as a further tranche of licences is still under consideration at the time of writing.

[232] P Carter, "The Regulator's Dilemma: how to regulate yet promote investment in the same asset base" – *the UK experience* [2007] IELTR 62 (hereinafter "Carter, *The Regulator's Dilemma*").

[233] These were issued on different terms to the current frontier area licences and are not be confused with them. These were a form of bespoke licence and are discussed further at para 4.70.

[234] For a discussion of the issues raised by this policy, see paras 4.49–4.51.

and an 18-year third term.[235] As before, the acreage rental of the licence is greatly reduced for the first 2 years of its existence,[236] and the expectation appears to continue to be that the licensee will let a large initial area, invest heavily in exploration, and relinquish a large proportion of the licensed area.

4.58   The new 9-year frontier licence is similar in most material respects to the 6-year frontier licence, but provides an even longer (9-year) initial term to take cognisance of the still greater difficulties associated with oil and gas exploration west of Scotland.[237] Again, the model clauses themselves are seriously lacking in detailed content relative to this licence variation and much is left to Sch 5, but the DECC has indicated that the licence will be available only in relation to work obligations presented on a "drill or drop" basis,[238] with the decision on whether to proceed to drill being taken within the first 6 years of the initial term.[239]

4.59   Limitations are imposed upon the number of blocks which may be held by a licensee on frontier terms,[240] and it appears that the DECC intends to continue with its previous policy of requiring large areas of the licence to be relinquished at a relatively early stage. In the case of both the 6-year and 9-year frontier licence, seven-eighths of the area initially let will have to be relinquished by the end of the initial term.[241] At the end of the second term, the surrender provisions come to mirror those which apply to a traditional production licence at the end of its second term.

4.60   These modifications to the traditional licence have been informed by a desire on the DECC's part to effect a balance between making the frontier licence attractive to industry and ensuring that it makes the most of the assets it regulates.[242] On the one hand, the licence

---

[235] DECC, *Licensing: Licence Types*.

[236] DECC, *Applications Guidance*, Annexe 1.

[237] DECC, *Licensing: Licence Types*

[238] *Ibid*. For a discussion of what is meant by "drill or drop", see para 4.44.

[239] DECC, *Licensing: Licence Types*.

[240] Licensees are not permitted to hold more than ten contiguous blocks per frontier licence, with an aggregate total of 40 blocks per applicant per round: DECC, *Applications for Production Licences General Guidance*, at para 29.

[241] DECC, *Licensing: Licence Types*. In each case the document states that 75% must be relinquished within 3 years of the licence's commencement, with a further 50% being relinquished at the end of the initial period.

[242] Carter, *The Regulator's Dilemma* at 62. In the UK's early years as an oil and gas province, the state acted in a manner which later led to the criticism that it had surrendered valuable acreage to the international oil and gas industry on poor terms: see, eg, P Cameron, *Property Rights and Sovereign Rights*, at 85–87; see also the debate of the Second Reading of the Petroleum and Submarine Pipelines Bill where, in response to allegations of naivety in business matters, the Labour Secretary of State for Energy, Eric Varley, accused his Conservative predecessors of "giving away licences like detergent coupons": *Hansard* HC (series 5), vol 891, col 518 (30 April 1975).

encourages companies to licence a large area by offering a generous abatement on rental; on the other hand, the state seeks to avoid tying up too large an area by imposing limits on the total area which a licensee can hold on frontier terms, and seeks to prevent promising areas from being tied up for an undue length of time by allowing only a limited amount of an additional time for initial exploration, and requiring the relinquishment of large areas at the end of that period. This encourages early and through exploration and permits the areas discarded to be recycled back into the licensing system quickly.[243] The introduction of the new 9-year version of the licence demonstrates that the state will continue to assess the licences it offers to ensure that they provide an adequate basis to encourage exploration in frontier areas.

Assessing the success of the frontier licence. At the time of writing, **4.61** 25 frontier licences have been granted since the licence form's introduction in 2004.[244] This is a very low figure when compared with either the promote or the traditional production licences, where over the same period there have been 266[245] and 419[246] grants respectively. However, it is dangerous to judge the success of this licensing variant purely on the strength of the number of licences granted. First, it has to be noted that the initial area let under a frontier licence will typically be much greater than that let on either traditional or promote terms. Moreover, it is generally accepted that, although substantial finds are by no means impossible in the well-explored areas of the UKCS,[247] there is a greater scope for making substantial

---

[243] The issues raised and legislative response are therefore similar to those discussed at para 4.49. However, the issues arise in a more acute form in the present context.

[244] Seven were offered in the 22nd Licensing Round, 6 in the 23rd and 6 in the 24th, 6 in the 25th and 1 in the 26th. See the webpages of each licensing round at DECC, *Oil and Gas: Licensing*, available at https://www.og.decc.gov.uk/upstream/licensing/index. htm (accessed 14 January 2011).

[245] Fifty-eight were offered in the 22nd Licensing Round, 75 in the 23rd and 65 in the 24th, 41 in the 25th and 27 in the 26th.

[246] Thirty-two were offered in the 22nd Licensing Round, 70 in the 23rd and 79 in the 24th, 124 in the 25th and 114 in the 26th: see DECC, *Oil is well*, read with the Written Ministerial Statement on the 22nd Round.

[247] J Munns, *Remaining potential and opportunities on the UKCS and the need for new entrants*, SHARP IOR Newsletter Issue 2, 2002, available for download at http://ior.senergyltd.com/issue2/talkingp/tp-2.htm (accessed 14 January 2011): "The recent PanCanadian Buzzard discovery in the North Sea demonstrates that giant oilfields can be discovered in mature areas." The Buzzard field, located at the fringes of the Moray Firth basin, is one of the largest discoveries within the last decade in the UKCS with estimated reserves of 300–400 million boe. It is hoped that the recently discovered Catcher field may be of a similar size: M Johnson, *North Sea oil find lifts groups*, *Financial Times*, 29 June 2010, available from http://www.ft.com/cms/s/0/25559a62-8301-11df-8b15-00144feabdc0. html#axzz1BzzqRlvu (accessed 23 January 2011).

discoveries in frontier areas than in the previously explored areas of the province.[248] If the frontier licence facilitates the discovery of only one or two substantial discoveries then, from a commercial perspective, at least, it will be adjudged a success.

4.62 **Promote licence.** The introduction of the promote licence followed a period of consultation, formally[249] begun in September 2002, between the Department and a broad cross-section of industry interests and stakeholders in the UKCS.[250] The purpose of the consultation was to assess the level of industry support for a licence tailored to meet the needs of the smaller or "niche" enterprise possessing considerable geo-technical ability but possibly lacking, at least in the first instance, the financial and/or technical and environmental capabilities which had hitherto been necessary to hold a production licence. The consultation document proposed that certain relaxations should be offered to such companies in order to attract them to the UKCS.[251] The Department received widespread (but not universal[252]) support for the proposal, and promote licences were first awarded during 2003 in the 21st Seaward Licensing Round.[253]

4.63 The promote licence comprises only a very slight variation to the traditional production licence. The initial term is divided into two parts by a break-point occurring on the second anniversary of the licence's grant; the work programme[254] is divided into Parts I and II; the licence survives beyond the break-point only if the licensee has taken all action described in Part I of the work plan, and has undertaken to complete before the expiry of the initial term the work described in Part II of the work programme; and the requirement found in the traditional production licence that, for a licence to continue into its second term, its "work programme" must be completed before the

---

[248] See, eg, Carter, *The Reguator's Dilemma* at 63 where frontier areas are described as "high risk/high potential".

[249] As the industry organisation PILOT had been involved in the formulation of the proposal in one sense the consultation process could be said to have started earlier.

[250] See DTI, *Possible Introduction of 'Promote' to Encourage Exploration Activity on the UKCS: Consultation Document* 2002 (hereinafter "DTI, *Possible Introduction of Promote*"), available for download from https://www.og.decc.gov.uk/consultations/consultation180902.htm (accessed 14 January 2011).

[251] DTI, *Possible Introduction of Promote*, paras 1–4. See also DTI, *Possible Introduction of "Promote" Licence to Encourage Exploration Activity on the UKCS: Open Consultation October/November 2002: Summary of Responses* (hereinafter "DTI, *Promote: Summary of Responses*"), available for download from https://www.og.decc.gov.uk/consultations/promconfind.htm (accessed 23 January 2011), paras 1 and 2.

[252] DTI, *Promote: Summary of Responses* at para 3.

[253] DTI press release, *Newcomers ready to embrace North Sea opportunities*, 2003, available for download from http://www.databydesign.co.uk/energy/ukdata/21_resul.htm (accessed 25 January 2011).

[254] See the further discussion of work programme at paras 4.42–4.43.

end of the first term, is in practice replaced by a reference to "Part II of the work programme". If a promote licence survives into a second term, it effectively converts into a traditional production licence.

These superficially modest departures from the traditional licence have been supplemented by ministerial guidance and practice. In particular, for the first 2 years of a promote licence, the annual rental rate is reduced by 90 per cent compared with a traditional production licence.[255] This is a dramatic reduction – one which the state has presumably been willing to make in order to make the promote licence affordable to its target market, on the basis that the benefits which will accrue by expanding the pool of players in the UKCS will outweigh the potential loss of acreage rental.[256]   **4.64**

In addition, the DECC has confirmed that an application containing a limited workscope restricted to activities such as data acquisition and evaluation will initially be acceptable during Part I of the work programme,[257] but that it expects by, the time Part II commences at the end of Year 2, there must be "a firm drilling (or agreed equivalent equally substantive activity) commitment".[258] The Department has also confirmed that while it requires full financial, technical and environmental capacity within the first 2 years,[259] it is not necessary – or indeed, appropriate[260] – for the promote licensee to possess these capabilities at the time of the grant. In practice, the initial promote licensee is unlikely, by itself, to attempt to attain the requisite technical capabilities, but will seek to import these into the licence either by entering into a joint venture with one or more established oil company players already possessing the requisite capacity, or by divesting itself of the asset entirely by selling it to a more established oil company after completing initial appraisal work.[261]   **4.65**

---

[255] DECC, *Applications Guidance*, Appendix 1, "Traditional Seaward Production Licence's rental Schedule", p 10, para 4.

[256] As was noted earlier, the contribution of acreage rental to the state's take from oil and gas production in the UKCS is relatively small: see paras 4.28–4.30.

[257] DECC, *Licensing: Licence Types*: https://www.og.decc.gov.uk/upstream/licensing/lictype.htm (accessed 25 January 2011).

[258] DECC, *Licensing: Licence Types*.

[259] *Ibid*; and DECC, *Applications Guidance*, para 21.

[260] If the licensee does possess such capabilities, the Department will expect it to seek a traditional licence, rather than a promote one: DECC, *Applications Guidance*, at 4, paras 18, 19, 20 and 21,. Where promote applications are in competition with frontier or traditional, the acreage will be awarded to the traditional/frontier applicant in all but the most exceptional circumstances, because of the confidence that the Secretary of State can draw from the proof of financial and operating capacity that a traditional/frontier applicant must provide.

[261] DECC, *Possible Introduction of Promote*, para 10. For an example of this occurring in practice, see the agreement between Reach Exploration and Petro-Canada relative to promote licence P1084. See the press release of 25 May 2004, available for download from http://www.reachexploration.co.uk/PR250504.pdf (accessed 25 January 2011).

4.66   Although the Government has been quick to use the perceived success of the promote licence to evidence the ongoing vitality of the UKCS,[262] it should be noted that the traditional licence is still the state's preferred production licensing vehicle. Where there is competition for acreage and one party offers to take a licence on traditional terms and the other on promote terms, the DECC will in general give precedence to the traditional application on the basis that it involves a firmer work programme, and therefore better serves the national interest.[263] The state's intention in offering promote licences is to attract players who would have found the barriers presented by the traditional production licence insuperable, not to allow established players who do not require the relaxations it offers to obtain new acreage "on the cheap".

4.67   The relaxations offered by this licensing variant provide the promote licensee with a set of concessions not available to the more established holder of a traditional licence. There is therefore unequal treatment between the two classes of licensee. However, there seems to be little or no disquiet about this among the more established companies.[264] This is less surprising than may at first appear. The super-majors who operate on the global scale may be disinterested in the relatively small developments which tend to attract the attention of the promote licensee and, as we have already seen, other established companies may perceive the promote licence initiative as an opportunity to permit them to in due course acquire, with at least a somewhat reduced risk, some of the fruits of the promote licensee's labours.[265] The built-in preference for the traditional licence referred to above also provides a degree of comfort to the established company, who will know that in the event of competition for acreage, a licensee offering to take on traditional terms will in all likelihood be allocated acreage ahead of a promote licensee.

4.68   *Assessing the success of the promote licence.* As has already been noted,[266] a relatively large number of promote licences have been awarded since the variant was introduced, although markedly fewer were awarded in the 26th Round than in any round since the

---

[262] DECC press release, *New Entrants Sink £90 million into North Sea*, available for download from http://webarchive.nationalarchives.gov.uk/+/http://www.dti.gov.uk/news/newsarticle101105b.html (accessed 14 January 2011).

[263] Although the decision is, strictly speaking, based on Marks Scheme, the more stringent criteria for traditional licence generally means higher marks. See DECC, *Applications Guidance*, at pp 7 and 8, paras 41–50.

[264] Daintith, *Discretion*, para 3326.

[265] See para 4.65.

[266] See para 4.61.

variant was introduced.[267] Moreover, we have already noted that the small number of licences granted does not of itself tell us all we need to know about the level of success of the frontier licence; by parity of reasoning, the large number of promote licences is not determinative either. It is in the nature of the promote licence that while the success rate of wells drilled under its aegis should be high, many, if not all, of the discoveries made will be small. Moreover, the number of such licences to continue after the 2-year break-point has been relatively low.[268] In addition, we can reasonably expect that the attracting small enterprises to the UKCS will almost inevitably lead to a higher level of business failure than we have been used to among licensee companies, which may in turn lead to knock-on difficulties for some within the contracting sector. None of the above is intended to suggest that the promote licence has been a failure, but simply to sound the warning that an initiative which encourages less well-resourced companies to engage in a risky but potentially profitable endeavour will have its ups and downs. For all that, there is sense in the Government's strategy. In the short life of the initiative wells have been drilled which would either not have been drilled at all, or which at least would not have otherwise been drilled so soon; promote licensees have discovered oil; and enterprises who would not otherwise been able to afford to enter into the UKCS as licensees have had an opportunity to do so.[269] The full extent of the contribution which will be made by oil produced under promote licences to the UK economy remains to be seen. But irrespective of the initiative's final assessment, the regulator is to be commended for its inventiveness and responsiveness.

Frontier licence on promote terms. The frontier licence on promote terms, discussed at para 3.69 of the first edition of this work, is no longer offered. The author is aware of no such licences having been awarded or indeed even applied for. The variant always appeared to be founded on a rather curious premise[270] and its disappearance is not therefore unexpected. By offering an extended period for exploration, the 9-year frontier licence referred to above might be thought to resemble the frontier licence on promote terms.[271] In reality, however, the licences differ markedly in that applicants for the

4.69

---

[267] See para 4.61.

[268] Thirty of the 54 promote licences granted in the 21st Offshore Round did not continue beyond the break-point: DTI press release, *New entrants sink £90 million into the North Sea* (2005).

[269] DECC, *New entrants sink £90 million into the North Sea.*

[270] The type of player who would require a promote licence is by definition unlikely to be interested in or capable of opening up frontier areas within a province.

[271] See paras 4.56–4.59.

9-year frontier licence require to demonstrate financial and technical and environmental capability from the outset.[272]

4.70 **Bespoke licences.** Given the discretionary nature of the system, it should come as no great surprise to note that the Minister is empowered to grant licences on non-standard terms. Section 4(1)(e) of the Petroleum Act 1998 provides that the Secretary of State shall make regulations prescribing the model clauses which shall be incorporated into petroleum licences "unless he thinks fit to modify or exclude them in any particular case". This discretion to tailor the terms of particular licences has been used on at least three occasions in recent times. First, when frontier area licences were granted in the May 1991 Licensing Round, this was done on an ad hoc basis, without the promulgation of a dedicated set of frontier area model clauses. Instead, the frontier area variations were advertised in advance[273] and incorporated into the six licences so awarded.[274] Second, as has already been noted, following consultation with the industry, all seaward production licences issued in the 20th and 21st Rounds were allocated on terms different from those contained in the model clauses then in force.[275] Third, at least one licence is known to have been issued which was tailored to accommodate the specific difficulties associated with re-developing a field which had already been relinquished and decommissioned by its previous operator.[276] The use of the power in the second-given example has been criticised by Daintith and Hill as being "of doubtful legality" on the basis that the "in any particular case" criterion cannot be legitimately used to effect a change of general application.[277] It is submitted that this criticism is a valid one, and that, although Daintith and Hill direct no criticism towards it, even the first-mentioned example might be thought to lie at the border of acceptability. The third-mentioned example, however, would seem to be a wholly legitimate use of the power to issue a

---

[272] DECC, *Licensing: Licensing Types*.

[273] DECC, *Notice Inviting Applications under the Petroleum (Production) (Seaward Areas) Regulations 1988, London Gazette*, 29 June 1990 at 11243–11245, available for download from http://www.gazettes-online.co.uk (accessed 4 June 2007). See particularly paras 2(b), 3(b) and 5–7.

[274] Daintith, Willoughby and Hill, para 1-602.

[275] See para 4.47.

[276] See DECC, *Licensing: Licence Types*. The Argyll field began producing oil in 1975 and was the first productive oilfield in the UKCS. It was decommissioned by its then operators, BHP, in 1992 but was re-opened by a joint venture led by Tuscan Energy (Scotland) Ltd in 2002: see DECC, *Ardmore Field Development Consent*, available for download from www.og.DECC.gov.uk/environment/permits/TuscanArdmore.htm (accessed 25 January 2011).

[277] Daintith, Willoughby and Hill, para 1-328/4; see also Daintith, *Discretion*, at para 3513.

licence on modified terms. The fact that, post-2008, the model clauses no longer detail the licence's term and leave much key content to be stipulated by the DECC in Sch 5 may make it less likely that the Department will have to issue bespoke licences in the future.

Landward licences

For a time, the main UK[278] landward licensing regime differed markedly from that applied in seaward areas. Three separate licences – exploration, appraisal and development – were awarded in succession as operations within the licensed area progressed from one phase to the next.[279] This regime was abandoned for new licences by the 1995 Regulations[280] which created the petroleum, exploration and development licence (PEDL), the current model clauses for which are to be found in the 2004 Regulations as amended.[281] The PEDL is the principal landward licence in current issue.[282] The PEDL shares the same structure and philosophy as the seaward production licence.[283] The duration of the terms of the licence differs from that of the traditional production licence;[284] the licences' Model Cl 2, although identical in function, are given different titles;[285] and the

4.71

---

[278] The caveat given at para 4.2 above, relative to Northern Ireland and the Isle of Man, also applies here. Nor is this chapter concerned with methane drainage licences or the specialities associated with coal bed methane. For a short discussion of these issues, see Daintith, Willoughby and Hill, paras 1-312 and 1-313 respectively.

[279] Daintith, Willoughby and Hill, para 1-312. For a fuller discussion of the early onshore regime (which continues to be relevant for pre-1995 licences), see J Salter, *UK onshore oil and gas law: a practical guide to the legal regime relating to United Kingdom onshore oil and gas operations* (1986), Chapter 3.

[280] Petroleum (Production) (Landward Areas) Regulations 1995 (SI 1995/1436), Sch 3.

[281] Ie in the Petroleum Licensing (Exploration and Production) (Seaward and Landward Areas) Regulations 2004, at Sch 6, as the same has been amended by the Petroleum Licensing (Exploration and Production) (Seaward and Landward Areas) (Amendment) Regulations 2006.

[282] The holder of a PEDL or one of its predecessor licence types may in addition apply for a supplementary seismic survey licence (SSSL) to authorise the undertaking of seismic surveys in an area which will be specified in Sch 1 to the licence but which must in any event be adjacent to the principal licence (see Model Cl 2). These licences last for a period of 1 year (Model Cl 3) but are subject to automatic termination on certain grounds specified in Model Cl 4. The licence contains a number of stipulations as to the circumstances in which seismic surveys may be undertaken (Model Cl 6) and imposes obligations to keep records (Model Cl 7) and make returns (Model Cl 8) which are broadly analogous to those contained in the seaward production licence (discussed at paras 4.38–4.53).

[283] The licences are divided into terms, and progress from one term to the next is contingent upon meeting certain conditions and relinquishing territory.

[284] Model Cl 1 provides for an initial term of 6 years, a second term of 5 years and a production period of 20 years.

[285] "Grant of licence" in the case of the traditional seaward production licence and "right to search and bore for and get petroleum" in the case of the PEDL.

PEDL omits as unnecessary several of the provisions which deal with the regulation of marine matters. The licences otherwise closely resemble each other.

4.72   Like seaward production licences, PEDLs are generally offered in rounds, although out-of-rounds applications are possible.[286] At the time of writing, there have been 13 landward licensing rounds in all and a 14th is about to open.[287] PEDLs are available on promote terms,[288] but not on frontier ones and, as with seaward licences, prospective licensees may, if the circumstances of an individual case permit, be able to persuade the Minister that a PEDL should be issued on bespoke terms.

4.73   There is no denying that oil obtained under the seaward production licence has been of much greater significance to the UK economy than that obtained under landward licences. In the period from the beginning of production to end 2009, a total of 3,133,397,511 tons of oil have been produced from the offshore UKCS. In the same period, 65,337,974 tons of oil have produced onshore, the overwhelming majority from one field; Wytch Farm in Dorset.[289] The offshore total therefore exceeds the onshore by a factor of 48 to one. Nevertheless it would be wrong to ignore the contribution to the UK economy of a cumulative quantity of oil which rivals the amount produced by all but the most massive offshore fields.[290] Onshore licensing will continue to have a role to play for years to come. Developments in directional and extended reach drilling mean that it is possible for a well commenced in an onshore borehole to be deviated a significant distance offshore. Thus oil and gas reserves which lie beneath environmentally sensitive areas within relatively close proximity to the coast may be reached by a rig located on an onshore location.[291] This approach may also appeal to a licensee for simple reasons of economics. Onshore drilling avoids the requirement for expensive offshore pipeline construction or tanker

---

[286] DECC, *Licensing: Award of Licensing.*

[287] DECC, *14th Licensing Round*: https://www.og.decc.gov.uk/upstream/licensing/onshore_14th/index.htm (accessed 25 January 2011).

[288] See the Petroleum Licensing (Exploration and Production) (Seaward and Landward Areas) Regulations 2004, as amended by the Petroleum Licensing (Exploration and Production) (Seaward and Landward Areas) (Amendment) Regulations 2006, Sch 7.

[289] The statistics are taken from DECC, *UKCS Oil Production*, available for download from https://www.og.decc.gov.uk/information/bb_updates/appendices/Appendix9.xls (accessed 25 January 2011).

[290] Claymore has produced some 76,000,000 tons of oil over its lifespan and Cormorant North some 55,000,000. No-one would argue that these were insignificant discoveries.

[291] Rigzone, *Reach Exploration Awarded 16 Blocks In UK Licensing Round*, available for download from http://www.rigzone.com/news/article.asp?a_id=25174. At the time of writing, production is scheduled to commence from Reach Petroleum's Lybster field, an offshore discovery drilled from onshore.

use and provides the licensee with the option either of constructing an onshore pipeline[292] or transporting oil by tanker, an option which may very well be the most economic when seeking to exploit a small field.

---

[292] Onshore pipelines are cheaper to lay than offshore ones. However, the licensee may experience difficulties in overcoming the property law rights of the proprietors of onshore land: see Chapter 17.

CHAPTER 5

MATURE PROVINCE INITIATIVES

Greg Gordon and John Paterson

As a hydrocarbon province such as the UKCS matures, industry and   5.1
government must play close attention to the changing economics of
both existing operations and new developments.

From the point of view of government, it is important to extend   5.2
the life of existing fields for as long as possible, to encourage exploration for new fields and to encourage the development of known
but perhaps marginal discoveries. There are two principal reasons
for this. First, there is the question of energy security. While some
observers believed that this issue had essentially disappeared from
the political agenda at the end of the last century, with the liberalisation of energy markets,[1] there is no question but that it is now
once again a major concern for governments.[2] Second, there is the
impact on the national economy: whether one is a net importer or
exporter of oil and gas may make a significant difference to the
balance of payments.

From an industry standpoint, the maturing of a province alters   5.3
its relative attractiveness compared with others. Thus, for a major
company, well used to operating on the global stage, the smaller
return on investment available, whether from the smaller discoveries
likely to be made or during the downward slope of an existing field's

---

[1] See, eg, J Mitchell, 'Energy Security', in Mitchell *et al* (eds), *The New Economy of Oil:
Impacts on Business, Geopolitics and Society* (2001), pp 176–208.

[2] For example, the Government's 2050 Pathways Anaylsis notes that the "pathways
show an ongoing need for fossil fuels in our energy mix, although the precise long term
role of oil, coal and gas will depend on a range of issues, such as development of CCS":
Department of Energy and Climate Change, *2050 Pathways Analysis* (URN 10D/764, July
2010), p 35. See also Chapter 3 above.

production profile,[3] may mean that bigger rewards are possible in the context of frontier provinces elsewhere in the world where larger discoveries may still be made.[4] Such companies may have little interest either in exploring for new fields, in developing marginal discoveries or in taking steps to extend the life of existing fields. There may still be money to be made from such ventures, but the same investment in a frontier province that results in a commercial discovery is likely to produce a bigger yield. On the other hand, smaller and often newer companies may perceive rich pickings in the same circumstances, perhaps due to variations in risk appetite, or perhaps making use of innovative technology.

5.4   A range of government policies may, therefore, have an impact on decisions taken by the industry in such a context. Government must walk a fine line if it is to encourage exploration, development and the extension of the life of existing fields while at the same time ensuring that it satisfies legitimate societal expectations regarding the nation's take from such activity.

5.5   These issues were recognised by government and industry as early as 1998, not least because they became particularly pressing in a high-cost province such as the UKCS in the context of the low oil prices then prevailing. The Oil and Gas Industry Task Force (OGITF) was established at that time with the "overall objective ... to create a climate for the UKCS to retain its position as a pre-eminent active centre of oil [and] gas exploration, development and production and to keep the UK contracting and supplies industry at the leading edge in terms of overall competitiveness".[5] This group established the so-called "Vision for 2010": "The UK Oil and Gas Industry and Government working together in partnership to deliver quicker, smarter, sustainable energy solutions for the new century. A vital UK Continental Shelf is maintained as the UK is universally recognised as a world centre for global business."[6] In order to realise this vision, a list of deliverables was established, including the following: a production level of 3 million boe/d beyond 2010; £3 billion of industry investment per annum; and prolonged self-sufficiency in

---

[3] "Average discovery size since 2000 has been 267 million boe per field, with two thirds of all discoveries less than 15 million boe (these should be compared with early UKCS fields each containing hundreds of million boe and, in some cases, 1 to 2 billion boe)": Oil & Gas UK, Economic Report 2010, p 7.

[4] "The UKCS has, therefore, to compete with less mature and less costly provinces, where the size of discoveries is much larger": Oil & Gas UK, Economic Report 2010, p 42.

[5] PILOT, *About PILOT: What is PILOT?*: http://www.pilottaskforce.co.uk/data/aboutpilot.cfm (accessed 16 December 2010).

[6] PILOT, *About PILOT: What is PILOT?: PILOT Vision* (hereinafter "PILOT, *Vision*"): http://www.pilottaskforce.co.uk/data/pvision.cfm (accessed 16 December 2010).

oil and gas for the UK.[7] The OGITF continued in existence until 1999 and was succeeded in 2000 by the PILOT initiative, which was established both to monitor progress towards the vision for 2010 and to identify what else might need to be done to ensure that it is realised.

As will be seen in this chapter, the work of PILOT has led to   5.6
significant initiatives aimed at responding to the challenges thrown up by a mature province. The first of these is the Fallow Areas Initiative, which aims to deal with the problem both of allocated but unexplored acreage and of undeveloped discoveries; the second is the so-called Brownfields Initiative, which aims to maximise the economic recovery of hydrocarbons from existing developments and which includes most notably, for present purposes, the Stewardship Initiative. As will be seen, these initiatives are noteworthy not only because of their innovative approach to the complex of technical, economic and political challenges posed by the mature province, but also because (at least in the case of Fallow Discoveries and Stewardship) they reveal a willingness on the part of the industry to acquiesce in schemes for which there is at best a relatively flimsy legal basis.

THE FALLOW AREAS INITIATIVE

Background and introduction

As has already been seen, in the early days of exploration for oil and   5.7
gas in the UKCS, production licences were granted which were of a lengthy duration and which contained very little in the way of provisions designed to control or incentivise exploration or production activity within the acreage let.[8] As Daintith has observed, "the idea that licensees might make significant discoveries but then not develop them does not appear to have occurred to those who first drafted the offshore licensing arrangements in 1964–1965".[9] Although one should not rush to criticise draftsmen who were operating under significant pressure of time and with little experience of the industry they sought to regulate, the fact remains that the offshore licensing system put in place in 1965 left the state powerless to control the pace either of exploration or production. Major legislative

---

[7] PILOT, *Vision*.
[8] Early licences had production periods of up to 40 years and were based upon "the very limited landward experience gained to 1964": T Daintith, G Willoughby and A Hill, *United Kingdom Oil and Gas Law* (looseleaf, Release 53, February 2007) (hereinafter "Daintith, Willoughby and Hill"), para 1–107. See also para 4.51 above.
[9] T Daintith, *Discretion in the Administration of Offshore Oil and Gas* (2006) (hereinafter "Daintith, *Discretion*") at para 4104.

amendments made in 1975[10] and further measures adopted in 1988[11] and 1996[12] went some way towards ameliorating the problem. However, at least in practice, there remained in the areas of exploration and production something of a regulatory black hole into which licences were wont to disappear once they had completed their initial term.[13] By 2002, it was estimated by the PILOT Progressing Partnership Work Group (PILOT PPWG) that there were 247 blocks in the UKCS where no significant exploration activity had taken place for an extended period, and 250 discoveries where no significant progress had been made to produce hydrocarbons.[14] While it was believed that in around half of these cases there was good cause for this lack of progress, that still left a large number of blocks and

---

[10] The Petroleum and Submarine Pipelines Act 1975 made substantial unilateral changes to all existing licences with retroactive effect. See Daintith, Willoughby and Hill at paras 1–330 to 1–331. The 1975 Act introduced the Minister's power to serve an additional or supplementary work programme at any time: this power continues to be incorporated into current licences by Model Cl 16; and to exercise controls over development and production, which controls are now incorporated into current licences by Model Cll 17 and 18). The legislation was passed in the face of considerable industry opposition: Daintith, *Discretion*, para 5107. The retroactivity of the Bill, and the fact that it offered no compensation to the industry in respect of any diminution in value between the licences as granted and as they would be after the legislation entered into force, drew particular criticism in Parliament: see, eg, *Hansard* HC (series 5), vol 891, cols 486 and 503 (30 April 1975) and Standing Committee D, Official Report (1974–1975), vol V, cols 1106 and 1146–1172.

[11] The Petroleum (Production) (Seaward Areas) Regulations 1988 (SI 1988/1213) replaced the two-term licence which had previously been in use with a three-term licence by splitting what had previously been a 30-year second term into a 12-year second term and an 18-year third term and providing that the licence would be permitted to progress into a third term if a field development plan has been approved or consented to.

[12] A 1996 Fallow Field Initiative (on which see Daintith, Willoughby and Hill (looseleaf, Release 62, Feb 2010), para 1–605) led to the Petroleum (Production) (Seaward Areas) (Amendment) Regulations 1996 (SI 1996/2946), which provided for a short initial term which could be extended in the event that the licensee undertook additional exploration activity and linked the amount of acreage which could be retained beyond the initial term to the number of wells drilled. A number of licences issued on these terms continue in existence but the amendments were not adjudged a success and, as shall be seen, were abandoned for future licences in 2002.

[13] The initial term of the licence is less problematic because of the need for the initial work programme to be carried out if the licence is to continue.

[14] PILOT, *The Work of the Progressing Partnership Work Group* (2002) (hereinafter "PILOT PPWG, *Work*"), para 3.1.2: http://www.pilottaskforce.co.uk/files/workgroup/422. doc (accessed 16 December 2010). *Prima facie*, the position seems to have been worse than estimated: in a little over 2 years of operation, the initiative identified 660 fallow blocks or parts of blocks and 240 fallow discoveries: PILOT, *Annual Report 2004–2005* (2005), p 6: http://www.pilottaskforce.co.uk/templates/relay/communicationrelay.cfm/1653 (accessed 16 December 2010). However, the large disparity between the position reported in 2005 and the 2002 estimate may at least in part be explained by the fact that the 2005 figures include not just blocks, but parts of blocks.

discoveries lying fallow for reasons which had nothing to do with the blocks or discoveries themselves but on other grounds, chiefly those connected with the choices and priorities of the licensees.[15] This would be unfortunate at any time for a state such as the UK, which obtains the vast majority of its oil and gas revenue by taxing the profits made on produced hydrocarbons.[16] But the criticality of this situation increased as the UKCS matured as an oil and gas province and the production from existing fields started to decline,[17] less and less virgin acreage became available to let outside of frontier areas, and the average size of new discoveries became progressively smaller.[18]

PILOT PPWG was established in 2002 to identify, report upon and make recommendations concerning "all commercial [and] behavioural barriers to development"[19] which existed in the maturing UKCS. The deficiencies within the licensing regime discussed above were one of a number of issues[20] PILOT PPWG identified when reporting upon its work to date: 5.8

> "The standard UKCS approach of long licence terms and low annual rentals combined with both limited relinquishment and limited activity obligations provides an environment where there is too little pressure on licensees to deliver value from their licences. Under these conditions, misalignments between co-licensees, decisions on marginal or high-risk economic activities, or divestment can be repeatedly deferred and remain unresolved, potentially indefinitely."[21]

---

[15] Many oil and gas companies have a portfolio containing assets in diverse locations throughout the world. They will not necessarily wish or be able to press on with the development of all those assets at an even pace but may decide, perhaps for strategic reasons or because of a lack of financial or other resources, to prioritise an asset or group of assets in one province over those in another. They may, for example, wish to retain assets in a relatively stable but high-cost province, such as the UK, as "insurance" while they undertake higher-risk, but potentially more profitable, activity elsewhere.

[16] See para 4.30 and Chapter 6.

[17] See DECC, *Digest of United Kingdom Energy Statistics (DUKES) 2010: long–term trends*, Table 3.1.1: *Crude oil and petroleum products: production, imports and exports 1970 to 2009*. Note that total annual production has steadily dropped from a peak of 137,099 tonnes in 1999 (of which 132,814 tonnes were offshore production) to 68,199 tonnes in 2009 (of which 67,018 tonnes were offshore production). Also see Figure 3.1 above.

[18] P Carter, *The Regulator's Dilemma: how to regulate yet promote investment in the same asset base – the UK's experience* [2007] IELTR 62 at 62.

[19] PILOT PPWG, *Work*, para 1.2.

[20] Among the other problem areas identified by this influential report were the need to place controls upon rights of pre-emption (PILOT PPWG, *Work*, Chapter 6, discussed further at para 18.13), and the commercial and supply chain Codes of Practice (PILOT PPWG, *Work*, Chapters 4 and 11 respectively).

[21] PILOT PPWG, *Work*, at para 3.1.2

5.9   The work of PILOT PPWG led to significant changes to the production licence Model Clauses which were implemented in the 2002 Licensing Round and which continue to form the basis of the current standard production licence's term and relinquishment structure.[22] As has already been seen, however, in the absence of primary legislation having retroactive effect, amendments to the Model Clauses affect only new licences incorporating those Model Clauses.[23] In consequence, Pilot PPWG also had to consider how to remedy the same weaknesses in the context of existing licences. The Work Group decided against recommending retrospective changes to existing licences on the basis that such a measure would be "disproportionate given the willingness of the exploration community to address the issue".[24] However, the Work Group did not have sufficient faith in the community's professed willingness to allow it to recommend a purely voluntary approach. Instead it recognised that "a voluntary scheme was already effectively in place and had failed to fully galvanise activity".[25] Given what has already been said about the number of fallow blocks and discoveries in existence at the time when PILOT PPWG was reporting, this might be thought to be a considerable understatement.[26] Be that as it may, the Work Group was satisfied that the most satisfactory result would be achieved by a scheme which was essentially voluntary in nature, but which was "underpinned by licence powers and the discretion of the Department".[27]

5.10   In formulating the detail of the scheme, the Work Group adopted two guiding principles: "that a group of licensees doing all that a fully resourced and skilled group could reasonably be expected to do should not be disadvantaged and that no group should have reasonable grounds to feel that they had not been given full opportunity to create value from their licence."[28] While the Work Group chose to express its findings in a positive manner, the principles could also be couched in a more negative way: the initiative will not protect a group of licensees who are not doing all that could reasonably be expected; and a group of licensees who have had the opportunity to exploit their acreage but who have not availed themselves of it cannot expect to retain it indefinitely.

5.11   The Government adopted PILOT PPWG's recommendations. The Fallow Areas Initiative is made up of two separate but related

---

[22] See para 4.47.
[23] See para 4.17.
[24] PILOT PPWG, *Work*, para 3.2.3.2.
[25] *Ibid.*
[26] See para 5.7 above.
[27] PILOT PPWG, *Work*, para 3.2.3.3.
[28] *Ibid.*

schemes: the Fallow Blocks Process and the Fallow Discovery Process. Although conceptually similar, the two programmes differ somewhat in detail. They will be discussed in turn.

The Fallow Blocks Process

A fallow block is defined as a block where the initial term of the **5.12** licence has expired and there has been no drilling, dedicated seismic or other significant activity for a period of 3 years.[29] The Revised Fallow Blocks Guidance does not define the term "block" but an earlier set of Clarification Notes issued by the DTI states that a block "will be assigned an area agreed between the Department and Licensees" and that determinations made for field or Petroleum Revenue Tax purposes are not relevant to this issue.[30] Information provided by the Department on the progress and operation of the process discloses that, in practice, the Department commonly sub-divides blocks into two or more constituent areas. Areas on the block that are producing hydrocarbons are by definition excluded from the ambit of the Fallow Blocks Initiative, as are areas in which a discovery has been made.[31] However, if there is a fallow area within the block it will be isolated from the non-fallow areas and subjected to the Fallow Blocks Process.[32] As the way in which "block" is to be understood has a considerable bearing upon the scheme's operation and extent,[33] it is perhaps unfortunate that the main items of published guidance are less than explicit on how the scheme is implemented in practice.

The Department assesses the status of blocks annually and, having **5.13** made a provisional determination of all blocks' status, issues a list

---

[29] DTI, *Revised Guidance for the Fallow Blocks Process* (July 2005) (hereinafter "Revised Fallow Blocks Guidance"), B. Definitions: https://www.og.decc.gov.uk/UKpromote/fallow/FallowBlocksGuidance.doc (accessed 16 December 2010). When the scheme was first introduced the triggering period was defined differently: 4 years plus 2 of no other significant activity: see PILOT PPWG, *Work*, Appendix 1(a) at 42, n 2 to para 1.

[30] DTI, *Fallow Blocks Process – Clarification Notes* (2004) (hereinafter "Fallow Block Clarification Notes") p 3, n 1.

[31] However such areas may respectively be subjected to the Stewardship Process (discussed at paras 5.35ff) and the Fallow Discovery Process (discussed at paras 5.23ff).

[32] See DECC, *UK Fallow Assets and Process – 11 January 2010*: https://www.og.decc.gov.uk/UKpromote/fallow/fallow_assets.htm (accessed 16 December 2010). See the discussion under the heading "2010 Fallow Blocks": "Many of [the fallow blocks published today] have producing fields or discoveries on the block, but it is the area outside the field or discovery area that now needs significant activity."

[33] As the *Revised Fallow Blocks Guidance* (and all antecedent guidance on the topic) is expressed in terms of blocks, not parts of blocks, one might reasonably have expected the fact that there was a producing area somewhere within the block to save the block as a whole from the ambit of the regime.

to the licence-holders of all the blocks it considers fallow. Licensees are provided with an opportunity to meet with, and make representations to, the Department before the formal classifications are issued.[34]

5.14   Blocks which have been classified as fallow are then allocated one of two classes: A and B.[35] A block will be designated Class A Fallow if "the current licensees are doing all that a technically competent group with full access to funding could reasonably be expected to do" to progress towards activity.[36] In such cases the Department accepts that the lack of activity is not attributable to the licensee. The block will be noted as Fallow A on the Department website and in the instances where a "technical barrier to progress" has been identified, the Department may request that details of that barrier be communicated to LOGIC and/or ITF for the purposes of guiding those organisations' programmes of technical research and development. Beyond this, the Department requires no action from the licensee. The block's status will be reviewed annually.[37]

5.15   In addition to the standard route to Fallow A status, described above, a newly fallow block which has not already been formally classified and which would otherwise be classified Fallow B will be deemed to be Fallow A if:

- a field has commenced production within the previous year; or
- there has within the previous year been a change of operator, and the Department has approved that change; or
- there has been a substantial change in ownership within the previous 3 months, and the Department has approved that change.[38]

5.16 A block is designated Class B Fallow if "the current licensees are unable to progress towards activity due to a misalignment within the partnership, a failure to meet economic criteria, [and/or] other commercial barriers".[39] Although the scheme as initially proposed by PILOT PPWG and the Guidance subsequently issued by the

---

[34] *Fallow Block Clarification Notes* at 3, n 2.

[35] In practice the Department further divides these classes into several numbered sub-classes. These sub-classes are of no legal consequence: a block classified A1 is not subjected to a different legal regime to an A5, but they do provide some insight into the particular issues which can arise to frustrate activity. For a summary of some of the sub-categories, see the *Fallow Block Clarification Notes*, at 4*ff*.

[36] *Revised Fallow Blocks Guidance*, "B – Definitions".

[37] *Ibid*, "C – Fallow Blocks Process: Fallow A Blocks", superseding the biennial assessment programme which subsisted when the scheme was first introduced: see PILOT PPWG, *Work*, Appendix 1a, para 2.

[38] *Revised Fallow Blocks Guidance*, "D – Change of Interest".

[39] *Ibid*, "B – Definitions".

DTI scrupulously avoids the language of blame, it is implicit in this definition and from the consequences which flow from Fallow B classification (discussed in the paragraphs that immediately follow) that this designation is applied where the Department believes that the current licensees have, for reasons which cannot be justified, made a less than acceptable level of progress.

After a block has been classified as Fallow B, unless divestment of **5.17** the asset is under serious consideration, in which case certain relaxations to the process are applied,[40] it will be entered into a process which, in broad terms, is designed to prompt the licensee either to start making use of the asset, sell it to (or otherwise involve the enterprise of) someone who will, or relinquish it back to the state. After formal designation of a block as Class B Fallow, the licensees are given an initial 3-month period in which to report to the Department on what activity could feasibly be carried out on the block to alter its Fallow B status. Licensees are specifically asked to consider whether a re-allocation of interests would assist in this process.[41] If no adequate proposals are received by the end of that period, the block will be publicly listed as Fallow B on the Department's website[42] for a period of 1 year.[43]

During that period the licensee is at liberty to market the **5.18** block itself,[44] and/or may submit a significant activity plan to the Department. If such a plan is agreed by the Department, the block will be re-classified as "rescued" and the licensee will be given a period of 1 year, which may be extended at the Minister's discretion, to implement the works specified.[45] Once the work has been undertaken, the block will revert to non-fallow status and, therefore, cannot be brought back into the Fallow Blocks Process for at least 3 years.[46]

An intermediate checkpoint is encountered after 9 months of **5.19** the Fallow B period have elapsed. At this point, licensees and any

---

[40] In such cases the block will be temporarily classed Fallow B Hold (if Fallow B status has not yet been formally assigned) or Rescued (if Fallow B status has been assigned and the block released on the Department's website) to permit the transfer to take place: *Fallow Block Clarification Notes*, 1f, per the note to numbered point 4.

[41] *Fallow Block Clarification Notes* at 1: see para 3.

[42] Initially the scheme stipulated that the listing would be on the LIFT website. This has been replaced in the most recent Guidance by a reference to the Department's own website, although LIFT (now known as UKLIFT) is still recommended as "a good shop window" for fallow blocks: *Fallow Block Clarification Notes* at 2: see the note to para 6.

[43] *Revised Fallow Blocks Guidance*, "C – Fallow Blocks Process: Fallow B Blocks", para 4.

[44] *Ibid.*

[45] *Ibid*, para 6.

[46] *Ibid*, para 7.

interested third parties[47] should report to the Department any plans
for significant activity, and any licensee not having a firm plan at
that time is expected to assign its interest to any co-licensees or third
parties having such a plan if requested by them to do so.[48]

5.20   If no satisfactory significant activity plan is agreed by the end of
the 12-month Fallow B period, the published guidance provides that
the licensee "will relinquish the block".[49] The language would suggest
that the licensee is under a firm obligation so to do. However, this is
rather misleading. As has already been seen, the scheme is essentially
a voluntary one, underpinned only by existing licence powers.[50] Thus
the Department has no free-standing legal right to demand the relinquishment of the licence at the process's end, but may do so only if a
power within the licence permits. The licence term that is of greatest
relevance in this regard is Model Cl 16(2),[51] which was discussed at
para 4.46. As has already been seen, the clause provides the Minister
with a right to serve notice upon a licensee requiring the licensee
to prepare and submit an appropriate programme for exploring
the licensed area and provides a rather elaborate procedure, which
includes the possibility of arbitration, in the event that the licensee
does not comply. While it is true that this process may ultimately
result in revocation of all or part of the licensed area, such a result

---

[47] Usually, parties which propose to acquire an interest in the asset.
[48] *Revised Fallow Blocks Guidance*, "C – Fallow Blocks Process: Fallow B Blocks",
para 5.
[49] *Ibid*, para 8.
[50] See paras 5.9–5.11 above. See also *Revised Fallow Blocks Guidance*, "F – DTI
Regulatory Position", which states: "If it appears to DTI at any stage in the process that
there is a firm activity plan that is not being progressed on a commercial basis, the DTI
will consider using its powers under the PSPA to require the licensees to drill the block
or forfeit the licence (or part thereof)." This piece of guidance appears to be a cryptic
reference to the Minister's willingness to use licence powers, but is poorly drafted in
two respects. Instead of referring to ministerial powers under the licence it refers to the
"PSPA" (presumably the Petroleum and Submarine Pipelines Act 1975), which (while it
effected important changes to the terms of existing licences) does not of itself contain
the relevant powers. Second, its description of the Minister's powers under the licence is
rather imprecise, and makes them sound rather stronger and less equivocal than they in
reality are.
[51] Standard production licence, current numbering, as specified by the Petroleum Licensing
(Production) (Seaward Areas) Regulations 2008 (SI 2008/225). This provision being one
of the ones inserted with retroactive effect by the Petroleum and Submarine Pipelines Act
1975 a like term can be found in all previous iterations of the Model Clauses. However,
the numbering of the sets of clauses varies. For instance, it was Model Cl 12 in the
2004, and Model Cl 16 in the 1988, Seaward Production Licence Model Clauses: see
the Petroleum Licensing (Exploration and Production) (Seaward and Landward Areas)
Regulations 2004 (SI 2004/352), Sch 4, and Petroleum (Production) (Seaward Areas)
Regulations 1988, Sch 4, respectively.

is by no means the inevitable outcome of the procedure,[52] and even if that were to be the outcome in a given case, the process could take considerable time to complete, particularly if the licensee chose to arbitrate. Model Cl 16(2) gives the Minister significant powers but is by no means a straightforward right to effect an immediate revocation upon the end of the Fallow Blocks Process.

The Department has stated that fallow blocks adjacent to median **5.21** lines will be brought into the Fallow Blocks Process but has acknowledged that median line issues may impact upon a licensee's ability to comply with the initiative by stating that it "fully recognises" the potential implications of such issues.[53] Licensees of median line blocks can therefore expect a degree of latitude in the scheme's operation if a cross-border issue can be shown to have hindered progress within the block.

The Department has publicly confirmed that the Fallow Blocks **5.22** Process is a voluntary one and has committed to applying its rules "in a fair and reasonable manner".[54] On its own, this might be read as no more than an undertaking to follow procedural fairness in applying the process's rules. However, it appears that more is intended. No formal dispute resolution mechanism or right of appeal is provided for within the process, but the Revised Guidance states that licensees should raise their concerns with senior Department officials if they believe that their case has not been fully understood or if the rules are not being applied properly "or are producing an unreasonable outcome".[55] The last-mentioned ground for referral is perhaps the most significant as it strongly suggests that the rules of the scheme are in the final analysis intended to be flexible and that there may be scope for relaxations in their application in any given case.

The Fallow Discovery Process

The Fallow Discovery Initiative is conceptually similar to the Fallow **5.23** Blocks Scheme but is directed not towards encouraging exploration of blocks but towards promoting the exploitation of individual discoveries[56] which have been made during exploration activity but which

---

[52] For instance, the Minister may be taken to arbitration, and may lose.
[53] *Revised Fallow Blocks Guidance*, "E – Median Line Blocks".
[54] *Ibid*, "G. Right of Appeal".
[55] *Ibid*.
[56] Defined as "any well where hydrocarbons were encountered": DTI, *Revised Guidance for the Fallow Discovery Process (July 2005)* (hereinafter "Fallow Discovery Revised Guidance") "B – Definitions": https://www.og.decc.gov.uk/UKpromote/fallow/ FallowDiscoveriesGuidance.doc (accessed 16 December 2010). Initially the scheme applied only to discoveries having no or only one appraisal well: PILOT PPWG, *Work*, Appendix 1b, p 46.

have been left lying dormant. The central philosophy of the process is again to require, or at least encourage, oil companies to surrender unused acreage or to engage in significant activity or transfer their interests or otherwise involve those who will. And, again, the Fallow Discovery Process is essentially a voluntary system.[57]

5.24   The Fallow Discovery Process follows broadly the same pattern as that for fallow blocks. As with blocks, discoveries are allocated into two categories, A and B, with Fallow A representing a fallow discovery where the current licensees are doing all that may be reasonably expected and Fallow B representing the situation where the present licensees could reasonably have done more to develop the discovery.[58] In addition, the provisions on appeals and dispute resolution, median line discoveries and the Department's regulatory position[59] are all *mutatis mutandis* the same as those discussed above in the context of the Fallow Blocks Process. There are, however, some material differences between the two schemes. These are noted in the paragraphs which follow.

Material differences between the two schemes

5.25   When the Fallow Areas Initiative was introduced, one of the more significant differences between the two constituent schemes was the absence in the Fallow Discovery Process of a provision equivalent to the Fallow Block Process's stipulation that the licence would be relinquished if at the end of the process the licensee had failed to commit to significant activity. As with the extended timeframe, this was said to be justified on the basis of the significant degree of investment which would have been involved in progressing activities to the point where a discovery had been made.[60] However, the Clarification Notes issued in 2004 incorporated a provision confirming that the Department expected the relinquishment of discoveries which continued to be fallow at the end of the process. This requirement was initially expressed in a rather weak way when first introduced: whereas the published Clarification Notes stated that at the end of the process a fallow block "will" be relinquished,[61] the equivalent guidance for the discovery process stated only that a fallow discovery "should" be relinquished[62] – phrasing which would

---

[57] See paras 5.9–5.11 above; also *Fallow Discovery Revised Guidance*, "H – Right of Appeal".

[58] For the full definition of each of the categories, see *Fallow Discovery Revised Guidance*, "B – Definitions".

[59] Ie the matters which were respectively discussed above in the fallow blocks context at paras 5.21–5.22 above.

[60] PILOT PPWG, *Work*, para 3.2.5.2.

[61] *Fallow Block Clarification Notes*, 2, numbered para 8.

[62] *Ibid*, 3, numbered para 8.

tend to suggest that there was scope for dialogue about the matter. The Revised Guidance of 2005 is firmer, and uses the word "will" in respect of both categories of fallow asset. The extent to which this apparently firm obligation can be enforced is discussed at paras 5.28–5.32 below.

The current Discoveries Guidance divides the Fallow A class into 5.26 three sub-classes: "linked", "stranded" and "active". The guidance recognises a variation upon the standard process for "linked" Fallow A discoveries.[63] However, nothing of legal consequence appears to turn on the "stranded" and "active" designations; these sub-classes are defined by the Guidance but not mentioned again, and seem to be used for administrative purposes only.

The Fallow Discovery Process, although noticeably similar in 5.27 structure to the Fallow Blocks Process, takes place over the significantly longer timescale of 27 months.[64] This difference has arisen because licensees are likely to have invested considerably more time, energy and resources in a fallow discovery than a fallow block.[65] The authors of the scheme recognised that in these circumstances fairness required the licensee of a fallow discovery to be afforded a greater opportunity to extract value from his licensed interests than the licensee of a fallow block.

Because, as noted at para 5.23 above, the Fallow Discovery 5.28 Process is directed towards a different phase of operations than is the Fallow Blocks Process, the licence terms that can be used by the Minister to enforce the processes differ. Model Cl 16 is not relevant to the Fallow Discoveries Initiative; the licence provisions of greatest consequence are the Minister's power under Model Cl 17 (as supplemented by Model Cl 18) to exercise control over the production

---

[63] "Linked" Fallow A discoveries are those which are "explicitly included" in an investment plan pertaining to a neighbouring development: *Fallow Discovery Revised Guidance*, "B – Definitions". Certain relaxations in the fallow process are offered in these circumstances: *Fallow Discovery Revised Guidance*, "C – Fallow Discoveries Process: Fallow A Discoveries", para 2.

[64] As opposed to 15 in the case of fallow blocks: see para 5.17 above. Like the Fallow Blocks Process, an initial warning that the Department intends to class an asset as fallow is followed by an opportunity to make representations. This in turn is followed by formal intimation of the status of the asset; a 3-month period during which a plan can be presented, and then a formal notification that the asset is fallow. There then follows a 2-year period in which the discovery is advertised on the Department's website and during which the licensees can present a significant activity plan and/or market the asset: *Fallow Discovery Revised Guidance*, "C – Fallow Discoveries Process".

[65] See PILOT PPWG, *Work*, para 3.2.5.2: "Fallow discoveries differ from fallow blocks significantly in that licensees will generally have invested heavily in the exploration activity and the resulting discoveries are likely to have substantial emotional or even 'book value.' In addition, the transition from discovery to development involves, in most cases, a far greater financial commitment and exposure."

phase of operations by approving, declining to approve, or varying the licensee's development and production programme. One may, however, query the extent to which these clauses are well suited to underpin the Fallow Discovery Process. Daintith raises a fundamental issue by observing: "the drafting of [Model Cl 17] assumes that the licensee, not the Minister, initiates the development process, and is not well designed to compel development."[66] Certainly, Model Cl 17 contains no direct equivalent to Model Cl 16(2), which, as has been seen, specifically provides that the Minister may "by notice in writing" require the licensee to submit a work programme "at any time".[67] Does the Minister have the power to initiate the development process? Model Cl 17(6) does provide the Minister with the power to prepare a production programme and serve it upon a licensee, but only *after* the licensee had a proposed programme rejected by the Minister and has failed satisfactorily to avail itself of the opportunity to submit a modified programme.[68] Model Cl 17(1) provides the Minister with no assistance in this regard: it contains not a forcing obligation to produce a development and a production plan within a certain period of time, but a prohibition upon carrying out relevant work except in accordance with an approved programme or ministerial consent.[69] Moreover, Model Cl 17(2) opens with words that strongly suggest that the licensee initiates the process.[70] It does, however, go on to state that the programme must be submitted "in such form and by such time and in respect of such period during the term of this licence as the Minister may direct". Although those words are capable of alternative construction,[71] and while it would certainly have been preferable for wording equivalent to that used in Model Cl 16 to be used, it is suggested that this provides sufficient authority to enable the Minister to request, through a direction issued to a licensee, that a programme be submitted. Certainly, it does appear that those who promoted the Petroleum and Submarine Pipelines Bill, which introduced what is now Model Cl 17, intended the Minister to have such a power.[72]

---

[66] Daintith, *Discretion*, at para 4311.
[67] See paras 4.46 and 5.14.
[68] Model Cl 17(6) read together with Model Cll 17(4) and 17(5).
[69] Model Cl 17(1).
[70] Ie, "The Licensee shall prepare and submit to the Minister ...".
[71] One could seek to argue, for example, that they do no more than provide the Minister with the power to make stipulations concerning matters of form and timescale in the event that a licensee chooses to submit a production and development programme.
[72] See, eg, the speech of Under-Secretary of State for Energy (John Smith) on 8 July 1975: Standing Committee D, Official Report (1974–1975) vol V, col 1278: "We believe it is a necessary part of depletion controls that the Secretary of State should be able to require a licensee to submit a programme or different programmes for different parts of the area.

Even if the specific example given by Daintith is not made out, 5.29
he is certainly correct to observe that Model Cl 17 is not a sound
foundation for the Fallow Discovery Process. Like Model Cl 16,
Model Cl 17 dates from legislation passed in 1975,[73] a time when
the UKCS was in the early stages of its development as an oil
and gas province. Enough lessons had been learned to allow the
Government to appreciate that the early licences had been granted
in terms which were deficient, at least from the standpoint of the
State;[74] however, petroleum policy was dominated by considerations
substantially different from those the UKCS now faces as an increasingly mature province. This is perhaps best demonstrated by the fact
that Model Cl 18, entitled "Provisions supplementary to clause 17",
is primarily concerned not with *maximising* recovery but with the
circumstances in which it may be appropriate for the state to impose
a *limit* upon it;[75] something that seems almost unthinkable in the
present production-hungry climate. Moreover, the Act was politically controversial and extensively amended in its passage through
Parliament. Several amendments were made in order to meet the
concerns of the international oil industry who were reluctant to cede
control over their licensed interests to the state.[76] In these circumstances, it is hardly surprising either that Model Cl 17 is not as
explicitly focused upon maximising recovery as one would expect of
a like clause drafted today, or that it does not contain broad statements of ministerial power but a more modest and detailed system
of checks and balances.

Bearing this background in mind, when considering the utility of 5.30
Model Cl 17 as an underpin to the Fallow Discovery Initiative, at

---

Otherwise, the licensee could sit on commercially exploitable discoveries and the nation
would lose the benefits of these reserves...we think it important that the Secretary of
State should have this power to require, through the programme, the licensee to exploit
the find."

[73] Ie the Petroleum and Submarine Pipelines Act 1975, on which see para 5.7 above.
The numbering of this model clause has changed from time to time. For instance, it was
Model Cl 13 in the 2004, and Model Cl 17 in the 1988 Seaward Production Licence
Model Clauses: see the Petroleum Licensing (Exploration and Production) (Seaward and
Landward Areas) Regulations 2004 (SI 2004/352), Sch 4 and the Petroleum (Production)
(Seaward Areas) Regulations 1988, Sch 4.

[74] See para 4.60.

[75] See also the so-called Varley assurances, discussed by Daintith, Willoughby and Hill
(looseleaf, Release 59, March 2009) at para 1–704.

[76] The debate in the Select Committee on what are now Model Cll 16–18 spans more than
370 columns: 1106–1383. None of these model clauses escaped amendment and Model Cl
18 was, in the face of stark opposition from the oil industry and its financiers, withdrawn
in its entirety and replaced with a clause which sought to strike a more careful balance
than had the original between "effective depletion control and the legitimate commercial
interests of the industry": per Under-Secretary Smith at col 1307.

least two further issues seem to require discussion. Does the scheme of the clause envisage that the Minister is entitled to demand the preparation of one development programme, or a succession of them? And on what basis is the Minister entitled to refuse to accept a programme submitted to him? These issues will be considered in turn.

5.31 **One programme, or a succession?** As has already been seen,[77] Model Cl 17(2) provides that "The Licensee shall prepare and submit to the Minister, in such form and by such time and in respect of such period during the term of this licence as the Minister may direct, a [production] programme". Model Cl 17(3) provides that the Minister may direct the licensee to prepare separate programmes in respect of separate parts of the licensed area[78] or, where the submitted programme relates only to a particular period within the term of the licence, to prepare a further programme in respect of additional periods.[79] Powers to vary, generally by *limiting*, the amount of petroleum to be produced, are contained in Model Cl 18.[80] Beyond this, however, the Minister has no obvious power to demand a succession of production programmes. Applying the above to the present context, it is suggested[81] that the Minister will be in a strong position against a licensee who, having been directed to do so, has not prepared a development and production programme for the licensed area at all. However, in the absence of a clear and unequivocal right to serve notice "at any time",[82] what is more doubtful is the Minister's position in a scenario where he has been provided with a programme, approved it without making any Model Cl 17(3) qualifications, and then subsequently come to the view, perhaps years later, that the programme is inadequate. At best, the open-textured nature of the drafting provides ample opportunity for an obdurate licensee to delay matters. At worst, Model Cl 17 provides no meaningful regulatory underpin to the Fallow Discovery Process in such cases.

5.32 **The grounds for rejecting a programme.** Given the amount of discretion that is generally afforded to the Minister by the licensing system, the grounds on which the Minister may reject a programme

---

[77] See para 5.28 above.

[78] Model Cl 17(3)(a).

[79] Model Cl 17(3)(b).

[80] Limitation is permissible in the national interest provided that the Minister has served an appropriate notice and further notice; the Minister may require an increase in quantity of petroleum which the licensee is required to get from the licensed area only by reason of a national emergency: Model Cl 18(4).

[81] *Quaere* Daintith, *Discretion*, para 4311; see para 5.28.

[82] Present in Model Cl 16(2) for work programmes: see paras 5.20 and 4.46.

submitted in accordance with Model Cl 17(2) may seem surprisingly narrow.[83] There are only two grounds: that the proposals are contrary to good oilfield practice,[84] or that they are, in the opinion of the Minister, not in the public interest.[85] No other factors will suffice. "Good oilfield practice" is not defined within the Model Clauses but is generally taken to relate "largely to technical matters within the disciplines of geology and reservoir, petroleum and facilities engineering and to the impact of the development on the environment".[86] Thus the term is generally considered to carry technical, rather than economic or policy-related connotations. The national interest criterion would seem to provide the Minister with surer grounds for rejecting a programme. However, while it is clear that at the macro level the national interest is served by a timely and thorough recovery of oil and gas reserves, it is by no means clear to the present authors that an individual programme which does not offer to develop a fallow discovery of small to medium potentiality can seriously be stated to be contrary to the national interest.

Conclusion on the Fallow Assets Initiative

There can be no doubting the impact of the Fallow Assets Initiative. **5.33** In the first 3 years of its operation "over 660 blocks and 240 discoveries [were] identified as inactive or 'fallow'".[87] Statistics released by the Department in early 2010 show that the scheme continues to be effective in stimulating exploration, drilling and other significant activity, promoting the transfer of assets or causing licensees to relinquish blocks, either in whole or in part. Perhaps most eye-catching of all is the large number of blocks and part-blocks that have been re-licensed following relinquishment. Of those blocks that were designated as Fallow B, 85 were re-licensed by the end of the 23rd Licensing Round offered in 2005. The next licensing round witnessed the re-licensing of an additional 52 blocks relinquished under the Fallow Process.[88]

---

[83] The extent of ministerial discretion in licensing matters is discussed throughout Chapter 4 and forms one of the major themes in Daintith, *Discretion*.

[84] Model Cl 17(4)(c)(i).

[85] Model Cl 17(4)(c)(ii).

[86] DECC, *Offshore Field Development Guidelines*, (hereinafter "Field Development Guidance"): https://www.og.decc.gov.uk/regulation/guidance/reg_offshore/reg_offshore_guide.doc (accessed 16 December 2010).

[87] *PILOT Annual Report 2004–2005* at 6. See also further information to similar effect in the PILOT Report relative to 2005–2006, available for download from http://www.pilottaskforce.co.uk/templates/relay/communicationrelay.cfm/1839 at 11.

[88] See the summary of activity in formerly fallow blocks contained at DECC, *UK Fallow Assets and Process – 11th January 2010*, at "Relicensing of Fallow B Blocks": https://www.og.decc.gov.uk/UKpromote/fallow/fallow_assets.htm (accessed 17 December 2010).

In the Department's latest release in 11 January 2010, 17 new Fallow
B blocks that "must have significant activity or be relinquished by 31
December 2010"[89] are added to the list, as well as six new Fallow B
discoveries that "must have significant activity or ... be relinquished by
31 December 2011".[90]

5.34   The scheme has therefore been, by any practical measure of
achievement, a remarkable success. But this should not blind us to the
fact that the initiative is, from a regulatory perspective, a very curious
animal. The scheme seeks to compel parties to engage in expensive
and risky commercial activities, and/or to divest themselves of assets
for which they have paid substantial sums of money and which
could potentially realise millions of pounds of revenue, under pain
of losing those assets without receiving a penny in compensation.
Moreover, it does so on the flimsiest of legal foundations. One might
have imagined that the industry would resent such a scheme and
resist it with great force; instead, it has gone along with it volun-
tarily. The practical consequences of the disconnections between
what the licence empowers the Minister to do and what the scheme
purports to require have gone untested. Nor is there evidence that
the delaying tactics that could have been used to frustrate the scheme
without openly challenging it have been utilised. The substantial
tightening up which has taken place, particularly in the Fallow
Discovery Process, since the scheme was brought into effect has
not been seriously opposed by the industry. Why? The fact that the
process is underpinned by the provisions of the licence is frequently
referred to.[91] The fact that it is also a process which takes place in the
shadow of the licensee's desire to remain in good standing with the
Department, which is in a position quite legitimately to discriminate
against the licensee when allotting new licenses,[92] is less frequently
discussed but must surely provide at least as great an incentive to
the licensee to co-operate in the scheme's operation.[93] But the desire
to remain in good standing can only be relied upon to moderate the

---

[89] DECC, *Fallow Blocks 11th Release – 11 January 2010*, note: https://www.og.decc.gov.
uk/UKpromote/fallow/FallowBBlocks_2010.doc (accessed 17 December 2010).

[90] DECC, *Fallow Discoveries 11th Release – 11 January 2010*, note: https://www.
og.decc.gov.uk/UKpromote/fallow/ReleaseBDiscoveries_2010.doc (accessed 17 December
2010). Note that these six Fallow B Discoveries are added to the already existing 27
Fallow B Discoveries from the immediately preceding release, the licensees of which ought
to carry out significant activity before 31 December 2010 in order to avoid the issue of
relinquishment.

[91] PILOT PPWG, *Work*, para 3.2.3.3; *Revised Fallow Blocks Guidance*, "F – DTI
Regulatory Position; *Revised Fallow Discoveries Guidance*", "G – DTI Regulatory
Position".

[92] See paras 4.32 and 4.44.

[93] See Daintith, *Discretion*, para 3421 and the discussion at para 4.32.

behaviour of individual licensees for so long as they obtain a benefit for so doing. As the UKCS becomes progressively more mature and the number of new or recycled fields to be let dwindles, and their relative size and value decrease, certain licensees may take the view that they are prepared to retain their existing acreage, but that they have no interest in bidding for new lets. When this point is reached, the threat of loss of good standing will lose its sting. It becomes much more likely that at least some licensees will start to act in a less co-operative manner and test the boundaries of the scheme.[94] The Fallow Areas Initiative has been a notable and welcome success, but its success is by no means guaranteed to continue.

STEWARDSHIP

While PILOT's Progressing Partnership Work Group was developing   5.35
the ideas that would lead to the Fallow Areas Initiatives, another had the task of considering issues related to existing fields, also known as brownfields. In 2002, this Brownfields Work Group launched a benchmarking exercise in order to establish the contribution that could be made to the attainment of the Vision for 2010 by mature fields.[95] This study considered 23 mature fields, which together accounted for half of the production and reserves contributed by such fields. Reporting in 2003, it concluded that the development of brownfields could help in "closing the gap to the PILOT targets". It also noted, however, that this would "require a concentrated effort on moving brownfield projects forward".[96]

Building on this foundation, PILOT launched the so-called   5.36
Brownfield Studies in 2004, which reported their findings in March 2005.[97] This report has resulted in some important new industry and regulatory initiatives. This part of the chapter considers some of the key findings of the March 2005 Report before looking in some more

---

[94] The industry's tendency to conduct operations jointly, discussed at Chapter 12 below, may mitigate this problem. It is possible that unco-operative participants in a JOA may find themselves outvoted. However, there are arguments that for some in the industry, specifically among the independents, this point of willingness to challenge the status quo may have already been reached and that it is only a matter of time before the UKCS witnesses similar action to the challenges mounted to the industry's regulators in the United States. See E Üşenmez, "Increase in Influence: How the Independents are Challenging the Authority of the US Government and Why the UK Government Should Take Note", 2009 5 IELR, pp 171–181.

[95] See para 5.3.

[96] Aupec, *2002 Brownfield Benchmark Study*, June 2003, p 1.

[97] PILOT, *Maximising Economic Recovery of the UK's Oil and Gas Reserves: Context for the Brownfields Challenge* (Report of the PILOT 2004 Brownfields Studies), March 2005 (hereinafter "Brownfield Studies Report").

detail at the most significant regulatory development to emerge from it: the Stewardship Process.

The Brownfield Studies Report

5.37 The Report identifies three "levers" to be used in realising the Vision for 2010: "(1) Increase the size of the resource base. (2) Ensure that oil and gas is extracted as efficiently as possible while the infrastructure exists. (3) Extend the life of the infrastructure."[98] As regards the first "lever", and in line with the observations above regarding the nature of a mature province, the Report's focus is particularly on maximising the recovery from existing fields and developing discoveries around them rather than on looking for new discoveries. Whereas the preceding benchmarking study mentioned above had noted that a "concentrated effort" would be required to move brownfield projects forward, the Report is more direct, suggesting that progress towards the Vision for 2010 will require "a change of mindset across the industry".[99]

5.38 The received wisdom of the industry has been that in so far as maximising the recovery from a field is principally about ensuring that the right assets are in the right hands, the focus must be upon facilitating asset transfer if it is always to be possible to increase investment when required. There is certainly a great deal of truth in this belief, and the Government is clearly playing a role in this regard with the Fallow Blocks and Fallow Discovery Initiatives discussed previously in this chapter.[100] But the Brownfield Studies reveal that a focus on asset transfer with regard to producing fields could be obscuring the important insight that similar increases in investment (and thus in recovery) as were achieved with the involvement of a new operator or owner were also possible where only the existing joint venture (JV) partners were involved.[101]

5.39 That said, however, the research conducted in the course of the Brownfield Studies reveals a wide variation between the best and worst performance in this regard. In view of this finding, the Report indicates that the key issue for existing fields is not transfer of assets, but rather ensuring that existing JV partners are applying the standards of *stewardship* displayed by those operating the best-performing fields. This concept of stewardship is understood, *inter alia*, to be about the "asset owners consistently doing the right

---

[98] Brownfield Studies Report, p 4.
[99] *Ibid*, p 6.
[100] See in particular para 5.17.
[101] Brownfield Studies Report, p 11.

things to identify and exploit opportunities".[102] While at first sight it may thus appear that stewardship is primarily concerned with the voluntary activities of the JV partners in implementing good oilfield practice, the Report makes clear – indeed from the outset – that intervention by the regulator is envisaged where problems exist in this regard. The first of its four recommendations highlighted in the Introduction is "Improving stewardship – screening all fields to focus more detailed annual reviews on those fields where stewardship could be a concern".[103]

The apparent willingness of the industry to agree to enhanced regulatory scrutiny of, and even intervention in, its affairs is thus a very striking feature of this report. A Brownfields Work Group dedicated to stewardship set about developing a model for the screening process, the basic detail of which is outlined in the Report.[104] This gives a first indication of why the industry has behaved in what may appear to be a counterintuitive way. The model aims to reduce the administrative load on the vast majority of JVs, first, by introducing a simplified approach to the annual reporting of field data and, second, by focusing the detailed attention of the regulator only on those fields where, in its view, "further conversation" is necessary.[105] In short, a similar attitude on the part of the industry as was apparent in respect of fallow blocks and discoveries[106] is evident here: there is no sympathy for JV partners who are not doing all that they could to maximise the recovery from the assets they have been entrusted with. It remains to consider, however, how this basic model has been developed and implemented by the Department.

The Stewardship Process

The Stewardship Process is not a creature of statute or even of regulation. In common with the treatment of fallow blocks and fallow discoveries, stewardship is dealt with on the basis of the Secretary of State's powers under the licence. One will hunt in vain, however, among even the most recent iteration of model clauses for details of the process. Instead the details are elaborated in the Department's *Offshore Field Development Guidelines*. In so far as this guidance indicates that the regulator's "*overall aim* is to maximise the economic benefit to the UK of its oil and gas resources" and that

5.40

5.41

---

[102] Brownfield Studies Report, p 11.
[103] *Ibid*, p 5.
[104] *Ibid*, p 24.
[105] *Ibid*.
[106] See para 5.16.

its first policy objective is "ensuring the recovery of all economic hydrocarbon reserves",[107] it may readily be seen how stewardship, as a process of checking to see that asset owners are "consistently doing the right things to identify and exploit opportunities", fits into this picture. And indeed these sentiments are repeated practically verbatim in the section of the guidance dedicated to stewardship.[108] The Department is at pains to emphasise that there will usually be alignment between its objectives in terms of maximising economic recovery for the nation and the commercial interests of the JV partners.[109] It notes, however, that there are instances where there could be divergence, including the following:

- "Where a field covers more than one block, with different owners. Attempts to gain higher shares in total output (i.e. capturing other companies' reserves) could damage reservoirs and result in needless expenditure.
- Where production is via a floating production system [and] high operating costs [produce] ... an incentive to cream off high early production and move to the next location, rather than produce all the economic oil.
- Where company capital constraints points them towards a lower cost, but less economic, development option which could leave potentially economic reserves unproduced.
- Where severe cash constraints lead Licensees to prefer options which emphasise the need for early cash at the expense of additional recovery, or result in additional gas flaring.
- Where partners disagree amongst themselves."[110]

The first four of these are clear cases of a lack of alignment between the commercial interests of the JV and the state's interests as represented by the regulator. Some, however, as well as producing a situation which takes the JV out of alignment with the regulator may also be examples of a divergence among the interests of the partners in an individual JV. This indicates perhaps the most compelling reason for the industry's willingness to countenance the enhanced regulatory scrutiny and intervention that stewardship seems to involve: the very threat might be enough to persuade recalcitrant partners that they must either agree to further investment or divest. And indeed, in addition to the idea that stewardship is about asset owners consistently doing the right thing, the guidance notes mention an additional "key factor": that "[a]ssets are in the hands

---

[107] *Field Development Guidance*, s 2.1 (emphasis in original).
[108] *Ibid*, s 6.1.
[109] *Ibid*.
[110] *Ibid*, Appendix 3.

of those with the *collective will, behaviours and resources* to achieve this".[111] The Department's discussion on licence extension policies[112] mentions this threat more directly:

"Where a field is not being operated to DECC's satisfaction, [the Department] will press the existing licensee to raise his game to the level expected. If it continues to fall below the required standard and reaches the end of the licence's lifespan, the Secretary of State reserves the right to refuse an extension, *and instead to invite competitive bids for a new licence over the field.*"[113]

Thus, the philosophy of asset transfer discussed at para 5.38, has not wholly been left behind in this initiative.

The Stewardship Process is described as involving two stages. In   5.42 the first, the operator, acting on behalf of the licensee(s), prepares an annual return which summarises "key aspects of the field's performance".[114] This return is to be completed during February and covers the previous calendar year, together with some forecasting for the year ahead.[115] Running in parallel with this exercise is a requirement for a further return relating to Production Efficiency, the results of which may be fed into the stewardship process. This is also the responsibility of the operator with the same deadline for submission of February.[116] The general idea is that the reporting burden is reduced for most fields.[117] Once the data is submitted, the guidance states that it will be screened quickly by the Department to identify "those fields where more detailed discussions are required".[118] As regards the screening process, the Department will focus upon "simple, objective, performance indicators based on reserves replacement, production decline, facilities performance,

---

[111] *Field Development Guidance*, s 6.1 (emphasis added).
[112] In September 2010, the offshore licences awarded in the 1st Licensing Round expired. The licences from the 2nd Round will expire on 24 November 2011.
[113] DECC, *Licence Extensions*, at "Poorly-stewarded Fields" (emphasis added): https://www.og.decc.gov.uk/upstream/licensing/licextent.htm (accessed 17 December 2010).
[114] *Field Development Guidance*, s 6.1.
[115] *Ibid*, Appendix 11.
[116] *Ibid*, Appendix 12. Note that the Production Efficiency Review Process is also the product of a joint government-industry initiative, this time involving the DECC–Oil & Gas UK Production Efficiency Work Group.
[117] Note, however, that there is some confusion in this regard in the published information. Whereas the Brownfield Studies Report, p 24, suggested that the "Annual Field Report is replaced by a simplified and more focused data request", the Department's website notes that while there has been since 2005 a waiver until further notice of "the requirement for periodic reports on licensed activities … [t]his waiver has no effect on any other reporting requirement, such as … Annual Field Reports" DECC, *Upstream: Reporting*, at "Other Reports" https://www.og.decc.gov.uk/upstream/field_reporting/index.htm (accessed 17 December 2010).
[118] *Field Development Guidance*, s 6.1.

investment levels and well utilisation".[119] If further clarification of the data submitted is required, then the regulator will discuss this informally with the operator. It is anticipated that feedback on the submission will be made in May. This brings the first stage to a close – and indeed brings the whole Stewardship Process to a close for most operators.

5.43   The second stage thus involves only those fields where issues have been identified during the first. It begins with formal written notification to the operators concerned and will involve discussions between the Department and the JV partners as to how these issues may be resolved. It may also involve audit of specific aspects of field management or indeed a full audit of the field as a whole. Third-party experts may be involved "to help resolve technical issues".[120] The Department expects that in so far as good stewardship equates to attractive economic investment, then in most cases "improvement can be secured by normal commercial means by the JV; perhaps by realignment, the introduction of 3rd party investment or, possibly, divestment".[121]

5.44   If, however, the discussions (and perhaps audits and the involvement of technical experts) do not lead to alignment between the Department and the JV, then the guidance indicates that the regulator will use its powers under the licence "to require the JV to improve its Stewardship of the field".[122] The text of the guidance mentions two possibilities, namely the specification of a development and production programme requiring the JV to carry out economic investment, and the replacement of the operator in cases where this party is identified as being the cause of the problem. The diagram illustrating the process mentions additionally, somewhat menacingly, "other sanctions".[123] Presumably, in the absence of any further specification, this is a reference to the possibility that in the ultimate the Department may revoke the licence.

5.45   It is one thing to say that Stewardship fits into the regulator's policy aims and objectives. It is quite another to say that there is a legal basis for the process. In so far as it is the forerunner to Model Cl 17[124] that is extracted in the Appendix to the guidance where the Department lists the "most relevant" Model Clauses,[125] it would appear that the regulator assumes that this clause provides it with

---

[119] *Field Development Guidance*, Appendix 11, at "Stewardship Process Timing".
[120] *Ibid*, s 6.1.
[121] *Ibid*, s 6.1 and Appendix 11.
[122] *Ibid*, s 6.1.
[123] *Ibid*, s 6.1 and the associated diagram.
[124] That is, cl 15. Only sub-cll (1) and (2) are included in the Appendix.
[125] *Field Development Guidance*, Appendix 2.

the necessary power. The guidance certainly notes that in reviewing Field Development Plans the Department "will need to be satisfied ... that the proposals address all the recoverable reserves of a field and do so over a long enough time period" and that "Licensees take into account implications for other developments in the area".[126] In other words, in describing its approach to Model Cl 17, the regulator clearly has in view precisely the sorts of issues covered by Stewardship. But while this clause may be read as giving the regulator the power to consider these issues *at the outset*, it is a question whether it allows him to *revisit* these issues in later years as the Stewardship Process assumes. As has been noted above in relation to the discussion of fallow blocks and discoveries, it is by no means clear that Model Cl 17 may be read in this way.[127] There is nothing in that clause that explicitly allows the regulator to serve a development notice (as envisaged by the guidance) in the absence of a new programme. It is then a question of whether the regulator could get round this problem by requiring a new development programme. Once again as noted above, the fact that Model Cl 17(2) refers only to "a programme" singular raises doubts in this regard. It might be argued that the reference in Model Cl 17(3) to the Minister directing the licensee "to prepare a programme or programmes ... in respect of a further period or further periods" during the term of the licence could be taken to imply that the regulator may act in this way, but this would appear to be excluded in cases where the original programme related to the entire term of the licence. It might thus be a matter of arguing that the regulator would have to rely on a purposive interpretation of the Model Clauses in order to prevail in the service of a development notice where a JV raises objections.

On the other hand, if one assumes, as the regulator clearly does, that it *does* possess the required powers under the licence to impose the "sanctions" listed in the guidance at the end of the second stage of the Stewardship Process, it could be argued that the process itself is actually a sign of the Department's moderation and forbearance. Inasmuch as the licence requires no such discussion before the service of notices, the regulator could be said to be going further to accommodate problem JVs than strictly it is required to. The fact that one can reach two such divergent conclusions, however, is surely a confirmation of the legal uncertainty surrounding this issue.

5.46

---

[126] *Field Development Guidance*, s 2.2.
[127] See in particular para 5.31.

Conclusion on Stewardship

5.47 It may be said, then, that Stewardship is in many respects a logical progression from the treatment of fallow blocks and discoveries. Whereas the latter aims to ensure that allocated acreage is actually explored and assessed and that discoveries are actually developed, the focus of Stewardship is on ensuring that producing assets fulfil their potential. The apparent willingness of the industry to countenance the enhanced regulatory scrutiny and intervention involved can at first sight appear counterintuitive. Closer inspection, however, reveals that this willingness is essentially motivated by self-interest. At the most basic level, the simplified reporting required by the Stewardship Process means that the vast majority of fields experience a reduced administrative burden. More importantly, where there are misaligned JVs, the more dynamic partners can use the threat of intervention by the Department as a lever to encourage the more recalcitrant either to agree to investment or to divest themselves of their stake. Finally, where either this threat does not work or the JV as a whole is simply underperforming, then the regulator will indeed take steps to enforce the changes necessary to maximise recovery.

5.48 It is important to note, however, that this apparent win–win scenario may mask problems. In common with the situation pertaining to fallow blocks and discoveries, the precise legal basis for the Stewardship Process is far from clear. This is not a problem at the level of the industry overall where there is broad agreement with the Department on the need for the process. But it is a question what would happen should a recalcitrant JV partner on the receiving end of the Department's attentions challenge the legitimacy of any demands made by the regulator. Vague references to licence powers would not then be of any avail and a court may struggle to see how Model Cl 17 justifies the sort of action that the Department's guidance suggests it may be minded to take when "further conversations" do not result in an alignment of views between it and the JV. The analysis above suggests that the Department may have to rely on a purposive interpretation of the model clauses in order to prevail in such a situation. The fact that courts have not so far been required to consider such clauses only serves to mask the holes that appear to exist.

5.49 This absence of court action up to this point can of course be explained by the fact that companies that might have been minded to litigate are "repeat players". In other words, knowing that they have to deal with the Department on an ongoing basis means that they are unlikely to take any action that would be calculated to incur the regulator's wrath. Whether this calculus will continue to apply as the province matures further must be open to question.

CHAPTER 6

THE UKCS FISCAL REGIME

Emre Üşenmez

During the first four licensing rounds on the UK Continental Shelf 6.1
(UKCS), that is, from 1965 until the end of 1974, only those actors
who were "citizens of the United Kingdom ... and [were] resident in
the United Kingdom or who [were] bodies corporate incorporated
in the United Kingdom" could apply for an exploration or production
licence.[1] The Minister even had the power to revoke a licence if the
licensee ceased to be a citizen of or a resident in, or ceased "to have
its central management and control in", the UK.[2]

This residency requirement was largely due to the then newly 6.2
introduced Corporation Tax. It was introduced in 1965 with effect
from the financial year (FY) 1964–65 and was payable on the
profits of UK-resident companies.[3] For non-UK resident companies,
Corporation Tax was applicable only if they were "carrying on
a trade in the United Kingdom through a branch or agency".[4]
Therefore, any non-resident would-be licensee essentially had to carry
on offshore operations in the UKCS through a branch or agency. This
imposed a heavy burden on overseas companies as UK Corporation
Tax was charged on worldwide profits,[5] and "they were frequently

---

[1] Petroleum (Production) (Continental Shelf and Territorial Sea) Regulations 1964
(SI 1964/708), reg 4; Petroleum (Production) Regulations 1966 (SI 1966/898), reg 4, as
amended by the Petroleum (Production) (Amendment) Regulations 1971 (SI 1971/814)
(hereinafter "1966 Regulations").
[2] 1966 Regulations, Sch 4, Model Clause 33. For discussion of licensing regimes, see Chapter 4.
[3] Finance Act 1965, s 46.
[4] *Ibid*, s 50. Note that this requirement was not oil industry specific but was applicable
to all non-UK resident companies. This requirement was reinforced in 1970, under the
Income and Corporation Taxes Act 1970, s 246.
[5] Finance Act 1965, ss 49 and 50; and Income and Corporation Taxes Act 1970, ss 243(1)
and 246(1).

prevented from obtaining tax relief for their expenditure in their base territory".[6] In recognition of this burden, in 1975, from the 5th Licensing Round onwards, this residency requirement was removed.[7]

6.3   In so far as the service companies and other contractors operating for the licensees were concerned, it was not until FY 1973 that their activities in the UKCS were brought into the Corporation Tax net.[8] Although the scope of Corporation Tax was extended to include UKCS activities only in 1973, this did not mean that licensees were not subject to Corporation Tax prior to that point; rather, this was one of the main reasons why the licences had the UK residency requirement.[9]

6.4   In 1975, the licences were also retrospectively amended[10] to include a 12½ per cent royalty payment on the semi-annual production.[11] Unlike Corporation Tax, this tax was not targeting the profits, but rather the gross production under a licence. In this way, the Government could ensure tax receipts from petroleum production without waiting for the company to recover its costs and make a profit. However, the royalty set-up was insensitive to variation in field sizes and in costs of production. As such, it was deemed to be a regressive tax, capable of deterring the development of marginal fields.[12] In fact, the decline in both the oil price and in development activity in the early 1980s not only highlighted the increasing importance of marginal fields in the UKCS but also eventually led to the abolition of the royalty regime,[13] first, for those fields that received development consent after 31 March 1982[14] under those licences

---

[6] Peat Marwick, *A Guide to UK Oil & Gas Taxation* (1986) (hereinafter "Peat Marwick, *A Guide to UK Oil & Gas Taxation*"), para 12.3. Further discussion on pre-1975 taxation of oil and gas production is beyond the scope of this chapter. For a concise account, see R F Hayllar and R T Pleasance, *UK Taxation of Offshore Oil and Gas* (1977) (hereinafter "Hayllar and Pleasance, *UK Taxation of Offshore Oil and Gas*"), Chs 18 and 19.

[7] Petroleum and Submarine Pipe-lines Act 1975, s 17, read together with s 14(1)(b) and Sch 2, Pt I. Note that Sch 2, Pt II provides the amended version of the 1966 Regulations. Model Clause 39 of this Part retains the Minister's right of revocation if the company ceases "to have its central management and control" in the UK. For further discussion of licensing, see Chapter 4.

[8] Finance Act 1973, s 38.

[9] Hayllar and Pleasance, *UK Taxation of Offshore Oil and Gas*, para 18.06.

[10] Petroleum and Submarine Pipe-lines Act 1975, s 18.

[11] *Ibid*, s 2 and Sch 2, Pt I. This section amends Sch 4 to the 1966 Regulations and reproduces the final amended version in Sch 2, Pt II. The royalty provision corresponds to s 9 of this Part.

[12] C Nakhle, *Petroleum Taxation: Sharing the oil wealth: a study of petroleum taxation yesterday, today and tomorrow* (2008) (hereinafter "Nakhle, *Petroleum Taxation*") at para 2.8.

[13] Nakhle, *Petroleum Taxation* at paras 2.8 and 4.2.3.

[14] Petroleum Royalties (Relief) Act 1983, s 1, read together with Finance Act 1983, s 36(2).

that incorporated the 1982 Model Clauses,[15] then entirely from 1 January 2003.[16]

Also in 1975, petroleum-specific taxation began with the intro- **6.5** duction of Petroleum Revenue Tax (PRT)[17] and the Ring Fence Corporation Tax (RFCT).[18] Under the "ring fence" concept, if "any oil extraction activities" were undertaken, or any "acquisition, enjoyment or exploitation of oil rights" was assumed by a company, then these activities were to be treated as a "separate trade, distinct from all other activities" carried out by that company.[19] In other words, for tax purposes, "oil extraction activities"[20] were isolated from a company's other activities, such as refining. This was to prevent artificial reductions in income from these fenced-in extraction activities by setting off the losses from those other activities – hence the term "ring fence". Hayllar and Pleasance likened the concept to a valve "in that it act[ed] one way only; thus, if the ring fence show[ed] a loss, it [could] be set off against profits earned outside the ring fence subject to the usual rules and restrictions", but not vice versa.[21]

This petroleum-specific taxation is the focus of this chapter.[22] **6.6** The discussion excludes the political and policy environment within

---

[15] Petroleum Royalties (Relief) Act 1983, s 1(2)(a); the 1982 Model Clauses are set out in Petroleum (Production) Regulations 1982 (SI 1982/1000), Sch 5.

[16] See the announcement: DECC, *Outcome of Consultation Paper on Appropriate Timing of Abolition of North Sea Royalty*, available at https://www.og.decc.gov.uk/consultations/royresp.pdf (accessed 14 June 2010).

[17] Oil Taxation Act 1975 (hereinafter "OTA 1975"), Pt I.

[18] *Ibid*, s 13. This section has been repealed under Income and Corporation Taxes Act 1988 (hereinafter "ICTA 1988"), s 32 and Sch 29, and re-enacted under ICTA 1988, s 492(1); which itself has recently (3 March 2010) been repealed under Corporation Tax Act 2010 (hereinafter "CTA 2010"), s 62 and Sch 1 and re-enacted under CTA 2010, s 279. Reliefs and allowances under ring-fence Corporation Tax are further discussed at paras 6.9–6.18.

[19] OTA 1975, s 13; ICTA 1988, s 492(1); CTA 2010, s 279, read together with ss 274 and 277.

[20] The term "oil extraction activities" refers to those activities that were carried out in searching for, or in extracting, oil in the UK or in a "designated area", ie the UK Continental Shelf (UKCS), as well as in transporting the oil to "dry land in the United Kingdom" and in "effecting ... the initial treatment or initial storage of oil". By definition, any downstream activities, or activities carried out outside the UK, are thus not within the scope of ring fence. See OTA 1975, s 19; ICTA 1988, s 502(1); and CTA 2010, s 272. The scope also includes those activities "in making available an asset in a way which gives rise to tariff receipts or tax-exempt tariffing receipts of the participator"; see CTA 2010, s 291(6). Note that "oil" is defined as "any substance won or capable of being won under the authority of a licence granted under ... the [1934] Petroleum (Production) Act 1934", thus including natural gas.

[21] Hayllar and Pleasance, *UK Taxation of Offshore Oil and Gas* at para 20.01.

[22] For an excellent and concise account of the early development of taxation of petroleum production and the political events surrounding that development, see J Paterson, *Behind the Mask: regulating health and safety in Britain's offshore oil and gas industry* (2000) (hereinafter "Paterson, *Behind the Mask*"), pp 113–117, 171–177 and 291–296.

which certain changes were applied, and starts with the Ring Fence Corporation Tax, followed by the relatively recently introduced concept of Supplementary Charge (SC) and, finally, by the Petroleum Revenue Tax.

RING FENCE CORPORATION TAX (RFCT)

6.7   RFCT is the same as the standard Corporation Tax to which all the companies in the UK are liable, albeit applied only within a ring fence. As mentioned,[23] the ring fence restriction is in place to avoid reducing the taxable profits from oil extraction activities by accounting in the losses accumulated elsewhere, or from other business activities.[24]

6.8   When the taxation of petroleum production began, the main Corporation Tax rate was 52 per cent.[25] This rate remained at the same level until FY 1983, when it was reduced to first 50 per cent, then 40 per cent for 1984 and 1985, and finally 35 per cent for 1986 where it plateaued for 4 years.[26] (See Table 6.1.) Although initially the main rate for FY 1990 was also set at 35 per cent,[27] this rate for FY 1990 was reduced by a single percentage point a year later.[28] Also for that next financial year, 1991, the rate was further reduced by a percentage point to 33 per cent,[29] where it remained unchanged until 1998. With the Finance Act 1998 the gradual reduction in the Corporation Tax continued first to 31 per cent for the FY 1998,[30] then to 30 per cent for the following year.[31] Finally, in 2008, the standard Corporation Tax and the Ring Fence Corporation Tax diverged for the first time. While the former was further reduced to 28 per cent,[32] the applicable Corporation Tax rate for the profits accrued from ring fence activities remained at 30 per cent.[33]

---

[23] See para 6.5.
[24] HM Revenue and Customs, *International Guide to the North Sea Fiscal Regime* (January 2008), under '*Ring fence Corporation Tax*', para 6.1
[25] Finance Act 1976, s 25. Note that, until 2008, the main Corporation Tax rate and the Ring Fence Corporation Tax rate were the same.
[26] Finance Act 1984, s 18.
[27] Finance Act 1990, s 19.
[28] Finance Act 1991, s 24 reduced the Corporation Tax rate charged for the financial year 1990 to 34%.
[29] Finance Act 1991, s 23.
[30] Finance Act 1998, s 28.
[31] *Ibid*, s 29.
[32] *Ibid*, s 6(2)(a).
[33] *Ibid*, s 6(2)(b).

Table 6.1 Gradual reduction of Ring Fence Corporation Tax rate

Legislation	Financial year	RFCT rate
Finance Act 1976 onwards	1975–1983	52%
Finance Act 1984, s 18	1983	50%
	1984	45%
	1985	40%
	1986	35%
Finance Act 1987 onwards	1987–1990	35%
Finance Act 1990, s 19	1990	35%
Finance Act 1991, s 24*	1990*	34%*
Finance Act 1991, s 23 onwards	1991–1997	33%
Finance Act 1998, s 28	1998	31%
Finance Act 1998, s 29 onwards	1999–2007	30%
Finance Act 2008, s 6	2008–Present	28%

*Finance Act 1991, s 24 reduced the Corporation Tax rate charged for the financial year 1990 to 34%.

Allowances and reliefs

Losses

Under the standard Corporation Tax, when a company accrued a **6.9** trading loss, that loss could be set against its trading income so that the amount of loss was deducted first from the profits in the same accounting period, then from the previous accounting periods within the immediate past 12 months (carry-back),[34] and finally from the consecutive taxable incomes (carry-forward).[35] The ring fence, on the other hand, restricted this tax relief. For the purposes of Corporation Tax calculations, the taxable profits gained within a ring fence could be reduced only if the losses were sustained from those ring-fence activities.[36] However, this did not mean the losses arising from ring-fence activities could only be set off against the ring-fence profits. Those losses could be deducted against the profits gained from the non-ring fence activities on the condition that, had there been no ring fencing, those activities from which the profit was gained and

---

[34] CTA 2010, s 37.
[35] *Ibid*, s 45.
[36] *Ibid*, s 304.

those from which the loss was suffered would have "constitute[d] a single trade".[37]

6.10   Although the losses could be carried forward indefinitely, initially the losses could be carried back only as far as the amount of time equal to the accounting period(s) in which the loss was suffered.[38] In 1991, the carry-back period was increased to 3 years.[39] This, however, did not last long, for in 1997 the period was reduced to 1 year,[40] which is still applicable today;[41] though within the ring fence, carry-back is re-extended to 3 years.[42] This 3-year extension is also applicable in the event of a cessation of trade or when a terminal loss is incurred.[43]

Interest payments

6.11   Likewise, under the standard Corporation Tax, interest payments can be deducted from profits as a tax relief.[44] However, for this relief to be applicable for the ring-fence profits the money borrowed on which the interest was paid must be used in financing the ring-fence activities.[45]

Expenditures

6.12   As mentioned,[46] the rules under the standard Corporation Tax apply, in principle, under RFCT as well. As such, the distinction between revenue and capital expenditures is rather important. When calculating the profits of a trade, capital expenditures are not allowed as a deduction.[47] However, there are no clear-cut rules on separating capital from revenue. Rather, it is a question of law, to be

---

[37] CTA 2010, s 304(4).

[38] ICTA 1988, s 393(3).

[39] Finance Act 1991, s 73(1). This section inserted s 393A into ICTA 1988, applicable for the accounting period ending on or after 1 April 1991.

[40] Finance (No 2) Act 1997, s 39. In addition to the change in the carry-back period (which is effective from 2 July 1997), this section inserted subss (2A)–(2C) into ICTA 1998, s 393A.

[41] CTA 2010, s 37(3)(b).

[42] *Ibid*, ss 40 and 42.

[43] *Ibid*, s 39. Note that if there are still unrelieved losses remaining after setting them against the profits from the previous 3 years, the relief period can be carried back even further, until the accounting period beginning after 16 April 2002 is reached. See CTA 2010, s 42.

[44] Corporation Tax Act 2009 (hereinafter "CTA 2009"), Pt 5, particularly s 307(3)(b) read together with s 297. This deduction was previously found in ICTA 1988, s 338.

[45] CTA 2010, ss 286 and 287; previously ICTA 1988, s 494.

[46] See paras 6.7 and 6.9.

[47] CTA 2009, s 53; previously ICTA 1988, s 74, which itself was previously ICTA 1970, s 130.

determined on a case-by-case approach.[48] In so far as UKCS upstream activities are concerned, the majority of expenditures in all phases, ie exploration and appraisal, development and production, and decommissioning and abandonment, are capital in nature.[49]

Capital allowances Although capital expenditures are not allowed 6.13 in calculating trading profits, there is a capital allowance system in place, which recognises the "need for an allowance in respect of the amortisation [and depreciation]".[50]

Plant and machinery Under this capital allowance system, expen- 6.14 ditures on certain capital are allowed for tax relief. For plant and machinery expenditures, a company receives a 25 per cent first-year writing-down allowance.[51] For the long-life assets, ie for the plant and machinery that has a "useful economic life of at least 25 years",[52] this allowance is 6 per cent.[53]

These figures, though, have changed for ring-fence activities 6.15 from 17 April 2002 onwards.[54] Any expenditure incurred from that date onwards on plant and machinery to be employed for a ring-fence activity qualifies for a 100 per cent first-year allowance.[55] For long-life assets within the ring-fence qualification, the allowance was 24 per cent for the first year[56] and 6 per cent thereafter.[57] However, for ring-fence activities, the long-life asset separation was removed so that costs on plant and machinery – regardless of the long-life distinction – incurred from 12 March 2008 onwards qualify for 100 per cent first-year allowance.[58]

---

[48] See the explanatory notes for CTA 2009, s 53, where it provides the judicial authority for this approach: "... the words of Brightman J on page 173 of ECC Quarries Ltd v Watkins (1975), 51 TC 153 Ch D: ... unchallenged evidence, or a finding, that a sum falls to be treated as capital or income on principles of correct accountancy practice is not decisive of the question whether in law the expenditure is of capital or an income nature". See also S Deeks (updated by), Chapter 10: "Trading Income", in N Lee, *Revenue Law – Principles and Practice* (27th edn), at para 10.75.

[49] See HM Revenue and Customs, *Oil Taxation Manual: OT20203 – Overview of the Main Types of Costs Incurred in Oil Exploration and Production – Exploration; OT20204 – Overview of the Main Types of Costs Incurred in Oil Exploration and Production – Production;* and *OT20205 – Overview of the Main Types of Costs Incurred in Oil Exploration and Production – Decommissioning and Abandonment*

[50] Hayllar and Pleasance, *UK Taxation of Offshore Oil and Gas* at para 19.10.

[51] Capital Allowances Act 2001 (hereinafter "CAA 2001"), ss 56(1) and 418(1)(b).

[52] CAA 2001, s 91.

[53] *Ibid*, s 102.

[54] Finance Act 2002, Sch 21.

[55] *Ibid*, Sch 21 and ss 3, 6 and 10. This Schedule inserts ss 45F and 416D and amends s 52(3) of CAA 2001.

[56] Finance Act 2002, s 6 and Sch 21; CAA 2001, s 52(3).

[57] CAA 2001, s 102.

[58] Finance Act 2008, s 108 amended CAA 2001, s 52(3).

6.16 *Mineral extraction* Similarly, a company can write off 25 per cent of its capital expenditure[59] on "mineral exploration and access";[60] or 10 per cent of the same expenditure[61] if it was spent on "acquiring mineral assets",[62] ie on the acquisition of mineral deposits or mineral rights over those deposits.[63] As in the case of plant and machinery expenditure, from 17 April 2002 onwards the capital costs incurred on mineral extraction (but not on acquisition of mineral assets[64]) within the ring fence do qualify for 100 per cent first-year allowance.[65]

6.17 *R&D* In addition, capital expenditures on hydrocarbon exploration and appraisal activity qualify for research and development allowances.[66] This allowance is equal to the amount of the expenditure, ie 100 per cent.[67] It should be noted, however, that a company cannot claim relief for both research and development allowances and the mineral extraction allowance, but is allowed to choose between them.[68]

6.18 *Decommissioning* In so far as decommissioning costs are concerned, they are essentially 100 per cent allowable. However, the definition of decommissioning expenditure has evolved over time. For the demolition expenditures incurred after 30 June 1991 and before 7 August 2000, s 62A of CAA 1990 was applicable.[69] From that date onwards, the term "demolition" was replaced with "decommissioning"[70] and CAA 2001, ss 164 and 165[71] became applicable. However, for decommissioning expenditures incurred on or after 12 March 2008, this special allowance was replaced with

---

[59] CAA 2001, s 418(1)(b).

[60] *Ibid*, s 395(1)(a); subject to CAA 2001, ss 400–402. "Mineral exploration and access" itself is defined at CAA 2001, s 396.

[61] CAA 2001, s 418(1)(a).

[62] *Ibid*, s 395(1)(b).

[63] *Ibid*, ss 397 and 398.

[64] *Ibid*, s 416B(2) and (3). Note that these still qualify for 10% write-down. Finance Act 2002, Sch 21 inserted ss 416A–416E into CAA 2001.

[65] CAA 2001, s 416D.

[66] *Ibid*, s 437. The term "research and development" was introduced in Finance Act 2000, Sch 19(1). It inserted s 837A into ICTA 1988. Section 837A(6) states that "Unless otherwise expressly provided, 'research and development' does not include oil and gas exploration and appraisal". CAA 2001, s 437(1)(b) expressly includes oil and gas exploration and appraisal.

[67] CAA 2001, s 441.

[68] *Ibid*, ss 7 and 8.

[69] As amended by Finance Act 1990, s 60.

[70] Finance Act 2001, s 68 and Sch 20, Pt 1.

[71] As amended by Finance Act 2001, Sch 20, Pt 2. If the decommissioning expenditure related to post-cessation of trading then s 165, otherwise s 164 applies.

"general decommissioning expenditure".[72] These additionally include expenditures incurred in providing decommissioning guarantees;[73] reimbursements to a guarantor for providing those guarantees;[74] in meeting the decommissioning liabilities of a defaulting party;[75] and those reimbursements of the defaulting party to the party that contributed in lieu.[76]

SUPPLEMENTARY CHARGE (SC)

Though it is not a Corporation Tax,[77] Supplementary Charge is **6.19** almost identical to a Corporation Tax. Applicable from 17 April 2002, it is charged in addition to the RFCT on the profits accrued from ring-fence activities.[78] Its administration procedure is the same as that for Corporation Tax and so are the provisions on returns, assessment, collection and receipt of Corporation Tax, appeals and "administration, penalties, interest on unpaid tax and priority of tax in cases of insolvency".[79]

When it was introduced in Finance Act 2002 the SC rate was set **6.20** at 10 per cent.[80] The justification in introducing this charge was that the pre-SC tax regime did not ensure a "fair return" to the state. The then Economic Secretary, Ruth Kelly, summarised the Government's rationale:

> "It is clear that oil companies are generating excess profits, and ours is the only major oil-exporting economy that does not have a special regime to reflect that ... It is [also] abundantly clear that the regime is not securing a fair deal for the nation from this national resource, and the changes introduced in the Bill will remedy that for the future. We have listened to industry, and the package that we are introducing ... focuses on investment. Companies that invest in the North Sea will receive full and immediate [100 per cent] relief against any tax

---

[72] HM Revenue and Customs, *Oil Taxation Manual: OT28100 – Decommissioning and Abandonment: General Decommissioning Expenditure: Relief for expenditure incurred before cessation of ring fence trade and on or before 11 March 2008.* See also Finance Act 2008, ss 109 and 110.

[73] CTA 2010, s 292.

[74] *Ibid*, ss 293 and 294.

[75] *Ibid*, s 297. See also Chapter 12 on Joint Operating Agreements and Chapter 10 on Decommissioning.

[76] CTA 2010, s 298

[77] HM Revenue and Customs, *Oil Taxation Manual: OT21219 – Corporation Tax Ring Fence: The Supplementary Charge – No Supplementary Charge losses or adjusted ring fence losses,*

[78] CTA 2010, s 330; previously ICTA 1988, s 501A; as inserted by Finance Act 2002, s 91.

[79] CTA 2010, s 332; previously ICTA 1988, s 501B(1); as inserted by Finance Act 2002, s 92(1).

[80] ICTA 1988, s 501A.

liability, while those which do not do so will rightly pay a higher share of Corporation Tax, together with a Supplementary Charge. In future, therefore, the Government will take a much greater share of the risk of investing in the future of the North Sea. It is right that, as a consequence, the nation should take a higher share of the profits of that investment."[81]

From 1 January 2006 onwards, however, the rate of SC was increased to 20 per cent[82] as a response to the then "recent significant rises in oil prices".[83]

6.21   The difference between SC and RFCT lies in the calculation of adjusted ring-fence profits. Supplementary Charge does not take into account the financing costs in calculating the profits arising from ring-fence activities.[84] The legislation refers to financing costs as meaning the "costs of debt finance",[85] the calculation of which uses rather broad definitions.[86] These include:

"•   loan relationship debits in respect of debtor relationships
-    forex differences arising in relation to debt finance
-    trading profits or losses on derivative contracts in relation to debt finance
-    the financing cost implicit in a payment under a finance lease
-    any other costs arising from what would be considered a financing transaction in accordance with generally accepted accounting practice (GAAP)".[87]

6.22   This limitation on the allowance for financing costs is intended to "prevent companies manipulating their levels of borrowing between ring fence and non-ring fence activities to minimise the impact of the SC".[88]

6.23   In 2009 a system of allowances was introduced in order to reduce the adjusted ring-fence profits calculated for SC for certain eligible

---

[81] *Hansard*, HC, vol 385, Pt 144; R Kelly, cols 359, 360 and 361 (9 May 2002).

[82] Finance Act 2006, s 152. See also CTA 2010, s 330(1).

[83] HM Treasury, *Pre-Budget Report 2005: Britain meeting the global challenge: Enterprise, fairness and responsibility*, 5 December 2005, Chapter 5: *Building a Fairer Society*, para 5.129. Note that crude oil prices rose above $50 per barrel in mid-2005: Energy Information Administration, *Petroleum Navigator: Weekly All Countries Spot Price FOB Weighted by Estimated Export Volume (Dollars per Barrel)*. As this book was going to press, the SC was, very controversially, raised to 32%: HM Treasury, Budget 2011, HC 836, March 2011, paras 1.146 and 2.101.

[84] CTA 2010, s 330(3); previously ICTA 1988, s 501A(2) and (3).

[85] CTA 2010, s 331(2); previously ICTA 1988, s 501A(4).

[86] CTA 2010, s 331(3); previously ICTA 1988, s 501A(5) lists the "matters to be taken into account" when "calculating the debt finance".

[87] HM Revenue and Customs, *Oil Taxation Manual: OT21206 – Corporation Tax Ring Fence: The Supplementary Charge: The Meaning of "Finance Costs"*.

[88] HM Revenue and Customs, *International – Guide to the North Sea Fiscal Regime*, Section 7: *Supplementary Charge*, January 2008.

companies.[89] Although the SC applies to all the adjusted profit derived from ring-fence activities, the allowances were based on field eligibility. If a company was a licensee in a small oilfield,[90] in an ultra-heavy oilfield[91] or in an ultra-high-pressure/high-temperature field[92] that received its development consent after 21 April 2009[93] than it became eligible for a share of the "field allowance" ranging from £75 million to £800 million[94] in proportion to its equity in the field.[95]

PETROLEUM REVENUE TAX (PRT)

Introduced at the same time as RFCT, Petroleum Revenue Tax is charged on the profits accrued from oil and gas activities.[96] Like RFCT, PRT has a similar ring fence concept albeit applicable only on a field basis. That is, while RFCT is applicable to a company's profits arising from all the upstream activities in the UKCS, PRT is charged on the income arising from an individual field.[97] Upon its introduction, PRT was regarded as a "completely new concept in UK taxation – a self-contained piece of legislation separate and distinct from the main corpus of the law of income tax (IT), Corporation Tax (CT) and capital gains tax (CGT)".[98]

6.24

As shown in Table 6.2, initially the PRT rate was set at 45 per cent.[99] This rate was first increased to 60 per cent from 1 January

6.25

---

[89] Finance Act 2009, s 90 and Sch 44, amending ICTA 1988, s 501A. Note that this allowance has been repealed and re-enacted under CTA 2010, Pt 8, Ch 7. Additionally, see HM Revenue and Customs, *2009 Pre-Budget Report Notes*, 9 December 2009 (hereinafter "HM Revenue and Customs, *PBRN*") at PBRN03.

[90] Field with reserves equal to or less than 3,500,000 tonnes: CTA 2010, s 353 and Finance Act 2009, Sch 44, para 21.

[91] Field with oil at less than 18 degrees API gravity and more than 50 centipoise viscosity at reservoir temperature and pressure: CTA 2010, s 354 and Finance Act 2009, Sch 44, para 22.

[92] Field with oil at more than both 1034 bar pressure and 176.67 degrees Celsius in the reservoir formation: CTA 2010, s 355; and Finance Act 2009, Sch 44, para 23. Note that the Government proposes to reduce these thresholds to 862 bar and 166 degrees Celsius. See HM Revenue and Customs, *PBRN*, at PBRN03.

[93] CTA 2010, s 350; and Finance Act 2009, Sch 44, para 1(1).

[94] This figure depends on the type and qualification of the field: CTA 2010, s 356; and Finance Act 2009, Sch 44, para 24.

[95] Detailed discussion of "field allowance" is beyond the scope of this chapter, but see E Üşenmez, "Stability of the UK Tax Regime for Offshore Oil and Gas: Positive Developments and Potential Threats", 2010 21(1) ICCLR.

[96] OTA 1975, s 1(1).

[97] *Ibid*, s 1(2). Note that the definition and the determination of a field are given in OTA 1975, Sch 1.

[98] Hayllar and Pleasance, *UK Taxation of Offshore Oil and Gas*, p 15.

[99] OTA 1975, s 1(2).

1979,[100] then to 70 per cent a year later[101] and finally to 75 per cent from 1 January 1983 onwards.[102] The Finance Act 1993 also introduced the concepts of "taxable" and "non-taxable" oilfields in terms of PRT, distinguishing fields by the date development consents were received.[103] If a development consent was received before 16 March 1993, then the field was referred to as a "taxable field" and was still liable to the PRT charge albeit at a reduced rate of 50 per cent,[104] whereas if a field received the said consent after that date, it would be deemed "non-taxable" as this Act abolished PRT from this day forward.[105] Therefore, for taxable fields, the PRT rate was set at 50 per cent charged every 6 months[106] – which approach is still applicable today.[107]

6.26   For each 6-month chargeable period, a company liable to a PRT charge on a given field has to return the details of the income arising in that period from its share in that field.[108] At the same time, a "responsible person" for the oilfield[109] has to prepare returns detailing the oil production within that period and the share of each licensee.[110]

PRT calculation

6.27   The charge base for calculating the PRT is not a company's share of the gross income from a field, but its "assessable profit" as provided under OTA 1975, s 2.[111]

6.28   Essentially, PRT liability does not arise until the payback period is reached and an assessable profit has risen. When calculating the PRT liability, the relevant rate is applied on a given assessable profit only after it is reduced by allowable losses and oil allowance.[112] However,

---

[100] Finance (No 2) Act 1979, s 18.

[101] Finance Act 1980, s 104.

[102] Finance Act 1982, s 132(1).

[103] Finance Act 1993, s 185.

[104] *Ibid*, s 186(1).

[105] *Ibid*, s 185.

[106] OTA 1975, s 1. PRT is charged on 30 June and 31 December of every year.

[107] Note that the reduction in PRT charge was not applicable to the accounting periods ending before 30 June 1993.

[108] OTA 1975, Sch 2, s 2.

[109] *Ibid*, Sch 2, s 4. "Responsible person" is a "body corporate or partnership" appointed for the purposes of preparing returns detailing the particulars of that field, including the interests of the licensee and the oil produced within the subject chargeable period.

[110] Sch 2, s 5.

[111] Assessable profit is further discussed at para 6.39.

[112] OTA 1975, s 1(2). Allowable loss reduction is provided under OTA 1975, s 7; and oil allowances under OTA 1975, s 8. Oil allowance is further discussed at para 6.31. Note that the terms "oil allowance" and "volume allowance" are used interchangeably in the literature but, for the sake of clarity, it is referred to as "oil allowance" in this chapter.

Table 6.2 Petroleum Revenue Tax rates

Legislation	Financial year	PRT rate
Oil Taxation Act 1975, s 1	1975–1978	45%
Finance (No 2) Act 1979, s 18	1979	60%
Finance Act 1980, s 104	1980–1982	70%
Finance Act 1982, s 132	1983–1992	75%
	–	TF* NTF*
Finance Act 1993, s 185, s 186	1993–Present	50% Nil
*TF= Taxable field, NTF = Non-taxable field		

the PRT payable amount is further limited by what is referred to as "safeguard".[113] These elements of the calculation will be discussed in turn below.

For example, assume that Company X has a 10 per cent interest in a Northern Basin field, called Northern Alpha, which received its development consent in 1992, and started production in June 1993. Also assume that the total oil won and saved from the field during the chargeable period between 1 July and 31 December 1993 totalled 2 million metric tonnes of oil equivalent (toe).[114] The gross profit of Company X from this production was £2,500,000; and the assessable profit was £1,800,000. The allowable loss carried from the previous period was £600,000. The profit PRT would be charged on is shown in Table 6.3.   6.29

PRT would then be charged at the rate of 50 per cent rate on this amount of £1.2 million less the oil allowance. This PRT liability of Company X, however, may be further limited by "safeguard" under OTA 1975, s 9. The oil allowance and safeguard are discussed in turn below.[115]   6.30

Oil allowance
Recognising the inequitable burden PRT would otherwise impose on the "smaller, more marginally economic fields",[116] the OTA 1975 provides for a certain level of PRT-free production. For   6.31

---

[113] OTA 1975, s 9.
[114] 1 metric tonne of oil equivalent is approximately 7.2 barrels of oil equivalent.
[115] For the breakdown of PRT assessments made by end February 2010 for the whole of the UK and the UKCS for the each chargeable period from the second chargeable period of 2002 to the first chargeable period of 2009, see HM Revenue and Customs, Table 11.12 – profits from oil and gas production, available at http://www.hmrc.gov.uk/stats/corporate_tax/menu.htm (visited 16 June 2010).
[116] HM Revenue and Customs, *Oil Taxation Manual: OT17025 – PRT: Oil Allowance – Background*.

Table 6.3 PRT calculation

Add	Subtract	Amount in £
Assessable profit		1,800,000
	Allowable loss	600,000
	Oil allowance	α
Chargeable profit		*£1,200,000 – α*

each chargeable period, a licensee is allocated an oil allowance proportional to its share of the oil "won and saved" during those 6 months.[117] In other words, a participant in a field would be liable for PRT only after its field profits exceed the monetary value of its share of the oil allowance in a given chargeable period.[118]

6.32   Currently there are three different volumes applicable as an oil allowance, depending on the date development consent was granted for a given field. For fields that received development consent before 1 April 1982 (old fields), the allowance for each field is 250,000 metric tonnes (t) per chargeable period, with an aggregate limit of 5,000,000 t.[119] For those fields that were given development consent after that date (new fields) the volume was increased to 500,000 t per 6-month period.[120] The third level of oil allowance was introduced in 1988. From the second chargeable period of 1988 forwards,[121] for new fields located either in the Southern Basin or onshore the oil allowance volume was reduced to 125,000 t.[122] For other new fields the allowance remained the same at 500,000 t per chargeable period. In parallel with the changes in the oil allowance volumes, the

---

[117] OTA 1975, s 8(2).
[118] The monetary value is calculated by the formula £(A x B/C), where A is the licensee's gross profit, B is its share of the allowance in metric tonnes, and C is its share of the oil won and saved (ie produced) in metric tonnes – all in a given chargeable period: OTA 1975, s 8(3).
[119] Note that the original amount in OTA 1975, s 8 was 500,000 t per chargeable period, with an aggregate limit of 10,000,000 t until the end of 1978. Finance (No. 2) Act 1979, s 21(1) reduced these amounts for the same fields to 250,000 t for the chargeable periods beginning in 1979 with an aggregate limit of 5,000,000 t, thus maintaining the aggregate limit of 20 chargeable periods (ie 10 years, assuming that all the available allowances for each chargeable period are used). Also note that 40,000 cubic feet of gas is deemed equivalent to 1 metric tonne of oil for the calculation of oil allowance: OTA 1975, s 8(7). This figure was also changed in Finance (No 2) Act 1979, s 21 from 40,000 cubic feet to 1,100 cubic metres in 1979.
[120] Finance Act 1983, s 36.
[121] Chargeable period beginning with 1 July 1988 and onwards.
[122] Finance Act 1988, s 138.

aggregate limits were adjusted accordingly so that it was maintained at 20-fold of the volume per period.[123]

Continuing with the example of Company X above, the Northern **6.33** Alpha field is categorised as a non-Southern Basin new field for oil allowance purposes. The cash equivalent of the oil allowance would then be:

$$£2,500,000 \times \frac{(500,000 \times 10\%)}{(2,000,000 \times 10\%)} = £625,000$$

Hence, "α" in Table 6.3 would be £625,000; which in turn would reduce the "chargeable profit" to £575,000. At a 50 per cent PRT rate, the total PRT charge would then be £287,500.

The oil allowance was undoubtedly designed noticeably to reduce **6.34** the PRT liability. The aggregate limit, consequently, was designed to ensure that this reduction was limited to the relatively early life of a field. If a participant used all of the allowance for each chargeable period, the aggregate limit would give a breathing space for the first 20 chargeable periods, or 10 years of its initial production.[124]

Safeguard

In addition to the oil allowance, safeguard is the second device **6.35** that recognises that PRT may inequitably burden marginal fields.[125] It guarantees a certain return by limiting the total amount of tax payable under PRT. The calculation does not involve a deduction from profits, but instead is carried out separately. In general, if the "adjusted profits"[126] are more than 30 per cent of "accumulated capital expenditure"[127] then the PRT liability is capped at 80 per cent of that excess.[128] However, this is applied only after all the reliefs and expenditures are computed.

Up until 1 January 1981, the calculation was on an annual basis. **6.36** Thereafter it was computed with reference to PRT chargeable periods.[129] The same year, this 30 per cent threshold was reduced

---

[123] In other words, the aggregate limit for the new fields in Southern Basin and onshore was 2,500,000 t, and for the rest of the new fields 10,000,000 t.

[124] The duration can be longer if the licensees don't use the full amount each chargeable period.

[125] HM Revenue and Customs, *Oil Taxation Manual: OT17525 – PRT: Safeguard*.

[126] As defined at OTA 1975, s 9(2). It is essentially calculated in the same way as assessable profit/allowable loss (see para 6.39).

[127] As defined at OTA 1975, s 9(3). This is essentially the total expenditure incurred up to and including the current period that would also qualify for uplift. For a discussion of uplifts, see para 6.51.

[128] OTA 1975, s 9(1), as it was originally enacted. Note that if the adjusted profits are less than 30% of accumulated capital expenditure then the PRT liability is nil.

[129] Finance Act 1981, Pt VII.

to 15 per cent, while the 80 per cent PRT limit was maintained.[130] At the same time a limit to the number of safeguard periods[131] was introduced.

6.37   Continuing the example of Company X, and assuming, first, that accumulated capital expenditure is calculated to be £10 million, and, second, that the net profit period has been passed so that no supplement is applicable, then the safeguard calculation is as shown in Table 6.4.

6.38   Since £240,000 is less than the £287,500 charge calculated under "normal" PRT rules, safeguard PRT applies. However, had the charge been less under the "normal" PRT rules, then that calculation would have prevailed.

Assessable profit/allowable loss

6.39   Under OTA 1975, s 2, a company's field profit, for PRT purposes, is calculated by subtracting certain expenditures from the income derived from that field in proportion to the company's share in that field. If the result is negative, ie income is less than the expenditure, then it is an allowable loss; otherwise it is an assessable profit.[132] The allowable losses can also be set against profits accrued in any preceding or future chargeable periods, further reducing the PRT liable assessable profit for that future period.[133] This calculation has been considered to be "the greatest contrast with Corporation Tax" because "[a]ccounts are completely ignored and instead the profit or loss for each field in which a participator is interested is arrived at by aggregating positive amounts and negative amounts".[134]

6.40   Initially, these "positive amounts" were gross profit, licence credit and "credit in respect of expenditure";[135] while the "negative

---

[130] Finance Act 1981, s 114(1).

[131] The limit is one and a half times the number of chargeable periods from commencement to the "net profit period": Finance Act 1981, s 114(1). This was further amended in Finance Act 1985, s 91 for the chargeable periods ending after 30 June 1985 so that the limit now became the number of chargeable periods from commencement to the net profit period "plus one half of those [chargeable periods] in which the amount of oil won and saved from the field exceeded 1,000 metric tonnes". See HM Revenue and Customs, *Oil Taxation Manual: OT17600 – PRT: Safeguard.*

[132] OTA 1975, s 2(2). Note that the terms "positive amounts" and "negative amounts" used in the legislation are "basically incomings (positives) and expenditure and certain specific reliefs (negatives)": HM Revenue and Customs, *Oil Taxation Manual: OT03150 – PRT Overview of PRT – Computation of PRT Charge.* The calculation of amount of expenditure to be debited/credited is provided under OTA 1975, s 2(8), (9), (10) and (11). The rules and procedures surrounding allowance of expenditure claims are provided under OTA 1975, Schs 5, 6 and 7.

[133] OTA 1975, s 7.

[134] Peat Marwick, *A Guide to UK Oil & Gas Taxation*, para. 4.1 (emphases removed).

[135] OTA 1975, s 2(3)(a).

Table 6.4 Safeguard calculation

Add	Subtract	Amount in £
Assessable profit		1,800,000
	15% of Acc Capex	1,500,000
		300,000
Total safeguard PRT charge		*240,000*

amounts" were gross loss, licence debit, and "debit in respect of expenditure".[136] The Finance Act 1981 introduced an additional item into positive/negative amounts. From 1 January 1981 onwards, any amount paid in relation to a licence – with the exception of royalty payments – either to the Secretary of State or from him, were to be included in the assessable profit/allowable loss calculation.[137] This item was added in order to "deal with refunds to licensees in respect of conveying and treating costs of royalties satisfied in kind".[138]

From the second PRT-period of 1982 onwards a further two items 6.41 were included in the computation: tariff receipts[139] and receipts from asset disposals.[140] Both of these items were to be added into the "positive amounts" only. The assessable profit/allowable loss calculation would thus be carried out as shown in Table 6.5.

Allowances and reliefs

Whereas the computation of chargeable income for PRT purposes is 6.42 relatively straightforward, the allowance system is rather complex.

Expenditures

When calculating the assessable profit for PRT, no distinction 6.43 is drawn between capital and revenue expenditure in so far as allowances are concerned.[141] Instead, field expenditures are categorised into three groups: (a) those incurred on long-term assets;[142]

---

[136] OTA 1975, s 2(3)(b).
[137] Finance Act 1981, s 118.
[138] Peat Marwick, *A Guide to UK Oil & Gas Taxation*, para. 4.37.
[139] OTA 1983, s 6. Calculation of this is in OTA 1983, s 9. Tariff receipts are essentially the income derived from third-party access charges. At the same time, OTA 1983, s 9 introduces tariff receipts allowance so that the cash equivalent of the first 250,000 tonnes is exempt from PRT liability. For regulatory discussion of third-party access to infrastructure, see Chapter 7 on Access to Infrastructure.
[140] OTA 1983, s 7. Calculation of this is in OTA 1983, s 10.
[141] *Ibid*, s 3(1): "any expenditure (whether or not of a capital nature)".
[142] *Ibid*, s 4.

Table 6.5 Assessable profit/allowable loss calculation

Add (*positive amounts*)	Subtract (*negative amounts*)	Amount in £
Gross profit		X
Licence credit		X
Expenditure credit		X
Tariff receipts		X
Disposal receipts		X
	Gross loss	Y
	Licence debit	Y
	Licence payments bar royalty	Y
	Expenditure debit	Y
Assessable profit / allowable loss		$\Sigma X - \Sigma Y$

(b) exploration and appraisal expenditure;[143] and (c) all other qualified expenditure.[144]

6.44   However, not all the field expenditures are allowed. Interest payments or other costs on loans;[145] costs of buying land;[146] costs of buying or constructing onshore buildings;[147] any payment – with the exception of those made to the Secretary of State – in acquiring a "direct or indirect interest" in production from a field;[148] and those expenditures "determined by reference to the quantity, value or proceeds of, or the profits from, oil won from the field"[149] are not allowable.

6.45   *Long-term assets (s 4) expenditures* Initially, s 4 defined long-term assets as those "whose useful life continues after the end of the claim period [of 6 or 12 months][150] in which it is first so

---

[143] OTA 1983, s 5.

[144] *Ibid*, s 3.

[145] *Ibid*, s 3(4)(a).

[146] *Ibid*, s 3(4)(b).

[147] *Ibid*, s 3(4)(c). The exceptions to this rule are listed in OTA 1975, s 3(4)(c)(i)–(iv).

[148] *Ibid*, s 3(4)(e).

[149] *Ibid*, s 3(4)(d). "The apparent purpose of these provisions is to simplify collection of the tax by ignoring fragmentation of profits which amy arise under various royalty and other agreements": Peat Marwick, *A Guide to UK Oil & Gas Taxation*, Appendix II, para II.4.

[150] The first claim period is defined in OTA 1975, Sch 5, para 1(1) as the period that ends on either 30 June or 31 December with 6- or 12-month duration of each subsequent period. Both choices are left to the "responsible person" to decide on. If the responsible person fails to provide a written choice, the default duration of a claim period is 12 months.

used".[151] With some exceptions,[152] costs incurred in order to acquire or bring into existence these assets, or incurred simply to increase their value, were allowable in their entirety. In 1983, s 4 was amended for expenditures incurred from 1 July 1982 onwards[153] to clarify the definitions and "to obviate difficulties with the old rules and in recognition of the increased use of tariff arrangements".[154] However, in a broad sense, the definitions of long-term assets[155] and the 100 per cent expenditure allowance[156] remained essentially the same,[157] so that the full relief was still available.

E&A (s 5) expenditures Initially, only the expenditure incurred   **6.46**
"wholly and exclusively" in the UK or UKCS after 31 December 1959 on unsuccessful, or "abortive" exploration was allowable.[158] This meant that the expenditure had to be incurred within the licence area but outside an area that would/could be determined as a field.[159]

However, the Finance Act 1983 restricted the abortive explo-   **6.47**
ration expenditure allowance to the expenditures incurred up to and including 15 March of the same year.[160] For expenditures incurred after that date the scope was widened under s 5A to include all the exploration and appraisal expenditures as long as they were incurred before the approval of field development.[161]

Other (s 3) expenditures These are also referred to as the "ordinary   **6.48**
expenditure rules".[162] Under these ordinary rules, the expenditure is allowable only if it is incurred for any of the following purposes: "searching for oil" within 5 km of a field; licence fee; "ascertaining the extent or characteristic of ... or what the reserves of oil" are in the field; "winning oil"; "measuring the quantity of oil"; transporting the produced oil to the land, "initial treatment or initial storage" of the produced oil; arm's-length sale of produced oil and "closing down the field or any part of it, but only if and to the extent

---

[151] OTA 1975, s 4(1).
[152] Expenditures on "brought-in assets" and on mobile assets are excluded: OTA 1975, s 4(3).
[153] Oil Taxation Act 1983 (hereinafter "OTA 1983"), s 3.
[154] Peat Marwick, *A Guide to UK Oil & Gas Taxation* at para 5.4.
[155] OTA 1983, s 3(8).
[156] *Ibid*, s 3(4).
[157] Though there were changes to the exceptions. These changes are beyond the scope of this chapter but, for further information, see OTA 1983.
[158] OTA 1975, s 5.
[159] The condition is that the expenditure "is not, and is unlikely to become, allowable under section 3 or 4 ... for any oil field": OTA 1975, s 5(c).
[160] Finance Act 1983, s 37.
[161] OTA 1975, s 5A(1). See para 6.53.
[162] Peat Marwick, *A Guide to UK Oil & Gas Taxation*, para 5.36.

that the expenditure is incurred for the purposes of safety or the prevention of pollution".[163]

6.49   In 1991, the last of these purposes was repealed and replaced with three further purposes in order to incorporate decommissioning provisions.[164] These additional purposes are: "obtaining an abandonment guarantee";[165] "closing down, decommissioning, abandoning or wholly or partially dismantling or removing any qualifying asset"; and "carrying out qualifying work[166] consequential upon the closing down of the field or any part of it."[167]

6.50   Apart from these expenditure purposes, any losses arising from decommissioning are treated as any other field losses,[168] ie the losses will first be carried forward, then the remaining will be carried back.[169] If there are still allowable losses remaining, it is possible under s 6 to set them against income from another field.[170]

6.51   *Expenditure supplement* Under the PRT regime, interest and loan costs are not deductible.[171] In order to reflect these costs a further allowance called supplement, or an "uplift", is introduced.[172] It is additional to the allowances provided to qualifying expenditure. In broad terms, the items that are classified as capital expenditure in usual accountancy principles would qualify for this uplift. However, "there may also be items which, on an accountancy basis, would be revenue but which nevertheless qualify for supplement, and vice versa".[173] OTA 1975, s 3(5) provides the criteria for qualification. Effectively, all the devel-

---

[163] OTA 1975, s 3(1).

[164] Finance Act 1991, Pt III. For detailed discussion of the regulatory framework, see Chapter 10 on Decommissioning.

[165] As defined in Finance Act 1991, s 104. These would typically include "fees, commission or incidental costs" incurred in obtaining this guarantee: HM Revenue and Customs, *Oil Taxation Manual: OT10300 – PRT: Decommissioning – Allowable Expenditure: Abandonment Guarantees.*

[166] As defined in OTA 1975, s 3(1B).

[167] OTA 1975, s 3, as amended by Finance Act 1991, s 103.

[168] See para 6.39.

[169] OTA 1975, s 7(3).

[170] See para 6.53.

[171] OTA 1975, s 3(4)(a). See para 6.44.

[172] HM Revenue and Customs, *A Guide to UK and UK Continental Shelf: Oil and Gas Taxation – January 2008*, para. 4.9. However, note that although it is intended to reflect these costs, the rate is not directly related to it but calculated as a fixed percentage of expenditure.

[173] HM Revenue and Customs, *Oil Taxation Manual: OT12025 – PRT: Supplement – Outline.*

opment costs,[174] "initial field appraisal costs",[175] expenditure that would "substantially" improve the production rate[176] and expenditure associated with "providing any installation for the initial treatment or initial storage of oil won from the field"[177] qualify for the "uplift".

The initial rate of uplift was 75 per cent.[178] This was reduced to 35 per cent for expenditures incurred after 31 December 1978.[179] Although initially there were no limitations as to when the qualifying expenditure was incurred, in 1981 a cut-off point, referred to as "the net profit period", was introduced.[180] This cut-off point is the period in which the aggregate cash flow turns positive, ie the payback period. Essentially, any expenditure incurred after this period would not qualify for the uplift – even if it was a qualifying expenditure.[181]   6.52

Non-field expenditures Although PRT is a field-based regime, there are certain exceptions where particular expenditures not relating to that field could also be allowed. The first of these exceptions is "unrelievable field losses". This applies when production from a field permanently stops and a company still holds allowable field losses that cannot be relieved under s 7 against profits from that field in other periods.[182] These losses, then, can be claimed against profits accrued in another field.[183]   6.53

The second exception is the "abortive exploration expenditure" allowance.[184] Any expenditure incurred after 31 December 1959 in order "wholly and exclusively" to explore for oil in the UK that is   6.54

---

[174] HM Revenue and Customs, *Oil Taxation Manual: OT12100 – PRT: Supplement – Bringing about the Commencement of Winning or Transporting Oil.*

[175] HM Revenue and Customs, *Oil Taxation Manual: OT12250 – PRT: Supplement – Ascertaining the extent of Oil-Bearing Area.* These would include seismic surveys, appraisal drilling and "ongoing re-appraisal expenditure".

[176] OTA 1975, s 3(5)(c). See also HM Revenue and Customs, *Oil Taxation Manual: OT12300 – PRT: Supplement – Substantially Improving the Rate at which Oil can be Won.*

[177] OTA 1975, s 3(5)(d). Note that this would cover most of the expenditure that qualifies under item (vii) of Field expenditure allowance.

[178] *Ibid*, s 2(9).

[179] Finance (No 2) Act 1979, s 19. Note that the transitional rate was 66⅔%.

[180] Finance Act 1981, s 111

[181] Note that this was further amended in 1985. For the chargeable periods ending after 30 June 1985, the net profit period is the earliest of "(a) the amount of oil won and saved from the field exceeds 1,000 metric tonnes … ; and (b) a net profit from the field accrues to the participator": Finance Act 1985, s 91(3).

[182] OTA 1975, s 6, as amended by Finance Act 1995, s 146 and by Finance Act 2001, s 101.

[183] *Ibid.*

[184] OTA 1975, s 5.

"unlikely to become" deductible in any field can be claimed against that company's PRT-liable field.[185] As the expenditures ought to be incurred before 15 March 1983,[186] this allowance is not applicable today.

6.55   From that day onwards, the third exception was introduced where the scope of this cross-field allowance was expanded to include all exploration and appraisal expenditure regardless of the outcome as long as the expenditure was incurred before the development programme was approved by the Secretary of State.[187] With this third exception a company would "get 100 per cent PRT relief for exploration and appraisal expenditure against the income of any field in which [that company] has an interest. The relief may be claimed at any time, thus enabling it to be set against the income from fields that are paying PRT, or would do so but for the relief".[188]

6.56   The fourth exception was introduced in the Finance Act 1987. It provides relief for expenditures incurred on research into the winning of oil.[189] The typical research could be on "the respective advantages of steel and concrete platforms, coating systems for pipelines, and mathematical modelling of reservoirs".[190] In order to qualify, the research expenditure has to be incurred after 16 March 1987, and must not have become allowable in any field within 3 years from the moment it was incurred.[191]

6.57   The Finance Act 1987 also introduced the fifth exception, the cross-field allowances,[192] in order to "give oil companies a financial incentive to develop smaller second generation fields".[193] Essentially, for any expenditure incurred in a "relevant new field" after 16 March 1987 that would otherwise qualify for the "supplement"[194]

---

[185] OTA 1975, s 5(1). The expenditures would typically include "the cost of shooting preliminary seismic surveys and their interpretation, drilling, supplies and well testing": HM Revenue and Customs, *Oil Taxation Manual: OT13950 – PRT: Non-Field Expenditure – Abortive Exploration Expenditure: Basic Conditions*.

[186] Finance Act 1983, s 37 and Sch 8, Pt II, s 3.

[187] *Ibid*, Sch 8, Pt I. This Part inserts s 5A into OTA 1975. See OTA 1975, s 5A(1)(c) and (7).

[188] HM Revenue and Customs, *A Guide to UK and UK Continental Shelf: Oil and Gas Taxation – January 2008*, para 4.29.

[189] Finance Act 1987, s 64 and Sch 13, Pt I. This section and this Part insert s 5B into OTA 1975.

[190] HM Revenue and Customs, *Oil Taxation Manual: OT14100 – PRT: Non-Field Expenditure – Research Expenditure: Outline*

[191] OTA 1975, s 5B(1). The 3-year requirement is in place to "ensure that only expenditure that does not relate to a specific field or fields will qualify": HM Revenue and Customs, *Oil Taxation Manual: OT14100*.

[192] Finance Act 1987, s 65 and Sch 14.

[193] HM Revenue and Customs, *Oil Taxation Manual: OT13020 – PRT: Cross Field Allowances – Outline*.

[194] Finance Act 1987, s 65(2)(c).

but not for the exploration and appraisal allowance,[195] above, a company can "elect" to offset up to 10 per cent of that cost against PRT liability in another field.[196] The restriction of "relevant new field" effectively excludes onshore fields, the offshore Southern Basin fields and those fields that received development consent before 17 March 1987.[197]

PRT–RFCT INTERACTION

Under the Corporation Tax regime any PRT paid by a company can be set off against the ring-fence income in the same accounting period when calculating the RFCT charge, reducing the profit to which the 30 per cent tax rate applies.[198]   **6.58**

CONCLUSION

According to the most recent statistics there are 77 fields in the UKCS with gross profits over £1 million to which the PRT regime applies, but only 29 of them actually paid any PRT in the first PRT-chargeable period of 2009.[199] For the remaining fields either the gross profits were covered by allowable losses and expenditures, or the assessable profits were reduced to nil by oil allowances and safeguards. In terms of the total tax the industry paid during the financial year 2009–10, the Government received approximately £0.9 billion in PRT, £3.3 billion in RFCT and £2.3 billion in SC payments.[200]   **6.59**

This chapter has explained the main legislation and method-ologies behind those figures. This, however, does not mean that it is a comprehensive or a historical review. The discussions have focused on the tax regime solely applicable to offshore oil and gas producers. Discussions of Supplementary Petroleum Duty, Advance Corporation Tax and the Gas Levy have deliberately been omitted   **6.60**

---

[195] Finance Act 1987, s 65(2)(d).

[196] *Ibid*, s 65(1).

[197] *Ibid*, s 8 and Sch 14. The Southern Basin is the "area to the East of the United Kingdom and between latitudes 52 and 55 North". See paras 6.31–6.34.

[198] CTA 2010, s 299; previously ICTA 1988, s 500.

[199] HM Revenue and Customs, *Table 11.13 – oil and gas fields assessed for Petroleum Revenue Tax*, available from http://www.hmrc.gov.uk/stats/corporate_tax/menu.htm (accessed 16 June 2010). Note that the chargeable period to 30 June 2009 is the latest available statistic.

[200] HM Revenue and Customs, *Table 11.11 – Government revenues from UK oil and gas production*, available from http://www.hmrc.gov.uk/stats/corporate_tax/menu.htm (accessed 16 June 2010).

because they are inapplicable in today's regime and their inclusion would have further complicated what is already a complex system.

6.61   This chapter also did not include any discussion of the political and economic environment within which the tax policies were implemented. However, from the frequency of the changes to the tax regime applicable to offshore oil and gas production, it is surely not unreasonable to conclude that the Government's thinking that it can "merrily dip into profits every time oil prices rise"[201] may be institutionalised. In so far as that is the case, one might also reasonably anticipate further changes in future, perhaps also in the direction of a stricter tax regime for the offshore oil and gas industry.

6.62   That is by no means the whole story, however. As many of the other chapters in this volume have highlighted, the maturity of the UKCS as a hydrocarbon province means that the Government cannot assume that the industry will continue to invest so as to achieve its desired aim of maximum economic recovery come what may. If there is any perception that the tax burden is so heavy as to compromise the return on investment, resources may well be diverted to other parts of the world. That the equation is a complex one, however, is exemplified by the difficulties the industry currently confronts in otherwise geologically attractive regions in terms of political instability, environmental concerns and, at the time of writing, a number of moratoria on deepwater drilling. In that context, might the UK Government conclude that the relatively benign situation on the UKCS justifies a robust attitude to the state's take? Time will tell.[202]

---

[201] *Hansard*, HC, vol 385, Pt 144; Mr Flight, col 329 (9 May 2002). Mr Flight was commenting on the introduction of SC.

[202] See n 83 above for the latest developments as this book went to press.

CHAPTER 7

ACCESS TO INFRASTRUCTURE

Uisdean Vass

As we saw in Chapter 5, the fact that the UKCS is a mature province 7.1 raises challenges for industry and government if economic recovery of the remaining hydrocarbons is to be maximised. Reserves of petroleum are useless to both the licensee and the state unless there exists some economic means of extracting the hydrocarbons and thereafter transporting them to a place where they can be processed and put to use. The permanent and semi-permanent physical objects used in the hydrocarbon transportation process can be described as infrastructure. Having access to infrastructure is therefore fundamental to the successful exploitation of reserves of petroleum. When developing very large discoveries, access to infrastructure, although important, is not especially problematic: you build your own, typically in the form of pipelines and associated elements. Doing so will be a very large capital expense, but this is justified if the economics of the venture permit it. However, as we have already seen,[1] nowadays very few new developments in at least the established parts of the UKCS are very large, or even large. The great majority are now satellite or "tie-back" developments which only have a realistic prospect of succeeding economically if they can utilise the infrastructure which already exists. The regulator[2] has put the matter thus:

> "Access to infrastructure on fair and reasonable terms is crucial to maximising the economic recovery of the UK's oil and, particularly,

---

[1] See, eg, para 5.3 above.
[2] Now the Department of Energy and Climate Change; previously the Department for Business, Enterprise and Regulatory Reform, which itself previously was the Department of Trade and Industry; hereinafter referred to as the "Department".

gas because many fields on the UKCS do not contain sufficient reserves to justify their own infrastructure but are economic as satellite developments utilising existing infrastructure."[3]

7.2   In this regard, the maturity of the basin offers both threats and opportunities. In so far as the North Sea is one of the most intensively developed offshore hydrocarbon provinces anywhere in the world, there exists a relatively well-developed infrastructure, meaning that, at least within the established part of the province,[4] few discoveries are far from a potential means of transportation. A moment's consideration, however, reveals the potential problems. While market forces, changes to licensing practices and mature province initiatives all combine to mean that many new developments will be carried out by new entrants, the major elements of the existing infrastructure were constructed – at considerable expense – by the established players with the principal intention of transporting oil and gas from the discoveries made within the areas licensed to them. In large measure, the infrastructure continues to be owned by those players. Moreover, it is ageing and the production from the fields which it was built to support is decreasing as those fields approach the end of their economic lives. How do the new entrants ensure that they can have access to the established infrastructure at a cost that is not prohibitive – and that they can do so before the infrastructure falls out of use? Nor is this a matter of indifference to the Government. If its mature province and licensing initiatives are to bite, and if its general objective of recovering as much of the UKCS's hydrocarbon reserves as is possible is to be met, then the problem of access to infrastructure needs to be solved. But how far is it legitimate for the state, which did not incur the expense associated with the construction of infrastructure, to seek to control its use? It can therefore be seen that the issues which surround access to infrastructure are not straightforward ones.

7.3   This chapter considers the three legs upon which access to infrastructure rests: the legislative framework (the Petroleum Act 1998[5] together with the Energy Act 2008); the Industry Code of Practice; and the Department's Guidance.

---

[3] DECC, *Guidance on Disputes over Third Party Access to Upstream Oil and Gas Infrastructure* (April 2009), available for download from https://www.og.decc.gov.uk/upstream/infrastructure/TPA_Guide.pdf (accessed 13 March 2011) (hereinafter the "Department's Guidance"), at para 9.

[4] This proposition does not hold true for frontier areas: see the discussion at para 4.54.

[5] As amended by the Gas (Third Party Access and Accounts) Regulations 2000 (SI 2000/1937), Sch 4; and by the Petroleum Act 1998 (Third Party Access) Order 2007 (SI 2007/290).

THE LEGISLATIVE FRAMEWORK
The Petroleum Act 1998

The basic approach to the issue of access to offshore infra- **7.4** structure by third parties is contained in s 17F of the Petroleum Act 1998.[6] Put shortly, this provides that third parties may, if negotiations with infrastructure owners fail,[7] petition the regulator, the Secretary of State at the Department, to serve a notice determining the applicant's access rights.[8] Such a notice may be granted only where the Secretary of State is satisfied that the pipeline "could be operated in accordance with the notice without prejudicing its efficient operation" as a means of satisfying the owner's own transportation requirements.[9] Moreover, such a notice "may contain such provisions as the Secretary of State considers appropriate" to secure to the applicant the right to connect a pipeline of its own into that of the owner and to convey through the owner's pipeline certain quantities of hydrocarbon without prevention or hindrance.[10] The notice may also regulate the charges made by the owner in consideration of the rights granted, and authorise the recovery of those charges from the applicant by the owner.[11]

Even though the Secretary of State has broad discretion in **7.5** awarding access rights, s 17F(8) of the Petroleum Act 1998 requires him to take the following seven factors into account when considering any such application for access:

"(a) capacity which is or can reasonably be made available in the pipeline in question;

(b) any incompatibilities of technical specification which cannot reasonably be overcome;

---

[6] The Petroleum Act 1998, s 17F substantially re-enacts s 10E(5) of the Pipelines Act 1962. Similar provisions apply to onshore gas processing terminals (s 12(1F) of the Gas Act 1995) and to pipelines connecting processing terminals to the National Transmission System (NTS) or to large gas users (s 10C(7) of the Pipelines Act 1962). It should be noted that any controlled petroleum pipeline which is, as a result of the Framework Agreement on cross-boundary co-operation made between the UK and Norway on 4 April 2005, subject to the Norwegian access system is regulated not by s 17F but by ss 17GA and 17GB. For further discussion on the Framework Agreement, see paras 13.61–13.63.

[7] The Petroleum Act 1998, s 17F(2) provides that an application must be made to the owner of the pipeline before any application is made to the Secretary of State. Section 17F(6) states that the Secretary of State "shall not entertain" any such application unless the parties have had a reasonable time to reach agreement themselves.

[8] Section 17F(5) read together with s 17F(9).

[9] Section 17F(9).

[10] Section 17F(10).

[11] Section 17F(11).

(c)   difficulties which cannot reasonably be overcome and which could prejudice the efficient, current and planned future production of petroleum;

(d)   the owner's reasonable needs for the transport and processing of petroleum;

(e)   the interests of all users and operators of the pipeline;

(f)   the need to maintain security and regularity of supplies of petroleum; and

(g)   the number of parties involved in the dispute."

7.6   If the third party provides falsified information either purposefully or "recklessly" in the application to persuade the Secretary of State to "issue any authorization"; or, following the regulator's notice, if the infrastructure owner breaches any of the provisions of that notice, he "shall be guilty of an offence and liable on summary conviction to a fine not exceeding the statutory maximum or on conviction on indictment to a fine".[12] Moreover, when the offender is a "body corporate" and there is a proof that the offence was "committed with the consent or connivance of, or to be attributable to any neglect on the part of, any director, manager, secretary or other similar officer of the body corporate or any person who was purporting to act in such capacity", then both that person and the "body corporate" will be considered as guilty.[13]

The Energy Act 2008

7.7   There had been some criticism, including in the first edition of this book,[14] of the legislation's fixation upon "pipelines" when defining the infrastructure. It was not clear whether the existing legislation covered each and every aspect of offshore infrastructure, to which an applicant might reasonably require access, and not just the pipelines.

7.8   The Energy Act 2008 goes a long way towards addressing these criticisms by extending the powers of the Secretary of State to "determine third party access rights to *all* upstream petroleum infrastructure".[15] First, it amends s 26 of the Petroleum Act 1998 to expand the definition of a "pipeline" to "a pipe or system of pipes (excluding a drain or sewer) for the conveyance of any thing, together with all apparatus, works and *services* associated with the

---

[12] Section 21(1).

[13] Section 22(6).

[14] See U Vass, "Access to Infrastructure" in G Gordon and J Paterson (eds), *Oil and Gas Law – Current Practice and Emerging Trends* (2007) at para 5.6.

[15] Energy Act 2008, Explanatory Notes, *Third Party Access: Summary and Background*, http://www.opsi.gov.uk/ukpga/2008/32/notes/contents (accessed 13 March 2011) (hereinafter the "2008 Explanatory Notes"), at para 398 (emphasis added).

operation of such a pipe or system", while removing the subsection defining what the apparatus and works are.[16] The aim is to include services like "the provision of fuel or power needed to operate third party equipment on or from the host facility" in the definition along with the works and apparatus associated with both the pipeline and the operation of it.[17]

Second, it simultaneously amends s 28 of the 1998 Act[18] and s 12 of the Gas Act 1995 to widen the definition of "gas processing operation". On top of the initial definition provided in the 2000 Regulations, it also includes the operations of "separating, purifying, blending, odorising or compressing gas" for the purpose of "converting it into a form in which a purchaser is willing to accept delivery from a seller, or enabling it to be loaded for conveyance to another place".[19] It additionally provides for the operations of "loading gas" as part of the gas processing operations.[20] These amendments, both to the Gas Act 1995 and to the Petroleum Act 1998, are intended to align the two with respect to third-party access. While the latter Act deals with the access to the majority of infrastructure, s 12 of the former specifically deals with access to facilities that carry out gas processing operations. By broadening the definition and aligning the two Acts, it is, therefore, intended to "increase the scope of the Secretary of State's powers over third party access" not only to the means to convey the gas but also to the facilities that process it.[21]   7.9

Third, the 2008 Act introduces a dispute resolution process for third-party access to facilities that carry out oil processing operations,[22]   7.10

---

[16] Energy Act 2008, s 78(3) (emphases added).

[17] 2008 Explanatory Notes, para 403.

[18] The Petroleum Act 1998, s 28 was initially amended under the 2000 Regulations, Sch 4, para 9, which introduced, among other things, the definitions of "downstream pipeline", "gas", "gas processing facility" and "gas processing operation".

[19] Energy Act 2008, s 78(4)(a).

[20] *Ibid.*

[21] 2008 Explanatory Notes, para 404. The definition of the "gas processing operation" has been broadened in a similar way by amending both the Pipelines Act 1962 and the Gas Act 1995 under the Energy Act 2008, s 78(1) and (2).

[22] "Oil processing" operations are defined as including "any of the following operations": (a) "initial blending and such other treatment of petroleum as may be required to produce stabilised crude oil and other hydrocarbon liquids to the point at which a seller could reasonably make a delivery to a purchaser of such oil and liquids; (b) "receiving stabilised crude oil and other hydrocarbon liquids piped from an oil processing facility carrying out operations of a kind mentioned in paragraph (a), or storing oil or other hydrocarbon liquids so received, prior to their conveyance to another place (whether inside or outside Great Britain);" and (c) "loading stabilised crude oil and other hydrocarbon liquids piped from a facility carrying out operations of a kind mentioned in paragraph (a) or (b) for conveyance to another place (whether inside or outside Great Britain)" (Energy Act 2008, s 81(8)).

similar to that of the controlled petroleum pipeline.[23] Under this process the third party, ie the applicant, seeking access to oil processing facilities[24] should, first, request the right from the owner of such facilities.[25] The request should include the type and quantity of the subject petroleum, and the processing duration sought.[26] If the parties fail to come to an agreement, only then may the applicant bring the issue to the regulator's attention.[27] As the regulator, the Secretary of State has to be "satisfied that the parties have had a reasonable time in which to reach agreement"[28] before he can consider the applicant's request.

7.11   Unlike s 17F(8) of the 1998 Act, which relates to pipelines,[29] the 2008 Act does not list factors for the Secretary of State to take into account in relation to a dispute concerning access to oil processing facilities. There are only three broad limitations to his discretionary powers where his decision cannot prejudice:

"(a)   the efficient operation of the oil processing facility,
(b)   the processing by the facility of the quantities of petroleum which the owner or an associate of the owner requires or may reasonably be expected to require to be processed by the facility for the purposes of any business carried on by the owner or associate, or
(c)   the processing by the facility of the quantities of petroleum which another person with a right to have petroleum processed by the facility requires to be processed in the exercise of that right."[30]

7.12 The regulator can either reject or suspend the application to "enable further negotiations between the parties" and notify the applicant of such decision; or, if he decides to give further consideration to the application, he can notify the owner together with "any person with a right to have petroleum processed at the facility, and the Health

---

[23] See paras 6.41–6.51. Note that a "controlled petroleum pipeline" is defined as pipelines or a network of pipelines within the UKCS "operated or constructed as part of a petroleum production project or used to convey petroleum from the site of one or more such projects" either directly back to the premises to be used for "power generation or for an industrial process"; or directly to a location "outside Great Britain"; or directly or indirectly to a terminal: Petroleum Act 1998, ss 28(1) and 14.

[24] These are facilities that carry out oil processing operations.

[25] Energy Act 2008, s 80(1). The "owner", in the context of an oil processing facility, "includes a lessee and any person occupying or controlling the facility": Energy Act 2008, s 81(8). The latter section also provides the definition of "oil processing operations".

[26] Energy Act 2008, s 80(4).

[27] Ibid, s 80(5).

[28] Ibid, s 80(6).

[29] See para 7.7.

[30] Energy Act 2008, s 80(9); the term "associate" is defined in the Energy Act 2008, s 82.

and Safety Executive" of such decision "and give them the opportunity to be heard in relation to the application".[31]

When serving his decision, the Secretary can also specify the 7.13
terms of the agreement the applicant and the owner should enter
into and "require the owner" to agree to these terms.[32] This is to
ensure the applicant receives the right he had requested without any
obstruction or delay; and in order to regulate the charges and secure
to "the applicant such ancillary or incidental rights as [he] considers
necessary or expedient, which may include the right to have a
pipeline connected to the facility by the owner."[33] The Secretary can
additionally specify the price, or the method of calculating that price,
the owner can charge for the right to use his processing facility.[34]

Similar to his authority regarding the controlled petroleum 7.14
pipelines, the Secretary can also request further information from
either the applicant or the owner, or both, including "financial information ... with respect to oil processing operations".[35]

Compliance with the Secretary's decision is "enforceable by civil 7.15
proceedings by the Secretary of State for an injunction or interdict
or for any other appropriate relief".[36]

A significant problem with the legislation in practice has been 7.16
the fact that its operation depends upon the initiative of the third
party seeking access.[37] In this regard, it is noteworthy that up until
very recently no third party had been willing to go so far as to
require the Secretary of State to issue a formal s 17F notification for
access.[38] A number of factors are responsible for this. First, it should
not be overlooked that in many cases the infrastructure owner
and the party seeking access have been able to come to a mutually
satisfactory commercial arrangement without outside assistance.

---

[31] Energy Act 2008, s 80(7) and (8) (emphasis added).
[32] Ibid, s 81(1)(a), read together with s 81(1)(c).
[33] Ibid, s 81(2).
[34] Ibid, s 81(1)(b).
[35] Ibid, s 81(3) and (4).
[36] Ibid, s 81(6).
[37] See para 7.4.
[38] Anecdotal evidence suggested that there had been a number of instances where third
parties had given very serious consideration to making such a referral but had drawn
back from doing so. However, in May 2010, the DECC was asked for the first time to
issue a determination on access rights. The dispute is between Endeavour International
Corporation and the infrastructure owners Nexen Inc, ExxonMobil, Premier Oil plc
and Suncor Energy Inc over charges of access to Scott platform. See: M Johnson,
Arbitration sought on North Sea pipe costs, Financial Times, 23 May 2010; and M
Johnson, *Tensions escalate over North Sea access*, Financial Times, 23 May 2010. At
the time of writing, it is understood that the DECC has informally indicated what it
thinks an appropriate tariff would be, and given the parties further time to resolve the
matter.

However, in many other cases the party wishing access has drawn back from petitioning for a s 17F notification for less satisfactory reasons: a shame factor based on the notion that oilmen should be able to sort things out on a direct basis; a fear that the Secretary of State's decision might actually prejudice the third party; and fear of "retaliation" in some fashion by the infrastructure owner, whether on the UKCS or elsewhere. While talk of shame and fear may appear somewhat melodramatic, it should be borne in mind that the upstream oil and gas industry is made up of a limited number of players operating in a global marketplace.[39] Moreover, most UKCS pipelines have been operated by major oil companies and many third parties seeking access have been independents or even small independents. The power differential should not be underestimated.

CODE OF PRACTICE ON ACCESS TO UPSTREAM OIL AND GAS INFRASTRUCTURE ON THE UKCS ("ICOP")

7.17 In 1994, the Government, concerned that the legislative approach[40] was not working well, voiced explicit concerns to the industry, focusing on the "lack of transparency in the terms of gaining access to oil and gas infrastructure, particularly offshore, and the delays in new field developments and the increased costs that this imposed".[41] The response was an early example of an approach that has become commonplace in addressing difficult regulatory issues within the industry:[42] the formation of a committee (the D'Ancona Committee), which was composed of representatives from government, infra-structure owners and those who sought access to infrastructure.[43] The committee required to consider whether the answer lay in more extensive regulation or in a new industry code of practice. The committee favoured the second option, and in February 1996 UKOOA (now Oil & Gas UK)[44] accepted the Rules and Procedures Governing Access to Offshore Infrastructure (RPGA).[45] The RPGA established many of the principles subsequently reiterated in 2004

---

[39] This is a factor which informs not just this issue but the industry's whole approach to dispute resolution: see Chapter 18 below.

[40] At that point contained in s 10E(5) of the Pipelines Act 1962.

[41] T Daintith, G Willoughby and A Hill, *United Kingdom Oil & Gas Law* (3rd edn, looseleaf, 2000–date) (hereinafter "Daintith, Willoughby and Hill, *United Kingdom Oil & Gas Law*"), para 1–733.

[42] See also the discussion at paras 5.7–5.9.

[43] Daintith, Willoughby and Hill, *United Kingdom Oil & Gas Law*, para 1–733.

[44] At the time Oil & Gas UK was known as the UK Offshore Operators Association (UKOOA). Throughout the chapter, both names will be used to refer to the same organi-sation, reflecting the original name at the relevant time.

[45] The rules and procedures were also commonly referred to as a "code of practice" but

by the Industry Code of Practice ("ICOP").[46] These principles, such as non-discriminatory access, separation of services, transparency, standardisation and timelines, were intended to be observed by infrastructure owners and third parties when conducting discussions in the shadow of the Secretary of State's statutory powers. Additionally, in 2001, the Department produced a Guidance Note[47] in an attempt to explain the considerations it might use to decide a third-party application for infrastructure access if it were called upon to do so. However, neither RPGA nor the 2001 Guidance Note succeeded in bringing a seismic shift in culture. Third parties declined to use their statutory rights and the principles established in RPGA were honoured more in the breach than the observance. As this century dawned and activity levels on the UKCS fell to historic lows, the licensing and administration system as a whole was subjected to rigorous analysis by the Department and other industry groups. Among other difficulties, potential new entrants identified the lack of transparency regarding access to offshore infrastructure as a factor which inhibited investment in the UKCS.[48] UKOOA, working closely with the Department, drafted a highly detailed response, the ICOP, which came into force in August 2004. In March 2005, the Department published new Guidance Notes,[49] which replaced the original Guidance Notes issued in 2001. These 2005 Guidance Notes, in turn, were replaced by the latest version in April 2009.[50] Along with the underlying legislation, the ICOP and the Guidance Notes (which are, of course, not laws, but are intended as guides to good practice within the industry and act as an indication of how the Secretary of State would exercise his powers under s 17F of the 1998 Act should he be called upon so to do) are central to issues of third-party access to offshore infrastructure on the UKCS.

---

the term "RPGA" will be preferred here, to distinguish this instrument from the 2004 ICOP and subsequent updates.

[46] Oil and Gas UK, *Code of Practice on Access to Upstream Oil and Gas Infrastructure on the UK Continental Shelf* (January 2009) (hereinafter "ICOP"), available for download from http://www.oilandgasuk.co.uk/publications/viewpub.cfm?frmPubID=243 (accessed 13 March 2011). Note that this is the updated version of the 2004 document, taking into account the creation of the Department of Energy and Climate Change. The principles and the paragraphs are otherwise identical.

[47] DTI, *Consideration of Applications for Resolution of Disputes over Third Party Access to Infrastructure: Guidance to Parties in Dispute* (2001).

[48] See, eg, the PILOT press release announcing ICOP: PILOT, *Oil and Gas Industry Agree to Boost Pipeline Access to Promote New North Sea Development* (15 September 2004), available for download from http://www.pilottaskforce.co.uk/data/presscentre. cfm/135/1/1 (accessed 13 March 2011).

[49] DTI, *Guidance on Disputes over Third Party Access to Upstream Oil and Gas Infrastructure* (2005).

[50] See n 3 above.

7.18   Developed by UKOOA,[51] the ICOP is essentially guidance for the negotiation process of third-party access to infrastructure on the UKCS.[52] It is non-statutory, but, by "their endorsement of this Code, parties make a commitment to be guided by its principles and procedures".[53]

Relevant infrastructure

7.19   The ICOP is stated to apply to "all UK oil and gas infrastructure throughout the hydrocarbon production and supply chain from wellhead through to receiving terminals and initial onshore processing facilities".[54] The ICOP ceases to apply at *onshore* receiving terminals and initial processing facilities. In the case of oil, the ICOP has onshore application up to the point where the oil is stabilised (that is, at the point it could be delivered to an independent buyer). In the case of gas, the ICOP has onshore application until the gas: (a) enters the National Transmission system (NTS); (b) enters a pipeline distribution system operated by a gas transporter; or (c) enters a downstream interconnector. The ICOP does not govern the access of gas to LNG import terminals, the NTS or interconnectors.[55]

Relevant parties

7.20   The ICOP applies to all owners of relevant infrastructure and all owners of capacity in relevant infrastructure. It is also intended to apply to all parties interested in acquiring access to relevant infrastructure.[56] The ICOP, however, has no applicability to hydrocarbons that are subject to prior transportation and processing agreements.[57]

General principles

7.21   All adherents to ICOP agree to comply with two "overarching principles", namely to uphold infrastructure safety and integrity and to protect the environment and to abide by the general offshore Commercial Code of Practice (which is intended to encourage fair

---

[51] UKOOA consulted the Department and other stakeholders in developing ICOP. It "supersedes the previous Offshore Infrastructure Code of Practice (agreed in 1996) and became effective in August 2004". See ICOP, para 1(4).

[52] ICOP, para 1(1).

[53] *Ibid*, para 1(2).

[54] *Ibid*, para 4(1).

[55] *Ibid*.

[56] *Ibid*, para 4(2).

[57] *Ibid*, para 4(3). Thus, parties to ICOP are not expected to dishonour existing contractual arrangements.

and efficient dealing).[58] In addition, parties also agree to comply with a further set of principles more specific than the Infrastructure Code of Practice, namely that meaningful information will be promptly provided to prospective users of infrastructure, and that the key commercial terms agreed be published; that parties resolve conflicts of interest; that transparent and non-discriminatory access be offered; that tariffs be unbundled (where this is requested and practicable); that tariffs be offered for unbundled services, where this is requested and practicable; that fair and reasonable tariffs are charged, where the rewards derived reflect the degree of risk under-taken; that access be negotiated quickly, and that ultimately recourse to the Secretary of State be available as a matter of course if these principles are violated.[59] Each of these principles will be discussed in turn.

Provision of meaningful information to prospective infrastructure users
This provision intends to give the third parties an "informed view" on the feasibility of using the infrastructure.[60] Individual infrastructure owners are responsible for preparing and providing information on their facilities. However, this task may be carried out by the relevant operator on behalf of the various owners.[61] Costs of providing and updating the information are the infrastructure owners' responsi-bility. Such information should be provided in good faith but on a no-liability basis.[62] The ICOP envisages the provision of three levels of information for interested parties. These will be discussed in turn.   **7.22**

High-level capacity information. Basic information, such as available capacity in any particular section of infrastructure, must be available on the appropriate corporate website, interlinked with UKOOA's (now Oil & Gas UK's) DEAL portal.[63] The information should be given for a minimum of 5 years' forward projection, and distinctions   **7.23**

---

[58] See ICOP, para 5, bullet points 1 and 2. The Commercial Code of Practice is a short but influential document, attached to the ICOP as Annex C, comprising 12 bullet points. It states its mission to be to "Promote Co-operative Value Generation". It then lists six principles of best practice process (among them the wise injunction: "ensure personal issues do not become a barrier to progress") and five principles for senior management commitment, two of which are "ensure appropriate use of tactics" and "adopt a non-blocking approach".

[59] These principles are introduced in ICOP, para 5 under the heading "Principles of the Infrastructure Code of Practice".

[60] ICOP, para 6.1(1).

[61] *Ibid*, para 6.1(3).

[62] *Ibid*, para 6.1(2).

[63] *Ibid*, para 6.2. The DEAL portal can be accessed at http://www.ukdeal.co.uk (accessed 13 March 2011).

should be made between firm and interruptible capacities. A sample format for the provision of information is provided at Annex E, para 1 of the ICOP, but other formats are acceptable.

7.24 **Further specific information.** The ICOP provides that any prospective user has the right to acquire further specific information "to permit it to find out more about the infrastructure system's capacity and other relevant technical data".[64] Ideally, such information should be posted on a corporate website, but at a minimum it should be provided in written form. The format is within the discretion of the provider as long as it is provided within a reasonable time (the example of 2 weeks as a reasonable response time is mentioned).[65] The minimum requirements for this kind of more detailed information are listed in Annex E, para 2 of the ICOP, covering entry and exit product specifications, details of primary separation, processing and gas treatment facilities, and oil export, gas compression, gas lift, produced water handling, dehydration, H_2S removal and water injection capacities. The provision of this additional material should not require the owner/operator to carry out "material incremental study activities".[66] UKOOA's 2006 Review Report[67] disclosed that there had been a very high degree of compliance with the obligation to make available both the high-level information referred to at para 5.23 above and the further information discussed in this paragraph.[68] However, it did identify certain deficiencies, generally associated with the technical set-up of websites but in some instances arising from the information provided, which it expected parties to put right.[69]

7.25 **Bona fide enquiry.** The types of public information discussed above can be obtained anonymously, or at any rate through a nominee. However, when prospective users reach the stage of negotiating access to particular infrastructure, a fuller exchange of information is needed between the parties. The ICOP refers to the prospective user at this initial negotiating stage as a "bona fide enquirer", that is, a company seeking to transport hydrocarbons from a discovery. The bona fide enquirer is obligated to provide full information on its discovery and requirements to the infrastructure owner (including location, licence, equity owners, reserves, development timetable,

---

[64] ICOP, para 6.3(1).

[65] *Ibid*, para 6.3(2).

[66] *Ibid*, para 6.3(4).

[67] UKOOA, *Infrastructure Code of Practice 2006 Review Report* (hereinafter "2006 Review"). The code charges UKOOA (now Oil & Gas UK) "with the support of the [Department]", with the task of maintaining and periodically reviewing the code: see ICOP, para 14(1).

[68] See the 2006 Review, at paras 2 and 26.

[69] ICOP at paras 2, 12–13, 26 and 28.

services required, and so on).[70] After receiving this information the infrastructure owner should respond with any further commercial information from its side that may be needed.[71] At this stage, all information provided by either party, while it should be provided in good faith and be relevant and material to the discussions,[72] will still be expressly on a no-liability basis. The parties can subsequently deal with liabilities in formal agreements.[73] The 2006 Review stated that while infrastructure users felt that ICOP had improved access to infrastructure, some continued to feel that this phase of the process was attended by unwarranted delay and demands for unreasonable levels of technical information.[74] In fact, together with the issues of liabilities and indemnities, the issue of delay was one of the main underlying reasons in developing the new Guidance Notes for ICOP.[75]

Publication of key commercial terms
In addition to the three levels of information discussed above, infra- 7.26
structure owners are required to publish short summaries of "newly concluded construction and tie-in agreements, transportation and processing agreements and/or operating services agreements" within a month of these becoming binding.[76] This information should be posted on the infrastructure owner/operator's website, or on the DEAL website.[77] A pro-forma for this information is attached to the Code of Practice as Annex H. The goal is to provide adequate disclosure of the main commercial provisions of any relevant agreement, including pricing. Additionally, the cumulative posting of commercial terms may serve to create a "market" for offshore infrastructure services. The 2006 Review reports poor compliance with this obligation but suggests that this may be more attributable to a time-lag which occurs as a result of a delay between deals being entered into and its becoming effectual. At this stage, the issue is being seen as a teething problem;[78] however, this is an important obligation which may assist greatly in expediting negotiations and,

---

[70] ICOP, para 6.4(1).
[71] *Ibid*, para 6.4(2).
[72] *Ibid*, para 6.4(3).
[73] *Ibid*, para 6.4(4).
[74] See the 2006 Review at paras 24–25.
[75] Oil & Gas UK, *Code of Practice on Access to Upstream Oil and Gas Infrastructure on the UK Continental Shelf: Guidance Notes* (2009) (hereinafter "ICOP Guidance Notes"). These Guidance Notes are the result of the "Changing Gear" initiative of PILOT. See ICOP Guidance Notes at para 1.
[76] ICOP, para 13(1).
[77] *Ibid*, para 13(2).
[78] See 2006 Review at para 3, read together with para 26.

if compliance rates do not pick up, infrastructure owners can expect to come under pressure from Oil & Gas UK and/or the Department to obtemper their obligations under this provision. Finally, it should also be noted that owners of onshore "gas processing terminals and relevant pipelines" are required under the Gas Act to publish their principal commercial terms for access on an annual basis. The effect of this provision is to enhance transparency relative to gas infrastructure.

Conflict of interest issues

7.27   The tendency of upstream oil and gas companies to work together in joint ventures[79] means that a situation may well arise where the same party is both an owner of relevant infrastructure and a bona fide enquirer. In such cases it can only be a negotiator in one capacity.[80] The same principle applies where the same party has ownership interests in two or more infrastructure systems that might provide service to a bona fide enquirer.[81] Dropping out as a negotiator, however, does not constitute any kind of waiver of rights to approve a particular agreement.[82]

Non-discriminatory access

7.28   The fundamental principle of the ICOP is that access should be transparent and non-discriminatory. The principle is expressly stated to apply to "all infrastructure coming within the scope of this Code".[83] Like cases must be treated alike but, equally, different cases should be treated differently: infrastructure providers are not required, or encouraged, to have a fixed set of prices for particular services "since different terms and conditions may be applied where there are differences in the service provided or the cost of risk of supply".[84] In a provision which builds upon s 17F(8)(d) of the Petroleum Act 1998,[85] the ICOP expressly permits infrastructure owners to reserve capacity to make reasonable provision for their own and their affiliates' needs.[86] This important concept is further developed in the ICOP, Annex D. Three examples of "reasonable provision" are detailed: (1) to allow for upsides in production or extensions of existing fields; (2) where the infrastructure owner has new field

---

[79] Discussed in greater detail in Chapter 12.
[80] ICOP, para 9(1).
[81] *Ibid*, para 9(2).
[82] *Ibid*, para 9(3).
[83] *Ibid*, para 10(1).
[84] *Ibid*, para 10(2).
[85] Discussed at para 6.5.
[86] ICOP, para 10(3).

developments which are under plan or are expected to be developed within a reasonable time (5 years is mentioned in this regard); or (3) where new developments were foreseen by the infrastructure owner before the infrastructure was built, and such potential new developments were part of the reason to build the infrastructure. This is a relatively broad interpretation of "reasonable provision" and may serve to frustrate a number of bona fide enquirers' requests.[87] It is interesting to note, however, that the ICOP, para 12.1(3) provides that the bona fide enquirer can require the infrastructure owner to expand its capacity to handle the new production, providing that the bona fide enquirer is willing to cover the entire cost.[88]

Separation of services ("unbundling")

Paragraph 11(1) of the ICOP requires that infrastructure owners   **7.29** offer terms for various services on an unbundled basis where this is "practical and requested". The principal reason is that this will facilitate competition where there are competing service providers. The ICOP also notes that unbundling may be appropriate when parts of a single service chain have different ownership. Perceived technical objections to unbundling should be discussed with prospective users with a view towards finding solutions which enable separation.[89]

Tariffs, liabilities and indemnities

Exclusion and indemnity clauses[90] are sometimes thought of as if   **7.30** they were mere "boilerplate" clauses.[91] If that is ever true, it is not in the context of access to infrastructure.[92] The ICOP recognises this and expressly links tariffs and liabilities and indemnities.

Tariffs. The ICOP's key provision on the tariff charged for use of   **7.31** infrastructure is that it should be "fair and reasonable, where risks taken are reflected by rewards".[93] Thus, the ICOP tries to strike a fair balance between the parties. It does not countenance profiteering

---

[87] While this result may obtain, that is not to say that the provision is necessarily unreasonable. It is not inappropriate that the company that took the commercial risk of building the infrastructure should make the first call upon its capacity.

[88] However, the Secretary of State's powers under the Petroleum Act 1998 do not appear to extend to compelling the infrastructure owner to extend its facilities. Thus, there appears to be no mechanism beyond reputational fall-out (the impact of which should not be underestimated in the oil and gas industry) to compel compliance.

[89] ICOP, para 11(2).

[90] For a general discussion on indemnities and other risk allocation clauses, see Chapter 14.

[91] See, eg, E McKendrick, *Contract Law: Cases, Text and Materials* (4th edn, 2010) at p 406. McKendrick does, however, note that such clauses are "one of the most contentious boilerplate clauses".

[92] See para 14.24.

[93] ICOP, para 12.1(1).

by the infrastructure owner,[94] but neither does it require the infra-structure owner to absorb risk without being rewarded for so doing.

7.32 **Liabilities and indemnities.** Agreement on liabilities and indemnities is an important part of the commercial deal between the parties.[95] The ICOP states that "the parties should bear appropriate risks having regard for [sic] the respective rewards expected to be enjoyed by each".[96] This much may seem uncontroversial, even obvious, but the reality is that the parties will commonly disagree on the level of risk it is appropriate for them to bear, particularly when, as is often the case with infrastructure agreements, their commercial interests are not closely aligned.[97] The scope for disagreement is only increased by the code's call for infrastructure owners to bear in mind the fact that "the capacity of bona fide enquirers investing in smaller fields to bear risks may be more limited than for those investing in large fields".[98] While this assertion may very well be true, an infrastructure owner might think itself justified in asking why such matters should prompt it to take a more benign negotiating stance concerning a project in respect of which it has a tangential financial interest at best, but which has the potential to jeopardise one of its strategic assets.[99] The ICOP states that liabilities and indemnities should be targeted for early negotiation, prior to the issuance of the ARN.[100] This is a wise provision as the indemnities and liabilities clause is often a controversial one in negotiations which can take some considerable time to resolve.

7.33 *Tie-in/modification phase.* The Code provides that if the parties agree that the bona fide enquirer should indemnify infrastructure owners against liabilities arising out of tie-in/modification works,[101] then the owners should be willing to concede reasonable liability

---

[94] Such as one commonly encounters in land law when a right of access is required over a so-called "ransom strip". See Chapter 17.

[95] This is expressly recognised in the code itself: see ICOP, para 12.2.1(1): "The liability and indemnity regime forms an important part of the overall risk–reward balance with consequent impact upon reward levels."

[96] ICOP, para 12.2.1(1).

[97] See the discussion at para 14.24.

[98] ICOP, para 12.1(1).

[99] The answer may be no more elegant than "because the government wants you to, and if you don't, they may put in place a regime which is more draconian than the present, so play nicely".

[100] ICOP, para 12.2.1(2). For ARN, see para 6.36.

[101] Note that the Code does not say that such an indemnity will always be appropriate: this will depend upon factors such as the level of tariff and the potential exposures of the infrastructure owners: see ICOP, para 12.2.2(1). Where an indemnity is agreed, the Code encourages parties to be specific about the type of economic losses involved.

caps.[102] Parties should agree reasonable liquidated damages to cover production losses arising from shutdowns solely caused to facilitate hook-up.[103] The 2006 Review notes that the liability cap approach has not always been followed in practice and strongly deprecates the practice of placing uncapped, and therefore uninsurable, liabilities upon the bona fide enquirer, a practice which it states can act as a "blocker" to access negotiations.[104] This is clearly a matter which Oil & Gas UK is monitoring closely: the 2006 Review states that this area "may require further effort as properly apportioning the risk and reward involved in deals is a key principle of the code".[105] Consequently, the 2009 ICOP Guidance Notes are closely focused on liability caps. They recognise that obtaining a liability insurance coverage for over £100 million for the risks arising from a construction and tie-in project is not only difficult, but, if a potential coverage is found, it will also require "more detailed data disclosure, negotiation, and possible justification".[106] The Guidance, therefore, suggests that, in the event the infrastructure requires over £100 million indemnity cap, "it is more important for the bona fide enquirer" that the infrastructure owner explains how this cap is set by disclosing the "supporting details of the credible potential losses" used in the calculations.[107] This suggestion intends to aid the bona fide enquirer in negotiating with the insurer. It is envisaged that this way the bona fide enquirer will not be "priced out of the deal" even though it can potentially agree to the access tariff.[108] However, it is not clear if this suggestion will really avoid uncapped indemnity requests by the infrastructure owner; or even address the underlying reasons for such requests.

Transportation and processing phase. With regard to the transportation and processing phase, ie the post tie-in phase, the normal rule should be the traditional "knock for knock", subject to wilful misconduct exclusions. Delivery of non-standard product or the provision of non-standard services will need special provisions; otherwise it is expected that the parties adhere to the "mutual hold harmless" principle.[109]   7.34

---

[102] ICOP, para 12.2.2(1).

[103] *Ibid*, para 12.2.2(1).

[104] See the 2006 Review at para 3.

[105] See the 2006 Review at para 27.

[106] ICOP Guidance Notes, para 8.2.2(b). "For the avoidance of doubt" it also explicitly states that uncapped liability exposure will not be insured.

[107] ICOP Guidance Notes, para 8.1.2.

[108] This was one of the issues raised in the 2006 Review. See the 2006 Review at para 3.

[109] ICOP, para 12.2.3. For "mutual hold harmless" principle, see Chapter 14.

Timely negotiation with automatic recourse to the Secretary of State

7.35 **Timeliness.** Given that one of the state's key objectives in securing third-party access to infrastructure is to facilitate the full recovery of economic oil and gas reserves before an ageing infrastructure system passes out of use,[110] it should come as no surprise to learn that one of the prime goals of the ICOP is to encourage rapid negotiations directed towards a "fair, reasonable and technically sound outcome".[111] Accordingly, the bona fide enquirer and the infrastructure owner(s) are required to agree a "framework for negotiations" at the outset, which must include a time schedule, specifying the technical, operational, legal and commercial matters which will need to be agreed in order to reach a successful deal.[112] A best practice negotiating process is provided at Annex F to the ICOP. It falls to the bona fide enquirer to indicate when it envisages the submission of an automatic referral notice (ARN).[113] The ARN is not, in and of itself, a request to the Secretary of State to use his statutory powers[114] to determine access, but rather *obligates* the bona fide enquirer to request the Secretary of State to use such powers 6 months after the issuance of the ARN.[115] The indicated date for the issuance of an ARN should be within 6 months of the projected conclusion of negotiations.[116] The bona fide enquirer should issue this ARN as early as preliminary negotiations will allow.

7.36 **The automatic referral notice (ARN).** The ARN process noted above was a major innovation on the part of the ICOP. It means that there is, from the start of serious negotiations, the certainty of involving the Secretary of State's legal dispute resolution powers in the event of a negotiating failure. The parties are compelled by the Code to involve the Secretary of State; it is therefore no admission of defeat or weakness to involve him. This is intended to get around the "shame factor" involved in calling on the Secretary of State. Once issued, the ARN is stated to be irrevocable unless the bona fide enquirer advises the Department that access to the relevant infrastructure has either been agreed or is no longer required.[117] However,

---

[110] See paras 7.1 and 7.2.

[111] ICOP, para 7(1).

[112] *Ibid*, para 7(4).

[113] A pro-forma is provided in Annex G to the ICOP.

[114] Ie, the statutory powers discussed at paras 6.4–6.16.

[115] ICOP, para 8(1) and 8(7).

[116] *Ibid*, paras 7(4), 8(1) and (4).

[117] *Ibid*, para 8(2). The exceptions thus carved out of the word "irrevocable" leave it unrecognisable from its dictionary definition, but presumably it has been used by the drafters of the Code to reinforce and normalise the ARN process.

if initial negotiations are complex but proceeding satisfactorily, the bona fide enquirer may, with the approval of the Department, extend the 6-month period specified in the ARN.[118] An ARN may be issued in respect of each relevant section of infrastructure, and the dates need not be the same.[119] It is important to note that the 6-month period specified in the ARN is a maximum period and does not affect the bona fide enquirer's right to request the Secretary of State to use his statutory powers earlier.[120] Equally, after the bona fide enquirer has formally requested that the Secretary of State use his statutory powers, the former may form the view that negotiations are proceeding satisfactorily but that more time is needed. In this case, the bona fide enquirer and the Department will agree a date on which the bona fide enquirer may again request that statutory powers should be employed.[121]

The 2006 Review suggested that the ARN process was experiencing some difficulties in bedding down. In particular, it noted that in a number of cases deals had been concluded without ARNs having been issued at all; conversely, some ARNs had been issued prematurely and had required to be extended as a result. It considered that the incidence of such cases would decrease in the future as the process became better understood.[122] However, the Review also noted that in some cases infrastructure owners had declined to engage with the bona fide enquirer, leaving the enquirer to submit an ARN at an earlier stage of negotiations than would have been desirable in order to compel the infrastructure owner to engage with the process. The Review notes that, in these cases too, ARNs may require to be extended, but does not deprecate this practice on the part of bona fide enquirers and warns infrastructure owners that "the [Department is] still strongly minded to determine any ARN which necessitates a statutory determination".[123] However, the Review also notes the bona fide enquirers' concern that when their service request is rejected unreasonably by the operators "there is no formal means

7.37

---

[118] ICOP, para 8(2). The ICOP Guidance Notes provide that the extension request is not a one-time submission but can be requested again if it is justified. The requests, however, should "ideally have the support of the Infrastructure Operator". However, the operator is not obligated to support the extension request and "may not wish to do so". See ICOP Guidance Notes, paras 3.4 and 2.4 respectively.

[119] ICOP, para 8(6).

[120] *Ibid*, para 7(4) and 8(7).

[121] *Ibid*, para 8(2) and (10).

[122] See the 2006 Review at paras 3 and 26.

[123] See the 2006 Review at para 3.

of resolution or judgment to resolve any issues" except to seek one from the Secretary of State.[124]

7.38   The 2009 ICOP Guidance Notes address these issues. They provide that the Code of Practice Champion[125] of the bona fide enquirer should be informed of "*any deviations* that would affect the ability to conclude agreements" within the timetable set in ARN.[126] Separately, when the 4-month mark from the issue of the ARN is reached, he should also consider whether "intervention is required" to adhere to the timetable. If intervention is needed, it should initially come from the Code of Practice Champions of each party. If they cannot resolve the issue, then senior management should be involved. This escalating step-by-step approach is an "extremely important part of the [intervention] procedure". It is explicitly intended that the bona fide enquirer should exhaust all possible avenues for resolving the issue "before making any application to the Secretary of State". If the alternative routes fail, only then should the Secretary of State be brought into the matter.[127]

7.39   **Determination by the Secretary of State.** Another crucial issue is how the Secretary of State would go about resolving access disputes if requested to do so. The Department's Guidance Notes will be considered below,[128] but it is important to note here that the ICOP itself offers broad guidance as to the methodology that the Secretary of State would use. Thus, it suggests that the Secretary of State is likely to try to determine the terms that would have been offered by the infrastructure owner if there had been "effective competition".[129] It further suggests that infrastructure owners are entitled to honour existing bona fide contractual commitments, make reasonable provision for their own production, and "take into account any realistic impact of prospective new business on their system".[130] According to para 12, tariffs and terms should be "fair and reasonable" and rewards should reflect risks taken. The ICOP

---

[124] See the 2006 Review at para 26.

[125] The Code of Practice Champion "should be someone at senior level within the organisation, chosen by and endorsed by the UK-based MD/CEO, who is committed to good negotiating practice and has the authority to ensure that both the Commercial and Infrastructure Codes of Practice, CCOP & ICOP, are understood and adopted by the organisation as the basis for all relevant UKCS negotiations". See ICOP Guidance Notes, para 4.7.

[126] ICOP Guidance Notes, para 3.4 (emphasis added).

[127] *Ibid*.

[128] See para 7.41.

[129] ICOP, para 2(3).

[130] *Ibid*, para 12. See, for further discussion, para 6.50.

rightly opines that the ideal situation is where there are two or more available infrastructure options.[131]

Competition
Prior to final agreement on the ICOP, UKOOA sought informal advice   **7.40**
as to whether the proposed ICOP's provisions could be in violation of the Competition Act 1998 or of EC competition law. Concern focused on the information sharing provisions. The informal and non-binding advice of the Office of Fair Trading, attached to the ICOP as Annex B, is that there are no grounds for concern.

THE DEPARTMENT'S GUIDANCE ON DISPUTES OVER THIRD-PARTY ACCESS

Introduction

The Department's Guidance provides essential support to the ICOP.   **7.41**
It seeks to state how the Department would actually resolve a dispute if an ARN required determination. Interestingly, the Guidance states that "the Department's main objective in operating its petroleum legislation is to ensure the recovery of all economic hydrocarbon reserves".[132] The direction is clear: new discoveries are becoming smaller and thus more dependent on access to existing infrastructure which is in turn getting older, serving declining fields which may need additional third-party income to remain economic.

Guiding principles

The general guiding principles on the setting of terms are outlined by   **7.42**
the regulator as follows:

> "While acknowledging that it is reasonable for owners to safeguard capacity for their own reasonably anticipated production, the Department supports the principle of non-discriminatory negotiated access to upstream infrastructure on the UKCS, encourages transparency and promotes fairness for all parties concerned since it is important that prospective users have fair access to infrastructure at competitive prices. At the same time, the Department is of the view that any terms determined by the Secretary of State would reflect a fair payment to the owner for real costs and risks faced and for opportunities forgone. It recognises that, for example, spare pipeline capacity has a commercial value and that the owner, having borne the cost and risks of installing, operating and maintaining the pipeline

---

[131] ICOP, para 12.1(1).
[132] Department's Guidance, paras 9 and 31.

systems, should be entitled to derive a fair commercial consideration for that value."[133]

7.43 The Department's Guidance also quotes assurances given by the then Labour Government in the House of Lords on 15 October 1975, relating to any decision by the Secretary of State imposing access:

> "• there were no circumstances in which, in those cases where the Secretary of State was called upon to intervene, the owner of a pipeline would be financially worse off through the admission of a third party;
> • pipeline owners would have all costs reimbursed, including indirect ones (e.g. the cost of interruption to the owner's throughput while a line is modified to enable third party use);
> • the tariff would be set so that the third party would bear a fair share of the total running costs incurred after his entry;
> • unless the supply in question were marginal or the pipeline owner had already made other sufficient arrangements to recover the full capital costs, the financial arrangements proposed would normally be expected to take account of the basic (historic) capital costs as well as the costs arising from the entry of the third party."[134]

The Department stands by the assurances, except that it observes that in contemporary circumstances it may be appropriate to allocate a part of upfront risk to the infrastructure owner so as to maximise future reward.[135] This might, depending on the circumstances of an individual case, involve some degree of derogation from the last principle.[136]

7.44 Significantly, the Guidance also notes that because there are typically so many factors to be considered in any given offshore access situation, it is impossible to specify in detail how each will be dealt with. The guidance is accordingly in general terms and sets forth principles which will be applied to any given situation through sound judgement.[137] That said, however, the Department does try to provide greater clarity through a discussion at para

---

[133] Department's Guidance, para 34.

[134] *Ibid*, para 36.

[135] *Ibid*, para 36, read with para 37.

[136] However, infrastructure owners should take some comfort from the observation that "infrastructure owners have a key role to play in ensuring maximum economic recovery of the UK's petroleum resources and that too narrow a focus on setting terms on a cost-reflective basis would reduce the incentive for them to bear risk, keep their infrastructure in operation and available, invest in innovative solutions and offer added value services. It anticipates that the Secretary of State would consider these factors in making a determination." See the Department's Guidance, para 38.

[137] Department's Guidance, para 35.

39 of what it regards as four of the most likely scenarios – while stressing that published guidance cannot serve to fetter the exercise of discretion under s 17F of the 1998 Act and s 80 of the Energy Act 2008.

Under *Scenario 1*, ullage is available in infrastructure relative to which capital costs have already been recovered (including a reasonable return, taking into account the risks originally incurred). In that case, the Department would usually set a tariff reflecting incremental costs. However, if infrastructure is part of a field development nearing the end of its economic life, the tariff may need to be higher to ensure continuing maintenance, and "the terms set by the Secretary of State would need to provide for appropriate cost sharing arrangements".[138]   **7.45**

In *Scenario 2*, the owner constructs infrastructure with a view to capturing third-party businesses. In this case, the Department would require the tariff to cover capital costs plus a reasonable rate of return given the level of third-party throughput expected when the decision to invest was made. If this is not the only infrastructure available to third parties, the rate of return could well be higher "to reflect incremental costs and risks".[139]   **7.46**

Under *Scenario 3*, third-party users are competing for access to the same infrastructure. The Department is very unlikely to force the owner to accept a lower bid.   **7.47**

In the *fourth and final Scenario*, there is insufficient ullage to accommodate the third party's production, given the owner's production and prior third-party commitments. Given the need to respect property rights and prior contractual commitments, it is unlikely that the Department would compel access. If it did, the tariff would have to reflect displacement costs.[140]   **7.48**

Statutory interpretation

As noted above, the Secretary of State is obligated to take into account the seven factors mentioned in s 17F(8) of the Petroleum Act 1998.[141] The Department's Guidance makes the following comments on some of these factors: **7.49**

"Reasonable" available capacity
The Department notes that the legislation is directed towards capacity "which is or can *reasonably* be made available". Infrastructure   **7.50**

---

[138] Department's Guidance, para 39.
[139] *Ibid.*
[140] *Ibid.*
[141] See para 7.5.

owners have the right to reserve "reasonable" capacity for their own needs and this clearly covers reasonably projected production from already producing fields and discoveries already made and to be developed within a reasonable period. On the other hand, it is not reasonable to hold on to capacity merely because the owner may (or may not) have some additional throughput at some time in the future.[142]

Incompatibilities of technical specification

7.51 An infrastructure owner may not be obligated to accept additional throughput for both qualitative and quantitative reasons. The examples given on the qualitative side are where a small new field would consume all the de-propanising capacity at an oil treatment facility, thus reducing overall throughput, or where sour gas from a new field would "pollute" a sweet system. In quantitative terms, an infrastructure owner will not be obligated to accept a new small volume when this additional volume would prevent acceptance of another larger volume.[143]

Interests of all users and operations

7.52 The Department will not impose third-party access where any such order would displace prior third-party volumes. Prior legal obligations must be respected.[144]

Other issues

Effect of determination

7.53 After the determination had been made, it would still be up to the third party to accept it. If the third party fails to accept the determination during the period of time specified by the Secretary of State, the owners of the infrastructure in question would cease to have any obligation to offer access on the terms mentioned in the determination.[145]

Disputes relating to the transnational infrastructure

7.54 The Department's Guidance notes that there may be special rules governing access to transnational infrastructure, and that these would govern.[146]

---

[142] Department's Guidance, para 29, n 1 (emphasis added).
[143] *Ibid*, para 29, n 2.
[144] *Ibid*, para 29, n 3.
[145] *Ibid*, para 43.
[146] *Ibid*, para 7.

Competition

Both the Department and Oil & Gas UK (relative to ICOP) have   **7.55**
given consideration to what impact EU and UK competition law
may have on UKCS infrastructure. Article 81 of the European
Community Treaty prohibits anti-competitive agreements and
Art 82 legislates against dominant position abuse. The Competition
Act 1998 directly introduces the same concepts into UK law. These
provisions apply to the UKCS. The OFT has never issued guidelines
on how it interprets the Competition Act 1998 to apply to upstream
oil and gas but, according to the Department, the OFT has stated
that it is not likely to find an abuse of a dominant position if infrastructure owners adhere to the principles for setting terms contained
in the Department's Guidance.[147]

CONCLUSION

The current UK system for third-party access to offshore infra-   **7.56**
structure might be said to have three closely interlinked legs: (i)
the statutory provisions; (ii) the ICOP; and (iii) the Department's
Guidance. While the "meat" of the system is found in the ICOP and
the Department's Guidance, these provisions are dependent on the
statutory provisions for their effect.

As we have seen, UKOOA issued a 2006 Review on the ICOP.   **7.57**
By and large, UKOOA found that the information programmes
mandated by the ICOP were operative, though the publication of
commercial terms has been slower. From the ICOP's introduction, in
August 2004, to May 2006 there were 38 ARN submissions relating
to 19 separate fields. Four deals were concluded. No ARN has yet
gone to the Department for resolution.[148] *A crucial observation is that
not all third parties are using the ICOP.* A weakness of the ICOP is
that non-Oil & Gas UK members are not required to subscribe, and
it is difficult for the Department to "enforce" the ICOP without full
third-party user participation and without a sanction. Moreover, and
as we have already seen, bona fide enquirers expressed dissatisfaction
about excessive indemnities which, because uncapped liabilities are
often uninsurable, can be as important as tariff levels. Although the
2009 ICOP Guidance Notes provide further suggestions addressing
the issues surrounding liability caps, it is not clear if those suggestions are sufficient to prevent uncapped indemnity requests by the
infrastructure owner; or even to address the underlying reasons for
such requests. So the ICOP has not by any means resolved all access

---

[147] Department's Guidance, paras 13–17.
[148] But see n 38, above, for recent developments.

to infrastructure issues which exist. Overall, however, the UKOOA Report's conclusions are positive: "the consensus from third party systems operators is that the code is fit for purpose and is showing signs of working well".[149] It is important to note this fact. However, the present author's own view is that in the final analysis the efficacy of the ICOP is held back both by the imperfections of its underlying legislation and by the legal nature of the instrument itself, and its terms. There is still too much leeway for evasion and foot-dragging. Given the importance of this issue to the Government's stated policy objectives, this is an area which we can expect to see kept under close review in the future.

---

[149] The 2006 Review, at p 4.

CHAPTER 8

HEALTH AND SAFETY AT WORK OFFSHORE

John Paterson

The UKCS is among the most hostile environments in which the 8.1
offshore oil and gas industry operates anywhere in the world. The
substances it produces are naturally volatile. The nature of the
activity means that the workforce lives in very close proximity to
the workplace. Travel to and from the workplace is by helicopter.
The industry has been characterised by a constant striving for newer
and better technology to allow it to operate in deeper water or to
cope with higher-temperature and higher-pressure reservoirs. All of
these issues very obviously impact upon health and safety at work.
They also raise profound questions for those charged with regulating
occupational health and safety in the offshore industry. How should
a regulator do the things that it would traditionally be expected to
do? How does it draft regulations for a novel setting that is then
characterised by constant change? How does it monitor and inspect
when the regulated area is remote and relatively inaccessible?

It is not surprising, then, that the regulatory approach to health 8.2
and safety at work offshore has seen a constant evolution throughout
a history that is now into its fifth decade. There have been severe
setbacks along the way – serious accidents that have revealed
regulatory shortcomings – and it is perhaps only in recent years that
it could be said with any confidence that the regulatory regime is
well adapted to the challenges presented by the industry. Even as that
position is reached, however, the realisation dawns that the character
of the regulated area is changing again. The UKCS is now described
as a mature province, which brings with it a new set of challenges:
the gradual withdrawal of the major oil companies and the arrival
of new entrants with innovative ideas but perhaps less experience;
infrastructure at or beyond its design life which the Government
is keen to take full advantage of to maximise the recovery of the

hydrocarbon resources; the decommissioning of platforms, pipelines and other equipment that has become redundant; the search for new reservoirs in deeper water that has previously been less attractive due to the difficulties and costs involved. All of these features of the mature province have the potential to impact upon occupational health and safety.

8.3   This chapter traces the evolution of the regulatory approach to health and safety at work offshore. The evolution is divided into three phases. The Early Phase covers the period when health and safety at work was dealt with under the licence and focuses upon, first, the Continental Shelf Act 1964 and, then, the findings of the Inquiry into the Sea Gem accident. The Middle Phase covers the period during which the detailed prescriptive regime recommended by the Sea Gem Inquiry was gradually developed and implemented. It accordingly considers: the Mineral Workings (Offshore Installations) Act 1971; the tension in due course between this Act and the Health and Safety at Work, etc Act 1974; and the findings of the Burgoyne Committee on Offshore Safety. The Late Phase covers the period during which the permissioning approach now in place was developed. Thus, it considers the Piper Alpha disaster and the findings of the subsequent public inquiry, the Offshore Safety Act 1992 and the subsequent safety case and goal-setting regulations; and, finally, the latest Offshore Installations (Safety Case) Regulations 2005. This treatment of the issue of health and safety at work offshore serves a number of purposes. By contrasting the current permissioning approach with the foregoing approaches it highlights the particularity of the means by which health and safety at work offshore is now regulated. This is of interest not only to those based in the UK, but also to the increasing number from other jurisdictions who are involved in the development of the regulation of health and safety in the offshore industry and who are looking to the UK for inspiration. Second, it reveals the extent to which the problems that the current approach seeks to deal with were evident from relatively early on but never adequately dealt with in the recommendations of inquiries or in the discussions of legislators. This serves also to bolster the new approach in the face of criticism from those who regret the passing of the prescriptive regime. Finally, it allows an appraisal of the ability of the permissioning approach to respond to the emergent challenges posed by the UKCS as a maturing province. In this last regard, the troubling findings of an investigation into asset integrity published just after the first edition of this book appeared in late 2007, as well as the questions raised by the Deepwater Horizon accident in 2010 (in particular by the European Parliament and European Commission), render such an appraisal all the more important. In such a demanding environment, recent changes to general health and safety law in the form of provisions relating to corporate killing and to increased penalties for breaches may take on particular significance.

EARLY PHASE: THE LICENSING APPROACH

The Continental Shelf Act 1964

The early days of the oil and gas industry in the North Sea coincided   8.4
with a period of economic difficulty for the UK. As a result, the possibility that there may be reserves of oil and gas on the UKCS almost seemed an answer to prayer as the country struggled with a crippling balance of payments deficit.[1] It has been suggested that this pressing need goes a long way to explaining the speed with which the Government then acted to ensure that the legal framework was in place to allow the industry to explore for and in due course to exploit oil and gas.[2] The presence of developed and politically stable markets around a geologically interesting location made the North Sea particularly attractive to the industry, but the financial investment involved meant that without a firm legal framework, work would not proceed. The Continental Shelf Act 1964 was accordingly passed, based on the United Nations Convention on the Continental Shelf of 1958 which had conferred "sovereign rights" in the continental shelf on coastal states.[3] It would be going too far to say that at this time no attention was paid to the question of occupational health and safety, but it would nevertheless be true to say that this issue was by no means uppermost in the minds of lawmakers. In so far as the whole point of the 1964 Act was to assert the UK's sovereign rights over the continental shelf, the assumption was that the general law, including statute law, could be extended offshore, which s 3 purported to do. This, however, fell foul of the accepted canon of statutory interpretation that holds that statutes are assumed to extend only to Great Britain unless otherwise stated.[4]

---

[1] For an indication of the extent to which this issue dominated government thinking at the time, see Sir Alec Cairncross, "Devaluing the Pound: the Lessons of 1967", *The Economist*, 14 November 1992, 25–28.

[2] See, eg, W G Carson, *The Other Price of Britain's Oil: Safety and Control in the North Sea* (1981), pp 141*ff*; see also L Turner, *Oil Companies in the International System* (3rd edn, 1983); G-P Levy, "The Relationship between Oil Companies and Consumer State Governments in Europe, 1973–1982" (1984) 19 *Journal of Energy and Natural Resources Law* 9.

[3] The Convention granted states "sovereign rights for the purpose of exploring [the continental shelf] and exploiting its natural resources" (Art 2(1)) and entitled them "to construct and maintain or operate ... installations" to that end (Art 5(2)). See also para 4.8.

[4] For a discussion of this point, see Daintith, Willoughby and Hill, para 1–510.

Accordingly, this section could not have the effect of extending, for example, existing factory legislation to cover offshore installations – even if the definitions in such onshore legislation could be stretched to accommodate these novel structures, which was by no means certain.

8.5   With the option of simply extending onshore occupational safety legislation offshore thus effectively ruled out, the treatment of this issue at the time under the legal regime explicitly dedicated to the offshore industry looks, with the benefit of hindsight, decidedly inadequate. In this regard, the Government, again perhaps motivated by the concern to allow rapid exploration and development in the North Sea, drew extensively upon the approach taken some 30 years earlier when the legal framework had been put in place for the nascent (and never more than marginally important) *onshore* oil and gas industry under the Petroleum (Production) Act 1934. This Act vested mineral resources in the Crown and required that those who wished to exploit them must obtain a licence. Regulations governing the grant of licences were promulgated in 1935 under the authority of the 1934 Act, with Model Licence Clauses annexed.[5] These regulations and model clauses were essentially repeated with minimal modification for offshore licences in the Petroleum (Production) (Continental Shelf and Territorial Sea) Regulations 1964.[6] The whole issue of occupational health and safety then fell to be dealt with in one clause of the licence where it was provided that: "[t]he Licensee shall comply with any instructions from time to time given by the Minister in writing for securing the health, safety and welfare of persons employed in or about the licensed area".[7] In practice, the Minister wrote to each licensee, instructing them in this regard to carry out operations: "in accordance with such provisions of … the Institute of Petroleum Model Code of Safe Practice in the Petroleum Industry issued in October, 1964, as relate to the safety, health and welfare of persons employed".[8] It is important to realise, therefore, that although a licensing approach may be regarded as a very interventionist form of regulation,[9] this was by no means the case in the context of the licences issued under the 1964 Regulations in so far as they applied to health and safety. This issue was simply not subject to any detailed regulatory stipulations or inspections, but

---

[5] Petroleum (Production) Regulations 1935 (SR & O 1935/426).

[6] SI 1964/708.

[7] Sch 2, cl 18.

[8] For details of this letter of instruction and the Institute of Petroleum Code, see Ministry of Power, *Report of the Inquiry into the Causes of the Accident to the Drilling Rig Sea Gem* (Cmnd 3409, 1967) (hereinafter "Sea Gem Inquiry"), pp 17–22.

[9] See, eg, A I Ogus, *Regulation: Legal Form and Economic Theory* (1994), pp 214*ff*.

rather was left to the industry itself to deal with. Even if the Minister did become aware of a shortcoming in the treatment of health and safety, the contractual nature of the licence limited both the remedies open to him and the individuals against whom they could be applied. The only remedy available would be a revocation of the licence, which would presumably be countenanced only in the case of the most egregious behaviour, while the only party against whom the Minister could in any event take action in this regard would be the licensee – a significant limitation in the context of an industry so characterised by subcontracting.[10]

The Sea Gem Inquiry

It was only a short time before the deficiencies of this approach to health and safety offshore became evident. In April of 1965 the first commercial gas field on the UKCS was discovered by the jack-up drilling rig Sea Gem, justifying the Government's and the industry's optimism with regard to the North Sea.[11] In December 1965, the same rig collapsed and sank with the loss of 13 lives.[12] This tragedy did not necessarily mean, of course, that there was a problem with the law. The fact that the Minister of Power discovered that he had no statutory authority to set up an inquiry into the accident because the rig fell into no category recognised by law did, however, set alarm bells ringing. An Inquiry was, nevertheless, established but it "was without statutory authority, had no power to compel the attendance of witnesses, nor was it empowered to administer oaths".[13] The Inquiry was presided over by a lawyer sitting with two assessors with engineering expertise and its recommendations led in due course to the establishment of the prescriptive regulatory approach that characterised the Middle Phase of the evolution described below. It is worth considering the approach of the Sea Gem Inquiry in a little more detail, however, in order to understand the reasoning that lay behind these recommendations.

8.6

While the Inquiry's ultimate recommendations certainly dealt with the difficulties attending the licensing approach to health and safety outlined above, its motivations were actually quite different. The Inquiry focused in no small measure upon the difficulties posed for *the law* by a code of practice that had been drafted by *the industry*. For example, the Inquiry considered the following paragraph of the

8.7

[10] For more detail, see R W Bentham, "The United Kingdom Offshore Safety Regime: Before and After Piper Alpha" (1991) *Journal of Energy and Natural Resources Law* 273.
[11] See *Petroleum Press Service* (April 1965), 127.
[12] See "Triumph and Tragedy in the North Sea" *Petroleum Press Service* 1966, 5.
[13] See Sea Gem Inquiry, p 1.

Institute of Petroleum Code: "[o]nly persons, who, in the opinion of the supervisor, are essential to the safe raising and lowering of a self-elevating type of mobile drilling platform, should be on the unit when this is being done. They should wear a lifejacket at all times while any phase of the raising and lowering operation is being carried out".

The Institute of Petroleum clearly had no problem with this wording, but the Sea Gem Inquiry was not impressed: "This paragraph would, if it had legislative force, be a prescription for unlimited litigation." Furthermore, a "court of law might have considerable difficulty in determining what" was meant.[14] That said, however, the Inquiry had earlier acknowledged that the "authors of the code emphasise that it deals with recommendations regarding safe practice only and does not necessarily include anything issued in the form of regulation or instructions by the appropriate national authorities".[15] Nevertheless, concern with the imprecision of the language in the Code led to the Inquiry recommending "a code of [statutory] authority with credible sanctions".[16]

8.8   This recommendation is entirely justified given the clear short-comings of the licensing approach generally, but it is surprising that it was not qualified in any way, given the Inquiry's own findings about the difficulty of legislating for such a complex area. "The field over which the Inquiry ranged is so large and the evidential material so complex" that "generalisations could well be both inapt and dangerous".[17] And, indeed, it could be suggested that the Inquiry had implicitly recognised the impossibility (or at least the difficulty) of trying to produce a comprehensive regulatory code for such a complex and rapidly changing field. Most of the deaths on the Sea Gem had actually been caused by strict adherence to the Code where it was unequivocal in its terms. The Code required personnel to muster on the helicopter deck in the event of an emergency, but this instruction had relevance only in the event of a fire and when helicopter evacuation had been arranged, not in the circumstances of a structural collapse when escape to the sea via life-boats or rafts (of which the Sea Gem had plenty for all the crew on board) was the appropriate response.[18] It is by no means clear that "a code of [statutory] authority with credible sanctions" would have avoided this problem.

8.9   Furthermore, it could also be suggested that the Inquiry accurately identified the extent to which the operation of the industry in the

---

[14] Sea Gem Inquiry, para 8.8.
[15] *Ibid*, para 8.2.
[16] *Ibid*, para 10.2(i).
[17] *Ibid*, para 10.1.
[18] *Ibid*, 9.2.

North Sea would inevitably be a learning process. As the Inquiry put it: "In terms of North Sea drilling the SEA GEM represented a pioneering, not to say an experimental project."[19] In so far as in 1965 it was already clear that what had taken place to date was only the first tentative step into uncharted territory, the idea that this would stop being a learning process anytime soon was surely a naïve one. That it was appropriate to call for a detailed regulatory code in such circumstances must accordingly be questioned. But that is what the Inquiry did. It thus revealed a fundamental belief, first, that responsibility for ensuring safety lay with the Government and, second, that the law could come to terms with the problems identified so as to provide a comprehensive regulatory code which, if enforced, could ensure safety in the industry.

It might thus be said that the Inquiry actually had quite profound **8.10** insights into the nature of the problems confronting regulation in this area, but did not follow through on those insights when it came to making its recommendations. It could be offered in the Inquiry's defence that it had few, if any, regulatory alternatives to turn to in 1965. It could also be suggested that the Inquiry's confidence in the appropriateness of its recommendations was unduly bolstered by the reliance it placed on the comparison it drew between an offshore installation and a ship to which the Merchant Shipping Acts applied. In this last regard, it is significant that of the six recommendations made, no fewer than five drew a direct comparison with those Acts.[20]

MIDDLE PHASE: THE PRESCRIPTIVE APPROACH

The Mineral Workings (Offshore Installations) Act 1971

Despite the urgency of the Sea Gem Inquiry's recommendations **8.11** when it reported in July 1967, it was another 4 years before any kind of legislative response was in place. The lapse of time is perhaps an indication of the difficulty confronted by the Labour Government and the subsequent Conservative Government in drafting the sort of

---

[19] Sea Gem Inquiry, para 10.1.

[20] In its other recommendations the Inquiry called for an accepted discipline and chain of command similar to those of the Merchant Navy (Sea Gem Inquiry, paras 10.2(ii) and (iii)); loudspeakers so that orders could be communicated (para 10.2(iv)); the keeping of records of, for example, increases and decreases of loading on the rig, and other matters affecting the rig as a structure (para 10.2(v)); and a daily round equivalent to that of a ship's master designed to keep "everybody up to scratch" (para 10.2(vi)). "Interestingly, however, while this new regulatory code was directly related to the UK experience of legislating for the control of merchant shipping (and installations had obvious similarities to ships), no attempt was made to apply merchant shipping laws directly to installations": B Barrett, and R Howells, "Safe Systems for Exploiting the Petroleum Resources of the North Sea" (1984) 33 *International and Comparative Law Quarterly* 811 at 817.

statutory code with credible sanctions that would meet the requirements of the Inquiry.

8.12   The Mineral Workings (Offshore Installations) Bill began life
in the Lords and moved in due course to the Commons. In both
Houses, the influence of the Sea Gem Inquiry can be seen, with
legislators broadly accepting its assessment of the problem and of
the appropriate solution. Thus, Earl Ferrers in the Lords acknowledged the problem of the lack of any sanction short of revocation
of the licence.[21] The Under Secretary of State for Trade and Industry
in the Commons, Nicholas Ridley, noted the problems arising from
the fact that the regime under the 1964 Act was contractual rather
than mandatory.[22] In place of this approach, a detailed code was
to be established which would set out clear requirements for the
industry, enforceable by the regulator and attracting graded penalties.[23] Flexibility was, however, to be a feature of this new approach,
not least in recognition of the fact that the industry was new and
developing rapidly.[24] The starting point for the new approach would
be the registration of every installation. The approach would then be
characterised by three means by which control could be exercised:
certification as fit for use of all installations by Certifying Authorities,
with those already active in the certification of shipping envisaged
in this role; the *appointment of masters*, later designated installation
managers, as the focal point of responsibility; and *regulations* to be
made in due course within the framework of the Act.[25]

8.13   The regulations in particular were seen to be the way in which the
regime could keep pace with technological change. This flexibility
and adaptability to change did not in any way mean, however, that
the regulations would not be comprehensive. It was foreseen that
they would cover the safety both of the installation itself and of
the operations on it and provide the basis for detailed inspection
and enforcement.[26] Furthermore, the framework Act would allow
coverage of both existing installations and those not yet designed or
built.[27] The need for the regulations to keep pace with change was
clearly understood: concern was expressed that they should neither
cramp development nor cause waste and extravagance for no good

---

[21] Earl Ferrers, *Hansard*, HL (series 5), vol 315, cols 741–746 and 742–743 (18 February
1971).

[22] Hon Nicholas Ridley (Under Secretary of State for Trade and Industry), *Hansard*, HC
(series 5), vol 816, cols 645–649 and 647 (28 April 1971).

[23] Ferrers at col 743; Ridley at col 647.

[24] Ferrers at col 743; Ridley at col 648.

[25] Ferrers at cols 744–745.

[26] Ferrers at col 744.

[27] *Ibid*; Ridley at col 648.

reason.[28] Furthermore, Parliament envisaged that regulators would not adopt a heavy-handed approach to their task: enforcement was foreseen as being "benevolent" and "advisory", with prosecution as a last resort.[29] In this regard, there was recognition from both Government and Opposition of the fact that the industry had offered ready co-operation.[30]

While there was, then, little disagreement between Government and Opposition about the nature of the new regime, a tension was evident between, on one hand, a desire to allow flexibility by leaving more to the regulators to determine and, on the other, a desire to restrict that flexibility by laying down more rules at the level of the Act. Thus, there was concern that matters seen to be fundamental, such as the provision of radio and radar, were not being set out in the Act but rather being left to regulations.[31] Equally, there was concern that the terms in which authority was delegated to the Secretary of State to make regulations assumed a great deal and lacked specification.[32] The Government position in each case was to insist on the need for flexibility in view of the uncertainty surrounding future developments.[33]

8.14

The Mineral Workings (Offshore Installations) Act 1971 was fully in force by 31 August 1972,[34] but the history of the eventual promulgation of regulations under it appears somewhat different to what was envisaged by Parliament. Far from there emerging quickly a comprehensive range of regulations which were then updated as and when required by the rapid pace of change, it was actually 1980 before the full set of regulations – in the form of 11 statutory instruments – was in place.[35] While the issue of registration was swiftly

8.15

---

[28] Ferrers at col 746; Ridley at col 648.
[29] Ferrers at col 746.
[30] Ridley at col 648.
[31] Lord Brown, *Hansard*, HL (series 5), vol 315, col 748 (18 February 1971).
[32] Mr David Mudd, *Hansard*, HC (series 5), vol 816, col 654 (28 April 1971).
[33] Ferrers at col 750; Ridley at col 648.
[34] Mineral Workings (Offshore Installations) Act 1971 (Commencement) Order 1972 (SI 1972/644).
[35] The regulations introduced under the 1971 Act in this period were: Offshore Installations (Registration) Regulations 1972 (SI 1972/702); Offshore Installations (Managers) Regulations 1972 (SI 1972/703); Offshore Installations (Logbooks and Registration of Death) Regulations 1972 (SI 1972/1542); Offshore Installations (Inspectors and Casualties) Regulations 1973 (SI 1973/1842); Offshore Installations (Construction and Survey) Regulations 1974 (SI 1974/289); Offshore Installations (Public Inquiries) Regulations 1974 (SI 1974/338); Offshore Installations (Operational Safety, Health and Welfare) Regulations 1976 (SI 1976/1019); Offshore Installations (Emergency Procedures) Regulations 1976 (SI 1976/1542); Offshore Installations (Life-saving Appliances) Regulations 1977 (SI 1977/486); Offshore Installations (Fire-Fighting Equipment) Regulations 1978 (SI 1978/611); Offshore Installations (Well Control) Regulations 1980 (SI 1980/1759).

dealt with (regulations in this regard appeared in 1972), it was 1976 before regulations relating to what might be regarded as core issues of health and safety at work were produced.[36] Furthermore, issues relating to emergency response were not covered by regulations until after that point. It is not insignificant that some of the North Sea's major fields began producing in the period before 1980, that is, before all the regulations were actually in place.[37] That said, however, by the time the last statutory instrument was promulgated, the regulations did present the appearance of the sort of comprehensive code that the Sea Gem Inquiry had envisaged some 13 years before, covering as they did everything from the construction and survey of installations and well control, through fire-fighting and life-saving equipment. Furthermore, while the regulations under the 1971 Act were centred on the installation itself, regulations were also promulgated under the Petroleum and Submarine Pipelines Act 1975 in relation to offshore pipe-laying operations.[38]

8.16   As important as the regulations, however, was the identity of the *regulator* itself. Although the responsibility for safety in the offshore industry under the 1971 Act passed between several different government departments, it is regarded as significant by many commentators that the body responsible for health and safety was always the same as that which was responsible for licensing and thus for ensuring the efficient exploitation of the nation's hydrocarbon resources.[39] For the majority of the period from 1971 to the end of what is referred to in this chapter as the Middle Phase, the responsibility for safety lay with the Petroleum Engineering Division (PED) of the Department of Energy (DEn).[40] This location of responsibility

---

[36] It later transpired that even this delay did not preclude the 1976 Regulations having been introduced "hurriedly" and with "inadequate consultations". See the Department of Energy's submission to the Burgoyne Committee, J H Burgoyne, *Offshore Safety: Report of the Committee* (Cmnd 7866, 1980) (hereinafter the "Burgoyne Report"), Submission 37, para 7.

[37] For example, Forties in September 1975, Brent in November 1976, Piper in December 1976 and Ninian in December 1978.

[38] Submarine Pipe-lines (Diving Operations) Regulations 1976 (SI 1976/923); Submarine Pipe-lines (Inspectors, etc) Regulations 1977 (SI 1977/835).

[39] For example, Carson, n 2 above, p 163; Bentham, n 10 above, 276; K Miller, "Piper Alpha and the Cullen Report" (1991) *Industrial Law Journal* 176 at 178–179.

[40] The administrative history of the regulators responsible for offshore health and safety is somewhat complicated. Initially, responsibility lay with the Petroleum Division of the Ministry of Power. In 1969, responsibility was transferred to the Ministry of Technology and a Petroleum Production Inspectorate was set up as a subdivision of the Petroleum Division. Only a year later, however, the function was moved to the Department of Trade and Industry where the responsible division became the Petroleum Production Division. In 1974, the Department of Energy was founded and the Petroleum Production Division became a part of that Department. It was this move in particular which concerned critics

for safety within the industry's "sponsoring" department very soon set offshore oil and gas at odds with the general trend in health and safety regulation in the UK. No regulatory regime is likely to last forever,[41] but few are already profoundly in question before they are even in force. That, however, was essentially the position of the 1971 Act.

Tension with the Health and Safety at Work, etc Act 1974

While the 1971 Act was passing through Parliament, a committee   8.17
set up by the Government under the chairmanship of Lord Robens was examining the whole question of the regulation of health and safety at work. In its report,[42] which was published in June 1972 (and thus before the 1971 Act was fully in force at the end of August 1972), the Committee came down firmly against precisely the sort of prescriptive regulatory approach that had just been mandated for the offshore industry. The Robens Committee had three main problems with this sort of approach. First, it took the view that there existed too much law relating to health and safety at work and the detailed prescription of every aspect of work had the effect of persuading people that health and safety was purely a matter of government regulation and not of individual responsibility. Second, it believed that too much of the existing law was irrelevant to real problems. Finally, it contended that there was a major disadvantage in attempting to address the problem of health and safety with the wide array of administrative agencies then engaged in the field.[43] Summing all of this up, the Committee concluded that:

> "[t]here are severe practical limits on the extent to which progressively better standards of safety and health at work can be brought about through negative regulation by external agencies. We need a more effectively self-regulating system. This calls for the acceptance and exercise of appropriate responsibilities at all levels within industry and commerce. It calls for better systems of safety organisation, for more management initiatives, and for more involvement of work people themselves. The objectives of future policy must therefore

---

who saw safety subordinated in a Department "for which energy production was the primary concern". In 1977, the Petroleum Engineering Division was established and most safety functions became its responsibility. See Carson, n 2 above, pp 161–163; Burgoyne Report, Appendix 7.

[41] Though even an Opposition Member of Parliament at the time of the passage of the 1971 Act believed its inherent flexibility meant it would last 100 years: Mr Eric Ogden, *Hansard*, HC (series 5), vol 821, col 678 (14 July 1971).

[42] Lord Robens, *Safety and Health at Work: Report of the Robens Committee* (Cmnd 5034, 1972) (hereinafter the "Robens Report").

[43] Robens Report, paras 28, 30 and 41.

include not only increasing the effectiveness of the state's contribution to health and safety at work but also, and more importantly, creating conditions for more effective self-regulation".[44]

The tension between this approach and that of the Sea Gem Inquiry some 5 years earlier is abundantly clear. And the two reports produced quite different results. As has been seen, the Sea Gem Inquiry led to the 1971 Act and in due course to a comprehensive set of detailed regulations specific to the offshore oil and gas industry. In stark contrast, the result of the Robens Report was the Health and Safety at Work, etc Act 1974 (HSWA 1974) which:

> "introduced a broad goalsetting, non-prescriptive model, based on the view that 'those that create risk are best placed to manage it'. In place of existing detailed and prescriptive industry regulations, it created a flexible system whereby regulations express goals and principles, and are supported by codes of practice and guidance. Based on consultation and engagement, the new regime was designed to deliver a proportionate, targeted and risk-based approach".[45]

Furthermore, the regulatory function was centralised in the Health and Safety Commission (HSC) and the Health and Safety Executive (HSE) instead of the broad array of industry-specific agencies that had existed previously. Perhaps because the 1971 Act was just emerging as the Committee deliberated, Robens did not discuss offshore safety in any depth. Instead, the 1971 Act was noted as one of a category of statutes that, though not considered in detail, the Committee thought capable of, on the face of it, being brought within the proposed unified system perhaps after the main arrangements had been made.[46] But that did not happen.

8.18   It would be going too far to say that the Robens approach was greeted uniformly with open arms at the time,[47] or that the subsequent HSWA 1974 was thereafter regarded by all as an unalloyed good.[48] But a measure of the perceived differences in the value of this approach as opposed to detailed regulation enforced by the

---

[44] Robens Report, para 41.
[45] HSE, *Thirty Years On and Looking Forward* (2004), p 3.
[46] Robens Report, para 109
[47] See, eg, A D Woolf, "Robens Report: The Wrong Approach?" (1973) 2 *Industrial Law Journal* 88.
[48] See, eg, R Kinnersley, *The Hazards of Work: How to Fight Them* (1973), pp 228–230; R Baldwin, "Health and Safety at Work: Consensus and Self-Regulation" in Baldwin and McCrudden (eds), *Regulation and Public Law* (1987), pp 132–158; S Dawson, P Willman, A Clinton and M Bamford, *Safety at Work: The Limits of Self-regulation* (1988); P James, "Reforming British Health and Safety Law: a framework for discussion" (1992) *Industrial Law Journal* 83; Ogus, n 9 above, p 188; S Tombs, "Law, Resistance and Reform: 'Regulating' Safety Crimes in the UK" (1995) 4 *Social and Legal Studies* 411.

offshore industry's "sponsoring" department may be gained from the numerous calls there were in the succeeding years for responsibility for offshore safety to be transferred to the HSE.[49]

Even if the offshore industry was not, then, brought within the **8.19** ambit of the 1974 Act at this time in the way that Robens anticipated, that Act did have an impact. Responsibility for offshore safety remained with the DEn and was not transferred to the HSE, but the general duties contained in the HSWA 1974 were in due course expressly extended offshore,[50] including the duty on the employer to ensure, so far as is reasonably practicable, the health, safety and welfare of employees.[51] The provisions relating to workforce involvement, such as safety committees and safety representatives, were not, however, similarly extended. The point has been made that the two different regimes (that under the 1971 and 1975 Acts and that under the 1974 Act) operated on the basis of different enforcement procedures. The former relied on criminal penalties and, in the ultimate, the power to suspend operations, while the latter relied on a more flexible system of improvement notices, prohibition notices and lastly criminal penalties. It has also been emphasised that the two regimes each envisaged different inspectorates and that the industry was concerned that the HSE would not understand the special problems faced in the offshore situation, including the extreme cost of delays.[52] Questions accordingly arose as to how the spirit of the 1974 Act could survive *without* the workforce involvement envisaged by that Act and precisely *with* the sort of inspectorate that the Robens Committee had criticised.

The Burgoyne Committee

If, however, the regulatory situation for the offshore oil and gas **8.20** industry was, to put it at its most charitable, extremely complicated by the end of the 1970s, an opportunity arose at that time to review it in detail and to recommend any necessary changes. This occurred as a consequence of the blow-out on the Ekofisk Bravo platform in

[49] For example, by the dissenting members of the Burgoyne Committee (see Note of Dissent, para 13, Burgoyne Report p 60) and by the Trades Union Congress (see Submission 62, para II(b), Burgoyne Report, p 292), in contrast to the opposition of the industry put forward by UKOOA (see Submission 43, Burgoyne Report, pp 241 and 247–249).
[50] Health and Safety at Work, etc Act 1974 (Application Outside Great Britain) Order 1977 (SI 1977/1232). The PED carried out the HSE's inspection function under an agency agreement between the HSC and the DEn. For the agency agreement, see Burgoyne Report, Appendix 11.
[51] Section 2.
[52] Daintith, Willoughby and Hill, para 1–857.

the Norwegian Sector of the North Sea in April 1977. Recognising that this could have been a major disaster resulting in significant loss of life, the UK Government established a further committee, under the chairmanship of Dr J H Burgoyne, to consider, among other things: "so far as they are concerned with safety, the nature, coverage and effectiveness of the Department of Energy's regulations governing the exploration, development and production of oil and gas offshore and their administration and enforcement".[53] The Report of this Committee, published in March 1980, is an important document that took on renewed significance in the context of events some 8 years later. It follows the line adopted by the Sea Gem Inquiry in some respects but departs from it, significantly, in others. It too, however, can be read, admittedly with the benefit of hindsight, as having had profound insights into the nature of the problems confronting the regulation of health and safety offshore but then as having failed to follow through on those in the form of recommendations.

8.21 Burgoyne agreed with the Sea Gem Inquiry that the ultimate responsibility for ensuring safety lay with the Government, and also that this end could be achieved through monitoring and enforcement by the regulator.[54] But Burgoyne departed from its predecessor when it came to the role that the law would play in this regard. The Sea Gem Inquiry wanted "a code of statutory authority with credible sanctions". Parliament, in passing the 1971 Act, was clearly of the view that the framework statute would allow regulations to keep pace with developments in the industry. But Burgoyne basically withdrew from the idea that law could ever be flexible enough to provide detailed safety regulations for the totality of this complex and evolving industry. The Committee's proposal was that the role of government was "to *set objectives* designed to achieve a uniformly high standard of safety throughout the Industry".[55] It is possible to detect resonances of the Robens Committee in this statement, resonances that only become clearer when Burgoyne states that "[t]he Government shall discharge its responsibility for offshore safety via a single Government agency whose task it is to *set standards* and to ensure their achievement",[56] and that "[m]ethods of implementation should be advised as fully and flexibly as possible in guidance notes, which should be recognised as being non-mandatory".[57] But if those resonances seemed to indicate that

---

[53] Burgoyne Report, para 1.1.
[54] *Ibid*, para 6.5.
[55] *Ibid*, 6.2 (emphasis added).
[56] *Ibid*, para 6.5 (emphasis added).
[57] *Ibid*, para 6.15.

Burgoyne was minded to place the offshore industry squarely under the 1974 Act, then they were misleading.

It seems instead that the Committee's apparent rejection of 8.22 prescription at the level of the regulations stemmed from its recognition that a tension existed between the law and the regulated area. But whereas the Sea Gem Inquiry was troubled by the inability of the law to understand a Code of Practice which had been drafted by the industry, the Burgoyne Committee was confronted by evidence that the converse problem had now arisen and that difficulties were being encountered *by the industry* in dealing with regulations drafted in accordance with the needs *of the legal system*. As the PED expressed it in its submission to Burgoyne:

> "[i]t is ... difficult to draft regulations which can be readily understood by a person without legal training. We accept, however, that legal conventions must be respected and that, in the ultimate, regulations must be able to stand up in a court of law. We think that the regulations under the 1971 Act are now understood by the offshore oil industry, largely through explanation and interpretation from the Inspectorates to educate the industry through guidance notes".[58]

Burgoyne thus appears to have accepted the PED's contention that it could make the regulations understandable to the industry. While the union members of the Committee expressed strong opposition, the majority decided in favour of leaving the PED in charge of safety rather than handing responsibility to the HSE.[59] It would be wrong to say, however, that the Committee was sanguine about the PED's abilities in this regard or that it was unaware of the extent to which the offshore industry had fallen behind developments onshore under the 1974 Act. Accordingly, it recommended that the PED should strengthen its relations with the HSE in order to benefit from the latter's expertise in occupational health and safety,[60] and it made a series of recommendations in relation to workforce involvement.[61] These latter reflected to some extent the terms of the Safety Representatives and Safety Committees Regulations 1977 applying onshore,[62] but there was no call for their extension offshore nor

---

[58] Submission by the Department of Energy, Petroleum Engineering Directorate to the Burgoyne Committee. See Burgoyne Report, Submission 37, para 8, p 228. It is worth noting that lawyers themselves were not enthusiastic about the comprehensibility of the 1971 Act. See W Dale, "Statutory Reform: The Draftsman and the Judge" (1980) 30 ICLQ 141 at 147.
[59] Burgoyne Report, para 6.6.
[60] *Ibid*, para 4.24.
[61] *Ibid*, para 5.94.
[62] SI 1977/500, made under the HSWA 1974.

did Burgoyne "consider it essential to embody these principles in mandatory regulations".[63]

8.23   These issues contributed to the union members of the Committee issuing a Note of Dissent. As regards the question of safety representatives and safety committees, they pointed out that the tripartite Offshore Industry Advisory Committee had recently reached agreement in principle regarding the extension of the onshore regulations.[64] Whatever the actual reasons for the Burgoyne Committee's position, its refusal to recommend the extension of the onshore regulations may have been an acknowledgement that these operated so as to allow employers who did not recognise trade unions to avoid the mandatory involvement of safety representatives,[65] a very relevant point in the context of an industry with a very low level of unionisation.[66] With regard to the role of the PED, the Note of Dissent mentioned fears of the "possibility of shared values and membership of closed groups"[67] as between industry and regulator. But that assessment must be read in the light of the difficulties in communication perceived by the PED mentioned above.

8.24   Burgoyne revealed that the orientation of the law envisaged by Parliament at the time of the passing of the 1971 Act was in fact difficult to implement. Regulators were unable to keep pace with developments in the offshore industry at the level even of secondary legislation and had instead to resort to guidance in order to achieve the necessary flexibility. They were also experiencing difficulties in communicating legal requirements to the industry. In view of the fundamental nature of these issues, it might be expected that these would have figured largely in the extensive parliamentary debate that followed publication of the Burgoyne Report.[68] In fact, these issues were not mentioned at all. Instead the focus was mainly on where responsibility for safety offshore should ultimately lie, with the DEn or the HSE. The Conservative Government took the view that it should remain with the DEn on the basis that those administering safety should have an intimate knowledge of this

---

[63] Burgoyne Report, para 5.97.

[64] See the Note of Dissent, para 25, Burgoyne Report, p 63.

[65] See D M Kloss, *Occupational Health Law* (3rd edn, 1998), p 137.

[66] See S S Andersen,, *British and Norwegian Offshore Industrial Relations: Pluralism and Neo-Corporatism as Contexts of Strategic Adaptation* (1987); C Woolfson, J Foster and M Beck, *Paying for the Piper: Capital and Labour in Britain's Offshore Oil Industry* (1996), pp 44ff. It is also worth noting that the original intention was to allow safety representatives to be appointed by either the workforce or trade unions. This provision in the HSWA 1974 was, however, repealed by the Employment Protection Act 1975 as part of the Social Contract between the then Labour Government and the TUC (see James, n 48 above, 90).

[67] See the Note of Dissent, para 8, Burgoyne Report, p 59.

[68] *Hansard*, HC (series 5), vol 991, cols 1472–1546 (November 1980).

complex field, and indeed have immediate access to the related expertise within other units of the Department.[69] Nevertheless, it was explicitly recognised that there was a danger in isolating the offshore from health and safety developments onshore and, therefore, the Secretary of State for Energy was to take over the responsibilities of the Employment Secretary under the HSWA 1974 – the matters which had previously been the subject of the agency agreement between the two Departments.[70] The former would still seek the advice of the HSE but ultimate responsibility would now rest with him. Whereas unions were concerned that this gave rise to an unacceptable conflict of interest, the Government's view was that the risks actually lay in splitting the various responsibilities of the Department of Energy given the limited number of experts at its disposal.[71] The Government acknowledged that there was room for new safety initiatives in the offshore industry, but maintained that the new administrative arrangements would be able to respond to this need efficiently and effectively.[72]

The Government's confidence in an arrangement that ran counter to practically every other industry was not shared by the Opposition, who regarded it as a "dog's breakfast".[73] It was also concerned, first, by the Burgoyne Committee's finding that none of the safety committees visited during their investigations had ever been contacted by the PED and, secondly, by the PED's view that they had never had the need to speak to such a committee.[74] The Opposition was accordingly clear that the responsibility for offshore safety should be transferred to the HSE.[75] **8.25**

Whatever the difference of view between Conservative and Labour on this issue, what is more significant in view of the issues highlighted in this chapter is the fact that legislators of all persuasions remained convinced of a direct correlation between the promulgation and enforcement of prescriptive regulation, on one hand, and improved occupational health and safety, on the other. Labour saw the conflict of interest within the DEn between safety and production as having the potential to reduce overall safety, whereas the Conservatives saw any increase in the distance between the technical experts of the DEn and the safety regulators as having the potential to reduce overall safety. But, crucially, all legislators **8.26**

---

[69] Mr Hamish Gray (Minister of State, Department of Energy) at cols 1476–1480.
[70] Gray at col 1479.
[71] Gray at cols 1479 and 1482.
[72] Gray at col 1484.
[73] Dr David Owen at col 1492.
[74] Mr Harold Walker at col 1533.
[75] Dr David Owen at cols 1489–1492.

appear to have adhered to the rationale they deployed in 1971 as regards the appropriate regulatory approach. It could be objected that the Robens approach upon which the 1974 Act is based would have resulted in a move away from prescriptive regulation and hence that the Labour programme by this time must be seen as fundamentally different,[76] but it is significant that neither side once mentioned this point during the course of the debate. The *orientation* of the law (prescriptive or goal-setting) was not an issue for legislators whereas the location of responsibility was. Whatever the Burgoyne Committee had discovered about difficulties of communication and about the limitations of prescription, this was not apparently visible to legislators. It is ironic that if the Opposition had focused on these aspects of the Burgoyne Committee's findings, the Government would have found it much more difficult to resist the calls for a transfer of responsibility to the HSE.

LATE PHASE: THE PERMISSIONING APPROACH

The Piper Alpha disaster and the Cullen Inquiry

8.27 The extent to which the Burgoyne Report and the subsequent parliamentary debate represented a missed opportunity to bring offshore health and safety into line with the most advanced thinking on the subject became all too clear 8 years later. On 6 July 1988 the Piper Alpha production platform was almost entirely destroyed by a series of explosions and subsequent fires: 167 men lost their lives, making this by far the worst accident in the history of the offshore industry. A public inquiry was set up[77] under the chairmanship of a senior Scottish judge, Lord Cullen. This was charged principally with providing answers to two questions: "[w]hat were the causes and circumstances of the disaster ...? and What should be recommended with a view to the preservation of life and the avoidance of similar accidents in the future?"[78]

8.28 The Inquiry became, at the time, the longest and most thorough ever seen in the UK. Its two-volume Report is a damning indictment of the state of safety in the UK sector of the North Sea in the late 1980s. The main cause of the disaster was a failure of the permit to work (PTW) system, especially as it related to communication between

---

[76] This point can, however, be overstated. There is evidence that even up to the mid-1980s the development of the approach to regulation onshore proposed by Robens and provided for by the HSWA 1974 was still relatively in its infancy. See Baldwin, n 48 above, p 145.
[77] By the Secretary of State for Energy under the Offshore Installations (Public Inquiries) Regulations 1974 (SI 1974/338).
[78] Lord Cullen, *The Public Inquiry into the Piper Alpha Disaster* (Cm 1310, 1990) (hereinafter the "Cullen Report"), para 1.1.

the different shifts on the platform. On the night in question, this led to equipment being used that was in fact subject to maintenance. A gas escape and explosion resulted.[79] What was already a serious incident was made much worse by a number of other factors, each one sufficient to raise profound questions about the adequacy of the regulatory regime in place at this time. First, the Claymore platform, to which the Piper Alpha was connected, continued to pump oil, thus feeding the fires that followed the initial explosion.[80] Second, the Offshore Installation Manager, such a focus of attention in the Sea Gem Inquiry's recommendations, "took no initiative in an attempt to save life".[81] Third, emergency systems, for which specific regulations had finally been passed in the late 1970s, failed as a result of the intensity of the explosion. Fourth, the platform's stand-by vessel, the *Silver Pit*, proved ineffective in the circumstances[82] as did the *Tharos* fire-fighting vessel, which was actually on hand at the time of the disaster.[83] The platform's owners, Occidental Petroleum, were severely criticised by Lord Cullen for this state of affairs. They were said to be unprepared for this sort of emergency and to have adopted a superficial attitude to such risks. Adequate safety arrangements were frequently not in place and where they were they were often ignored, as exemplified by the PTW system.[84]

Lord Cullen's criticism did not, however, stop with the operator. **8.29** The PED was also singled out. In Lord Cullen's view, the inspections carried out by the PED were "superficial to the point of being of little use as a test of safety on the platform"[85] and not really an effective means of assessing the *management* of safety.[86] This litany of criticism went to the core of the existing regulatory approach and completely undermined existing assumptions: the Government's faith in the regulation of safety by the "sponsoring department", specifically reiterated despite the opportunity to revisit the issue in the aftermath of the Burgoyne Report; the regulator's adherence to a mode of regulation and inspection that had already been called into question by Robens in 1972, and its questionable grasp of core occupational health and safety, so tellingly already exposed in its evidence to the Burgoyne Committee;[87] and the industry's ability to

---

[79] Cullen Report, Chapter 11.
[80] *Ibid*, paras 7.37–7.40.
[81] *Ibid*, para 8.35.
[82] *Ibid*, para 9.42.
[83] *Ibid*, paras 9.49–9.57.
[84] *Ibid*, Chapter 14.
[85] *Ibid*, para 15.48.
[86] *Ibid*, para 15.50.
[87] See n 36.

prepare for and respond to emergencies, which had been expressed so confidently in its submission to Burgoyne.[88]

8.30   Lord Cullen's trenchant criticisms of both the operator and the regulator were translated into no fewer than 106 recommendations which, taken together, constituted a radical re-orientation of occupational health and safety regulation offshore. Some of the issues that had emerged already at the time of the Burgoyne Committee a decade earlier were again apparent in the Cullen Report. Now, however, they were followed through to their logical conclusion and worked into a comprehensive and coherent system. As regards the regulator, Cullen adopted the proposal made by the authors of the Note of Dissent to the Burgoyne Report – albeit for different reasons – in recommending that responsibility for health and safety offshore should be transferred from the "sponsoring department" to the Health and Safety Executive. The approach to regulation would similarly see radical reform. The proposal was that the operator of each and every installation on the UKCS should submit to the regulator a safety case, that is, a document making the case that the installation is safe in both its construction and operation. The safety case would demonstrate that certain objectives have been met, including the following: that the Safety Management System (SMS) of the company and that of the installation are adequate to ensure that the design and the operation of the installation and its equipment are safe; that the potential major hazards to the installation have been identified and appropriate controls provided; and that adequate provision is made for ensuring, in the event of a major emergency affecting the installation, a temporary safe refuge for personnel and their safe and full evacuation, escape and rescue.[89] Superficially, it may be wondered whether there was anything dramatically different here from the recommendations made by the Sea Gem Inquiry in 1967. But whereas it too had called for a comprehensive approach, what Cullen had in mind was quite distinct.

8.31   As troubling as it may have appeared to lawyers and regulators, Cullen essentially abandoned any idea that law, even in its most flexible forms such as secondary legislation, could provide a detailed and comprehensive code covering all the aspects of the industry. Rather, he placed a considerable degree of responsibility on *the operator*: to identify risks to occupational health and safety, whether at the level of issues with a catastrophic potential or at that of the more mundane slips, trips and falls; to demonstrate, by means of

---

[88] "UKOOA has full confidence in the ability of the industry ... to cope with any emergencies that may arise", Burgoyne Report, Submission 43, para 5.3. For the full Code of Practice and Plan for Offshore Emergencies, see Appendix A to Submission 43.
[89] Cullen Report, para 23.2.

Quantified Risk Assessment (QRA) where appropriate, that these risks had been minimised; and to show how this risk minimisation had been (or was to be) achieved. He thus very significantly departed from the views on the location of responsibility expressed by both the Sea Gem Inquiry and the Burgoyne Committee, stating that "a regulator cannot be expected to assume direct responsibility for the on-going management of safety ... this is and remains in the hands of the operator".[90] As far as he was concerned, an operator may depart from procedures outlined either in regulations or in official guidance provided that this was justified in the Safety Case.

Such a position accordingly implied a reorientation of the regula-　8.32 tions themselves. Thus, Cullen called for prescriptive regulations as far as possible to be replaced with goal-setting regulations.[91] He argued, indeed, that prescriptive regulation could actually be part of the problem rather than a solution, as this approach encouraged a compliance mentality rather than a wider consideration of safety[92] and was unable to cope with the overall interaction of components.[93] The extent of his departure from the position both of the Sea Gem Inquiry and indeed of the legislators at the time of the passing of the Mineral Workings (Offshore Installations) Act 1971 can perhaps best be seen when he associated himself with the remarks of one witness to the Inquiry who claimed that safety could not be legislated.[94]

This change in the orientation of the regulations naturally implied　8.33 a different notion of compliance as well as a change in the role of the regulator. Lord Cullen's view in this regard was that the operator under the new regime must satisfy itself by means of audits that the Safety Management System was being adhered to and that the regulator should review the operator's audit and ensure that the

---

[90] Cullen Report, para. 21.4.

[91] The recommendation was that the Construction and Survey Regulations, the Fire Fighting Regulations, the Life-Saving Appliances Regulations and the Emergency Procedures Regulations should be revoked and replaced by: (i) Construction Regulations, covering *inter alia* the structure and layout of the installation and its accommodation; (ii) Plant and Equipment Regulations, covering *inter alia* plant and equipment on the installation and in particular those handling hydrocarbons; (iii) Fire and Explosion Protection Regulations, covering *inter alia* both active and passive fire protection and explosion protection; and (iv) Evacuation, Escape and Rescue Regulations, covering *inter alia* emergency procedures, life-saving appliances, evacuation, escape and rescue. Each of these sets of regulations should include goal-setting regulations as their main or primary provisions and should be supported by guidance notes giving advice which is non-mandatory: Cullen Report, para 21.69.

[92] Cullen Report, para 21.51.

[93] *Ibid*, para 21.42.

[94] *Ibid*, para 21.4. The witness was Mr R E McKee, the Chairman and Managing Director of Conoco (UK) Ltd.

output from the SMS was satisfactory.[95] This shift in responsibility away from the regulator and towards the operator was also evident in the degree of freedom that the latter would have in the regime envisaged by Cullen with regard to the specification of the standards to be used to demonstrate compliance with the goal-setting regulations.[96] This fitted in, however, with Cullen's view that the primary function of the safety case was to ensure that every operator produces a Formal Safety Assessment (FSA) to assure itself that its operations are safe. Only secondarily would it be a matter of demonstrating this to the regulators, albeit that this would meet the legitimate expectations of the workforce and the public and provide a sound basis for regulation.[97] There could perhaps be no clearer indication than this of the extent of Cullen's departure from a traditional view of the process and function of regulation.

8.34   The recommendations regarding the use of FSA, QRA and other such procedures are another interesting feature of Cullen's approach. He was explicitly impressed by the HSE's use of such methods in relation to onshore industries under the Control of Industrial Major Accident Hazard (CIMAH) Regulations 1984[98] – indeed this was one of the factors that helped him decide which agency should be given responsibility for regulating offshore safety.[99] His assessment of the value of this approach appeared to be based in part on its contribution to successful communication between industry and regulator, which, as has been seen, was a concern to both the Sea Gem Inquiry and the Burgoyne Committee. Cullen found no evidence to support the concerns expressed by the authors of the Note of Dissent to the Burgoyne Report regarding the closeness of the PED and the industry or a conflict of interest between safety and production in the DEn.[100] Rather, he seems to have shared the PED's concerns as

---

[95] Cullen Report, para 21.60.

[96] *Ibid*, para 21.70.

[97] *Ibid*, para 17.35. It is worth noting that the idea of a formal safety assessment was mentioned at the second reading stage of the Mineral Workings (Offshore Installations) Bill in 1971. Mr David Watkins raised the issue or "damage control ... a technique whereby it is possible for experts to examine thoroughly any place where people are subject to any possible form of hazard arising from their work and, by reporting fully, enable steps to be taken to eliminate many of the causes of accident": *Hansard*, HC (series 5), vol 816, col 663 (28 April 1971).

[98] SI 1984/1902, implementing the so-called Seveso Directive (Council Directive 82/501/EEC of 24 June 1982 on the major-accident hazards of certain industrial activities) and now replaced by the Control of Major Accident Hazard (COMAH) Regulations 1999 (SI 1999/743) which in turn implement the Seveso II Directive (Council Directive 96/82/EC of 9 December 1996 on the control of major-accident hazards involving dangerous substances, as amended by Directive 2003/105/EC).

[99] Cullen Report, paras 22.28 and 22.34.

[100] *Ibid*, para. 22.38.

expressed in the evidence to the Burgoyne Committee as regards the difficulty in achieving communication between law and the regulated area. Whereas the Burgoyne Committee took some steps towards addressing this problem in its recommendations of non-mandatory guidance and flexibility, Cullen met the problem head-on and recommended an approach that would allow the regulators to speak to the industry in a language that it could understand. In evidence to the inquiry the HSE explained that it used QRA as a means of founding "legal or political judgements as firmly as possible on a rigorous scrutiny of the facts" because the "technologically based industries or scientifically numerate organisations" it dealt with expected "a structured and logical approach".[101] Cullen was clearly impressed by this.

The issue that caused such contention for the Burgoyne Committee 8.35 and indeed for Parliament thereafter was, of course, the involvement of the workforce in health and safety. While the inquiry was ongoing, the DEn brought in a set of regulations that provided for workforce involvement.[102] This was not an extension of the corresponding onshore regulations but rather reflected the approach recommended by the Burgoyne Committee. As a result, in the course of the Piper Alpha Inquiry, there were calls for these to be amended to incorporate trade union involvement.[103] While Cullen was sympathetic to the view that the appointment of representatives by trade unions could be beneficial with regard to credibility and the ability to resist pressure, he concluded that the particular circumstances of the offshore workforce in terms of its low level of unionisation and its fragmentation meant that such a change would have the effect of removing representation from a large number of workers.[104]

The Offshore Safety Act 1992 and the Safety Case Regulations 1992

Just as the recommendations of the Sea Gem Inquiry and the 8.36 Burgoyne Committee had been almost unequivocally accepted, so did the Government accept without demur Cullen's 106 proposals for change.[105] The foundation was laid with the passing of the

---

[101] Cullen Report, para 17.53.
[102] Offshore Installation (Safety Representatives and Safety Committees) Regulations 1989 (SI 1989/971).
[103] Details of trade union evidence to the Cullen Inquiry can be found in the Cullen Report, paras 21.78–21.80.
[104] Cullen Report, para 21.85
[105] For the parliamentary debate, see *Hansard*, HC (series 6), vol 180, cols 329–345 (12 November 1990); vol 187, cols 472–567 (7 March 1991).

Offshore Safety Act 1992 in March of that year, which served to extend fully the Health and Safety at Work, etc Act 1974 offshore and allowed regulations to be made repealing those made under the Mineral Workings (Offshore Installations) Act 1971 and the Submarine Pipelines Act 1975. The Health and Safety Commission announced that it would set about the reform of offshore safety on three fronts: the development of new regulations specific to the offshore environment in line with Cullen's vision for a goal-setting approach; ensuring that the offshore environment was subject to new regulations being made to implement European Directives on health and safety at work; and the extension of offshore of existing health and safety regulations as appropriate.[106]

8.37   In November, the Offshore Installations (Safety Case) Regulations 1992 were made,[107] coming into force on 31 May 1993. These required operators of fixed installations to prepare a safety case prior to completion of the design and to send it to the HSE so as to allow time for any concerns raised to be taken account of in the design.[108] Further, operation of a fixed installation was not permitted unless the safety case had been accepted by the HSE.[109] Owners of mobile installations were not permitted to move such installations into UK waters (as defined) with a view to operation without prior acceptance of a safety case.[110] Where combined operations involving a fixed and a mobile installation were to be carried out, a separate safety case would be required.[111] Finally, the 1992 Regulations required an operator of a fixed installation to prepare a safety case in relation to the proposed abandonment of an installation.[112] In each case (except combined operations), the operator or owner had to include sufficient particulars to demonstrate that (a) the management system was adequate to ensure that relevant statutory provisions would be complied with; (b) adequate arrangements were in place for auditing and reporting; (c) all hazards with the potential to cause a major accident had been identified; and (d) risks had been evaluated and measures taken to reduce them to the lowest level that is reasonably practicable.[113] In each case, schedules to the regulations provided further detail on what the safety case was to contain.[114]

---

[106] For details of the HSC's statement, see Daintith, Willoughby and Hill, para 1–932.

[107] SI 1992/2885.

[108] Reg 4(1).

[109] Reg 4(2).

[110] Reg 5.

[111] Reg 6.

[112] Reg 7.

[113] Reg 8. The ALARP standard (As Low As Reasonably Practicable).

[114] Sch 2 for fixed installations, Sch 3 for mobile installations, Sch 4 for combined operations and Sch 5 for abandonment.

Regulation 9 embodied Cullen's vision that the safety case should be a "living document" in so far as it provided that an operator or owner should revise it as often as required. Where any such proposed revision would render the safety case "materially different" from the version last seen by the HSE, the regulation required that the regulator should accept it before it be made. Regulation 9 also required the triennial resubmission of the safety case. Without renewed acceptance by the HSE, continued operation was not permitted. An indication of the radical nature of the safety case approach was to be found in reg 10 which imposed a duty on the operator or owner to ensure that health and safety procedures and arrangements contained in the safety case were actually followed. Criminal liability could arise from a breach of that duty. It was also incumbent on every person to whom the regulation applied to co-operate with the operator or owner so as to enable the latter to comply with the Regulations.[115] Transitional provisions allowed the 200 or so installations already operating on the UKCS to continue to do so after the coming into force of the Regulations, provided that a safety case was submitted within 6 months of that date and provided the HSE had accepted the case within 30 months of that date.[116] The HSE announced in November 1995 that it had achieved the successful assessment and acceptance of all safety cases for existing installations before the deadline. The HSE at this time also indicated just how far the understanding of the locus of responsibility for safety had changed since the Sea Gem Inquiry and the Burgoyne Committee. It stated that acceptance of a safety case "cannot guarantee" that safety management systems are working effectively but rather allows inspectors to "target their continuing intervention".[117]

The goal-setting regulations

The process of introducing the new goal-setting regulations was also efficiently completed. The first of these, the Offshore Installations (Management and Administration) Regulations 1995,[118] deals with the following matters: notification of entry into or departure from relevant waters of an installation and of any change in the duty holder of an installation;[119] the appointment of an installation

8.38

---

[115] Reg 14.
[116] Reg 13.
[117] See HSE Press Release E180:95, 22 November 1995.
[118] SI 1995/738, as amended by the Offshore Safety (Miscellaneous Amendments) Regulations 2002 (SI 2002/2175).
[119] Reg 5. "Duty holder" is defined by reg 2(1) as meaning the operator in relation to a fixed installation and the owner in relation to a mobile installation.

manager, his powers of restraint and putting ashore and the duty
of others to co-operate with him;[120] the keeping of records of those
on the installation;[121] the use of PTW systems;[122] the availability
and comprehensibility of health and safety instructions;[123] arrangements for communications with the shore, other vessels, aircraft
and other installations;[124] helicopter operations;[125] gathering of
meteorological and related information;[126] availability of contact
details for the Health and Safety Executive;[127] health surveillance
of workers;[128] supply of drinking water and provisions;[129] identification of the installation;[130] the possibility of exemptions;[131]
and the application of the Employers' Liability (Compulsory
Insurance) Act 1969.[132] Reading through this list, the level of
detail may give the impression that these are really prescriptive
rather than goal-setting regulations. Closer inspection of the
specific provisions reveals, however, that, while some elements
of prescription remain, important issues are indeed dealt with
on the basis of goal-setting. For example, reg 6(b) requires that
the duty holder ensure that "the installation manager is provided
with appropriate resources to be able to carry out effectively
his function", but offers no further specification of what these
resources might be. Similarly, reg 10 requires that a PTW system
be utilised where this is required by the nature of the work or the
circumstances in which work may be carried out, but provides no
detail on the work or circumstances envisaged. The duty holder's
response to these regulations will be determined by the Formal
Safety Assessment they carry out under the safety case regulations.

8.39   The same approach is found in the second set of regulations
usually referred to under the goal-setting heading: the Offshore
Installations (Prevention of Fire and Explosion, and Emergency
Response) Regulations 1995.[133] These begin by imposing a general
duty on the duty holder to take appropriate measures to protect

---

[120] Regs 6, 7 and 8.
[121] Reg 9.
[122] Reg 10.
[123] Reg 11.
[124] Reg 12. There are particular requirements in respect of helicopter landings on
"not-normally-manned" installations.
[125] Reg 13.
[126] Reg 14.
[127] Reg 15.
[128] Reg 16.
[129] Regs 17 and 18.
[130] Reg 19.
[131] Reg 20.
[132] Reg 21.
[133] SI 1995/743.

persons on the installation from fire and explosion and to secure effective emergency response.[134] The means by which this duty is fulfilled is principally via an assessment covering: the identification of events which could cause a major accident involving fire or explosion or the need for evacuation, escape or rescue to avoid such an accident; "the evaluation of the likelihood and consequences of such events" (that is, a risk assessment); the establishment of performance standards for evacuation, escape, recovery and rescue equipment; and "the selection of appropriate measures".[135] Thereafter a series of more specific requirements are listed in regs 6–21, but none of these affects the generality of the duty in reg 4(1).[136] The more specific provisions relate to preparation for emergencies (including helicopter emergencies) and preparation of an emergency response plan;[137] prevention of fire and explosion;[138] detection of incidents;[139] communication in, and the control of, emergencies;[140] mitigation of fire and explosion;[141] muster areas, arrangements for evacuation, means of escape and arrangements for recovery and rescue;[142] suitability of personal protective equipment for use in an emergency;[143] suitability and condition of plant;[144] life-saving appliances;[145] and information regarding plant.[146] Once again, while there are elements of prescription in these more specific provisions, most make reference to the duty holder taking "appropriate measures" or making "appropriate provision" without specifying in detail what these measures or provisions should be.

The third set of "goal-setting" regulations is the Offshore Installations and Wells (Design and Construction, etc) Regulations 1996.[147] The principal parts of this statutory instrument (relating respectively to integrity of installations[148] and wells[149]) each start by imposing a general duty. In the case of integrity of installations, the duty is imposed on the duty holder to ensure that "an installation at

8.40

---

[134] Reg 4(1).
[135] Reg 5.
[136] Reg 4(2).
[137] Regs 6, 7 and 8.
[138] Reg 9.
[139] Reg 10.
[140] Regs 11 and 12.
[141] Reg 13.
[142] Regs 14, 15, 16 and 17.
[143] Reg 18.
[144] Reg 19.
[145] Reg 20.
[146] Reg 21.
[147] SI 1996/913.
[148] Pt II.
[149] Pt IV.

all times possesses such integrity as is reasonably practicable".[150] In the case of wells, the duty is imposed on the well operator[151] to ensure that a well is utilised at all stages of its life in such a way that "so far as is reasonably practicable, there can be no unplanned escape of fluids" and that risks to health and safety are as low as is reasonably practicable.[152] In each case, more specific provisions follow which are expressly without prejudice to the generality of these duties.[153] In the case of integrity of installations, the more specific provisions relate to the design of, and work to, an installation;[154] operation of an installation;[155] maintenance of integrity;[156] reporting of danger to an installation;[157] and decommissioning and dismantlement.[158] In the case of wells, the more specific provisions relate to assessment of conditions below ground;[159] design with a view to suspension and abandonment;[160] fitness for purpose of materials;[161] well control;[162] arrangements for examination by independent persons of the well;[163] provision of drilling and other information relating to a well;[164] imposition of a duty of co-operation with the well operator on persons concerned in an operation relating to a well;[165] information, instruction, training and supervision.[166]

8.41　　Three other sets of regulations follow the same goal-setting approach as that contained in the instruments described above – the Pipelines Safety Regulations 1996;[167] the Diving at Work Regulations

---

[150] Reg 4(1).

[151] Defined by reg 2(1) as the person appointed by the concession owner to organise and supervise well operations, or in the absence of such an appointment the concession owner.

[152] Reg 13(1).

[153] Regs 4(2) and 13(2).

[154] Regs 5 and 6. Note that, uniquely among the regs in this instrument, a defence is provided by reg 22 to a person charged with contravention of these provisions. The defence is to the effect that the commission of the offence was the fault of another person (not being one of his employees) and that he took all reasonable care and exercised all due diligence to avoid the commission of the offence.

[155] Reg 7.

[156] Reg 8.

[157] Reg 9.

[158] Reg 10. Note that Pt III of and Sch I to the Design and Construction Regulations impose further requirements relating to installations, for example, with regard to the design and construction of helicopter landing areas.

[159] Reg 14.

[160] Reg 15.

[161] Reg 16.

[162] Reg 17.

[163] Reg 18.

[164] Reg 19.

[165] Reg 20.

[166] Reg 21.

[167] SI 1996/825. These revoke the Offshore Installations (Emergency Pipe-line Valve)

1997;[168] and the Lifting Operations and Lifting Equipment Regulations 1998[169] – but these will not be discussed in further detail here.

The goal-setting regulations discussed above also served in part 8.42 to give effect to the requirements of European Law in the shape of the Framework Directive on Safety at Work[170] and the Extractive Industries Directive.[171] Further general regulations covering both onshore and offshore industries were also introduced in 1992 to implement European requirements.[172]

All of this activity clearly indicates that, if nothing else, the 8.43 regulation of health and safety offshore during the 1990s changed out of all recognition. Now referred to as a *permissioning*

Regulations 1989 (SI 1989/680), the Regulations requiring the installation of emergency valves in the immediate aftermath of the Piper Alpha disaster.

[168] SI 1997/2776.

[169] SI 1998/2307.

[170] Council Directive 89/391/EEC of 12 June 1989 on the introduction of measures to encourage improvements in the safety and health of workers at work.

[171] Council Directive 92/91/EEC of 3 November 1992 concerning the minimum requirements for improving the safety and health protection of workers in the mineral-extracting industries through drilling (eleventh individual Directive within the meaning of Art 16(1) of Directive 89/391/EEC)

[172] Management of Health and Safety at Work Regulations 1992 (SI 1992/2051) (now replaced by SI 1999/3242) implementing the Framework Directive (n 173), Council Directive 92/85/EEC of 19 October 1992 on the introduction of measures to encourage improvements in the safety and health at work of pregnant workers and workers who have recently given birth or are breastfeeding (tenth individual Directive within the meaning of Art 16(1) of Directive 89/391/EEC) and Council Directive 94/33/EC of 22 June 1994 on the protection of young people at work; Provision and Use of Work Equipment Regulations 1992 (SI 1992/2932) (now replaced by SI 1998/2306) implementing Council Directive 89/655/EEC of 30 November 1989 concerning the minimum safety and health requirements for the use of work equipment by workers at work (second individual Directive within the meaning of Art 16(1) of Directive 89/391/EEC) itself amended by Directive 95/63; Manual Handling Operations Regulations 1992 (SI 1992/2793) implementing Council Directive 90/269/EEC of 29 May 1990 on the minimum health and safety requirements for the manual handling of loads where there is a risk particularly of back injury to workers (fourth individual Directive within the meaning of Art 16(1) of Directive 89/391/EEC); Personal Protective Equipment at Work Regulations 1992 (SI 1992/2966) implementing Council Directive of 30 November 1989 on the minimum health and safety requirements for the use by workers of personal protective equipment at the workplace (third individual directive within the meaning of Art 16(1) of Directive 89/391/EEC) (89/656/EEC); Personal Protective Equipment Regulations 1992 (SI 1992/3139) implementing Council Directive 89/686/EEC of 21 December 1989 on the approximation of the laws of the Member States relating to personal protective equipment; Health and Safety (Display Screen Equipment) Regulations 1992 (SI 1992/2792) implementing Council Directive 90/270/EEC of 29 May 1990 on the minimum safety and health requirements for work with display screen equipment (fifth individual Directive within the meaning of Art 16(1) of Directive 89/391/EEC)

approach,[173] it appeared to many to represent a significant step forward for what had been a problematic industry sector. And, indeed, during those years there was a tendency to suggest very much that a corner had been turned and that a cultural change had occurred in the industry's approach to safety. Some commentators, however, were less enthusiastic. Woolfson, Foster and Beck, for example, writing in 1996, suggested that this perception was due more to efforts on the part of the offshore industry to project a new safer image and to divert attention from ongoing health and safety problems.[174] These authors contended, indeed, that the new permissioning regime was inherently flawed. They had three principal concerns. first, safety cases placed the major burden of responsibility on line management in a highly technocratic way that few understood, especially because external consultants had often produced them. Second, the handling of compliance was also technocratic because the HSE now audited processes rather than checking to see if its regulations were being observed. The authors believed that goal-setting regulations could be effective only if anchored in genuine workforce involvement, and this was affected by their third concern, namely that there was a lack of trade union support for the safety representatives who formed the cornerstone of workforce involvement.[175]

The Offshore Installations (Safety Case) Regulations 2005

8.44   As evidence both that these criticisms may carry some weight and equally that the HSE adopts a proactive stance to the regulation of health and safety offshore, the 1992 Safety Regulations were repealed and replaced with an updated set in 2005.[176] That said, however, the appearance of new regulations might seem surprising, given that the 1992 Regulations explicitly envisaged change, with the safety case being understood as a living document that would evolve through the lifetime of an installation. The HSE noted, however, that the system in place under the 1992 Regulations was increasingly perceived to be excessively bureaucratic. Equally, while it was seen to have produced a significant change in the health and

---

[173] See, eg, Health and Safety Commission, *Policy Statement: Our Approach to Permissioning Regimes* (2003).

[174] Woolfson, Foster and Beck, n 66 above, pp 360–361.

[175] *Ibid*, p 346. For further critical comment, see D Whyte, "Moving the Goalposts: the Deregulation of Safety in the Post-Piper Alpha Offshore Oil Industry" (1997) *Contemporary Political Studies* 1148.

[176] Offshore Installations (Safety Case) Regulations 2005 (SI 2005/3117), which came into force on 6 April 2006.

safety situation offshore in the early years, each subsequent 3-year cycle of safety case resubmissions appeared to have produced less in the way of improvement.[177]

Thus, as regards the focus of the new regulations on bureaucracy, **8.45** a triennial resubmission of the safety case is no longer required, with this requirement replaced by a 5-yearly "thorough review" (or as directed by HSE).[178] Providing that specific safety cases are no longer required for combined operations, design, or decommissioning also reduces the burden of bureaucracy. In the first two instances, simpler notification procedures are in place,[179] while in the last a modification of the existing safety case is all that is required, albeit that this must be accepted by the HSE.[180] Note also that a right of appeal to the Secretary of State against a refusal to accept is introduced.[181]

Turning to the focus on diminishing returns, there are changes **8.46** to the requirements relating to workforce involvement and the demonstration of compliance. As regards workforce involvement, while this was already a feature of the 1992 Regulations, the revised approach requires that the safety case summarises consultation with the workforce not only with regard to its preparation but also its revision and review.[182] In other words, by these means, the regulator seeks to ensure that the workforce is directly engaged in the safety case process on an ongoing basis. As regards the demonstration of compliance, while the 1992 Regulations required a demonstration that major hazard risks had been reduced to a level "as low as reasonably practicable" (ALARP), the 2005 Regulations require that they are identified and evaluated, and that relevant statutory provisions will be complied with.[183] At first sight, this can appear to be a

---

[177] See generally: Health and Safety Commission, *Proposals to replace the Offshore Installations (Safety Case) Regulations 1992* (2004); and Health and Safety Commission, *A strategy for workplace health and safety in Great Britain to 2010 and beyond* (2004).

[178] 2005 Regulations, reg 13. Note that there is an exception to this rule where there are "material changes" which will still require to be accepted (reg 14). For further detail, see HSE, *Offshore Installations (Safety Case) Regulations 2005 Regulation 13: Thorough Review of a Safety Case*, Offshore Information Sheet No 4/2006; also HSE, *Procedure for dealing with thorough review summaries submitted under regulation 13 of the Offshore Installations (Safety Case) Regulations 2005* (2007).

[179] Regulation 10 (Notification of combined operations), reg 6 (Design and relocation notification for production installation) and reg 9(1) (Design notification in respect of a non-production installation). Note that the terms "fixed" and "mobile" used in the 1992 Regulations are thus replaced in the 2005 Regulations by "production" and "non-production" respectively.

[180] Reg 11 (Safety case for dismantling fixed installation).

[181] Reg 24.

[182] Sch 2, para 3. The Offshore Installations (Safety Representatives and Safety Committees) Regulations 1989 (SI 1989/971) are consequently amended.

[183] Reg 12.

retrograde step. In fact, the change reflects the recognition that the safety case regulations were not the appropriate location for the setting of standards. In so far as Lord Cullen had called for the replacement of the previous prescriptive regulations with goal-setting regulations, it is in these latter that standards should appear. Furthermore, in so far as there continue to be some prescriptive elements setting absolute standards,[184] there was actually a contradiction between these and the 1992 Regulations.[185] ALARP has not, therefore, disappeared from the offshore health and safety environment; rather it is now to be found only in the goal-setting regulations.[186]

8.47   In recognition of the changing character of the UKCS as a maturing province with the appearance of new and perhaps less experienced entrants,[187] the 2005 Regulations place a new duty on the licensee in respect of health and safety – a curious echo of the position in the Early Phase of the evolution of health and safety regulation offshore, albeit of a quite different nature. Thus, reg 5 provides that the licensee must ensure that "any operator appointed by him is capable of satisfactorily carrying out his functions and discharging his duties under the relevant statutory provisions" and then "take all reasonable steps to ensure" that the operator does indeed behave in this way. As the HSE's guidance makes clear, if in its opinion "the operator appointed by the licensee is unable to discharge the management and control functions, the duty to submit the safety case and other related duties will revert to the licensee".[188] The licensee will accordingly have to take particular care in the appointment of the operator if it is not to be faced with a considerable regulatory burden that it itself may struggle to cope with.

8.48   Similar concerns arising from the changing character of the maturing province lie behind the alteration in the definition of "operator" in the 2005 Regulations. Whereas in the 1992 Regulations, this was defined in relation to a fixed installation as "the person appointed by a concession owner to execute any function of organising or supervising any operation to be carried out by such installation", this is now defined in relation to a production installation as "the person appointed by the licensee to manage and control directly *or by any other person* the execution of the main

---

[184] As discussed previously. See paras 8.38–8.39.

[185] See HSE, *Offshore Installations (Safety Case) Regulations 2005 Regulation 12: Demonstrating compliance with the relevant statutory provisions*, Offshore Information Sheet No 2/2006.

[186] As discussed previously. See paras 8.38–8.41.

[187] See further in Chapter 5.

[188] HSE, *Offshore Installations (Safety Case) Regulations: Guidance*, Operations Notice 71, May 2006. See also the definition of "operator" in reg 2.

functions" of such an installation.[189] The net effect is to emphasise to operators that while they can delegate functions to contractors, this does not absolve them of their responsibilities under health and safety legislation and regulations.

A further change is to be found in new guidance issued by the 8.49 HSE with regard to risk assessment.[190] Here the regulator notes that the 1992 Regulations focused attention on QRA, which often required specialist consultants to be involved.[191] While this is seen to have been useful in the post-Piper Alpha era, the regulator believes that the understanding of offshore risks is now mature. Accordingly, it believes that risk assessment should focus on adding value and be management owned rather than consultant owned.[192] The guidance notes that risk assessment should be proportionate to the complexity of the problem in hand and the magnitude of risk. QRA thus features only where the risk level and the complexity of a problem are high, with qualitative and semi-quantitative approaches being identified as appropriate for lower level situations.[193] Lest this should be read as a lessening of the level of responsibility rather than just a lessening of the regulatory burden, the guidance makes clear, first, that the main purpose of risk assessment is to decide whether more needs to be done to reduce risk and, second, that the duty holder must demonstrate that risks are controlled and are not intolerable.[194]

With the appearance of the 2005 Regulations, therefore, it 8.50 could have been assumed that the regulatory regime for health and safety at work offshore had reached a stage of maturity commensurate with the challenge of the maturing province. As the concluding sentence of this chapter in the first edition of this book warned, however, the characteristics of the mature province might only have been beginning to test the ability of the permissioning approach. And, within a very short time, significant doubts were indeed raised.

---

[189] Reg 2 (emphasis added).

[190] HSE, *Guidance on Risk Assessment for Offshore Installations*, Offshore Information Sheet No 3/2006 (hereinafter "Guidance on Risk Assessment").

[191] It is a question whether this is a problem unique to the offshore oil and gas industry. Recall that the reasoning behind Lord Cullen's recommendation of QRA was evidence from the HSE that it used this approach as a means of founding legal or political judgements as much as possible on a rigorous scrutiny of the facts because the technologically based industries or scientifically numerate organisations it dealt with expected a structured and logical approach. See n 82 above.

[192] Guidance on Risk Assessment, p 2.

[193] *Ibid*, p 3.

[194] *Ibid*, pp 8–9.

Key Programme 3: Asset Integrity

8.51   While conducting a major effort from 2000 to 2004 to reduce hydrocarbon releases offshore, the HSE "became increasingly concerned
about an apparent general decline in the condition of fabric and
plant on installations".[195] As a consequence a further initiative was
set up to run between 2004 and 2007, focused on the issue of asset
integrity, designated "Key Programme 3 (KP3)". Around 100 installations (or 40 per cent of the total on the UKCS) were inspected, with
the concentration on the maintenance management of safety-critical
elements. The HSE defined *asset integrity* as "the ability of an asset
to perform its required function effectively and efficiently whilst
protecting health, safety and the environment" and *safety-critical
elements* as "the parts of an installation and its plant ... whose
purpose is to prevent, control or mitigate major accident hazards
... and the failure of which could cause or contribute substantially
to a major accident", while *maintenance management* in relation
to safety critical elements was understood to be "the management
systems and processes which should ensure that [such elements]
would be available when required".[196]

8.52   Given the very close connection between these issues and the idea
of the safety case as a "living document" designed to ensure the
ongoing safe operation of an installation, KP3's findings are sobering
to say the least. With regard to maintenance management, there was
considerable variation both across the industry and between installations within the same company. Problems arose because there
was difficulty in keeping track of which equipment was defective
or overdue for maintenance.[197] Very strikingly, given the claimed
advances in the years following the Piper Alpha disaster, the HSE
found that there was "a poor understanding across the industry
of [the] potential impact of degraded, non-safety-critical plant and
utility systems on safety-critical elements in the event of a major
accident"[198] and that "the role of asset integrity and [the] concept of
barriers in major hazard risk control" was "not well understood".[199]
A finding that might have cheered observers of safety on the UKCS
in the seventies, to the effect that monitoring by management tended
to focus on occupational safety, was nevertheless problematical in

---

[195] Health and Safety Executive, *Key Programme 3: Asset Integrity Programme: A Report
of the Offshore Division of the HSE's Hazardous Installations Directorate*, November
2007 (hereinafter "KP3"), p 5.
[196] *Ibid*, p 5.
[197] *Ibid*, pp 11–13.
[198] *Ibid*, p 6. See also p 13.
[199] *Ibid*, p 6.

so far as it thus served to mask the significance of "major accident precursors".[200]

As regards the condition of the infrastructure as a whole, the HSE was heartened to find that structural integrity was "well controlled" and the main hydrocarbon boundary "reasonably well controlled", but concerned that other parts of the hydrocarbon infrastructure such as pipes and valves were in decline – again a very striking finding given the resonance with the circumstances of Piper Alpha disaster.[201] There was also evidence of the low oil price having prompted deferrals in maintenance that had not been reversed, especially where there were plans to sell on assets in due course. Not surprisingly, this state of affairs was having an adverse effect on workforce morale.[202] Again calling into question the ongoing significance of the safety case as a "living document", the HSE also found that there was insufficient testing of safety-critical elements leading to diminished reliability.[203]   8.53

By way of an explanation for these deficiencies, the HSE identified three underlying problems relating to *learning*, the *engineering function* and *leadership*. As regards the first of these, there was seen to be a problem both of inadequate auditing and monitoring and of a lack of processes to allow learning to be embedded.[204] In so far as auditing and monitoring are supposed to be integral parts of the sort of safety management system prioritised in the setting of the safety case, this appears to indicate a significant failure of the permissioning approach to safety offshore. As regards the second underlying problem, the issue here was the relative strength of the engineering function in companies which was seen to have declined "to a worrying level".[205] While the report was not explicit as to which other functions engineering had lost out to, it may be inferred that these are related to finance – a conclusion borne out by the third underlying problem identified above. With regard to leadership, the HSE noted that senior management in setting priorities for spending had to balance safety and financial risks and often did not properly understand the impact on these risks of operating with "degraded [safety critical elements] and safety-related equipment".[206] This lack of understanding, coupled with the HSE's findings that well-publicised findings during KP3 were not being acted upon even as the   8.54

---

[200] KP3, p 6.
[201] *Ibid.*
[202] *Ibid.*
[203] *Ibid*, p 7.
[204] *Ibid*, p 8.
[205] *Ibid.*
[206] *Ibid.*

programme proceeded,[207] does raise the possibility that cost factors were predominant in a way that the safety case approach might have been supposed to have made impossible given its emphasis on risk and safety assessment on an ongoing basis.[208] It is one thing for such a problematical balancing of safety and financial risks to emerge in the context of a review such as KP3. It would be quite another were it to emerge in the context of a prosecution or litigation following a serious accident. In this regard, the fact that the HSE's concerns about the relative weights accorded safety and financial risks are now on the record is not insignificant. Furthermore, this observation takes on increased importance given two statutory developments affecting health and safety at work since the first edition of this book was published: the Corporate Manslaughter and Corporate Homicide Act 2007 and the Health and Safety (Offences) Act 2008.

The Corporate Manslaughter and Corporate Homicide Act 2007

8.55 Even before this Act came into force on 6 April 2008 it was possible for a company to be prosecuted in the event that a person had died as a result of the company's activities. The law was, however, criticised in so far as the requirement that the "directing mind" of the company be identified meant that prosecution of small companies was considerably easier than that of large companies, notwithstanding that the activities of the latter perhaps had greater potential to result in more serious accidents and multiple fatalities.[209]

---

[207] KP3, p 6.

[208] That such an interpretation is by no means unreasonable may be inferred from the comments of the Chief Executive of Petrofac, Ayman Asfari, at the Oil and Money Conference in October 2008, where he indicated that "his company had seen installations which were in bad need of repair", that he feared "firms will fail to spend enough in improvements" and that he was "concerned that the industry would end up in a situation where budgets were curtailed, leading to more risk of accidents". Oil and Gas UK disagreed with this sentiment whereas the offshore arm of the RMT Union indicated that this served to confirm its warnings in this regard. See BBC news online at http://news.bbc.co.uk/1/hi/scotland/north_east/7696232.stm (accessed 26 April 2011). The fact that the offshore industry was criticised by the Chair of the HSE at this time in relation to its accident statistics for problems relating to the "control of potential major incident risks" would tend to suggest that the Chairman of Petrofac and the RMT had a point. See HSE Press Release E039:08, 13 August 2008.

[209] The first successful prosecution was precisely of a small company with only one director: R v Kite and OLL Ltd (1994) (unreported). For an accessible discussion of this case, see M G Welham, Corporate Killing: A Manager's Guide to Legal Compliance (2002), pp 51–59. See also G Slapper, "Litigation and corporate crime" (1997) Journal of Personal Injury Litigation, 220–233. For the preceding position in Scotland, see Transco plc v HM Advocate 2004 SLT 41. For a discussion, see J Chalmers, "Corporate culpable homicide: Transco plc v HM Advocate" (2004) 8 Edinburgh Law Review 2, 262–266.

An organisation[210] is guilty of the new offence (corporate   8.56
manslaughter in England and Wales or Northern Ireland, corporate
homicide in Scotland[211]) "if the way in which its activities are
managed or organised (a) causes a person's death, and (b) amounts
to a gross breach of a relevant duty of care owed by the organisation
to the deceased".[212] The offence is only committed if the way in
which the organisation's "activities are managed or organised by its
senior management is a substantial element" in the breach of duty.[213]

There are clearly a number of concepts within this definition of the   8.57
offence which require further clarification. A "relevant duty of care"
includes duties owed by the organisation under the law of negligence
(or under a supervening statutory provision[214]) "to its employees
or to other persons working for the organisation or performing
services for it",[215] thus readily covering the situation on an offshore
installation where in addition to the employees of the operator there
may be many workers present who are employed by a range of
contractors and subcontractors. With regard to the potential liability
of contractors or subcontractors in the same setting, it is significant
that the concept of a "relevant duty of care" is further defined *inter
alia* to include "the supply by the organisation of goods or services",
"the carrying on by the organisation of any construction or maintenance operations", "the carrying on by the organisation of any other
activity on a commercial basis", or "the use or keeping by the organisation of any plant, vehicle or other thing".[216] A breach of a relevant
duty of care is a "gross breach" where the conduct in question "falls
far below what can reasonably be expected of the organisation in
the circumstances".[217] This raises intriguing possibilities should there
ever be a prosecution for a fatality on an offshore installation given
that this is an industry where an operator will have set out in detail
how it is going to behave in an installation's safety case.[218] The court
will thereby be provided with a ready guide as to what the operator
itself (and by implication the HSE through the fact of acceptance

---

[210] An "organisation" for the purposes of the Act includes a corporation and a partnership:
Corporate Manslaughter and Corporate Homicide Act 2007, s 2. "Corporation" is defined
in s 25 to include a "body corporate" and is thus broad enough to encompass a limited
liability partnership.
[211] 2007 Act, s 1(5). Note that the Act applies in relation to offshore installations by virtue
of s 28(3)(e).
[212] 2007 Act, s 1(1).
[213] *Ibid*, s 1(3).
[214] *Ibid*, s 2(4).
[215] *Ibid*, s 2(1)(a).
[216] *Ibid*, s 2(1)(c).
[217] *Ibid*, s 1(4)(b).
[218] See the 2005 Regulations, discussed at paras 8.44–8.50.

of the safety case[219]) would have regarded as reasonable in the circumstances. As regards "senior management", this is defined as the persons in an organisation who "play significant roles in (i) the making of decisions about how the whole or a substantial part of its activities are to be managed or organised, or (ii) the actual managing or organising of the whole or a substantial part of those activities".[220] Note that the individuals themselves are not the target of the Act – only an organisation can be prosecuted[221] – but the behaviour of the senior management will be subject to close scrutiny because it is ultimately this that will determine whether there has been the required breach of duty.[222]

8.58   Where it is established that a relevant duty of care is owed, it is then a matter for the jury to decide whether or not there has been a gross breach of that duty. In so doing, the Act specifies that there are certain issues which the jury *must* consider and certain that it *may* consider or have regard to. With regard to the former, these are stated to be "whether the evidence shows that the organisation failed to comply with any health and safety legislation that relates to the alleged breach, and if so (a) how serious that failure was; (b) how much of a risk of death it posed".[223] As regards the latter, the jury may "consider the extent to which the evidence shows that there were attitudes, policies, systems or accepted practices within the organisation that were likely to have encouraged any [such failure] or to have produced tolerance of it" (again raising questions related to the HSE's findings, for example, of a problematical balancing of financial and safety risk in KP3) and may "have regard to any health and safety guidance that relates to the alleged breach".[224] The jury may also have regard to any other factor which it considers relevant.[225]

8.59   Note that an organisation charged under the 2007 Act may simultaneously face charges under health and safety legislation.[226]

8.60   As regards the penalty which may be imposed in the event of conviction, this takes the form of an unlimited fine.[227] Since 15 February 2010, sentencing guidelines have been in place for

---

[219] 2005 Regulations.

[220] 2007 Act, s 1(4)(c).

[221] See also 2007 Act, s 18 in this regard.

[222] It remains open to the prosecution, of course, to bring separate charges against any individual in connection with the death, including members of the senior management.

[223] 2007 Act, s 8(2).

[224] *Ibid*, s 8(3).

[225] *Ibid*, s 8(4). See also s 8(5) for the broad definition of "guidance" in this context.

[226] See also para 8.63.

[227] 2007 Act, s 1(6).

convictions for corporate manslaughter in England and Wales.[228] These guidelines provide courts with criteria with which to judge the seriousness of the offence they are dealing with, including the foreseeability of serious injury, the extent to which the defendant has fallen short of the appropriate standard, whether this is an isolated or more common event, and the level within the organisation at which the breach occurs.[229] Other factors are additionally offered in a non-exhaustive list as potentially aggravating the offence, including multiple deaths, deliberate failures, and injuries to the vulnerable.[230] Among the factors included in this second list, two stand out as particularly relevant to the offshore oil and gas industry in light of the findings of the KP3 Asset Integrity Programme discussed in the foregoing section of this chapter, namely "cost-cutting at the expense of safety" and "failure to heed warnings or advice", especially from HSE inspectors and health and safety representatives, or failure "to respond appropriately to 'near misses'".[231] On the other hand, where a convicted organisation has accepted responsibility without delay, co-operated in the investigation, tried genuinely to put right what has gone wrong, or has "a good health and safety record" or "a responsible attitude to health and safety", these factors are likely to have a mitigating effect.[232] As regards the fixing of the fine, the courts are reminded that it "must be punitive and sufficient to have an impact on the defendant."[233] As an indication of what this will mean in practice, the guidelines suggest that for corporate manslaughter the appropriate fine "will seldom be less than £500,000 and may be measured in millions of pounds".[234] The courts may consider the impact of any fine on the employment of the innocent, but the impact on directors or shareholders will not normally be taken into account.[235] It is noteworthy that the 2007 Act also makes provision for publicity orders[236] and remedial orders[237] and the guidelines also offer assistance to the courts in deciding whether and how to make

---

[228] Sentencing Guidelines Council, *Corporate Manslaughter and Health and Safety Offences Causing Death: Definitive Guideline*, February 2010 (hereinafter "Sentencing Guidelines"), available online at: http://www.sentencingcouncil.org.uk/docs/web__guideline_on_corporate_manslaughter_accessible.pdf (accessed 26 April 2011).
[229] Sentencing Guidelines, para 6.
[230] *Ibid*, para 7.
[231] *Ibid*.
[232] *Ibid*, para 8.
[233] *Ibid*, para 22.
[234] *Ibid*, para 24.
[235] *Ibid*, para 19.
[236] 2007 Act, s 10.
[237] *Ibid*, s 9.

such orders.[238] While there is no such guidance in Scotland, it must be assumed that the Scottish courts would take similar issues into account in sentencing following a conviction for corporate homicide under s 1 of the 2007 Act.

8.61   It is not yet clear how the Act will work out in practice. The progress of the first prosecution to be brought has been delayed by the ill health of the managing director who had also been charged with gross negligence manslaughter. The trial of both the company and the managing director was initially adjourned, but the medical condition of the latter has now led to the court agreeing to stay the prosecution against him permanently. The trial of the company will now recommence in early 2011,[239] but there must be doubts that the prosecution of what is a very small company in circumstances where someone who is evidently a key member of the senior management will be unavailable will really provide a clear indication of the way in which the courts are likely to interpret the 2007 Act.

The Health and Safety (Offences) Act 2008

8.62   Section 1 of this Act, which came into force on 16 January 2009, amends s 33 of the Health and Safety at Work, etc Act 1974. Section 33 specifies the offences which may be committed under the 1974 Act and the amendments to that section give effect to a new Schedule[240] which sets out the mode of trial and the maximum sentence which applies in the case of each of the offences listed in s 33(1). With regard to prosecution for breach of the key duty under s 2 of the 1974 Act,[241] the penalty on summary conviction rises from a fine not exceeding £20,000 to imprisonment for a period not exceeding 6 months or a fine not exceeding £20,000 or both, while the penalty for conviction on indictment rises from an unlimited fine to imprisonment for a period not exceeding 2 years or an unlimited fine or both.[242]

8.63   With regard to the prosecution of bodies corporate under the 1974 Act for offences causing death, while imprisonment is of course not a possibility, it is very important to note that the sentencing guidelines discussed in the previous section of this chapter will also apply. Accordingly, even where a body corporate is not charged with

---

[238] Sentencing Guidelines, paras 30–32 and 33–36.

[239] L Ponting, "First Corporate Manslaughter Trial Delayed Again", 15 October 2010, available online at: http://www.healthandsafetyatwork.com/hsw/Eaton-charges (accessed 26 April 2011).

[240] Sch 3A.

[241] The employer's duty "to ensure, so far as is reasonably practicable, the health, safety and welfare at work of all his employees".

[242] Sch 3A, para 1.

corporate manslaughter or corporate homicide under the 2007 Act, but only with offences under the 1974 Act causing death,[243] the possibility of very substantial fines must be considered.[244]

Furthermore, in so far as s 37 of the 1974 Act provides that where 8.64 an offence committed by a body corporate "is proved to have been committed with the consent or connivance of, or to have been attributable to any neglect on the part of, any director, manager" or other corporate officer, that individual shall also be guilty of the offence and liable to be dealt with accordingly, it is clear that the 2008 Act also has very profound implications for senior management.[245]

Taken together, the 2007 and 2008 Acts have radically altered the 8.65 health and safety landscape for bodies corporate and their senior managers, with considerably more severe penalties now available to the courts. Quite how these will play out in practice remains to be seen, but the HSE made its intentions clear when the 2008 Act came into force, stating that it would "continue to target those who knowingly cut corners, put lives at risk and who gain commercial advantage over competitors by failing to comply with the law".[246]

Possible effects of the Deepwater Horizon accident on UK offshore safety regulation

While the legislative changes discussed in the foregoing sections have 8.66 radically altered the health and safety landscape of the offshore oil and gas industry for bodies corporate and their senior management in terms of the penalties for breaches of duties, the Deepwater Horizon accident in the Gulf of Mexico in April 2010 has the potential to produce effects on the very orientation of health and safety regulation on the UKCS.

In the immediate aftermath of the disaster, the Secretary of State 8.67 for Energy and Climate Change announced a review of relevant legislation and regulation in the UK, which found relatively quickly that the existing regime was "fit for purpose".[247] That there is no complacency, however, is evident from the fact that further investigations are ongoing, both on the side of the regulators and that of the industry. The HSE, for example, has established a Deepwater Horizon Review Group which is reviewing the findings of the investigation

---

[243] Or, of course, is charged under the 2007 Act and under the 1974 Act in the alternative.
[244] Sentencing Guidelines, para 24.
[245] For further discussion of the 2008 Act generally, see B Barrett, "The Health and Safety (Offences) Act 2008: The Cost of Behaving Dangerously at the Workplace", *Industrial Law Journal*, vol 38, March 2009, 73–79.
[246] HSE Press Release E011:09, 15 January 2009.
[247] DECC Press Release: PN10/067, UK increases North Sea rig inspections, 8 June 2010.

into the accident and which will inter alia "make recommendations as necessary with regard to the control of wells and the safety of the exploitation of offshore oil and gas in the UK".[248] Meanwhile, Oil & Gas UK has set up the Oil Spill Prevention and Response Advisory Group (OSPRAG), which brings together industry, regulators and trade unions "to provide a focal point for the sector's review of the industry's practices in the UK, in advance of the conclusion of investigations into the Gulf of Mexico incident".[249] Finally, the House of Commons Energy and Climate Change Select Committee has heard oral evidence and received written submissions from a range of stakeholders in relation to deepwater development.[250]

8.68   Whether all of this activity will result in any changes to the UK's regulatory approach to offshore safety remains an open question at the time of writing, but the clear impression being given by both industry and government is that the safety case approach makes the occurrence of a Deepwater Horizon-style event much less likely on the UKCS. Whether that confidence is shared by the EU institutions who have also taken a very close interest in the wider implications of events in the Gulf of Mexico is a moot point. Both the European Parliament in its resolution of 7 October 2010[251] and the European Commission in its communication of 12 October 2010[252] indicate that legislative action is necessary at a European level – perhaps in the form of (but by no means necessarily restricted to) an amendment of the Extractive Industries Directive.[253] One might be tempted to read references in these documents to existing best practice[254] as an indication that other Member States will be expected to adopt the UK's approach, but in so far as the Parliament refers specifically to only one Member State in its resolution and in so far as that is a negative reference to the latest serious injury and fatality statistics

---

[248] Details online at: http://www.hse.gov.uk/offshore/deepwater.htm (accessed 26 April 2011).
[249] Details online at: http://www.oilandgasuk.co.uk/knowledgecentre/OSPRAG.cfm (accessed 26 April 2011).
[250] Interestingly, this committee is not only concerned with the adequacy of the regulatory regime, but also with knowing more about the contribution that will be made by deepwater resources to the UK's energy security and with understanding whether such development will actually be necessary in the context of the objective of transition to a low-carbon economy. Details online at: http://www.parliament.uk/business/committees/committees-a-z/commons-select/energy-and-climate-change-committee/inquiries/uk-deepwater-drilling/ (accessed 26 April 2011).
[251] European Parliament resolution of 7 October 2010 on EU action on oil exploration and extraction in Europe (hereinafter "Parliament Resolution").
[252] European Commission, Communication from the Commission to the European Parliament and the Council: Facing the challenge of the safety of offshore oil and gas activities, SEC(2010) 1193 final (hereinafter "Commission Communication").
[253] Directive 92/91/EEC. See para 8.42.
[254] For example, Commission Communication, pp 3 and 5.

reported by the HSE,[255] then that might be a dangerous temptation to give in to. The wording of Parliament's resolution is much more emotive and the action it calls for is much more far-reaching than in the Commission's communication, but it would be naïve to think that the latter communication sets out anything other than a very comprehensive programme of evaluating the status quo across the EU and a robust attitude to legislative action should that prove to be necessary. The Commission's intentions in this regard also need to be read in the context of its growing interest in the question of an integrated maritime policy and its enthusiasm for a much more coherent approach than currently exists.[256] Given the potential impact of an event on the scale of Deepwater Horizon, it is likely to prove very difficult to suggest that the regulation of offshore safety should lie outside of any new integrated approach.

CONCLUSIONS

The regulation of health and safety at work offshore has had a long, complex and sometimes troubled history. Three distinct approaches have been successively adopted, ranging from what amounted to self-regulation in the Early Phase, through detailed prescriptive regulation in the Middle Phase, to the permissioning approach of the Late Phase. This chapter has deliberately adopted an historical approach to this subject because the significance of the current approach is more easily appreciated if what has gone before is understood. It is also striking to note how early on in the process the particular problems the current approach seeks to deal with were recognised but not acted upon. The appropriateness of the permissioning approach becomes more apparent when that point is grasped. Be that as it may, the fact that the character of the UKCS is changing quite profoundly in the context of a maturing province will challenge the permissioning approach. In so far as that maturity must increasingly be read to include not only the ageing of assets but also the push into deeper water and the engagement with more demanding reservoirs, the challenges become all the clearer – not least when one considers the possible impact of the Deepwater Horizon accident

8.69

---

[255] Parliament Resolution, para 25. See also HSE, Offshore Safety Statistics Bulletin 2009/2010, available online at: http://www.hse.gov.uk/offshore/statistics/stat0910.htm (accessed 26 April 2011).
[256] Commission Communication, para 4. See also Communication from the Commission to the European Parliament, the Council, the European Economic and Social Committee and the Committee of the Regions, An Integrated Maritime Policy for the European Union, COM(2007) 575 final. For updated details, see http://ec.europa.eu/maritimeaffairs/ (accessed 26 April 2011).

and the renewed interest of the European Commission in the way that offshore health and safety are regulated. If the permissioning approach is felt by the Commission to be lacking in any way, will this inevitably mean a return to greater prescription? If so, what does the UK's past experience with that approach say about the wisdom of any move in that direction? The story of health and safety at work offshore is far from over.

CHAPTER 9

ENVIRONMENTAL LAW AND REGULATION ON THE UKCS

Luke Havemann

"When the North Sea was first opened up for exploration and production, the Government did not consider it necessary to put in place any special legislation to protect the environment ... the environmental impact of the offshore industry was not obvious; exploration and production activity was not seen as a serious source of pollution."[1]

While the attitude of government revealed in the opening quotation **9.1** has given way in due course to a quite different appreciation of the environmental risks involved and a veritable "raft of regulatory provisions governing the environmental aspects of offshore oil – and gas – activities",[2] it is surely true that offshore exploration and production activities on the UKCS in and of themselves have not figured prominently in the public or indeed political imagination as significant potential sources of pollution – in contrast, for example, to tanker operations.[3] The events in the Gulf of Mexico in 2010, however, have surely profoundly changed that situation.[4] The leak of an unprecedented volume of oil from a BP-operated well, following an explosion aboard the drilling rig Deepwater Horizon

---

[1] J Rowan Robinson, "Environmental and Planning Law" in A Hill (ed), *Daintith, Willoughby and Hill: United Kingdom Oil and Gas Law* (2000) at 1281.

[2] J Kearns, "Environmental Management" in J Wils and E C Neilson (eds), *The Technical and Legal Guide to the UK Oil and Gas Industry* (2007), p 537.

[3] Notable spills from tankers in UK waters include the *Torrey Canyon* in 1967, *Braer* in 1993 and *Sea Empress* in 1996. For details, see J Sheail, *An Environmental History of Twentieth-Century Britain* (2002), pp 221*ff*; and M Regester and J Larkin, *Risk Issues and Crisis Management in Public Relations: A Casebook of Best Practice* (4th edn, 2008), pp 176*ff* and 180*ff*.

[4] For up-to-date information on the incident, see http://www.deepwaterinvestigation.com (accessed 11 April 2011).

which claimed 11 lives, may not have been the first time that hydro-carbons have flowed uncontrolled from a well into the sea,[5] but the last significant event was sufficiently long ago to have persuaded both the industry and its regulators that technology and procedures were now adequately developed and embedded as to justify confidence in existing regulatory arrangements. This situation has been questioned in the US in so far as the same government body that was responsible for managing oil, gas and other mineral reserves on the US Continental Shelf is no longer responsible also for the safety of operations and their possible impact on the environment,[6] but it is interesting to note that this apparent problem of regulatory architecture is not such a feature of the UKCS approach – the body responsible for the safety regulation of hydrocarbon operations in the UK is separate from the industry's sponsoring department. This is not the case, however, with environmental regulation. The evidence from the regulators to the Energy and Climate Change Select Committee considering the implications of the Gulf of Mexico oil spill was nevertheless to the effect that the current arrangements are fit for purpose and the committee was not minded to depart from that assessment.[7] Whether the European Commission is equally sanguine remains to be seen. It will be interesting to see whether this initiative recommends any changes to what has hitherto been regarded as a comprehensive regulatory regime – not least because of the way in which it dovetails with the goal-setting safety case approach to health and safety offshore, discussed in Chapter 8. As this chapter will demonstrate, the indications are that the regime is robust and that, provided the obligations imposed continue to be taken seriously by both regulator and industry, the prospects are good. The one issue in particular that threatens this optimistic conclusion (and indeed that looms over so many of the issues discussed in this volume) is the fact of the maturity of the province. It will be a matter of considering whether and how this issue may undermine the very good record enjoyed by the industry on the UKCS over the past 20 years with regard to environmental protection. Before that point is reached, however, this chapter will provide an overview of the key legislative and regulatory instruments that address the environmental impact of the industry's offshore exploration, development and production

---

[5] The Santa Barbara oil spill off California in 1969 was a turning point in the attitude of US authorities to offshore drilling. See A J Hoffman, *From Heresy to Dogma: An Institutional History of Corporate Environmentalism* (2001), pp 57–58.

[6] For details of the role of the Minerals Management Service in environmental stewardship, see http://www.mms.gov/eppd/index.htm (accessed 11 April 2011).

[7] Available at: http://www.publications.parliament.uk/pa/cm201011/cmselect/cmenergy/ 450/45002.htm (accessed 11 April 2011).

activities. The following section deals with the environmental aspects of petroleum licences generally, already touched upon in Chapter 4, as well as the regulations affecting licensing. The remainder of the chapter is then divided into two broad sections, the first of which considers the environmental regulations that have an impact on activities carried out under an exploration licence (that is, surveying and shallow drilling), while the second considers those that touch on activities carried out under a production licence.[8] Conclusions are then drawn in the final section.

THE ENVIRONMENTAL ASPECTS OF PETROLEUM LICENCES GENERALLY

As discussed in Chapter 4, oil and gas exploration, development and production activities on the UKCS proceed on the basis of licences issued by the Secretary of State under powers granted to him by s 3(1) of the Petroleum Act 1998. In so far as such licences may be granted on such terms and conditions as the Secretary of State thinks fit, the starting point in any consideration of the environmental obligations to which those engaged in offshore hydrocarbon operations are subject must be the Model Clauses which are published from time to time.   9.2

Petroleum Licensing (Exploration and Production) (Seaward and Landward Areas) Regulations 2004[9]

The Exploration Regulations are divided into Schedules according to the type of licence to which they apply.[10] Exploration licences are governed by the model clauses contained in Sch 1,[11] while production licences, which were issued prior to the advent of the Production Regulations on 6 April 2008, are governed by the model clauses contained in Schs 2 through 5.[12] In so far as the Model Clauses for production licences issued after that date are now the subject of later regulations to be discussed in the next section,[13] the discussion here will be confined to those relevant to exploration licences.   9.3

---

[8] The decommissioning phase of course presents its own environmental challenges. These are considered separately in Chapter 10.

[9] SI 2004/352.

[10] See Model Cl 3(1)–(8). In accordance with Model Cl 3(7) and (8), read with the definition of "petroleum exploration and development licence" contained in Model Cl 2, Schs 6 and 7 apply to landward licences and will therefore not be discussed.

[11] Model Cl 3(2).

[12] Model Cl 3(3)–(6).

[13] See paras 9.10–9.13.

9.4   Perhaps the first noteworthy model clause of Sch 1 is Model Cl
1(2), which provides that, whenever the licensee is more than one
person, all obligations are joint and several. Thus, although it is not
an expressly environmental clause, joint and several liability is a
positive enforcement mechanism as it ensures that, should persons
renege on the terms of their licence (including any environmental
obligations), others who are party thereto can be held accountable.
Additionally, obligations may be enforced against whoever is the
most suitable of the persons constituting the licensee: for example,
where there are two companies constituting the licensee, the election
may be made to pursue the wealthier company, which may be far
more capable of ensuring adherence to the obligations attached to
the relevant exploration licence. Concomitantly, where a licensee
is more than one person, such persons are unable to allocate the
obligations among themselves and thus to choose a potential
"scapegoat" should they renege on their obligations. In other words,
such persons are prohibited from arranging that the Minister has
access to only the "shallowest pocket". This may appear to be a very
obvious point, but such joint and several liability is not a feature of
the petroleum licences of every jurisdiction, potentially exposing the
states in question to the risk that they will be left to deal with the
aftermath of any unfulfilled obligations.[14]

9.5   Model Cl 7(1) and (2) provide that a licensee may not commence
(or recommence) the drilling of a well, or abandon a well, without
the written consent of the Minister, the environmental benefit of
which is that all drilling and abandonment activities are brought to
the attention of the relevant authorities. It is only once the DECC is
aware of a licensee's desire to undertake such activities that it is able
to take steps to ensure that they are conducted in accordance with
the relevant environmental regulations.[15] There are two noteworthy
instances where, in relation to abandonment, a lack of written consent
from the Minister is not sufficient cause not to commence with the
plugging of wells.[16] First, there is an obligation on a licensee to plug
all the wells in the exploration area to which the licence applies not
less than 1 month prior to the expiry (or further determination) of

---

[14] At the time of writing, this is the case, for example, in South Africa.

[15] Notably, Model Cl 7(4) provides that where the granting of ministerial consent in
accordance with Model Cl 7(1) is conditional upon the position, depth or direction or
casing of the well to be drilled, the Minister may direct that the well and all records
relating thereto be examined by persons of his choosing. Likewise, Model Cl 7(4) provides
that when determining whether or not to grant consent to plug or seal a well in accordance
with reg 7(2), the Minister may direct that the well and all records relating thereto are
examined by persons of his choosing.

[16] Model Cl 7(2), read with Model Cll 2, 7(5) and (6).

its licence rights, unless the Minister determines otherwise.[17] Second, where a licence is already in force in a particular area, an exploration licence for that area may be granted only through agreement between the prospective licensee and the original licence-holder. Where such an agreement results in the original licence-holder's rights ceasing to be exercisable for the time being, or when the agreement between the original and prospective licensee terminates, the licensee must plug its wells within 1 month after the date on which its rights cease to be exercisable, unless the Minister determines otherwise.[18] Irrespective of whether the abandonment and plugging of wells occurs with or without ministerial consent, Model Cl 7(7) provides that "[t]he plugging of any well shall be done in accordance with a specification approved by the Minister ... and shall be carried out in an efficient and workmanlike manner".

Abandonment and plugging of wells aside, exploration   9.6
licensees are bound to maintain in "good repair and condition" all apparatus, appliances and wells which have not been abandoned or plugged[19] and carry out all operations in a "proper and workmanlike manner in accordance with methods and practice of exploration customarily used in good oilfield practice".[20] However, the phrases "proper and workmanlike manner" and "good oilfield practice" are problematic, having been described as "simplistic and vague".[21] The DECC has, however, stated that good oilfield practice "relates largely to technical matters within the disciplines of geology and ... engineering and to the impact of ... [oil and gas] development[s] on the environment".[22] This statement does not, however, constitute a binding definition and fails to address the issue of how competing interests are balanced. For example, from a geological and reservoir engineering perspective it may be highly appropriate to conduct extensive seismic surveys, yet from

---

[17] Model Cl 7(6).

[18] Model Cl 7(5).

[19] Model Cl 9(1).

[20] Model Cl 9(2).

[21] Z Gao (ed), Environmental Regulation of Oil and Gas (1998), p 13. See also T Daintith and G Willoughby UK Oil and Gas Law (1996), para 5386, who note, for example, that "[t]he expression 'good oilfield practice' is widely used ... but no indication is given of where such practice may be found". See generally: M A G Bunter, The Promotion and Licensing of Petroleum Prospective Acreage (2002), pp 309–310; and I L Worika, "Environmental Terms and Concepts in Petroleum Legislation and Contracts" in Z Gao (ed), Environmental Regulation of Oil and Gas at pp 393–413.

[22] DECC, Guidance notes on procedures for regulating offshore oil and gas developments, https://www.og.decc.gov.uk/upstream/field_development/programme.htm (accessed 11 April 2011).

an environmental impact point of view such conduct may be highly inappropriate.[23]

9.7   In addition to carrying out operations in accordance with good oilfield practice (or perhaps in furtherance thereof), licensees are required to take all steps practicable in order, *inter alia*, to prevent the escape of waste or petroleum into the exploration area, its waters, or any waters in the vicinity thereof.[24] Failing to do so requires the licensee immediately to give notice thereof to the Minister and the Maritime and Coastguard Agency.[25] Another noteworthy environmental consideration of the Exploration Regulations is the stipulation that licensees "shall not carry out any operations ... in or about the Exploration Area in such manner as to interfere unjustifiably with navigation or fishing in the waters of the Exploration Area or with the conservation of the living resources of the sea".[26] Despite the environmental purport of this stipulation, it is submitted that there are two problems therewith. First, what constitutes unjustifiable interference is not defined; and the problem is compounded by the fact that there has not been any judicial interpretation of this concept. From the perspective of the fishing and shipping industries, the fact that, by implication, there can be justifiable interference, yet there is no guidance provided regarding when such interference becomes unjustifiable, may be a point of concern. It is submitted that this may also be a point of concern for the offshore industry in that it may be in the offshore industry's interests to have its relationships with the fishing and shipping industries based on clearly defined concepts, thereby reducing the possibility of disputes pertaining thereto. The second of the aforementioned problems is the fact that the phrase "in the waters of the Exploration Area" appears to be an unnecessary geographical limitation on a licensee's obligation not to have its operations interfere with navigation or fishing. It may be possible to argue that this limitation falls away in relation to fish and other living marine resources by means of the phrase "or with the

---

[23] On the issue of the phrase "good oilfield practice" failing to address competing interests adequately, see Worika (n 21 above) at p 401. Notably, s 6 of Australia's Offshore Petroleum Act 2006, which defines good oilfield practice, provides the following particularly vague definition that does not address competing issues: "'good oilfield practice' means all those things that are generally accepted as good and safe in (a) carrying on of exploration for petroleum; or (b) petroleum recovery operations". Additionally, Bunter (n 21 above) makes the point that what may be considered "good and safe" today may be considered particularly harmful in the future; the example of diesel oil-based drilling mud is a case in point.

[24] Model Cl 9(1). Note that Model Cl 1 defines the "exploration area" as "the area for the time being in which the Licensee may exercise the rights granted by this licence".

[25] Model Cl 9(3).

[26] Model Cl 10.

conservation of the living resources of the sea"; however, this argument fails to cure the fact that licensees do not appear to be obliged not to interfere unjustifiably with navigation outside their exploration areas. Nevertheless, despite the foregoing concerns, the Exploration Regulations do require licensees to appoint fisheries liaison officers, whose task it is to promote good working relationships between the owners and masters of vessels (including seismic survey vessels) employed by the licensee and organisations representing the local fishing industry.[27] Licensees are furthermore required to consult with local fisheries organisations regarding the sea routes to be used by the licensees' vessels and to ensure that such sea routes are adhered to.[28] What is more, should licensees' activities result in debris, they are obliged, without reasonable delay, to locate and remove such debris.[29] As for the method of removal, they are required to consult with the relevant fishing organisations and to inform the Secretary of State thereof.[30] Importantly, should fishing gear be lost or damaged, or a loss of fishing time result from reported debris, a licensee is obliged to deal with any such loss promptly.[31] What, specifically, a licensee is obliged to do when dealing with loss promptly is, however, not set out.[32] Nevertheless, it is submitted that the abovementioned provisions are, from an enviro-legal perspective, generally praiseworthy as they provide fairly detailed obligations aimed at negating the occurrence of pollution in the form of interference with fishing and shipping activities during the operations under an exploration licence.

In addition to the foregoing, the Exploration Regulations contain various record-keeping provisions of environmental significance. First, a licensee must maintain accurate records of the drilling, deepening, plugging or abandonment of wells,[33] and, on or before the 15th day of each month, for the duration of the licence, supply the Minister with a return containing, *inter alia*, "a statement of

9.8

---

[27] Model Cl 23(1).

[28] Model Cl 23(a) and (c). Note that Model Cl 23(c) disallows non-adherence to agreed sea routes unless safety of navigation or security of cargo dictate otherwise. After consultation with local fisheries organisations, licensees are to inform the Secretary of State for Environment and Rural Affairs (as well as the Scottish Government Minister of Environment and Rural Affairs) of the results of the consultations and then to agree on the measures to be employed to minimise interference with fishing activities.

[29] Model Cl 23(2).

[30] *Ibid.*

[31] *Ibid.*

[32] See, however, in this regard the UK Fisheries Offshore Oil and Gas Legacy Trust Fund Limited at http://www.ukfltc.com/ and, as an example of one of its initiatives, FishSAFE at http://www.fishsafe.eu/en/home.aspx (both accessed 11 April 2011).

[33] Model Cl 11(1).

the areas in which any geological work, including surveys by any physical or chemical means, has been carried out".[34] Second, an annual return must be submitted showing the situation of all wells, as well as all works executed.[35] Third, all records, papers and so forth kept in pursuance of an exploration licence may be inspected by duly appointed persons.[36] Logically, the creation and consideration of such records may assist in combating environmental harm caused by, amongst other things, seismic surveys, interference, oil and offshore chemicals. Although the information that licensees submit to the Minister may not be disclosed to any person who is not in the service or employment of the Crown,[37] there are, from an environmental perspective, two noteworthy exceptions. First, the Minister may furnish the Natural Environment Research Council ("NERC") with, *inter alia*, any records, returns, samples, and information obtained from a licensee.[38] Second, the Minister and NERC may use the information submitted by the licensee to prepare and publish reports and surveys of a geological, scientific, technical and general nature.[39] It should also be noted that a consequence of the Environmental Information Regulations 2004 may be that such information could become public in some shape or form, albeit subject to protections for, *inter alia*, commercial confidentiality.[40]

9.9   Aside from the abovementioned record-keeping provisions, the Exploration Regulations also entitle the Minister to authorise persons to inspect a licensee's installations and equipment and to examine the state of repair and condition thereof.[41] In doing so, such persons may, in certain circumstances, execute any works or provide and install any equipment.[42] For example, where a licensee reneges on its obligation to maintain equipment in good repair and condition so as to prevent the escape of petroleum into the waters of the exploration area, the Minister may, after reasonable notice, execute any works, including the installation of any equipment, which in the Minister's opinion are necessary to secure performance of the obliga-

---

[34] Model Cl 12(1)(a).

[35] Model Cl 12(2).

[36] Model Cl 15(a).

[37] Model Cl 14.

[38] Model Cl 14(b). Notably, the Minister may also furnish any other body that conducts substantially similar geological activities to those conducted by NERC with the said information.

[39] Model Cl 14(c) and (d). The right to use such information is also extended to any additional bodies that have been furnished therewith.

[40] SI 2004/3391, reg 12(5)(e).

[41] Model Cl 16(a).

[42] Model Cl 16(b).

tion.[43] In addition to executing works and installing equipment, the Minister is also entitled to revoke an exploration licence where there has been breach or non-observance of any of the terms and conditions thereof.[44] Notably, bankruptcy and liquidation are specifically mentioned as instances when the Minister may revoke a licence,[45] which, it is submitted, may help to ensure that companies that are financially unable to meet the various environmental obligations attaching to exploration licences are forbidden from operating offshore.[46]

Petroleum Licensing (Production) (Seaward Areas) Regulations 2008[47]

As with the Exploration Regulations, the first environmentally noteworthy provision of the Production Regulations is that, whenever the licensee is more than one person, all their obligations are jointly and severally applicable.[48] A provision with obvious environmental significance is the stipulation that a licensee may not erect or carry out any relevant works without ministerial consent or approval having been obtained by means of the submission of a programme specifying what works it intends to erect or carry out, the purpose and location thereof, as well as when such works will commence and be completed.[49] Although the Minister maintains the ability to reject a programme if it would be contrary to good oilfield practice or if it would not be in the national interest, the proviso of a programme having to be in the national interest relates only to the maximum and minimum quantities of petroleum that the licensee proposes to acquire[50] and not, for example, whether a proposed operation may detrimentally affect major fishing or mariculture activities which arguably might be in the national interest.[51] Additionally, as previ-

9.10

---

[43] Model Cl 17, read with reg 9(1)(e).

[44] Model Cl 20(2)(a).

[45] See Model Cl 20(2)(c), (e) and (f).

[46] In this regard, see also now Model Cl 20A, inserted by the Energy Act 2008, s 77 and Sch 3, which grants the Minister the power partially to revoke a licence in respect of a person who has become bankrupt etc.

[47] SI 2008/225.

[48] Model Cl 1(2).

[49] Model Cl 17(1)(a) and (b). Notably, Model Cl 17(9) defines "relevant works" as "any structures and any other works whatsoever which are intended by the Licensee to be permanent and are neither designed to be moved from place to place without major dismantling nor intended by the Licensee to be used only for searching for Petroleum". There is no equivalent provision in the Exploration Regulations, as such activity is not in contemplation where only surveying or shallow drilling is permitted.

[50] Model Cl 17(4)(c)(ii), read with Model Cl 17(2)(c) and (1)(b).

[51] Model Cl 18(6) does, however, grant the Minister the discretion to determine what may

ously discussed, the phrase "good oilfield practice" is not defined and the uncertainty surrounding how competing interests will be considered in relation thereto begs the question whether activities that are potentially harmful to the marine environment would ever be sufficient for the Minister to reject a programme on that basis alone when faced with favourable economic considerations.

9.11   The Production Regulations contain various provisions pertaining to the drilling, plugging and abandonment of wells that essentially mirror those of the Exploration Regulations.[52] The only noteworthy distinction is that the Minister may direct that upon expiration of production licensees' rights they need not plug and seal a well; instead they must leave it "in good order and ... fit for further working".[53] There is, however, no explanation as to whether leaving a well in "good order" incorporates environmental concerns. Accordingly, it must be assumed that the concept of "good order" incorporates environmental concerns.[54]

9.12   The Production Regulations specifically govern development wells, which are those wells that will be used, not merely for the searching for petroleum, but for the actual getting thereof from the licence area.[55] Any work, such as the installation of a casing or equipment, for the purpose of bringing a well into use as a development well is referred to as "completion work".[56] Although licensees may not undertake any completion work except in accordance with a programme approved by the Minister,[57] the Production Regulations do not stipulate that such programmes ought to take note of environmental concerns. They do, however, dictate that all operations be conducted in a "proper and workmanlike manner in accordance with methods and practice of exploration customarily used in good oilfield practice" while taking all steps practicable, *inter alia*, to prevent the escape of petroleum into the waters of the licence area.[58] The concerns that were raised against the same provisions of the Exploration Regulations can again be raised here. There are two unique provisions in the Production Regulations which attract praise rather than concern: first, flaring may not be

---

or may not be within the national interest as regards his interpretation of Model Cl 17 in relation to minimum and maximum quantities of petroleum.

[52] Model Cl 19.

[53] See Model Cl 19(12)(a) and (b).

[54] Note, however, that DECC directs operators, in this regard, to guidance prepared by Oil & Gas UK: OP006 – *Guidance on Suspension and Abandonment of Wells/North Sea Well Abandonment Study* (2009).

[55] Model Cl 21.

[56] Model Cl 21(4).

[57] *Ibid.*

[58] See Model Cl 23.

undertaken without ministerial consent;[59] and, second, licensees are bound to comply with any reasonable instructions from the Minister that are aimed at ensuring that funds are available "to discharge any liability for damage attributable to the release or escape of [p]etroleum".[60]

Aside from those provisions discussed above, the noteworthy **9.13** environmental considerations contained in the Production Regulations, such as those pertaining to fishing and record-keeping, are practically identical to those of the Exploration Regulations and thus will not be reconsidered. In sum, it is submitted that the environmental considerations contained in the Exploration Regulations and Production Regulations are generally praiseworthy as they are fairly detailed and the few criticisms thereof that have been raised pertain mostly to the fact that certain concepts could have been more appropriately defined. That these definitional issues may not be as troubling as might be feared becomes evident, however, when the significant amount of additional legislation and regulation directed specifically at the environmental dimension of offshore hydrocarbon operations is taken into consideration. In short, the licence is but one layer in the complex legal and regulatory arrangements that seek to ensure environmental protection offshore, as the remainder of this chapter reveals.

General environmental regulations affecting licensing in the UK

The environmental considerations contained in the Model Clauses **9.14** are, as previously mentioned, not the only regulatory measures to which regard must be had but, whereas most of the latter are of particular relevance only after licences have been granted, there are also regulations which have an impact before this point, some directed at the Secretary of State and some at prospective licensees. Particularly noteworthy in this regard are the Offshore Petroleum Activities (Conservation of Habitats) Regulations 2001 (as amended)[61] (the "Conservation Regulations") and the Offshore Petroleum Production and Pipe-lines (Assessment of Environmental Effects) Regulations 1999 (as amended)[62] (the "Assessment Regulations"). Each of these is considered in turn.

---

[59] Model Cl 23(3)(a). There are, however, certain exceptions to this stipulation, such as where there is a risk of injury to persons: see Model Cl 23(7)(a).
[60] Model Cl 23(9).
[61] Offshore Petroleum Activities (Conservation of Habitats) (Amendment) Regulations 2007 (SI 2007/77).
[62] The Offshore Petroleum Production and Pipe-lines (Assessment of Environmental

Offshore Petroleum Activities (Conservation of Habitats) Regulations 2001[63]

9.15   In essence, the Conservation Regulations are designed to ensure the protection of specific habitats and species from the potentially harmful activities of the offshore industry. So as to achieve this objective, the Conservation Regulations require an assessment to be made of any activity that is likely to have a significant effect on a "relevant site", prior to the granting of a licence by the Secretary of State in terms of the Petroleum Act.[64] A "relevant site" is defined as one of the following: (i) a special area of conservation;[65] (ii) a site of European Community ("EC") importance as listed in terms of Art 4(2) of Council Directive 92/43/EEC on the Conservation of Natural Habitats and of Wild Fauna and Flora (the "Habitats Directive");[66] (iii) a site hosting a priority natural habitat type or priority species;[67] (iv) an area classified in terms of Art 4(1) or (2) of Council Directive 79/409/EEC on the Conservation of Wild Birds (the "Birds Directive");[68] (v) a site included in the list of sites submitted to the European Commission (the "Commission") by the UK in accordance with Art 4 of the Habitats Directive;[69] and (vi) a site which the Secretary of State, after consultation with the appropriate nature conservation body,[70] believes would be likely to be included in the list of sites submitted to the Commission in accordance with Art 4 of the Habitats Directive.[71]

9.16   In making an assessment as to whether or not an activity is likely to have a significant effect on a relevant site, the Secretary of State is obliged to consult with the appropriate nature conservation body.[72] Surprisingly, however, the Regulations fail to make provision for

---

Effects) (Amendment) Regulations 2007 (SI 2007/933) introduced various relatively minor amendments aimed at increasing public access to environmental information and allowing for greater public participation in the environmental decision-making process.
[63] SI 2001/1754.
[64] Reg 5(1).
[65] Reg 2(1)(a).
[66] Reg 2(1)(b).
[67] Reg 2(1)(c).
[68] Reg 2(1)(d).
[69] Reg 2(1)(e).
[70] The "appropriate conservation body" is defined under reg 2(1) as "such body with responsibilities for providing relevant advice on nature conservation in relation to the land or waters within or adjacent to the relevant site, which the Secretary of State considers appropriate". In practice, this would often be the Joint Nature Conservation Committee (the "JNCC"), which is the statutory adviser to the UK Government on national and international nature conservation. See http://www.jncc.gov.uk/ (accessed 11 April 2011).
[71] Reg 2(1)(f).
[72] Reg 5(2).

consultation with special interest and conservation groups. What is more, the Secretary of State need take into account the opinion of the general public only if he considers it to be appropriate to do so.[73] Nevertheless, once the Secretary of State has consulted with the Joint Nature Conservation Committee (and possibly the general public), any assessment that demonstrates that the proposed activity is likely to have an adverse effect on the integrity of a relevant site will prohibit the Secretary of State from authorising the activity.[74] However, authorisation may be granted despite the likelihood of the proposed activity having adverse effects on a relevant site if, in the opinion of the Secretary of State, there is no satisfactory alternative[75] and the Secretary of State certifies that the activity should be carried out for reasons of overriding public interest, including reasons of a social or economic nature.[76] Fortunately, where the Secretary of State gives a certification in support of overriding public interest, he is obliged to consult with the appropriate nature conservation body so that suitable compensatory measures may be taken to ensure that the overall coherence of Natura 2000 is protected. Natura 2000 is the European network of protected sites established under the Habitats and Birds Directives aimed at protecting rare, endangered or vulnerable species.[77] The Habitats Directive requires the establishment of Special Areas of Conservation ("SACs") and the Birds Directive requires the creation of Special Protection Areas ("SPAs"); and, together, SACs and SPAs make up the Natura 2000 series.

Where the Secretary of State is satisfied that something pursuant **9.17** to a licence, authorisation, or approval has or may have adverse effects on the integrity of a relevant site, he may give a direction to the person concerned to take certain steps to avoid, reverse, reduce or eliminate such effects, and to submit a plan of the steps to be taken.[78] Notably, before issuing any such direction, the Secretary of State is again obliged to consult with the appropriate nature conservation body.[79]

The Conservation Regulations also specifically provide for the **9.18** protection of certain creatures and birds. To this end, it is forbidden to carry out oil and gas activities in such a way as, *inter alia*, to harm any creatures (as well as their eggs or breeding sites) that are

---

[73] Reg 5(2).
[74] Reg 5(4), read with reg 5(1), (2) and (3).
[75] Reg 6(1)(a).
[76] Reg 6(1)(b).
[77] See Natura 2000, http://www.natura.org/ (accessed 11 April 2011).
[78] Reg 7(1)(a) and (c) and (2)(a).
[79] Reg 7(3).

members of any of the species listed in Annex IV(a) of the Habitats Directive,[80] or of the species listed in Art 1 of the Birds Directive.[81] The Secretary of State may, however, consent to such activities where, in his opinion there is not only an overriding public interest in the activity being carried out but also a lack of a satisfactory alternative and, having consulted with the JNCC, the activity will not be detrimental to the maintenance of the populations of the species.[82]

9.19   Offences under the Conservation Regulations are constituted by failure to comply with a direction by the Secretary of State[83] or by breaches of the regulations protecting certain creatures, birds or plants[84] or of those prohibiting certain methods of killing or capturing specified species.[85] Conviction in relation to a failure to comply with a direction may attract a fine,[86] whereas other convictions in relation to other offences under these regulations may attract a fine or imprisonment.[87] The protection offered by the corporate veil is avoided by means of the fact that where an offence is committed by a body corporate with the consent, connivance, or neglect of a director, manager, secretary or other similar officer, or a person purporting to act in such capacity, both the body corporate and the person in question shall be guilty of an offence.[88] In sum, the Conservation Regulations demonstrate that, during the licensing process, the UK has clearly forced potential licensees to see to it that the potential effects of their activities are fairly stringently assessed in relation to certain habitats and species.

Offshore Petroleum Production and Pipe-lines (Assessment of Environmental Effects) Regulations 1999[89]

9.20   Throughout the European Union it is mandatory under Directive 85/337/EEC (as amended) to conduct environmental assessments of any proposed offshore oil and gas activities.[90] This obligation

---

[80] Regs 10 and 11.

[81] Reg 11(a).

[82] Reg 14. Note that, up until the Conservation Regulations were amended in 2007, all references to "appropriate nature conservation body" used to be to the JNCC. For some reason, however, the amendments did not alter the reference to the JNCC in reg 14.

[83] Reg 7.

[84] Regs 10, 11 and 12.

[85] Regs 16, 17 and 18.

[86] Reg 19(2).

[87] Reg 19(3).

[88] Reg 19(4).

[89] SI 1999/360 (hereinafter the "Assessment Regulations").

[90] Council Directive on the Assessment of the Effects of Certain Public and Private Activities on the Environment (85/337/EEC), as amended by Council Directive 97/11/EC.

is transposed into UK law by the Assessment Regulations, which require offshore operators to assess the environmental impact of offshore activities prior to their authorisation.[91] The conclusions of any such environmental assessment ("EA") must be submitted to the Environmental Management Team ("EMT") within the Offshore Environment and Decommissioning Unit ("OED") of the DECC, in the form of an environmental statement ("ES") or a Petroleum Operation Notice ("PON 15"),[92] and demonstrate whether there will be a significant impact on the environment.[93] Although, surprisingly, the concept of "a significant impact" is not defined, failure to demonstrate that no significant environmental impact will occur may result in the DECC refusing to grant a licence or possibly imposing conditions to mitigate or remedy any negative effects that might occur.[94] In order to get a sense of how the Assessment Regulations affect the industry, as well as how they seek to protect the environment, the following subsections will consider the following issues: (i) when an ES or a PON 15 should be employed; (ii) the required content of an ES and a PON 15; (iii) the various consultation processes and publicity requirements of the Regulations, as well as an explanation of the concept of "scoping"; and (iv) the potential penalties for failing to adhere to the Assessment Regulations.

When an ES or a PON 15 should be employed. In determining   9.21
whether an ES or a PON 15 should be submitted, it is useful to begin by establishing the situations in which the Assessment Regulations indicate that an ES will be required. These are: (i) the getting of more than 500 tonnes of oil or 500,000 cubic metres of gas per day;[95] (ii) the construction of a pipeline of 800 mm in diameter and 40 kilometres or more in length;[96] (iii) the application for the extension of a consent for a particular project that would amount to a variation allowing for either the getting of more than 500 tonnes of oil or 500,000 cubic metres of gas per day, or the construction of any structure that is likely to produce such amounts, or the construction of a pipeline of 800 mm in diameter and 40 km or

---

[91] See generally Rowan Robinson (n 1 above), paras 1284–1289 and DECC, *Guidance Notes for Industry: Guidance Notes on the Offshore Petroleum Production and Pipelines (Assessment of Environmental Effects) Regulations 1999 (as amended)*, https://www.og.decc.gov.uk/environment/EIAGuidanceNote.pdf (accessed 11 April 2011).

[92] Reg 5(1)(a); DECC (n 91 above). Note that an ES must be accompanied by a PON 16 which is a form that briefly describes the activities for which consent is being sought.

[93] Reg 5(2); DECC (n 91 above).

[94] Reg 5(7).

[95] Reg 6(5)(a) and (b).

[96] Reg 6(5)(c).

more in length;[97] and (iv) where there are transboundary interests in the form of the participation by either another EU Member State or a signatory to the Convention on Environmental Impact Assessment in a Transboundary Context (the "Espoo Convention").[98] Where the proposed offshore activity will not involve one of the afore-mentioned instances and will not have a significant effect on the environment, an operator may submit a PON 15 summarising the likely level of environmental impact.[99] If DECC agrees, on the basis of the information submitted in a PON 15, that there will not be any significant impact on the environment, then it will issue a Direction that an ES need not be prepared.[100] The PON 15 has thus been referred to as a "mini ES" to be employed for the assessment of "less significant activities"[101] such as the drilling of wells and the construction of small pipelines.[102]

9.22   **The required content of an ES.** Schedule 2 to the Assessment Regulations explains in some detail the required content of an ES, which can essentially be divided into five points. First, an ES must describe the site, design and size of the project,[103] including: the seabed use requirements during the construction and operational phases;[104] a description of the production processes including the nature and quantity of the materials used;[105] and an estimate by type and quantity of the expected residues and emissions resulting from the proposed project.[106] Second, an ES must describe measures that will be employed to avoid, reduce and, where possible, remedy signif-icant adverse effects on the environment.[107] Third, an ES, with regard to current knowledge and methods of assessment, must contain the necessary data to assess the effects that the proposed project is likely to have on the environment including, in particular, "fauna, flora, water including the sea and any aquifers under the seabed, air, climatic factors, the landscape or the seascape ... and the interaction between any of the foregoing".[108] Moreover, the data contained in the ES must also include a description of the likely significant effects on the environment arising from the existence of the project, the

---

[97] Reg 6(5A).
[98] Reg 6(5)(d).
[99] Reg 6(1).
[100] DECC (n 91 above).
[101] *Ibid.*
[102] *Ibid.*
[103] Sch 2(a).
[104] Sch 2(a)(i).
[105] Sch 2(a)(ii).
[106] Sch 2(a)(iii).
[107] Sch 2(b).
[108] Sch 2(c)(i).

use of natural resources, the emission of pollutants, the creation of nuisances and the elimination of waste,[109] as well as details of the forecasting methods used to assess such effects.[110] Fourth, the main alternatives to the proposed activity together with the environmental implications thereof and the reasons for the relevant operator's choice must also be provided.[111] Fifth, an ES must also contain a non-technical summary ("NTS") of all the information required by the previous four points[112] so that a non-specialist reader will be able to understand the principal environmental impacts of a proposed activity without having to refer to the main ES.[113]

This approach to the preparation of the ES has a number of 9.23 advantages. First, it ensures that an ES not only describes all the foreseeable potential environmental impacts of a proposed offshore operation but also identifies solutions to eliminate or mitigate such impacts.[114] Second, it requires explicit acknowledgement in the ES of any *lacunae* in environmental information and any other difficulties (including technical difficulties and lack of know-how) encountered by the operator in compiling the required information.[115] What is more, strategies to address such *lacunae* or difficulties should also be acknowledged in the ES.[116] Third, this explicit recognition of uncertainties, coupled with the requirement that alternatives must also be described together with the reasons for the ultimate selection among them, provides the Secretary of State with a better view of the extent to which environmental considerations are being given due priority. It is also noteworthy that the exact content of every individual ES is to a large extent influenced by formal and informal consultation processes which are, respectively, mandated and strongly recommended by the Assessment Regulations.

The consultation processes, publicity requirements, and scoping. 9.24 The DECC requires operators to participate in formal consultations with certain environmental authorities,[117] while also strongly recommending that they participate in various informal consultations with interested parties such as special interest and conservation groups as well as users of the sea.[118] As regards participation in formal

---

[109] Sch 2(c)(ii).
[110] *Ibid.*
[111] Sch 2(d).
[112] Sch 2(e).
[113] DECC (n 91 above); Rowan Robinson (n 1 above) at p 1287.
[114] DECC (n 91 above).
[115] Sch 2(f).
[116] DECC (n 91 above).
[117] Reg 5(4)(a).
[118] DECC (n 91 above).

consultations, all ESs and PON 15s must be submitted to various environmental authorities, which are entitled to make representations in relation thereto to the DECC,[119] including: the JNCC and, depending on the location of the proposed activity, either the Scottish Government Environment and Rural Affairs Department ("SGERAD") and its agency the Fisheries Research Services ("FRS"), or to the Department of Environment, Food and Rural Affairs ("DEFRA") and its agency the Centre for Environment, Fisheries and Aquaculture Science ("CEFAS").[120] Additionally, if the activity which is the subject of an ES is within 40 km of the coast then that ES must be submitted to various other authorities, including, *inter alia*, the Countryside Council for Wales ("CCW") for Welsh waters; Natural England for English waters; Scottish Natural Heritage ("SNH") and the Scottish Environment Protection Agency ("SEPA") for Scottish waters; and one, or possibly more, of the 12 Sea Fisheries Committees for English and Welsh waters.[121] The importance of such formal consultations is highlighted by the fact that consent to a project will not be granted unless consideration has been given to the representations made by any environmental authority to which a copy of the ES was required to be sent.[122]

9.25   As regards informal consultations, the DECC has acknowledged that a "fundamental concept of environmental legislation is to involve, as far as possible, the general public and its specialist representative organisations in the decision making process".[123] Accordingly, the DECC strongly recommends that informal consultations take place between licensees and interested parties such as conservation groups and users of the sea.[124] Although they are not compulsory, the fact that the relevant guidance notes produced by the DECC stress that they are "strongly recommended" suggests that an ES or PON 15 that fails to reflect an informal consultation process may well fail to obtain DECC approval. In the same vein as formal and informal consultation processes, companies wishing to undertake offshore projects are bound to meet detailed requirements aimed at granting the general public access to relevant information such as a description of the proposed activity and, where applicable, the content of an ES.[125] It must be acknowledged that, since the Brent Spar case in the mid-1990s, the industry has become much more

---

[119] Reg 9.
[120] DECC (n 91 above).
[121] See Rowan Robinson (n 1 above) at p 1288.
[122] Reg 5(4)(b)(ii).
[123] DECC (n 91 above).
[124] *Ibid*.
[125] See, generally, reg 9 (as amended).

aware of ensuring proactive dialogue with potentially interested stakeholders.[126]

In contrast to the detailed requirements set out for publicity in relation to an ES, there are no equivalent arrangements for PON 15s. They are merely listed on the DECC website and published in the *Edinburgh, Belfast* and *London Gazettes.*[127] In this regard, it is interesting to note that despite the fairly recent publication of the Offshore Petroleum Production and Pipe-lines (Assessment of Environmental Effects) (Amendment) Regulations 2007, which were designed to enhance the public access to environmental information and public participation provisions of the Assessment Regulations, the opportunity was not taken to make any mention of PON 15s. This can, of course, be explained by the need first and foremost for the Assessment Regulations and the amending regulations to transpose European Directives which make reference only to ESs, and also by the fact that by definition a PON 15 will in all probability relate to an activity without a significant environmental impact. But there is surely an argument, based on the bitter experience of the Brent Spar, that industry and regulator satisfaction with the technical soundness of a decision is no guarantee of its social acceptance. Thus, even if the spirit of the amended regulations was not regarded as persuasive in requiring anything more proactive with respect to PON 15s, the pragmatic desire to avoid controversy might be. 9.26

As regards the concept of "scoping", this simply refers to an operator's right to obtain information that will assist it in the preparation of an ES where such information is held by the DECC or another environmental authority and the operator has been unable to obtain such information through normal published sources or via commercial means.[128] Should the DECC not possess the necessary information, it may serve on another authority that it thinks may have such information a notice requiring such authority to furnish the operator therewith.[129] Although operators are not bound to obtain information by means of scoping, the DECC considers that, when required, scoping for information can be considered best practice, particularly in relation to large projects and those in sensitive locations.[130] 9.27

Potential penalties. Significantly, the submission of false or misleading information, or the breaching of conditions aimed at reducing or 9.28

---

[126] See the discussion in Chapter 10.
[127] See, generally, reg 9 (as amended).
[128] Reg 8.
[129] Reg 8(2) and (3).
[130] DECC (n 91 above).

eliminating any significant adverse effects on the environment, or the carrying out of any offshore activity without the necessary approval, constitutes an offence.[131] In terms of being able to identify a responsible party in a context dominated by corporate actors, reg 18(6) stipulates that where the perpetrator of an offence is a body corporate and the offence is proved to have been committed with:

> "[t]he consent or connivance of, or to have been attributable to any neglect on the part of any director, manager, secretary or other similar officer of the body corporate or on the part of any person purporting to act in such capacity, he as well as the body corporate shall be guilty of that offence and shall be liable to be proceeded against and punished accordingly."

Nor is the corporate veil any protection where the affairs of a body corporate are managed by its members. In such circumstances the above penalty applies in relation to the acts or omissions of a member in connection with his or her management functions as if he or she were a director of the body corporate.[132] The Assessment Regulations thus cast a fairly wide net for ensuring the liability of those who commit offences – and this net is enlarged further by virtue of reg 18(10), which disallows application of s 3 of the Territorial Waters Jurisdiction Act 1878 (TWJA 1878). The crux of s 3 of TWJA 1878 is that (with the exception of certified consent from one of Her Majesty's Principal Secretaries of State, evidencing the expediency thereof) it prohibits the institution of proceedings in any court in the United Kingdom against persons who, although they have committed offences under the law of the United Kingdom, are not subjects of Her Majesty. Continuing the theme of reg 18(10), reg 18(11) specifically states that, for all incidental purposes, an offence under the Assessment Regulations may be taken as having been committed in any place in the United Kingdom. Only two possible defences may be raised by anyone charged with an offence. The first is to argue that reasonable steps were taken to avoid the commission of the offence,[133] while the second is to argue that in order to secure the safety of a person the offence had to be committed as a matter of urgency.[134] It is accordingly perhaps not surprising that the Assessment Regulations, among the various steps that must be taken during the licensing phase so as to prevent the

---

[131] Reg 18(1) and (2).
[132] Reg 18(7).
[133] Reg 18(4)(a).
[134] Reg 18(4)(b).

possibility of marine pollution, have been described as "[p]ossibly the most significant preventative step".[135]

In sum, it may be said that the foregoing discussion of the   9.29
Conservation, Assessment, Exploration and Production Regulations has demonstrated that UK law (albeit in many instances implementing European obligations) takes cognisance of the potentially adverse environmental effects of its offshore oil and gas activities even before the licensing process commences. We will now go on to consider the environmental obligations to which the industry is subject once a licence has been granted and activity begins, looking first, and more briefly, at those relating to exploration licences, and then, at greater length, at those relating to production licences.

SURVEYING AND SHALLOW DRILLING

As previously explained, before there is any environmental   9.30
impact as a consequence of the actual extraction of oil and gas, the activities associated with the exploration phase will themselves have environmental consequences. These include not only geological surveys but also shallow drilling for the purposes of obtaining geological information. The UK law that has been designed to curb the potential harm that may arise from such activities comes in the form of the previously discussed Conservation Regulations. These regulations will be revisited below with particular regard to the manner in which they regulate surveying and shallow drilling. Thereafter, the Food and Environment Protection Act 1985 (FEPA 1985) and the Coast Protection Act 1949 (CPA 1949) will be considered, as they, too, have a bearing on such activities.

Offshore Petroleum Activities (Conservation of Habitats) Regulations 2001

The Conservation Regulations dictate that offshore operators may   9.31
not carry out certain geological surveys (including seismic surveys) or shallow drilling, or test any equipment to be used for those purposes, unless the Secretary of State has granted prior written consent thereto.[136] The relevant application form, which must be submitted to the DECC's EMT in order to obtain such consent, is

---

[135] Rowan Robinson (n 1 above) at p 1284.
[136] Reg 4(1)(a), (b) and (c). See, generally, DECC, *Guidance Notes for Oil and Gas Surveys and Shallow Drilling*, https://www.og.decc.gov.uk/regulation/pons/PON14a_guide_110906.doc (accessed 11 April 2011).

the PON 14A.[137] It must be borne in mind that obtaining consent to survey or shallow drill is independent from any form of permission granted under exploration and production licences.[138] Accordingly, an unlicensed area cannot be subjected to a survey or to shallow drilling without both an exploration licence and an approved PON 14A. Similarly, where production licences apply, those areas may not be surveyed or shallow drilled unless an approved PON 14A has been obtained.

9.32　　Importantly, the submission of a PON 14A must be supported by an EA in those instances where: (a) there is any likelihood that the proposed activities could disturb marine mammals or adversely affect other protected species; or (b) the activity in question involves the use, in sensitive sea areas, of seismic surveys, high-resolution seismic site surveys or any other survey that employs airguns, waterguns or vibroseis; or (c) the relevant activity could affect the integrity of a relevant site or other sensitive area, for example shallow drilling on a reef habitat.[139]

9.33　　The importance of conducting an appropriate EA must not be underestimated as the DECC stresses that, in combination with a PON 14A, an EA "will form the basis for deciding whether consent/agreement should be granted".[140] To this end, an EA should include, among other things: (a) an assessment of possible environmental sensitivities including, for example, fish spawning areas and marine mammals; (b) a description of the survey or shallow drilling operation and how the specific technique to be employed may interact with the environmental sensitivities of the specific location;[141] (c) information regarding measures that will be employed to mitigate adverse environmental effects, such as the use of marine mammal observers to detect the presence of cetaceans in the vicinity of a seismic survey;[142] and (d) the details of any other surveys or shallow drilling operations or activities that

---

[137] DECC (n 136 above) at 13.

[138] *Ibid* at 6–7.

[139] *Ibid* at 10.

[140] *Ibid* at 11.

[141] For example, in relation to shallow drilling the description should refer to the potential smothering of seabed species.

[142] Notably, the DECC (n 136 above, at 18), has stipulated that seismic surveys must be conducted in accordance with the most recently published guidelines for minimising acoustic disturbance to marine mammals. However, the relevant guidelines, namely the JNCC guidelines for minimising the risk of disturbance and injury to marine mammals from seismic surveys, http://www.jncc.gov.uk/PDF/Seismic%20Guidelines%20 June%202009_ver01.pdf (accessed 11 April 2011), have recently been criticised for relying on commonsense measures rather than firm science or proven efficacy, and for, *inter alia*, failing to "mitigate against the chronic degradation of habitat caused by repeated use of this far-travelling and high-intensity noise". See C M Parsons *et al*, "A critique of the UK's

may have the potential to interact with the proposed activity and result in cumulative impacts.[143] Notably, the DECC has pointed out that these considerations do not constitute a closed list and thus an EA narrative should include but not necessarily be limited thereto.[144]

In addition to the EA carried out by the prospective licensee, where a proposed activity will have a "likely significant effect" on the environmental sensitivities of a relevant site, DECC will also conduct a so-called appropriate assessment (an "AA").[145] It does not matter whether the relevant activity will in fact occur within the boundary of the relevant site or not. Instead, what is of cardinal importance is simply that the activity will have a significant effect on the relevant site's environmental sensitivities.[146] The DECC stresses that the term "significant effect" must be understood in light of a document produced by the Commission, entitled *Assessment of plans and projects significantly affecting Natura 2000 Sites – Methodological guidance on the provisions of Article 6(3) and 6(4) of the Habitats Directive 92/43/EEC* (the "Commission Guidance").[147] The Commission Guidance states that whether or not there will be a "significant effect" may be determined through one of two approaches.[148] The first is through what is essentially a judgement of the possible impacts of a proposed activity, irrespective of whether they may be adverse or beneficial. Such judgements will be made through a process of assessment that is based on numerous factors including, *inter alia*, the magnitude, spatial extent and duration of anticipated change; the resilience of the environment to cope with change; the existence of environmental standards against which the proposal could be assessed; the degree of public interest; and the scope for mitigation, sustainability, and reversibility.[149] The second approach for determining whether or not a proposed activity will have a significant effect focuses on the adverse consequences thereof through reference to sets of significance criteria which relate specifically to various aspects of the environment.[150] This approach

9.34

JNCC seismic survey guidelines for minimising acoustic disturbance to marine mammals: Best practice?" (2009) 58 *Marine Pollution Bulletin* 643–651.

[143] DECC (n 136 above) at 11.

[144] DECC (n 136).

[145] *Ibid* at 12; reg 5.

[146] DECC (n 136) at 12.

[147] DECC (n 136 above). A copy of the Commission Guidance is available online at http://ec.europa.eu/environment/nature/natura2000/management/docs/art6/natura_2000_assess_en.pdf (accessed 11 April 2011).

[148] Commission Guidance (n 147 above) at 62.

[149] *Ibid*.

[150] *Ibid*.

has been adopted in Australia where, for example in relation to migratory species, an impact is considered significant if it: (a) modifies, destroys, or isolates an area of habitat important to the survival of the species; (b) introduces invasive species into an important habitat of the species; or (c) seriously disrupts the lifecycle of an ecologically meaningful proportion of the population of the species. Irrespective of which of these two approaches may be adopted to determine whether a proposed survey or shallow drilling operation may have a likely significant effect on a relevant site, to date, only five fairly small areas of the UKCS have been identified as candidates for the designation and there is no indication that these sites are in areas which might become of interest to the offshore industry.[151] Thus, it would appear that AAs are presently not required for the vast majority of offshore surveys and shallow drilling operations in the UK. Nonetheless, the DECC has adopted a precautionary approach and is prepared to treat areas of the UKCS that may be selected as relevant sites as if they were already selected as such.[152] Accordingly, where the proposed activities of those wishing to conduct offshore surveying or shallow drilling operations in the UK may interact with the environmental sensitivities of what may one day be considered to be a relevant site, AAs may be required.

9.35   It is noteworthy that, in accordance with PON 9 (Record and Sample Requirements for Seaward Surveys and Wells),[153] upon completion of seismic surveys, what is generally referred to as a "close-out" form must be completed and submitted to DECC, which will then be used by the UK Government to report seismic survey statistics in furtherance of the objectives of the Agreement on Small Cetaceans of the Baltic and North Seas ("ASCOBANS").[154] The information will also be submitted to Digital Energy Atlas and Library ("DEAL"), which is an initiative sponsored by Oil & Gas UK that provides a web-based service designed to facilitate access to information relevant to the exploration and production of hydrocarbons on the UKCS.[155] The DECC has stated that the submission of survey information to DEAL will inform the future environmental assessments to be made by the Government and offshore industry.[156] Finally, it should be noted that, in addition to

---

[151] JNCC, "Designated Offshore SACs and Candidate SACs", http://www.jncc.gov.uk/page-4534 (accessed 11 April 2011).

[152] DECC (n 136 above) at 12.

[153] DECC, "PON 9: Record and Sample Requirements for Seaward Surveys and Wells", https://www.og.decc.gov.uk/regulation/pons/pon_09.pdf (accessed 6 June 2010).

[154] DECC (n 136 above) at 18. See ASCOBANS, http://www.ascobans.org/ (accessed 11 April 2011).

[155] DEAL, http://www.ukdeal.co.uk (accessed 11 April 2011).

[156] DECC (n 136 above) at 18.

a close-out form, each operator must also submit a survey report together with all related marine mammal observations to the JNCC.[157]

The Food and Environment Protection Act 1985 and the Coast Protection Act 1949

In addition to the aforementioned Conservation Regulations, FEPA 1985 and CPA 1949 contain certain permitting requirements that may need to be met by prospective surveyors and shallow drillers and which, if met, reduce the risk of environmental harm arising.   9.36

In accordance with FEPA 1985, ss 5 and 7, a licence is required for all deposits (whether temporary or permanent) that are to be made in the sea or under the seabed, unless they can be specifically exempted by virtue of the Deposits in the Sea (Exemptions) Order 1985.[158] Accordingly, it may be necessary for those wishing to conduct geological surveys or shallow drilling operations to obtain a licence for any deposits that may be made during the course of their activities, such as the abandonment of sacrificial anchors that secured equipment to the seabed. Logically, these requirements help to reduce the risk that harm in the form of interference, such as the snagging of fishing gear on sacrificial anchors, will arise.   9.37

Similarly, CPA 1949 dictates that consent is required to: (i) construct, alter or improve any works in or on the seashore below the level of mean high water springs; or (ii) deposit any object or materials there; or (iii) remove any objects or materials from the seashore below the level of mean low water springs (for example, through the process of dredging).[159] In essence, these requirements are applicable to shallow waters within the limits of the territorial sea where the aforementioned actions could have navigational consequences.[160] However, s 4(1) of the Continental Shelf Act of 1964 has extended the ambit of points (i) and (iii) so that they are now applicable in any part of the UKCS where oil and gas exploration and development is designated to take place.[161] Thus, the DECC recommends that potential surveyors and shallow drillers whose actions may result in temporary or permanent deposits on   9.38

---

[157] DECC (n 136 above) at 18.

[158] SI 1985/1699.

[159] CPA 1949, s 34.

[160] See, generally, Marine and Fisheries Agency ("MFA"), "The Coast Protection Act (CPA) 1949": http://www.mfa.gov.uk/environment/works/licensing-cpa.htm (accessed 11 April 2011).

[161] DECC, "Guidance to the Coast Protection Act 1949": https://www.og.decc.gov.uk/environment/Guidance_cpa1949.pdf (accessed 11 April 2011).

the seabed, contact and obtain authorisation from the relevant authorities in accordance with CPA 1949.[162]

DRILLING AND PRODUCTION

9.39 Thus far, in considering the environmental law governing offshore upstream activities on the UKCS, this chapter has discussed the law pertaining to licensing, as well as surveying and shallow drilling. What follows is an analysis of those environmental considerations in the UK legislation that pertain to the various forms of pollution that arise during the operations possible under a production licence.

Oil pollution

9.40 The UK legislature has over the years fashioned regulations aimed at protecting the marine environment from oil pollution occasioned by the offshore industry, not least in response to international obligations. These take the form of the Merchant Shipping (Oil Pollution Preparedness, Response and Co-operation Convention) Regulations 1998[163] (the "Merchant Shipping (OPRC) Regulations"), the Offshore Installations (Emergency Pollution Control) Regulations 2002[164] (the "EPC Regulations") and the Offshore Petroleum Activities (Oil Pollution Prevention and Control) Regulations 2005[165] (the "OPA Regulations"). The relevance of these regulations has been thrown into sharp relief by the events in the Gulf of Mexico in 2010 discussed in the introduction to this chapter. It is therefore pertinent to ask how these regulations might have been engaged by similar events on the UKCS.

---

[162] DECC (n 136 above). It is perhaps worth pointing out that the Marine Works (Environmental Impact Assessment) Regulations 2007 (SI 2007/1518), which provide a framework for carrying out environmental impact assessments in relation to, *inter alia*, the removal or disposal of articles, and the construction or alteration of certain works within the UK marine environment, do not apply to such articles or works resulting from surveying or shallow drilling. The reason for this is that the two annexes of Council Directive 85/337/EEC, which list the various projects in relation to which environmental impact assessments may be conducted, fails to list any surveying or shallow drilling related works. This is the situation despite the fact that the marine works to which these regulations apply are defined as those works for which regulatory approval is required, which in turn are defined to include the pertinent provisions of FEPA 1985 and CPA 1949 – see reg 2(1).

[163] SI 1998/1056.

[164] SI 2002/1861.

[165] SI 2005/2055, as amended by SI 2011/983.

Merchant Shipping (Oil Pollution Preparedness, Response and
Co-operation Convention) Regulations 1998
Created under the provisions of the Merchant Shipping Act 1995,   **9.41**
the Merchant Shipping (OPRC) Regulations were the means for the
UK Government to introduce into law the oil spill planning and
reporting requirements of the OPRC Convention. Importantly, the
Merchant Shipping (OPRC) Regulations define an "oil pollution
incident" broadly enough to incorporate discharges of oil from
offshore installations. To this end, an oil pollution incident is
defined as:

> "an occurrence or series of occurrences having the same origin, which
> results or may result in a discharge of oil and which poses or may
> pose a threat to the marine environment, or to the coastline or related
> interests of the United Kingdom and which requires emergency action
> or other immediate response".[166]

In order to deal effectively with any such incident, every operator of
an offshore installation must have an oil pollution emergency plan.[167]
Such plans must be submitted to the Secretary of State at least
2 months prior to the commencement of drilling or production,[168] and
must be reviewed and resubmitted within 5 years after submission.
Additionally, should any major change affecting, or possibly
affecting, such plans arise, operators are required, within 3 months
of knowledge thereof, to submit a new or an amended pollution
emergency plan.[169] However, what constitutes a "major change"
is not defined under the Merchant Shipping (OPRC) Regulations.
Nevertheless, where an operator fails to submit, re-submit, maintain
or implement an oil pollution emergency plan when required to
do so, it shall be guilty of an offence.[170] At the time of writing, it
appears that the difficulties encountered by BP in the Gulf of Mexico
in controlling the leak and thus shutting off the source of the oil
pollution arose in the main from the depth at which the operation
was being conducted. It is not immediately evident that there are
lessons to be drawn for oil pollution emergency plans on the UKCS,
given that the deepest developments so far in the UK waters lie at
about one-third of the depth in the vicinity of the leak in the Gulf
of Mexico,[171] but it is by no means inconceivable that in due course

---

[166] Reg 2.
[167] Reg 4(1)(c).
[168] Reg 3(a), read with reg 4(a)(iii) and (iii)(bb) as well as (7).
[169] Reg 4(5)(b).
[170] Reg 7(1).
[171] Existing fields west of Shetland, such as Schiehallion, lie beneath waters of a maximum
depth of around 450 m, whereas the leak in the Gulf of Mexico in 2010 occurred in water
over 1,500 m deep.

the experience gained from this event may require to be incorporated into emergency plans on this side of the Atlantic.[172]

9.42   Notably, although the Merchant Shipping (OPRC) Regulations do not incorporate a provision allowing for circumvention of the "corporate veil", s 277 of the Merchant Shipping Act 1995 contains the requisite provision, which is applicable "[w]here a body corporate is guilty of an offence under this Act or any instrument made under it". A related environmental consideration is the Secretary of State's right to authorise any person to inspect any offshore installation to which the Merchant Shipping (OPRC) Regulations apply,[173] which is every offshore installation in the UK waters and in any area designated under the Continental Shelf Act 1964.[174]

9.43   A final point for consideration is the fact that the Merchant Shipping (OPRC) Regulations contain certain noteworthy reporting obligations, including the requirement that should masters of UK ships become aware of events involving the discharge of oil from offshore installations, they are bound to report such events either to the Maritime and Coastguard Agency, if the event occurred in UK waters, or to the nearest coastal state, if the event occurred outside UK waters.[175] Similarly, where an individual in charge of an offshore installation is aware of any event involving the discharge of oil at sea from another installation, he must report the incident to the Maritime and Coastguard Agency.[176]

Offshore Installations (Emergency Pollution Control) Regulations 2002

9.44   Crafted in accordance with s 3 of the Pollution Prevention and Control Act 1999, the EPC Regulations grant the UK Government certain powers of intervention following an accident involving an offshore installation so as to prevent and reduce possible pollution. Although an "accident" is defined as "any occurrence causing material damage or a threat of material damage to an offshore installation",[177] a definition of what constitutes "material damage" is not provided. Nevertheless, a definition of "pollution" is provided which specifically refers to oil that may, *inter alia*, harm living

---

[172] Note that the seismic survey recently ordered by Chevron to the west of Shetland will take place in depths of up to 1,200 m.
[173] Reg 8.
[174] Reg 3(2).
[175] Reg 5(1).
[176] Reg 5(2).
[177] Reg 2.

resources and marine life, or interfere with other legitimate uses of the sea.[178]

In order to achieve the objective of the EPC Regulations, the **9.45** Secretary of State is granted the broadly phrased authority to give directions to the operator or manager of an offshore installation (as well as any servant or agent of the operator)[179] that "may require the person to whom they are given to take, or refrain from taking, any action of any kind whatsoever".[180] Somewhat more specifically, the Secretary of State is also entitled to direct the relevant person to, *inter alia*: relocate the installation, or any part thereof; not discharge any oil or other substance; and take remedial measures.[181] If the Secretary of State is of the opinion that any such directions are inadequate, he may take "any action of any kind whatsoever"[182] including taking over control of the relevant offshore installation,[183] or sinking or destroying the offshore installation or part thereof.[184] Importantly, however, it must be borne in mind that the Secretary of State may only exercise such powers where an accident has occurred and, in the opinion of the Secretary of State, the use of such powers is urgently needed as the accident will cause "significant pollution".[185] Neither the EPC Regulations nor the Pollution Prevention and Control Act 1999 provide an explanation of what constitutes significant pollution.

The Minister accordingly has very extensive powers to direct how **9.46** an operator or manager should respond to an accident that may give rise to pollution and indeed to intervene himself. While these powers are undoubtedly necessary to allow steps to be taken in the case of some egregious failure on the part of the operator or manager, it might be suggested that the events in the Gulf of Mexico in 2010 would give any Minister pause for thought before intervening in a way that may in due course raise questions as to his competence to make such decisions.

Lastly, it should be noted that it is an offence to fail to comply **9.47** with a direction,[186] which is, among other things, punishable on summary conviction to a fine not exceeding £50,000.[187] It might be

---

[178] Reg 2.
[179] Reg 3(2).
[180] Reg 3(3).
[181] Reg 3(3)(a), (b) and (c).
[182] Reg 3(4).
[183] Reg 3(4)(c).
[184] Reg 3(4)(b).
[185] Reg 3(1)(a), (b) and (c).
[186] Reg 5(2).
[187] Reg 5(4).

suggested that this fine may not be substantial enough relative to the harm that may be occasioned by a corporation that has unambiguously opted not to comply with a direction.

Offshore Petroleum Activities (Oil Pollution Prevention and Control) Regulations 2005

9.48 At the heart of the OPA Regulations is a ban on the discharge of oil, except in accordance with a permit.[188] The definition of "oil" is particularly broad and covers:

> "any liquid hydrocarbon or substitute liquid hydrocarbon, including dissolved or dispersed hydrocarbons or substitute hydrocarbons that are not normally found in the liquid phase at standard temperature and pressure, whether obtained from plants or animals, or mineral deposits or by synthesis".[189]

The broad nature of the above definition clearly outlaws the release of any form of oil from an offshore installation without a permit.[190] An operator of an offshore installation who is desirous of obtaining a permit to discharge oil bears the responsibility of furnishing the Secretary of State with information describing, *inter alia*, the installation, its location, the relevant oil, the circumstances in which the oil is to be discharged, and the measures that will be employed to monitor the discharge.[191] The submission of false or misleading information may result in any permit that has been granted, being revoked.[192]

9.49   Upon receipt of the requisite information the Secretary of State may not only determine whether to grant or refuse the application[193] but also the time period for which it will be valid[194] and what conditions, if any, ought to be attached thereto.[195] Such conditions may relate to, among other things, the concentration,

---

[188] Reg 3(1).

[189] Reg 2.

[190] There are, however, two exceptions. First, in accordance with reg 3(2)(a), (b) and (c), discharges that are either regulated by the Offshore Chemical Regulations 2002 or by the Merchant Shipping (Prevention of Oil Pollution) Regulations 1996 and 1998 do not require a permit under the EPC Regulations. Second, in accordance with reg 3(3)(a), where an existing exemption applies and oil is being discharged, a permit need not be granted until such time as the Secretary of State specifies by notice in writing that such a permit is required.

[191] Regs 3(4), 4(1) and 5(1)(a), (b) and (c). Note that, in accordance with reg 5(2), the Secretary of State is also empowered to call upon the operator to furnish him with any additional information that he may require.

[192] Reg 9(1)(a).

[193] Reg 4(1).

[194] Reg 4(3).

[195] Reg 4(2) and (4).

frequency, quantity, location and duration of the discharge, measures to minimise pollution, and appropriate monitoring techniques and procedures,[196] as well as any condition that the Secretary of State thinks fit.[197] Importantly, the Secretary of State is entitled to review the conditions attached to any permit and to revoke a permit where there has been a breach of its conditions.[198] Additionally, where the Secretary of State is of the opinion that the operation of an offshore installation involves imminent risk of serious pollution as a consequence of any discharge of oil, a prohibition notice may be served on the permit holder.[199] Significantly, the risks for which prohibition notices may be served need not relate to the contravention of a permit issued under the OPA Regulations, but to any aspects of the operation of an offshore installation.[200]

With a view to securing compliance with the OPA Regulations, the Secretary of State may appoint inspectors to investigate compliance therewith including the monitoring of any discharge of oil.[201] Such inspectors may, *inter alia*, board offshore installations and inspect relevant records, as well as make such examinations or investigations as they consider necessary, including the taking of samples.[202] Failure by, *inter alia*, corporations or their directorial and managerial staff to comply with the requirements of the OPA Regulations constitutes an offence.[203] Defences that can be raised are either that the contravention arose as a consequence of something that could not reasonably have been prevented, or that the contravention was due to something done as a matter of urgency for the purpose of securing the safety of a person.[204] Significantly, where a defendant wishes to rely on the latter of these two defences, he is prohibited from doing so if the necessity to do the thing in question was due to the fault of the defendant.[205]

9.50

---

[196] Reg 4(2).
[197] Reg 4(a).
[198] Regs 7(1) and (2) and 9(1)(b). Note that, in accordance with reg 8, should a permit holder wish to assign his permit to another person, the permit holder and the proposed assignee must both make application to the Secretary of State.
[199] Reg 14(1).
[200] Reg 14(2).
[201] Reg 12(1)(a) and (b).
[202] See, generally, reg 12.
[203] See, generally, reg 16.
[204] Reg 16(2)(a) and (b).
[205] Reg 16(3)(b).

Drilling fluids and drill cuttings

9.51　The UK regulates the environmental threat posed by the adherence of hydrocarbons to drill cuttings by means of the OPA Regulations. In view of the fact that the OPA Regulations have already been discussed above, there is no need for repetition in relation to this issue. Suffice to state that any contamination of drill cuttings by hydrocarbons will require a permit under the OPA Regulations if such cuttings are to be discharged overboard or reinjected into the well.

9.52　　As for the various chemicals that adhere to the drill cuttings, the relevant law in the UK is the Offshore Chemical Regulations 2002[206] (the "OC Regulations"). FEPA 1985 also plays a regulatory role in relation to drill cuttings, in so far as a licence is required in terms thereof for the export of cuttings from one field to another for reinjection.[207] Additionally, as will be discussed in Chapter 10, which considers the environmental regulation of decommissioning, certain obligations arising from the provisions of the OSPAR Convention also have a bearing on the environmental threat posed by drill cuttings.[208] For present purposes, however, the specific roles of the OC Regulations and FEPA 1985 will be discussed in more detail below.

Offshore Chemical Regulations 2002

9.53　The OC Regulations forbid the use or discharge of offshore chemicals, save in accordance with one of two possible permits granted by the Secretary of State.[209] Significantly, there are currently no exceptions to this stipulation and the term "offshore chemicals" is broadly defined so as to encompass "any chemical, whether comprising a substance or a preparation, intentionally used in connection with offshore activities".[210] The relevant permits are either "production permits", which pertain to instal-lations that use or discharge chemicals, or "term permits" which cover time-limited use and discharge of chemicals during such activities as the drilling of wells and decommissioning activities.[211] Importantly, in determining whether or not to grant a permit the

---

[206] SI 2002/1355.

[207] Oil & Gas UK, "Reinjection of Mud and Cuttings", http://www.ukooaenvironmental legislation.co.uk/Contents/Topic_Files/Offshore/Reinjection.htm (accessed 11 April 2011).

[208] See Chapter 10.

[209] Reg 3(1), read with reg 4(1).

[210] Reg 2.

[211] See DECC, *Guidance Notes on the Offshore Chemical Regulations 2002* at 15: https://www.og.decc.gov.uk/regulation/legislation/environment/chemregs2002.doc (accessed 11 April 2011).

Secretary of State must have regard to any opinion expressed by CEFAS or the FRS (as appropriate), any State that is party to OSPAR which may be affected by the use or discharge of the chemicals,[212] and the general public.[213] Moreover, the Secretary of State may not grant a permit where certain publicity requirements have not been met, including making the permit application available for public inspection and publishing the details thereof in newspapers on occasions when it is likely to come to the attention of persons interested in, or affected by, the use or discharge of the relevant chemicals.[214]

It is noteworthy that a permit application must include not only a description of the relevant offshore installation and the proposed technology and techniques to be used for the prevention and reduction of the use and discharge of chemicals, as well as measures that will be employed to monitor the use or discharge of such chemicals, but also an assessment of the possible risk to the environment as a consequence of the use or discharge of the chemicals.[215] As to the conditions that may be attached to a permit, these can take almost any form as the Secretary of State is given an overriding discretion to attach such conditions as he thinks fit.[216] More specifically, however, he is entitled to attach conditions relating to, *inter alia*, the quantity of the discharge and measures to prevent both pollution and accidents that may affect the environment.[217] Where a permit is subject to a time limit and an operator wishes to renew it, an application for renewal must be made 3 months before the expiry date of the permit and the Secretary of State is bound to consult once more with CEFAS or the FRS, as well as any State that is party to OSPAR and which may be affected by the use or discharge

9.54

---

[212] Reg 4(1)(a), read with reg 2. Whether or not the Secretary of State consults with CEFAS or FRS depends on the relevant area to which the permit would relate.

[213] Reg 4(1)(b). Note that reg 7(2) states that the Secretary of State need not consult with the general public if the permit application is made:

"(a) in connection with a relevant project for which the Secretary of State gives a direction, pursuant to Regulation 6 of the Offshore Petroleum Production and Pipelines (Assessment of Environmental Effects) Regulations 1999, that no environmental statement need be prepared; (b) in connection with a discharge for a pipeline, being a discharge to which the Secretary of State gives a consent pursuant to an authorization issued under Part III of the Petroleum Act 1998; or (c) in connection with activities carried out in accordance with an abandonment programme approved by the Secretary of State under Part IV of the Petroleum Act 1998".

[214] Regs 4(2) and 7(1) and (3).

[215] Reg 6(1)(a)–(d).

[216] Reg 5(1).

[217] Reg 5(2).

of the chemicals.[218] Interestingly, however, the Secretary of State is not bound to take into account representations made by the general public, as he is required to do in relation to the application for a new permit. Nevertheless, not only may renewed permits be subject to such further terms and conditions as the Secretary of State thinks fit,[219] all permits, together with the terms and conditions that attach to them, are to be kept by the Secretary of State[220] in a register which must be open for public inspection.[221]

9.55   Once granted, permits are not set in stone and may be varied by means of an application from the operator or by means of a review by the Secretary of State.[222] Applications for substantial variations may be refused,[223] while applications for other variations require the Secretary of State to take into account any relevant representations from CEFAS or the FRS, as well as any State that is party to OSPAR and which may be affected by the use or discharge of the offshore chemicals.[224] Again, however, no provision is made for taking the opinion of the general public into account. As regards the reviewing of permits, the Secretary of State is bound to undertake reviews where pollution, or the risk thereof, is of such significance that restrictions on the use or discharge of offshore chemicals ought to be revised or new restrictions ought to be included.[225] Interestingly, it is only in such instances that the Secretary of State has the discretion to take into account any relevant representations from CEFAS or the FRS, as well as any State that is party to OSPAR and which may be affected by the use or discharge of the offshore chemicals.[226]

9.56   Bearing in mind the fact that the submission of false or misleading information, or the breach of permit conditions, entitles the Secretary of State to revoke the relevant permit,[227] it is interesting to note that operators are bound to provide details of any incident or accident involving an offshore chemical, including the breach of permit

---

[218] Reg 10(1), (2) and (3), read with reg 2. Surprisingly, the Secretary of State may issue permits that do not have time limits, which from an environmental perspective may not be advisable. For example, where it transpires that particular chemicals have previously unforeseen harmful effects on the marine environment, an operator may nonetheless use these chemicals until such time as the Secretary of State opts to review the relevant permit in the light of this new knowledge and issue new restrictions in relation thereto.
[219] Reg 10(5).
[220] Reg 14(1).
[221] Reg 14(2).
[222] Regs 11 and 12.
[223] Reg 11(4).
[224] Reg 11(2), read with reg 2.
[225] Reg 12(2).
[226] Reg 12(7).
[227] Reg 13(1).

conditions or "where there has been, or may be, any significant effect on the environment".[228] Although the term "effect" is given a broad definition, in that it "includes any direct, indirect, cumulative, short, medium or long-term, permanent or temporary, or positive or negative effect[s]",[229] that which constitutes a "significant effect" remains an unanswered question. Breach of permit conditions constitutes an offence for which certain employees of juristic persons, such as directors, can in certain instances (such as their having consented thereto) be punished.[230] The possibility of detecting breaches of permit conditions is augmented by the fact that the OC Regulations allow for the appointment of inspectors who, when monitoring the use or discharge of offshore chemicals, may board offshore installations and, *inter alia*, take samples found thereon or in the atmosphere, water, and seabed.[231]

Food and Environment Protection Act 1985
As previously mentioned, FEPA 1985 mandates that a licence is 9.57 required for the deposit of any substances or articles in the sea or under the seabed.[232] In relation to drill fluids and drill cuttings, however, the Deposits in the Sea (Exemptions) Order 1985 exempts the deposit on site or under the seabed of any chemicals, drilling muds or drill cuttings from the FEPA licensing requirement.[233] Nevertheless, the export of cuttings from one field to another for reinjection is not exempt from the FEPA licensing requirement.[234] As such exportation for reinjection is not commonplace, only the most cardinal of FEPA 1985's environmental provisions pertaining thereto will be discussed. First, a licence under FEPA 1985 must, where the licensing authority thinks it necessary or expedient, include provisions to protect, among other things, the marine environment and the living resources which it supports.[235] Second, compliance with such provisions may be achieved through enforcement officers, who may board vessels, aircraft, hovercraft and marine structures if they have reasonable grounds for believing that they contain drill cuttings that are to be deposited in the sea or under the seabed.[236] Third, FEPA licences may be varied or revoked if, among other things, there has been a breach of any of their provisions, or a

---

[228] Reg 15(1)(a) and (b).
[229] Reg 15(2).
[230] Reg 18(4). As regards offences and penalties see, generally, reg 18.
[231] Reg 16.
[232] Section 5.
[233] Sections 14, 15 and 15A.
[234] Oil & Gas UK (n 207 above).
[235] Section 8(3).
[236] Section 11.

change in circumstances relating to the marine environment or the living resources it supports, or an increase in scientific knowledge relating thereto.[237] Fourth, persons who act without a licence when one is required, or cause or permit another person to do so, are guilty of an offence.[238] Fifth, and finally, FEPA 1985's provisions governing liability of persons specifically refers to bodies corporate and the like, thus essentially mirroring the relevant provisions of the OC Regulations, save, however, for the fact that FEPA 1985 does not provide that where the commission of an offence is due to the act or default of some other person, that other person may be charged therewith, irrespective of whether or not proceedings are taken against the first-mentioned person.[239]

Produced water

9.58   Produced water is water that is extracted from the subsurface along with oil and gas, which may have originated in the reservoir or through injection into the formation so as to maintain pressure and a particular rate of production. Produced water consists of, among other things, a mixture of oil droplets, trace metals, dissolved organic compounds and production chemicals.[240] The key items of legislation governing produced water from the UK's offshore oil and gas operations, are twofold, namely the OPA Regulations and FEPA 1985. As both of these have been discussed at length above, the present discussion will simply provide a brief synopsis on how they apply to produced water.

Offshore Petroleum Activities (Oil Pollution Prevention and Control) Regulations 2005

9.59   As previously discussed, the OPA Regulations aim to reduce the quantities of hydrocarbons discharged during the course of offshore operations and they do so via, *inter alia*, introducing a permitting system for oil discharges[241] and strengthening the powers of inspection and investigation into such discharges.[242] The definition

---

[237] Sections 8(10) and (11)(b) and 9(11)(a).

[238] Section 9(1)(a) and (b). See also s 21(6). Persons guilty of an offence under this section shall, in accordance with s 21(2A)(a) and (b), be liable: on summary conviction, to a fine of an amount not exceeding £50,000; and, on conviction on indictment, to a fine or to imprisonment for a term not exceeding 2 years or to both.

[239] See reg 18(6) of the OC Regulations.

[240] See IMO Joint Group of Experts on the Scientific Aspects of Marine Environmental Protection, *Impact of oil and related chemicals and wastes on the marine environment*, (GESAMP Reports and Studies No 50, 1993), p 170.

[241] Reg 3(1).

[242] Reg 12(1)(a) and (b).

of "oil" under the OPA Regulations is broad enough to include hydrocarbons found in produced water[243] and thus any discharge of produced water will require a permit under the OPA Regulations.

It is by means of the OPA Regulations that the UK Government implemented its obligations under OSPAR Recommendation 2001/1 and achieved, by the end of 2006, compliance with a 30mg/l monthly average dispersed oil in water discharge, as well as a 15 per cent reduction in oil tonnage discharged in produced water, when compared with discharges from 2000.[244] Interestingly, until recently, regulation of produced water in the UK was based on a system of allowances regulated by the Dispersed Oil in Produced Water Trading Scheme (the "DOPWTS") which was, in essence, a cap-and-trade scheme in terms of which DECC issued discharge allowances out of an overall discharge allowance pot.[245] Although the DOPWTS has been revoked, DECC is considering various proposals for the future management of produced water, which include maintaining certain aspects of the status quo such as the 30mg/l monthly average of dispersed oil in produced water discharge limit, the 100mg/l maximum dispersed oil concentration limit, and the fact that operators' predictions of annual discharge tonnage of dispersed oil in produced water must take into account the principles of Best Available Technique ("BAT") and Best Environmental Practice ("BEP").[246] Notably, one of the new proposals for the management of produced water is the so-called Risk Based Approach that the OSPAR Commission is in the process of preparing and which will place greater emphasis on risk assessment and furtherance of the objectives of OSPAR Recommendation 2001/1, in particular reaching the ultimate goal of zero harmful discharge.[247]

9.60

---

[243] Reg 2.

[244] Oil & Gas UK, "Produced Water", http://www.ukooaenvironmentallegislation.co.uk/Contents/Topic_Files/Offshore/Produced_water.htm#newdevelopments (accessed 11 April 2011); DECC, "Oil Discharged with Produced Water 2006 – 2008", https://www.og.decc.gov.uk/information/bb_updates/chapters/Table3_2.htm (accessed 11 April 2011).

[245] The allowance pot for 2006/2007 was approximately 4,888 tonnes of dispersed oil to sea in produced water discharges and was based on the aforementioned OSPAR stipulation of a 15% reduction of oil tonnage discharged in produced water, relative to the discharges of the year 2000 – see Oil & Gas UK (n 244 above).

[246] See the letter from Sarah J Kydd, DECC, Head of Environmental Operations, to the UK offshore industry, entitled "Response to Consultation on the Future of the UK Dispersed Oil in Produced Water Trading Scheme", dated 31 July 2008: https://www.og.decc.gov.uk/environment/opaoppcr_letter_310708.pdf (accessed 11 April 2011).

[247] Oil and Gas UK (n 244 above); Sarah J Kydd (n 246 above).

Food and Environment Protection Act 1985

9.61   FEPA 1985 regulates produced water only in so far as the export thereof to another field for reinjection requires a licence.[248] Thus, the discussion above regarding the need for a FEPA 1985 licence in relation to the export of drill cuttings from one field to another for reinjection is equally applicable to produced water. Nevertheless, it should perhaps be pointed out that applications for a FEPA 1985 licence must include a description of, *inter alia*: how the production water is to be transported; how the reinjection operation will be undertaken (including a technical explanation in support of how containment of the disposed produced water will be undertaken); and an assessment of alternative means of disposal must also be provided so as to demonstrate that offsite reinjection is in line with BAT and BEP.[249]

Pipeline and production chemicals

9.62   The cardinal environmentally oriented regulations governing pipeline and production chemicals in the UK are the OC Regulations.[250] This is not to say that the EPC Regulations, discussed above, do not play an important role in the regulation of offshore chemicals – they do, but apply only in so far as they grant the UK Government certain powers of intervention following an accident involving an offshore installation. Although the numerous provisions of the OC Regulations have already been discussed in detail in relation to the chemicals that may be found in drilling fluids and adhering to drill cuttings, there are certain general provisions governing the many other types of offshore chemicals that warrant further elucidation.

9.63   The thrust of the OC Regulations is that they are only intended to apply to chemicals used and discharged through exploration, exploitation, offshore processing and decommissioning.[251] Thus, non-operational chemicals that might otherwise be used on an offshore installation, such as paints, are not subject to the OC

---

[248] See s 5(a) and (b) of FEPA 1985 and regs 14, 15 and 15A of the Deposits in the Sea (Exemptions) Order 1985 (SI 1985/1699); and Oil & Gas UK (n 244 above).

[249] Oil & Gas UK (n 244 above).

[250] The OC Regulations implement, in UK law, OSPAR Decision 2000/2 on a Harmonised Mandatory Control System for the Use and Reduction of the Discharge of Offshore Chemicals, which operates in conjunction with two OSPAR Recommendations which are fundamental to the implementation of the Decision, namely, OSPAR Recommendation 2000/4 on a Harmonised Pre-Screening Scheme for Offshore Chemicals and OSPAR Recommendation 2000/5 on a Harmonised Offshore Chemical Notification Format.

[251] Reg 2; DECC, *Guidance Notes on the Offshore Chemicals Regulations 2002*, 9: https://www.og.decc.gov.uk/regulation/legislation/environment/chemregs2002.doc (accessed 11 April 2011).

Regulations.[252] When an offshore operator applies for a permit under the OC Regulations, irrespective of whether it is a production or term permit, not only must the application list the chemicals and the amounts thereof that will be discharged,[253] it must also contain a risk assessment of the effects thereof on the receiving environment.[254] Notably, applications for permits by operators may only include those chemicals that have been assessed by CEFAS and listed on its website.[255] Where such so-called pre-screening has identified a chemical as hazardous, less hazardous substitutes must be sought.[256] Surprisingly, however, operators are not obliged to choose the least hazardous alternative.[257] Consequently, it is submitted that although the aforementioned pre-screening procedure is praiseworthy in that it possesses the possibility of negating the introduction of hazardous chemicals into the marine environment, it is nonetheless flawed by virtue of the fact that operators are not obliged to choose less hazardous alternatives.

Aside from the abovementioned pre-screening procedure, it is   9.64
significant to note that DECC provides a specific list of particular offshore activities that require permits under the OC Regulations. These activities have been divided into three groups, namely: new and existing producing developments; wells, pipelines, and decommissioning of installations; and unforeseen use and spillage.[258]

New and existing producing developments
New offshore developments are, in accordance with the previously   9.65
discussed Assessment Regulations, subject to mandatory environmental impact assessments.[259] Additionally, however, operators are required to submit PON 15D applications for production permits, except where new developments will be tied back to existing installations because in such instances the operators of host platforms may then simply apply to have their permits varied to allow for

---

[252] See DECC (n 251 above) at 9, where it is explained, for example, how "corrosion inhibitors added to fire-fighting drench systems are included [as discharges under the OC Regulations], as they are used in open systems discharging to the sea. [Whereas] [f]ire-fighting foams are not included, as they are contained in closed systems and only used in an emergency".

[253] *Ibid* at 5.

[254] *Ibid.*

[255] *Ibid.*

[256] See DECC (n 251 above) at 5, where it is stated that "[i]t should be borne in mind that the underlying thrust of the [OSPAR] Decision [2000/2] is to seek the use of less hazardous chemicals wherever that is possible".

[257] *Ibid.*

[258] See, generally, DECC (n 251 above) at 11–12.

[259] See para 9.20.

the additional use and discharge of offshore chemicals. Notably, PON 15D permits are required for the day-to-day use and discharge of chemicals as a consequence of normal production activities and are issued on the basis of discharge sites, which means that each offshore installation in a particular field will require a permit, except for those installations that are tied back to a host installation and undertake combined discharges as these will require only one production permit for the host installation. If granted, PON 15D permits are issued on an open-ended basis but will be reviewed every 3 years and are subject to quarterly reporting which must cover actual use and discharge.

Wells, pipelines, and decommissioning of installations

9.66   The use and discharge of offshore chemicals during the drilling of a well requires a term permit to be issued under the OC Regulations. In order to obtain such a permit, a PON 15B must be submitted. Interestingly, the PON 15B is dual purpose as it includes both a request for a direction that an environmental statement need not be prepared as well as the application for a permit to use and discharge chemicals. Where, however, an environmental statement is deemed necessary, the PON 15B may again be used to apply for the necessary term permit. In those instances where offshore chemicals are to be used for, among other things, the installation or decommissioning of pipelines, a term permit is required for which a PON 15C must be submitted. Similarly, when an offshore installation is to be decommissioned and chemicals are to be employed in that regard, the operator must apply for a term permit. In this instance, however, a PON 15E must be submitted.

Unforeseen use and spillage

9.67   There are two situations that may involve the unforeseen use of offshore chemicals. First, certain chemicals may need to be used on a contingency basis, such as those that are utilised in the event of drilling problems being encountered. Second, situations may arise on very short notice where unforeseen use is necessary. In such situations it may be impractical for operators to apply for the necessary permits and so provision is made for them to receive emergency permission telephonically or electronically, provided that DECC is satisfied that the environmental consequences of such use has been considered. If emergency permission is granted the operator must, as soon as possible, submit a request for a variation of his existing permit so as to maintain proper records.

9.68   Where there has been an accidental spillage of offshore chemicals, DECC stresses that the incident must be reported immediately and that the relevant operator must complete a PON 1 within 24 hours of the release. It is in such situations where there has been a chemical spill that the EPC Regulations come into play. As previously mentioned, these Regulations grant the UK Government certain powers of intervention when there is, or may be, a risk of significant pollution, or where the operator has failed to implement proper control and preventative measures.

Atmospheric emissions

The law of the UK governing atmospheric emissions from offshore installations is the subject-matter of various sets of regulations and consequently it is outside the scope of this chapter to consider all of them. Those that will be considered here are those regulations that govern the cardinal sources of atmospheric pollution arising from offshore installations, namely power generation and flaring.

9.69

Merchant Shipping (Prevention of Air Pollution from Ships) Regulations 2008[260]

Section 128(1)(e) of the Merchant Shipping Act 1995 was specifically formulated so as "to provide a power to make secondary legislation regarding air pollution from ships ... [that] would implement Annex VI [of MARPOL 73/78]",[261] which, among other things, sets limits on the emission of SO_x and NO_x while also prohibiting the emission of certain ozone-depleting substances such as CFCs. It was not until 8 December 2008, however, that the requisite regulations, namely the Merchant Shipping (Prevention of Air Pollution from Ships) Regulations 2008 (the "PAPS Regulations"), came into force.

9.70

As a starting point, the PAPS Regulations specifically apply to any vessels "of any type whatsoever including ... a platform, which is operating in the marine environment".[262] The thrust of the PAPS Regulations is that they implement a certification procedure for the regulation of atmospheric emissions from such vessels. In relation to offshore installations, the relevant certificates may take one of two possible forms. The first is an International Air Pollution Prevention Certificate (an "IAPP Certificate") which applies to "a platform which is or will be engaged in voyages to waters under the sovereignty of a Contracting Government other than the United Kingdom",[263] a Contracting Government being any government bound by

9.71

---

[260] SI 2008/2924, as amended by the Merchant Shipping (Prevention of Air Pollution from Ships) (Amendment) Regulations 2010 (SI 2010/895).
[261] Lord Davies of Oldham, *Hansard*, HL, vol 672, col 1130 (14 June 2005).
[262] Reg 2(1).
[263] *Ibid.*

MARPOL 73/78.[264] The second is a United Kingdom Air Pollution Prevention Certificate (a "UKAPP Certificate") which applies to "a platform which is not or will not be engaged in voyages to waters under the sovereignty or jurisdiction of a Contracting Government other than the United Kingdom".[265] A concern in relation to the applicability of these two forms of certificate is that they apply to platforms "engaged in voyages", yet the term "voyage" is not defined and there is not an equivalent regulatory requirement for platforms when stationary. To this end, the *Oxford English Dictionary*'s definition of a "voyage" is that it is a "long journey involving travel by sea or space", which implies that the relevant certificates are not of application to stationary platforms. Fortunately, however, a "platform" is described as including "fixed and floating platforms and drilling rigs".[266] Nevertheless, an inconsistency clearly exists between the definition of a platform and the definition of when the relevant certificates apply to platforms. Presumably, the PAPS Regulations apply to platforms only when they are in motion and thus, to some extent, take on the characteristics of a ship. Given that in the usage of the industry "platform" generally applies to a fixed structure, while "rig" is used to describe a mobile installation, the wording of these provisions could usefully be clearer.

9.72 The PAPS Regulations dictate that platforms must, on various occasions, be surveyed by a Certifying Authority, which must be satisfied that, *inter alia*, the equipment and systems thereof are such that they will fully comply with particular regulations pertaining to, among other things, the control of emissions of SO_x and NO_x, failing which platforms will not be permitted to proceed to, or remain at, sea.[267] The consequent burden of appropriately maintaining platforms and their equipment falls expressly on the owners and managers thereof and, notably, they are bound to ensure that platforms will not present "an unreasonable threat of harm to the marine environment".[268] What constitutes "an unreasonable threat" is, however, undefined.

9.73 Regulations specifically applying to particular forms of atmospheric pollution can be found in Pt 3 of the PAPS Regulations. As regards ozone-depleting substances, the deliberate emission thereof is expressly prohibited.[269] Surprisingly, however, the installation of new equipment, systems and so forth, which involve the intro-

[264] Reg 2(1).
[265] *Ibid.*
[266] *Ibid.*
[267] See regs 5–15.
[268] Reg 9(1), read with reg 2(5)(b).
[269] Reg 20(1). The term "deliberate emission", in accordance with reg 20(2), "includes

duction onto a platform of ozone-depleting substances, other than hydrochlorofluorocarbons, is prohibited, but only in relation to platforms that do not belong to UK-based operators.[270] In relation to NO_x, the emission thereof from diesel engines is, subject to certain exceptions, prohibited where, in line with the procedures set out in the NO_x Technical Code, such emissions exceed either: 17.0g/kWh when the rated engine speed (crankshaft revolutions per minute) is less than 130 rpm; or, $45.0 \times n^{-0.2}$ g/kWh when the rated engine speed is 130 or more but less than 2,000 rpm; or, 9.8g/kWh when the rated engine speed is 2,000 rpm or more.[271] Notably, however, the PAPS Regulations do not apply to any emissions from diesel engines that are "solely dedicated to the exploration, exploitation and associated offshore processing of seabed mineral resources".[272] As far as the emission of SO_x is concerned, the relevant stipulation is that the content thereof in any fuel oil used onboard a platform, subject to certain exceptions, may not exceed 4.5 per cent by mass.[273] The most noteworthy exception is the fact that stricter emission limits are placed on platforms within a SO_x emission control area ("SECA"), with only 1.5 per cent by mass being permitted.[274] Interestingly, the North Sea SOX Emission Control Area (the "North Sea SECA") is such that most of the offshore installations in the UK's waters fall within its borders.[275] Nevertheless, there are numerous installations that fall outside the geographical ambit thereof which would thus be subject to less stringent emissions standards. It is submitted that this disparity is unfortunate and that the PAPS Regulations should be amended so as to apply the stricter emissions of the North Sea SECA to all offshore installations in UK waters.

As regards volatile organic compounds, it appears that the PAPS Regulations do not apply to offshore installations but rather to oil or chemical tankers as well as to terminal operators or harbour authorities operating vapour emission control systems.[276] As regards the regulation of emissions arising from incineration, the PAPS 9.74

---

an emission occurring in the course of maintaining, servicing, repairing or disposing of systems or equipment".

[270] Reg 20(3) and (4). Note that the hydrochlorofluorocarbon exclusion will expire on 1 January 2020.

[271] Reg 21.

[272] Reg 3(13)(e).

[273] Reg 22. In accordance with reg 2(1), "fuel oil" refers to "such substances as may be specified by the Secretary of State in a Merchant Shipping Notice".

[274] Reg 22(3)(a) and(b).

[275] The North Sea SECA lies southwards of latitude 62°N and from the North of Scotland it falls eastwards of longitude 4°W, while South of England it falls eastwards of 5°W.

[276] Reg 23, read with reg 2(1).

Regulations dictate that, subject to certain exceptions, the incineration of, among other things, polychlorinated biphenyls, garbage containing more than trace amounts of heavy metals and refined petroleum products containing halogen compounds is prohibited.[277] Although "garbage" is defined so as to include "all kinds of ... operational wastes generated during the normal operation of a ship and liable to be disposed of continuously or periodically",[278] the incineration of "substances that are solely and directly the result of exploration, exploitation and associated offshore processing of sea-bed mineral resources"[279] is excluded from the ambit of the PAPS Regulations. Such specifically excluded activities include flaring, as well as the burning of drill cuttings, muds and stimulation fluids during well completion and testing operations.[280] Finally, as regards fuel oil, the PAPS Regulations dictate that such fuel must meet particular specifications, including the fact that it may not exceed the appropriate SO_x content, or cause an engine to exceed stipulated NO_x emission levels, or include any added substance or chemical which causes additional air pollution.[281] Notably, however, hydrocarbon produced and used on platforms as fuel, if that use has been approved by the Secretary of State, is excluded from the relevant fuel oil regulations.[282]

9.75 The PAPS Regulations contain various enforcement provisions. Notably, the submission of false information, or the use of equipment that is damaged or defective, entitles the Secretary of State to cancel a certificate.[283] The appointment of inspectors to monitor compliance is also provided for. Enforcement provisions of particular significance are the detention provisions that allow for the fact that a UK-registered platform may be detained until such time as "a surveyor of ships is satisfied that it can proceed to sea without presenting any unreasonable threat of harm to the marine environment".[284]

Offshore Combustion Installations (Prevention and Control of Pollution) Regulations 2001[285]

9.76 The OCI Regulations are designed to control atmospheric pollution arising from so-called "qualifying combustion installations" ("QCIs")

---

[277] Reg 24(4).
[278] Reg 24(5).
[279] Reg 3(13)(c).
[280] Reg 3(13)(c)(i).
[281] See, generally, reg 25.
[282] Reg 25(1)(c).
[283] Reg 18.
[284] Reg 28(1), read with regs 3(5)(a) and 16(1).
[285] SI 2001/1091.

which are permanently installed on a platform and that singularly, or in combination with any other such installation installed on the same site, have rated thermal inputs exceeding 50 megawatts.[286] Notably QCIs are:

> "any technical apparatus in which fuels are oxidised to use the heat thus generated and includes gas turbines and diesel and petrol-fired engines and any equipment on a platform connected to such apparatus which could have an effect on emissions from that apparatus or could otherwise give rise to pollution but does not include any apparatus the main use of which is the disposal of gas by flaring or incineration".[287]

The operation of a QCI requires a permit, and applications for such permits must stipulate, *inter alia*, the nature and quantities of foreseeable emissions from the relevant installation, the significant effects they may have on the environment, and measures to monitor the emissions.[288] Note that an application for a permit may not need to contain all of the above where an ES regarding the effects of the operation of the QCI in question already exists. In such instances the application for a permit, when submitted, must simply be accompanied by a copy of the ES.[289]

When considering an application for a permit, the Secretary of State must not only take into account any relevant ES but also any public representations as well as any representations made by States that are party to the Agreement on the European Economic Area ("EEA States") and that are affected by the operation of the combustion installation.[290] Moreover, the Secretary of State must be satisfied that various publicity requirements have been complied with, including the submission of a copy of the application to any EEA State whose environment is likely to be significantly affected.[291] However, what constitutes a significant effect is not defined under the OCI Regulations or under the Pollution Prevention and Control Act 1999 in terms of which the OCI Regulations were created. Nevertheless, the Secretary of State is bound to attach specific environmentally orientated conditions to all permits, which must ensure, *inter alia*, that: appropriate measures are taken to prevent pollution, in particular through the use of BAT;[292] no significant

9.77

---

[286] Reg 2.
[287] *Ibid.*
[288] Regs 3 and 5.
[289] Reg 5(3), read with reg 2.
[290] Reg 4(1), read with reg 2.
[291] Reg 7(3) and (4).
[292] Notably, in relation to the concept of BAT, reg 2 defines "available techniques" as those "which can be implemented on platforms under economically and technically viable conditions, balancing the costs of their implementation against the benefits to

pollution occurs; there are controls on the emission of pollutants;[293] and there are provisions to minimise long-distance or transboundary pollution.[294]

9.78 When it comes to enforcement of the OCI Regulations, it is worth noting that not only is the Secretary of State entitled to review, update, and revoke permits,[295] he is also empowered to appoint inspectors, serve enforcement and prohibition notices and to take further action in the event that such notices are not complied with.[296] The OCI Regulations create various offences, including: the operation of a combustion installation without, or in breach of a condition attached to, a permit; and failure to comply with an enforcement or prohibition notice.[297] Notably, a body corporate, as well as particular officers thereof, such as directors who through consent, connivance or neglect allow the commission of an offence, may be held liable for any such offence.[298]

Petroleum Licensing (Production) (Seaward Areas) Regulations 2008

9.79 In the UK, flaring contributes substantially to the offshore industry's atmospheric emissions, with venting providing a nominal contribution.[299] Flaring is regulated by the previously discussed Production Regulations, and the National Emission Ceilings Regulations 2002[300] (the "NEC Regulations"). As for venting, the regulation thereof falls under the Energy Act 2008.

9.80 The Production Regulations forbid a licensee from flaring any gas unless written consent has been obtained and any conditions attached thereto have been adhered to.[301] Exceptions thereto include instances where there is a risk of injury to persons, or where it is

---

the environment". In relation to such techniques, the terms "best" and "techniques" are respectively defined as "the most effective in achieving a high general level of protection of the environment as a whole" and "the technology used and the way in which the installation is designed, built, maintained, operated and decommissioned".

[293] Such controls may include emission value limits (reg 4(2)(g)(i)), equivalent parameters or technical measures (reg 4(2)(g)(ii)), or a combination of emission value limits and equivalent parameters and technical measures (reg 4(2)(g)(iii)).

[294] Reg 4.

[295] Regs 9 and 10.

[296] Regs 13–16.

[297] Reg 18.

[298] Reg 18(4).

[299] See The World Bank, "Overview of Onshore and Offshore Gas Flaring and Venting in the United Kingdom": http://siteresources.worldbank.org/INTGGFR/Resources/united-kingdom.pdf (accessed 11 April 2011), where it is noted that in 2001, 20% of the offshore CO_2 emissions arose from flaring while only 0.05% arose from venting.

[300] SI 2002/3118.

[301] Reg 23(3)(a).

necessary to maintain a flow of petroleum from the well.[302] If flaring without consent has occurred, the licensee is obliged to inform the Minister thereof; and, where it was done so as to maintain the flow of petroleum, the licensee must stop flaring when directed to do so.[303] It is surprising that operators may be permitted to flare gas until such time as they are requested to stop as it would make greater sense if, for example, they were obliged to stop as soon as reasonably possible based on objective scientific criteria related to the flow of petroleum. Similarly, when a licensee wishes to apply for consent to flare, a written submission specifying the date of proposed commencement thereof is required,[304] but the licensee is not required to specify a date for the cessation thereof.

National Emission Ceilings Regulations 2002
The NEC Regulations require that the Secretary of State must **9.81** ensure that, in 2010 and every year thereafter, the emission of certain pollutants, namely sulphur dioxide (SO_2), nitrogen oxides (NO_x), volatile organic compounds (VOC) and ammonia (NH_3), do not exceed the permitted amounts thereof as stipulated in the Schedule to the NEC Regulations.[305] So as to achieve this objective, the Secretary of State is bound to prepare a programme for the progressive reduction in emissions of the relevant pollutants.[306] Although the NEC Regulations apply to emissions from land, the territorial sea and the continental shelf,[307] Oil & Gas UK notes that the UK Government is of the belief that it will be able to meet the targets of the NEC Regulations without having to apply these targets offshore.[308] Whether or not the targets will be met solely through onshore application remains to be seen. However, as Oil & Gas UK point out, "this does not preclude future targets for offshore operations".[309]

---

[302] Reg 23(7)(a) and (b). This is, however, subject to the proviso in reg 23(7) that such exceptional flaring should only occur as a consequence of an event that the licensee did not foresee in time to deal therewith in an alternative manner.

[303] Reg 23(7).

[304] Reg 23(4).

[305] Reg 3, read with reg 2. Presently, the national emission ceilings in the Schedule are: 585 kilotonnes for SO_2; 1,167 kilotonnes for NO_x; 1,200 kilotonnes for VOCs; and 297 kilotonnes for NH_3.

[306] Reg 4(1).

[307] Reg 2(2)(a) and (b).

[308] Oil & Gas UK, "Atmospheric Emissions – Offshore Cargo Loading": http://www. ukooaenvironmentallegislation.co.uk/contents/Topic_Files/Offshore/VOC.htm (accessed 11 April 2011).

[309] Oil & Gas UK (n 308 above).

Sewage and garbage

9.82 Having come into force on 1 February 2009, the Merchant Shipping (Prevention of Pollution by Sewage and Garbage from Ships) Regulations 2008[310] (the "PPSGS Regulations") are the UK Government's domestic manifestation of Annexes IV and V of MARPOL 73/78 which address pollution from ships by sewage and garbage respectively. Importantly, the concept of a "ship" includes fixed or floating platforms operating in the marine environment.[311] Unfortunately, the use of the word "operating" raises the question whether the PPSGS Regulations apply to non-operational offshore installations which, although they may for some reason not be involved in the drilling and production of oil and gas, are nonetheless present in the marine environment with personnel onboard who will certainly be producing sewage and garbage. Leaving this point aside, the definitions of "garbage" and "sewage" under the PPSGS Regulations are particularly broad. What constitutes "garbage" includes:

> "all kinds of victual, domestic and operational wastes generated during the normal operation of a ship and liable to be disposed of continuously or periodically, but does not include fresh fish and parts thereof, sewage, or any other substance the disposal of which is prohibited or otherwise controlled under an Annex to the Convention other than Annex V."[312]

"Sewage" is defined as including, among other things, drainage and other wastes from any form of toilet or urinal, as well as other waste waters that may be mixed with any such drainage.[313]

9.83 With regard in particular to sewage, the PPSGS Regulations prohibit the discharge thereof into the sea[314] and provide for surveys to be conducted of offshore installations and their compulsory sewage management systems as well as for the certification thereof.[315] There are some notable exceptions to the prohibition on discharging sewage. First, sewage discharge may take place if it has been through a sewage treatment plant that complies with the requirements of the Merchant Shipping (Marine Equipment) Regulations 1999,[316] the said plant has been tested and the results thereof are reflected in the relevant sewage certificate, and, there will be no visible solids

---

[310] SI 2008/3257, as amended by SI 2010/897.
[311] Reg 2(1).
[312] *Ibid.*
[313] *Ibid.*
[314] Reg 23(1).
[315] Reg 7.
[316] SI 1999/1957.

or discolouration of the seawater.[317] Second, treated sewage may be discharged more than 3 nautical miles from the nearest land if it has been through a comminuting and disinfecting system approved by the Maritime and Coastguard Agency ("MCA") which meets the standards set out in Merchant Shipping Notice MSN No 1807.[318] Third, untreated sewage may be discharged at a specific rate at a distance of more than 12 nautical miles from land where offshore installations are en route and proceeding at not less than 4 knots.[319] Fourth, the general prohibition on the discharge of sewage does not apply to "old ships", a term which indirectly incorporates offshore installations constructed before 2 October 1983.[320] The owners of such installations are, however, bound to ensure that they are "equipped, so far as is practicable" to discharge sewage through a sewage treatment plant that complies with the requirements of the Merchant Shipping (Marine Equipment) Regulations 1999 or a comminuting and disinfecting system approved by the MCA which satisfies the standards set out in Merchant Shipping Notice MSN No 1807.[321]

As regards the aforementioned sewage certification require- **9.84** ments, offshore installations may not "be put into service, or … continue in service" unless an "initial survey" has been conducted, the relevant equipment has been deemed to be satisfactory, and a Sewage Certificate has been issued.[322] When Sewage Certificates require renewal, the PPSGS Regulations dictate that offshore installations may not "proceed to sea, or … remain at sea" without a "renewal survey" having been conducted and a new Sewage Certificate having been issued.[323] Notably, the responsibility of appropriately maintaining offshore installations and their sewage equipment falls on the owners and managers thereof, who are specifically bound to ensure that offshore installations "remain fit to proceed to sea without presenting an unreasonable threat of harm to the marine environment".[324] As with the aforementioned PAPS Regulations, however, what constitutes "an unreasonable threat" is undefined.

The relevant sewage management equipment must consist of **9.85** either: a sewage treatment plant, which, as previously mentioned,

---

[317] Regs 24(a), (b) and (c) and 21(1)(a).

[318] Regs 25(1)(a)(b) and 21(1)(b).

[319] Reg 25(2) and (3), read with reg 2(1).

[320] Reg 23(3), read with reg 2(1) and (4).

[321] Reg 21(2), read with regs 24 and 25.

[322] Reg 7. Reg 2(1) defines a Sewage Certificate as "an International Sewage Pollution Prevention Certificate referred to in Regulation 5 of Annex IV".

[323] Reg 8.

[324] Reg 9(1), read with reg 2(6)(b).

must comply with the requirements of the Merchant Shipping (Marine Equipment) Regulations 1999; or a comminuting and disinfecting system approved by the MCA which meets the standards set out in Merchant Shipping Notice MSN No 1807; or a holding tank that is, among other things, constructed in accordance with standards set out in Merchant Shipping Notice MSN No 1807, and of sufficient capacity relative to, *inter alia*, the number of persons on the installation.[325] Notably, owners of installations constructed before 2 October 1983[326] need only ensure that they are "equipped, so far as is practicable" to discharge sewage through a sewage treatment plant that complies with the requirements of the Merchant Shipping (Marine Equipment) Regulations 1999, or a comminuting and disinfecting system approved by the MCA and meeting the standards set out in Merchant Shipping Notice MSN No 1807.[327]

9.86   As regards garbage, its disposal into the sea from offshore installations is prohibited,[328] with the exception of food wastes that have been ground or comminuted and disposed of from an installation which is 12 nautical miles or more from the nearest land.[329] Offshore installations are also bound to carry garbage management plans and garbage record books that comply with guidelines developed by the IMO and set out, respectively, in Schs 3 and 4 to Merchant Shipping Notice MSN No 1807.[330]

9.87   In relation to the enforcement of the PPSGS Regulations, provision is made for the inspection of offshore installations so as to verify, for example, the existence and validity of a Sewage Certificate.[331] It is noteworthy that provision is made for the detention of offshore installations until, *inter alia*, the relevant surveyor is satisfied that they "can proceed to sea without presenting an unreasonable threat of harm to the marine environment".[332] Unfortunately, guidance is not provided as to what a surveyor's subjective assessment of "an unreasonable threat" may be based on. Aside from the fact that the PPSGS Regulations repeatedly fail to provide an explanation of this particular concept, it is submitted that they go a long way towards satisfying the objectives of Annexes IV and V of MARPOL 73/78.

---

[325] Reg 9(1), read with reg 2(6)(b).
[326] Reg 2(4), read with reg 2(1) and 21(1).
[327] Reg 21(2), read with regs 24 and 25.
[328] Reg 29, read with reg 2(1). Under reg 26(1) the disposal of plastics is specifically prohibited.
[329] Reg 29(2).
[330] Reg 32.
[331] Reg 36.
[332] Reg 38.

Interference with other users of the sea

What follows is a brief discussion of those laws that address the 9.88
possibility of interference with fishing and navigation caused by the
presence of offshore installations and pipelines. The cardinal statutes
addressing this form of pollution are the previously discussed
CPA 1949 and the Petroleum Act 1998.

Coast Protection Act 1949

In accordance with s 34 of CPA 1949, the consent of the 9.89
Secretary of State is required, not only in relation to the location
of offshore installations and pipelines, but also in relation to any
construction or alteration of any works on, under or over any
part of the seashore lying below the level of mean high water
springs, or the depositing of any object or any materials thereon,
or removing any object or any materials from any part of the
seashore lying below the level of mean low water springs, where
such operations may result in obstruction or danger to navigation.[333] Notably, s 4(1) of the Continental Shelf Act 1964 has
extended the application of s 34 of CPA 1949 to all areas of the
UKCS.

    Obtaining the abovementioned consent requires the submission to 9.90
the Secretary of State of "such plans and particulars of the proposed
operation as he may consider necessary".[334] The plans and particulars
that the Secretary of State will consider as necessary will be those
that enable him to evaluate the risk to navigation.[335] Every proposed
location and each installation will be evaluated in relation to, among
other things, shipping movements close to a proposed location and
the danger of passing vessels colliding with the installation.[336] The
Secretary of State's consent will also depend on the deployment of
specified navigation aids such as flashing obstruction lights, foghorns
and buoys, which will be subject to regular seaward inspections
by the General Lighthouse Authority (the "GLA").[337] Additionally,
obtaining consent in relation to mobile rigs requires notification of
the movements thereof being sent, generally 48 hours beforehand,
to the consent issuing office and the relevant Coastguard Maritime

---

[333] Section 34(1)(a), (b) and (c).
[334] Section 34(2).
[335] Oil & Gas UK, http://www.ukooaenvironmentallegislation.co.uk/contents/Topic_Files/
Offshore/Fishing_Navigation_Installation.htm (accessed 11 April 2011).
[336] Oil & Gas UK (n 335 above).
[337] Section 36A; DECC, "Guidance to Coast Protection Act 1949": https://www.og.decc.
gov.uk/environment/Guidance_cpa1949.pdf (accessed 11 April 2011).

Rescue Co-ordination Centre as well as the Hydrographer to the Navy.[338]

9.91   Where the Secretary of State is of the opinion that the location of a proposed offshore installation or pipeline may obstruct or pose a danger to navigation, he will either refuse to grant his consent thereto or grant consent subject to such conditions as he thinks fit.[339] Any person who fails to obtain the requisite consent, or fails to comply with any conditions subject to which consent has been granted, shall be guilty of an offence.[340]

9.92   Prior to considering the relevant provisions of the Petroleum Act 1998, it should be borne in mind that DECC considers proposed operations in Deep Water Routes and Traffic Separation Schemes, as well as the approaches thereto, to be such that they will usually obstruct and endanger navigation.[341]

9.93   The foregoing discussion of the CPA 1949 demonstrates that the UK possesses particularly detailed legislation aimed at addressing pollution in the form of interference with fishing and navigation. As will be demonstrated below, the Petroleum Act also plays a significant role in relation to offshore pipelines.

Petroleum Act 1998

9.94   Under the Petroleum Act, no person may construct or use such pipelines without the Secretary of State's prior authorisation.[342] This prohibition applies to any pipeline in, under, or over controlled waters which are defined as the territorial sea adjacent to the UK and the sea in any area designated under s 1(7) of the Continental Shelf Act 1964.[343] Importantly, authorisations to construct or use pipelines (commonly referred to as Pipeline Work Authorisations) may contain conditions pertaining to the route and the design thereof, as well as steps that must be taken to avoid or reduce interference with fishing or other activities connected with the sea or the seabed or subsoil.[344]

9.95   The Petroleum Act provides that persons who construct or use a pipeline without the Secretary of State's authorisation, or fraudulently

---

[338] DECC (n 337 above).

[339] Section 34(3).

[340] Section 36(1).

[341] DECC (n 337 above).

[342] Section 14(1)(a) and (b).

[343] Section 14(2). Note that s 26(1) defines a "pipeline" as meaning, except where the context otherwise requires, "a pipe or systems of pipes (excluding a drain or sewer) for the conveyance of any thing, together with any apparatus and works associated with such a pipe or system".

[344] Section 15(3)(c)(i), (iii) and (iv).

obtain such authorisation, shall be guilty of an offence.[345] Notably, operators may be particularly apprehensive about constructing or utilising a pipeline without the requisite consent in view of the fact that, should they do so, the Secretary of State may serve upon them a notice requiring the removal of any relevant works and, should they fail to do so, the Secretary of State may attend thereto and recover any expenses reasonably incurred.[346] The Petroleum Act contains additional deterrents including provisions relating, where appropriate, to the institution of criminal and civil liability.[347]

CONCLUSION

The economic benefits of oil and gas to the UK's economy cannot   9.96
be gainsaid. Whatever the broad environmental effects of burning the hydrocarbons produced from the UKCS, the oil and gas operations themselves (excluding tanker operations) have not produced adverse environmental effects of the sort that have excited significant public or political concern. The extent to which this is a function of the legislative and regulatory approach that has progressively been introduced by the UK Government, frequently with the impetus of international or, specifically, European legal obligations, is an open question, but it is true to say that there is an observable difference between the regulatory architecture on the UKCS and that which was until recently present in the Gulf of Mexico. Whereas in the US the sponsoring department for the offshore industry (the Minerals Management Service) was also responsible for safety, these functions have been separated in the UK since 1992. In the aftermath of the catastrophic oil spill in the Gulf of Mexico in 2010, while there have been some guarded suggestions to the effect that the UK's regulatory approach makes such an event less likely,[348] there has been a more significant effort to avoid complacency and to institute a joint industry/regulator/trade union review of existing practices (the Offshore Spill Prevention and Response Advisory Group) to ensure that nothing requires attention.[349] Given the overarching concern of this volume with the impact of maturity on the law and regulation that relates to the UKCS, it is surely pertinent to suggest

---

[345] Section 21(1)(a) and (c)(i).

[346] Section 21(2) and (3).

[347] Sections 22 and 23.

[348] See Oil & Gas UK Press Release, "Oil & Gas UK Comments on UK Safety Regulation to Minimise Risk of Oil Spills", 13 May 2010: http://www.oilandgasuk.co.uk/news/news. cfm/newsid/500 (accessed 11 April 2011).

[349] For details, see: http://www.oilandgasuk/knowledgecentre/OSPRAG.cfm (accessed 11 April 2011).

that this factor must be a key concern for OSPRAG. In so far as the UKCS is characterised by ageing infrastructure, where the decision on decommissioning looms large and where joint industry and government initiatives are endeavouring to extend the life of reservoirs with a view to maximising economic recovery, there must be concern that the tension between this entirely legitimate objective and environmental protection may be increased problematically. That complex balance will certainly be in the minds of those charged with reviewing the UK environmental regulatory regime under the auspices of OSPRAG. The Health and Safety Executive's findings in relation to asset integrity in the maturing province discussed elsewhere in this volume[350] raised concerns in relation to occupational safety – it may equally be suggested that they raise concerns for environmental protection that OSPRAG will surely also bear in mind.

---

[350] See Chapter 10.

CHAPTER 10

DECOMMISSIONING OF OFFSHORE
OIL AND GAS INSTALLATIONS

John Paterson

In contrast to the pioneering nature of field start-up, whether from 10.1
the engineering or the legal perspective, the processes relating to
field abandonment can appear at first sight to be considerably less
glamorous. Yet the technical challenges involved in decommissioning[1]
installations and pipelines are increasingly regarded as comparable
to, if not indeed greater than, those associated with construction and
installation.[2] Similarly, the legal treatment of the decommissioning
process, whether in terms of environmental protection, taxation or
ongoing liabilities, is now understood not simply as part of a tidying
up exercise but rather as a crucial component in the continued
success of what is a mature province. Nor is it clear that all the
questions have yet been answered in this regard.[3] The most recent

---

[1] Note that the terms "abandonment" and "decommissioning" can be used interchangeably. While the Petroleum Act 1998 (discussed below at para 10.38) uses
"abandonment", both the regulator (formerly the Department of Trade and Industry,
then the Department for Business, Enterprise and Regulatory Reform and now the
Department of Energy and Climate Change, hereinafter the "Department") and the
industry generally avoid this term. The Department notes simply in its Guidance Notes
for Industry (discussed below at para 10.48) that "decommissioning" is the "preferred
and generally accepted term" (para 2.1). Industry sources suggest that there is concern
that "abandonment" conveys the wrong image of what is involved. This sensitivity
to public perceptions of the terminology is explained in large part by the Brent Spar
case (discussed below at para 10.17). For a discussion, see A D M Forte, "Legal
Aspects of Decommissioning Offshore Structures" in D G Gorman and J Neilson (eds),
Decommissioning Offshore Structures (1997) (hereinafter "Gorman and Neilson"),
pp 125–140, 126–127.
[2] Comments by C Gray, Conoco, at the *Decommissioning: Facing the Future* seminar
organised by Shepherd and Wedderburn, Solicitors, Aberdeen, 20 March 2007.
[3] For an indication of the growing awareness of the significance of decommissioning in oil

Activity Survey from Oil & Gas UK informed the Government that uncertainty in relation to the fiscal treatment of decommissioning as well as the advent of Phase III of the EU Emissions Trading Scheme could "result in premature cessation of production for many assets".[4] In so far as this would be entirely at odds with the Government's stated objective of maximising economic recovery,[5] some of the most important legal developments affecting the offshore oil and gas industry in the near future may well occur in the area of decommissioning. The need for these developments may be appreciated from the fact that while the removal of redundant installations and infrastructure has already started, what has so far occurred[6] will pale into insignificance compared with what will happen in coming years.[7] It is true to say that decommissioning dates have frequently been pushed back, but Oil & Gas UK suggest that 2010 sees this trend halted and indeed perhaps in some cases reversed.[8] Does this mean that a surge of decommissioning is imminent? The Department would appear to be sceptical, suggesting that industry predictions have frequently turned out to be pessimistic.[9]

---

and gas development globally, as well as of the extent to which many governments have not yet or inadequately addressed the issue, see World Bank, "Environmental Governance in Oil-Producing Developing Countries", Extractive Industries for Development Series #17, June 2010, p 17. It is noted there that "[i] In less than half of the countries surveyed, governments pay little or no attention to liability and the decommissioning of oil and gas facilities". For a discussion of the approach taken in a range of developed and developing countries, see P Park and M O Igiehon, "Evolution of international law on the decommissioning of oil and gas installations" (2001) 9 *International Energy Law and Taxation Review* 199–212.

[4] Oil & Gas UK, *2010 Oil and Gas UK Activity Survey* (2010 (hereinafter "Oil & Gas UK), p 17. See also See M Tholen, "Decommissioning liabilities cast shadow on UKCS investment", (2007) 67 *Offshore* (http://www.offshore-mag.com/articles/article_display. cfm?ARTICLE_ID=290866&p=9) (accessed 26 April 2011); and P Dymond, "Shadow cast by decommissioning liability" (2006) 8/9 *International Energy Law and Taxation Review* 222–225.

[5] See para 5.6.

[6] Approved decommissioning programmes are listed on the Department's website at http://www.og.decc.gov.uk/upstream/decommissioning/programmes/approved.htm.

[7] The fact that decommissioning dates appeared to be changing so often has prompted the Department to move away from publishing a graph of Estimated Decommissioning Dates and instead to replace it with a graph showing the number of fields projected to cease production in a given year together with data from previous years so as to allow the trend to be discerned. This is available online at http://www.og.decc.gov.uk/upstream/decommissioning/forecast_rem.htm (accessed 26 April 2011). Broadly speaking, this indicates that the years up to 2020 will see the greatest number of fields cease production although there would still be fields in double figures to be closed down after 2035.

[8] Oil & Gas UK, n 4 above, p 17. It is notable, however, that the Department's figures quoted above at n 7 do appear to show decommissioning dates being put back between 2008 and 2009, so it remains to be seen if Oil & Gas UK's 2010 claims are borne out in due course.

[9] Presentation by Keith Mayo, Head of the Offshore Decommissioning Unit, Bergen, 10–11 February 2009.

Whenever decommissioning begins in earnest, however, the scale   10.2
of the task facing the industry serves to provide an indication of the
importance of this issue. Precise figures for the number of installations and the length of pipeline to be removed vary from source to
source, but the Department's most recent figures suggest 552 installations on the UKCS. Of these, 21 are floating, 278 are subsea, 244
are fixed steel structures and eight are gravity-based concrete structures. As regards pipelines, the Department has indicated that these
measure in excess of 15,000 km.[10]

Perhaps more informative than the numbers of installations and   10.3
lengths of pipeline are the costs involved. Estimates of these also
vary, with the Department suggesting a figure of around £20 billion
against a backdrop of falling costs, but Oil & Gas UK quoting a
figure of £26 billion and specifically suggesting that decommissioning
is an exception to the rule of reducing costs.[11] The importance of the
legal treatment of decommissioning thus begins to be come clearer.
Precisely what the law requires to be removed, whether there will be
any tax breaks and what those involved may need to set aside for
future liabilities will have a significant impact on precisely what the
final costs will be.

It is worth noting at the outset that part of the reason for these   10.4
substantial sums is the fact that when the first generation structures
were designed and built the practicalities of decommissioning were
not considered. Notwithstanding that relatively detailed projections
of costs and returns were calculated associated with the lifetime
production profile of a reserve, decommissioning costs were notable
by their absence.[12] As time went on, however, this factor began to
loom larger in industry thinking,[13] though even then it is important
to bear in mind that structural engineers were often more focused
on responding to emergent problems as ongoing experience in the
North Sea threw up new challenges.[14] The deep water of the northern

---

[10] Presentation by Keith Mayo, Head of the Offshore Decommissioning Unit, Kuala
Lumpur, 1–2 October 2009. For full details of the installations on the UKCS, see
OSPAR Commission, 2009 Biennial Update of the Inventory of Oil and Gas Offshore
Installations in the OSPAR Maritime Area (OSPAR Publication No 334/2009). This lists
all the installations located within the sea area covered by the OSPAR Convention of 1992
(discussed below at para 10.12).
[11] Oil & Gas UK, n 4 above, p 17.
[12] For a view of field project calculations at this time, see F E Banks, The Political
Economy of Oil (1980), p 52.
[13] See, eg, P H Prasthofer, "Decommissioning Technology Challenges" (1998) III Offshore
Technology Conference 379.
[14] The industry entering the North Sea had assumed that experience gained in the Gulf of
Mexico could simply be transferred. The first 10–15 years, however, revealed that installation design assumptions based on maximum wave height were not sufficient and that
fatigue failure was more of a problem in the North Sea. No sooner had this been factored

North Sea is another reason that is often cited as an explanation for the high costs,[15] though some studies suggest that a variety of factors, including paradoxically the very flexibility of the UK's approach to decommissioning, contribute to the problem.[16]

10.5 The legal treatment of decommissioning therefore needs to be sensitive to these cost[17] and technical[18] issues. Equally, as the Brent Spar case of the mid-1990s demonstrated, it needs to take account of the potential for possibly considerable public interest in decommissioning decisions.[19]

10.6 This chapter is accordingly structured as follows. Following this introduction, the evolution of the international legal regime is considered, both at the global and regional levels prior to the Brent Spar case. There is thus consideration of the Convention on the Continental Shelf 1958, the London Dumping Convention 1972, the United Nations Convention on the Law of the Sea 1982 and the International Maritime Organization's Guidelines and Standards 1989, and the OSPAR Convention 1992. Thereafter the extraordinary events of the Brent Spar case and its implications are examined. This involves consideration of the initial regulatory approach, the Greenpeace protest, the Stakeholder Dialogue initiated by Shell and the impact of the case on OSPAR and the UK Government. This is followed by a review of international and domestic legal developments post-Brent Spar with particular attention paid to the 1996 Protocol to the London Convention, OSPAR Decision 98/3 and the Petroleum Act 1998 as amended by the Energy Act 2008. Noting that the Department has not utilised its regulatory powers under the 1998 Act but rather has preferred to operate on the basis of guidance, the chapter then examines its updated Guidance Notes for Industry in some detail, specifically the treatment of s 29 notices, decommissioning security agreements and the decommissioning

---

in than dynamic response emerged as an issue. For an overview of these problems, see R J Howe, "Evolution of Offshore Drilling and Production Technology" (1986) IV *Offshore Technology Conference* 593.

[15] Oil & Gas UK suggests that 44% of the total expected bill will be attributed to the northern North Sea, with the southern and central areas accounting for 24% and 15% respectively: n 4 above, p 17.

[16] P E O'Connor, B R Corr, S Palmer and R C Byrd, "Comparative Assessment of Decommissioning Applications of Typical North Sea and Gulf of Mexico Approaches to Several Categories of Offshore Platforms in the Middle East" (2004) *Proceedings of The Fourteenth International Offshore and Polar Engineering Conference* 460.

[17] See A G Kemp and L Stephen, "Economic and Fiscal Aspects of Decommissioning Offshore Structures" in Gorman and Neilson, n 1 above, pp 80–123.

[18] See P A Meenan, "Technical Aspects of Decommissioning Offshore Structures" in Gorman and Neilson, n 1 above, pp 23–56.

[19] See A G Jordan and L G Bennie, "Political Aspects of Decommissioning" in Gorman and Neilson, n 1 above, pp 141–162.

programme process. Two continuing areas of uncertainty related to decommissioning, namely residual liabilities and taxation, are then considered before concluding remarks are made.

THE EVOLUTION OF INTERNATIONAL LAW 1958–92

United Nations Convention on the Continental Shelf 1958

The starting point for any discussion of decommissioning outside of 10.7 territorial waters, involving as it does operations on the Continental Shelf, must be international law. The foundation document in this regard is the United Nations Convention on the Continental Shelf 1958. At the same time as this Convention granted states "sovereign rights for the purpose of exploring [the continental shelf] and exploiting its natural resources"[20] and entitled them "to construct and maintain or operate … installations" to that end,[21] it also provided in blunt terms that "[a]ny installations which are abandoned or disused must be entirely removed".[22] While this may have seemed to be an entirely reasonable proposition in 1958, bearing in mind that offshore operations were then only in their infancy and very much confined to shallow waters, it became apparent with the passage of time that this requirement might not always be realistic. This realisation posed no problems for states that were not party to the Convention, but for a country such as the United Kingdom the situation was different. It undoubtedly faced some of the most difficult challenges in complying with Art 5(5) given the fact that substantial structures were located in deep water on the UKCS. The Government argued in 1987, however, that the 1958 Convention needed to be interpreted purposively. This purpose could be discovered in Art 5(1) which stipulated that "[t]he exploration of the continental shelf and the exploitation of its natural resources must not result in any unjustifiable interference with navigation, fishing or the conservation of the living resources of the sea". Given that the circumstances of the industry had changed considerably since 1958 and that it was by 1987 difficult – if not indeed impossible – to meet the complete removal requirement, the UK would remove installations to the extent necessary to ensure that there was no unjustifiable interference with navigation, fishing or the conservation of the living resources of the sea.[23]

---

[20] 1958 Convention, Art 2(1).
[21] *Ibid*, Art 5(2).
[22] *Ibid*, Art 5(5).
[23] Daintith, Willoughby and Hill, para 1–1304. See also A D M Forte, "Legal Aspects of Decommissioning Offshore Structures" in Gorman and Neilson, n 1 above, pp 125–140 and 129.

UNCLOS 1982 and the IMO Guidelines 1989

10.8   Considerations such as these had in any event prompted the United Nations itself to revisit the issue of redundant installations. The 1982 Convention on the Law of the Sea (UNCLOS), the preamble to which explicitly recognises "that developments since … 1958 … have accentuated the need for a new and generally acceptable Convention on the law of the sea", thus stipulates a less draconian position:

> "Any installations or structures which are abandoned or disused shall be removed to ensure safety of navigation, taking into account any generally accepted international standards established in this regard by the competent international organization. Such removal shall also have due regard to fishing, the protection of the marine environment and the rights and duties of other States. Appropriate publicity shall be given to the depth, position and dimensions of any installations or structures not entirely removed."[24]

It may be wondered as a consequence why the UK Government needed to argue for a purposive interpretation of the 1958 Convention as late as 1987, in view of this more favourable provision in the 1982 Convention. This is explained by the fact that the UK did not accede to the latter Convention until 1997.[25] Nevertheless, with that accession, it is now UNCLOS 1982 that sets out the UK's international obligations with regard to decommissioning.

10.9   Given the wording of Art 60(3), it is important to know the identity of "the competent international organization" and whether it has established "any generally accepted international standards". In this regard, the body in question is the International Maritime Organization,[26] and in particular its Maritime Safety Committee.[27]

---

[24] 1958 Convention, Art 60(3), as applied to the Continental Shelf by Art 80.

[25] See D H Anderson, "British Accession to the UN Convention on the Law of the Sea" 1997 46(4) ICLQ 761–786.

[26] The IMO is an agency of the United Nations, established by the Inter-Governmental Maritime Consultative Organization Convention of 1948. Article 1 of the Convention (as amended) lists the purposes of the IMO, including "(a) To provide machinery for co-operation among Governments in the field of governmental regulation and practices relating to technical matters of all kinds affecting shipping engaged in international trade, and to encourage the general adoption of the highest practicable standards in matters concerning maritime safety, efficiency of navigation and prevention and control of marine pollution from ships; and to deal with administrative and legal matters related to the purposes set out in this Article".

[27] Its functions include consideration of "aids to navigation, construction and equipment of vessels, manning from a safety standpoint, rules for the prevention of collisions, handling of dangerous cargoes, maritime safety procedures and requirements, hydrographic information, log-books and navigational records, marine casualty investigation, salvage and rescue and any other matters directly affecting maritime safety": 1948 Convention, n 24 above, Art 29.

This body produced Guidelines[28] which were adopted by the IMO's Assembly in 1989[29] and which state that "[a]bandoned or disused offshore installations or structures on any continental shelf or in any exclusive economic zone are required to be removed, except where non-removal or partial removal is consistent" with the guidelines and standards it goes on to set out.[30] These Standards and Guidelines are not legally binding: the IMO Assembly resolution adopting them simply "recommends" that they be taken into account by "Member Governments ... when making decisions regarding the removal of abandoned or disused installations or structures".[31] Such whole or partial removal is to be carried out "as soon as reasonably practicable after abandonment or permanent disuse" of an installation or structure.[32] The Guidelines provide that the treatment of installations or structures should be on a case-by-case basis by the relevant coastal state. Where it is proposed to allow the whole or part of an installation or structure to remain in place, account must be taken of a range of factors including: potential effects on navigation; environmental effects; the costs, technical feasibility and risks to personnel involved in removal; and any new use or other justification for allowing all or part of the installation or structure to remain.[33] Notwithstanding the fact that the Guidelines allow for the possibility of only partial removal, the Standards provide that where an installation or structure stands in less than 75 m of water and weighs less than 4,000 tonnes in air (excluding topsides) it should be entirely removed.[34] For installations and structures put in place after 1 January 1998 the water depth is increased to 100 m.[35] The only exception permitted in the case of installations or structures falling within these parameters is where complete removal is "not technically feasible or would involve extreme cost, or an unacceptable risk to personnel or the marine environment".[36] It should be noted, however, that the Guidelines further provide that installations or structures located in certain defined areas important for navigation "should be entirely removed and should not be subject to any exceptions".[37] It should

---

[28] Guidelines and Standards for the Removal of Offshore Installations and Structures on the Continental Shelf and in the Exclusive Economic Zone (hereinafter "IMO Guidelines").
[29] Resolution A.672(16), adopted 19 October 1989.
[30] IMO Guidelines, para 1.1.
[31] Resolution A.672(16), n 27 above.
[32] IMO Guidelines, para 1.2.
[33] Ibid, para 2.1.
[34] Ibid, para 3.1.
[35] Ibid, para 3.2.
[36] Ibid, para 3.5.
[37] Ibid, para 3.7.

also be noted that para 3.13 of the Guidelines provides that no installation or structure should be emplaced on or after 1 January 1998
unless its "design and construction ... is such that entire removal
... would be feasible". It could thus be suggested that the increase
in the water depth criterion to 100 m for installations or structures
of 4,000 tonnes or less emplaced on or after 1 January 1998 in
para 3.2 is superfluous in so far as para 3.13 appears to impose a
more stringent standard for *all* installations or structures emplaced
after that date. In any case where there is partial removal with no
part of the installation or structure projecting above the surface, this
must leave an unobstructed water column of at least 55 m.[38] It should
be noted finally that as regards the situation where there is a new use
or other justification for allowing all or part of the installation or
structure to remain, the Guidelines specifically envisage their reuse as
artificial reefs where they can serve to enhance fisheries.[39]

London Convention 1972

10.10   It is one thing to remove an installation or structure, whether wholly
or partly; what happens to it thereafter is quite another. Reuse as
an artificial reef is clearly a possibility in some situations, but where
there is any proposal to dispose of an installation or structure in
the sea where no new use is intended, then this must be considered
in terms of the various dumping Conventions. In this regard, there
are both global and regional instruments to be considered. The first
global instrument is the London Convention on the Prevention of
Marine Pollution by Dumping of Wastes and Other Matter of 1972.
This divides wastes into three categories, in each case specifying what
action may be taken in relation to them: dumping of wastes listed
in Annex I to the Convention is prohibited;[40] dumping of wastes
listed in Annex II requires a prior special permit;[41] and the dumping

---

[38] IMO Guidelines, para 3.6.

[39] See *ibid*, paras 3.4.1 and 3.12. This approach has particularly been adopted in the
Gulf of Mexico where it has been overseen by the Minerals Management Service of the
US Department of the Interior under Title II of the National Fishing Enhancement Act of
1984 (PL 98-623) and the National Artificial Reef Plan (NOAA Technical Memorandum
NMFS OF-6, November, 1985, as amended) developed by the National Marine Fisheries
Service. At least 128 installations have been reused in this way. For further details, see:
http://www.gomr.boemre.gov/homepg/regulate/environ/rigs-to-reefs/artificial-reefs.html
(accessed 26 April 2011).

[40] The list in Annex I to the 1972 Convention includes, *inter alia*, certain heavy metals,
persistent synthetics, heavy oils and high-level radioactive substances.

[41] The list in Annex II to the 1972 Convention includes, *inter alia*, certain metals,
fluorides, pesticides and "Containers, scrap metal and other bulky wastes liable to sink to
the sea bottom which may present a serious obstacle to fishing or navigation".

of all other wastes requires a prior general permit.[42] No permit is
to be issued prior to careful consideration of factors mentioned in
Annex III.[43]

As regards offshore installations, these are specifically covered **10.11**
by Art III(1)(a)(ii) which defines "dumping" as including "any
deliberate disposal at sea of vessels, aircraft, platforms or other
man-made structures at sea". It would accordingly appear that as
far as the London Convention is concerned, provided a structure or
installation did not fall foul of the Annex I prohibition, its disposal
at sea would be possible subject to a prior special permit.

OSPAR 1992

The regional instrument on dumping affecting the United Kingdom **10.12**
is the Convention for the Protection of the Marine Environment of
the North-East Atlantic of 1992. This is more commonly known
as the OSPAR Convention, reflecting the fact that it combined
and updated the pre-existing Oslo Convention for the Prevention
of Marine Pollution by Dumping from Ships and Aircraft 1972
and Paris Convention for the Prevention of Marine Pollution
from Land-based Sources 1974. The extent of the Convention's
coverage is precisely defined in Art 1(a), but for present purposes
it is sufficient to note that the whole of the UKCS is included.
"Dumping" is defined so as to include specifically "any deliberate
disposal in the maritime area of ... (2) offshore installations and
offshore pipelines",[44] but it does not include "the leaving wholly
or partly in place of a disused offshore installation or disused
offshore pipeline, provided that any such operation takes place
in accordance with any relevant provision of the Convention and
with other relevant international law".[45]

The general obligations imposed on contracting parties are set out **10.13**
in Art 2. The principal obligation is:

"to prevent and eliminate pollution and ... take the necessary measures
to protect the maritime area against the adverse effects of human
activities so as to safeguard human health and to conserve marine
ecosystems and, when practicable, restore marine areas which have
been adversely affected".[46]

---

[42] 1972 Convention, Art IV(1).
[43] These factors include the characteristics and composition of the matter, the characteristics of the dumping site and the method of deposit, all as further defined.
[44] OSPAR Convention 1992, Art 1(f).
[45] *Ibid*, Art 1(g).
[46] *Ibid*, Art 2(1)(a).

In adopting "programmes and measures" to this end, the contracting parties are required to apply the precautionary principle[47] and the "polluter pays" principle.[48] They must also "ensure the application of best available techniques and best environmental practice", both of which terms they must define taking account of criteria set out in Appendix 1 to the Convention.[49]

10.14   The key provisions dealing with offshore installations are contained in Annex III to the Convention. Article 5(1) of that Annex provides:

> "[n]o disused offshore installation or disused offshore pipeline shall be dumped and no disused offshore installation shall be left wholly or partly in place in the maritime area without a permit issued by the competent authority of the relevant Contracting Party on a case-by-case basis".

Article 5(3) further provides that where a Contracting Party intends to issue such a permit for dumping after 1 January 1998 it "shall, through the medium of the [OSPAR] Commission, inform the other Contracting Parties of its reasons for accepting such dumping, in order to make consultation possible". This echoed pre-existing notification and consultation arrangements contained in Guidelines for the Disposal of Offshore Installations issued in June 1991 under the Oslo Convention.[50]

10.15   It should be noted that the Convention does admit of exceptions. First, the requirements relating to the disposal of offshore installations do not apply "in case of *force majeure*, due to stress of weather or any other cause, when the safety of human life or of an offshore installation is threatened".[51] Second, Arts 8 and 10 of Annex III envisage the possibility of leaving installations in place or emplacing them for purposes other than those for which they were originally intended – in other words, rigs-to-reefs[52] – albeit that this will only be where specifically authorised and in accordance with guidelines to be drawn up by the OSPAR Commission.

10.16   It might be suggested, then, that with the OSPAR Convention, a fairly sophisticated and robust international regime was in place, not least in the area including the UKCS, to deal with the removal and ultimate disposal of offshore installations and of pipelines. And yet even before the OSPAR Convention entered into force on 25 March 1998, the adequacy of this approach had been profoundly called into question in a remarkably public fashion.

---

[47] OSPAR Convention 1992, Art 2(2)(a).
[48] *Ibid*, Art 2(2)(b).
[49] *Ibid*, Art 2(3)(b).
[50] See Parliamentary Office of Science and Technology, "Oil Rig Disposal", POST Note 65, July 1995.
[51] OSPAR Convention 1992, Annex III, Art 6.
[52] See n 39 above.

BRENT SPAR

No account of the legal treatment of the decommissioning of **10.17** offshore installations would be complete without a discussion of the Brent Spar case, not only because it enjoyed such a high profile, but especially because it led directly to changes in the approach both of OSPAR and the UK regulator at the time, the DTI.

The original disposal plan

The Brent Spar was in many respects a unique structure in that it **10.18** was neither a rig nor a platform, but rather a floating oil storage buoy. It was intended as a temporary storage and tanker loading facility for the Brent field in the northern North Sea – operated jointly by Shell and Esso – until such time as a pipeline could be built. It weighed 14,500 tonnes, was 140 m tall and was composed of six huge storage tanks with a capacity of some 50,000 tonnes of oil and a displacement of some 66,500 tonnes. It was finally declared redundant in 1991.

Disposal options for the Brent Spar could be divided into two **10.19** broad groups. The first would involve its removal and dumping in deep water; the second, its removal and dismantling ashore. While the structure had been assembled practically in its entirety onshore then floated out to its location in the North Sea, a number of factors made the simple reversal of this process difficult. While the structure was stable where it stood, degradation of the tanks over time coupled with damage to two during operations meant that any attempt to refloat it or to rotate it to a towing position risked buckling or even rupturing the tanks. This was problematical because although the tanks had been drained of oil and filled with seawater, residual sludge that could not be pumped out remained.

The provisions of the relevant international instruments in **10.20** force at the time, namely the London Convention and the Oslo Convention, were enacted in the UK by the Food and Environment Protection Act 1985 and the Petroleum Act 1987. Under the 1987 Act, Shell, as the operator, was required to obtain a licence from the DTI for the disposal of the Brent Spar.[53] Grant of the licence was dependent on acceptance of the Abandonment Plan prepared by Shell. This Plan had to be proportionate, cost-effective and consistent with both international obligations and the precautionary principle. In addition, the Plan had to constitute the Best Practicable

---

[53] Where the operator proposed to dispose of an installation at sea away from the original site, there was also a requirement for licences to be obtained under the Food and Environment Protection Act 1985.

Environmental Option (BPEO), a concept proposed by the UK Royal Commission on Environmental Pollution in 1988.[54] Demonstrating that an option constituted the BPEO involved a number of factors including: ensuring that a full range of alternatives had been considered; specifying the origins of data used and their reliability; presenting scientific evidence objectively in order to assist the taking of decisions with social or political significance; and not regarding financial considerations as overriding.

10.21   Discussions between Shell and the DTI began in 1992, with some 13 disposal options initially being considered. Of these, six were regarded as viable, with two finally being considered in detail: deepwater disposal and horizontal dismantling. Between 1992 and 1994, different aspects of these two options were examined (including some 30 separate studies) until documentation was submitted to the DTI proposing deepwater disposal at one of three sites identified by SOAEFD[55] as the BPEO – a conclusion that had itself been subject to three independent evaluations. During the same period, surveys of those sites had been commissioned by Shell and SOAEFD. The DTI approved the Abandonment Plan on 20 December 1994 and in May 1995 granted Shell a licence to dispose of the Brent Spar at the North Feni Ridge in the North Atlantic. The deepwater disposal option was chosen over the horizontal dismantling on the basis that it involved significantly lower risks to personnel (by a factor of six), was cheaper (by a factor of four) and would have only a minimal environmental impact.

10.22   In view of what has been said above about the international regime for the removal and disposal of offshore installations, nothing in the Brent Spar case to this point should come as a surprise. Indeed, it is significant in this regard that the other Contracting Parties under the Oslo Convention had been notified on 16 February 1995 of the DTI's approval of the disposal plan in accordance with the Guidelines mentioned above[56] and had not raised any objections or concerns. But the story was far from over.

The Greenpeace protest

10.23   The environmental NGO, Greenpeace, took the view that the dumping of such a vast structure was unacceptable in all circumstances and set a dangerous precedent – albeit that the DTI was at

---

[54] Twelfth Report of the Royal Commission on Environmental Pollution, *Best Practicable Environmental Option* (Cm 310, 1988).

[55] The North Feni Ridge, the Rockall Trough and the Maury Channel, all located in the North Atlantic.

[56] See para 10.14.

pains to stress that it adopted a case-by-case approach in line with the IMO Guidelines.[57] In addition, it believed, following a suggestion from an ex-oil worker, that the inventory of toxic substances on the installation could be much more significant than had been admitted by Shell. It accordingly occupied the Brent Spar and took samples from the storage tanks. From this sample it concluded that perhaps as much as 5,000 tonnes of oil remained on board, in contrast to the nominal amount claimed by Shell. This claim, coupled with the dramatic video footage of the Greenpeace occupation of the installation transformed the Brent Spar case from a peripheral issue of technical interest only to regulators and industry into a major international issue touching the whole question of the attitudes of government and industry to ocean dumping specifically and environmental protection in general. The case became headline news across Europe and Shell became the target of public protest, ranging from a boycott of its products to the firebombing of its petrol stations in Germany. Meanwhile, the UK Government came under sustained pressure from its European partners, including previously quiescent Oslo Convention partners, to reverse the decision to allow deepwater disposal.[58]

The UK Government's response was extremely robust, 10.24 defending the regulator's decision on the basis that a rigorous process had identified deepwater disposal as the BPEO.[59] This tough stance was continued even as the issue came to dominate relations with its European partners, most notably at the G7 summit in June 1995. Shell, on the other hand, wavered in the face of the dramatic effects on its business across Europe and finally announced, even as the UK Prime Minister reiterated the Government's stance, that it was abandoning the deepwater disposal plan. Shortly afterwards, Norway granted Shell permission to moor the installation in the Erfjord while it was decided what should happen next. And what happened next was nothing short of extraordinary.

---

[57] See para 10.9.

[58] For a discussion of the extent to which the Brent Spar case involved continental European environmental norms overriding those applying in the UK, see S C Zyglidopoulos, "The Social and Environmental Responsibilities of Multinationals: Evidence from the Brent Spar Case" (2002) 36 *Journal of Business Ethics* 141.

[59] For a discussion of the relative unimportance of scientific rationality in this context as compared with the "symbolic capital" of the key players, see H Tsoukas, "David and Goliath in the Risk Society: Making Sense of the Conflict between Shell and Greenpeace in the North Sea" (1999) 6 *Organization* 499. See also A D M Forte, "Legal Aspects of Decommissioning Offshore Structures", n 1 above, p 127.

Shell's Stakeholder Dialogue[60]

10.25   Flying in the face of the Government's insistence that it carry out the approved Abandonment Plan, Shell reopened the whole question of how it would dispose of the Brent Spar, calling for proposals from contractors and setting up what was essentially an entirely new regulatory process. It first commissioned Det Norske Veritas (DNV), an independent, not-for-profit, foundation, to carry out an audit of the contents of the installation with the aim of resolving the dispute with Greenpeace. Before the publication of DNV's report, which supported Shell's assessment, Greenpeace admitted errors in its sampling.[61]

10.26   Shell also announced what it called the "Way Forward". It placed a notice in the *Official Journal* seeking expressions of interest from contractors regarding the disposal of the Brent Spar. These submissions together with some 200 other proposals that Shell had received were to be developed into a "long list" and the organisations involved then invited to meet pre-qualification criteria. A list of 21 contractors was eventually published, with those involved required to develop an outline of their disposal plans.

10.27   At this point, Shell also announced that there would be a Stakeholder Dialogue Process, which would play a role in identifying the ultimate solution. This process grew out of an earlier approach to the Environment Council[62] where it had begun to discuss options for the way forward as regards reaching a new disposal decision. The Environment Council first proposed a process by which a Europe-wide panel of 50–60 stakeholders would be established with a view to it being consulted throughout the technical process of developing a new disposal plan as a means of testing ideas and keeping in touch with the various interested constituencies. While Shell was agreeable to this proposal, the response from the UK Government was negative. The latter did, however, accept a modified plan – albeit stressing that whatever disposal option was eventually chosen had to be at least as good as deepwater disposal which the regulator had

---

[60] This section draws on work carried out in the context of the EU Framework Programme 5-funded RISKGOV project which involved interviews with individuals involved in the Brent Spar case, including representatives of Shell, Greenpeace, the DTI and the Environment Council. The Brent Spar Case Study is available in G Brownless and J Paterson, "Complex and contentious risk based decisionmaking in the field of health, safety and the environment: Comparative analysis of two UK examples", Health and Safety Executive, Research Report 448 (2006).

[61] See also M Saunders, "Environmental Protection: abandonment – study vindicates Shell over Brent Spar" (1995) 13(12) *Oil and Gas Law and Taxation Review* 145–146.

[62] The Environment Council is an independent charitable organisation that brings together stakeholders from all sectors to develop solutions to environmental problems.

identified as the BPEO. This modified plan was not vastly different from the first proposal and it is probably not insignificant that in the interim between the UK Government's initial rejection and ultimate acceptance the Energy Minister had left the Government. Equally, a report commissioned by the DTI from the National Environmental Research Council had concluded that "some means should be sought to take public acceptability into account in evaluating future marine environment impact assessments".[63]

The Environment Council next set about contacting parties who were likely to be interested in being involved in the process. This produced some 200 responses and it was then a matter of arriving at a balanced group of stakeholders who would be prepared to meet periodically, prior to the points at which key decisions about the disposal would have to be taken. These meetings were facilitated by the Environment Council and it was made clear from the outset, first, that the deepwater disposal option had to be considered, as this was what the regulators had decided was the BPEO, and, second, that the aim of the exercise was not to reach a consensus but rather to ensure that whatever decision was eventually reached emerged from an open and transparent process. The process itself began with the facilitator attempting to draw out from the participants what their concerns were with the various options on the table with a view to informing the engineering process. **10.28**

The first meeting in London on 1 November 1996 discussed a range of some 30 disposal options produced by the 21 pre-qualified contractors on the so-called "long list". As a result of that initial Stakeholder Dialogue, the list was reduced to 11 disposal options from six contractors by mid-January 1997. Those contractors were then given 4 months to develop detailed commercial projects. DNV was once again retained to provide an independent evaluation of the projects on technical, environmental and safety grounds. **10.29**

Over the next few months, Stakeholder Dialogue meetings were held in Denmark and the Netherlands and in June the six short-listed contractors presented nine detailed proposals. Then, in the autumn of 1997, the contractors' prices together with the findings of DNV's evaluations were published and further Dialogue meetings were held in the UK, Denmark, the Netherlands and Germany. On the basis of these interactions the choice was narrowed down to the original deepwater disposal option and a plan to reuse the Brent Spar in the construction of a quay extension at Mekjarvik near Stavanger in Norway. A final BPEO assessment was conducted and Shell announced in January 1998 that it had chosen the reuse option. **10.30**

---

[63] NERC, *Scientific Group on Decommissioning Offshore Structures: First Report* (1996).

This choice then had to be approved by the DTI, which approval was forthcoming in August 1998. The project was completed in July 1999.

10.31 The Stakeholder Dialogue process, dovetailing with the technical process, operated according to the BPEO approach. This meant that once the most technically feasible options had been identified, their environmental aspects were addressed first, then their safety considerations and finally their cost. The environmental evaluation covered such areas as energy balance, emissions to air, consumption of resources, waste disposal, containment, ecological effects, aesthetic impacts, local societal effects and the environmental management systems put in place by the contractors.

10.32 It is interesting to note that the stakeholders concluded that none of the options put forward would have a significant environmental impact, not even the original deepwater disposal plan which had caused so much controversy.[64] The issue was, therefore, how to choose among the options given that there were only very small differences between them in terms of environmental impact. Here the stakeholders in the dialogue process were able to agree criteria to be used in such circumstances. First, projects with a *positive energy balance* were to be favoured, that is, those in which more energy was saved than consumed. Second, projects coming higher up the *waste hierarchy* would be favoured over those lower down. This hierarchy, which aims at the minimisation of waste, ranks options as follows: first, reuse; second, recycling; third, disposal. Applying these criteria, the stakeholders favoured the quay extension proposal above others on the short list inasmuch as it had the best energy balance figure and would allow 80 per cent reuse. Turning next to safety, the quay extension and deepwater disposal options had the lowest potential for loss of life or a major accident. Finally, on cost, deepwater disposal was the lowest, with the quay extension coming next.

10.33 It is worth noting, however, that although the calculations of risk and cost allowed projects to be ranked according to the different criteria, the actual outcome for the quay extension fell short of expectations: it cost nearly twice as much as expected and failed to achieve a positive energy balance.

The impact of Brent Spar on OSPAR and the UK Government

10.34 The Brent Spar case was a wake-up call to those concerned with the legal treatment of the decommissioning of offshore installa-

---

[64] In this regard, see further P A Tyler, "Disposal in the deep sea: analogue of nature or *faux ami?*" (2003) 30 *Environmental Conservation* 26.

tions at both the international and at the domestic levels. Despite the apparently robust and comprehensive regime that was in place in 1995, the public reaction to the proposed dumping of the Brent Spar indicated that it suffered from two major shortcomings. First of all, whatever the scientific thinking about the possibility of deepwater disposal, this was evidently not an approach that was socially acceptable. Second, despite the UK Government's firm belief in the regulatory approach under the Petroleum Act 1987, the public perception was rather of a closed conversation between industry and regulator, with neither of these parties enjoying much in the way of public support. And while OSPAR did not have a high public profile in the case, it was acutely aware of the weaknesses in its position that Brent Spar had exposed. None of the contracting parties had been concerned initially by the plan to dump the installation in the North Atlantic – this was, after all, something that the Oslo Convention explicitly countenanced provided the relevant assessment had been carried out, which the DTI's notification manifestly demonstrated it had been. Crucially for OSPAR, nothing in the 1992 Convention, which was then shortly due to come into force, would have altered the position. The same dumping plan could have been approved and the same notification would have been made, presumably eliciting a similarly quiet agreement. For the DTI the main issue was the fact that its robust and considered regulatory approach had been completely rejected by the public, despite its own assurance about the sound scientific basis for the decisions made. By contrast, Shell's Stakeholder Dialogue, initiated in the face of strong opposition from both the DTI and the Government, had taken the considerable heat out of the situation and was widely regarded as a success, even by those, such as Greenpeace, who had initially been most critical of the company. Both OSPAR and the DTI drew lessons from this experience and, as will be seen below, the current approach to decommissioning at both the international and the domestic levels reflects this fact.[65]

INTERNATIONAL AND DOMESTIC LAW POST-BRENT SPAR

The 1996 Protocol to the London Convention

The situation with regard to dumping is modified somewhat by 10.35 the coming into force on 24 March 2006 of the 1996 Protocol to

---

[65] For a discussion of the impact of the Brent Spar case on the integration of environmental values into national and international policymaking, see L G Bennie, "Brent Spar, Atlantic Oil and Greenpeace" (1998) 51 *Parliamentary Affairs* 397.

the London Convention 1972.[66] While this adopts a different, and indeed stricter, approach inasmuch as it prohibits *all* dumping *with the exception of* wastes and other matters mentioned in Annex I to the Protocol (the so-called "reverse list"), the fact that this includes "vessels and platforms or other man-made structures at sea", means that the position is broadly the same for the question of decommissioning offshore installations as under the 1972 Convention. A special permit will still be required, and the grant of such a permit must be in accordance with the provisions of Annex II, which is headed "Assessment of Wastes or Other Matter that May Be Considered for Dumping". It is also provided that "[p]articular attention shall be paid to opportunities to avoid dumping in favour of environmentally preferable alternatives".[67] This, together with the Protocol's adoption of the precautionary principle[68] as well as the "polluter pays" principle,[69] means that anyone proposing to dump an installation or structure would have to demonstrate that there were no environmentally preferable options and that appropriate preventive measures were being taken "when there is reason to believe that wastes or other matter introduced into the marine environment are likely to cause harm even when there is no conclusive evidence to prove a causal relation between inputs and their effects".[70] Note that there is no mention in the London Convention or the 1996 Protocol of pipelines, although this omission is less important in the case of the UK, covered as it is by a regional instrument that specifically mentions pipelines.

OSPAR Decision 98/3

10.36   The preamble to OSPAR Decision 98/3 on the Disposal of Disused Offshore Installations,[71] adopted unanimously at the Ministerial Meeting in July 1998, contains an immediate indication of the impact of the Brent Spar case in so far as it recognises that "re-use,

---

[66] For more details, see E J Molenaar, "The 1996 Protocol to the 1972 London Convention" (1997) 12 *International Journal of Marine and Coastal Law* 396; E A Kirk, "The 1996 Protocol to the London Dumping Convention and the Brent Spar" (1997) 46(4) ICLQ 957–964; L de La Fayette, "The London Convention 1972: Preparing for the Future" (1998) 13 *International Journal of Marine and Coastal Law* 515. For a discussion of the issue of waste generally in the context of decommissioning, see J Rowan Robinson and L Cowie, "Decommissioning and the regulation of waste" (2003) 1 *International Energy Law and Taxation Review* 1–7.

[67] 1996 Protocol, Art 4(1.2).

[68] *Ibid*, Art 3 (1).

[69] *Ibid*, Art 3(2).

[70] *Ibid*, Art 3(1).

[71] Note that this Decision does not apply to pipelines.

recycling or final disposal on land will generally be the preferred option for the decommissioning of disused offshore installations in the maritime area". The precise way in which this recognition is given effect is through a general prohibition on the "dumping, and the leaving wholly or partly in place, of disused offshore installations within the maritime area"[72] followed by the opening up of the possibility of a derogation from that general prohibition in certain defined circumstances.[73] Derogations, involving leaving all or part of an installation in place or dumping as appropriate, may be permitted by the competent authority of a contracting party in the following cases:

(a) all or part of the footings of a steel installation weighing more than 10,000 tonnes in air emplaced before 9 February 1999;[74]

(b) a concrete installation (including a gravity-based concrete installation, a floating installation and any concrete anchor-base) which results, or is likely to result, in interference with other legitimate uses of the sea;

(c) any other disused offshore installation when exceptional or unforeseen circumstances resulting from structural damage or deterioration, or from some other cause presenting equivalent difficulties can be demonstrated.[75]

Any such permission may only be issued following, first, an assessment in accordance with Annex 2 to the Decision that satisfies the competent authority that there are "significant reasons why an alternative disposal ... is preferable to re-use, recycling or final disposal on land"[76] and, second, consultation with the other Contracting Parties in accordance with Annex 3 to the Decision.[77] Any permit must be in the form specified in Annex 4 to the Decision[78] and must be reported to the OSPAR Commission,[79] with a further report

---

[72] OSPAR Decision 98/3, para 2.

[73] Ibid, para 3.

[74] This would appear to be at odds with the IMO Guidelines which, recall, provide at para 3.13 that no installation or structure should be emplaced on or after 1 January 1998 unless its "design and construction ... is such that entire removal ... would be feasible" (emphasis added). See para 10.9. This raises the possibility of an installation having been placed on the UKCS after 1 January 1998 but before 9 February 1999 and being allowed under OSPAR to have its footings left in place at decommissioning despite the wording of the IMO Guidelines. The crucial issue here, of course, is that while Decision 98/3 is binding, the IMO Guidelines are not.

[75] OSPAR Decision 98/3, para 3 and Annex 1.

[76] Ibid, para 3.

[77] Ibid, para 4.

[78] Ibid, para 5.

[79] Ibid, para 9.

following completion of the disposal.[80] In view of the important role played by Det Norske Veritas in the Brent Spar case, it is interesting to note that one of the requirements of Annex 4 is that a permit shall "require independent verification that the condition of the installation before the disposal operation starts is consistent both with the terms of the permit and with the information upon which the assessment of the proposed disposal was based".[81]

10.37   The general prohibition on dumping in Decision 98/3 is certainly significant, although it might be contended that the envisaged derogations mean that in many respects there has been little change from UNCLOS 1982 where the practical difficulties involved in removal in many cases was first recognised. Two things indicate that such criticism would be wide of the mark. First, it is practically impossible to imagine an operator in a similar position to Shell pushing for dumping if another option was available, even if more difficult or more expensive. Second, OSPAR has clearly signalled that it does not want to be caught on the back foot again as it was in 1995. Paragraph 7 of the Decision provides that the Commission will seek to reduce the scope of derogations in the light of ongoing experience with decommissioning. While it was specifically envisaged that the Commission would consider possible amendments initially in 2003, it was noted at that time that "decommissioning activity has not developed as quickly as expected in 1998" and that consequently there was no substantive evidence either to suggest that any of the derogation categories was no longer needed or on which revised criteria for these categories could be based.[82] The Commission undertook to review this issue again at its meeting in 2008.[83] Once again, however, the conclusion was that "the number of projects involving concrete structures and substantial steel footings has been very low and there have been no significant developments in the technical capabilities of the industry which would support a reduction in the categories eligible for derogation".[84] The matter will be reviewed again in 2013, with OSPAR making it clear that the aim is to see whether the categories that may be considered for

---

[80] OSPAR Decision 98/3, para 10.

[81] Ibid, Annex 4, para 2.b.

[82] Annual Report of the OSPAR Commission, 2002–2003, vol 1, Chap 5, para 138.

[83] Ibid, para 139. For further discussion, see L de La Fayette, "New Developments in the Disposal of Offshore Installations" (1999) 14 International Journal of Marine and Coastal Law 523; E A Kirk, "OSPAR Decision 98/3 and the dumping of offshore installations" (1999) 48(2) ICLQ 458–464; J Woodcliffe, "Decommissioning of offshore oil and gas installations in European waters: the end of a decade of indecision?" (1999) 14(1) International Journal of Marine and Coastal Law 101–123.

[84] OSPAR Commission, Assessment of impacts of offshore oil and gas activities in the North-East Atlantic (OSPAR Commission, 2009), p 26.

derogation can be reduced such that "derogations from the dumping ban remain exceptional".[85]

Petroleum Act 1998, as amended by the Energy Act 2008

The impact of Brent Spar is not immediately obvious in the legislation **10.38** that now governs decommissioning on the UKCS, notwithstanding that this received the Royal Assent in 1998. This is because Pt IV of the Petroleum Act 1998 largely serves to consolidate the pre-existing provisions to be found in the Petroleum Act 1987, Pts I and II as well as other enactments. But the echoes of the case are certainly to be detected, as will be seen below, in the Guidance Notes that the Department has issued to supplement the legislation.

The UK's approach to decommissioning proceeds on the basis of **10.39** a notice that the Secretary of State is empowered by s 29(1) of the 1998 Act to serve upon a variety of parties requiring them to submit "a programme setting out the measures proposed to be taken in connection with the abandonment of an offshore installation[86] or submarine pipeline".[87] Such a s 29 notice will either specify the date by which the abandonment programme is to be submitted to the Secretary of State or, as is more usual in practice, provide for it to be submitted on or before a date to be specified in future.[88] Section 29(3) allows the Secretary of State to require in the notice that the person upon whom it is served must carry out such consultations as he may specify. The required contents of the abandonment programme are briefly listed by s 29(4) but, as will be seen below, this is now substantially supplemented by the Department's Guidance Notes.[89]

The parties upon whom such a notice may be served are listed in **10.40** s 30(1) and include:

(a) the person having the management of the installation or of its main structure [that is, the operator];

(b) the licensee;[90]

(ba) a person who has transferred his interest under a licence without the consent of the Secretary of State;[91]

---

[85] OSPAR Commission, *Assessment of impacts of offshore oil and gas activities in the North-East Atlantic* (OSPAR Commission, 2009), p 27.

[86] As defined by s 44.

[87] As defined by ss 26 and 45.

[88] Section 29(2).

[89] See para 10.48.

[90] As defined by s 30(5) and (6).

[91] Inserted by the Energy Act 2008, s 72(2)(a) to deal with a situation of which the Secretary of State had become aware in the context of increased transfers of assets in

(c) a person falling outside of the above categories who is party to a joint operating agreement or similar agreement;

(d) a person falling outside the above categories who owns any interest in the installation otherwise than as security for a loan;

(e) a body corporate[92] outside the above categories but which is associated with a body corporate within any of those categories.[93]

As regards pipelines,[94] the parties upon whom a s 29 notice may be served are listed in s 30(2) and include:

(a) a person designated as the owner by an order made by the Secretary of State under s 27;[95]

(b) a person falling outside the above category who owns an interest in the whole or substantially the whole of the pipeline, otherwise than as security for a loan; and

(c) a body corporate outside the above categories but which is associated with a body corporate within any of those categories.[96]

An amendment introduced by the Energy Act 2008 also extends the scope of those on whom a s 29 notice may be served to those who fall into one of the above categories and who are not yet actually engaged in relevant activities on an offshore installation but who intend to become so involved.[97] The same Act has also extended the list of parties on whom a s 29 notice may be served so as to ensure that installations used for gas storage and importation (which is

---

the mature province. See also Sch 5, para 10 for the concomitant duty to carry out an approved programme.

[92] The term "body corporate" is substituted for "company" here and in s 30(2)(c) by the Energy Act 2008, s 72(2)(b) and (3) to ensure that limited liability partnerships are covered as well as companies. This is another example of the way in which the law has had to adapt to keep pace with the changing profile of the actors on the UKCS as a mature province. The test for establishing whether one body corporate is associated with another is contained in s 30(8)–(8D), substituted by s 72(5) of the 2008 Act, once again with the intention of ensuring that limited liability partnerships are brought within the scope of those on whom a s 29 notice may be served.

[93] As defined by s 30(8) and (9).

[94] Note that the definition of "submarine pipeline" now includes a pipeline which is intended to be established, allowing earlier service of a s 29 notice in respect of pipelines than had heretofore been the case. See Energy Act 2008, Sch 5, para 11, amending s 45 of the Petroleum Act 1998.

[95] Section 27(1) provides that "'owner' in relation to a pipeline ... mean[s] the person for the time being designated as the owner of the pipeline ... by an order made by the Secretary of State".

[96] As defined by s 30(8) and (9).

[97] Section 30(5)(b), as amended by s 72(4) of the 2008 Act.

itself the subject of Chapter 2 of Pt 1 of the 2008 Act) are also subject to the same decommissioning regime.[98] Installations used for Carbon Capture and Storage (the subject of Chapter 3 of Pt 1 of the 2008 Act) will also be covered by the decommissioning provisions of the 1998 Act.[99] The comprehensive reach of the s 29 notice is enhanced by the ability of the Secretary of State to require any party appearing to fall within the s 30 categories to furnish him with the name and address of every other person whom that party believes to fall within those categories,[100] on pain of a criminal penalty.[101] The aim of this approach, bluntly stated, is to ensure that whoever else ends up having to foot the bill for decommissioning installations (which recall is likely to be in the region of £20–26 billion), it will not be the British taxpayer. This consideration explains why under s 31(1) persons falling into categories (d) and (e) will not have a s 29 notice served on them where the Secretary of State is satisfied that parties under categories (a)–(c) have made "adequate arrangements, including financial arrangements ... to ensure that a satisfactory abandonment programme which will be carried out". This provision will not apply, however, where a notice has not been complied with or where the Secretary of State has rejected a programme.[102] It is noteworthy, however, that a s 29 notice, once served, may be withdrawn.[103] This recognises the fact that as the UKCS matures as a hydrocarbon province there is increasing activity with regard to the transfer of assets. The Government is keen to encourage this so as to maximise recovery. It is accordingly willing to relieve a party divesting itself of assets of ongoing liabilities for decommissioning costs through withdrawal of a s 29 notice. That said, however, this will only happen where the Secretary of State is satisfied that the party acquiring the assets has the ability, technical and financial, to meet the decommissioning responsibilities. Where this is not the case, the parties will be required to enter into a financial security agreement.[104] Furthermore, it is important to realise that the fact that a s 29 notice is withdrawn does not mean that a further notice cannot be served at some future date.[105] Nor does it mean that a party who has had their s 29 notice withdrawn cannot be recalled, as will be seen below.[106]

---

[98] Energy Act 2008, Sch 1, paras 10 and 11.
[99] Petroleum Act 1998, s 30.
[100] *Ibid*, 30(3).
[101] *Ibid*, 30(4).
[102] *Ibid*, 31(3).
[103] *Ibid*, 31(5).
[104] See para 10.58.
[105] Petroleum Act 1998, s 31(5).
[106] See para 10.42.

10.41   The Secretary of State may approve or reject an abandonment plan,[107] or approve it with modifications or conditions.[108] In the case of a rejection or of a failure to comply with a s 29 notice, the Secretary of State may himself prepare an abandonment plan.[109] In so doing he may call on the recipients of a s 29 notice to provide records, drawings or other information[110] on pain of a criminal penalty[111] and to reimburse the costs of preparing the programme.[112]

10.42   In view of the fact that the circumstances surrounding an installation may change, whether from a technical perspective or from that of the parties having an interest in it, s 34 provides for the possibility that an approved programme may be revised. Thus, either the Secretary of State or the persons who submitted the abandonment programme may propose an alteration to it or to any condition attached to it.[113] Equally, they may propose that any person who has a duty to carry out the programme may be relieved of that duty or that another person may have the duty imposed upon them.[114] It is this seemingly innocuous provision that raises the possibility (not so far acted upon) that the Secretary of State may recall a party who has had a s 29 notice withdrawn and who has no current interest in the licence or the installation. Note that persons falling within the categories listed in s 30(1)(d) and (e) and s 30(2)(b) and (c) will not have such a duty imposed upon them unless in the Secretary of State's view another person already with that duty has failed or may fail to discharge it.[115] Where the Secretary of State proposes a change to the programme, then the persons having the duty to carry out the programme have an opportunity to make representations.[116] Where a proposal has been made to remove the duty from a person or to give it to another, then all the affected parties have a similar opportunity to make written representations.[117] The decision on any change to an approved abandonment programme lies with the Secretary of State who must give reasons for it.[118] It is also possible for one or more of those who submitted a programme to ask that the approval be

---

[107] Petroleum Act 1998, s 32(1).
[108] *Ibid*, s 32(2).
[109] *Ibid*, s 33(1).
[110] *Ibid*, s 33(2).
[111] *Ibid*, s 33(3).
[112] *Ibid*, s 33(4).
[113] *Ibid*, s 34(1)(a).
[114] *Ibid*, s 34(1)(b) and (2).
[115] *Ibid*, s 34(3).
[116] *Ibid*, s 34(5).
[117] *Ibid*, s 34(6).
[118] *Ibid*, s 34(7).

withdrawn.[119] Where this occurs and not all of the persons initially involved in the submission are now involved, the Secretary of State will notify the others and give them an opportunity to make written representations.[120] The Secretary of State's determination of any such application will be notified to all of those who made the initial submission.[121]

The duty to secure the carrying out of an approved abandonment **10.43** programme (as well as compliance with any conditions) is imposed by s 36 on *each* of the persons who submitted it, meaning that the duty is joint and several. If there is any default in this regard, then the Secretary of State may require any of those who submitted the programme to take such remedial action within such time as he may specify in a written notice.[122] In practice, therefore, one party – namely the one with the greatest assets – may be left to bear the full burden of the decommissioning costs and then to attempt to recover the shares due by the others. Failure to comply with such a notice is an offence, unless the party on whom the notice was served can demonstrate that they exercised due diligence to avoid it.[123] Equally, where there is non-compliance, the Secretary of State may carry out the required remedial action and recover the cost from the person on whom the notice was served,[124] with interest running at commercial rates from the date of notification of the sum due until payment.[125] Note, however, that the commercial realities of the UKCS, which see licences divided into separate sub-areas, mean that a party to a licence or to a JOA may have no commercial interest in an instal-lation located in one or another sub-area of the licensed area. This is now recognised in s 31(A1)–(D1) which prevents the Secretary of State from serving a s 29 notice on a party who has never derived a commercial benefit from the installation in question.[126]

The Government's concern to ensure that the taxpayer does not **10.44** end up footing the bill for decommissioning (beyond the amount that is borne indirectly through tax allowances)[127] is reflected in the provisions of s 38. First of all, even before a s 29 notice has been served, the Secretary of State may require a person to provide information relating to their financial affairs together

---

[119] Petroleum Act 1998, s 35(1).
[120] *Ibid*, s 35(2).
[121] *Ibid*, s 35(3).
[122] *Ibid*, s 37(1).
[123] *Ibid*, s 37(2).
[124] *Ibid*, s 37(3).
[125] *Ibid*, s 37(4) and (5).
[126] Inserted by s 72(7) of the Energy Act 2008. There is a concomitant adjustment to s 34 by virtue of s 72(8) of the 2008 Act.
[127] See para 10.77.

with supporting documentation.[128] Second, in order to allow the Secretary of State to confirm that a person is actually capable of fulfilling their obligations under an abandonment programme, he may at any time require such information and documentation as may be specified.[129] Failure to comply with such requests is an offence, as is the knowing or reckless supply of false information.[130] Note also that, given the sensitive nature of the information involved, it is also an offence for anyone to disclose such information as has been provided to the Secretary of State in these regards.[131]

10.45   The Secretary of State has very widely drawn powers where he is not satisfied that a person will be capable of fulfilling their duties under s 36 (that is, to carry out an approved abandonment plan and any conditions attaching thereto). Section 38(4) provides that he may require such a person to "take such action as may be specified ... within such time as may be specified". This includes the provision of financial security. Such a notice cannot be served without the person concerned having the opportunity to make written representations[132] but, once served, failure to comply is an offence.[133] It was previously the case that the Secretary of State could only take such action after an abandonment programme had been approved, but this can now be done as soon as a s 29 notice has been served.[134]

10.46   As may be imagined, the extent of the Secretary of State's powers in these regards has been the subject of some concern on the part of the industry. Given the increasing amount of transfers of assets that naturally accompany the maturing of a hydrocarbon province, the possibility that a party who has, with full consent of the Secretary of State, divested itself of its interests in a licence and an installation may be recalled to implement and bear the costs of an abandonment plan is seen as a potential obstacle to such transfers. The consultation period prior to the passing of the Energy Act saw lobbying on the part of the industry for the repeal of this aspect of s 34, but to no avail. The Department reminded the industry about the Ardmore case where the parties developing the field went into liquidation and although "[t]he decommissioning costs were very low at around

---

[128] Petroleum Act 1998, s 38(1)–(1B). The scope of this power was extended by s 73(1) and (2) of the 2008 Act which substituted these subsections for the original s 38(1).

[129] Section 38(2). The range of information that may be requested was extended by s 73(3) of the 2008 Act which amplified the wording of the original s 38(2).

[130] Section 38(3).

[131] Section 38(6).

[132] Section 38(5).

[133] Section 38(6).

[134] Section 38(4A), read with s 38(2A) as inserted respectively by s 73(5) and s 73(4) of the 2008 Act.

£5 million … considerable effort has been required to ensure the costs did not fall to the taxpayer".[135] The Government's view has been that the uncertainties associated with decommissioning costs at what is still a relatively early stage of the process are such that it requires to have this protection in place so that the interests of taxpayers may be ensured.[136] In this regard, one further change effected by the Energy Act 2008 requires consideration at this stage, namely the protection from creditors of funds set aside for decommissioning costs. As will be discussed further below, the industry had taken an initiative to establish a model decommissioning security agreement that would facilitate transfers of assets, but a remaining concern was whether such an arrangement would be proof against the claims of creditors in the event of the insolvency of one of the parties to the arrangement.[137] Any lingering uncertainty is removed by the disapplication of any provision of insolvency law which could interfere with the arrangement being used for its intended purpose of meeting decommissioning costs.[138] This matter will be returned to below in the context of the discussion on decommissioning security.[139]

The provisions of Pt IV of the Petroleum Act considered so far 10.47 concentrate especially on ensuring that there is clarity about who will be responsible for the preparation and implementation of an abandonment programme and that the financial burden will not fall on the tax payer. As regards the substantive content of an abandonment programme, s 39 empowers the Secretary of State to make regulations. It is envisaged that these may prescribe standards for dismantling, removal and disposal; standards and safety requirements where there is only partial removal; make provision for the prevention of pollution; and make provision for inspection. The Secretary of State is also empowered to charge fees[140] and to make it an offence to contravene any regulations.[141] The usual requirements are imposed regarding consultation before the making of any such regulations.[142] It is noteworthy, however, that no regulations have

---

[135] DTI, "Decommissioning Offshore Energy Installations: A Consultation Document" (June 2007), p33.
[136] *Ibid*, p 34.
[137] The joint opinion for UKOOA on this point by Gabriel Moss QC and Mark Arnold concluded that "a trust which functions as a security mechanism may be challenged by a liquidator. However, a carefully drawn trust mechanism should survive such a challenge".
[138] Section 38A, inserted by s 74 of the Energy Act 2008. Section 38B ensures that information is provided so that creditors and potential creditors are aware that such funds are protected in the case of insolvency.
[139] See para 10.58.
[140] Sections 39(2)(d) and (e).
[141] Section 39(3) and (4).
[142] Section 39(5) and (6).

ever been made. This is undoubtedly because the regulator is of the view that detailed prescriptive regulations would interfere with the case-by-case approach that it was at pains to stress it would take during the events surrounding the decommissioning of the Brent Spar.[143] It is also worth noting that, by the time of the 1998 Act, the problems caused by the attempt to produce detailed prescriptive regulations for health and safety at work offshore under the Mineral Workings (Offshore Installations) Act 1971 were fully recognised following the criticism in the Report of the Cullen Inquiry into the Piper Alpha Disaster.[144] Instead of regulations, the Department has produced extensive Guidance Notes, which in their current incarnation extend to over 130 pages.

THE DEPARTMENT'S GUIDANCE NOTES

10.48   The Department's Guidance Notes on Decommissioning were first produced in August 2000 and have been updated since, with the most recent version, the fifth, being issued in January 2010.[145] It is noteworthy that the introduction to the Guidance Notes states explicitly that they have been prepared taking account of "views expressed by operating companies and other interested parties" and that they "provide a framework and are not intended to be prescriptive".[146] The echoes of Brent Spar can also be heard in this introduction where it is stated that the approach adopted will allow "adequate time for full and considered consultation". But it is equally clear that the regulator has the interests of industry in mind with stress being laid on flexibility (within the constraints of law and policy) and on the avoidance of unnecessary delay.[147]

10.49   The influence of the Brent Spar case is evident too in the Government's overall policy on decommissioning. This seeks "to achieve effective and balanced decommissioning solutions, which are consistent with international obligations and have a proper regard for safety, the environment, other legitimate uses of the sea, economic considerations and social considerations".[148] The overall policy is further specified in a list of matters that the regulator will seek to ensure, including that "decommissioning decisions are

---

[143] See para 10.23.
[144] See para 8.31.
[145] Offshore Decommissioning Unit, DECC, *Guidance Notes: Decommissioning of Offshore Installations and Pipelines under the Petroleum Act 1998* (January 2010), available online at: https://www.og.decc.gov.uk/regulation/guidance/decommission.htm (hereinafter referred to as "Department's Guidance Notes").
[146] *Ibid*, p 1.
[147] *Ibid*.
[148] *Ibid*, para 1.1.

consistent with waste hierarchy principles[149] and are taken in the light of full and open consultations".[150] It is worth noting, however, that whereas earlier versions of the Department's Guidance Notes stated at the outset that the "Government will act in line with the principles of sustainable development", this is replaced in the current version with a recognition of the need to "maximise energy production as a contribution to UK energy security", on one hand, while taking account of "impacts on climate change",[151] on the other – a subtle, but perhaps not insignificant, shift in emphasis given the concerns discussed in Chapter 3. This change is amplified by the addition of the suggestion that the DECC will ensure that "decommissioning will be regarded as the last option after re-use of the facilities for energy or other projects has been ruled out" but equally that "comparative assessments of decommissioning options take account of impacts on climate change".[152]

The Guidance Notes then go on to flesh out the implementation of the provisions of Pt IV of the 1998 Act (as amended by the Energy Act 2008) and other relevant legislation[153] in accordance with the UK's international obligations, with particular reference to OSPAR Decision 98/3[154] and the IMO Guidelines and Standards 1989.[155] The following aspects of the Guidance Notes will be discussed in turn below: the treatment of s 29 notices; decommissioning liabilities; Decommissioning Security Agreements; and the decommissioning programme process.

10.50

Treatment of s 29 notices

The process for the service of s 29 notices commences when a field development is approved, with the Department sending the operator

10.51

---

[149] The waste hierarchy is discussed further in para 6.2 of the Department's Guidance Notes. It is a framework that prefers waste reduction ahead of any other option, failing which reuse and recycling in that order. Only where none of these options is possible will disposal be considered. Note that this approach was adopted in the Brent Spar Stakeholder Dialogue instituted by Shell. See para 10.25.

[150] Department's Guidance Notes, para 1.2.

[151] *Ibid*, para 1.1.

[152] *Ibid*, para 1.2.

[153] This includes the Coast Protection Act 1949, the Offshore Installations (Safety Case) Regulations 2005, the Pipeline Safety Regulations 1996, the Food and Environment Protection Act 1985, the Environmental Protection Act 1990 and the Radioactive Substances Act 1993. Note that the oil and gas operations already covered by the Petroleum Act 1998 and the Energy Act 2008 are exempt from the provisions of the Marine and Coastal Access Act 2009 and the Marine (Scotland) Act 2010.

[154] Discussed in detail in Section 7 of the Department's Guidance Notes.

[155] Discussed in detail in Section 8 of the Department's Guidance Notes.

a Facility Information Request. This asks the operator to confirm the accuracy of the information held by the Department with regard *inter alia* to the "companies"[156] involved in the field.[157] Thereafter, a so-called "warning letter" will be issued to the operator, the owner and "relevant licensees and JOA partners", advising them that the Secretary of State is considering serving a s 29 notice and giving each 30 days to make written representations as to why this should not happen.[158] Service of the notice will usually then follow. Prior to the amendments introduced by the Energy Act 2008, the involvement of parties other than the operator and the owner would have been possible only after production had started.[159] As regards pipelines, a similar procedure is followed, usually only in respect of the owner.[160] Whereas it was previously the case that the procedure would commence only once the pipeline is emplaced or production has started, it is now the case that this will happen "when the pipeline works authorisation is given and construction has commenced".[161] A considerable period of time may then elapse before the Secretary of State calls for the submission of an abandonment programme.[162] While the s 29 notice includes advice on the need to consult interested bodies in preparing an abandonment programme, nearer the point of decommissioning any party who received such a notice will also receive a list of the organisations they should consult in respect of their programme.[163]

10.52   As regards the possibility that a person who has had a s 29 notice withdrawn under s 31(5) may be "called back" under s 34, the Department stresses in the guidance that it regards this as a "measure of last resort ... which we endeavour to avoid by the use of prudent security arrangements".[164] While this situation has not so far arisen, the Department gives some indication of how it would act. In particular, it suggests that where more than one company is involved it would "aim to agree a fair and reasonable distribution

---

[156] Although this of course should now be read as "corporate bodies". See n 92 above.

[157] Department's Guidance Notes, para 3.3.

[158] *Ibid*, para 3.4. The Department also makes clear that where it has concerns about financial resources or other issues affecting the satisfactory achievement of decommissioning service may also be contemplated in respect of parents or associates in accordance with s 30 of the 1998 Act as amended, as discussed above at para 10.40.

[159] See n 97 above.

[160] Although, again, parents or associates may be included where there are concerns about financial resources or other issues that may have an impact on satisfactory decommissioning. See n 158 above.

[161] Department's Guidance Notes, para 3.6. This change is a consequence of the amended definition of "submarine pipeline". See n 94 above.

[162] Department's Guidance Notes, para 3.8.

[163] *Ibid*, para 3.7. See further para 10.64.

[164] *Ibid*, para 3.11.

of the liabilities in discussion with the companies concerned".[165] There is an interesting change in the wording at this point between the latest version of the Department's Guidance Notes and earlier versions. Whereas it used to be provided that a person who *has* had a notice withdrawn under s 31(5) would not usually be liable for any new installation emplaced in a field after assignment of their interest (although they may be liable for new equipment fitted to an installation in respect of which they had previously held a s 29 notice),[166] this is now expressed as applying in a situation where a s 29 notice is *not* withdrawn.[167] At first sight this seems contradictory until it is realised that in each case what is contemplated is the treatment of a party who has assigned their interest in an installation and who has no current financial involvement. The change in wording would thus appear to indicate that withdrawal of a s 29 notice is less likely than was previously the case. One might want to argue that the change in wording opens up the question of what happens when a s 29 notice *is* now withdrawn and then the recipient is called back under s 34, but there appears little doubt that they would be treated in the same way in this respect as if the notice had never been withdrawn. In any case, the Department's Guidance Notes also state that "[if a company [for which we should now presumably read "body corporate"] has concerns relating to a specific section 29 case they should contact DECC's Offshore Decommissioning Unit for further clarification".[168] All of this may give some comfort to the industry as regards the implementation of a provision that sometimes provokes strong criticism.

Some comfort may also be derived from the clarification that the latest guidance notes offer in terms of whether a range of parties might find themselves inadvertently and unexpectedly liable for decommissioning costs as a result of the complex contracting and infrastructure arrangements that characterise the UKCS. Thus, the industry has been worried about the position both of contractors offering management services to operators, and of the operator of a host installation in respect of a tieback. DECC has been at pains to offer reassurance in each case,[169] although in respect of the latter it has seen fit to set out some parameters that it considers in "determining when it is reasonable and proportionate to treat tiebacks as separate installations".[170]

10.53

[165] Department's Guidance Notes.
[166] *Ibid* (September 2006 edn), Annex F, para 11.
[167] *Ibid*, para 3.13.
[168] *Ibid*, para 3.14.
[169] *Ibid*, paras 3.15 and 3.16 respectively.
[170] *Ibid*, paras 3.17–3.21.

Decommissioning liabilities

10.54   The innovative licence arrangements discussed elsewhere in this
volume[171] which are designed to extend the life of the UKCS as a
hydrocarbon province have naturally encouraged new entrants.
Similarly, the changing economic incentives associated with a
maturing province have seen the assignment of licences from larger
and well-established companies to smaller and often less experienced
entities.[172] While the Government is wholly in favour of these developments, it is equally concerned that they raise the possibility of
default with respect to decommissioning obligations – either because
the companies involved may lack the required financial assets or
because such assets are overseas and thus beyond the Government's
enforcement powers.[173] As a consequence, a policy is in place to
ensure that adequate funds are available to meet the decommissioning costs for each field.[174]

10.55   The first point to consider in this regard is the approach that
the Department adopts in deciding whether to withdraw a s 29
notice under s 31(5) where a party's interest in a licence has
been assigned. In the previous version of the Guidance Notes,
the Department very reassuringly noted that it had agreed to do
this "in the majority of cases" in so far as it has always been
satisfied that at least one of the remaining parties to the JOA
has sufficient UK assets to cover the costs of decommissioning.[175]
While this language is not repeated in the current version of the
Guidance Notes, where instead it is emphasised somewhat less
reassuringly that "[i]t should be noted that such a withdrawal is
granted at the discretion of the Secretary of State",[176] the DECC
does state that it "aims to withdraw as many notices as possible",
albeit on the basis of an assessment of the level of risk to the
taxpayer. In this last regard, the current Guidance Notes represent
a departure from the previous version. Whereas the latter offered
a non-exhaustive list of the factors to be considered in reaching a
decision on withdrawal of a s 29 notice (including the estimated
decommissioning costs; the financial strength of the remaining
notice holders; the likelihood that they will remain as licensees;
their other UKCS interests; and whether security arrangements
have been established), the latest version of the Guidance Notes

---

[171] See para 4.62.
[172] See para 16.2.
[173] Department's Guidance Notes, para 4.1 and Annex F, para 3.
[174] *Ibid*, Annex F.
[175] *Ibid* (February 2008 edn), Annex F, para 12. Indeed, the point is even reiterated at
para 13.
[176] Department's Guidance Notes, Annex F, para 6.

now offers a flow-chart showing how the risk of default associated with a group of s 29 notice holders is calculated together with detailed notes on each of the steps followed by a series of worked examples.[177] It should be noted that the use of this risk assessment tool is not restricted to the point at which a party seeks to exit, but that it "is also used to review the risk of all section 29 groups on a periodic basis (every 6 to 12 months)".[178] Nor is this by any means an academic exercise in view of the ability of the Secretary of State under s 38(4), as amended by the Energy Act 2008, to require a body corporate to provide security at any time if it has received a s 29 notice. The details of this process are beyond the scope of this chapter. It is sufficient to note that where the risk associated with a group is considered to be high, a s 29 notice will not be withdrawn; where it is medium, withdrawal is said to be "probable" if costs are £25 million or less; and where the risk is low, withdrawal is said to be "probable" if costs are £100 million or less. It should be noted, however, that these threshold values are indicative.[179]

Where a Decommissioning Security Agreement (DSA) as described   10.56
in Annex G is in place the regulator is likely to be minded to release the exiting s 29 notice holder. This will not be possible, however, where the transfer of the interest in the licence will leave only one party holding the whole licence. In such circumstances the Department will not withdraw the notice of the last party to sell and instead will require them to remain to "police" the Agreement.[180]

Where the risk is assessed to be medium or high, the DECC will   10.57
first of all consider whether service of a s 29 notice on a parent or associate will serve to mitigate the situation.[181] Where the risks are regarded as "unacceptable" and such an approach will not suffice, then a s 29 notice holder can be required to provide security under s 38(4) as amended.[182] Bear in mind that this can happen as a result of a periodic review and not only when a notice holder seeks to exit. The DECC makes clear, however, that its assessment of risk will take due account of the existence of "any relevant security agreements" and a s 38(4) notice is unlikely to be issued "where there is a satisfactory security agreement in place".[183]

---

[177] Department's Guidance Notes, Annex F, paras 8–29.
[178] *Ibid*, Annex F, para 9.
[179] *Ibid*, Annex F, para 20.
[180] *Ibid*, Annex F, para 21 and Annex G, para. 5.
[181] *Ibid*, Annex F, para 22.
[182] *Ibid*, Annex F, para 23.
[183] *Ibid*, Annex F, para 24.

Decommissioning Security Agreements[184]

10.58   It is clear, then, that where a DSA is already in place it is likely to be easier for a s 29 notice holder to exit. Similarly, the presence of a DSA makes it less likely that a s 29 group will attract the adverse interest of the DECC on the basis of a periodic risk assessment. Recent years have seen important developments with regard to DSAs, not least the development of a model agreement by a working group established under the auspices of the Brownfield Studies Group.[185]

10.59   This group noted a variety of problems in connection with DSAs, including: negotiation costs arising due to the absence of a standard form of DSA; the possibility of demands for double security in some cases; uncertainty as to what form of DSA the Department would regard as acceptable; over-pricing of security in connection with the transfer of mature assets due to cautious calculations with consequent adverse impacts on the market; and concerns that where effective security was lacking "the historic licensees were in effect being required to underwrite the decommissioning of legacy assets".[186] The new model deed,[187] which, it is stressed, is "voluntary and subject to negotiation" seeks to resolve such problems and in particular to offer greater detail and clarity, not least in relation to calculating security and to the requirements for a DECC-compliant DSA; to reduce the risk of double security; and to ensure that the situation where an operator under a JOA is replaced is covered.[188] As regards the calculation of security, the formula most often used "is to multiply … estimated decommissioning costs by a risk factor to reflect the uncertainties … but then to deduct the expected future revenues from the field".[189] One area of uncertainty noted by the Group relates to the treatment of possible derogation cases under OSPAR Decision 98/3. Should the obtaining of a derogation be assumed in cases which appear to fall within the parameters mentioned therein? Or should a more conservative approach be adopted on the basis that the fact that an installation falls within the 98/3 parameters only means that a derogation may be sought but offers no guarantee that one

---

[184]   For the interaction between Decommissioning Security Agreements and Joint Operating Agreements, see para 12.64.

[185]   See para 5.6.

[186]   J Aldersey-Williams, "The Decommissioning Cost Provision Deed: facilitating assets transfers on the UKCS" 2008 IELR 169–177 at 171 (hereinafter "Aldersey-Williams, 'Decommissioning'"). See also M Hammerson, "Decommissioning offshore oil and gas facilities: industry contracts and security arrangements" (2009) 21(1) *Environmental Law and Management* 31–38.

[187]   See Oil and Gas UK, Decommissioning Security Agreement, OP021 (2009).

[188]   Aldersey-Williams, "Decommissioning" at 172.

[189]   *Ibid* at 173.

will be granted?[190] In so far as the model DSA allows negotiation, it "provides some options for discussion in this area".[191] As regards the form of security that would be acceptable, a letter of credit (irrevocable and unconditional) is the most common, though others (singly or in combination) are permitted by the model DSA, in each case with an annual reassessment.[192] At the time of the discussions leading to the production of the first model DSA (at that time referred to as the Decommissioning Cost Provision Deed), one of the key concerns for the industry was the robustness of the funds held in trust in the context of the insolvency of one of the parties.[193] As noted above, this issue has been dealt with by the disapplication of insolvency law to such agreements by the Energy Act 2008.[194] As regards the duration of a DSA, the model envisages that this will be "until a date defined as the end of the 12-month period following the submission of a close-out report to [DECC], assuming that no further work is required by [DECC] during that 12-month period".[195] The close-out report is discussed further below,[196] as is the possible significance of this limitation on the duration of the DSA.[197]

Decommissioning Programme Process

As mentioned above, the regulator characterises the process of approving a decommissioning programme as "flexible, transparent and subject to public consultation"[198] and envisages that it will typically have five main stages: preliminary discussions with the DECC; detailed discussions and submission of a consultation draft programme to the DECC, other interested parties and the public for consideration; formal submission of a programme and approval under the Petroleum Act 1998; commence main works and undertake site surveys; and monitoring of the site.[199]

10.60

---

[190] The fact that OSPAR is keen to reduce the categories that may be considered for derogation would certainly appear to be an argument in favour of a more conservative approach. See n 85 above.

[191] Aldersey-Williams, "Decommissioning" at 174.

[192] *Ibid* at 174–175.

[193] See n 137 above.

[194] See n 138 above.

[195] Aldersey-Williams, "Decommissioning" at 176.

[196] See para 10.68.

[197] See para 10.73.

[198] Department's Guidance Notes, para 5.2.

[199] See *ibid*, para 5.3. A useful overview of the process, both in straightforward cases and in those where a derogation from the general rule in OSPAR Decision 98/3 is sought, is provided in the form of a flowchart in Annex J to the Department's Guidance Notes. Earlier versions of the Department's Guidance Notes divided the process into six main stages, with what is now stage two being divided into two separate stages.

Preliminary discussions with the Department

10.61   The regulator stresses the importance of entering into discussions well in advance of the cessation of production, perhaps as much as 3 years in the case of multi-installation fields and even longer where a derogation under OSPAR Decision 98/3 is a possibility. The wording of s 29(2) of the 1998 Act may give the impression that an operator should wait until called upon by the Secretary of State to submit a decommissioning programme before taking any action, but the guidance makes clear that the "onus rests with the Operator to initiate these discussions".[200] The regulator's expectation at this initial stage is that the operator will outline the "likely timetable of future events to form a basis of agreement on when more detailed discussions should commence and what documentation should be prepared in advance".[201] The Department is keen to ensure that the burden on operators is as light as it can reasonably be and it accordingly will act as far as possible as a "one-stop shop" for the operator's contacts with government. While it will, thus, liaise with many of the other interested departments, there will be occasions when the operator must do this itself – perhaps most notably the Health and Safety Executive in respect of the modification of the safety case to take account of decommissioning.[202]

10.62   The expected content of the decommissioning programme is outlined in Section 6 and Annex C to the Guidance Notes.

Detailed discussions and submission of consultation draft programme to DECC, other interested parties and the public for consideration

10.63   In straightforward cases, it is envisaged that there will be little distinction between the first and second stages of the Decommissioning Programme process. Where a derogation from the general rule in OSPAR Decision 98/3 is sought, however, then the Department will be required at this stage to determine whether a case has been made out in accordance with the procedure specified in Annex 2 to the Decision. In this regard, the regulator encourages operators to use the criteria and methodology it has itself developed and which are contained in Annex A to the Guidance Notes. This essentially involves the completion of a matrix, which allows comparison of the safety and technical risks and the environmental, societal and economic impacts associated with different decommissioning options. While the matrix approach is not compulsory, the Department notes that

---

[200] Department's Guidance Notes, para 5.8.
[201] *Ibid*, para 5.10.
[202] See para 8.45.

its use "will help to provide a clear overall indication of the acceptability of the derogation case".[203]

While under previous versions of the Department's Guidance **10.64** Notes the Decommissioning Programme Process was divided into six rather than five main stages – with detailed discussion with the Department being placed prior to consultation with other interested parties and the public – it was always the case that such consultation could actually be required in parallel with discussions with the Department. Thus, even when the two stages were separated, stakeholder engagement was actually required earlier in a derogation case: the Notes accompanying Annex A in the February 2008 version of the Department's Guidance Notes already indicated that the completion of the matrix in respect of societal impacts would depend upon stakeholder engagement.[204] The merging of these two stages in the current version of the Guidance Notes means, however, that consultation will be required in parallel with discussions with the Department also in straightforward cases. At one level, these will be the statutory consultations with parties notified to the recipient of a s 29 notice, as provided for by s 29(3). The Guidance Notes contain more information in this regard in so far as Annex H lists those parties who are usually included in a notification.[205] Beyond that, the guidance indicates that operators will also be asked to announce proposals publicly and to make copies of the draft programme available for consultation. The results of such consultation should be discussed in the next draft of the programme.[206] In derogation cases, "operators will need to develop and manage a wide-ranging public consultation process", the "form and timing" of which is to be discussed with the regulator.[207] Interestingly, the wording of the guidance suggests that only where such a consultation indicates that a derogation should be sought will the Department then consult with the other OSPAR contracting parties.[208] This may be another indication that a derogation will not be sought where there is strong public feeling against the idea, unless, of course, there is some overriding consideration – safety of personnel, for example – which renders it necessary. Note also that the guidance places a responsibility on the operator to prepare documentation supporting the

---

[203] Department's Guidance Notes, Annex A, para. 6.
[204] In this regard, the Department directs operators to the Oil and Gas UK Guidelines on Stakeholder Engagement for Decommissioning Activities.
[205] Namely, the various fishing organisations as well as Global Marine Systems, which provides submarine cable laying and maintenance.
[206] Department's Guidance Notes, paras 6.25–6.26.
[207] *Ibid*, para 6.27.
[208] *Ibid*, para 6.28.

derogation case, even though it is the Department's responsibility to carry out the consultation with the other OSPAR contracting parties.[209]

10.65   It will also be necessary to carry out an Environmental Impact Assessment (EIA) and prepare an Environmental Statement (ES) at this stage, especially in a derogation case, in order to support the completion of the environmental impact aspects of the matrix in Annex A to the Department's Guidance Notes, but also in straightforward cases where the EIA will be restricted to addressing "the impacts of the proposed decommissioning activity on the environment".[210] The EIA and the ES are creatures of European law,[211] and are required in the case of certain public and private projects. Certain oil and gas projects are now subject to the mandatory preparation of an ES,[212] but this is *not* the case with the decommissioning of installations and pipelines. Notwithstanding the absence of any legal requirement, the Guidance Notes make clear that "a decommissioning programme will nevertheless need to be supported by an EIA".[213] An Environmental Impact Assessment will thus be required in respect of *all* decommissioning programmes.[214]

10.66   Finally, note that in derogation cases, while reputational issues are not to be included in the matrix in Annex A, the Guidance Notes make clear that these may well influence the final decision on whether a derogation will be permitted.[215] Implicit in the wording here is the fact that the Department is not only thinking about the reputation of the operator but also that of the Government.[216] It may thus be suggested that were there ever to be public antipathy to a decommissioning programme on the scale witnessed in the Brent Spar case, the Department might not be minded to argue on the basis of scientific rationality in the way that it did then, absent some overriding consideration such as safety.

---

[209] Department's Guidance Notes, para 6.29.

[210] *Ibid*, para 12.1.

[211] Council Directive 85/337/EEC on the Assessment of the Effects of Certain Public and Private Projects on the Environment as amended by Council Directive 97/11/EC. See paras 4.26 and 9.20.

[212] The Directives are transposed in the UK in respect of these projects by the Offshore Petroleum Production and Pipe-lines (Assessment of Environmental Effects) Regulations 1999 (SI 1999/360), as amended by the Offshore Petroleum Production and Pipe-lines (Assessment of Environmental Effects) (Amendment) Regulations 2007 (SI 2007/933).

[213] Department's Guidance Notes, para 12.1.

[214] *Ibid*, Annex C, para 10.

[215] *Ibid*, Annex A, para 7.

[216] "Companies and government will also wish to take account of reputational issues from their own perspective."

Formal submission of a programme and approval under the Petroleum Act 1998

The extent to which the decommissioning process goes forward on the basis of guidance rather than statutory or regulatory requirements is evident from the fact that it is only at this third stage, when the operator and the Department are in a position to agree a final version of the decommissioning programme, that the Secretary of State will call for its submission in terms of s 29(1) of the 1998 Act. **10.67**

Commencement of main works and conduct of site surveys

Stage four of the decommissioning process covers the implementation of the physical removal work together with the notification to the Department of the progress of that work. The means by which this notification will take place as well as the milestones for review of progress will be specified in the decommissioning programme.[217] Any variations of the programme require the Secretary of State's approval under s 34.[218] When the work is completed (including the clearing of any debris and the carrying out of any required surveys of the site), a Close-out Report must be submitted to the Department within 4 months. The content of the Report is detailed in Section 13 of the Guidance Notes and includes: the outcome of the process and how it was achieved; details of variations and consequent permits required; results of clearance operations and monitoring; results of post-decommissioning sampling; details of any future monitoring; measures taken to manage risks from any legacies; details of actual costs and explanations of differences from forecasts.[219] Note that the operator will be asked to place a copy of the Close-out Report on its website. **10.68**

Monitoring of the site

Where a derogation from the general position specified by OSPAR Decision 98/3 has been agreed and all or part of an installation remains in place, then the operator will be required to undertake ongoing monitoring of the site in order that the condition of the remains may be kept under review.[220] The precise monitoring regime will be agreed with the Department and the schedule will be included in the decommissioning programme.[221] Reports on the monitoring are to be submitted to the Department along with any proposals for remedial work. The operator must publish these monitoring reports **10.69**

---

[217] Department's Guidance Notes, para 5.15.
[218] As discussed above at para 10.42.
[219] Department's Guidance Notes, para 13.1.
[220] *Ibid*, para 5.17.
[221] *Ibid*, para 14.1.

(for example, on the internet) but there is ambiguity in the Guidance as to whether this requirement extends to proposals for remedial work. It would be safest to assume that it does.[222]

10.70 As discussed above,[223] Annex 4 of OSPAR Decision 98/3 requires that there be independent verification of the condition of the installation before work on the disposal begins. The Guidance indicates that "it will be for the Operator to propose a suitable organisation to carry out the independent verification".[224] The unspoken element here is that the Department will need to approve this proposal.

10.71 As regards the post-decommissioning report required by para 10 of Decision 98/3, the Guidance indicates that the Department will prepare this on the basis of the Close-out Report and will give the operator the opportunity to review it before submission to the OSPAR Commission.[225]

10.72 Where all or part of an installation is to remain in place, it is the operator's responsibility to ensure that the UK Hydrographic Office is informed so that navigational charts may be updated accordingly.[226] Where there is projection above the surface, the operator will also be responsible for the installation and maintenance of the appropriate navigational aids, in consultation with the relevant interested parties.[227]

AREAS OF UNCERTAINTY

Residual liabilities

10.73 One of the issues exercising the minds of those concerned with decommissioning is the question of residual liability for an installation left wholly or partly in place under a derogation from the general position described by OSPAR Decision 98/3. In case anyone should be under any illusions in this regard, the Department's Guidance Notes discussed in the foregoing part of this chapter inform readers that "[a]ny residual liability remains with the owners in perpetuity"[228] and that "[a]ny claims for compensation from third parties arising from damage caused by any remains will be a matter for the owners and the affected parties and will be covered by the general law".[229] In this regard, the position under both English and

---

[222] Department's Guidance Notes, para 14.2.
[223] See para 10.36.
[224] Department's Guidance Notes, para 14.3.
[225] *Ibid*, para 14.4
[226] *Ibid*, para 15.1.
[227] *Ibid*, para 15.4.
[228] *Ibid*, para 16.1.
[229] Department's Guidance Notes, para 16.3. Note that in terms of a UK seaward area

Scots law is that the owner of such an installation would be liable in damages for loss arising from his negligence in circumstances where a duty of care is owed to the other party. The test for the existence of a duty of care is laid down in *Caparo Industries Ltd* v *Dickman*.[230] There, Lord Bridge of Harwich stated that the test is threefold: is there sufficient proximity between the parties? Was the loss foreseeable? Is it fair, just and reasonable in the circumstances to impose the duty of care?[231] It may be said that in all of the most likely scenarios involving loss arising from the remains of a decommissioned installation, this test would be passed. For example, imagine a fishing boat snagging its nets on the remains and sinking. There would certainly be sufficient proximity between the owners of the remains and a legitimate user of the seas above them. The scenario suggested is entirely foreseeable. It does not appear unfair, unjust or unreasonable to impose a duty of care on the owners of remains, which by their very nature constitute a hazard to other users.

In so far as this is accepted to be the case, the question which then arises is how the owner may discharge his duty of care and thus avoid liability in the event that damage occurs in such circumstances. It may be suggested that in so far as the owner has fulfilled all of his obligations under Pt IV of the Petroleum Act 1998, had his Close-out Report accepted by the Department, notified the UK Hydrographic Office of the situation and conformed to the schedule of ongoing monitoring agreed in the decommissioning programme, then it is unlikely that any liability would arise. It is also the case that in derogation situations where there continues to be a projection above the surface, the 500-m safety zone will continue to exist around the remains.[232] In so far as anyone entering that area would be guilty of an offence,[233] then should they incur losses there would undoubtedly be a finding of contributory negligence. **10.74**

The prudent owner, accordingly, probably has little to fear with regard to residual liability – at least as far as the Scottish and English courts are concerned. It has been pointed out, however, that a problem may arise where a claim is raised in a foreign court "claiming extra-territorial jurisdiction and applying principles of **10.75**

---

petroleum licence, well casings and fixtures relating to wells that are not plugged and abandoned at the expiry or determination of a licensee's interest in a licence "shall be left in left in good order and fit for further working" and "shall be the property of the Minister". See the Petroleum Licensing (Production) (Seaward Areas) Regulations 2008 (SI 2008/225), Model Cll 12(b) and 14.

[230] [1990] 2 AC 605.

[231] At 617–618.

[232] See ss 21 and 22 of the Petroleum Act 1987. See also Department's Guidance Notes, paras 15.5 and 15.6.

[233] Petroleum Act 1987, s 23.

strict liability".[234] This issue, together with the sheer uncertainty involved in retaining residual liability for decades or longer, persuade some in the industry that an approach similar to that adopted in the Norwegian sector of the North Sea would be preferable. Section 5–4 of the Norwegian Petroleum Activities Act of 1996, as amended, states that:

> "In the event of decisions for abandonment, it may be agreed between the licensees and the owners on one side and the State on the other side that future maintenance, responsibility and liability shall be taken over by the State based on an agreed financial compensation."[235]

There are presently no indications that an exactly similar approach is on the cards in the UK, and it is in any case perhaps not insignificant that the wording of the Norwegian provision reads "*may* be agreed" rather than "*shall* be agreed".

10.76 This is not only an issue that concerns those who bear the residual liability, however. Other users of the waters above the UKCS face potential difficulties if they suffer harm as a result of negligence (however remote a possibility this may be) but the owners of the installation in question are then defunct. This is one of the drivers behind work undertaken within the PILOT Brownfields initiative to develop a Fisheries Legacy Trust Company.[236]

Taxation

10.77 The principal taxes affecting the production of hydrocarbons on the UKCS are Petroleum Revenue Tax (PRT) and Ring Fence Corporation Tax (RFCT). PRT was introduced by the Oil Taxation Act 1975 and applies to fields granted development consent prior to 16 March 1993. The Finance Act 1993 repealed PRT for fields granted development consent on or after that date. Such fields are accordingly only subject to RFCT. PRT fields are also subject to RFCT, with the former tax being deductible in the calculation of profits chargeable to the latter.

10.78 On the face of it, each of these taxes is organized in such a way as to recognise the costs incurred in decommissioning. As regards PRT, decommissioning costs are deductible for PRT purposes and, broadly speaking, any losses can be carried back without limit and set against profits from the field. Unused losses may be set against profits from

---

[234] Daintith, Willoughby and Hill, para 1–1326.
[235] Available in English on the Norwegian Petroleum Directorate's website at: http://www.npd.no/en/Regulations/Acts/Petroleum-activities-act/#Section 5–4 (accessed 26 April 2011).
[236] Department's Guidance Notes, para 16.4. See also http://www.ukfltc.com/ (accessed 26 April 2011).

another of the company's fields.[237] As regards RFCT, all expenditure related to an approved decommissioning programme qualifies for one hundred per cent allowances and may be carried back for 3 years.[238]

But those apparently benign arrangements mask problems as far as the industry is concerned and these have been the subject of discussions in recent years with the Treasury.[239] The basic problem with regard to PRT is that the industry fears that the Treasury may be minded to abolish this tax at the point at which it no longer makes economic sense to collect it. Were this to happen, the argument runs, the companies involved in fields subject to PRT would have no opportunity to offset their decommissioning costs.[240] As regards RFCT, the perceived problem is that premature decommissioning may occur where a company has insufficient profit streams on the UKCS against which it could set the costs.[241] **10.79**

In relation to the PRT problem, the Treasury so far has no answers. It notes that the options being proposed by the industry such as a field-by-field switch-off of the tax would require considerably more accurate projections of decommissioning costs than are currently available:[242] "Despite these complications Government remains keen to discuss the various policy options further with industry, and examine jointly whether there are solutions to the various issues that may exist."[243] **10.80**

As regards RFCT, the industry believes that allowing unlimited carry-back similar to the arrangements under PRT can solve the problem.[244] The Treasury remains to be convinced about this and wants further work to establish the real extent of the problem.[245] Indeed, earlier in the document the Treasury seems almost sanguine with respect to the RFCT problems, noting that given the long production tail of most fields "the result of this would be a small loss of overall oil and gas recovery".[246] This would appear to be out of step with the Government's overall efforts to maximise production from the UKCS, not simply in terms of the lost oil, but also in terms of understanding that installations may act as infrastructure nodes allowing step out developments which would otherwise be **10.81**

---

[237] For full details, see para 6.49.

[238] For full details, see the discussion at para 6.18. See also the discussion in HM Treasury, *The North Sea Fiscal Regime: a discussion paper* (2007) (hereinafter "Treasury Discussion Paper").

[239] Treasury Discussion Paper.

[240] *Ibid*, para 3.8.

[241] *Ibid*, para 3.15.

[242] *Ibid*, para 4.7.

[243] *Ibid*.

[244] *Ibid*, para 3.16.

[245] *Ibid*, para 4.13.

[246] *Ibid*, para 3.15.

uneconomical. Elsewhere, the Treasury is absolutely on message: "The Government is also looking at whether there are other, more targeted policy options, which would also resolve this issue and result in increased recovery of oil and gas."[247]

10.82　　There have been some developments in the recent past designed to offer reassurance to the industry. For example, tax provisions that may have deterred reuse of installations for renewable energy or carbon storage projects have been removed, while reassurance has been given that PRT relief will be available beyond the expiry of a licence. Crucially, however, the industry remains concerned. In its 2010 *Activity Survey*, Oil & Gas UK states that "there is continuing uncertainty on whether future Governments will meet its commitment regarding decommissioning tax relief".[248] And in case the Government was in any doubt as to what is at stake, Oil & Gas UK continues by pointing out that this may accelerate the pace of decommissioning, reduce the amount of oil and gas recovered and "needlessly threaten our security of supply and damage the future of our supply chain with a consequent loss of technology and highly skilled jobs in the UK economy".[249]

CONCLUSION

10.83　The approach to decommissioning on the part of the Department and of the industry has changed considerably in the 15 years since the Brent Spar case. The low public profile of this issue may be said to be a measure of the success of the current way of doing things. A striking feature of that approach is the extent to which it operates on the basis of guidance rather than regulation. That said, however, the alignment of the interests of the industry and of the regulator in avoiding the sort of adverse publicity that surrounded Brent Spar is probably sufficient to ensure that this approach is unlikely to be challenged.

10.84　　The environmental protection dimension of decommissioning accordingly appears to be relatively robust and uncontentious. But when the first edition of this book was published in 2007, the same could not be said for the financial dimension. Since then, however, there have been significant developments in the form of the model Decommissioning Security Agreement and of legislation to provide reassurance with respect to the protection of decommissioning funds in the event of insolvency. Questions about taxation and concerns over residual liability still exercise industry minds, but the extent

---

[247] Treasury Discussion Paper, para 4.15.
[248] Oil and Gas UK, n 4 above, p 4.
[249] *Ibid.*

to which these issues impact upon the issue of energy security may well see positive developments in the years ahead. It is absolutely clear that the Government cannot remain indifferent to problems which risk jeopardising initiatives aimed at securing the future of the maturing province.

One issue which continues to be mentioned on any occasion **10.85** when members of the industry gather to discuss decommissioning is the possibility that the recipient of a s 29 notice who has been successful in having it withdrawn under s 31(5) may be called back at some point in the future under s 34. It is hard to overestimate the extent to which this rankles with the industry and the question is not infrequently raised as to whether developments such as the DSA might lead to the repeal of s 34 call-back. The simple answer to that question is surely "no". The Government has made it abundantly clear on numerous occasions that whoever else ends up paying the decommissioning costs on the UKCS, it will not be the British taxpayer. Given the liabilities assumed by (or at least on behalf of) the taxpayer in recent years in the context of the banking crisis, it seems scarcely credible that the Government would countenance the risk of further liabilities which it simply need not assume. As galling as that may be for the industry, it is worth recalling that the DSA should provide the sort of reassurance for exiting JOA co-venturers that they have so dearly sought in the context of the repeal of s 34 call-back. It is surely the case that if the industry itself believes that the DSA does what it claims it does, then there is nothing to fear from s 34.

CHAPTER 11

COMPETITION LAW AND THE UPSTREAM OIL AND GAS BUSINESS

Judith Aldersey-Williams

WHY COMPETITION LAW MATTERS

Competition law is a serious matter: operators and contractors **11.1** are quite right to be wary of breaching the prohibitions, as the consequences can be significant. Both the UK and EU authorities have significant powers to fine parties up to 10 per cent of their annual worldwide group turnover.[1] Since fines are relatively rare, in practice a more significant sanction is likely to be the fact that agreements which breach the prohibition are void and unenforceable.[2] Increasingly, there is also the threat of damages actions from third parties who claim to have been the victims of anti-competitive conduct.[3]

---

[1] For more information on fining policy, see the EU Guidelines on the method of setting fines imposed pursuant to Art 23(2)(a) of Regulation No 1/2003 [2006] OJ C210/2, available for download at http://ec.europa.eu/comm/competition/antitrust/legislation/fines.html (accessed 13 March 2011), and the OFT Guidance 423, *OFT's Guidance as to the appropriate amount of a penalty* (2004), available for download from http://www.oft.gov.uk/shared_oft/business_leaflets/ca98_guidelines/oft423.pdf (accessed 13 March 2011); see also C Kerse and N Khan, *EC Antitrust Procedure* (5th edn, 2005), Chapter 7.
[2] See R Whish, *Competition Law* (6th edn, 2008) (hereinafter "Whish, *Competition Law*") at p 314.
[3] Third parties who suffer a loss as a result of a breach of EU competition law have a direct right in damages: see Joined Cases C–298 to 299/04 *Manfredi v Lloyd Adriatico Assicurazioni* [2006] 5 CMLR 17. In the House of Lords case of *Crehan v Inntrepreneur Pub Co* [2007] 1 AC 333, the claimant's attempt to win damages in respect of the defendant's breach of competition law failed. However, this was a very peculiar case which turned on its own facts. See further in relation to damages and other related issues: OFT, *Private actions in competition law: effective redress for consumers and business Discussion paper*, 2007, available for download from http://www.oft.gov.uk/shared_oft/

11.2   Although there is no power to fine employees or directors for breach of competition law, the Office of Fair Trading can apply to have a company director disqualified for up to 15 years if his company is found to have infringed competition law in situations where his conduct is considered to make him unfit to act as a director.[4] Senior managers responsible for cartel activity by their company may also be prosecuted and if convicted can be sent to prison for up to 5 years.[5] However, a recent decision suggests that a company will rarely be able to sue its own employees who have engaged in anti-competitive conduct for the resulting losses to the company.[6]

11.3   In addition to their powers of enforcement, it is important to bear in mind that the authorities have extensive powers of investigation and can even give rewards for whistle-blowing regarding cartels.[7] Even if a company is ultimately found to have committed no offence, an investigation may cause significant disruption to business and a drain on management time and resources. For instance, in May 2007, in a joint operation by US, UK and EU competition authorities, eight executives, including three from the UK, were arrested in the USA while "dawn raids" were carried out on a range of business and

---

reports/comp_policy/oft916.pdf (accessed 13 March 2011). The European Commission is endeavouring to make it easier for aggrieved parties to claim damages. In 2008, the Commission published a White Paper on Damages Actions for Breach of the EC anti-trust rules. The White Paper suggests specific policy options and measures that would help victims of EU anti-trust infringements access effective redress mechanisms so that they can be fully compensated for the harm they suffered. This is available for download from http://eur-lex.europa.eu/LexUriServ/LexUriServ.do?uri=CELEX:52008DC0165:EN:NOT (accessed 13 March 2011). It has also engaged in work to assist in the process of quantifying damages – details are available for download from http://ec.europa.eu/competition/antitrust/actionsdamages/index.html (accessed 13 March 2011).

[4] See ss 9(A)–(E) of the Company Directors Disqualification Act 1986 and the OFT's Guidance 510, *Director Disqualification Orders in Competition Cases*, available for download from http://www.oft.gov.uk/shared_oft/business_leaflets/enterprise_act/oft510.pdf (accessed 13 March 2011).

[5] Enterprise Act 2002, ss 188–189 and OFT's Guidance 515, *Powers for Investigating Criminal Cartels*, available for download from http://www.oft.gov.uk/shared_oft/business_leaflets/enterprise_act/oft515.pdf (accessed 13 March 2011).

[6] In *Safeway Ltd v Simon Twigger* [2010] EWCA Civ 1472, the Court of Appeal ruled that a corporate undertaking, upon which the OFT had imposed a penalty for breaches of competition law, could not sue its former directors, officers or employees for damages equivalent to that penalty or the costs of the OFT investigation that the claimant had had to bear. The Court of Appeal held that such liabilities were intended, under the relevant statutory scheme of the Competition Act 1998, to be personal to the corporate undertaking and any claim against its directors or employees was barred by the maxim *ex turpi causa non oritur actio* (ie a claimant cannot recover for the consequences of his own criminal or quasi-criminal act).

[7] See http://www.oft.gov.uk/OFTwork/cartels-and-competition/cartels/rewards (accessed 13 March 2011).

residential addresses in the UK and elsewhere – all of this activity was directed at uncovering a cartel in the market for marine hose used to transfer oil.[8] This investigation ultimately led to the prosecution of three executives and fines on the companies involved totalling over 131 million euros.[9] In 2008, the European Commission fined E.ON Energy AG ("E.ON") 38 million euros because a seal affixed by Commission inspectors to secure documents was broken during an inspection carried out at the premises of E.ON in May 2006. E.ON denied breaking the seal, but could not explain the reason for its having been broken.[10]

Briefly, the authorities may, among other things: **11.4**

- obtain interim injunctions to stop harmful conduct while investigations are carried out;
- on completion of investigations, order the conduct to cease permanently;
- arrive unannounced at business premises, search for and take copies of documents, question staff and remove computers;
- search home premises;
- fine or, in the UK, even imprison for up to 2 years persons who interfere with their investigation.[11]

However, competition law is sometimes used to justify behaviour   **11.5** which, on analysis, turns out to have nothing to do with competition law concerns. Often this results from poor understanding and an excess of caution. A basic understanding of competition law is therefore a useful tool in challenging such behaviour.

One of the difficulties of competition law is that the analysis is   **11.6** not simply a legal one. The rules are not "bright-line" legal requirements to which there is always a straightforward "yes" or "no"

---

[8] For further information, see OFT Press Release 70/07, OFT *launches criminal investigation into alleged international bid rigging, price fixing and market allocation cartel*, available for download from http://www.oft.gov.uk/news/press/2007/70-07 (accessed 13 March 2011).

[9] See OFT Press Release 72/08, *Three imprisoned in first OFT criminal prosecution for bid rigging*, available for download from http://www.oft.gov.uk/news-and-updates/press/2008/72-08 (accessed 13 March 2011) and Commission press release, "Antitrust: Commission fines marine hose producers €131 million for market sharing and price-fixing cartel", available for download from http://europa.eu/rapid/pressReleasesAction.do?reference=IP/09/137&format=HTML&aged=0&language=EN&guiLanguage=en (accessed 13 March 2011).

[10] For further information, see *Commission fine on E.ON for breach of seal during inspection – guide*, available at http://www.eubusiness.com/topics/competition/eon-fine-guide/ (accessed 13 March 2011).

[11] See ss 25–29 of the Competition Act 1998; also OFT Guidance 404, *Guidance on Powers of Investigation*, (2004), available for download from http://www.oft.gov.uk/shared_oft/business_leaflets/ca98_guidelines/oft404.pdf (accessed 13 March 2011).

answer. Invariably, an analysis of the competition law position requires an understanding of the market position of the parties. This is fundamentally an economic issue and requires advisers to be provided with facts and information which businesses often do not have readily available and commercial clients are certainly not used to having to provide to their lawyers. In addition to analysing the object and effect of the agreement and any restrictions it contains on competitors and customers, competition advisers will need to consider more "political" issues such as whether competitors or customers are likely to complain or whether this is a particularly high-value or high-profile contract likely to attract the attention of the authorities.

11.7　　It is not possible in one chapter to give a complete account of competition law in the UK. The purpose of this chapter is to give a brief overview of competition law to enable general practitioners to determine when specialist advice may be necessary.

THE BASIC PROHIBITIONS

11.8　These days, both UK and EU competition law are based on the same two prohibitions. The EC prohibitions are found in Arts 101 and 102 of the TFEU[12] and the equivalent UK prohibitions are found in Chapters I and II of the Competition Act 1998. The prohibitions are against:

- anti-competitive agreements and practices (Art 101/Chapter I); and
- abuse of dominance (Art 102/Chapter II).

These will be discussed further below.

Anti-competitive agreements

11.9　Article 101/Chapter I prohibits arrangements between undertakings[13] which:

- affect trade in the EU/UK (as appropriate); and
- have as their object or effect the restriction of competition in the EU/UK.

Examples of anti-competitive agreements include classic price-

---

[12] Treaty on the Functioning of the European Union (the "TFEU"), formerly known as the Treaty establishing the European Community.

[13] An undertaking for competition law purposes is any legal or natural person engaged in economic activity, including individuals, companies, state bodies and trade associations. However, corporate groups are viewed as a single entity for these purposes.

fixing[14] and market-sharing agreements[15] and some less obvious ones, such as customer boycotts, some trade association rules,[16] and exclusive purchasing or supply agreements.[17] Agreements may also be anti-competitive if they apply dissimilar conditions to equivalent transactions with other trading parties, thereby placing them at a competitive disadvantage, or if they make the conclusion of contracts subject to acceptance by the other parties of supplementary obligations which, by their nature or according to commercial usage, have no connection with the subject of such contracts.[18] Mergers may in some cases fall within Art 101 where they significantly impede competition. The issue of merger control is outside the scope of this chapter.[19]

Agreements do not have to be formal written contracts to fall **11.10** within the prohibition[20] – oral agreements, gentlemen's agreements,[21] rules and recommendations of trade associations[22] and concerted practices[23] can all fall within the prohibition.

Agreements which fall within the Art 101/Chapter I prohibition **11.11** are void and unenforceable, although if the anti-competitive clauses can be severed from the remainder of the agreement under the governing law of the contract then the rest of the agreement may survive.[24]

There is an exclusion under both EU and UK law for agreements **11.12** of minor importance, although it is unlikely that many agreements in the oil and gas sector will fall within these *de minimis* exclusions. The European Commission's Notice on Agreements of Minor

---

[14] Ie agreements which distort competition by directly or indirectly fixing purchase or selling prices or other trading conditions.

[15] On which see Whish, *Competition Law* at p 515.

[16] See, eg, OFT Guidance 408, *Trade associations, professional bodies and self-regulating bodies* (2004), available for download from http://oft.gov.uk/shared_oft/business_leaflets/ca98_guidelines/oft408.pdf (accessed 13 March 2011).

[17] See, eg, C–393/92, *Almelo v Energiebedrijf Ijsselmij* [1994] ECR I–1477.

[18] Competition Act 1998, s 2(2).

[19] For a general discussion, see Whish, *Competition Law*, Chapters 20, 21 and 22; and for an account directed specifically towards cross-border mergers and acquisitions in the energy sector, see P Cameron, *Competition in Energy Markets: Law and Regulation in the European Union* (2nd edn, 2007) (hereinafter "Cameron, *Competition in Energy Markets*"), Chapter 14.

[20] Although they may be, and even documents in the nature of compromise agreements may fall within the prohibition in certain circumstances: see *Re Penney's Trade Mark* [1978] OJ L60/19.

[21] Case 41/69, *ACF Chemiefarma NV v Commission* [1970] ECR 661.

[22] See para 11.9.

[23] Case 48/69, *ICI v Commission (The Dyestuffs Case)* [1972] ECR 619. See also the discussion at Whish, *Competition Law*, pp 104–107.

[24] Case 319/82, *Société de Vente de Ciments et Bétons de l'Est SA v Kerpen & Kerpen GmbH und Co KG* [1983] ECR 4173

Importance[25] sets out the European Commission's view that agreements between undertakings which affect trade between Member States do not appreciably restrict competition within the meaning of Art 101 if:

- the aggregate market share of the parties to the agreement (and their affiliates) does not exceed 10 per cent on any of the relevant markets affected by the agreement where the agreement is made between competing undertakings (ie undertakings which are actual or potential competitors on any of the markets concerned);[26] or
- the market share of each of the parties to the agreement (and their affiliates) does not exceed 15 per cent on any of the relevant markets affected by the agreement where the agreement is made between non-competing undertakings (ie undertakings which are neither actual nor potential competitors on any of the markets concerned).[27]

11.13   An agreement containing any of the restrictions set out in para 11 of the Notice on Agreements of Minor Importance does not benefit from the exemption. These include:

- in the case of an agreement between competing undertakings a provision which directly or indirectly fixes prices, shares markets or limits production; or
- in the case of an agreement between non-competing undertakings a provision which:
    - limits a buyer's ability to determine its resale price (except that a supplier may impose a maximum resale price or recommend a resale price, provided that pressure from the parties to the agreement does not result in that becoming a fixed or minimum price); or
    - restricts a buyer operating at a retail level from selling to any end-user in response to an unsolicited order (passive selling); or
    - restricts active or passive selling by authorised distributors

---

[25] Commission Notice on agreements of minor importance which do not appreciably restrict competition under Art 101(1) of the Treaty establishing the European Community (hereinafter "Notice") OJ 2001 C368/13.

[26] *Ibid*, Art 7(a).

[27] *Ibid*, Art 7(b). In both cases, these thresholds are reduced to 5 per cent where competition on the relevant market is restricted by the cumulative foreclosure effect of parallel networks of agreements having similar effects on the market – the agreements under which many petrol stations are affiliated to particular oil companies might constitute such a series of parallel networks: Notice, Art 8.

> to end-users or other authorised distributors in a selective distribution network; or
> — restricts, by agreement between a supplier of components and a buyer who incorporates those components in its products, the supplier's ability to sell the components as spare parts to end-users or independent repairers not entrusted by the buyer with the repair or servicing of its products.

The OFT is required to have regard to the Commission's notice and as a matter of practice the OFT is unlikely to find that an agreement falls within either Art 101 or the Chapter I prohibition when it is covered by the Notice. However, even agreements which exceed these thresholds may be found to have no appreciable effect depending on factors including the content of the agreement and the structure of the market, such as entry conditions or the strength of buyer power. The OFT has confirmed that, where an agreement does not have the object of restricting competition, its effect will be judged within its full market and economic context.[28] **11.14**

Agreements which on the face of it fall within the prohibition may also be exempt if they meet certain criteria set out in Art 101(3), discussed at para 11.16. Formerly, it was necessary to obtain an individual exemption from the authorities for such agreements or to fall within a so-called "block exemption" for certain categories of agreement. Now,[29] individual exemptions are no longer granted – the exemption applies automatically if the criteria are met, but it is up to the parties and their lawyers to decide whether they meet the criteria and ultimately any such decision may be challenged through the courts by an aggrieved party. However, the block exemption system continues in place and in practice many agreements – for instance, most vertical agreements,[30] research and development agreements[31] and specialisation agreements[32] – will continue to benefit from these **11.15**

---

[28] OFT Guidance 401, *Agreements and concerted practices*, available for download from http://oft.gov.uk/shared_oft/business_leaflets/ca98_guidelines/oft401.pdf at para 2.14 (accessed 13 March 2011).

[29] Ie since the coming into force on 1 January 2004 of the Council Regulation of 16 December 2002 on the implementation of the rules on competition laid down in Arts 101 and 102 of the Treaty – Regulation 1/2003 (hereinafter the "Modernisation Regulation") [2003] OJ L1/1.

[30] See Commission Regulation 330/2010 [2010] OJ L102/1 which replaced Regulation 2790/99 on Vertical Agreements with effect from 1 June 2010. See further below at paras 11.53–11.55.

[31] See Regulation 1217/2010 on research and development agreements [2010] OJ L 335/36.

[32] See Regulation 1218/2010 on specialisation agreements [2010] OJ L335/43. A speciali-

exemptions, albeit that future block exemptions will be issued in a revised, less formalistic style.

11.16   The criteria to be met for an individual exemption are that the agreement:

- contributes to improving the production or distribution of products or to promote technical or economic progress;
- allows consumers a fair share of the resulting benefit;
- imposes only restrictions which are indispensable to the attainment of the above listed objectives;
- does not afford the possibility of eliminating competition in respect of a substantial part of the products in question.[33]

Abuse of dominance

11.17   Article 102/Chapter II prohibits conduct which:

- amounts to the abuse of a dominant position; and
- affects trade in the EU/UK (as appropriate).

In order to fall within this prohibition a business must have a dominant position. This will usually involve the business having a significant market share, but this is merely evidence of dominance.[34] The key to a dominant position is not market share *per se* but having *market power*, which in essence means that the business can act in the marketplace without fearing that its competitors will take custom from it or that its customers will turn to other products or services.[35] In order to measure market power it is necessary first to determine on which market a business is active (discussed further at paras 11.23–11.24) and then what market share it has. Market share is an indicator (although not a foolproof one) of market power. Generally, a company with a market share of over 40 per cent may have a dominant position, depending on the structure of the market, while a company with a market share of over 50 per cent

---

sation agreement is, broadly speaking, one whereby one or more of the parties agrees either to refrain from producing a product or products, or to produce products jointly.

[33] See Art 101(3) of the Treaty of Rome; s 9 of the Competition Act 1998.

[34] For a detailed account, see Whish, *Competition Law*, Chapter 1, particularly at pp 25–47.

[35] See, eg, OFT Guidance 415, *Assessment of Market Power*, 2004, available for download from http://oft.gov.uk/shared_oft/business_leaflets/ca98_guidelines/oft415.pdf (accessed 13 March 2011) at 3.1: "Market power can be thought of as the ability profitably to sustain prices above competitive levels or restrict output or quality below competitive levels." For a discussion of various definitions which have been used from time to time, see S Bishop and M Walker, *The Economics of EC Competition Law: Concepts, Application and Measurement* (2nd edn, 2002) at para 3.04.

will generally be presumed to have a dominant position unless the contrary is shown.[36]

It is important to note that the prohibition does not make it illegal to *have* a dominant position, but only to *abuse* it. Abuses of dominance may take many forms, but include imposing unfair prices/conditions, operating loyalty rebates, refusing to supply a particular customer, making the purchase of one product or service conditional on taking another product or service ("tying"). A business may also have a dominant position in relation to the purchase of particular types of goods or services.[37] There are fewer exclusions available in relation to the Art 102/Chapter II prohibition than in relation to the Art 101/Chapter I prohibition, and no exemptions.

11.18

UK OR EC JURISDICTION – WHAT DIFFERENCE DOES IT MAKE?

The Competition Act 1998 requires the UK authorities to interpret the UK prohibitions consistently with EC law[38] and therefore interpretation of the two prohibitions should be broadly similar under both regimes. As we have seen,[39] both carry significant sanctions for breach, including substantial fines, but there are important differences between the two systems, for instance, concerning:

11.19

* procedures for dealing with complaints;
* investigative powers;
* the scope of exclusions for agreements of minor importance;
* the EC concern about agreements which put up barriers to a single market.

In addition, the political priorities of the competition authorities in the two jurisdictions may be different, leading to different risks of intervention in relation to certain activities.

So, how do you decide whether your contract or business activity is likely to fall under the jurisdiction of the UK or EC authorities? The key is whether there is any actual or potential effect on trade with other EU/EEA countries (EU rules apply also in the EEA).[40] For

11.20

---

[36] See Case 62/86, *AKZO Chemie BV* v *Commission* [1991] ECR I–3359.
[37] For a full account of these practices, see Whish, *Competition Law*, Chapters 17 and 18.
[38] See the Modernisation Regulation, Art 1
[39] See para 11.1.
[40] See the Commission's *Notice on guidelines on the effect on trade concept* OJ 2004 C101/101 and equivalent UK guidance: OFT Guidance 401, *Agreements and concerted practices* (2004), available for download from http://www.oft.gov.uk/shared_oft/business_leaflets/ca98_guidelines/oft401.pdf (accessed 13 March 2011).

instance, any agreement concerning the distribution of oil or gas is likely to have such an effect (however small) because oil is sold onto an international commodity market and gas is sold onto an increasingly European market as a result of the Interconnector between the UK and Belgium and the various pipelines which can divert gas between the UK and continental Europe.[41] However, there may be some *de minimis* exceptions such as an agreement by one offshore field to supply fuel gas to a neighbouring offshore field. Equally, a transport and processing agreement ("TPA") between a new satellite field and a nearby host operator is unlikely to affect trade between Member States since there was never any prospect of using an export route to another country but a TPA for a major new discovery may do so, if the owners could have chosen an export route to Norway or the Continent. Many offshore service and supply contracts could be performed by a supplier from Norway or Denmark as easily as by a UK supplier and therefore they also may be thought to affect trade between Member States. Onshore contracts may or may not affect trade, depending on the nature of the goods or services concerned and the likelihood of their being supplied from outside the UK. It should be noted that an agreement between two or more parties outside the EU can have an effect in the EU (for instance a cartel between a US manufacturer and an Asian manufacturer of particular goods supplied into the EU market).[42]

EU Members as at 1 January 2010	Austria, Belgium, Bulgaria, Cyprus, Czech Republic, Denmark, Estonia, Finland. France, Germany, Greece, Hungary, Ireland, Italy, Latvia, Lithuania, Luxembourg, Malta, Netherlands, Poland, Portugal, Romania, Slovakia, Slovenia, Spain, Sweden and UK
EEA Members as at 1 January 2010	EU Member States plus Norway, Iceland and Liechtenstein

11.21   Under the EU rules, agreements are unlikely to affect trade between Member States if the aggregate market share of the parties on any relevant market in the EU does not exceed 5 per cent and the aggregate annual Community turnover of the parties (in horizontal agreements) or of the supplier (in vertical agreements) in the products concerned does not exceed 40 million euros.

11.22   If in doubt, it is probably safer to assume that EU law applies since if a European exemption applies you will have a parallel exemption

---

[41] See para 11.3.

[42] The global reach of cartels has been identified as a major impediment to the implementation of competition law and policy and has led to increased co-operation between anti-trust authorities: see Whish, *Competition Law*, pp 490–495.

under UK law and, to date, the European Commission has shown more interest in the oil and gas sector than has the UK.

DEFINING THE RELEVANT MARKET

In order to analyse the impact of an agreement in competition terms it is necessary to conduct market analysis which aims at answering the following questions:[43] **11.23**

- What is the **product market**? This will include the particular product or service being provided under the agreement and any other goods or services which the customer views as a substitute for that product or service. In other words, if the price of the particular product or service went up by, say, 5 per cent, to what alternative would the customer turn? If there is such an alternative, it is likely to form part of the market.
- What is the **geographic market** in which it is provided? In determining the geographic market, the authorities will look at the area from which customers usually purchase the relevant goods and services. The growth of e-commerce and the global procurement marketplace may expand the market for some goods and services but the authorities will be interested in concrete examples of trade flows, not just theoretical options.
- What are the parties' **market shares** on the product and geographic market identified under steps 1 and 2 above, and, if the market is confined to the UK Continental Shelf ("UKCS"), what are their shares in the EU and worldwide?
- Who are the **principal competitors** and what is their turnover and market share in the UKCS, EU and worldwide?
- How easy would it be for a **new competitor** to enter the market? What are the barriers to entry – for instance, start-up costs, research and development issues, distribution network, intellectual property rights, reputation?
- Who are the **customers** for this product/service – for instance, operators, major contractors, small service companies? This will determine the degree of "buyer power" which may counterbalance any perceived power of the parties to the agreement.

---

[43] See the Commission's Notice on Market Definition [2001] OJ C38/13, and OFT Guidance 403, *Market Definition* (2004), available for download from http://oft.gov.uk/shared_oft/business_leaflets/ca98_guidelines/oft403.pdf (accessed 13 March 2011) and Whish, *Competition Law*, pp 25–47.

Example of market definition

For example, if an operator were to enter into a restrictive contract with a contractor for the supply of ROVs for rig positioning, what would be the relevant market? The first step would be to consider all suppliers of ROVs for rig positioning, but one would also have to consider whether there are any other ways of checking rig position accurately. If so, and these are comparable in cost and quality, such that the operator would turn to them if the cost of using ROVs increased by, say, 5 per cent, then they too will be part of the market. What if another supplier has ROVs but has traditionally used them only for seabed surveys – if the prices were attractive, could that supplier adapt its business? If it could enter the market within, say, a year, then it may be a potential competitor, and will be considered when assessing the market power of the ROV contractor, although it has no current market share on the rig-positioning market.

11.24   The market for transportation services is particularly difficult to determine. There is no case law on market share of offshore transportation and processing in the context of Art 101. In its merger decisions, the European Commission has assessed market shares in transportation of gas and oil by looking at the shares of capacity of each individual owner in all pipelines in which it has an interest in each of the Northern North Sea and Southern North Sea.[44] It has also looked at ullage in all pipelines in which each owner has an interest, on the assumption that each owner has a veto over new business and therefore each owner effectively controls all ullage and not just their own share. While this analysis may be adequate for merger purposes, if a particular agreement was challenged under Art 101 it seems likely that a different approach would be taken. From the perspective of one offshore field, needing to transport its gas to the beach, the overall share of the owners of the nearest pipeline in infrastructure in the Northern North Sea is of no relevance; all that affects its negotiations is whether it has any alternative method of exporting its gas; therefore the geographic market in that instance would seem to be essentially the same as the product market. In other words, it would consist of the potential export routes which were economic for that field.[45]

---

[44] See, eg, Decision M2745 of 4 April 2002 (Shell/Enterprise Oil), available for download from http://ec.europa.eu/comm/competition/mergers/cases/decisions/m2745_en.pdf (accessed 13 March 2011).
[45] See further Chapter 7.

HORIZONTAL AND VERTICAL AGREEMENTS

Horizontal agreements are agreements with one's trade competitors. **11.25**
The potential for such agreements to manipulate fair competition
is obvious and they have traditionally been viewed with greater
suspicion by the competition authorities than have vertical agreements.[46] Some of the principal types of horizontal agreements in
use in the industry are JOAs, joint procurement contracts and
joint sales contracts and these are considered in more detail at
paras 11.27–11.43.

A vertical agreement is one between two or more parties each of **11.26**
which acts at a different level in the supply chain for the purposes
of the agreement – even though they may be at the same level of
the chain in other contexts – and which relates to the conditions
under which goods or services may be purchased, sold or resold. A
vertical agreement would include an agreement between an operator
and a contractor, or a contractor and a subcontractor. Procurement
contracts entered into by individual operators are the most common
type of vertical agreement in the industry, although an agreement by
a single licensee for the sale of gas or oil is also a vertical agreement.
Generally, vertical agreements raise fewer competition issues than
the horizontal agreements. However, see paras 11.54–11.56 for an
analysis of vertical agreements and when they may cause competition problems.

COMMON COMPETITION ISSUES IN UPSTREAM AGREEMENTS

Joint operating agreements and unit operating agreements

As we have already seen, because of the enormous risks and capital **11.27**
involved in oil and gas development, oil companies spread their risk
by taking different levels of interest in different fields and developments.[47] This does require co-operation between companies which
are competitors in other markets but if it were not possible to share
risks in this way, development would be significantly restricted. A
Joint Operating Agreement or JOA is necessary in order to regulate
the sharing of risk and reward. However, JOAs in themselves do not
often raise significant competition concerns as they do not restrict
competition to any appreciable extent. First, JOAs rarely restrict the
parties in relation to matters outside the joint development itself –

---

[46] The Commission's approach to horizontal agreements can be seen in its Guidelines on
the applicability of Art 101 of the Treaty on the Functioning of the European Union to
horizontal co-operation agreements [2010] OJ C11/1.
[47] See para 12.1.

licensees are entirely free to engage in other joint ventures with other parties – their co-operation is restricted to the specific area covered by their licence which is unlikely in itself to represent a significant share of any oil or gas market. Second, joint development does not necessarily entail joint sale of the products of development. In the case of JOAs, the parties are keen to ensure for taxation and liability reasons that their JOA is not treated as a partnership, and therefore for this reason, even before the impact of competition law concerns was felt, it has been standard practice for JOAs to stipulate that each licensee owns its share of production separately and for the JOA not to encompass the sale of that production. In terms of competition analysis, a joint venture to develop an oil or gas field is therefore unlikely to have an appreciable impact on competition. Even if it did, it would be likely to benefit from an exemption under Art 101(3).

11.28   Even though there are no restrictive clauses in most JOAs, the mere existence of the JOA may give rise to concerns that the exchange of information could itself constitute a breach of Art 101. The exchange of information between competitors which leads to market co-ordination (on commercial strategy, on pricing, on sharing out of customers etc) or which could lead to competitors adopting similar approaches to the market is regarded as a violation of Art 101(1).

11.29   The exchange of collated and aggregated statistical information (most easily justified when it is of historic relevance) and technical information is permitted (see below on benchmarking). In a JOA this means that exchange of information pertinent to the continued safe operation of the system and associated activities (eg in relation in due course to abandonment cost expectations) would be permissible. This would include information on the state of equipment, assets and current use in order to deal with upkeep, maintenance and any development. The sharing of technical information on operational and maintenance issues should be non-controversial. However, information on price, on raw materials, production statistics, supplier arrangements, sales figures, terms of business, customer details, business strategy and input cost information have all been prohibited in certain contexts. In reality, in cases of jointly owned facilities there will inevitably be exchanges of information falling within some of these headings in so far as it relates to the joint venture. If the overall arrangement falls within Art 101(3) then these exchanges are likely to fall within the exemption also. However, any information exchange should be kept to the minimum necessary. The licensees will inevitably receive information about their competitors' costs in relation to the production from the individual joint venture (as each party will take its proportionate share of the venture's costs) – the concern would ordinarily be that this would enable the licensees to predict their partners' sale prices and therefore choose not to compete hard with them on price, but the production costs from one venture will in most cases represent only a small proportion of any licensee's overall costs and therefore will not necessarily give any indication as to the prices at which they will be prepared to sell their production. In any event, on a commodity market cost of production of a single seller has only an indirect impact on sale price.

One area where concerns do arise is in relation to "federal" **11.30** contracts under which operators enter into contracts for the supply of services to a number of joint ventures which they operate – operators may be concerned that they would be giving an anti-competitive advantage to their co-venturers by revealing to them the costs under these contracts, as they will also apply to other joint ventures to which those co-venturers are not party. The co-venturers, on the other hand, will legitimately query how they can be asked to pay their share of costs if they are not allowed to approve and audit those costs. These issues may be addressed by limiting rights of access to this information to audit rights only. Problems may also arise with regard to decisions to re-inject or shut in which have an appreciable effect on production, as these may amount to a joint decision to limit production.

UUOAs raise similar issues to JOAs. Bidding agreements or **11.31** AMIs, however, may raise more concerns as they may contain clauses preventing parties from bidding for assets in a particular area except through the consortium. This constitutes a restriction on competition and must therefore be analysed for compliance with competition law. In most cases, the area and duration are likely to be limited and the effect on competition is unlikely to be appreciable.

Joint procurement

In one sense all procurement by joint ventures is joint procurement **11.32** as it is carried out by the operator on behalf of, and often expressly as agent for, the co-venturers under the JOA. However, so long as this is limited to procurement required for the development then, as discussed above in relation to JOAs, it is unlikely to raise any competition concerns – it is an inevitable consequence of the joint development. Joint procurement by neighbouring fields is encouraged by various industry initiatives such as CRINE. Such joint purchasing is likely to produce economies of scale and may even enable the development of previously uneconomic fields. It is unlikely to be a problem under competition law unless the purchasing consortium reaches a size where it would be dominant in the relevant purchase market or the consortium imposes exclusive selling obligations on its chosen suppliers. For EU purposes, where the market shares of the parties on the purchasing market are less than 10 per cent and their share of the affected downstream market is also less than 10 per cent the agreement is unlikely to fall within Art 101 at all and if such shares are in each case less than 15 per cent the agreement is likely to fall within Art 101(3).

Joint selling of oil and gas

11.33 Generally, joint selling arrangements have not been viewed sympathetically by the competition authorities. The principal concerns of joint selling arrangements are that:

- they can facilitate the exchange of commercially sensitive information between the participants which could lead to a co-ordination of their behaviour within the market;
- price competition can be reduced since the group will collectively set prices for the goods or services sold and customers are unable to negotiate with suppliers on an individual basis and exploit price differentials between the various suppliers. This will be exacerbated if the group collectively holds a large market share;
- the collective setting of other trading terms in the joint selling arrangement can also distort competition. The participants of the group may be limited in the range or specification of goods or services offered, the length of agreements, ancillary products or services offered;
- smaller suppliers can be foreclosed from the market because of the power of the selling group;
- some joint arrangements require their members to abide by quotas, limit the development of new capacity of members, require members to notify each other when they intend to increase output or require some element of market allocation – all these elements will distort competition within a market as a result of the co-ordinated and prescribed behaviour of the participants;
- a combination of the above elements between participants in a joint selling group can be the basis of a wider industry cartel.

11.34 Oil is sold onto a commodity market and is movable around the world. Co-venturers in a particular development therefore generally sell on an individual basis. Joint sales rarely occur except in the case of small accumulations unlikely to represent an appreciable restriction on competition and individual sales rarely include any clauses restrictive of competition. Gas sales agreements are a different matter. Gas is not a commodity to the same extent. In order to reach the ultimate consumer it must be transported through a pipeline system. In the absence of a fully integrated global distribution system, gas field owners have almost always looked for a long-term contract for sale of their gas to a gas distributor – in the absence of such a contract any single co-venturer may veto a development. Although gas is owned separately and therefore in theory each seller could contract separately, there are a number of difficulties with this:

- the difficulty of negotiating lifting and gas balancing agreements;
- the need for consistency as regards technical considerations such as landfall, pipeline size, production profile and processing arrangements;
- the impact of swing factors, liquidated damages or other shortfall arrangements on the management of production;
- the need to offer economic volumes and ease of administration to buyers.

These factors have meant that joint selling was traditionally the norm in the UK. (Although each seller had an individual agreement with the buyer for the sale of its individual share of production, these contracts were negotiated on behalf of the co-venturers by the operator and were usually all on identical terms – from the competition law perspective, this constitutes joint selling.) This situation has altered as competition law concerns have come to the fore. The tendency to use long-term depletion contracts is also changing as the market for gas becomes more fragmented and shorter-term contracts become available, especially for small volumes. **11.35**

Competition decisions on oil and gas

Joint gas sales agreements benefited from a specific exemption from the old UK competition regime under the Restrictive Trade Practices Act 1976 and retained a transitional exemption until 2005. No such exemption exists under the Competition Act or EU law and therefore joint selling of gas by co-venturers will in many cases fall within the prohibition on anti-competitive agreements. **11.36**

There are no published decisions of the UK or EU authorities on the application of competition law to gas sales agreements and so one must turn to press releases to determine the European Commission's approach. The first decision in this area was the Britannia decision.[48] In this case, a consortium of gas field developers jointly developing the Britannia gas condensate field in the UKCS sought negative clearance **11.37**

---

[48] Commission Press Notice, *The Commission Clears a Notified Agreement Concerning the Britannia Gas Field* [1996] OJ C291/10.

or exemption from the Commission for the practice of joint selling of their gas. The only Interconnector operational at the time was between the UK and Ireland, and the Commission was satisfied that this was essentially a security of supply measure, designed to back up production in Ireland. The Commission therefore took the view that the agreement had no effect upon trade between Member States and did not issue a formal decision (since it took the view that at the time the arrangement did not fall within the jurisdiction of EC competition law), but only a brief press release. However, a very different course would have been likely to be followed if the Commission had taken the view that it had jurisdiction. It has been indicated in a commentary on competition law written by Commission officials that in this case the Commission did conclude that the joint selling arrangement would have amounted to a restriction of competition within the scope of Art 101 if there had been jurisdiction, despite the parties being able to withdraw from the arrangement at will.[49]

11.38   In 1995, the joint venture agreement for the construction and operation of the UK–Belgium Gas Interconnector received a comfort letter from the Commission.[50] The project as a whole was found to be pro-competitive, especially because it linked markets which previously for technical reasons were generally isolated. The JV company co-ordinates the activities of the participants in the construction and operation of the Interconnector, but the marketing and use of the capacity of the pipeline remains substantially within the individual companies' control. Ownership and capacity are shared in defined proportions. Capacity holders are free to provide transport capacity to others by assignment and by sub-lease. The Commission found that there was no indication that the market for the assignment and sub-lease of such capacity would not be competitive. As part of the arrangements, the JV company was, however, permitted to market spare transport capacity on behalf of the partners, which could lead to joint selling by the JV partners. The Commission found that such joint selling would occur only in limited circumstances (presumably because the parties would ask Interconnector UK Ltd ("IUK") to market on their behalf only scraps of capacity). Nevertheless this restriction could gain some significance given the fact that the JV partners, at least in the Interconnector's initial phase, would have 100 per cent of the relevant market for transport of piped gas

---

[49] European Commission, XXVIIth Report on Competition Policy, Part Two (Report on the application of the competition rules of the European Union) (1997), p 137.
[50] Commission Press Notice IP/95/550, 1 June 1995, *The Commission Gives its Approval to a Joint Venture that will Contribute to the Integration of the European Gas Market*, available for download from http://europa.eu/rapid/pressReleasesAction.do?reference=IP/95/550&format=HTML&aged=1&language= en (accessed 13 March 2011).

across the Channel. Despite finding this aspect of the joint venture to be a restriction of competition falling within Art 101(1), the Commission concluded that overall the pro-competitive effects of the JV outweighed the limited restrictions associated with it and thus issued a comfort letter.[51]

In April 2001, the Commission decided to close its examination in the Corrib case relating to the Corrib gas field off the west coast of Ireland, following the decision of the field owners to withdraw their application for an exemption to market the Corrib gas on a joint basis.[52] The Commission had been expected to refuse the request for an exemption. During the notification process, the Commission had expressed a number of concerns and had questioned whether joint marketing of gas brought about any or sufficient economic benefits which would justify an exemption being granted. Competition Commissioner Mario Monti stated: "This case also confirms the Commission's general policy not to tolerate joint selling, unless compelling reasons are provided as a justification." **11.39**

In June and July 2001, the Commission issued statements of objections[53] to all the companies producing gas in Norway, on the grounds that the joint sale of Norwegian gas carried out through the Gas Negotiation Committee (known as the GFU) was in breach of Art 101(1) as it fixed, among other things, the price and quantities of gas sold. The Commission welcomed the announcement by the Norwegian Government to discontinue the GFU joint sales. In its press release the Commission states: "As the European gas market is progressively being liberalised, it is of paramount importance that producers sell their gas individually so that those customers that can already choose their supplier benefit from real choice and competitive **11.40**

---

[51] In a later inquiry, also closed without a formal decision, the Commission investigated why the Interconnector reversed flow to export gas to the Continent during a period when UK prices were higher than on the continent. It found no evidence of collusion between the shippers: the cause of the reversal was rigidities in the nomination and flow transition procedures in the pipeline but IUK and its members had agreed alterations to their rules to make these processes more flexible and to increase transparency. See Commission Press Notice IP/02/401 of 13 March 2002, *Commission closes investigation into UK/Belgium gas interconnector*, available for download from http://europa.eu/rapid/pressReleasesAction.do?reference=IP/02/401&format=HTML&aged=1&language=EN&guiLanguage=en (accessed 13 March 2011).

[52] See Commission Press Notice IP/01/578 of 20 April 2001, *Enterprise Oil, Statoil and Marathon to market Irish Corrib gas separately*, available for download from http://europa.eu/rapid/pressReleasesAction.do?reference=IP/01/578&format=HTML&aged=1&language=EN&guiLanguage=en (accessed 13 March 2011).

[53] See Commission Press Notice IP/02/1084 of 17 July 2002, *Commission successfully settles GFU case with Norwegian gas producers*, available for download at http://europa.eu/rapid/pressReleasesAction.do?reference=IP/02/1084&format=HTML&aged=1&language=EN&guiLanguage=en (accessed 13 March 2011).

prices." In 2003, a similar joint investigation by the Commission and the Danish competition authorities into similar behaviour by the incumbent Danish gas supplier, DONG, and its main gas producers (acting through a consortium known as DUC) was settled when the producers in DUC agreed to market their production individually and DONG released the producers from their obligation to offer all gas first to DONG.[54]

11.41   Of the above cases only the UK–Belgium Interconnector decision related to joint selling of transportation, all the others concerning arrangements for the joint sale of gas. To date, there have been no other reported cases concerning the joint sale of capacity within an upstream gas pipeline or of processing services in relation to gas.[55] The downstream situation is complicated by the existence of the Gas Directive, part of the European Commission's liberalisation measures, which is outside the scope of this chapter.[56]

Conclusions on joint selling of oil and gas

11.42   The Commission's guidelines and case law make it clear that, in its view, joint selling will always fall under Art 101(1). However, joint activities falling short of joint selling may not fall within Art 101(1) where the parties' market share is below 10 per cent. Above 10 per cent, the impact of the joint activities would need to be considered on a case-by-case basis to determine, for instance, whether they either allow the exchange of sensitive commercial information (particularly on market strategy and pricing) or if they influence a significant part of the parties' final cost so that the actual scope for price competition at the final sales level is limited. The Commission's press releases on the Corrib field in the Irish Sea and on the Norwegian GFU arrangements give us a clear signal as to the Commission's approach: it will be difficult to convince the Commission that joint selling is essential. They may be prepared to permit some technical and production-related issues to be determined jointly but it is difficult to see why, in many instances, pricing negotiations could not take place separately.

---

[54] See Commission Press Notice IP/03/566 of 24 April 2003, *Commission and Danish competition authorities jointly open up Danish gas market*, available for download at http://europa.eu/rapid/pressReleasesAction.do?reference=IP/03/566&format=HTML&aged=1&language=EN&guiLanguage=en (accessed 13 March 2011).

[55] There are a number of other European cases, settled informally, in relation to gas distribution – these largely concern the Commission's efforts to eradicate territorial restrictions in gas sales contracts in order to create a single market in gas.

[56] For a discussion of the downstream position, see Cameron, *Competition in Energy Markets*, Chapter 13.

Transportation agreements – joint supply or purchase of capacity

Transportation agreements raise three potential issues under compe-   **11.43**
tition law:

- First, joint decisions of the infrastructure owners and/or
  shippers with regard to tariffs and other matters raise issues of
  joint selling similar to those raised by joint sales of oil or gas.
- Second, depending on the definition of the relevant market,
  infrastructure owners may be found to be in a dominant
  position and the infrastructure to amount to an "essential
  facility" which, under EU case law, imposes obligations on the
  owners to provide access on fair, transparent and non-discriminatory terms.
- Third, joint purchasing of capacity by the shippers may
  raise issues similar to joint procurement of other services as
  mentioned above, aggravated by the fact that the shipping
  takes place outside the scope of the JV, occurring after the
  point at which each party takes ownership of its individual
  share. It is therefore more analogous to joint purchasing by
  neighbours.

Discussions on joint selling of capacity in oil and gas pipelines and   **11.44**
processing facilities may crudely be separated into those which do
not affect price setting (chiefly technical issues) and those which
either directly fix prices (direct discussions on tariffs to be quoted
and/or agreed) or indirectly lead to the setting of tariffs (discussion
of acceptable margins, cost influences etc). In so far as discussions
either directly or indirectly concern the fixing of prices then whatever
the parties' market shares the starting point is that the arrangements
contravene Art 101(1). Very strong justification would have to be
found to allow this to continue.

It has been suggested that the specialisation block exemption[57]   **11.45**
might apply to these sales. The definitions of "product" and
"production" in this block exemption are wide and, as well as
covering the sale of gas, would appear to include the provision of
transportation and processing services. Although Art 4(a) of the
block exemption expressly states that the exemption provided for
by the block exemption does not apply to specialisation agreements
which, directly or indirectly, have as their object the fixing of prices
to third parties, there is an exception where in the context of a
joint venture which jointly distributes production the parties agree
provisions which fix the prices that the production joint venture
charges to its immediate customers. One might argue that joint sale

---

[57] Regulation 1218/2010, referred to at para 11.15.

of transportation capacity is analogous to the joint distribution of products by a group of manufacturers who have pooled their resources to make a product more efficiently than each is able to do on his own. However, there is no evidence to date that the specialisation block exemption has successfully been used to cover either the sale of gas by joint venturers or the construction and operation of infrastructure on which capacity is then jointly sold.[58] Even if this block exemption could be used to justify joint selling, Art 3 of the block exemption provides that agreements complying with the requirements of the block exemption will be exempt from Art 101(1) only where the combined market share of the parties does not exceed 20 per cent of the relevant market.

11.46   In so far as discussions neither directly nor indirectly fix prices nor do they include discussion of other sensitive commercial information, then the activities of the sellers will be presumed not to fall within Art 101(1) at all if the co-venturers' market shares are in aggregate below 10% of the relevant market (see above for the difficulties in definition of markets in this area) and may merit an exemption above that level.

11.47   There is a grey area in between these two, and the practice has been used in some cases of making an initial joint offer with an indicative tariff or range of tariffs and then agreeing all other terms, at which point the parties separate and conclude final tariff terms which are inserted in separate but otherwise identical contracts. The validity of this approach has not, so far as we are aware, been tested before the competition authorities but it is certainly preferable to agreeing prices jointly.

11.48   The question of dominant position in relation to control of oil and gas infrastructure has not been the subject of a decision by the EU authorities, although analogies could be drawn to cases in other sectors, such as those involving port facilities.[59] As the market has been defined by the European Commission in its merger cases, it seems unlikely that any such dominant position would be found in relation to a particular pipeline. However, as mentioned

---

[58] In the DONG case referred to at para 11.40, above, DUC attempted to argue that a previous block exemption for specialisation agreements covered their joint distribution activities – the press release states that DG Competition disagreed with the assessment of the parties and they – while maintaining their legal position – agreed to cease their joint marketing efforts.

[59] For instance, port fees may in some cases be analogous to tariffs applied for access to infrastructure: for a discussion on recent cases on allegedly excessive port fees as abuse of a dominant position, see M Lamalle, L Lindstrom-Rossi and A Teixeira, *Two important rejection decisions on excessive pricing in the port sector* [2004] 3 ECCPN at 40. See also the investigation into the port of Piraeus for alleged abuses of dominant position: P Aivatzidis, "Can Piraeus Keep Everyone Happy?" [2007] 360 *Fairplay* at 19–20.

above, the methods employed by the European Commission (an aggregation of UK capacity or ullage of individual pipeline owners split between NNS or SNS) may not represent a useful or accurate indicator of market power in the case of a complaint over access to an individual pipeline. A more useful indicator of market power particularly in relation to small accumulations would be to look at market power on a more localised and individual basis based on the geographical/economic/market context in which the pipeline and the relevant pipeline owners operate. If a subsea tie back to a particular platform is likely to be the only means of export for a satellite field then the owners of that potential host platform may be considered to be collectively dominant and the platform may be considered to be an "essential facility". If the owners were found to be in a dominant position, then compliance with Art 102 would require that access to the infrastructure must be offered on terms that would not be considered to be an abuse, ie access must be offered on reasonable terms and must not be unreasonably refused.

In practice, the focus of the debate over refusal of access to infra- **11.49** structure has shifted to the DECC-sponsored "Infrastructure Code of Practice" (the "ICOP"),[60] developed by DECC and Oil & Gas UK (and their predecessors) among others in response to the perceived difficulty of obtaining access on fair and transparent terms to existing infrastructure. Particularly for smaller discoveries, the cost of infrastructure access could be the critical factor in marginal economics of development. The Code requires tariffs to be fair, reasonable and non-discriminatory but there is little guidance on how these principles will be applied in practice. Moreover, it is voluntary and there is no penalty for failure to comply with it, other than the risk that a party may institute the procedure established by the ICOP in order to ask for terms to be imposed by DECC using its statutory powers. On the other hand, there are considerable costs and risks to using competition law in this situation. In its Guidance on Disputes over Third Party Access to Upstream Oil and Gas Infrastructure, DECC states:

> "Although the OFT has not issued specific guidance on the application of [the Competition Act 1998] to upstream oil and gas infrastructure (including on the definition of the relevant market), it considers that infrastructure owners are unlikely to have breached the Chapter II prohibition on abuse of a dominant position where they have had

---

[60] The ICOP is available from the Oil and Gas UK website at http://www.oilandgasuk. co.uk/knowledgecentre/InfrastructureCodeofPractice.cfm. (accessed 13 March 2011). The ICOP is also discussed extensively in Chapter 7.

due regard to the Secretary of State's principles for setting terms ... in arriving at the terms that they offer to, and agree with, third parties."[61]

The DECC Guidance continues with an apparent warning directed towards any party considering utilising the mainstream law on abuse of a dominant position in preference to the industry-specific ICOP mechanism: "investigation of any complaint is at the OFT's discretion and would be subject to resource constraints and priorities. Recourse to the sector specific legislation therefore provides a more certain process and is likely to give a speedier outcome."[62]

11.50   Therefore, although there is nothing to prevent a party bringing a claim under Art 102 to the OFT, the OFT may well take the view that if the Code has been applied, it would not be an appropriate use of its resources to investigate further. On the other hand, the OFT's advice on the Code stated clearly that it reserved the right to respond if a complaint was received about the way the Code operated in practice. Because of the obligations of national authorities with regard to the implementation of EC competition law under the Modernisation Regulation,[63] the OFT would need to engage in a proper investigation of any complaint which appeared well founded and there is the possibility that the OFT would engage more fully with this issue than it has done to date.

11.51   Issues regarding exchange of commercial information also arise in relation to joint selling of infrastructure capacity. The type of information which would fall into the "commercially sensitive" category can usefully be considered by reference to what would be commercially confidential were the co-venturers in fact selling on a divided rights basis, and therefore very conscious of their position as competitors, such as tariff terms with customers (including formulae and indexation provisions); volume of capacity in any contract (which raises some interesting questions about the role of the operator in dealing with nomination/allocation); specific terms of business not common to the operation of the pipeline; marketing strategies/business planning, for example, what customers are being approached on what terms, state of current negotiations; pricing policy (for example, in terms of the owner's group's approach to acceptable rates of return); other information which in normal conditions of competition a co-venturer would regard as confidential because to share it with a competitor would be to give that

---

[61] DECC, *Guidance on Disputes over Third Party Access to Upstream Oil and Gas Infrastructure*, April 2009 (hereinafter "DECC *Guidance*") at para 17. The Guidance is discussed further in Chapter 7.

[62] DECC Guidance, at para 18.

[63] Regulation 1/2003.

competitor an advantage over the co-venturer or could lead to collusion.

Benchmarking or industry data-gathering exercises?

The industry has a long history of collaboration, benchmarking and trade association activity designed to increase the efficient exploitation of the hydrocarbon resources of the UKCS.[64] However, it is very important not to be complacent about the potential competition law implications of these activities. Exchange of information between competitors can be anti-competitive because it can result in concerted practices or reveal a competitor's commercial strategies. As such, great care needs to be taken over the exchange of industry data. The following table sets out some of the factors which determine whether an exchange is likely to be permitted.

11.52

Safe	Dangerous
The relevant data is available publicly in any event	The relevant data is confidential
The relevant data is entirely technical	The relevant data is commercial
The data will be published in an aggregated form or it will be published anonymously and in such a way that no individual company 's data will be identifiable	The data will not be aggregated and the source of the data will be identified/identifiable
The data will be available only to regulatory authorities or to an industry task force set up to deal with a specific public interest issue	The data will be circulated freely around the industry
The data will be available only to potential customers	The data will be available to competitors
The data is historic	The data is current or relates to future plans

---

[64] Collaboration can be seen at every level in the industry: from licence-holding and JOA arrangements to the very way in which the Government regulates: by persuasion, committees and initiatives, rather than by direct rule. The Government actively encourages the sharing of information through and provision through such initiatives as UKDEAL and its involvement in groups like PILOT. Nor is such information sharing of purely technical material: consider, for example, the requirement to share key elements of commercial information in access to infrastructure situations, discussed in Chapter 7. Collaboration is seen as one of the industry's great strengths and crucial to its ongoing success.

Vertical agreements – are they ever a problem?

11.53 Many procurement contracts between an operator and a contractor contain no restrictions on competition at all. If there are any restrictions, particularly in the form of tying up large parts of the market or the capacity in the industry for a particular product or service for an extended period, then it will be necessary to consider whether the agreement will fall within a block exemption or qualify for an individual exemption. The EU has issued a block exemption for vertical agreements,[65] which under UK competition law applies also to agreements where the UK authorities have jurisdiction. It applies only where the parties have market shares not exceeding 30 per cent.[66] It has a number of other restrictions, the principal ones relevant in this context being those set out at para 11.55.

11.54 Because some of the limits to the exemption are technical and their interpretation is not yet fully understood, it is always best to have any vertical agreement reviewed by a competition lawyer if it restricts competition, ie it places any restrictions on the ability of the parties to do business with third parties. Examples of restrictions would include any limitations on the persons to whom, territories in which or prices at which goods may be on-sold, or provisions which directly or indirectly (eg through the use of pricing incentives) oblige a seller to sell all of its production of a particular product to the buyer, or a buyer to buy most or all of its requirements of a particular product only from the seller, or clauses requiring a seller to offer the buyer the best prices it offers other customers or to allow the seller to match prices offered to the buyer by other sellers.

11.55 Which vertical agreements may cause problems?

- Price-fixing agreements are not given the benefit of the block exemption (although maximum resale prices are allowed, as are recommended minimum prices where these are not binding).[67]
- Vertical agreements entered into by dominant companies may be exempted under Chapter I /Art 101 but still infringe the Chapter II /Art 102 prohibition.
- Market shares over 30 per cent agreements cannot benefit

---

[65] See Commission Regulation 330/2010 on the application of Article 101(3) of the Treaty on the Functioning of the European Union to categories of vertical agreements and concerted practices [2010] OJ L102/1 and the related Guidelines on Vertical Restraints [2010] OJ C130/1. This block exemption replaces Regulation 2790/99 on Vertical Agreements with effect from 1 June 2010, with a 1-year transition period for existing agreements.

[66] Regulation 330/2010, Art 3. The relevant market share for the purchaser is its share on the purchasing market, not the downstream market.

[67] *Ibid*, Art 4(a).

from block exemption and will need to be analysed to see if they qualify for individual exemption.

- Agreements where non-compete clauses on the buyer are for indefinite periods or for more than 5 years (including clauses which are tacitly renewable beyond 5 years) or where non-competes survive termination of the agreement.[68]
- Any restriction on the territory or customers to which the buyer can sell (with certain exceptions).
- Agreements between competitors (with certain exceptions).
- Agreements involving associations of businesses (with certain exceptions).
- Agreements whose primary object is the assignment or licensing of intellectual property.

---

[68] For these purposes, EU law treats any contract for the purchase of 80% or more of an undertaking's requirements as a non-compete obligation.

CHAPTER 12

JOINT OPERATING AGREEMENTS

Scott C. Styles

The joint operating agreement ("JOA") is the common means by 12.1
which businesses come together as a *joint venture* in their search
for and production of oil and gas, both within the United Kingdom
Continental Shelf (UKCS) and internationally. The need for a JOA
is primarily driven by the economics of oil exploration, which is a
high-risk, high-cost enterprise with a heavy frontloading of costs,
albeit one which offers high rewards to successful parties. There
are several benefits in entering into a JOA. Joint ventures allow oil
companies to come together to mitigate their risks and share in the
outlays required for capital-intensive exploration, development and
production activities. Joint ventures also facilitate cost savings and
economies of scale which enable the participating companies to
operate with fewer employees, permit the elimination of duplicate
facilities, equipment and functions and allow cost savings through
bulk purchases of supplies and materials. The joint venture is also
important in that it allows upstream oil and gas companies to
manage their portfolio of assets in a manner that seeks a balance
between minimising risk and maximising returns by allowing each
company to invest in several different prospects for the same capital
outlay.

The term "joint venture" is not a term of art[1] in English or 12.2
Scots law[2] and it can be used to refer to a specifically established

---

[1] The question of the legal nature of the joint venture is discussed further at para 12.6
onwards.
[2] In the UKCS, the vast majority of JOAs contain a choice of law clause stating that the
contract will be governed by English law and interpreted by the English courts should any
dispute arise between the parties. For this reason, while Scots law will be noted in passing
at points throughout this chapter, its principal focus will be on English law.

limited company, a partnership or an unincorporated contractual association for a given purpose. It is the unincorporated joint venture which is used by the oil industry in the UKCS (and most commonly throughout the rest of the world). But although the term "joint venture" is not a technical legal term, it has been recognised by the courts in numerous cases and the current judicial approach may legitimately be considered to be summarised by the Court of Appeal in Northern Ireland in *Sweeney* v *Lagan Developments*,[3] discussed further below.[4] The unincorporated joint venture has been favoured by the oil industry over other possible models, such as legal partnership or incorporation into a limited company, because of the tax advantages it provides and because of the lack of mutual liability which is possible under the JOA. Like many other aspects of oil industry practice, the use of the unincorporated joint venture as a means of pooling resources in the search for hydrocarbons has its origins in the United States.[5] By the 1950s there was a widely perceived need within the US oil industry for a standardised JOA which would minimise time spent in arguing over contractual matters. There soon developed a standardised US model form operating agreement: the American Association of Petroleum Landmen's Model Form Operating Agreement, also known as the AAPL Form 610 of 1956. The AAPL Form 610 has been revised several times since then[6] but remains very similar to the 1956 original. The AAPL Form 610 was an influential model on the early UKCS JOAs which were introduced in the wake of the First Licensing Round in 1964. Although no

---

[3] [2007] NICA 11.

[4] See para 12.5 below.

[5] See, eg, T Winsor and S Tyne, *Taylor and Winsor on Joint Operating Agreements* (2nd edn, 1992) (hereinafter "Taylor and Winsor") at xxiii. The reasons behind the adoption of unincorporated JV, rather than the partnership, as the commercial vehicle of choice for oil and mining companies seems to have arisen in the prohibition under US law against companies forming partnerships.

[6] The most recent revisions being in 1982 and 1989. The AAPL Form 610 is very much an American document and can be purchased through the AAPL's website (http://www.landman.org/ (accessed 22 April 2011)). It should be noted that Form 610 is for onshore JOAs. AAPL's Model JOAs for the US Outer Continental Shelf (Form 710) and deepwater (Form 810) are available for download from the OCS Advisory Board website (http://www.ocsadvisoryboard.org/ (accessed 22 April 2011)). In 1990 the Association of International Petroleum Negotiators produced a model JOA for the international context: the AIPN Model Form International Operating Agreement. A revised version was produced in 2002. For an account of the AIPN Model Form, see P Weems and M Bolton, "Highlights of Key Revisions – 2002 AIPN Model Form International Operating Agreement" (2003) IELTR 169. In Canada the standard JOA is the Canadian Association of Petroleum Landsmen's (CAPL) Operating Procedure. The 2007 edition is available for download from the CAPL website: http://www.landman.ca/pdf/operating_procedures/2007/final/2007%20Operating%20Procedure%20Text%20(Final%20Annotated%20Version%202008).pdf (accessed 22 April 2011).

absolutely standard form of UKCS JOA has ever emerged, a major step towards the standardisation in this regard occurred during the Fifth Round of UKCS licensing in 1977. Licences granted under the Fifth Round were given to consortia that had to include the then state-owned British National Oil Corporation (BNOC),[7] and the JOA had to be in terms acceptable to BNOC. BNOC took a model form JOA drafted by UKOOA[8] a year earlier, adapted it to its needs, and produced the BNOC Proforma Joint Operating Agreement for Fifth Round Licences. This pro-forma JOA (together with the very similar Sixth Round pro-forma which followed) proved to be a workable document which secured widespread industry acceptance. Its legacy continues to be seen in UKCS JOAs to this day, long after the nationalised BNOC itself has ceased to exist. In advance of the 20th UKCS Offshore Licensing Round in 2002, a group of industry lawyers working under the auspices of UKOOA used the BNOC pro-forma as a starting point to produce the UKOOA 20th Round Draft JOA. This 20th Round JOA was consequently revised in 2008 by a group of industry lawyers working under the auspices of Oil & Gas UK to bring it into line with the standard Decommissioning Security Agreement (DSA)[9] published by Oil & Gas UK Ltd,[10] and the new Oil & Gas UK Model JOA was published in February 2009.[11] This has proved to be an influential model for UKCS JOAs and frequent reference will be made to the new Oil & Gas UK Model JOA, hereinafter referred to in this chapter simply as the "2009 Model JOA".

As was noted earlier, while there has been movement towards standardisation, in practice no absolutely standard JOA has emerged. Standard documents such as the 20th Round and the 2009 Model JOAs are influential, but each oil company tends to have its own preferred style JOA and disagreements can arise between the parties over the finer points of certain terms of the JOA. For reference, it should be noted that there is a major policy difference between the US and the UK forms of JOA, namely that the US JOAs place the operator in a very strong, even dominant, position with regard to the non-operators, while under the UK JOAs non-operators have more rights and more say than they would have under a US JOA.[12]

12.3

---

[7] For a short discussion of the history of BNOC, see para 4.1.

[8] The United Kingdom Offshore Operators Association (UKOOA) was succeeded by Oil & Gas UK Ltd in April 2007.

[9] For DSAs, see paras 12.69–12.73 and also paras 10.58–10.59.

[10] This JOA may be purchased through Oil & Gas UK Ltd's website: http://www.oilandgas uk.co.uk/ (accessed 22 April 2011).

[11] See http://www.oilandgasuk.co.uk/news/news.cfm/newsid/379.

[12] See, eg, Taylor and Winsor at 11 and more generally throughout Chapter 2 of that work.

JOINT BIDDING AGREEMENT

12.4   Every JOA follows on from a Joint Bidding Agreement ("JBA") or an Area of Mutual Interest Agreement ("AMI"). These contracts are agreements between interested parties to bid for selected acreage under a UKCS licensing round, or to make an out-of-rounds bid, with the aim of securing from the Government the award of a production licence. In an AMI, the parties specify an area of licensing acreage within which they agree to work jointly and to the exclusion of any non-signatory third parties should any licensing possibilities arise. A JBA commits the parties to bid jointly for selected acreage in a particular licensing round (or out-of-rounds bid) and, if the application is successful, commits them to conclude a JOA as quickly as possible in order to conduct operations under the licence. It is now common practice to attach the whole of the proposed JOA to the JBA in order to facilitate its implementation without unnecessary delay. A JOA only comes into existence when a licence has been granted by the Government to the members of a successful JBA; the members of the JBA will then solidify their relations by executing the JOA.

12.5   The central right granted by a UK licence is to "search and bore for, and get" petroleum.[13] UKCS licences and model clauses generally refer to "licensee" in the singular and are also silent about the legal relations between any co-licensees.[14] As the whole purpose of the Bidding Agreement is to secure a licence then, obviously, all the members of the prospective JOA must satisfy the UK Government's criteria for the award of a production licence. These are that applicants must meet certain minimum standards of financial and technical capability and environmental management. Provided that these thresholds are met, then the key factors in determining the actual award of a licence are the geological rationale for the application and the programme of exploration work that is proposed. In short, the parties willing to spend the most in exploration are the ones who most likely to be awarded the licence.[15]

NATURE OF THE JOINT VENTURE

12.6   As mentioned above, the term "joint venture" is not a term of legal art in English or Scots law and to add further to the conceptual confusion the term is often used in quite different ways. When two

---

[13] Petroleum Licensing (Production) (Seaward Areas) Regulations 2008 (SI 2008/225) (hereinafter "2008 Regulations"), Model Cl 2(1). See further the discussion at paras 4.31–4.34.

[14] Under the 2008 Regulations, Model Cl 1, "Licensee" is defined as the "person or persons to whom this licence is granted, his personal representatives and any person or persons to whom the rights conferred by this licence may lawfully have been assigned".

[15] See further the discussion at paras 4.31–4.34.

or more parties choose to pool their efforts by setting up a limited company, that is often spoken of as an "incorporated joint venture". However, for lawyers at least, this terminology is confusing as, whatever the underlying commercial reality, the legal obligations constituted by such an "incorporated joint venture" are simply those of normal company law. The terminological confusion is exacerbated by the fact that the terms "joint venture" or "joint adventure" have been used in both Scots and English law[16] to designate partnerships for a fixed period or specific project, a designation which again *prima facie* would appear to govern the typical North Sea JOA. Perhaps it would be better if the JOA referred not to "joint ventures" and instead referred to "alliances" and "alliancing", terms which at least run no risk of having any implication, as the term "joint venture" does, of fixed-term partnerships, but the terminology of "joint venture" is so embedded in the usage and practice of the international oil industry that the use of that expression is likely to continue for many years to come. Moreover, the conceptual basis of the unincorporated joint venture is far from clear in English or Scots law. The concept of the joint venture seems to rest uneasily between two well-established legal concepts and institutions, namely contract and partnership. The concept of the joint venture seems slightly "fuzzy" because, in many ways, it seems to function as a partnership but – quite deliberately – lacks many of the key characteristics of a partnership. Some doubts still remain about the courts' attitude to the unincorporated joint venture. This issue will be discussed further at paras 12.14–12.18 below, under the heading "Partnership or not?".

The unincorporated joint venture is a form of contractual associ-   **12.7**
ation; that is, the relationship is created by contract – the JOA itself – and the terms of the joint venture will largely be prescribed and limited to those set out in the JOA. The JOA thus functions as the constituent contract of the commercial relations between the parties. Indeed, it is usual for the JOA to contain a clause reducing the entire terms of the contract to the JOA itself. The JOA needs to carry out a number of important functions. It will define the proportionate interests of the parties and allocate control mechanisms and rights: all the Joint Operations must be conducted in accord with the terms of the JOA. In addition to the agreement of the parties, because the creation or amendment of a JOA commonly entails the apportionment of at least some of the rights granted by a Petroleum Act licence, both its creation and amendment requires the consent

---

[16] See, for English law, Lord Mackay of Clashfern (General Editor), *Halsbury's Laws of England* (4th edn), 2003 Reissue (hereinafter "Halsbury"), vol 35, para 8; for Scots law, Bell, *Principles*, para 392.

of the Secretary of State, acting on behalf of the UK Government. As the JOA is a contract it may, of course, be amended only by the unanimous consent of the parties and therefore it is vital that the JOA be as well drafted and fit for purpose as is possible, because it may well have to endure for many years.

12.8   Notwithstanding the need for the Secretary of State's consent, the JOA is in essence a private contract between the licensees which governs the "horizontal" relations between the parties, and the purpose of a JOA is to allocate control, risk and reward between the licensees *inter se,* as distinct from their "vertical" relationship with the Government. That vertical relationship is governed by the terms of the licence.[17] The scope of the JOA is the exploration for and production of petroleum under the relevant licence, together with those activities which flow inevitably from that task, ie, the storage and transport of the petroleum product and so on.[18] Unless terminated at an earlier date by the parties, the JOA will terminate when all commercially available hydrocarbons have been extracted and the costs for the decommissioning of the field have been met. While it is extant, the JOA has two quite distinct legal functions: a *proprietorial* one and a *functional–relational* one. In other words, the contract both establishes the *property interests* of the parties and regulates the *rights and duties* of the parties. These respective functions will be discussed in turn.

---

[17] The licence lays down various obligations, most of which are contained in the model clauses. Examples of these obligations are discussed in Chapters 4 and 5 above. From the standpoint of the vertical relationship between the Government and the JOA members *qua* licensees, liability for any breach of these obligations is joint and several between all the licensees. As between the licensees/JOA members themselves, the extent of their liability will depend on the nature of the fault but most JOAs make provision that any civil liabilities arising under the licence will be allocated on a *pro rata* basis.

[18] Eg, the 2009 Model provides at cl 3.1.1:

"The scope of this Agreement shall extend to:

(a) the exploration for, and the appraisal, development and the production of Petroleum under the Licence;

(b) without prejudice to clause 18, the treatment, storage and transportation of Petroleum using Joint Property;

(c) [[without prejudice to clause 18, the consideration of technical and operational issues in connection with the treatment, storage and transportation of Petroleum using third party infrastructure;]]

(d) [[the consideration of technical and operational issues in connection with the use of Joint Property by third parties;]]

(e) the decommissioning or other disposal of Joint Property; and

(f) the conditions for the carrying out of Sole Risk Projects in the Licence."

Note that the sub-clauses 3.1.1(c) and (d) are new additions in the 2008 Draft to bring the third party access to infrastructure within the scope of JOA. For regulatory discussion on access to infrastructure, see Chapter 7.

Proprietorial functions – declaration of percentage interest and creation of tenancy in common

The proprietorial role of the JOA is to establish the *legal nature* **12.9** or *form* of the property interest of the parties and to allocate the *proportion* of that proprietary interest between them. Arguably the most important clause of all in any JOA is the one which specifies the respective proportional interests of the parties in the licence in any petroleum won, and in any property owned by the JOA. Such a clause is commonly known as the "interests clause". For instance, cl 4 of the 2009 Model JOA provides:

> "Subject to the provisions of this Agreement, the Licence, all Joint Property, all Joint Petroleum and all costs and obligations incurred in, and all rights and benefits arising out of, the conduct of the Joint Operations shall be owned and borne by the Participants in proportion to their respective Percentage Interests which at the date hereof are as follows ..."

The interests clause allocates the percentage property rights of each **12.10** member of the JOA under the licence. All other rights and duties of the JOA members are borne in proportion to the extent of their proprietary interest in the licence.[19] Furthermore, the declaration that joint property is to be held in proportion to the parties' respective percentage interests provides the all important "words of severance" which English law requires if the "joint tenancy"[20] granted to the licensees by the state by the award of the licence is to be replaced by a "tenancy in common".[21] In other words, the collective unitary form of ownership granted by the licence is transformed by the interests clause into individual ownership of proportions of the property, each owner having a separate undivided share of the JOA assets. The central form of reward under the JOA is the allocation of production in kind of any assets produced by the joint operation.[22] The undivided interest is a form of intangible personal property,[23] or

---

[19] The JOA may also provide for non *pro rata* sharing in certain circumstances, eg, where there are sole risk operations; see below at paras 12.41–12.42.

[20] Joint tenancy is a form of ownership by which two or more persons, called joint tenants, share ownership of the property in an equal and undivided manner. Obviously, oil companies do not wish to hold their interest in a licence in an equal and undivided manner.

[21] Tenancy in common is a form of ownership by which two or more persons have community of possession but distinct and several titles to their shares which need not necessarily be equal and which they may dispose of separately. See *Halsbury*, vol 39(2), para 208.

[22] That is, allocation not of equivalent monetary value but of the volume of hydrocarbon produced.

[23] "Personal property" is used here in its sense under English law; in Scots law it would be classified as "moveable property".

to put the matter more precisely, it is a chose in action,[24] and, subject to any restrictions on assignment, may be sold or mortgaged by its owner.

12.11   The transfer of an interest in a JOA and in a licence is done by a process of novation and assignment.[25] All and any such trading in licence interests is subject to consent being granted by the Government, but there is in place a system of open permission.[26] Furthermore, as regards securities, it is government policy not to allow them to be granted over licence interests unless they are used to finance offshore operations.[27]

Assignation and pre-emption rights

12.12   Until 2002 it was usual for JOAs to contain a clause restricting the assignment of a co-venturer's interest in the JOA.[28] The main argument in favour of pre-emption rights in a JOA is that they preserve the identity of the original group and can help to keep out undesirable new joint venture partners. This approach makes sense if a JOA is viewed primarily as a relational contract, like a traditional partnership, with a significant element of *delectus personae*.[29] An incoming party to a JOA is not just buying equity in a project (as, for example, a purchaser of shares in a limited company does), he is also

---

[24] See *Halsbury*, vol 6, para 1.

[25] See further on this topic Chapter 17.

[26] A copy of this Open Permission (Operating Agreements) is available from https://www. og.decc.gov.uk/upstream/licensing/OpenPermJOA.pdf (accessed 22 April 2011). Note, however, that the open consent "permits the several companies that together constitute the Licensee to novate an Operating Agreement (including both Joint and Unit Operating Agreements) in the course of implementing a Licence Assignment *that has already been approved by the Secretary of State*".

[27] A copy of this Open Permission (Creation of Security Rights over Licences) can be downloaded from https://www.og.decc.gov.uk/upstream/licensing/OpenPermChg.pdf (accessed 22 April 2011).

[28] For a discussion, see R Major, "A practical look at pre-emption provisions in upstream oil and gas contracts" (2005) IELTR 117.

[29] The courts tend to uphold pre-emption rights: see, eg, *Texas Eastern Corporation (Delaware) & Others v Enterprise Oil Plc*, CA, 21 July 1989 (unreported) in which the Court of Appeal effectively re-wrote the pre-emption clause in the joint operating agreement, which had become totally unworkable if given a literal meaning. The assignment clause in this case stated that the parties had pre-emption rights in the ratio to their percentage interest. Over 25 years, however, the contract area had been sub-divided into numerous sub-areas in which different parties had different percentage interests. It was, therefore, difficult to apply the clause. Nevertheless, the Court of Appeal felt that the parties were duty bound to give effect to the intention behind the clause and required the parties to work out a formula so that it could be applied. But, obviously, pre-emption rights will not apply to situations where the proposed transfer is permitted: see company law examples of *Scotto v Petch* [2001] BCC 899 and *Re Gunlegal Ltd* [2003] EWHC 1844 (Ch).

becoming liable for his share of expenditure, and the rest of the JOA participants would like to be reassured as to his solvency. On the other hand, if one views the JOA primarily as a proprietary contract granting a right to certain shares in production from the area of operations, then pre-emption rights can be seen as an unjustifiable restraint upon commerce. By the end of the 20th century, pre-emption rights were seen by the UK Government as a major impediment to the free trading of interests and as a factor which served to delay or even entirely prevent the introduction of new funds and resources into the UKCS.[30] Accordingly, the UK Government worked with the offshore industry[31] to bring in arrangements under a "Master Deed" to facilitate asset transfers under existing licences. It also announced that, other than in certain specially justified circumstances, JOAs in respect of licences granted from the 20th Round[32] onwards would not be approved if they contained pre-emption clauses, and that in all cases they must follow the Master Deed format.[33] The Master Deed greatly expedites the transfer of UKCS offshore licence interests and other agreements relating to associated assets and infrastructure. It also introduces a standard pre-emption regime to give confidence to incoming companies.[34]

Functional–relational aspect of the JOA

The JOA creates what contract theorists now refer to as a "relational" contract, which is to say a contract which seeks to govern an ongoing relationship between the parties which will typically last for several years.[35] The JOA creates a relationship between the parties of investors involved in the joint operation of exploring for and producing oil under the relevant licence. In more straightforward terms, the JOA creates contractual rights and duties of performance between the co-venturers.   **12.13**

---

[30] See PILOT's Progressing Partnership Working Group's *Operators Final Report*, PP/94/01, 18 December 2001, s 6, available from http://www.pilottaskforce.co.uk/files/workgroup/402.doc; see also C Kehoe and N Foate, "Pre-emption Clauses Under Attack", 9 July 2002, available at http://www.herbertsmith.com/Publications/archive/2002/enr9july2002.htm (accessed 22 April 2011).

[31] Through PILOT's Progressing Partnership Working Group (PPWG) and a number of other interested organisations.

[32] The 20th Round licences were granted in July 2002.

[33] S Gyaltsen and A Turton, "The Master Deed and Changes in the North Sea" (2003) 9 IELTR 258–260.

[34] Discussed further at paras 16.37–16.39.

[35] See I R Macneil, "Contracts: adjustments of long-term economic relations under classical, neo-classical, and relational contract law" (1977–78) 72 *NWULR* 854.

Partnership or not?

12.14 As mentioned earlier, for reasons of tax and minimising the liabilities of the members to the JOA *inter se*, all standard JOAs contain a clause denying that the agreement constitutes a partnership.[36] However, the English and Scottish courts take a somewhat ambivalent attitude to such clauses. There is a tension in the attitude of the courts between, on the one hand, a desire to give effect to the legitimate intentions of persons engaged in commerce as agreed by contract and, on the other, a desire to recognise that the mere label which is attached to a contract does not of itself determine its legal content and meaning. There is clear judicial authority that the courts will look beyond the wording of labelling or deeming clauses and towards the actuality of matters:

> "If a partnership in fact exists, a community of interest in the adventure being carried on in fact, no concealment of name, no verbal equivalent for the ordinary phrases of profit or loss, no indirect expedient for enforcing control over the adventure will prevent the substance and reality of the transaction being adjudged to be a partnership ...".[37]

This is so even where there is an express denial of partnership in the contract:

> "Two partners enter into a transaction and say, 'It is hereby declared that there is no partnership between us.' The court pays no regard to that. The court looks at the transaction and says, 'Is this, in point of law, really a partnership?' It is not in the least conclusive that the parties have used a term or language intended to indicate that the transaction is not that which in law it is."[38]

12.15 Thus, the courts will assess the question by reference to what the arrangement is, not how it is labelled. However, it is a strange fact that despite the increasing use of the unincorporated joint venture as a commercial vehicle beyond the oil industry and despite its near universal use in the UKCS as the commercial vehicle by which operations to the value of billions of dollars have been conducted, there have been only two cases where the actual legal nature of the unincorporated joint venture has been

---

[36] Eg 2009 Model JOA, cl 22.1 states: "The liability of the Participants hereunder shall be several and not joint or collective and each Participant shall be responsible only for its individual obligations hereunder. It is expressly agreed that it is not the purpose or intention of this Agreement to create, nor shall it be construed as creating, any mining partnership, commercial partnership or other partnership."

[37] *Adam* v *Newbigging* (1888) 13 App Cas 308 at 315, affirmed by LC Halsbury in the Scottish appeal of *McCosh* v *Brown & Co's Trs* (1889) 1 F (HL) 86 at 88.

[38] *Weiner* v *Harris* [1910] 1 KB 285 per Cozens-Hardy MR at 290.

recognised.[39] In the unreported English case of *Spree Engineering & Testing Limited* v *O'Rourke Civil & Structural Engineering Ltd*[40] the High Court expressly recognised the existence of the unincorporated joint venture,[41] as distinct from that of a partnership, in the instant case. In the course of his opinion the judge made the following observations:

"22 Mr Davis [counsel for O'Rourke], however, referred to me to Hewitt on joint ventures, and in particular to pages 55 to 58, and 79 to 81. He submits that the situation here fits with the description at page 56 of an unincorporated venture based on a simple contract between the parties, detailing their cooperation. Such an arrangement usually involves the sharing of costs and resources, and sometimes income, on terms which do not give rise to a legal partnership. A typical unincorporated venture is a bidding agreement, which was the essence of the joint venture agreement here. Mr Davis drew attention to a passage on page 81 which reads:

'In the absence of strong tax considerations or professional requirements, it is comparatively rare to find a commercial joint venture business organised in the UK on a partnership basis.'

23 He also referred to passages on pages 29 and 30 of Linklaters and Payne's work on joint ventures, and submits that the case here is a classic illustration of a non-integrated joint venture which is not a partnership. In analysing the situation here, I derive considerable assistance from passages on page 30 of this last work. It reads as follows:

'The participants in a non-integrated joint venture would typically assume the same joint and several liability to the employer for the performance of their obligations under the construction contract, as would parties to an integrated joint venture.

In a non-integrated joint venture on the other hand, no profit is struck at the level of the joint venture. Instead, the work is divided up into discreet segments which the participants carry out severally, each bearing their own costs of performance, and dividing between them the flow of payments from the employer

---

[39] That is, cases where the legal nature of an unincorporated joint venture was a disputed issue before the court. There are many reported cases involving joint ventures where the issue is something other than the nature of the joint venture itself.

[40] *Spree Engineering & Testing Ltd* v *O'Rourke Civil & Structural Engineering Ltd*, unreported, 18 May 1999, 1999 WL 33453546 (High Court of Justice Queen's Bench Division) (hereinafter "*Spree Engineering*").

[41] *Spree Engineering* per Mr T Stow QC at para 26: "I have reached the firm conclusion that the contractual arrangements between Kent and ROR amounted to a non-integrated joint venture, and did not consist of a partnership. Even if I had been in doubt about their status, I would have resolved this doubt in favour of ROR by reason of the clear terms of clause 18 of the joint venture agreement. As is pointed out in Lindley at paragraph 504, such a declaration may be of particular significance where the nature of the relationship does not appear clearly from the remainder of the agreement."

under the construction contract. Profit is thus taken, not at the level of the non-integrated joint venture, but severally by the participants, and it is possible for one participant to show a profit, and another a loss, on their respective parts of the work under a non-integrated joint venture.

It will be seen that the status of the two types of venture is very different for the purposes of the Partnership Act. An integrated joint venture generally satisfies the test of "the relation which subsists between persons carrying on business in common with a view to profit."

On the other hand, the non-integrated joint venture generally falls to be treated simply as an unincorporated association, since the participants generally share no more than the gross payments received from the employer under the construction of the contract – see the Partnership Act sub-section 2.2.'

24 I accept Mr Davis's submission that this description of a non-integrated joint venture is close to the situation we have in this case. One must be cautious about accepting at face value the opinions of authors, unsupported directly by authorities of the courts, but I find the analysis compelling, and likely to represent the views of professionals used to dealing with joint ventures on a regular basis."[42]

Spree is only a decision at first instance in the High Court, and is therefore not in itself of very high authority, but the approach of the court in *Spree* was confirmed in the Court of Appeal in Northern Ireland in *Sweeney* v *Lagan Developments*.[43] The court made the following important remarks:

"[13] Clause 3 of the Consortium Agreement makes clear that what the parties were setting out to establish was a joint venture. The term 'joint venture' does not have a precise legal significance not being a legal term of art. As Hewitt's 'Joint Ventures' 3rd Ed at para 1.11 makes clear it refers to a range of collaborative business arrangements, the fundamental characteristic of a joint venture being collaboration between the participants involving a significant degree of integration between the joint venturers. The key element to be considered and agreed by the joint venturers is the degree and nature of that collaboration. Joint ventures may take the form of a contractual alliance, a partnership or a corporate joint venture. As is pointed out in Lindley and Banks on Partnership 18th Ed at paragraph 5.07 although partnerships and joint ventures have a number of common characteristics, in some instances the two expressions appear to be used interchangeably whilst in others the joint venture is recognised as a relationship quite separate and distinct from partnership. Whilst it can probably be said

---

[42] *Spree* 1999 WL 33453546, paras 22–24.

[43] [2007] NICA 11 (hereinafter "*Sweeney*"). The case concerned potential building development where the parties had formed an incorporated joint venture with a view to establishing a company, ie an incorporated JV, if their bid for the land was successful.

that all partnerships involve a joint venture the converse proposition does not hold good. In *Spree Engineering* the court concluded that the particular arrangement between two companies in a joint venture did not involve a partnership because they specifically agreed provisions which avoided the degree of integration necessary to found a partnership. The companies carried out their own part of the work independently. The court concluded that:-

'An integrated joint venture generally satisfies (the partnership) test of "the relation which subsists between persons carrying on business in common with a view to profit." On the other hand a non-integrated joint venture generally falls to be treated simply as an unincorporated association since the participants generally share no more than gross payments received.'

[14] It is clear that joint venturers must be in agreement as to the model of the joint venture if they are to reach a consensus necessary for a contract since very different legal and financial consequences flow from the model adopted. There are clear legal differences between running a joint venture as a company and running it as a loose contractual alliance. These include the management framework, the decision making arrangements, the funding arrangements and the financial powers of the entity (a company, for example, having powers to raise money by way of floating charges). Clearly there will be different exit strategies and issues relating to the division of profits."[44]

It is submitted that the approach taken by the courts in *Sweeney* and *Spree Engineering* may legitimately be considered accurately to embody the current approach of the British courts on the issue of the nature joint ventures. Moreover, while there is a paucity of case law discussing the issue of whether or not a particular joint venture is a partnership, there are numerous cases where the courts have considered joint ventures in some other context and it would seem that the UK courts are increasingly comfortable with the notion of the unincorporated joint venture.

Any definitive answer confirming the separate existence of a joint venture will always presuppose that the concept can be meaningfully distinguished from a partnership. The question then becomes: what constitutes a partnership in English and Scots law? Unfortunately, the law here is far from clear. The Partnership Act 1890 defines "partnership" as "the relation which subsists between persons carrying on a business in common with a view of profit".[45] But this definition merely describes three necessary conditions of partnership: more than one party, in business and attempting to make a profit – it does not lay down sufficient conditions of partnership. Section 2 of the Act gives some more guidance and provides that neither

12.16

---

[44] [2007] NICA 11, paras 13–14.
[45] Partnership Act 1890, s 1.

co-ownership[46] nor the sharing of gross returns[47] will of itself constitute a partnership. It does, however, go on to provide that "the receipt by a person of a share of the profits of a business is *prima facie* evidence that he is a partner", but then gives five exceptions to that principle.[48] So the only things we can say for certain about a partnership is that, of themselves, sharing ownership or gross returns will not create a partnership, but there is a rebuttable presumption that the sharing of profits will create a partnership. The strongest accounts of the legal case against a court deeming a JOA to be a partnership are those given by M Crommelin,[49] and by G Lewis.[50] Crommelin argues that a JOA does not carry on a business in common with a view to profit, but rather each party is carrying on his own *distinct* business with a view of *separate* profits, even although admittedly some parts of that business are performed in common. In his comment on Crommelin's paper, Lewis states:

> "Now the normal joint operating agreement does not involve the sharing of gross returns, but it does involve that each participant is

---

[46] Partnership Act 1890, s 2(1) provides: "Joint tenancy, tenancy in common, joint property, common property, or part ownership does not of itself create a partnership."

[47] *Ibid*, s 2(2).

[48] *Ibid*, s 2(3): "The receipt by a person of a share of the profits of a business is prima facie evidence that he is a partner in the business, but the receipt of such a share, or of a payment contingent on or varying with the profits of a business, does not of itself make him a partner in the business; and in particular–

(a) The receipt by a person of a debt or other liquidated amount by instalments, or otherwise out of the accruing profits of a business does not of itself make him a partner in the business or liable as such.

(b) A contract for the remuneration of a servant or agent of a person engaged in a business by a share of the profits of the business does not of itself make the servant or agent a partner in the business or liable as such.

(c) A person being the widow or child of a deceased partner, and receiving by way of annuity a portion of the profits made in the business in which the deceased person was a partner, is not by reason only of such receipt a partner in the business or liable as such.

(d) The advance of money by way of loan to a person engaged or about to engage in any business on a contract with that person that the lender shall receive a rate of interest varying with the profits, or shall receive a share of the profits arising from carrying on the business, does not of itself make the lender a partner with the person or persons carrying on the business or liable as such. Provided that the contract is in writing, and signed by or on behalf of all the parties thereto.

(e) A person receiving by way of annuity or otherwise a portion of the profits of a business in consideration of the sale by him of the goodwill of the business is not by reason only of such receipt a partner in the business or liable as such."

[49] M Crommelin, "The Mineral and Petroleum Joint Venture in Australia" (1986) 4 JENRL 65–79 (hereinafter "Crommelin, *Joint Venture*"). Despite the Antipodean title, the arguments in this paper apply with equal force in the UK, as the Australian law in this area follows English law. This is the point that Lewis makes in his Comment.

[50] G Lewis, "Comment: The Joint Operating Agreement: Partnership or not?" (1986) 4 JENRL 80–84 (hereinafter "Lewis, *Partnership or Not?*").

entitled and bound to take in kind its share of the crude or the gas which is produced ... and to sell its share for its own account. There is much to be said for the view that these arrangements do not amount to a sharing of profits which the Partnership Act definition requires. In effect, the participants share the expenses of the production, but sell the products separately.

Ladbury has described the matter this way:

'...[it] is likely that the major difference between the mining joint venture and partnership is that in the joint venture the profit or gain will be derived by the venturers individually and will not be derived for their common or joint benefit. The mining joint venture is an expense sharing and production sharing agreement.'"[51]

This would suggest that the separate disposal of petroleum is an **12.17** essential component of the claim that a JOA does not amount to a partnership: because it is *production* not *profits* which are shared, and therefore the sharing does not fall within the ambit of s 2(3) of the Partnership Act. Notwithstanding the apparent clarity of this analysis, it is submitted that the waters are somewhat muddier than they may at first seem. This is so because even the sharing of gross returns, while not constitutive of partnership in the same way as is the sharing of profits, *may* nevertheless give rise to a presumption of partnership. For instance, in *Todd v Adams*,[52] a Court of Appeal case on share fishermen, Neuberger J stated:

"Although I am not saying that the arrangement in the present case was necessarily a partnership, it is interesting to note this observation in Lindley and Banks on Partnership (17th ed., 1995) at par. 5–27:

'Persons who agree to share the profits of a venture are prima facie partners, even though they may also have agreed between themselves that they will not be liable for losses beyond the amount of their respective contributions.'"[53]

It is not altogether easy to provide a settled and confident conclusion **12.18** on this issue, as the case law does not all pull in one direction. However, it is possible to say that it is extremely prudent to provide

---

[51] Lewis, *Partnerhip or Not?* at 82. The internal quotation is to R Ladbury, "The Joint Development of Resource Projects in Australia", a paper given at the SERL Singapore regional seminar on joint development of resources projects, September 1985.

[52] *Todd v Adams* [2002] 2 All ER (Comm) 97 (herinafter "*Todd v Adams*").

[53] *Ibid*, per Neuberger J at para 78. See also the *dictum* of Mance LJ at para 104: "Partnership, in contrast, is the relationship existing between two or more independent persons, contracting together to engage in a business in common with a view to making and sharing profit. Generally, a partner will contribute either property, skill or labour, but sleeping partners who contribute nothing are also not uncommon. Generally, partners share in any losses, but this too is not 'essential to the legal notion of partnership.' ... Whether a partnership exists is a mixed question of fact and law ... It is an inference from the primary facts."

in the JOA that each co-venturer has the right to take and dispose separately of its share of the petroleum obtained.[54] Such a provision makes it clear that the common enterprise of the joint venture is limited to the exploration for and/or the production of the oil or gas which the co-venturers hold in common. As each co-venturer is acting in the course of its own business when it comes to the disposal of the resulting product, then there is no mutual profit which could give rise to a partnership. But, notwithstanding the functional test listed above, it is submitted that most third parties working within the oil industry doing business with an operator could be reasonably expected to be aware of the nature of the unincorporated joint venture. Furthermore, comfort may be derived from the explicit recognition of the existence of an unincorporated JOA in the *Spree Engineering* and *Sweeney* decisions, and its implicit recognition in several other cases.[55] It is accordingly submitted that even *absent* a separate disposal clause, the courts might be slow to disrupt the long-established expectations of parties in the industry and to impose partnership. Obviously, the presumption might not be as strong if the operator deals with a third party whose primary business is not oil specific, for example a software specialist, and in those circumstances there may be a greater risk that a court might deem a partnership to exist. On the other hand, it must be stressed that even if partnership were to be found by a court, this would not of itself regulate the relations of the parties *inter se*, as partners are specifically allowed by the Partnership Act to order their internal relations as they agree between themselves.[56] The mandatory provisions[57] of the Partnership Act apply only to external relations with third parties. For parties participating in the oil industry, any risk of extra liabilities arising as a result of a JOA being deemed to be a partnership are therefore likely to be small or non-existent. However, the one major impact of a judicial decision which considered a JOA to be a partnership would probably be on the tax position of the parties.

---

[54] In practice, JOAs invariably contain language to this effect. The 2009 Model JOA, cl 18(a), for example, states that "each of the Participants shall have the *right* to take in kind and separately dispose of its Percentage Interest share in the total quantities of Petroleum available under this Agreement" while cl 18(b) provides that "each of the Participants shall have the *obligation* to take in kind and separately dispose of its Percentage Interest share in all Petroleum produced" (emphasis added).

[55] See para 12.15.

[56] Partnership Act 1890, s 19: "The mutual rights and duties of partners, whether ascertained by agreement or defined by this Act, may be varied by the consent of all the partners, and such consent may be either express or inferred from a course of dealing."

[57] *Ibid*, ss 5–18.

THE TWO CLASSES OF CO-VENTURER: THE OPERATOR AND THE NON-OPERATORS

There are two classes of member of any JOA: the "operator", who **12.19** actually executes the collective will of the members of the joint venture and is responsible for the day-to-day management of the joint operations; and the other members, who are simply designated as "non-operators". The institutional link between the operator and the non-operators is the Joint Operating Committee ("JOC", often referred to informally as the "Operating Committee" or, most commonly of all, the "Opcom") on which all the co-venturers sit.[58]

The operator

The operator is responsible for the day-to-day exploration, devel- **12.20** opment and production activities in the venture while the remaining interest holders are non-operating members who share in the costs and production (if any) of the joint venture activities. There is only ever a single operator, and the identity of the first operator in a given JOA will be specified in the agreement.[59] The JOA will also contain provisions for the possible removal of the operator and his replacement by another party.[60] The choice of operator is subject to Government approval with the Minister holding the right to revoke that approval.[61] The role of the operator is to act on behalf of the JOA members in the exploitation of any reserves which come to the JOA members under the licence. Although operatorship inevitability entails much work and responsibility for the operator, it is a central feature of the JOA that the operator works in that role gratuitously for the benefit of all members of JOA: that is, he gets no payment for his troubles in exercising his role of operator; rather, he simply takes his rewards, if any, *pro rata* from the production of the field. The question arises then as to why (other than for reasons of pure altruism) any JOA member would wish to act as operator. The answer is that traditionally the perception has been that the operator has *de facto* much more say over the entire project than the non-operators and is best positioned to take the initiative. Thus, the operator is rewarded with greater power, rather than greater potential profits. Usually, the JOA member with the largest percentage interest in the JOA will be the operator of the joint venture. During the negotiations, the operator will generally want to have operator removal provisions limited to those requiring good

---

[58] The JOC or Opcom is discussed further at paras 12.36–12.39.
[59] See, eg, 2009 Model JOA, cl 5.1.
[60] See, eg, 2009 Model JOA, cl 5.3.
[61] 2008 Regulations, Model Cl 24.

cause, for example default or wilful misconduct.[62] The operator will also seek to have a removal clause which requires unanimity among the JOA members, which of course allows the operator to veto any attempt to remove him. Conversely, the non-operators may seek to have a removal clause which is without cause and based on majority voting of the members. The actual outcome of these discussions will be dependent on the relative negotiating strengths of the parties and the extent to which they trust each other. The JOA will also contain clauses allowing the operator to resign, and which provide for the selection of a replacement.[63] This is an area where there may be tensions over the relevant pass mark for making this decision, as discussed further at para 12.38 below.

12.21   In recent years there has been a tendency towards delegating operating functions to professional contractors who are not actually members of the JOA. Such contractor–operators are not generally dealt with in the JOA. Rather, the tendency is for the JOA operator to delegate in turn much of his day-to-day management role to the contractor–operator. Such delegation would generally require the consent of the other members.

Duties and liabilities of the operator

12.22   Broadly speaking, the operator has the day-to-day responsibility for the conduct of the exploration and development operations. The operator is obliged to "conduct the Joint Operations by itself, its agents or its contractors under the overall supervision and control of the [JOC]".[64] Even "[i]f the Operator does not conduct any of the Joint Operations itself, it shall nevertheless remain responsible" for the joint operations as the operator.[65] The major duties of the operator include:[66]

(a) the preparation of programmes, budgets and AFEs;[67]
(b) the implementation of JOC-approved programmes;
(c) the provision to each of the co-venturers of reports, data and information.

12.23   As the *de facto* day-to-day manager of the project and agent of the JOA, the operator owes a duty of care to the other members in his capacity as operator. The nature of the duty is usually specified in the JOA as the duty to perform the role of operator in "a proper and

---

[62] "Wilful misconduct" is discussed further at para 12.24.
[63] See, eg, 2009 Model JOA, cl 5.2.
[64] *Ibid*, cl 6.1.1.
[65] *Ibid*, cl 6.1.2.
[66] But are not limited to these: 2009 Model JOA, cl 6.2.1.
[67] "Authorisations For Expenditure". AFEs are discussed further at para 12.40.

workmanlike manner" in accordance with "good oilfield practice" and "in compliance with the requirements of the Acts, the licence and any other applicable legislation" and to carry out, "with due diligence, all such acts and things within its control as may be necessary to keep and maintain the Licence in force and effect".[68] "Good oilfield practice" is defined as "the application of those methods and practices customarily used in good and prudent oil and gas field practice in the [UKCS] with that degree of diligence and prudence reasonably and ordinarily exercised by experienced operators engaged in the [UKCS] in a similar activity under similar circumstances and conditions".[69] Therefore, the exact nature of what counts as "good oilfield practice" will depend upon the circumstances and will also change as technology changes.[70] The corollary of the principle that the operator *qua* operator is not remunerated for his services is that he will usually only be liable *qua* operator to the non-operators if he is responsible for "wilful misconduct"[71] or fails to maintain insurance.[72] However, he will not usually be liable for an honest mistake, a misjudgement or a negligent act or omission.

"Wilful misconduct" is not a concept whose meaning is entirely clear under English common law.[73] However, there is some judicial guidance at to its meaning. In *Forder* v *Great Western Railway Co*,[74] Lord Alverstone CJ adopted the following definition given by Johnson J in *Graham* v *Belfast and Northern Counties Railway Co*:[75]

12.24

> "Wilful misconduct ... means misconduct to which the will is party as contradistinguished from accident, and is far beyond any negligence, even gross or culpable negligence, and involves that a person wilfully misconducts himself, who knows and appreciates that it is wrong conduct in his part in the existing circumstances to do, or to fail or

---

[68] 2009 Model JOA, cl 6.2.2.

[69] *Ibid*, cl 1.1. This is the definition of the term "good oilfield practice" in the JOA context. See the discussion below for the definition in the licensing context.

[70] In the litigation which will arise in the US courts out of the Deepwater Horizon explosion on 20 April 2010 at Macondo in the Gulf of Mexico, and the environmental harm caused by the consequential oil spill, much is likely to turn on whether BP had conducted the operation in accordance with good oilfield practice.

[71] 2009 Model JOA, cl 6.2.4. Though note that sub-cl (b) provides that non-operators should "defend, indemnify and hold the Operator harmless ... from and against any *Consequential Loss* ... even in the event of [the Operator's] negligence and/or breach of duty ... and/or Wilful Misconduct." (emphasis added). See also para 12.24.

[72] See further para 12.27.

[73] It is, however, to be found in certain UK statutes; see the discussion later in this paragraph.

[74] [1905] 2 KB 532 at 535–536.

[75] [1901] 2 IR 12.

to omit to do (as the case may be), a particular thing, and yet intentionally does or fails or omits to do it, or persists in the act, failure or omission, regardless of the consequences." The addition which I [Lord Alverstone] would suggest is 'or acts with reckless carelessness, not caring what the results of his carelessness may be.'"

In order to avoid any doubts as to the scope and meaning of "wilful misconduct" the standard practice is to define the term "wilful misconduct" in the JOA itself as a "deliberate or reckless action resulting in loss", a definition which is a much narrower concept than simple negligence, and one with a higher evidential burden resting on the party which seeks to rely upon it. The 2009 Model JOA, cl 1.1 defines "wilful misconduct" as:

> "an intentional, or reckless disregard by Senior Managerial Personnel of Good Oilfield Practice or any of the terms of this Agreement in utter disregard of avoidable and harmful consequences but shall not include any act, omission, error of judgement or mistake made in the exercise in good faith of any function, authority or discretion vested in or exercisable by such Senior Managerial Personnel and which in the exercise of such good faith is justifiable by special circumstances, including safeguarding of life, property or the environment and other emergencies."

In addition to any contractual definition contained within the JOA itself, there is also a growing body of case law on the statutory use of the term "wilful misconduct"[76] which, it is submitted, might be useful in any contractual dispute about the meaning of the terms. For example, in *Porter* v *Magill*[77] the House of Lords had to define the meaning of "wilful misconduct" under s 20 of the Local Government Finance Act 1982.[78] In so doing, the Lords reviewed and approved the existing case law in the following terms:

> "That expression [wilful misconduct] was defined by Webster J in *Graham v Teesdale* ... to mean 'deliberately doing something which

---

[76] The phrase is used in the Convention on the Contract for the International Carriage of Goods by Road (CMR) 1956 and there is a considerable body of case law on the meaning of the term in that context. In addition, the term is found in a number of statutory provisions, eg, Marine Insurance Act 1906, s 55(2); Local Government Finance Act 1982, s 20.

[77] [2001] UKHL 67, [2002] 2 AC 357 (HL).

[78] Section 20(1) of the Local Government Finance Act 1982 provided:

> "(1) Where it appears to the auditor carrying out the audit of any accounts under this Part of this Act ...
>
> > (b) that a loss has been incurred or deficiency caused by the wilful misconduct of any person,
>
> he shall certify that ... the amount of the loss or the deficiency is due from that person and, subject to subsections (3) and (5) below, both he and the [local authority] in question ... may recover that ... amount for the benefit of that [local authority]".

is wrong knowing it to be wrong or with reckless indifference as to whether it is wrong or not.' That definition was approved by the Court of Appeal [and the House of Lords] in *Lloyd v McMahon* ... It was adopted by the Divisional Court [and by the Court of Appeal] in the present case ... There was no challenge to this definition before the House and I would accept it as representing the intention of Parliament when using this expression."[79]

In a recent case, *TNT Global SPA v Denfleet International Ltd*,[80] on the meaning of "wilful misconduct" under the Convention on the Contract for the International Carriage of Goods by Road (CMR) 1956 the Court of Appeal gave a useful summary of the various authorities. The case concerned a lorry driver who fell asleep at the wheel, causing an accident, and the issue was whether this amounted to wilful misconduct. The court concluded that falling asleep at the wheel did not amount to wilful misconduct, partially for evidential reasons, and the case is a good example of the high degree of misconduct that is necessary before a court will consider it wilful. The court cited with approval[81] *Forder* (above) and also the passage in *National Semiconductors (UK) Ltd v UPS Ltd*,[82] where Longmore J, having considered various authorities on wilful misconduct – said:[83]

> "If I summarise the principle in my own words, it would be to say that for wilful misconduct to be proved there must be either (1) an intention to do something which the actor knows to be wrong or (2) a reckless act in the sense that the actor is aware that loss may result from his act and yet does not care whether loss will result or not or, to use Mr Justice Barry's words in *Horobin's case*, 'he took a risk which he knew he ought not to take' [1952] 2 Lloyd's Rep. at p 460."

Although most of these judicial definitions of "wilful misconduct" have been given in the context of statutory interpretation, there seems to be no need to restrict them to that setting, an approach confirmed by the Court of Appeal in *TNT Global* where the court did not restrict its search for authorities on the definition of wilful misconduct merely to cases on the CMR itself. It is submitted that this judicial exposition of the meaning of "wilful misconduct" by the Lords in *Porter v Magill*[84] as "deliberately doing something which is wrong knowing it to be wrong or with reckless indifference as to whether it is wrong or not" is one which well captures the concept of wilful misconduct as used in the oil industry generally and in JOAs in

---

[79] *Porter v Magill* [2002] 2 AC 357 HL per Lord Bingham of Cornhill at para 19.
[80] [2007] EWCA Civ 405, [2008] 1 All ER (Comm) 97, [2007] 2 Lloyd's Rep 504.
[81] Opinion of Court, paras 8–13 [2007] 1 CLC 710 at 714–715.
[82] [1996] 2 LL Rep 212.
[83] *Ibid* at 214.
[84] [2001] UKHL 67, [2002] 2 AC 357 (HL).

particular. An example of how important a wilful misconduct clause can be when a joint venture finds itself in difficulties is given by the Deepwater Horizon incident. In June 2010 one of BP's co-venturers, with a 25 per cent share in the Mocondo well, Anadarko Petroleum Corporation, announced that it would not contribute towards the massive compensation costs resulting from the oil spill on the ground that: "BP's behavior and actions likely represent gross negligence or wilful misconduct and thus affect the obligations of the parties under the operating agreement."[85] To put the matter concisely, Anadarko appear to be seeking, at the time of writing, to escape from its liability for 25 per cent of all costs arising out of the Deepwater Horizon blow-out and consequential massive oil spill by arguing that as BP's behaviour amounted to wilful misconduct, BP alone should bear the clean-up costs – costs which are estimated at between $15 billion and $40 billion.[86]

---

[85] From a press release issued by Anadarko Petroleum Corporation, Houston, June 18, 2010. This is a fuller extract:

"(BUSINESS WIRE) – Following this week's hearings in Washington regarding the Deepwater Horizon tragedy, Anadarko Petroleum Corporation (NYSE: APC) issued the following statement:

'The events surrounding the Deepwater Horizon explosion represent a terrible loss for the families of those who lost their lives and an unprecedented environmental tragedy,' Anadarko Chairman and CEO Jim Hackett said. 'Sadly, it also continues to have tremendous impacts on the livelihoods of many Gulf Coast families and their communities. We, along with others in the industry, have continued to support the Unified Command in its response with technical expertise and specialized equipment.

The mounting evidence clearly demonstrates that this tragedy was preventable and the direct result of BP's reckless decisions and actions. Frankly, we are shocked by the publicly available information that has been disclosed in recent investigations and during this week's testimony that, among other things, indicates BP operated unsafely and failed to monitor and react to several critical warning signs during the drilling of the Macondo well. BP's behavior and actions likely represent gross negligence or wilful misconduct and thus affect the obligations of the parties under the operating agreement,' continued Hackett.

Under the terms of the joint operating agreement (JOA) related to the Mississippi Canyon block 252 lease, BP, as operator, owed duties to its co-owners including Anadarko to perform the drilling of the well in a good and workmanlike manner and to comply with all applicable laws and regulations. The JOA also provides that BP is responsible to its co-owners for damages caused by its gross negligence or wilful misconduct. Importantly, any actions Anadarko may take under the agreement to protect its rights relative to BP's performance as operator in the drilling of the well will in no way shift any financial burden to the American taxpayer. Hackett also said, 'We recognize that ultimately we have obligations under Federal law related to the oil spill, but will look to BP to continue to pay all legitimate claims as they have repeatedly stated that they will do.'" (downloaded from http://www.anadarko.com/Investor/Pages/NewsReleases/NewsReleases.aspx?release-id=1439839 (accessed 22 April 2011)).

[86] "Early reckonings of those costs from Credit Suisse and Tudor, Pickering, Holt & Co Securities were not encouraging. Credit Suisse put the tally at $15 billion to $23 billion, not including a separate $14 billion of claims from the tourism industry and fisheries.

It is good practice explicitly to exclude any potential liability **12.25** by the operator for consequential losses, and if the formulation contained in the 2009 Model JOA is followed, then the operator has no liability whatsoever to the non-operators for any consequential loss suffered by them because of the acts or omissions of the operator, even should he be guilty of wilful misconduct.[87]

The operator will make contracts on behalf of the joint venture, **12.26** but contracts above a defined level of value may be made by the operator only with the consent of the JOC and after being put out to competitive tender.[88]

The operator is obliged to acquire and maintain all appropriate **12.27** insurances in compliance with the requirements of the licence and any other applicable legislation, or of "any contract entered into by the operator in furtherance of Joint Operations",[89] "except in respect of any insurance which the operator must take out in its own name". The cost of insurance is charged between the co-venturers in proportion to their respective percentage interests, unless a co-venturer chooses not to participate in the insurance.[90] The only required insurances are those for employee protection[91] (which will be carried in the operator's own name) and the pollution insurance provided by the Offshore Pollution Liability Agreement (OPOL)[92] which is required of the operator by all UKCS JOAs.[93] The operator will also take out on behalf of the entire joint venture

---

Tudor Pickering put the tally even higher: $35 billion to $40 billion:" Dow Jones online, 2 June 2010 (downloaded from http://www.nasdaq.com/aspx/company-news-story.aspx?storyid=201006021905dowjonesdjonline000674&title=debt-market-hammers-bppartners-for-second-day#ixzz0ylstDhsn (accessed 22 April 2011)).

[87] 2009 Model JOA, cl 6.2.4(b).

[88] *Ibid*, cl, 6.5.4–6.5.5.

[89] *Ibid*, cl 8.1.

[90] *Ibid*, cl 8.1.1.

[91] Under the Employers' Liability (Compulsory Insurance) Act 1969 employers must provide insurance for all employees working in the UK, and this legislation has been extended offshore.

[92] The most recent version, 1 January 2010, of OPOL is available from the Offshore Pollution Liability Association Ltd website at http://www.opol.org.uk/ (accessed 22 April 2011). Under OPOL, member operating companies agree to accept strict liability for pollution damage and the cost of remedial measures with only certain exceptions, up to a maximum of US $120 million per incident. As a result of the concerns arising in the wake of the Deepwater Horizon explosion on 20 April 2010 in the Gulf of Mexico, the UK signatories to the OPOL met on 18 August 2010 and agreed to raise the compensation limit from $120 million to $250 million per incident. These changes take effect from 1 October 2010. (Source: *Financial Times* 18 August 2010: see http://www.ft.com/cms/s/0/be351e8e-aaf6-11df-9e6b-00144feabdc0.html and private correspondence with OPOL.) Within this limit there may also be included the cost of remedial measures undertaken by the party to OPOL involved in the incident.

[93] 2009 Model JOA, cl 8.2.

any other insurance which the Joint Operating Committee thinks appropriate.[94] The most common form of optional insurance taken out by a JV is Construction All Risk (CAR) insurance to cover the construction of the installation and any other joint developments. The operator is also required to give notice to the non-operators of any incidents which may give rise to litigation. The operator is generally authorised to conduct any litigation arising out of the joint operations up to a low limit but otherwise generally may only conduct litigation with the approval of the Opcom.[95]

Agency of the operator

12.28 Unlike the position with partnership,[96] the typical JOA contains no clause expressly denying the agency of the operator with respect to the joint venture (obviously, there is no need to deny the agency of the non-operators). This is not surprising given that the relationship between the operator and non-operators is inevitably in the form of agency. When contracting on behalf of the joint venture the operator will, by definition, be acting *qua* agent for the group of principals who are the members of the JOA. Agency creates liability in the principal, ie, the non-operators – for the authorised contracts and actions of the agent. Accordingly, in the case of a typical JOA the operator will simultaneously be a joint principal along with the other JOA members and acting in a representative capacity as agent. In this sense at least, the role performed by the operator is analogous to that of a partner contracting on behalf of a partnership where the roles of agent and principal are performed concurrently.

12.29   Whether or not the agency of the operator is disclosed or undisclosed is a matter of varying practice. The 2009 Model JOA provides that all contracts made by the operator should disclose the fact that the operator is acting *qua* agent.[97] Where an operator does not disclose that he is contracting on behalf of the JV then this would be deemed by the courts to be an instance of undisclosed agency.[98] As regards a third party, the standard rule in undisclosed agency is that the third party must elect to sue either the agent or the principal, once the fact of the undisclosed agency has been disclosed to or discovered by the third party. However, this doctrine of election is irrelevant in the case of a JOA because the doctrine is based on the premise that the apparent principal was in reality only an agent and the undisclosed principal was the real principal, whereas in the case

---

[94] 2009 Model JOA, cl 8.1.1.
[95] *Ibid*, cl 8.3.
[96] See para 12.14.
[97] 2009 Model JOA, cl 6.5.8.
[98] *Watteau* v *Fenwick* [1893] 1 QB 346 is the leading case.

of undisclosed operatorship – ie, the operator contracting apparently as principal – the operator is both principal and agent. Accordingly, it would seem to follow logically that the third party would be able to sue both the operator and the undisclosed non-operators together if need arose. Likewise, in a situation of undisclosed agency the non-operators are entitled to sue the third party once the agency is disclosed. The 2009 Model JOA attempts to get round these complexities by the paradoxical provision that the operator should disclose his agency when making contracts but notwithstanding the disclosure of agency any rights and duties arising out of the contract may be claimed against or made by the operator alone.[99] The effect of such a provision is effectively to prevent the imposition on the operator of any agency duties which would arise under the common law of agency by means of a contractual agreement to exclude the application of any such duties. However, to be effective, the contents of this clause would have to be accepted by any third party contracting with the operator as the internal contractual arrangements of the co-venturers naturally cannot affect the position of a third party unless that third party explicitly accepts them. Even if a third party were to do so there must be some doubt as to whether these terms would be upheld by a court, as they seem to give the co-venturers all the benefits of being a principal (because through the mechanism of the JOA they can compel the operator to sue on their

---

[99] 2009 Model JOA, cl 6.5.8 provides:

"The Operator shall act as agent of the Participants in dealings with contractors and shall use all reasonable endeavours to include in all contracts made pursuant to this Agreement, a provision which ensures that the Operator makes the contract on behalf of all the Participants. The Operator shall use all reasonable endeavours to include in all such contracts provisions in the following or similar form for which purpose 'COMPANY' refers to the Operator and 'CO-VENTURERS' refers to the Non-operators:

The COMPANY enters into the CONTRACT for itself and as agent for and on behalf of the other CO-VENTURERS. Notwithstanding the above:

(a) the CONTRACTOR agrees to look only to the COMPANY for the due performance of the CONTRACT and nothing contained in the CONTRACT will impose any liability upon, or entitle the CONTRACTOR to commence any proceedings against any CO-VENTURER other than the COMPANY;

(b) the COMPANY and only the COMPANY is entitled to enforce the CONTRACT on behalf of all CO-VENTURERS as well as for itself. For that purpose the COMPANY shall commence proceedings in its own name to enforce all obligations and liabilities of the CONTRACTOR and to make any claim which any CO-VENTURER may have against the CONTRACTOR.

(c) all losses, damages, costs (including legal costs) and expenses recoverable by the COMPANY pursuant to the CONTRACT or otherwise shall include the losses, costs (including legal costs) and expenses of the COMPANY's CO-VENTURERS and AFFILIATES except that such losses, damages, costs (including legal costs) and expenses shall be subject to the same limitations or exclusions of liability applicable to the COMPANY or the CONTRACTOR under the CONTRACT."

behalf) but gives them apparent immunity from suit by third parties. It is submitted that, on the grounds of agency law, public policy and the terms of the Unfair Contract Terms Act 1977, a court might well strike down such clauses. In the case of tortious liability, as opposed to contractual liability, the agent is personally liable alone unless the wrongful act was in the course of his duties or authorised or ratified by the principal. In the case of a JOA it follows that the operator alone will be liable unless the Opcom authorised or ratified the wrongful act, or it was clearly within the scope of his responsibilities as agent. Should an operator be found liable in tort then the non-operators will be liable *pro rata* to the operator for any damages he has to pay in compensation.

Fiduciary duties

12.30   Some commentators have argued that joint ventures give rise to fiduciary duties because, rather than working at arm's length as in a normal commercial contractual situation, the co-venturers are working together towards the same goal: the finding of petroleum and maximising its extraction.[100] But the importance of the terms of the contract must be stressed in establishing whether or not there is a fiduciary duty.[101] This was a point made by Lord Browne-Wilkinson, giving the judgment of the Privy Council in *Kelly* v *Cooper*,[102] where, quoting with approval from the judgment of Mason J in *Hospital Products Ltd* v *United States Surgical Corp*,[103] he stated:

> "That contractual and fiduciary relationships may co-exist between the same parties has never been doubted. Indeed, the existence of a basic contractual relationship has in many situations provided a foundation for the erection of a fiduciary relationship. In these situations it is the contractual foundation which is all important because it is the contract that regulates the basic rights and liabilities of the parties. The fiduciary relationship, if it is to exist at all, must accommodate itself to the terms of the contract so that it is consistent with, and conforms to them. The fiduciary relationship cannot be superimposed upon the contract in such a way as to alter the operation which the contract was intended to have according to its true construction."[104]

---

[100] The most exhaustive account of this view can be found in G Bean, *Fiduciary Obligations and Joint Ventures: The Collaborative Fiduciary Relationship* (1995) (hereinafter "Bean, *Fiduciary Obligations and Joint Ventures*").

[101] The contracts used in the UKCS will often exclude or at least seriously curtail the possibility of fiduciary duties: see para 12.34.

[102] *Kelly* v *Cooper* [1993] AC 205 (hereinafter "*Kelly* v *Cooper*").

[103] (1984) 55 ALR 417 at 454–455.

[104] *Kelly* v *Cooper* per Lord Browne-Wilkinson at 215.

A useful definition of "fiduciary duties" was given by Millett LJ in **12.31** *Bristol and West Building Society* v *Mothew*:

> "A fiduciary is someone who has undertaken to act for or on behalf of another in a particular matter in circumstances which give rise to a relationship of trust and confidence. The distinguishing obligation of a fiduciary is the obligation of loyalty. The principal is entitled to the single-minded loyalty of his fiduciary. This coreliability has several facets. A fiduciary must act in good faith; he must not make a profit out of his trust; he must not place himself in a position where his duty and his interest may conflict; he may not act for his own benefit or the benefit of a third person without the informed consent of his principal. This is not intended to be an exhaustive list, but it is sufficient to indicate the nature of fiduciary obligations. They are the defining characteristics of the fiduciary ... he is not subject to fiduciary obligations because he is a fiduciary; it is because he is subject to them that he is a fiduciary."[105]

The difficulty of establishing when fiduciary duties occur was **12.32** highlighted by Lord Browne-Wilkinson in *Henderson* v *Merrett Syndicates Ltd*:

> "The phrase 'fiduciary duties' is a dangerous one, giving rise to a mistaken assumption that all fiduciaries owe the same duties in all circumstances. That is not the case. Although, so far as I am aware, every fiduciary is under a duty not to make a profit from his position (unless such profit is authorised), the fiduciary duties owed, for example, by an express trustee are not the same as those owed by an agent. Moreover, and more relevantly, the extent and nature of the fiduciary duties owed in any particular case fall to be determined by reference to any underlying contractual relationship between the parties. Thus, in the case of an agent employed under a contract, the scope of his fiduciary duties is determined by the terms of the underlying contract ... The existence of a contract does not exclude the coexistence of concurrent fiduciary duties (indeed, the contract may well be their source); but the contract can and does modify the extent and nature of the general duty that would otherwise arise."[106]

A fiduciary duty may therefore be summed up as the obligation not **12.33** to make a profit at the expense of, or hidden from, one's partners (using that term in a loose, non-technical sense). There are two possible grounds for arguing that a JOA gives rise to fiduciary duties. The first possible ground, which would apply equally to all the co-venturers, is that as the contractual relationship is joint, there is an element of mutuality which gives rise to a fiduciary relationship.

---

[105] *Bristol and West Building Society* v *Mothew* [1998] Ch 1 per Millet LJ at 18.
[106] *Henderson* v *Merrett Syndicates Ltd* [1995] 2 AC 145 per Lord Browne-Wilkinson at 206A–D.

The second possible ground stems from the law of agency and, on the basis that as the operator is an agent, he is automatically in a fiduciary relation to the non-operators. If a fiduciary duty were to apply to a JOA, it would logically apply with equal measure to all the co-venturers and not just the operator, although arguably the operator has more opportunities for the making of secret profits, for example by taking a secret commission from a contractor. That said, non-operators could abuse their position by, for instance, using confidential data confided to them *qua* JOA members.[107]

12.34   There has been some judicial support for the existence of fiduciary duties in various common law jurisdictions. In the US, for example, the Kansas Supreme Court has held that the parties to a JOA were in "fiduciary like" relations and owed a duty of fair dealing to each other.[108] Also, Alberta, Canada has proved especially welcoming of the application of fiduciary principles to JOAs.[109] But so far there is no case law to support this argument in English or Scots law. The concept of fiduciary duty is unlikely to have much application in UKCS JOAs, for three reasons. First, in almost all important decisions the operator can only act with the authority of his fellow co-venturers as given by the Opcom. The UKCS operator, therefore, has much less scope for independent decision-making than operators acting under the US AAPL Form 610, or under the Canadian CAPL Operating Procedure JOA which gives the non-operators far less say in the conduct of the operations, and gives the operator correspondingly greater freedom. Second, the tendency in the UKCS is to exclude (or at least substantially curtail the effect of) the application of fiduciary duties through the drafting of the JOA.[110] Third, UKCS

---

[107] A duty of confidentiality is in any case an explicit term of any well-drafted JOA.

[108] *Amoco Production Co* v *Wilson*, 976 P 2d 941. For an analysis of this case, see R James, "Kansas Oil and Gas Law: Defining the Duty between Participants in a Joint Operating Agreement" (1999) 39 Washburn LJ 128.

[109] See: *Bank of Nova Scotia* v *Société Générale (Canada)* (1988) 87 AR 133, 58 Alta LR (2d) 193 (Alberta CA); *Luscar Ltd* v *Pembina Resources Ltd* (1995) 24 Alta LR (3d) 305, [1995] 2 WWR 153 (Alberta CA); *Erewhon Exploration Ltd* v *Northstar Energy* Corp (1993) 147 AR 1, 15 Alta LR (3d) 200 9 Alberta QB).

[110] See 2009 Model JOA, cl 1.1 definition of "Consequential Loss":

"'Consequential Loss' means any indirect or consequential loss howsoever caused or arising whether under contract, by virtue of any fiduciary duty, in tort or delict (including negligence), as a consequence of breach of any duty (statutory or otherwise) or under any other legal doctrine or principle whatsoever whether or not recoverable at common law or in equity. 'Consequential Loss' shall be deemed to include, without prejudice to the foregoing generality, the following to the extent to which they might not otherwise constitute indirect or consequential loss:

(a) loss or damage arising out of any delay, postponement, interruption or loss of production, any inability to produce, deliver or process hydrocarbons or any loss of or anticipated loss of use, profit or revenue;

JOAs generally contain a clause reducing the entire agreement to the express written terms of the JOA.[111] Taken together, these three considerations would seem to exclude the potential importation of fiduciary duties into the agreement by the UK courts.

The non-operators

The role of the non-operators in the joint venture is one of non-operating, non-working, interest owners or, to put it more simply, the role is that of an investor. But non-operators are *active* investors, in that they have an active say in the managing of the project through the Joint Operating Committee.[112] The existence of the Opcom is one of the most significant differences between the typical UKCS JOA, such as the 2009 Model JOA, and a US JOA based on AAPL Form 610, where there is no provision for an Operating Committee. The most important duty of a non-operator is to provide its share of funds when faced with a cash call. Should any co-venturer fail to pay its share, when called upon to do so, then they will be deemed to be in default.[113]

12.35

(b) loss or damage incurred or liquidated or pre-estimated damages of any kind whatsoever borne or payable, under any contract for the sale, exchange, transportation, processing, storage or other disposal of hydrocarbons;

(c) losses associated with business interruption including the cost of overheads incurred during business interruption;

(d) loss of bargain, contract, expectation or opportunity;

(e) damage to any reservoir, geological formation or underground strata or the loss of hydrocarbons from any of them;

(f) any other loss or anticipated loss or damage whatsoever in the nature of or consequential upon the foregoing."

[111] See 2009 Model JOA, cl 3.2: "This Agreement represents the entire understanding of and agreement between the Participants in relation to the matters dealt with in this Agreement, and supersedes all previous understandings and agreements, whether oral or written, relating to such matters. Each Participant agrees that it has not been induced to enter into this Agreement in reliance upon any statement, representation, warranty or undertaking other than as expressly set out in this Agreement, and to the extent that any such representation, warranty or undertaking has been given, the relevant Participant unconditionally and irrevocably waives all rights and remedies which it might otherwise have had in relation to it ..."; as well as cl 31.2: "This Agreement represents the entire agreement of the Participants in relation to its subject matter and supersedes any prior understanding, agreements or undertakings in relation to it (other than the JOA)."

[112] This may be contrasted with the passive investor role of a shareholder in a corporation.

[113] For further discussion on "Default and Forfeiture", see para 12.43 onwards.

MANAGING THE JOINT VENTURE AND THE RELATIONSHIP BETWEEN THE MEMBERS: THE JOINT OPERATING COMMITTEE (THE OPCOM)

12.36 Ultimate responsibility for the management of the joint venture is entrusted to the Joint Operating Committee. The Opcom is composed of representatives of each of the members of the JOA. Usually the JOA will provide that each member is entitled to one representative on the Opcom but the representatives may send alternatives when necessary and likewise may invite other persons to attend to give technical advice as appropriate.[114] Voting on the Opcom is weighted, with each representative casting a voting interest equal to the percentage interest in the JOA held by the member he represents.[115] The Opcom will usually appoint area-specific subcommittees to deal with the major technical matters in more detail. Typical sub-committees would be technical, commercial and reservoir sub-committees. In practice often the decisions are substantially made by the experts in the sub-committees, which are then ratified by the Opcom itself.

12.37 The authority of the Opcom will encompass all major policy decisions involving the joint venture. The JOA will probably specify the powers of the Opcom in the broadest possible way and then add some specific examples of matters which are encompassed by that general authority such as the consideration, revision and approval or disapproval, of all proposed programmes, budgets and "Authorisations For Expenditure" (AFEs) and deciding upon the timing and location of any wells drilled.[116] There will also generally

---

[114] 2009 Model JOA, cl 9.2.

[115] *Ibid*, cl 9.8.1.

[116] For more detail on AFEs, see para 12.40. See 2009 Model JOA, cl 9.1:
"There is hereby established a Joint Operating Committee which shall exercise overall supervision and control of all matters pertaining to the Joint Operations. Without limiting the generality of the foregoing, but subject as otherwise provided in this Agreement, the powers and duties of the Joint Operating Committee shall include: –
(a) the consideration and determination of all matters in general relating to policies, procedures and methods of operation hereunder with the intent that all such operations should be undertaken in a manner consistent with Good Oilfield Practice and in compliance with best practice standards in respect of health and safety and of the environment; and
(b) the consideration, and, if so required, determination of inter alia the following:
  (i) exploration, appraisal, development and production strategies;
  (ii) contract strategy;
  (iii) decisions as to cessation of production, strategies for Decommissioning and the disposal of Joint Property; and
  (iv) any other matter relating to the Joint Operations which may be referred to it by the Participants or any of them (other than any proposal to amend this

be a provision in the JOA authorising the operator to act without agreement or consultation in the case of an emergency.

As mentioned above, voting in all Opcom decisions is *pro rata* **12.38** to the interest of the participating members. However, the effective value of any percentage voting right will be affected by the "pass mark" laid down in the JOA. The pass mark is the percentage interest share of votes which must be obtained before the Opcom may make a binding decision. Obviously, the pass mark cannot be less than 50 per cent, but often it is much higher, 70 per cent being a common level. Decisions as to the size of the pass marks tend to be one of the most hotly contested matters when a JOA is being negotiated. A low pass mark will give the largest interest holder dominant position, while a higher pass mark will give smaller interest holders more influence on the management of the joint venture. The JOA is a private contract, not an experiment in participatory democracy, and the actual pass mark is a matter for negotiation and agreement between the parties, the outcome being dependent on the relative contractual strengths of the parties and the degree of trust they have in each other. It is also possible to have different pass marks for different types of decision, for example a lower pass mark for the comparatively low-cost exercises of exploration and appraisal than for the much more expensive activity of development. Certain major decisions will typically be specified as requiring unanimity, for example, relinquishment of the licence.

As the operator is very much in control of day-to-day opera- **12.39** tions, one of his major duties to the non-operators is to keep them informed of developments and this will be done by providing the Opcom representatives with reports and data.

Expenditure

As mentioned above, the day-to-day control of joint operations **12.40** rests with the operator. In practice this reduces the position of the non-operators to one major duty and one major right. The major duty is to pay *pro rata* for all expenditure authorised by the Opcom and to contribute *pro rata* towards any liabilities incurred by the joint operations. The non-operators' major right is to uplift *pro rata*

Agreement) or which is otherwise designated under this Agreement for reference to it;

(c) the approval of Programmes and Budgets;

(d) the amendment of the monetary limits set out in this Agreement from time to time either generally or in respect of particular operations or particular phases of operations, to take account of the general level of inflation and (if appropriate) the prevailing costs of relevant goods and services, at the request of the Operator or any Participant."

their share of any production arising out of the joint operations.[117] In practice, the main way the non-operators exercise influence over the development of the joint operations is through the Opcom's control of the approval of programmes and budgets, a procedure which is generally done annually.[118] The programme will outline any work which the joint venture plans to undertake and the budget is the estimate of how much those works will cost. The budget is usually divided into a capital budget to cover drilling and developments costs and an operating budget for staff costs and overheads.[119] It is generally recognised that both programme and budget are "living documents" and may require amendment as events unfold. A budget is in the way of an estimate of costs, but does not of itself authorise the operator to demand financial contributions form the JOA members; rather, this is done by the eponymous "Authorisation For Expenditure", generally referred to simply as "AFE".[120] The need for the operator to secure agreement on AFEs greatly strengthens the influence of the non-operators over the development of joint operations, as it means there can be no cash call on the non-operators without sufficient consent to make the stipulated pass mark.[121]

Sole risk and non-consent

12.41   In an ideal world there would be unanimous agreement among the members on all significant decisions. In practice, there will from time to time be disagreements among the members and usually these disputes will be resolved within the Opcom by means of decisions taken which secure a pass mark. Where, however, for some reason there is a disagreement on a fundamental decision of policy as to whether to engage in further operations, disputes may be resolved by the use of "sole risk" or "non-consent" clauses, each of which allows for the non participation of one or more members.

12.42   The difference between the two types of clause is essentially between the amount of support a proposal has obtained at the JOC. A *sole risk* project is one which has failed to obtain the pass mark in the Opcom, but which the defeated member(s) nevertheless wish to go ahead. A *non-consent* project, by contrast, is one which succeeds in obtaining the pass mark in the Operating Committee, but where the outvoted minority nevertheless elect not to participate in the proposed project. Both sole risk and non-consent clauses

---

[117] 2009 Model JOA, cl 18.
[118] *Ibid*, cll 10–13.
[119] *Ibid*, cl 14.3.
[120] *Ibid*, cll 10.2, 11.2, 12.2 and 12.2, read together with cl 14.1.5.
[121] For discussion of the "pass mark", see para 12.38 above.

are in a very real sense inimical to the very *raison d'être* of a joint venture: mutual decision-making with the aim of sharing of risk, costs and production. In practice, sole risk clauses are much more common in UKCS JOAs than non-consent clauses.[122] Where a project proceeds on a sole risk basis, the sole risking members will bear all the costs of the operation,[123] and will be entitled to the entirety of any production that should result from the sole risk operations. In principle, and legal and economic logic, the non-sole risk members should not be entitled to any production which ensues from the sole risk operation. However, most JOAs which contain a sole risk clause will also provide measures which allow the non-sole risk members to buy themselves back into a share of the production, but only on the basis of a large premium.[124] The most likely member to be a sole risker is the operator, but where it is a non-operator then the JOA will allow the operator to carry out the sole risk project on behalf of the sole risker, or to cease acting as operator either by volunteering to do so or on the request of the sole risk members.[125] Where sole risk operations are in progress the JOA will usually provide that they will be managed by an operating committee comprising only sole risk members.[126]

Default and forfeiture

The most important duty of all members of a JOA is to provide funds when requested under a cash call. Each JOA is built on the founding presumption that the burden of financing operations will   12.43

---

[122] For example the UKOOA 20th Round Draft JOA provides for a sole risk clause (cl 14) but not a non-consent one. However, the 2009 Model JOA, cl 11.1.4 provides a non-consent option with respect to amending "Development Programmes and Budgets": "Upon the Secretary authorising ... the commencement of the development, any of the Participants may, if [the JOC approved Development Programme and Budget] has been or is required to be amended ... elect not to proceed with the development ... [In such an event the] provisions of clause 15.8.6 shall apply." Clause 15.8.6, in turn, states that "In the event that, following the Secretary authorising ... the commencement of a development in which all the Participants are participating, any of the Participants elects not to proceed with the development under clause 11.1.4, the other Participants shall be entitled to proceed with the development in accordance with the approved development Programme and Budget (as amended) ...."
[123] The sole risker will also solely bear any liability to third parties arising out of the sole risk operations by means of indemnifying and holding harmless the non-sole risk members. See 2009 Model JOA, cl 15.2.5.
[124] For the premium on acquiring information and data, see 2009 Model JOA, cll 15.4.5 and 15.7.6; for buying back into a discovery as a result of sole risk drilling, see 2009 Model JOA, cl 15.6; and for development, see 2009 Model JOA, cl 15.8.
[125] 2009 Model JOA, cl 15.2.9.
[126] *Ibid*, cl 15.2.10(a).

be shared. Any co-venturer failing to fulfil his financial obligations under an AFE has, therefore, breached his most basic duty under the JOA. Moreover, such failure may cause real financial difficulties to the other members of the JOA, who will have to make good the shortfall. The standard remedy under a JOA for failure to honour a cash call is forfeiture.[127] All JOAs will provide that monies due must be paid up after notice has been given within a set time limit. After the time limit expires without payment the operator will issue the defaulting party with a default notice and, if the default continues for more than a short defined period (typically between 6 and 12 days), then, upon service of the default notice, the defaulter loses his rights under the JOA to attend meetings of the JOC and his right to his share of production.[128] At the same time, the non-defaulting members of the JOA will have to make up the financial shortfall *pro rata*. The defaulting party will have the right to remedy the default at any time prior to forfeiture of his interest by payment of the sums due plus interest. If, however, the defaulting party fails to remedy the situation within the specified time – typically 60 days – then, in the case of a total forfeiture clause, each of the non-defaulting parties has the right to have the defaulting party's interest forfeited to them in proportion to their interest.[129] If the non-defaulting parties do not wish to acquire the defaulter's interest, the JOA will usually provide that operations be abandoned, the licence surrendered and decommissioning (if appropriate) commenced, with each party remaining liable *pro rata* for its share of the decommissioning costs.

12.44   Up until now, default has been quite rare within the UKCS, but as the UKCS petroleum and gas industry winds down it may well become more likely, for two reasons. First, there is a current tendency in the UKCS for the major operators – the multinational giants such as Shell and BP – to divest themselves of their smaller assets in favour of smaller independent oil companies. Small companies, however, are much more likely to go bankrupt than major ones as they, by definition, do not enjoy the same financial strength to weather emergent problems. Second, when a field is at or near exhaustion a co-venturer has little financial incentive to stay in the licence because the licence now constitutes a liability, not an asset, in which circumstance far from being a penalty, forfeiture might well be seen as a benefit by a party.

---

[127] Note, however, that there is more than one type of forfeiture clause: see, eg, the discussion on withering interest clauses, a specific sub-category of forfeiture clause, at para 12.51.

[128] 2009 Model JOA, cl 17.

[129] *Ibid*, cl 17.4. See para 12.51 for a discussion on the consequences of defaulting upon a withering interest clause.

Both of these trends came together in the case of the development **12.45**
of the Ardmore field by Tuscan Energy, who became insolvent in
2005.[130] Thus, one major practical weakness with forfeiture as a
remedy for default on obligations, even assuming such clauses are
upheld as valid,[131] is that while such a sanction is of value before or
during the productive life of the joint operation acreage it is of no
effect once the field has ceased producing, when all the members of
the JOA can look forward to is paying the costs of abandonment.
Ultimately, the best protection a joint venturer can have is to choose
his co-venturers wisely from those parties who are competent, trust-
worthy and, above all, solvent and who are likely to remain so.

Although the contractual provisions regarding forfeiture of **12.46**
licence interests on default are very clear, there has always been
some concern within the industry as to whether such a forfeiture
clause would be enforceable in court if default should occur in
the production phase of the operations.[132] This is because in these
circumstances the defaulting party would lose everything after
having already incurred a substantial expenditure towards the joint
operations. Given that the whole purpose of a joint venture is the
joint sharing of costs and liabilities, it is only reasonable that some
sort of sanction be applied to defaulting parties. However, the issue
of the validity of forfeiture for default has always been a contentious
one. In the absence of direct authority in English law, aid is sought
from analogous cases, such as forfeiture of leases. There are two
possible threats to the validly of forfeiture clauses. First, they might
be struck down as being *de facto* penalty clauses. Second, they may
be held to breach the general law of insolvency by creating an unfair
preference in favour of the JOA members. Each of these possibilities
will be considered below in some detail.

Forfeiture clauses may be penalty clauses
Strictly speaking, forfeiture and penalty clauses are different types of **12.47**
sanction: forfeiture is the *negative* sanction of loss of property rights,
while a liquidated damages/penalty clause is a *positive* obligation to
pay money to the innocent party; however, in practice they have the
same economic effect – a point well made by Atiyah:

> "… it is worth noting that penalties and forfeiture are closely related.
> In essence they are the same thing, the only difference between them
> being that the role of plaintiff and defendant are reversed. In the case

---

[130] As there were no other parties from whom to seek recompense, the decommissioning
costs have had to be covered by the Government.

[131] See the discussion on the validity of forfeiture clauses from para 12.46 onwards.

[132] See G Willoughby, "Forfeiture of Interests in Joint Operating Agreements" (1985)
3 *JENRL* 256–265.

of penalties, one party is seeking to recover money from the other
beyond the value of the damage he has actually suffered; in the case
of forfeiture, he already has the money and is seeking to keep it while
the other party is trying to recover it."[133]

12.48   This tendency to equate forfeiture with liquidated damages/penalty
clauses has found increasing favour with courts.[134] The general law
on the issue of penalties and liquidated damages was laid down by
Lord Dunedin in a pair of House of Lords cases in the early 20th
century: *Commissioner of Public Works* v *Hills*[135] and *Dunlop
Pneumatic Tyre Co Ltd* v *New Garage & Motor Co Ltd*.[136] In the
former judgment, Lord Dunedin defined the distinction between
liquidate damages and penalty clauses thus:

> "The general principle to be deduced ... is ... that the criterion of
> whether a sum – be it called penalty or damages – is truly liquidated
> damages, and as such not to be interfered with by the Court, or is
> truly a penalty which covers the damage if proved, but does not assess
> it, is to be found in whether the sum stipulated for can or can not
> be regarded as a 'genuine pre-estimate' of the creditor's probable or
> possible interest in the due performance of the principal obligation."[137]

12.49   The distinction between a sanction clause being found to be liquidated damages or a penalty[138] is of crucial importance because, while
a liquidated damages clause can be enforced, a contractual term
found to be a penalty clause is treated by the courts as invalid. Lord
Dunedin, in the second judgment, laid down the criteria by which
the courts make the distinction between legitimate enforceable liquidated damages clauses and unenforceable penalty clauses:

> "1. Though the parties to a contract who use the words 'penalty' or
> 'liquidated damages' may *prima facie* be supposed to mean what they
> say, yet the expression used is not conclusive. The Court must find
> out whether the payment stipulated is in truth a penalty or liquidated

---

133 P Atiyah, *An Introduction to Contract* (2nd edn) at 269. Interestingly, this passage does
not appear in the most recent (6th) edition of this work.

134 See, for instance, *Jobson* v *Johnson* [1989] 1 All ER 621 (CA) (hereinafter "*Jobson* v
Johnson"), discussed further at para 12.53.

135 *Commissioner of Public Works* v *Hills* [1906] AC 368 (hereinafter "*Commissioner
of Public Works*"); see also (for the position in Scots law) *Clydebank Engineering and
Shipbuilding Co Ltd* v *Don Jose Ramos Yzquierdo y Castaneda* (1904) 7 F (HL) 77.

136 *Dunlop Pneumatic Tyre Co Ltd* v *New Garage & Motor Co Ltd* [1915] AC 79
(hereinafter "*Dunlop Pneumatic Tyre Co Ltd*").

137 *Commissioner of Public Works* at 375f.

138 For a full discussion, see Law Commission for England and Wales Working Paper
on *Penalty Clauses and Forfeiture of Monies Paid* (WP No 61, 1975); for a Scottish
perspective, see Scottish Law Commission *Report on Penalty Clauses* (Scot Law Com No
171).

damages. This doctrine may be said to be found *passim* in nearly every case.

2. The essence of a penalty is a payment of money stipulated as *in terrorem* of the offending party; the essence of liquidated damages is a genuine covenanted pre-estimate of damage.

3. The question whether a sum stipulated is penalty or liquidated damages is a question of construction to be decided upon the terms and inherent circumstances of each particular contract, not as at the time of the breach.

4. To assist this task of construction various tests have been suggested, which if applicable to the case under consideration may prove helpful, or even conclusive. Such are:

(a) It will be held to be [a] penalty if the sum stipulated for is extravagant and unconscionable in amount in comparison with the greatest loss that could conceivably be proved to have followed from the breach.

(b) It will be held to be a penalty if the breach consists only in not paying a sum of money, and the sum stipulated is a sum greater than the sum which ought to have been paid. This though one of the most ancient instances is truly a corollary to the last test...

(c) There is a presumption (but no more) that it is [a] penalty when 'a simple lump sum is made payable by way of compensation, on the occurrence of one or more or all of several events, some of which may occasion serious and others but trifling damage'...

(d) It is no obstacle to the sum stipulated being a genuine pre-estimate of damage, that the consequences of the breach are such as to make precise pre-estimation almost an impossibility. On the contrary, that is just the situation when it is probable that pre-estimated damage was the true bargain between the parties."[139]

A straightforward example of the application of these criteria is **12.50** *Campbell Discount Co Ltd v Bridge*,[140] where the House of Lords struck down as a penalty a clause in a hire purchase agreement, requiring the hirer to pay compensation for premature termination on the ground that the clause provided a sliding scale which operated in the wrong direction: the less the depreciation of the vehicle, the greater was the compensation payable.

In the 1970s and 1980s, there was widespread concern within **12.51** the industry that a total forfeiture clause[141] might be deemed by the courts to be a penalty clause[142] and this resulted in some parties

---

[139] *Dunlop Pneumatic Tyre Co Ltd* per Lord Dunedin at 86–88.

[140] *Campbell Discount Co Ltd v Bridge* [1962] AC 600.

[141] Ie, one where if the default continued after the expiry of the due notice and the opportunity to redress the fault then the defaulting party lost their entire interest in the JOA and to their share of production.

[142] These fears seem to have been promoted by the opinion of Lord Wilberforce in *Shiloh Spinners Ltd v Harding* [1973] AC 671. The case concerned the forfeiture of a lease.

adopting a so-called "withering interest" forfeiture clause.[143] Under such a clause the interest of the defaulting parties "withered away", ie, decreased in proportion to the increasing amount by which the party was in default. However, withering interest clauses are very complex to apply and in any case all such clauses do is moderate the degree of the punishment, not eliminate the element of forfeiture. In recent years withering interest clauses seem to have become less common in UKCS JOAs.[144]

12.52   By contrast with the above situation, however, a trio of cases in the 1980s[145] indicated that the courts would be reluctant to grant relief against forfeiture. This rather more robust approach to the issue provided the oil industry with some reassurance that forfeiture clauses, whether withering or total, would be upheld. The old fears of unenforceability were re-awoken, however, at least to some extent, by an Australian case, *Mosaic Oil NL v Angaari Pty Ltd*,[146] where the judge made some *obiter* remarks to the effect that such clauses might be unenforceable as being *de facto* penalty clauses. But almost simultaneously, the industry in Britain was given further reassurance that JOA forfeiture clauses would be upheld at least in part by *Jobson v Johnson*.[147]

12.53   *Jobson v Johnson* concerned a share sale agreement for a football club which provided for the sale of shares to the defendant's nominee

---

Although, on the facts, the House of Lords was satisfied that forfeiture was appropriate, certain *dicta* suggested that the court reserved the right to grant relief in cases where the default had not been wilful, and where (a) the primary function of the contract was to procure a certain result; (b) that result could still be attained at the time when the matter came before the court; and (c) the forfeiture provision acted as a security against the obtaining of that result. Legal advice given in the light of that case to parties negotiating the JOA for the Thistle Field was influential in promoting the fear, and therefore the move towards withering interest clauses. See G Willoughby, "Forfeiture in Joint Operating Agreements" (1985) JENRL 256 at 258–259.

[143] J Waite and D Dawborn, "Contractual Forfeiture of Joint Venture Interests: are such clauses enforceable?" [1990] 11 OGLTR 389.

[144] The 2009 Model JOA reinstates the defaulting party at the original share and not at a lower rate. 2009 Model JOA cl 17.3.2 says ".. the Defaulting Participant shall ... have restored to it the right to take in kind and dispose of its Percentage Interest share of the Petroleum subject to any lifting procedures ...". However, UKCS JOA forfeiture clauses often contain a provision that where a defaulting party is reinstated on remedy of the default the party will be reinstated with a lower interest. This is in order to discourage opportunist withholding of funds.

[145] *Scandinavian Trading Tanker Co AB v Flota Petrolera Ecuatorina (The Scaprade)* [1983] QB 529; *Sport International Bussum BV v Inter-Footwear Ltd* [1984] 1 WLR 776; and *BICC plc v Burndy Corp* [1985] Ch 232.

[146] (1990) 8 ACLC 780 (New South Wales Supreme Court). But a decision regarding a mining JV that went in the opposite direction in a different Australian state the previous year was *CRA v NZ Goldfields Investments* [1989] VR 873 Supreme Court (Victoria). In *CRA* a clause which required a defaulting party to sell its interest to the non-defaulting party at fair market value less 5% was upheld and not considered as a penalty.

[147] [1989] 1 All ER 621 (CA), [1989 1 WLR 1026 (CA).

for £40,000. By a side letter, the defendant agreed to pay additional sums for the shares by half-yearly instalments. The additional sum of just under £311,000 was to be paid by six instalments of just under £52,000 each. A paragraph in that side letter provided that if there was a default in the first instalment, the defendant would re-transfer 49 per cent of the share capital of the football company. For any defaults in later instalments there was a provision that he would transfer the shares subject to a payment to him of £40,000. There was a default and the question arose whether the obligation to transfer the shares subject to a payment of £40,000 was a penalty or forfeiture clause. The Court of Appeal held that a forfeiture clause and a penalty clause shared similar characteristics. Both were subject to equitable jurisdiction. Such clauses would not be enforced without giving a proper opportunity for relief, but they were enforceable to the extent that they provided the innocent party with compensation for his loss. On the facts of this particular case, the court ordered a sale of the shares with an obligation to pay the plaintiff the amount of the unpaid instalments. The court also confirmed that an excessive deposit in the form of a large initial instalment could be regarded as a penalty.

An illuminating case in this respect is *Philips* v *Attorney-General of Hong Kong*.[148] Here, the Privy Council upheld the decision of the Hong Kong Court of Appeal that the liquidated and ascertained damages clause in a construction contract was valid and enforceable. It was held that the fact that in certain circumstances a party to a contract might derive a benefit in excess of his loss did not outweigh the very definite practical advantages of the present rule upholding a genuine estimate of probable loss, formed at the time the contract was made. **12.54**

A good general overview of the robust approach of the English courts was provided in the more recent case of *Alfred McAlpine Capital Projects Ltd* v *Tilebox Ltd*.[149] The background to this case was that on 27 April 2001, Tilebox and McAlpine entered into a written building contract. Clause 24 of the contract conditions provided that McAlpine should pay liquidated and ascertained damages for delay at the rate of £45,000 per week or part thereof. The Contract Completion Date was 14 August 2002, but the building works were not completed by that date, and not expected to be complete until June 2005 (ie, some 2½ years late). Against this background, McAlpine became concerned about its potential liability (of something approaching £6 million) **12.55**

---

148 [1993] 61 BLR 41.
149 [2005] EWHC 281 (TCC): 25 February 2005.

to liquidated and ascertained damages under cl 24 of the contract conditions. McAlpine took legal advice and, having done so, formed the view that the rate of liquidated and ascertained damages specified in the building contract was excessive, and was a penalty clause and was therefore invalid. Tilebox denied that cl 24.2 was a penalty clause. In his opinion the judge, Mr Justice Jackson, considered the authorities and made the following general observations:

> "(1) There seem to be two strands in the authorities. In some cases judges consider whether there is an unconscionable or extravagant disproportion between the damages stipulated in the contract and the true amount of damages likely to be suffered. In other cases the courts consider whether the level of damages stipulated was reasonable ... I accept, that these two strands can be reconciled. In my view, a pre-estimate of damages does not have to be right in order to be reasonable. There must be a substantial discrepancy between the level of damages stipulated in the contract and the level of damages which is likely to be suffered before it can be said that the agreed pre-estimate is unreasonable.

> (2) Although many authorities use or echo the phrase 'genuine pre-estimate', the test does not turn upon the genuineness or honesty of the party or parties who made the pre-estimate. The test is primarily an objective one, even though the court has some regard to the thought processes of the parties at the time of contracting.

> (3) Because the rule about penalties is an anomaly within the law of contract, the courts are predisposed, where possible, to uphold contractual terms which fix the level of damages for breach. This predisposition is even stronger in the case of commercial contracts freely entered into between parties of comparable bargaining power.

> (4) Looking at the bundle of authorities provided in this case, I note only four cases where the relevant clause has been struck down as a penalty ... In each of these four cases there was, in fact, a very wide gulf between (a), the level of damages likely to be suffered, and (b), the level of damages stipulated in the contract."

Based upon the above, and the circumstances of this case, Mr Justice Jackson formed the view that the liquidated damages clause in question was not a penalty clause, and therefore would be enforced.

12.56   Another case which illustrates the English courts' robust approach to this matter, and one which, while having its origins in a very different set of facts from those found in a UKCS JOA, is nevertheless strongly analogous to the economic realities and legal structure of a JOA, is *Nutting* v *Baldwin*.[150] This case stemmed from a

---

[150] *Nutting* v *Baldwin* [1995] 1 WLR 201 (hereinafter "*Nutting*").

professional negligence litigation pursued by 986 Lloyd's members against a managing agent of Lloyd's. An association was formed by the members to co-ordinate and finance legal proceedings against the agent by pooling of claims and the levying of subscriptions to cover the costs of litigation. The association was controlled by a committee elected by the members. The committee of the association was empowered to levy additional subscriptions from members, subject to the passing of a supporting resolution by two-thirds of the members present and voting at a general meeting. Such a resolution was duly passed and members were given written notice requiring them to pay an additional subscription by 1 February 1991. By 5 July 1991, despite reminders sent out in April, 19 members had failed to pay their additional subscriptions, and accordingly the committee purported to exercise its power under the rules to declare them to be defaulting members, with the result that they were no longer entitled to share in anything which the association might recover from the managing agent and the members' agents. Two actions were brought by the association which eventually resulted in an agreement by the syndicate agent to pay £116 million to the association's solicitors on trust for the committee to apply in paying the association's outstanding liabilities and distributing the balance among members of the association other than defaulting members. The committee sought and obtained a court declaration that it was authorised to distribute the amount recovered, on the footing that no defaulting member was entitled to a share of the award. The High Court held that the essence of the contract between the members of the association was that there should be a pooling of the members' claims and of individual contributions required to meet the risks of the proposed litigation; that it was an essential part of that arrangement that if a member ceased to contribute to the cost of pursuing the claims he should cease to share in the pool of benefit represented by the proceeds of such claims, and accordingly the exclusion from benefit was not a penalty for breach of contract; that, while the exclusion of a defaulting member from the sharing in the proceeds was a "forfeiture" of his share, the object of the power to exclude a member was to ensure that all those who were going to share in the fruits of the litigation should also share in the risks involved and it would be wrong, whatever the individual circumstances, for the court to grant relief against forfeiture to those who had not shared in the risks involved.

The court found that when payment at a given time was an **12.57** essential part of the contract the forfeiture of rights would not be considered a penalty:

> "… In my judgment the essence of the contract between the members of the association is that the burden and benefit of enforcement of the

members' claims against the agents should be shared between all the members. There is a pooling of all such claims and a pooling of contributions in the form of subscriptions for the purpose of financing the enforcement of such claims. It is an essential part of the arrangement that if a member ceases to contribute to the pool of financial contributions to the cost of pursuing the claims there should be power for the committee on behalf of all the members to determine that he shall cease to share in the pool of benefit represented by the proceeds of such claims. In other words a member who fails to shoulder his share of the burden of this essentially multilateral arrangement runs the risk of being excluded from his share of the benefit of the arrangement. *This is not a penalty for breach of contract. It is an essential part of the pooling arrangement thereby effected.*"[151]

This clear statement by Rattee J is a further clear indication that the courts will be predisposed towards enforcing contractual duties and slow to find ground for relief. A further quotation from the judgment will perhaps serve to demonstrate why:

"… To allow a member who has not undertaken his share of the risk by paying his subscriptions on time to come in after the litigation has been successfully concluded, so that there is no longer any risk, and still share in the fruits of the litigation on payment of his overdue subscription would, in my judgment, undermine rather than attain the object of the forfeiture provision against which relief is sought, and indeed one of the fundamental objectives of the constitution of the association. This being so, whatever the individual circumstances of the defendants, and whatever the reasons for their default, it would in principle be wrong for the court to grant relief against forfeiture. However hard the result may bear on individual defaulting members they must, in my judgment, be held to the arrangement constituted by the rules of the association to which they expressly agreed when they signed their application to join the association."[152]

12.58   The parallels between the association in *Nutting* and a JOA are striking. In each case an association is formed to bear the high costs of a high-risk/high-reward operation: litigation and oil exploration. In each case, the finances of the group are based on contractually agreed cost-sharing, and in each case failure to contribute results in the loss of any right to the proceeds of the operation: monetary award and oil respectively. It is submitted that this case gives good grounds to believe that the courts will uphold forfeiture clauses and, indeed, following the logic of *Nutting*, they should uphold total forfeiture clauses, not just withering interest ones. More generally it can be said that the English courts are usually strongly inclined

---

[151] *Nutting* per Rattee J at 208 (emphasis added).
[152] *Ibid*, per Rattee J at 210.

where possible to uphold contractual terms that have been freely agreed between the parties. Furthermore, another strong argument against a forfeiture clause in a JOA being considered a penalty clause is that it is a clause which applies equally to all the parties, while generally the contractual clauses which the courts have considered to be penalty clauses were those which were designed to benefit only one party to the contract.

Thus, taking all the above factors into consideration it would seem that, other than in the most exceptional of cases, the courts are very unlikely to find a liquidated damages clause to be a penalty clause.   **12.59**

In practice the risk of a forfeiture clause being struck down by the courts is small because the only relief which the courts will be likely to grant in those rare occasions when they see fit to intervene is to give the debtor time to pay his debt and, arguably, the time periods provided by most JOAs already provide a reasonable time to make payment. So even if relief from forfeiture were to be granted by the courts, the actual effect would be minimal. Ironically, the real danger from a dispute over the validity of a forfeiture clause comes not from any remedy which might be granted by the courts but rather from the high costs and long delays associated with a court action which could well have a negative impact upon the conduct of the joint operations. Rather more problematic is the effect of English insolvency law, discussed below.   **12.60**

Forfeiture clauses and insolvency law

It is a longstanding principle[153] of English law that a private contract cannot thwart the operation of the general law of insolvency: "there cannot be a valid contract that a man's property shall remain his until his bankruptcy, and on the happening of that event shall go over to someone else, and be taken away from his creditors".[154] This rule is often referred to, for conciseness, as the "anti-deprivation principle". In the context of the provisions of a petroleum JOA there is thus a possibility that a forfeiture clause might be struck down as an unfair provision which is contrary to the anti-deprivation principle on the ground that it deprives the insolvent co-venturer's non-JOA member creditors of their right to share in his assets, including his share of production under the JOA. But while the rule is clear, its application is not: "The scope of this common law rule of   **12.61**

---

[153] See *Higinbotham v Holme* (1812) 19 Ves 88, where Lord Eldon laid down the principle that no-one can be allowed to derive benefit from a contract that is in fraud of the bankruptcy laws.

[154] *Ex p Jay; In re Harrison* (1880) 14 Ch D 19, per Cotton LJ at 26.

public policy is, however, notoriously uncertain."[155] The case law is certainly not entirely easy to follow either. However, one case in this line of authority, which is striking in its similarities to the position of a JOA with a defaulting member, is the case of *Whitmore* v *Mason*.[156]

12.62   In *Whitmore*, a certain Mr Mason had been granted a mining lease that he held on trust for himself and four partners in shares based on the amounts they each had subscribed to the capital of the partnership. The partnership deed included a provision that in the event of the bankruptcy of any of the partners his share of the assets would be forfeited to the remaining partners. On Mason's bankruptcy the court deemed this provision to be void and unenforceable.

12.63   A similar approach was taken in *Ex p Jay; In re Harrison*,[157] where a building agreement provided that the contractor was to erect 40 houses and was to be granted leases as and when the houses were completed. The agreement provided that, in the event of the contractor's insolvency, all the improvements on the land not demised to the builder as well as all the building materials which had been placed upon that land by the builder should become absolutely forfeited to the landlord. The Court of Appeal held that the agreement was unenforceable so far as it related to the building materials:

> "a simple stipulation that, upon a man's becoming bankrupt, that which was his property up to the date of the bankruptcy should go over to someone else and be taken away from his creditors, is void as being a violation of the policy of the bankrupt law ... I think we cannot escape from applying that principle to the present case."[158]

12.64   However, a case on very similar facts the very next year, *Ex p Newitt; In re Garrud*[159] was decided differently and a forfeiture clause upheld as valid, sowing seeds of confusion which have persisted to the present day.[160] For example, clauses preventing the transfer of shares to creditors in a private company have been upheld where they are valueless or transferred for value,[161] and the imposition of restrictions upon transfer of membership to creditors

---

[155] J Armour, "The Uncertain Flight of *British Eagle*" [2003] CLJ 39–42 at 39.

[156] *Whitmore* v *Mason* (1861) 2 J & H 204 (hereinafter "*Whitmore*").

[157] *Ex p Jay, In re Harrison* (1880) 14 Ch D 19 (hereinafter "*Ex p Jay*").

[158] *Ibid* per James LJ at 25.

[159] (1881) 16 Ch D 522.

[160] The contrast between the outcomes of *Ex p Jay* and *Ex p Newitt; In re Garrud* was described as "rather surprising" by F Oditah in "Assets and the Treatment of Claims in Insolvency" (1992) 108 LQR 459 at 476.

[161] See *Borland's Trustee v Steel Bros & Co Ltd* [1901] 1 Ch 279.

of an unincorporated non-profit-making association has also been upheld as valid.[162]

The leading modern case on this is the House of Lords decision in **12.65** *British Eagle International Airlines Ltd* v *Cie Nationale Air France*.[163] The plaintiff and defendant were members of the International Air Transport Association ("IATA"), which established a clearing house arrangement contractually binding on all its members, with the object of providing machinery for the settlement of debits and credits arising where members performed services for one another. Under those regulations the members could not claim payment directly from one another, but only from IATA on the basis of the balances due to them under the clearing house scheme. In IATA's clearing house manual of procedure, it was expressly stated that it was to "be deemed to be an express term of every contract agreement or arrangement for the time being subsisting between any two members" that any "debit or credit shall be payable or receivable by and through the medium of the clearing house in accordance with the regulations and current clearing procedure and not otherwise in any manner". The House of Lords held that such a contracting out was contrary to public policy, and the rules of the general liquidation should prevail over the clearing house arrangements.

British Eagle can hardly have been said to clarify the law in **12.66** this general area.[164] In *Money Markets International Stockbrokers Ltd (in liquidation)* v *London Stock Exchange Ltd*,[165] the High Court wrestled with the conflicting authorities, and the opinion of Neuberger J contains a magisterial review of the conflicting case law in this area. In the instant case it was concluded that a term which forfeited an insolvent party's membership of the London Stock Exchange was valid and not in breach of insolvency law on the grounds that a membership of the LSE was personal in character, and not proprietary. So if a court were to be persuaded that a membership of a JOA was essentially personal in character there might be grounds for arguing that a forfeiture clause be upheld. However, it is clear that, as stated at the beginning of this chapter, a JOA does possess a dual function, and it has a proprietary character as well as a personal one.[166]

---

[162] *Bombay Official Assignee v Shroff* (1932) 48 TLR 443 (PC).

[163] [1975] 1 WLR 758.

[164] G McCormack commented, with some understatement, "The result in *British Eagle v Air France* has not been the subject of universal approbation": see *Proprietary Claims and Insolvency* (1997) at 18.

[165] [2002] 1 WLR 1150.

[166] See the discussion at paras 12.9–12.18.

12.67   Another recent case, *Fraser* v *Oystertec plc*,[167] concerned a company, Easyrad, which owned a patent that had been bought from its inventor, Mr Davidson. The contract granting ownership to Easyrad contained a clause which provided that if the company became insolvent then the ownership of the patent would automatically be assigned back to Mr Davidson in return for payment of any expenditure by Easyrad in securing the patent protection. The Patents Court deemed this clause to be invalid in terms which, if followed by a court considering the validity of a JOA forfeiture clause, might indicate that it would strike down a JOA forfeiture clause:

> "[W]here a business owns an asset of substantial independent value, whose existence lies at the heart of the venture, and that asset is held out to the outside world as the property of the business without qualification, an agreement entered into by that business according to which it may be peremptorily deprived of that asset on the grounds of its insolvency, by unilateral action to be taken pursuant to that agreement, does not constitute a relevant exception to the principle [that insolvency law prevails over private contracts]. Thus such an agreement is to that extent null and void."[168]

12.68   Further support for the validity of forfeiture clauses can be found in the conjoined cases of *Perpetual Trustee Co Ltd* v *BNY Corporate Trustee Services Ltd* and *Lehman Brothers Special Financing Inc; and Butters* v *BBC Worldwide Ltd*.[169] The Court of Appeal had to consider the effect of the anti-deprivation rule in two separate cases. The *Lehman* case concerned a credit-linked note issued by a Lehman Brothers' structured issuance vehicle and the BBC case concerned a licence issued under an incorporated joint venture agreement between BBC World and the Woolworths Group. So both cases were about the effectiveness of a contractual priority or forfeiture provision in the context of the defaulter's insolvency. In the *Lehman* case the court had to consider whether a clause in a security trust deed which provided that a swap counterparty (*Lehman*) was to be paid in priority to noteholders, unless an event of default occurred under the swap agreement, in which case the priority "flipped" so that noteholders would be paid in priority to LBSF (the so-called "flip clause"), infringed the anti-deprivation principle. The court held it did not. In the BBC case, which is more directly analogous to default under a JOA, the court had to consider whether clauses in a licence of intellectual property rights granted to an incorporated

---

[167] [2004] BCC 233 (hereinafter "*Fraser*").
[168] *Fraser*, per Prescott QC at para 124.
[169] [2009] EWCA Civ 1160, [2010] 3 WLR 87, [2010] Bus LR 632, [2010] BCC 59.

JV company which operated to terminate the licence to certain intellectual property rights on the insolvency of a contracting party were effective. The agreement provided that in the event of the insolvency of a joint venture partner (or the parent company of a joint venture partner) the joint venture agreement and the licence would terminate and the solvent joint venturer would have a pre-emption right over the insolvent party's share in the JV company. These clauses were not considered to be penalties and were upheld by the Court of Appeal.

There has yet to be a UK case on the validity of a JOA forfeiture clause, but when an Australian court, in *Mosaic Oil NL v Angaari Pty Ltd*,[170] had to consider the specific issue of the relationship between a forfeiture clause under a petroleum JOA and insolvency law it was held that the latter would prevail and that such a forfeiture clause would not be upheld. Taken overall, then, the authorities indicate that while there must be a possibility that a forfeiture clause might possibly be deemed unenforceable on the ground that it gives an unfair preference to the co-venturers the tendency in the recent case law from the English courts, not least *Perpetual Trustee*, seems to indicate that the courts would uphold forfeiture clause under a JOA as valid.

DECOMMISSIONING

In the initial years of the North Sea oil industry neither the oil industry nor the British Government gave much, if any, thought to the issue of the removal and disposal of redundant installations and infrastructure when the recoverable reserves of a field had been exhausted.[171] Accordingly, the JOAs agreed in the 1960s and 1970s gave little or no thought to the issue of decommissioning and when the issue was eventually considered it was almost always dealt with in a separate decommissioning agreement. This was generally referred to as an abandonment security agreement, agreed by the co-venturers several years after the JOA had been agreed. However, since the 1980s as many oil and gas fields began to approach the end of their productive lifespan the industry began to take the issue of decommissioning increasing seriously. At the same time developments in international law which have been transposed into UK domestic law[172] meant that the issue of potential decommissioning costs is one that has become increasingly onerous. Accordingly, the

12.69

---

[170] (1990) 8 ACLC 780 (New South Wales Supreme Court), discussed at para 12.52 above.
[171] See para 10.4.
[172] See especially para 10.38 onwards.

Government now requires that all fields have decommissioning plans and it is now best practice to agree a Decommissioning Security Agreement at the same time or shortly after the JOA is agreed. Decommissioning Security Agreements, as the name implies, are an attempt by the co-venturers to supply some sort of financial security in the form a guaranteed source of funds that may be accessed if the need arises in order to pay for the actual costs of decommissioning installations. Financial security becomes a paramount issue in the final stage of an oil or gas field's productive life as, by definition, the time for making a profit out of the field's assets has passed and the field now represents a financial liability rather than a financial asset. The industry in the early 21st century is very aware of the need to make provision for decommissioning and the 2009 Model JOA makes provision for decommissioning in Arts 13 and 26 and in Sch C where it is presumed that the provision for decommissioning will take the form of the Oil & Gas UK 2009 Model Decommissioning Security Agreement.[173] However, of course, the parties are free to make whatever arrangement they like provided they meet with Government approval.

12.70   As discussed in greater detail in Chapter 10 in this volume, the nature and extent of the decommissioning obligations laid upon the co-venturers are largely determined by international law. Article 60(3) of the United Nations Convention on the Law of the Sea of 1982 ("UNCLOS") provides that "any installations or structures which are abandoned or disused shall be removed to ensure safety of navigation, taking into account any generally accepted international standards established in this regard by the competent international organisation". The "competent international organisation" mentioned in Art 60(3) is the International Maritime Organization ("IMO") and, in 1989, the IMO adopted Resolution (A.672(16), 19 October 1989) with an annex on Guidelines and Standards for the Removal of Offshore Installations and Structures on the Continental Shelf and in the Exclusive Economic Zone. These guidelines require the removal of: (i) all installations standing in less than 75 metres of water and weighing less than 4,000 tonnes; (ii) all installations placed on the sea bed after 1 January 1998, standing in less than 100 metres and weighing less than 4,000 tonnes; and (iii) installations located in primary navigational routes. However, neither UNCLOS nor the IMO Guidelines give explicit direction on how to dispose of disused installations and during the early 1990s the oil industry and the British Government believed that in certain

---

[173] Available from http://www.oilandgasuk.co.uk/publications/index.cfm (hereinafter referred to as the "2009 Model DSA").

circumstances deep-sea disposal of assets remained a lawful option. However, the political mood regarding the acceptability of deep-sea disposal changed in the wake of the Brent Spar incident in 1995. The regional international body responsible for environmental regulation of the North Atlantic and the North Sea, the Convention for the Protection of the Marine Environment of the North-East Atlantic (OSPAR), effectively banned deep-sea disposal of installations by means of OSPAR Decision 98/3.[174] The obligation to remove almost all installations entirely has significantly increased the costs of decommissioning.[175]

As a matter of international law under UNCLOS and OSPAR, **12.71** the UK Government has the primary obligation to ensure the appropriate removal of decommissioned offshore installations. However, the British Government, by virtue of internal domestic law, notably the Petroleum Act 1998, has transferred the primary liability for decommissioning from itself onto the oil companies, although obviously the British Government remains ultimately liable for decommissioning in the event that the relevant oil company licensees should all default on their obligations. This imposition of primary liability upon the licensees may be seen as a classic example of the implementation of the "polluter pays" principle in environmental law. If international law determines the extent of the decommissioning obligations of the parties, the liability to pay those costs is determined by a mixture of contract, the terms of the JOA and the DSA and statute, the Petroleum Act 1998. This liability for decommissioning costs may be described as contractual primary *several pro rata* liability, undergirded by a potential statutory secondary *joint* liability.

The Decommissioning Security Agreement

The 2009 Model JOA presumes that the 2009 Model DSA will be **12.72** annexed to the JOA as a schedule. This can be done at the same time as the JOA is agreed or it can be agreed later and added to the JOA. For obvious reasons, it is envisaged that the DSA be agreed prior to the filing of a field development plan. In order to ensure that there will be sufficient funds available to pay for the decommissioning costs of a given field the DSA provides that a trust fund be establish to pay for the decommissioning when a time known as the "trigger date" is reached. The trigger date occurs when the net value of reserves remaining in the field is equal to or less than

---

[174] Which came into force on 25 March 1998. For further details, see para 10.36.
[175] See para 10.3.

the estimated remaining net costs, including those associated with decommissioning, as escalated by a risk factor to be agreed between the parties. The risk factor, which is commonly 120–150 per cent, is an attempt to cope with the double financial risk that decommissioning works entails. First, the costs of decommissioning may well fluctuate, generally in an upwards direction. Second, given the high volatility of oil and gas prices, it is always difficult actually to estimate how much *in situ* reserves will be required to pay for the decommissioning of a given field. The decommissioning trust will be constituted with a third party as trustee and each party will be required to contribute a sum (the "provision amount") to the trust on an annual basis from the "trigger date" until the "end date". The end date is defined as occurring after decommissioning is completed, and when 12 months after the submission to the Secretary of a "close-out report" have elapsed. The period between the trigger date and the end date is known as the "run-down period". The calculations for net cost and net value are made by the operator in accordance with the decommissioning plan, which the operator is obliged to provide annually beginning the year before the run-down period commences. The decommissioning plan will include the calculations for net cost and net revenue and must be approved unanimously by the parties or be referred to an expert. The purpose of the trust is that any funds residing in it can act as security for payment of the costs of decommissioning the field, but the primary method of collecting funds to pay for the decommissioning plan remains AFEs issued in the usual way under the JOA and the intention is that the funds in the decommissioning trust are security for payment. The strength of financial protection provided to the co-venturers and the Government by the DSA has been greatly enhanced by the insertion of s 38A in the Petroleum Act 1998 by the Energy Act 2008, which provides that all sums set aside as security for decommissioning under a DSA will be protected from any creditors of any of the co-venturers in insolvency and will thus remain available for the purposes of paying decommissioning costs.[176]

Alternative security and default

12.73   While the 2009 Model DSA envisages cash for security purposes being held by a decommissioning trust, it also allows that the parties may provide alternative security. The Model DSA "alternative provision" for security allows for several different forms of security, which include the provision of a letter of credit, corporate bond or a parent company guarantee (PCG) in the forms annexed

---

[176] See para 10.46.

to the DSA. The UK Government requirements for letters of credit are for a credit rating equivalent to AA (Standard and Poors) or Aa2 (Moodys) It should be noted that the Government does not accept PCGs or parent bonds due to issues of enforceability against foreign companies and EU state aid rules for UK domestic companies. Default on a DSA is triggered by the failure to provide or maintain the security to the requisite amount or credit rating. However, a default under the parent JOA itself will also trigger default under the DSA. The usual remedy of forfeiture of participating interest in the JOA and licence applies, subject to rights to remedy a default. This will entail the defaulting party's interest being transferred to the non-defaulting parties in addition to any sum held by the trustee as security. But obviously, as mentioned earlier,[177] forfeiture is not much of a penalty at a stage when a field represents liabilities rather than potential profits.

CONCLUSION

The unincorporated JOA has proved to be a flexible and cost **12.74** effective means by which parties who wish to shares the risks and rewards of oil and gas exploration may come together and it is likely to remain the dominant form of alliancing in the oil and gas industry both within and outwith the UKCS for the foreseeable future.

---

[177] See discussion on default and forfeiture: from para 12.43 onwards.

CHAPTER 13

UNITISATION

Nicola MacLeod

Oil and gas deposits are typically composed of porous rock bounded   13.1
by impermeable strata which serve to trap the oil and gas under
conditions of high pressure. Drilling through the impermeable cap
decreases the pressure of the reservoir and allows the oil and gas to
migrate through the porous rock to the source of lower pressure (in
most cases the drilled well) in order to be extracted.[1] Thus oil and
gas behave quite differently to other minerals such as coal, stone
and metal ores, which exist in strata in solid state and in a fixed
position. As we will see, petroleum's migratory (sometimes described
as "fugacious") characteristics pose some particular challenges for
the law.

As we have already seen in Chapter 4, in the UK oil and   13.2
gas production is generally permitted and governed primarily by
(in seaward areas) production licences and (in landward areas),
petroleum exploration and development licences (PEDLs). Such
licences are granted in respect of areas known as blocks.[2] In many
cases the boundaries of an oil or gas field will be contained wholly
within the area of one block. In such a case, the field can be developed
by the parties who are entitled to produce oil from that block by
virtue of licence from the state and the terms of the contractual
arrangements they have entered into with their co-venturers.[3]
However, there are many examples of fields which do not lie wholly
within one block but instead extend either into vacant territory, into

---

[1] T Reynolds, "Delimitation, Exploitation, and Allocation of Transboundary Oil and Gas
Deposits Between Nation-States" (1995) *ILSA Journal of International and Comparative
Law*, Spring (hereinafter "Reynolds, 'Delimitation'") at 136.
[2] See para 4.18.
[3] Joint operating agreements ("JOAs") are discussed in Chapter 12.

blocks where licences have already been granted to different parties, or across a line of international maritime delimitation into parts of the Continental Shelf controlled by other another state. In all such situations, careful thought must be given as to how the reserves are to be extracted.[4] This is so chiefly because petroleum deposits "are characterized by a complicated 'equilibrium of rock pressure, gas pressure and underlying water pressure,' so that extracting natural gas or petroleum at one point unavoidably changes conditions in the whole deposit".[5]

13.3   The fugacious character of oil and gas raises a host of legal questions. For instance: who can be said to own or otherwise control a mineral that migrates? Can the person who owns or otherwise holds exclusive rights appertaining to one particular area of the subsoil legitimately complain if drilling activities carried out at a remote location reduce the amount of oil and gas within that person's area of entitlement? Is ownership of oil and gas in situ even an appropriate legal concept? These will be considered throughout this chapter.

PREVENTING WASTE AND MAXIMISING RECOVERY: THE CASE FOR UNITISATION AND RELATED CROSS-BOUNDARY CONTROLS

13.4   On first discovering that a field within one's own licensed area continues into another licensee's block, assuming that there is an absence of any legal controls prescribing what kind of development is and is not legitimate, at first sight the most economically beneficial strategy seems clear: to develop the field as aggressively as possible in order to cause as much oil and gas as possible to migrate from neighbouring areas into one's wells, thereby maximising one's own take from the common field. This approach was taken in the United States of America in the early days of oil and gas production there.[6] At this point there was no systematic control over the exploitation of common fields, and property in oil and gas was governed by the rule of capture, which is the "legal rule of non-liability for (a) causing oil

---

[4] B Taverne, *Co-operative Agreements in the Extractive Petroleum Industry* (1996) (hereinafter "Taverne, *Co-operative Agreements*"), p 70; see also B Taverne, *Petroleum, Industry and Government: An introduction to petroleum regulation, economics and government policies* (2000) (hereinafter "Taverne, *Petroleum, Industry and Government*") at paras 11.3.1–11.3.2.

[5] D Ong, "Joint Development of Common Offshore Oil and Gas Deposits: 'mere' state practice or customary international law?" [1999] 93 Am J Intl L 771 (hereinafter "Ong, 'Joint Development'") at 778. The internal quotation is from N Ely, "The Conservation of Oil" (1937–38) 51 Harv L Rev at 1209.

[6] See, eg, *Kelly v Ohio Oil Co*, 49 NE 399 (Ohio, 1897).

or gas to migrate across property lines and (b) producing oil or gas which was originally in place under the land of another, so long as the producing well does not trespass".[7] Wells were commonly drilled at or close to the boundary of a block in order to draw as much oil and gas in from deposits underlying neighbouring areas. However, this in turn tended to encourage the proprietors of neighbouring areas to engage in similar behaviour in order to seek to maximise their own recovery.[8] This practice was known as competitive drilling and, due to the rule of capture, was legally legitimate.[9] However, studies in the United States[10] have shown that such competitive production leads to a proliferation of wells and associated infrastructure and higher subsurface costs. Subsurface pressures are prematurely and unnecessarily depleted, oil recovery is reduced[11] and ultimately the field will be abandoned sooner as it is not commercially profitable in its later stages.[12] This form of drilling can also result in unnecessary duplication of expenditure[13] and protracted court proceedings.[14]

---

[7] T Daintith, G Willoughby and A Hill, *United Kingdom Oil and Gas Law* (3rd edn, looseleaf, 2000–date) (hereinafter "Daintith, Willoughby and Hill") at para 1–724. See also *Kelly v Ohio Oil Co*, 49 NE 399 (Ohio, 1897). As we shall see at para 13.10, the rule of capture also has a role to play in UK oil and gas law.

[8] See, eg, J Lowe, O Anderson, E Smith and D Pierce, *Cases and Materials on Oil and Gas Law* (4th edn, 2002) (hereinafter "Lowe *et al*, *Cases and Materials*"), p 786.

[9] It should be noted here that the rule of capture has not been confined to the past. As a principle of property law, it is still extant. However, property law is no longer the *only* source of regulation of these matters. On the grounds of conservation and enhanced recovery, most states in the USA now impose significant controls on cross-boundary developments, including well spacing, pooling and compulsory unitisation provisions. For a detailed review, see Lowe *et al*, *Cases and Materials*, Chapter 6. For an overview, see Reynolds, "Delimitation", at 138 and/or J Weaver, D Asmus *et al*, "International Unitization of Oil and Gas Fields: The Legal Framework of International Law National Laws and Private Contracts" (Association of International Petroleum Negotiators Research Paper, 2005) (hereinafter 'Weaver *et al*, 'International Unitization'") at 12. Texas does not have a compulsory unitisation statute: see P Murray and F Cross, "The Case for a Texas Compulsory Unitization Statute" (1992) 23 St Mary's LJ 1099.

[10] See, eg, G Libecap and D Wiggins, "Oil Field Unitization: Contractual failure in the presence of Imperfect Information" (1985) 75 *American Economic Review* 368; "The Influence of Private Contractual Failure on Regulation: The Case of Oil Field Unitization" (1985) *Journal of Political Economy* 670; "Contractual Responses to the Common Pool: Prorationing of Crude Oil Production" (1984) 74 *American Economic Review* 87.

[11] Reynolds, "Delimitation", at 139. The promotion of recovery and the reduction of waste is a matter of concern not just to licensees but also to the state: see the discussion at para 4.1 and throughout Chapter 5.

[12] Weaver *et al*, "International Unitization" at 7.

[13] P Deemer, "Unitisation Agreements", Conference Paper, University of Dundee, September 2004 (hereinafter "Deemer, 'Unitisation Agreements'") at 2.

[14] E Poitevent, "Oil – proceeds from unitised field" 2000 IELTR N10. See also R Pound, *Law Finding through Experience and Reason* (1960), pp 63–64.

13.5 Unitisation is one of a number of legal devices[15] which seek to remove the destructive competitive element stimulated by the rule of capture. The field is developed as a whole, expenditure is reduced and recovery is maximised. Libecap and Wiggins summarise the position thus:

> "The potential aggregate gains from unitized, single firm production are large: extraction rates can more fully consider user costs and follow rent-maximizing patterns; capital costs can be reduced through elimination of excessive wells and subsurface storage; and total oil recovery can be increased since subsurface pressures can be better maintained through controlled oil withdrawal."[16]

INTRODUCTION TO THE CONCEPT OF UNITISATION

13.6 Unitisation is the process whereby the oil and gas reserves of a reservoir that does not sit within an area covered by a single licence are treated as a single *unit* (hence the term "unitisation") for the purposes of development and operation, with the resulting production from the field divided between the licensees in agreed proportions irrespective of from where within the unitised area the oil and gas has been produced.[17] The licensees of the areas containing the reservoir enter into a unitisation and unit operating agreement (UUOA) to regulate how the reservoir will be developed.

Alternatives to full unitisation

13.7 As we have already seen, one alternative to regulating by way of unitisation is quite simply not to regulate, and to leave matters to

---

[15] See also the alternatives to unitisation discussed at paras 13.7–13.10.

[16] G Libecap and D Wiggins, "The Influence of Private Contractual Failure on Regulation: The Case of Oil Field Unitization" (1985) *Journal of Political Economy* 670 at 712. See also Taverne, *Co-operative Agreements*, p 82: "Co-operation in the exploitation of a straddling (single, continuous) petroleum reservoir is not only a legal necessity when so instructed by the competent authority but also, generally speaking, a technical necessity, assuming the respective (adjacent) rightholders aim or are obliged in the context of good oilfield practice to aim at a maximum efficient recovery of petroleum. The alternative, i.e. independent, non-co-operative exploitation of the separate parts of a straddling reservoir, will lead to costly defensive or competitive drilling." The principle of joint development has also received support at the highest international level from the International Court of Justice, which has held that joint development is particularly appropriate to preserve the unity of a deposit: see *The Continental Shelf Cases* (1969) ICJ Reports at 52, paras 97–99.

[17] M Taylor and S Tyne, *Taylor and Winsor on Joint Operating Agreements* (2nd edn, 1992) (hereinafter "Taylor and Winsor"), p 110. See also Weaver *et al*, "International Unitization" at 1, where the process is described as the joint, co-ordinated operation of a petroleum reservoir by all the owners of rights in the reservoir, a process of combining the separately held portions of the reservoir or field into a large unit.

be governed by property law concepts, most notably the rule of capture.[18] However, again, as we have seen, there are good reasons to reject such an approach. It will not be further considered here. However, depending on the factual circumstances, there may very well be occasions when approaches other than full unitisation are merited. For instance, where the field is found to extend beyond the boundary of the licence-holders' block into unlicensed territory, it may, in some jurisdictions, be possible for the licence group to make an out-of-rounds application.[19] If such an application is granted, then both parts of the field will be licensed to the same group of licensees and the need for unitisation will therefore have been obviated.

Even when a field extends into territory which has already **13.8** been let to another licensee or, more likely, group of licensees,[20] unitisation is not inevitable. Another alternative is for one licence group to purchase the adjoining acreage from the other, and then develop the field under their existing joint venture agreement. Such an arrangement has the benefit of simplicity. It is, however, likely to be attractive to either group only if the extension into the adjoining area is very clearly a small one. If it is sizeable, then commercial factors[21] are likely to push the parties towards unitisation,[22] or at least one of the cognate agreements discussed below.

There are also some variations on full unitisation, such as fixed- **13.9** interest agreements and cross-licence agreements. "Fixed interest" is where the percentage interests of the parties are agreed at the outset of development to avoid the requirement for complicated and costly redeterminations.[23] In this situation the parties need to agree the technical parameters without having drilled any development wells.

---

[18] See para 13.4.

[19] This is possible in the UK: see T Daintith, *Discretion in the Administration of Offshore Oil and Gas* (2006) (hereinafter "Daintith, '*Discretion*'"), para 5406; see also the discussion at paras 4.22 and 13.10. Canadian petroleum law also provides for this type of situation, although not in an identical manner to that of the UK: see Daintith, *Discretion*, para 5412. Neither Australia nor the United States has equivalent provisions: see Daintith, *Discretion*, paras 5401 and 5415 respectively.

[20] See Chapter 12 for a discussion of why oil and gas companies generally explore for and develop assets jointly.

[21] For instance, the purchasers may not be able to afford the purchase price, or at least be unwilling to run the commercial risks associated with paying a capitalised sum for an asset of uncertain size and volatile value. Similarly, the selling licence group will be unlikely to wish to run the risk of selling out at too low a price, or of discovering that the asset sold was significantly larger than they initially believed it to be.

[22] W English, "Unitisation Agreements" in M David, *Upstream Oil and Gas Agreements* (1997) (hereinafter "English, '*Unitisation Agreements*'") at p 115.

[23] See English, "Unitisation Agreements" at p 115. Redetermination is discussed at paras 13.26–13.38.

This requires a leap of faith by the parties, one, moreover, which may have significant financial implications, which is why this alternative is generally agreed only in the case of small developments.[24] "Cross-licensing" involves the licensees taking an assignment of each other's licences and becoming parties to the entire unitised area.[25] This also has the requirement that the parties reach agreement on the split of reserves and is, in practice, uncommon for much the same reasons as have already been discussed.

UNITISATION AND RELATED PRACTICES WITHIN THE UNITED KINGDOM

The legal regime in the UK

13.10   As has already been noted, s 1(1) of the Petroleum (Production) Act 1934 expressly vested "property in petroleum, existing in its natural condition in strata in Great Britain" in the Crown.[26] Thus oil and gas reserves under the landmass of Scotland, England and Wales and their associated territorial seas are owned by the Crown; one might therefore think that, because licensees do not take original ownership, but instead derive ownership from the state, there is no scope for the operation of the rule of capture here. That, however, would be an over-simplification. Model Cl[27] 2 of both a seaward production licence and a landward PEDL[28] provides the licensee with "exclusive licence and liberty during the continuance of this licence and subject to the provisions hereof to search and bore for, and get, Petroleum under [the licensed area]". The responsible government department[29] formerly interpreted this to mean that licensees had a vested right to such petroleum as underlay their licensed area.[30] However, that

---

[24] However, English does refer to "at least two major fields" in the UKCS which proceeded on this basis: English, "Unitisation Agreements" at p 115.

[25] English, "Unitisation Agreements" at p 115.

[26] See para 4.7.

[27] Sets of model clauses which are incorporated into new seaward licence grants can be found in the Petroleum Licensing (Production) (Seaward Areas) Regulations 2008 (SI 2008/225). Unless the context requires otherwise, references throughout this chapter to a "model clause" will be to the standard seaward production licence Model Clauses. See, however, the discussion at para 4.17.

[28] The model clauses for new PEDLs are to be found in the Petroleum Licensing (Exploration and Production) (Seaward and Landward Areas) Regulations 2004 (SI 2004/352), as amended by the Petroleum Licensing (Exploration and Production) (Seaward and Landward Areas) (Amendment) Regulations 2006 (SI 2006/784), Sch 6.

[29] Previously the Department for Business, Enterprise and Regulatory Reform – and the Department of Trade and Industry prior to that – and now the Department of Energy and Climate Change (hereinafter referred to as the "Department").

[30] See Daintith, Willoughby and Hill, para 5–2732.

interpretation was disagreed with by a number of commentators[31] and has subsequently been departed from, at least in relation to the UKCS.[32] Moreover, as we have already seen, in the UKCS outside the territorial sea the Crown has only a sovereign right to exploit resources, not a full right of ownership.[33] If the state does not own oil and gas in situ, it cannot pass title on to its licensees. Instead, its licensees obtain original title upon extraction.[34] This is the rule of capture in its purest form. However, competitive drilling of the nature described at para 13.41 is inherently unlikely to occur in the UKCS. The dangers of competitive drilling have been identified and legislated for from the earliest days of the UK's development of its petroleum law.[35] The Secretary of State therefore enjoys a number of licence powers designed to prevent competitive drilling. The provisions most specifically directed towards this purpose[36] are the general prohibition upon the drilling of wells less than 125 metres from any of the boundaries of the block,[37] provisions relative to the development of fields which cross international lines of maritime demarcation,[38] and the Minister's power, in certain circumstances, to compel unitisation.[39] In addition to the Minister's powers under the licence, it should also be recalled[40] that where the field is found to extend beyond the boundary of the licence-holders' block into unlicensed territory the licensees may make an out-of-round application[41] for a licence to the adjacent block. If such an application

---

[31] See, eg, Daintith, Willoughby and Hill, para 1–347; Daintith, *Discretion*, para 5408; English, "Unitisation Agreements", p 98.

[32] Daintith, *Discretion*, paras 5408 and 5421. No similar declaration appears to have been made in relation to landward licences or those within the territorial sea, although, as has been noted above, the clause granting the licence in these cases is identical in all material respects.

[33] See para 4.8.

[34] In Scotland, this is as a result of the principle of *occupatio*; in England and Wales, of ownership by occupancy. See (for the position in Scotland) W Gordon, "Corporeal Moveable Property" in K Reid (ed), *The Law of Property in Scotland* (1996), para 539; (for the position in England and Wales) see Lord Mackay of Clashfern (General Editor), *Halsbury's Laws of England* (4th edn, 2003, reissue), vol 35, para 1236.

[35] See Daintith, Willoughby and Hill at para 1–103.

[36] Other Model Clauses, including the Model Cll 17 and 18 powers of the Secretary of State to exercise control over production discussed at paras 5.28–5.30, although not so specifically directed towards the issue, are also relevant: see, eg, Daintith, *Discretion* at para 5408.

[37] Model Cl 20. The Minister does, however, reserve an unfettered discretion to consent to such drilling.

[38] Model Cl 28, discussed further at para 13.48.

[39] Model Cl 27. This power will be discussed further at para 13.11.

[40] See para 13.7.

[41] Out-of-rounds applications are discussed above at paras 4.22 and 13.7.

is approved,[42] the need for unitisation will be eliminated. However, even if the application is not approved, given what has been said in this paragraph about the Department's present views on the stage at which property rights to petroleum vest, there would seem to be no reason in principle why the Department should not approve a production and development programme the effect of which would be to drain hydrocarbons from an area outside the licensed area, as long as it was satisfied that the operations carried out under the programme would not damage the underlying reservoirs, reduce overall recovery or otherwise be contrary to good oilfield practice.

Unitisation in practice

13.11 Where he is satisfied that a petroleum field in one block extends into another block in respect of which a UK production licence is extant, and if he considers "that it is in the national interest in order to secure the maximum ultimate recovery of Petroleum and in order to avoid unnecessary competitive drilling that the Oil Field should be worked and developed as a unit",[43] then the Minister is entitled to serve a notice in writing compelling the preparation by all the relevant licensees of a unitised development scheme.[44] The Minister is entitled to himself design and impose a "fair and equitable" unitised development programme upon the licensees if they cannot agree on one within the timescale he has set out or if the Minister does not approve the scheme submitted to him,[45] although this is made subject to the licensees' right to arbitrate.[46] Although the Secretary of State has never served a notice to unitise under these powers, the mere existence of his ability to do so, along with some encouragement from the Department, is thought enough to ensure that licensees take the appropriate measures to gain approval.[47]

13.12 If a field extends into a neighbouring licensee's area the Department will need to be satisfied that the development plan for that area is the one most likely fully to exploit the recovery of economic reserves before any approval will be given. The Department states that:

> "The most efficient way to satisfy these requirements and therefore avoid any possible delay in the authorization process is for the

---

[42] And if the Minister is satisfied that "geological or production considerations" (see para 4.23) justify it, this is the likely outcome.
[43] Model Cl 27(1).
[44] Model Cl 27(2).
[45] Model Cl 27(4).
[46] Model Cl 27(5), read with Model Cl 43.
[47] English, "Unitisation Agreements", p 100; Deemer, "Unitisation Agreements" at 3.

Licensees to discuss their plans with their neighbours at an early stage and propose an agreed Field Development Plan. The Proposal ... should allow an optimum Field Development Plan and demonstrate that there would be no risk of unnecessary competitive drilling."[48]

Unitisation is becoming increasingly prevalent within the UKCS. One **13.13** of the reasons for this is the decreasing size of the acreage available for lease. States who license on the basis of a grid pattern determined before specific discoveries have been made are always likely to encounter situations where fields extend outside the discovery block.[49] The frequency with which that situation is encountered will only increase as the average size of block falls. When licensing first began in the UKCS the average size of licence blocks was 250 square kilometres. This figure has been gradually reduced over time, principally as a result of the sub-division of blocks, relinquishment of acreage and the drawing of the median lines "carving up" the Continental Shelf into exclusive economic areas associated with individual states.[50] As a result of these developments, oil and gas reservoirs are increasingly found to underlie more than one block.

The unitisation and unit operating agreement ("UUOA")
The unitised area is treated as a single unit for development purposes **13.14** as if merged into one single licence. The practical effect of unitisation is that the licensees will have to negotiate a new type of operating agreement – a unitisation and unit operating agreement ("UUOA") – to govern the conduct of operations in the unitised area. UKCS fields will generally be unitised prior to development because of the necessity of Department approval.[51] The Department will want to be satisfied that the agreement provides for the maximum recovery of petroleum, that no company has an unfair advantage and that there are appropriate arrangements in place to deal with abandonment (including the financial or security provisions between the parties).[52] While, at least in the context of an intra-national unitisation, the Department is not directly concerned as to how the reserves are shared out among the licensees,[53] as we have already seen, Model

---

[48] DECC, *Offshore Field Development Guidelines*, available for download from http://www.og.decc.gov.uk/upstream/field_development/index.htm (accessed 13 March 2011) at para 2.5.1.
[49] Daintith, *Discretion*, para 5400.
[50] Daintith, Willoughby and Hill at para 1–723. See also UN Convention on the Law of the Sea 1982, Part V.
[51] The parties must prepare a unitisation scheme and apply for an "Annex B" approval from the Department: English, "Unitisation Agreements", p 100.
[52] See paras 10.54–10.59.
[53] The Department will take a different view of these matters in the international context: see para 13.46.

Cl 27(4) allows the Secretary of State to prepare a development scheme which is "fair and equitable to the licensee and all other licensees" if the scheme originally submitted is unacceptable. The scheme submitted must therefore be reasonable and, as long as the Department's main concern of maximum recovery of reserves is satisfied, the plan should be approved.[54]

13.15   Due to the time it takes to negotiate the full UUOA and gain Department approval, the UUOA will often be preceded by a pre-unitisation agreement between the members of the licence groups in order to allow preliminary work to be carried out in the area.[55] The size and scope of pre-unitisation agreements vary enormously;[56] however, they will often provide for the conducting of seismic surveys, the establishment of a common database of results pertaining to the reservoir, and for a joint programme to appraise and evaluate any drilling. The results of these preliminary studies will determine whether there is a case for developing the field on a unitised basis. The pre-unitisation agreement is viewed as beneficial even if it is ultimately found that there is no case for unitisation, as the parties will have made financial savings by jointly conducting these studies. If a case for unitisation is established, the Department will usually require that the UUOA is signed prior to or at the time of development consent (also known as Annex B approval).[57]

13.16   The UUOA will essentially include all the main features of a joint venture or joint operating agreement[58] (and may be based on one of the licence groups' current agreements) including: the appointment of an operator; the establishment of a unit operating committee; voting provisions; sole risk provisions; work programmes and budgets; default clauses; procedures for the disposal of petroleum; and accounting mechanisms. Many of the clauses and issues of contention discussed in Chapter 12 are therefore equally relevant here. In addition, however, a UUOA will also contain some special provisions applicable to a unitised field. These provisions are discussed more fully later in this chapter, the most important ones being the declaration that the field will be operated as a single unit, the tract participations (these are the percentage interests held by each of the licence groups in the unit) and detailed redetermination

---

[54] English, "Unitisation Agreements", p 100.

[55] Entry into such an agreement has been endorsed as a best practice which helps to avoid delay at full unitisation stage by senior officials within the Department: see Taylor and Winsor, p 113.

[56] Weaver et al, "International Unitization" at 49; Taylor and Winsor, p 113.

[57] See, eg, DECC, "Redetermination of Oil Field Boundaries on Economic Grounds: Explanatory Note and Guidance for Licensees" (2009), available for download from: https://www.og.decc.gov.uk/regulation/guidance/fld_bound_redet.pdf (accessed 13 March 2011).

[58] English, "Unitisation Agreements", p 97.

provisions.[59] It is possible to have separate agreements for the unitisation and operation of the unit area, as is often the case in the United States; however, in the United Kingdom the two are almost always combined.[60] This does not mean that the UUOA will effect a termination of the joint operating agreements (JOAs) between each of the licence groups. These agreements will continue to be fully operative in the parts of the relevant licence areas that lie outside the unitised area, with the UUOA governing the unit area only.[61] It is also possible for the UUOA to cover only certain substances or certain depths and in these cases the JOAs will continue to govern with respect to those substances and/or depths that are not unitised. The existing JOAs will require to be amended either directly or through the UUOA to exclude the area, substances or depths subject to the unitisation.

The JOAs may also continue to govern the relationships   **13.17** between the licensees within each licence group with regard to such areas as withdrawal, assignment and default. For example, if a party wishes to assign its unit share, that party will usually have to follow the assignment provisions in both the UUOA and its own licence group's JOA.[62] It is therefore important when drafting the UUOA to consider how the provisions relate to the underlying JOAs. In order to resolve any potential conflict between the UUOA and the JOAs the UUOA will commonly contain a clause stating that in the event of conflict between the two the UUOA shall prevail.

COMMON ISSUES IN UNITISATION

Tract participations; determination; re-determination; and dispute resolution

Tract participation
Typically, a UUOA will contain a clause to the effect that: **13.18**

> "all rights and interests of the Parties under the Licences are hereby unitised in accordance with the provisions of this Agreement insofar as such rights and interests pertain to the Unitised Zone and each of the Parties shall own all Unit Property and Unitised Petroleum in undivided shares in proportion to its Unit Equity".[63]

It follows that wherever in the field the unitised oil and gas comes

---

[59] Deemer, "Unitisation Agreements", at 1.
[60] See Taylor and Winsor, pp 113f; also English, "Unitisation Agreements", p 97.
[61] Daintith, Willoughby and Hill, para 1–741.
[62] *Ibid.*
[63] English, "Unitisation Agreements", p 97.

from, the owners will have claim to such production in their unitised shares. Each individual licensee's unitised share will be a function of their equity holding in their own licence group JOA and the percentage interest in the unit held by each of the separate licence groups, or, as it is known, each licence group's "tract participation".[64]

Determination

13.19   The characteristic provisions of a unitisation agreement and those that distinguish it from an ordinary JOA are the determination of the tract participations and the subsequent re-determination provisions.[65] The tract participation provisions determine the percentage interests held by each of the separate licence groups in the unit. Once determined, each of the parties will be entitled to its tract participation percentage of unitised production, regardless of from where within the unit it is produced, and will also be liable for that same undivided percentage of costs and liabilities.[66] Due to the significant sums involved, each of the licensees has an interest in maximising its share of the reserves and therefore its licence group tract. At the same time, parties do not wish to be responsible for up-front costs for a greater area than estimated, especially as they will have no revenue stream from the field at this point.[67] It is not surprising, therefore, that these provisions are often the subject of lengthy negotiations.

13.20   In the early stages of development there will be insufficient technical data to calculate precisely each party's share of reserves. The tract participations will therefore be determined on a provisional basis. The two or more licence groups will agree the participations based on a best estimate of the percentage of the hydrocarbons underlying each of the separate licence areas. As the parties will at this point have at least a somewhat imperfect knowledge of the physical characteristics and extent of the reserves,[68] this will be a negotiated figure rather than a technical one and may well have been concluded in a pre-unitisation agreement. This allocation will then be maintained until the first re-determination.[69]

---

[64] See Daintith, Willoughby and Hill at para 1–742.

[65] *Ibid.*

[66] Weaver *et al*, "International Unitization", at 58.

[67] English notes that in a development costing £1 billion, each 1% share is worth £10 million and as such can have a significant impact on a company's finances: English, "Unitisation Agreements", p 105.

[68] Although with modern improved seismic and other surveying and modelling techniques the parties are nowadays likely to have much better information on which to base their "best guess" than was formerly the case.

[69] English, "Unitisation Agreements", p 105.

As mentioned earlier, the determination of the tract participations **13.21**
is one of the most lengthy and difficult areas to bargain, particularly where the formula for the original calculations is also to be
used for the re-determinations.[70] There are several methods used
for determining tract participation and re-determinations, the three
most common being "stock tank oil originally in place" (STOOIP),
"recoverable reserves" and "moveable oil originally in place"
(MOOIP).[71]

STOOIP relates to the total volume of oil originally in the reservoir. **13.22**
This is generally considered to be the easiest method to determine
and one which can be determined with finality as soon as development drilling has been completed.[72] However, this method may
not be completely equitable, as some of the oil will never actually be
produced. In addition, it makes no distinction between the reserves
that are produced and those which are left in the reservoir.[73]

Recoverable reserves are simply those reserves which are recovered. **13.23**
In theory this method is arguably the most equitable, however in
practical terms it cannot be finally determined until the reservoir has
been completely depleted and at this point there are no reserves left
for making final equitable adjustment of quantities.[74]

MOOIP relates to the oil originally in place minus the theoretical **13.24**
oil left in the reservoir once depleted. This is no more equitable
than STOOIP and has more uncertainties, therefore the majority of
unitisations in the UKCS have been based on the STOOIP method.[75]
English states that:

> "As the methods become progressively more complicated they will in
> theory become more equitable, but there will also be greater scope
> for disagreement. There tends therefore to be a preference within the
> industry for opting for one of the more straightforward methods,
> providing that it will give an equitable result."[76]

In contrast, unitisations in the United States commonly use complex **13.25**
formulae taking into account factors such as well productivity,

---

[70] Taylor and Winsor, p 114.

[71] These are by no means the only methods currently available; nor is the terminology
used to describe any given basis uniform. See also the list of potential bases offered by
English: English, "Unitisation Agreements", p 105.

[72] Daintith, Willoughby and Hill, para 1–742; see also Taylor and Winsor, p 115.

[73] Daintith, Willoughby and Hill, para 1–742.

[74] This point is developed in the discussion on re-determination below at
paras 13.26–13.32.

[75] Daintith, Willoughby and Hill, para 1–742. The equivalent method to STOOIP for a
gas field is called "initial gas in place" or IGIP.

[76] English, "Unitisation Agreements", p 106.

well density, reservoir penetration and acre-feet of reservoir rock.[77] Derman and Derman state that more sophisticated geophysics has allowed the industry to understand better the subsurface of the reservoir. As a result of these improvements they argue that re-determination methods should advance accordingly. They assert that the typical re-determination process is both ambiguous and contentious and advocate a new mathematical formula based on the Nigerian offshore model.[78] With a marked increase in the incidence of unitisations in the UKCS and elsewhere, and the problems associated with the re-determination process (discussed below), it is possible that the industry may at least experiment with these and other new methods for handling this difficult and contentious process.

Re-determination

13.26   As the development proceeds the parties will learn more about the characteristics of the field and gain a much greater technical understanding of the reservoir. By the time of first production the parties will have a much firmer idea of the extent to which the field underlies each of the blocks. The UUOA will therefore usually contain provisions for parties to be able to request a re-determi-nation (or series of re-determinations) of the tract provisions at certain stages throughout the development.[79] As re-determination is an expensive and time-consuming process,[80] the UUOA will usually place at least some restriction upon the circumstances in which a re-determination is permitted.[81] For instance, re-determination may be permitted only after a specific number of wells have been drilled or after the lapse of a certain period of time. Some UUOAs will only permit re-determinations after all development drilling has been completed, or when significant new geological data is available, or even only after the unitised area has been expanded.[82] If based only

---

[77] Weaver *et al*, "International Unitization" at 60.

[78] P Derman and A Derman, "Unitization? A mathematical formula to calculate redetermi-nations" OGEL Issue 1 (January 2003) (hereinafter "Derman and Derman, 'Unitization'").

[79] It should, however, be noted that UUOAs in the United States do not often contain re-determination provisions: Derman and Derman, "Unitization", at 2.

[80] See para 13.30.

[81] Critical as the process of re-determination is, fatigue can sometimes set in. In the case of the Statfjord Field discussed at para 13.60, the UUOA provided for a series of re-determinations to be carried out, initially every 2 years and then at 3- and 4-year intervals. In the event, however, a number of these re-determinations were waived by the parties: see Daintith, Willoughby and Hill, para 1–743.

[82] Deemer, "Unitisation Agreements" at 7. Daintith, Willoughby and Hill cite the example of a medium field whereby 30 wells are to be drilled requiring the first re-determination after 15 wells have been drilled and then a second after the field is fully developed. They also state that a larger field may require more than two re-determinations during the life of the field: see para 1–743.

on time or the number of wells drilled, it would be possible for several re-determinations to be requested throughout the life of the field. As such there is usually a limit placed on the total number of re-determinations that can be conducted, and a minimum time limit between each one. In addition, the agreement may provide that in the event that a re-determination is found to be "frivolous" – for instance, if it results in less than a certain agreed percentage shift in tract interests – then the licence group who requested the re-determination may be responsible for meeting all or a proportion of the other licence groups' costs.[83]

The UUOA will also set out in detail the procedure for conducting re-determinations. In some instances the operator will be charged with carrying out the re-determination, reporting to a re-determination committee made up of the licensees. More commonly, the re-determination committee and sub-committees will themselves carry out the process, or the re-determination may be contracted out to a specified third party. Whichever method is used, all interested parties will be involved throughout the process.[84]   **13.27**

The financial consequences of a re-determination can be very substantial.[85] As a result of each re-determination the tract participations of the licence groups will either increase or decrease, and each licence group will receive a new entitlement to petroleum from the field. Once the re-determination has been agreed, the UUOA will contain provisions for the adjustment of costs and/or production, the principle being that the participants should, so far as possible, be put in the position in which they would have been had the new tract participations prevailed from the outset.[86] Thus the re-determination will ordinarily be intended to have retroactive effect, meaning that "the performance by participants of all their rights and obligations which are dependent on or determined by reference to their respective unit percentage interests have to be revised and the appropriate adjustments have to be made".[87]   **13.28**

The re-determination provisions will generally provide a mechanism for re-allocating past capital expenditures, operating costs and past production of oil and gas. Capital expenditures are usually handled by immediate cash payments from those parties   **13.29**

---

[83] Weaver *et al*, "International Unitization" at 63.
[84] See English, "Unitisation Agreements", pp 107f.
[85] The editors are aware of one relatively recent re-determination on a relatively small field where a move of less than a quarter of one percentage point on an individual licensee's unit share cost that licensee a sum in the order of £10 million.
[86] Taylor and Winsor, p 118.
[87] Taverne, *Co-operative Agreements*, p 89.

whose tract participation has increased to those whose share has reduced.[88] The licence group whose tract participation is increased will have received an inadequate share of production from the field prior to the re-determination. This is usually dealt with under the UUOA by providing that the deficient parties can lift their share of production each year and in addition lift a percentage of their deficient amount. They are not usually allowed to lift their entire deficient amount at one time as this could cause severe financial disruption to the other parties; however, if production is not sufficient for make-up to be accomplished in the required time, this percentage may be increased. If make-up is still not possible over the life of the field, for example in the case of substantial re-determinations or re-determinations late in the life of the field, the UUOA may require the other licence groups to make a cash payment to the deficient licence group. This produces a number of issues in itself, such as how to value the oil and whether interest should be payable. There may also be significant negative tax implications with regard to a cash pay-back.[89] These are all significant issues that must be considered when negotiating the re-determination provisions in the UUOA, and are among the issues which led Derman and Derman to argue that a new mathematical formula is required.[90]

13.30   Re-determinations are extremely time-consuming and very expensive to conduct. Taylor and Winsor, writing in 1992, stated that on average it is estimated that a re-determination will keep 12 people employed for 2 years and cost £2 million.[91] In addition, re-determinations will also involve a considerable amount of management time and financial planning. It has been observed that "the human resource cost, particularly the opportunity cost, associated with protracted unitisation and re-determination procedures and negotiations may be larger than the actual benefits accruing from minor increases in unit interests".[92]

13.31   Despite these difficulties, re-determinations are still deemed necessary by most companies in the UKCS. The prime reason for this is that determination and re-determination bear directly upon the

---

[88] See English, "Unitisation Agreements", p 111; Taylor and Winsor, pp 117f.

[89] Deemer, "Unitisation Agreements" at 11.

[90] Derman and Derman, "Unitization" at 2.

[91] Taylor and Winsor, p 116. Weaver et al cite the admittedly extreme example of the Prudhoe Bay re-determination in the US which was estimated to have cost between $50 and $100 million due to the number of complications involved and litigation spanning 5 years: see Weaver et al, "International Unitization" at 63–67.

[92] P Jones, "Unitisation and redetermination – key issues/corporate responses", Conference paper, London, November 1994 (hereinafter "Jones, 'Unitisation and redetermination'") at 2.

value of the asset. There is an argument that advances in technology have reduced the need for re-determinations as parties are now more knowledgeable about the reservoir from the outset; however, many companies have to date been unwilling to take this "risk". This may change as the average size of fields discovered in the UKCS decreases.[93] Companies may take the view that they do not wish to waste precious time and resources conducting an exercise which may not be worth the candle.[94]

Whichever method is used, it can be seen that re-determinations are difficult and time-consuming to negotiate. They are also the reason for most disputes arising under UUOAs.[95] Given the huge sums involved and the potential for discord, it is common for parties to insert dispute resolution methods into the UUOA in an effort to manage, prevent or limit such disputes.[96] These methods often provide for the use of an independent expert procedure which, rather perversely, can often itself transpire to be the cause of litigation.[97]   **13.32**

Dispute resolution: the independent expert
The general intent of a UUOA is that re-determinations will be reached by consensus. If, in the process of reaching agreement on the new tract participations, the parties are unhappy with any element in the calculation, the UUOA will often have a provision for the matter to be referred to an independent expert. In negotiating the expert procedures in the UUOA, a number of issues commonly arise. These include: the matters that can be referred to an expert, who can request a referral, how the expert is selected; what data they have access to; and what procedure the expert should follow.[98] The parties will be concerned that the procedure is fair and that any referral will be carried out within a limited period of time and with a minimum of expense.   **13.33**

---

[93] English, writing in 1997, noted that as field size decreases in the UKCS, "the potential advantage to be gained by a change in equity is unlikely to be much greater in value [than the costs of the exercise]": English, "Unitisation Agreements", p 108.

[94] Daintith, Willoughby and Hill note that in a number of recent unitisations the co-venturers have opted to have no re-determination provisions except in cases where the field is extended considerably: see para 1–745. Deemer also cites one example whereby the re-determination process was so difficult that the parties stuck with the original tract participations: Deemer, "Unitisation Agreements" at 7.

[95] English, "Unitisation Agreements", p 106.

[96] A Steele-Nicholson, "Unitisation Disputes: Do Pendulum Procedures Offer Fairness in Equity Redeterminations?" 2001 IELTR 234 (hereinafter "Steele-Nicholson, 'Pendulum Procedures'") at 234.

[97] See para 13.37.

[98] Deemer, "Unitisation Agreements" at 8.

13.34   The expert will usually be an independent company with the necessary expertise to carry out the work. Their role will be somewhere between that of a traditional expert, who will provide an opinion by which the parties will agree to abide, and an arbitrator who will look at the merits of the competing claims.[99]

13.35   An increasing trend in dispute resolution is for the expert to adopt the "pendulum procedure" method – a procedure commonly used in United States labour disputes. This is where the expert is required to adopt the position of one or other of the parties in dispute and is barred from settling for anything between the two positions. It is argued that this method strongly encourages parties to put forward more reasonable positions as, without it, the parties, suspecting that the expert will adopt the middle ground, will tend to put forward extreme cases. The Department favours this method, although Taylor and Winsor contend that it is draconian in its nature.[100] Steele-Nicholson has studied this procedure[101] and has concluded that it can be a useful tool to help limit disputes. He notes that while the procedure does have some pitfalls, these can be avoided with careful draftmanship.[102]

13.36   Some recent UUOAs provide for the independent expert to be involved in all stages of the re-determination process in order to settle disputes as they arise.[103] This is sometimes referred to as the "guided owner" approach. The expert will have observed all of the discussions and will be aware of the circumstances of the case and the positions of both parties and as such will be able to make an informed decision. Although this approach will involve greater involvement by the expert and increased costs, considerable savings can be gained in the overall time taken by the re-determination if a dispute is successfully avoided.[104]

13.37   Most UUOAs contain detailed provisions for the selection and remit of the expert. A number of cases have been brought concerning the role of the expert and the mechanics of the procedure. In *Amoco (UK) Exploration Co v Amerada Hess Ltd*,[105] the underlying UUOA contained complicated "guided owner" provisions which identified 21 key steps which would take place

---

[99] English, "Unitisation Agreements", p 109.
[100] Taylor and Winsor, p 117.
[101] Steele-Nicholson, "Pendulum Procedures", provides a detailed account of the advantages and disadvantages of the pendulum procedure including case studies of how it has been used.
[102] Steele-Nicholson, "Pendulum Procedures" at 240.
[103] Jones, "Unitisation and redetermination" at 4.
[104] Daintith, Willoughby and Hill, para 1–743.
[105] [1994] 1 Lloyd's Rep 330.

in accordance with an agreed timetable and without being inter-rupted by court proceedings. During one of these steps, one of the parties referred to, and the expert made use of, data which was not expressly included in the guided owner provisions. The plaintiffs sought a court order determining the data and material which could be referred to and utilised in the determination process. The defendants contended that the guided owner provisions contained a mechanism for objecting to the data which the plaintiffs had failed to use, and that, having so failed, it was inappropriate to seek the relief of the court. The court agreed with the defendant's analysis and held that, as the guided owner provisions contained a complex dispute resolution mechanism which did not envisage interruption by the court, the plaintiff's application should be stayed. In *Shell UK Ltd* v *Enterprise Oil plc*,[106] a dispute arose over the computer program used to re-determine tract participation. The agreement between the parties and the expert specified that a certain computer program would be used for most purposes and that a second program would be used for one limited purpose. In the event, however, the expert, apparently as a result of an honest misinterpretation of the degree of freedom afforded to him by the contract, used the second program far more broadly than the contract envisaged. It was held that this was a material departure from his instructions likely to put the defendants at a disadvantage, as they did not have access to the second program. The decision issued by the expert was therefore vitiated and rendered contrac-tually ineffectual. In *Neste Production Ltd and Another* v *Shell UK Ltd and Others*,[107] a dispute arose between the parties as to whether the expert should issue his judgment in accordance with the second interim operating agreement, or a somewhat different provision contained in a variation which had at least been under contemplation but which, by the time it came for the expert to issue his determination, some parties contended had never been formally agreed to. It was held that the independent expert provisions could not be construed so as to oust the jurisdiction of the court,[108] and, moreover, that the question of whether the parties had agreed to vary the contractual provisions did not fall within the expert's remit.[109] The twin issues of which set of provisions governed, and

---

[106] [1999] 2 Lloyd's Rep 456.
[107] [1994] 1 Lloyd's Rep 447.
[108] In this respect *Amoco (UK) Exploration Co* v *Amerada Hess Ltd* [1994] 1 Lloyd's Rep 330 was distinguished.
[109] *Neste Production Ltd and Another* v *Shell UK Ltd and Others* [1994] 1 Lloyd's Rep 447 at 453.

how those provisions were to be construed, were therefore determined by the court.

13.38　　It follows that provisions governing the appointment of an independent expert, describing his powers (and the extent to which he is to be subject to controls by the court) and narrating the procedure through which he is to reach his decision should be carefully drafted and unequivocal if unnecessary and costly litigation is to be avoided. These are all matters which will turn on the construction of the relevant contract, whether that be the UUOA itself or an ancillary agreement entered into to regulate the expert determination itself. Moreover, if difficulties are to be avoided, the terms and construction of the relevant contractual provisions should be borne in mind by both the parties while the determination process is ongoing.

Non-unit operations and sole risk

13.39　The UUOA applies to all areas within the unit area; however, it is only the *unitised zone* which will be exploited jointly. If a licence group wishes to drill an exploration well outside the unitised zone, the UUOA may provide for the conduct of non-unit operations on approval from the other parties.[110] While unit operations under the UUOA will always take priority over non-unit operations,[111] the UUOA may allow the use of unit facilities for the conduct of a non-unit operation.[112]

13.40　　The licensees may wish to use any spare capacity in the unit facilities for their own interests, either for the production and transportation of oil and/or gas from an adjoining field or from an accumulation discovered as a result of a non-unit operation.[113] Such spare capacity can usually be used without additional cost if total usage by the licence group is not in excess of its tract participation interest. If it is in excess then a payment may have to be made to the other licence groups.

13.41　　Sole risk operations may also be permitted under the UUOA. These are operations which the unit operating committee has rejected but which a party or parties wish(es) to carry out themselves. These are usually only permitted to enable a licence group to obtain data on its tract, at its own expense, for use in future re-determinations. This work will be carried out by the unit operator and, as with the

---

[110] English, "Unitisation Agreements", p 114.
[111] Taylor and Winsor, p 119.
[112] Daintith, Willoughby and Hill, para 1–745.
[113] English, "Unitisation Agreements", p 114.

non-consent provisions, such operations will not be permitted to take precedence over any unit operations.[114]

Operatorship, voting and control

The UUOA involves two or more groups of parties; as such, two 13.42 different decision-making structures are possible. The first, and the one used for most decision making, is individual voting by each unit party. The second structure, usually restricted to re-determination decisions, is decision making by each licence group.[115] The party with the largest share will usually become the operator and they, along with the other parties with a large interest in the field, will not want their operations to be vetoed by an owner with a smaller interest. The smaller interest holders, on the other hand, will not want to be pressurised into accepting a decision with which they do not agree. This can lead to contentious debate in the negotiation process and is usually resolved by agreement that no licence group will be forced into a decision by the vote of the others unless that licensee's share is minimal: otherwise, at least one vote from each licence group.[116] This is due to the cost and value of offshore developments and companies not being prepared to be voted into anything with which they do not agree.[117] To ensure that deadlock does not occur, the matter may sometimes be referable to the independent expert.

Default and forfeiture of interest

Taverne states that the principal obligation of any party is to 13.43 make payments in response to cash calls from the unit operator in accordance with the provisions of the UUOA.[118] Non-payment of the monies required by these cash calls will constitute default under the UUOA.

Due to the nature of unitisation, the formal default mechanisms 13.44 contained in a standard JOA[119] are not usually carried through into the UUOA.[120] There is some dispute as to what is the ordinary

[114] Daintith, Willoughby and Hill, para 1–745.
[115] Weaver et al, "International Unitization", at 72.
[116] English, "Unitisation Agreements", p 103. See also Taverne, Co-operative Agreements, p 91.
[117] Taverne, Co-operative Agreements, p 107.
[118] Taverne, Petroleum, Industry and Government, para 11.3.4.14.
[119] On which, see paras 12.43–12.68.
[120] English, "Unitisation Agreements", p 113. See also Taylor and Winsor, p 121. The issue which makes a straightforward JOA-style forfeiture clause inappropriate is that, if such a clause operated at the level of the UUOA, forfeiture would be to all the participating

practice in the event of default. English states that if a party is in default under the UUOA its share of costs will ordinarily be borne by its own licence group, who will then in turn seek recompense under the provisions of its JOA,[121] and that the JOA will also usually provide for forfeiture or some lesser form of redress in the event that the default is not remedied within a certain time period.[122] The non-defaulting parties will be able to force this forfeiture if the default is not remedied and subsequently acquire the defaulting party's share under the JOA and thence on to the UUOA. Taylor and Winsor admit of this possibility, but also suggest that the practice of including a default clause in the UUOA which provides not for a transfer of interest but simply a suspension of the rights of the defaulting party is an appropriate solution to the problem relatively commonly encountered.[123]

CROSS-BORDER UNITISATION

International laws and treaties

13.45 Unitisation agreements may also be required at an international level where a reservoir is found to straddle an international boundary or, in the case of the UKCS, a line of international maritime delimitation. In this situation the reservoir will fall partly under the jurisdiction of two different states. The national rules of the states on joint exploitation will be insufficient, as the Governments will not have the jurisdiction to require the licensees of the other state to co-operate in the development of the field. Instead, an agreement must be reached between the states concerned. This agreement will then be used to form the basis of a further UUOA between all of the licensees.[124]

13.46   It has been argued that the successful sharing of cross-border reserves relies on difficult bilateral negotiations backed up with the political will of both countries to reach an agreement.[125] These negotiations are so protracted because the Governments face a number of potential problems in coming to such an agreement. In the first instance the Governments will be mindful of their respective goals to ensure that the field is developed in such a way as to

---

parties, not just those within the defaulter's own licence group. This would not usually be the commercial intention of the parties.

[121] English, "Unitisation Agreements", p 113.

[122] As to the enforceability of such provisions, see the discussion in Chapter 12.

[123] Taylor and Winsor, p 121.

[124] S Chatterjee, "Unitisation: Certain Policy Issues" [1986/87] 12 OGLTR 309.

[125] D Pike, "Cross-border hydrocarbon reserves" in R Schofield, *Territorial Foundations of the Gulf States* (1994) at p 187.

maximise the recovery of petroleum. They will also wish to retain the power to control the unitisation process, such as the right to approve the operator and the determinations. Third, they will be concerned as to how they can ensure the maximum financial return from the field through royalties[126] and/or taxation.[127] In the case of a field wholly within one jurisdiction the Government will not be overly concerned as to the equity split as it will receive its tax take irrespective of the percentage shares of each licensee. However, when a field straddles an international boundary line, the interests of each Government become aligned to those of the "home" licence group, ie the Government has an interest in the licence group which holds its licensed interests from it obtaining the maximum tract partici-pation possible so that the Government can maximise its tax take.[128] Consequently, Governments will be keenly interested in the terms not only of the bilateral treaty but also of the agreement negotiated between the licence groups.[129]

As exploration in the UKCS expanded in the 1960s and 1970s, **13.47** certain countries contiguous to the North Sea, such as Germany, Denmark, Norway, the United Kingdom and the Netherlands, mandated by treaty the manner in which a field found to be straddling their borders should be most efficiently exploited.[130] The agreements between the United Kingdom and the Netherlands, and the United Kingdom and Norway, are discussed in more detail later in this chapter; however, in general they follow the template of a standard UUOA with some additional provisions required to protect the Governments' interests in the development. These include such matters as the reservation of the right to approve the initial determination and re-determination; applicable law and arbitration; health and safety; movement of personnel across the international median line; transpor-tation; and taxation issues.[131]

The agreements are between the respective Governments and **13.48** as such are not binding directly on the interest holders; however,

---

[126] Royalty continues to exist in some jurisdictions but is no longer relevant in the UK where it has been abolished, at least in practice if not strictly in law. See para 4.29.

[127] Deemer, "Unitisation Agreements" at 3.

[128] English, "Unitisation Agreements", p 100.

[129] This may explain why most countries, excepting the US and Canada, require licence groups to submit "all the detailed operating agreement terms to the host government for approval, when such approval of unitization by the host government is required": J L Weaver and D F Asmus, "Unitizing Oil and Gas Fields Around the World: A Comparative Analysis of National Laws and Private Contracts" (2006) 28(1) *Houston Journal of International Law* 71, available from Association of International Petroleum Negotiators (AIPN).

[130] Steele-Nicholson, "Pendulum Procedures" at 234.

[131] English, "Unitisation Agreements", p 101.

they will be made binding through the application of the countries' national legislation. In the United Kingdom this is achieved through the application of the model clauses. Model Cl 28 provides that where the Minister is satisfied that any strata in the licensed area form part of a field which extend into an area controlled by another jurisdiction, and the Minister is satisfied that it is expedient[132] that the field should be unitised, the Minister may serve the licensee with a notice providing "such directions as the Minister may think fit, as to the manner in which the rights conferred by this licence shall be exercised".[133] The licensee is under an obligation to observe and perform all such requirements in relation to the licensed area as may be specified in the direction.[134] The model clause specifically provides that any such direction may add to, vary or revoke the provisions of a unit development scheme.[135]

13.49   It has been argued that international state practice may have led to the emergence of a customary rule of international law that would require states to co-operate in the exploitation of cross-boundary reservoirs.[136] There is certainly some evidence of this, for example the principles of co-operation exhibited by many states reflect those embodied in the 1982 Convention on the Law of the Sea which provides that "States bordering an enclosed or semi-enclosed sea should cooperate with each other in exercise of their rights and in the performance of their duties".[137] Reynolds comments that if this Convention was stronger in its wording as to require unitisation between states the result would be "maximized recovery (value) for all concerned parties, minimized waste and minimized environmental concerns and operating costs".[138] Ong reviewed UN General Assembly resolutions, the Convention and relevant case law to assess whether there is an international obligation for states to co-operate. He concluded that while the obligation to co-operate does not extend so far as to require states actually to participate in the joint development of shared reserves, many examples can be found

---

[132] Note that the test in this instance is expedience. Compare this to the rather stricter test which applies in domestic law: see para 13.11.

[133] Model Cl 28(1).

[134] Model Cl 28(2).

[135] Model Cl 28(3).

[136] R Lagoni, "Oil and Gas Deposits Across National Frontiers" (1979) 73 Am J Intl L 215.

[137] Art 123, as noted in Ong, "Joint Development" at 782.

[138] He comments that the Convention has been criticised for being too vague in parts, possibly as a result of trying to get the agreement ratified by all parties: Reynolds, "Delimitation" at 140.

whereby the joint development of international common zones is standard practice.[139]

The UK/Netherlands example

On 6 October 1965 the United Kingdom and the Netherlands signed   13.50
a bilateral delimitation agreement to establish the boundaries of
the Dutch Continental Shelf.[140] At the same time as the boundary
agreement the countries entered into an agreement to govern the
exploitation of any field which crossed the international border.[141]
Article 1 of this agreement provides that where a field extends across
the border the States "shall seek to reach agreement as to the manner
in which the structure or field shall be most effectively exploited
and the manner in which costs and proceeds relating thereto shall
be apportioned, after having invited the licensees concerned, if any,
to submit agreed proposals to this effect". Article 2 provides that if
the parties fail to reach an agreement the parties shall appoint an
arbitrator and be bound by his decision.[142]

The Markham field was the first cross-border field to be developed   13.51
between the United Kingdom and the Netherlands as a unitised
field. In 1985, under an exploration licence awarded to Ultramar
Exploration (Netherlands) BV, a reservoir of approximately
700 billion cubic feet was discovered to straddle the international

---

[139] Ong, "Joint Development" at 788. In addition to the three examples discussed at paras 13.50–13.60, Deemer notes also that, outside the UKCS, whether concession agreements, production sharing contracts or risk service contracts are the standard form of agreement used, "those documents frequently contain provisions giving government the power to require unitisation": Deemer, "Unitisation Agreements" at 1. For a detailed discussion of co-operation in the development of resources in international law, see P D Cameron, "The rules of engagement: Developing cross-border petroleum deposits in the North Sea and Caribbean" (2006) 55 ICLQ 559–586. For a discussion of joint development in the absence of agreement on international boundaries, see Y M Yusuf, "Is joint development a panacea for maritime boundary disputes and for the exploitation of offshore trans-boundary petroleum deposits?" (2009) 4 IELR 130; and also C W Dundas, "The impact of maritime boundary delimitation on the development of offshore mineral deposits" (1994) 20(4) *Resources Policy* 273.

[140] Neth Treaties Series (Tractatenblad) 1965, no 191 and (Tractatenblad) 1966, no 130. This treaty was amended on 28 January 1971 following the signing of delimitation agreements between the Netherlands, Germany and Denmark.

[141] Agreement between the Government of the United Kingdom of the Netherlands and the Government of the United Kingdom of Great Britain and Northern Ireland relating to the exploitation of single geological structures extending across the dividing line on the Continental Shelf under the North Sea, 6 October 1965 (Tractatenblad) 1965, no 192, as amended on 25 November 1971 (Tractatenblad) 1972, no 139.

[142] M Roggenkamp, "The Markham Field: Joint Exploitation by the Netherlands and the United Kingdom" [1992] 7 OGLTR 193 (hereinafter "Roggenkamp, 'The Markham Field'") at 194.

border.[143] The discovery was named the Markham Field Reservoirs. The countries signed the Markham Agreement on 26 May 1992[144] to govern the joint exploitation of the field.

13.52   The Markham Agreement was based on the unitisation agreements signed between the United Kingdom and Norway (as discussed in detail below) for the joint exploitation of gas fields straddling the United Kingdom–Norway border.[145] Under the Markham Agreement the Governments of both countries required their relevant licence groups to enter into a UUOA to govern the exploitation of the reservoir. We have already seen how UUOAs differ from JOAs. The Markham Agreement contains all these particular provisions, including the apportionment of petroleum and re-determination provisions.[146] A further variation, particular to cross-border UUOAs such as the Markham Agreement, is that each of the countries involved retains jurisdiction over that part of the field on its side of the border. In order to avoid conflict between the two jurisdictions the agreement contains special "umbrella" provisions declaring whether specific provisions of national laws are applicable or not. New obligations can also be created under the agreement, such as the requirement of approval by the Governments of both countries for any new unit operator or for any development plan, neither of which is usually required under Dutch law.[147]

13.53   Following Art 2 of the 1965 Agreement, the Markham Agreement contains provisions for dispute resolution.[148] In the first instance the parties must try to resolve the dispute through the Markham Commission, established for the purposes of implementing the agreement. If unresolved the two Governments must then enter into negotiations and it is only if these fail that the dispute may be submitted to an arbitral tribunal.

13.54   Other jurisdictional issues addressed by the agreement include safety and taxation. Both Governments may determine the safety measures they wish to apply in their own jurisdiction; however, uniform standards were required to make the operations workable. Article 10 of the Agreement provides standard safety regulations which include, among others, those recommended by the Cullen Report (discussed extensively in Chapter 7). In addition, both the

---

[143] Roggenkamp, "The Markham Field" at 194.
[144] Ie the Agreement relating to the Exploitation of the Markham Field Reservoirs and the Offtake of Petroleum Therefrom (hereinafter "Markham Agreement")
[145] Taverne, *Co-operative Agreements*, p 82.
[146] Arts 5 and 16 respectively.
[147] Roggenkamp, "The Markham Field" at 195.
[148] Art 23.

Health and Safety Executive of the United Kingdom and the equivalent body in the Netherlands[149] have access to all installations and information pertaining to the field. The United Kingdom and the Netherlands each have their own taxation regimes and all profits gained from the exploitation of the field are taxed in accordance with these regimes and also the applicable conventions on double taxation.

Roggenkamp concludes that the negotiation of agreements such as **13.55** the Markham Agreement is a time-consuming and difficult process; however, once agreed, they provide a framework for the successful development of the field and can be used as a template for any future unitisations between the countries.[150]

The UK/Norway example

The United Kingdom and Norway suite of agreements provides an **13.56** excellent example of successful trans-boundary unitisation and the progress that can be achieved by countries with a strong bilateral relationship. The United Kingdom and Norway signed a bilateral delimitation treaty on 10 March 1965. This agreement contained the first explicit provision for the action to be taken in the event of a cross-border discovery of petroleum. The treaty, as amended in November 2009, stipulated that:

> "If any single geological petroleum structure or petroleum field ... extends across the dividing line and the part of such structure or field which is situated on one side of the dividing line is exploitable, wholly or in part, from the other side of the dividing line, the Contracting Parties shall, in consultation with the licensees, if any, seek to reach agreement as to the manner in which the structure or field shall be most effectively exploited and the manner in which the proceeds deriving therefrom shall be apportioned."[151]

Although the treaty does not specify that the reservoir should be **13.57** exploited as a unit, this was the procedure followed by the states party. The treaty provided the foundation for the three cross-border unitisation agreements subsequently entered into, namely the Frigg, Statfjord and Murchison Field Agreements signed in 1976, 1979 and 1979 respectively.[152] The first of the agreements signed (the

---

[149] The Staatstoezicht op de Mijnen.

[150] Roggenkamp, "The Markham Field" at 197.

[151] Agreement between the Government of the United Kingdom of Great Britain and Northern Ireland and the Government of the Kingdom of Norway relating to the delimitation of the continental shelf between the two countries, 10 March 1965, as amended on 22 December 1978 and in November 2009 (hereinafter "UK–Norway Delimitation Treaty of 1965"), Art 4.

[152] Frigg Field Agreement (Cmnd 6491); Statfjord Field Agreement (Cmnd 8288); and

Frigg Agreement) and the agreement pertaining to the largest area of United Kingdom–Norway unitised reserves (the Statfjord Agreement) are outlined briefly below. The UK–Norway 2005 Framework Treaty is then considered in more detail.

Frigg Agreement

13.58 The Frigg field was initially discovered in 1969 and in 1972 it was found to straddle the international line of maritime demarcation between the UK and Norway. In accordance with Art 4 of the United Kingdom–Norway Delimitation Treaty the countries were obliged to agree on how the field should be developed and how the proceeds from such development should be apportioned. In this particular arrangement it was the United Kingdom and Norwegian licensees who made the first moves towards unitisation. In conjunction with their respective Governments, the licensees signed a series of agreements to unitise the Frigg field. These included: the Frigg Field Main Agreement, the Frigg Field Operating Agreement and the Frigg Field Expert Agreement. The host Governments then confirmed these arrangements in the Frigg Field Agreement dated 10 May 1976.[153] This agreement stated that "[t]he two Governments shall consult with a view to agreeing to a determination of the limits and estimated total reserves of the Frigg Field Reservoir and an apportionment of the reserves therein ... For this purpose the licensees shall be required to submit to the Governments a proposal for such determinations".[154]

13.59   The Agreement went on to state that a single operator acting for all licensees should develop the single unit and the countries should share the proceeds from the field in accordance with the proportion of the deposit within their jurisdiction. A commission was established to supervise the operations and administration of the field. Weaver *et al* note that to mitigate the potentially conflicting effect of the involvement of two separate jurisdictions the Agreement provided for consultation between the Governments on issues such as uniform safety and installation standards.[155]

Statfjord Agreement

13.60 The most important example, in terms of volume of oil and gas, is the Statfjord Agreement signed on 16 October 1979.[156] Taverne

---

Murchison Field Agreement (Cmnd 8270) (as amended by Cmnd 8577).

[153] Weaver *et al*, "International Unitization" at 109.

[154] Frigg Treaty, Art 2.

[155] Weaver *et al*, "International Unitization" at 111.

[156] Known as the Agreement between the Government of the United Kingdom of Great

notes that this agreement followed the form of the Frigg Field Agreement.[157] As with the Frigg Agreement, it contains the basic principle that the field should be exploited as a single unit. Unlike the Frigg Agreement, however, it contains no provisions on the manner in which the reserves should be exploited, the specific means of transportation to be used or the destination for the oil and associated gas. This is left to the individual licensees to agree in accordance with the provisions of the inter-state agreement. The Governments did, however, ensure that they retained control of important areas such as the right to approve the unit operator, the determination of the limits of the reservoir and the apportionment of reserves between the United Kingdom and Norwegian parts of the continental shelf. Either Government may also request a review of the reservoir and the apportionment of reserves in order to arrive at a re-determination.[158] Another issue reserved by the Governments is that of taxation. The Agreement states that profits from the field will be taxed in accordance with the laws of the United Kingdom and Norway respectively, and that the jurisdiction of each country over the continental shelf remains unaffected by the Agreement.

The 2005 UK–Norway Framework Treaty
On 4 April 2005, the United Kingdom Energy Minister and his **13.61** Norwegian counterpart finally agreed the text of the long-awaited new framework treaty on cross-border petroleum co-operation.[159] The Treaty covers the construction and operation of pipelines carrying oil and gas from Norway to the United Kingdom; the joint exploitation of reservoirs straddling the borderline; and the joint use of infrastructure. It also aims to harmonise regulations and simplify the administration of cross-border projects, one of the hopes being to remove the need for separate agreements, such as the Frigg, Statfjord and Murchison Agreements discussed above.

The Treaty contains specific provisions with regard to uniti- **13.62** sation. These include an obligation on each Government to unitise in accordance with the terms of the Framework Agreement, unless they mutually decide not to,[160] and to require their licensees to enter into a Licensees' Agreement to regulate the exploitation of a trans-

---

Britain and Northern Ireland and the Government of the Kingdom of Norway relating to the Statfjord Field Reservoirs and the Offtake of petroleum therefrom.
[157] Taverne, *Co-operative Agreements*, p 83.
[158] *Ibid*, p 84.
[159] The treaty is available for download from http://www.og.decc.gov.uk/upstream/infrastructure/frametext.htm (accessed 13 March 2011).
[160] Framework Agreement, Art 3.1(1).

boundary reservoir.[161] This agreement must be submitted to both Governments for their approval[162] and must contain provisions to the effect that, in the event of a conflict between the Licensees' Agreement and the Framework Agreement, the latter will prevail.[163] Government approval is also required for the appointment of the unit operator,[164] any development plan,[165] cessation of production,[166] and the decommissioning of installations associated with cross-boundary projects.[167] The Framework Agreement also contains provisions relevant to the determination[168] and re-determination of reserves and the provision of an independent expert in the event of disagreement.[169] It is noteworthy that the provisions relative to the expert's role and the basis on which he is to carry out a re-determination are remarkably open-textured and vague in comparison with the corresponding provisions in many UUOAs within the UK.[170] In addition to the provisions specific to unitisation, it should be noted that there are provisions for the establishment of a framework forum involving members of each Government to facilitate the implementation of the agreement,[171] and mechanisms for the settlement of disputes.[172]

13.63   It is clear that both Governments are seeking to simplify the process,[173] especially in the case of smaller fields that cannot justify

---

[161] Framework Agreement, Art 3.2(1).

[162] *Ibid*, Art 3.2(2).

[163] *Ibid*, Art 3.2(1).

[164] *Ibid*, Art 3.7.

[165] *Ibid*, Art 3.9(1).

[166] *Ibid*, Art 3.12.

[167] *Ibid*, Art 1.14.

[168] *Ibid*, Art 3.3.

[169] *Ibid*, Art 3.4, read with Annex D.

[170] *Ibid*, Art 3.4 provides for the appointment of a single expert "within 60 days" of Governments notifying each other of the disagreement, who should "act in accordance with the terms of Annex D". Annex D, para 2 then defines expert, and his role, as the person who can "provide undertakings in respect of any conflict of interest"; while Annex D, para 5 obliges him to provide a "preliminary decision" within "12 weeks of his appointment". Finally, Annex D, para 4 puts the condition that every communication with and from the expert must be shared with the other party if the other party is not already present at the joint-Governmental meetings. However, apart from these provisions there are no other specifics as to the expert's role and/or the basis on which he is to carry out re-determination.

[171] Framework Agreement, Art 1.15.

[172] *Ibid*, Art 5.

[173] Clear evidence of this came even before the Framework Agreement was finalised, when the UK Government agreed to waive its interest in the mainly Norwegian Boa Field and the Norwegian Government similarly waived its interest in the mainly British Playfair Field. (See Exchange of Notes dated 30 September and 4 October 2004 relative to the Boa and Playfair Fields (Cm 6412) at 4, para c.) In each case the extension into the other's territory was small and it was a condition of the arrangement that in neither

protracted governmental negotiations.[174] Both Governments also hope that these new arrangements will make the North Sea more attractive to potential investors and maximise the opportunities for renewed activity and use of existing infrastructure. This is a wise policy and one which is in keeping with the UK Government's general approach of taking a flexible and in many respects licensee-driven approach to regulation in order to prevent petroleum law and administration from acting as a barrier to attracting new investment.[175] Early indications are that the Framework Agreement is achieving its objectives. The first fields to make use of the Framework Agreement's provisions were Enoch and Blane, which had development plans approved on 1 July 2005, having lain undeveloped for a number of years "mainly because of the perceived trans-boundary complications and the difficulty of reaching commercial agreement between UK and Norwegian partners".[176]

CONCLUSION

This chapter has discussed the issues that arise when a reservoir is found to underlie more than one block or to straddle an international boundary. Unitisation is by no means a process without its imperfections. It is, however, widely regarded as being one of the most efficient contractual methods for the development of cross-boundary reservoirs, both by Governments who have implemented   **13.64**

---

case would active works be undertaken in respect of the area made subject to the waiver. The Agreement was made in order to simplify and accelerate the development project, and was made subject to a specific right to reconsider the manner in which these projects were governed in the event that one or another of the extensions turned out to be larger than anticipated. See also Norwegian Ministry of Petroleum and Energy, "UK and Norway open way for two new North Sea projects", available for download from http://www.regjeringen.no/en/archive/Bondeviks-2nd-Government/ministry-of-petroleum-and-energy/Nyheter-og-pressemeldinger/2004/uk_and_norway_open_way_for_two.html?id=254176 (accessed 13 March 2011).

[174] One of the principal objectives of the joint PILOT and Kon-Kraft Report, *Unlocking Value Through Closer Relationships*, one of the main proponents of the Framework Agreement, was to streamline cross-border working practices and improve efficiencies. It was felt that the impact of this effort would be "particularly material at the field scale. This improved competitiveness will be especially attractive for smaller UK and Norwegian companies and new entrants targeting niche opportunities adjacent to the median line". See PILOT and Kon-Kraft, *Unlocking Value Through Closer Relationships* (2002), p 11.

[175] See also, eg, the introduction of the frontier and promote licences, discussed at paras 4.54–4.61 and 4.62–4.68 and the mature province initiatives discussed in Chapter 5.

[176] See DTI, "First Strike for UK-Norway Deal", available for download from http://www.eeegr.com/news/info.php?refnum=938&startnum=1477 (accessed 13 March 2011).

measures for compulsory unitisation and by the individual licensees who are happy to embrace this method without such force.

13.65   To be successful in its implementation, sufficient care must be taken when drafting the UUOA. If the parties are pragmatic in their negotiations and considerable investment is made when drawing up the UUOA, unitisation can be an exceptionally useful method for the joint development of reserves.

CHAPTER 14

RISK ALLOCATION IN OIL AND GAS CONTRACTS

Greg Gordon

As has already been noted, the oil and gas industry is an inher- **14.1** ently hazardous one.[1] Exploring for, producing, transporting and processing volatile hydrocarbons is attended by a whole host of risks: to people, property, the environment, and to the valuable commodity itself. The degree of difficulty associated with these operations, and therefore the level of risk which attends them, is only heightened when – as is commonly the case in the United Kingdom[2] – oil and gas reserves are located offshore.

The oil and gas industry has developed a number of contracting **14.2** practices to allow it to regulate and manage these physical[3] risks. Generally speaking, and subject to certain important exceptions,[4] up- and midstream oil and gas contracts seek to depart quite radically from the common law's presumptions about how such risk should be allocated. Three vehicles are commonly used to achieve this risk re-allocation: (a) indemnity and hold harmless clauses; (b) clauses which exclude or limit liability for what are commonly, if rather loosely, described as "consequential losses"; and (c) overall limitations on liability. Each will be discussed in turn.

---

[1] See the discussion at para 8.1.
[2] As we have already seen, the UK is primarily an offshore oil and gas province: see, eg, para 4.73.
[3] Sometimes also described as "insurable" risk.
[4] See para 14.24.

INDEMNIFICATION

Introduction to the concept of indemnification

14.3   An indemnity is a contractual provision whereby the indemnifying party agrees to make a payment to the party having the benefit of the indemnity in the event that the indemnified party suffers loss as a result of the occurrence of a specified event. As we shall see, indemnification is – at least in some contexts – a contractual device which the courts have tended to treat with considerable suspicion.[5] It is nevertheless a commonly encountered legal concept, by no means particular to oil and gas contracts. Indemnification lies at the heart of the law of marine[6] and fire[7] insurance. It also features in construction contracts, where contractors will commonly provide their employer with indemnities against personal injury or death, or damage to property, in any way associated with the work contracted for.[8] The concept will also be familiar to the company lawyer: in a corporate acquisition and disposal, the seller will frequently be asked to provide an indemnity in respect of liabilities incurred by the company in the period between the deal's conclusion and its completion.[9] Many other examples could be given.[10] For the remainder of this chapter, the one-sided[11] indemnity clauses just described will be referred to as simple indemnity clauses in order to differentiate them from mutual indemnity clauses, which will be discussed below.

Indemnity and hold harmless clauses

14.4   As we shall see in greater detail below, the oil and gas industry makes extensive use of a particular form of wording in its risk allocation

---

[5] See paras 14.10 and 14.37.

[6] Marine Insurance Act 1906, s 1: "A contract of marine insurance is a contract whereby the insurer undertakes to indemnify the assured, in manner and to the extent thereby agreed, against marine losses."

[7] *Castellain* v *Preston* (1883) 11 QBD 380 per Brett LJ at 386.

[8] See the Joint Contracts Tribunal *Standard Form of Contract*, cll 6.1 and 6.2 respectively, discussed at J Uff, *Construction Law* (9th edn, 2005) at 380f. For an illustration of cl 6.1.2 in operation, see *Scottish & Newcastle plc* v *G D Construction (St Albans) Ltd* [2003] EWCA Civ 16.

[9] See, eg, J Young and J Kitching, "Buying and Selling a Business: Warranties and Indemnities" 1995 6(10) ICCLR 336. For a discussion in the specific context of the sale and purchase of and oil and gas business, see Chapter 17.

[10] For instance, one of the leading cases on the construction of indemnities (discussed further at para 14.34) is concerned with a lease: *Canada Steamship Lines* v *The King* [1952] AC 192.

[11] The term "one-sided" is here used not to suggest that simple indemnity clauses are necessarily unfair or biased, merely to denote the fact that in a simple indemnity clause, the indemnity travels in one direction only – from the indemnifier to the indemnified party. No reciprocal indemnity is provided.

clauses. A party will very often offer not merely to indemnify, but to indemnify and hold harmless, the other party.[12] Before the UK Supreme Court decision in *Farstad Supply AS* v *Enviroco Ltd*,[13] commentators on the industry's risk allocation practice generally considered the words "and hold harmless" to add little or nothing to the content of such clauses, which were simply described as "indemnity clauses".[14] It is submitted that this approach accurately mirrored that of the industry. The oil and gas industry routinely used the terms "indemnify", "hold harmless" and "indemnify and hold harmless" interchangeably in its risk allocation arrangements. Thus, in the LOGIC Standard Contracts for the Oil and Gas Industry, clauses by which a party indemnifies and holds harmless the other are described simply as "Indemnities".[15] Similarly, while the industry's attempt to put in place a contractual risk allocation regime between offshore contractors who would not otherwise have a contractual relationship[16] is known as throughout the industry as the Industry Mutual Hold Harmless Deed,[17] the Deed is formally entitled the "Mutual Indemnity and Hold Harmless Deed".[18] Although the Deed's central risk allocation clause uses the wording "indemnify and hold harmless", the clause is entitled "Indemnities by the Signatories"[19] and the Deed is itself referred to in the Deed of Adherence (by which parties other than the original signatories can enter the scheme) as the "Indemnity Deed". However, in *Farstad* v *Enviroco* the Supreme Court held that a clause whereby the owner of a vessel under charter agreed to "indemnify and hold harmless" the charterer against all liability resulting from loss of or damage to the vessel was not a pure indemnity clause but a mixed

---

[12] That said, clauses which utilise the word "indemnify" are not unknown in an oil and gas context, particularly in contracts relating to maritime matters such as towage: see, eg, TOWCON cl 18 referred to in *A Turtle Offshore SA* v *Superior Trading Inc* [2008] EWHC 3034 (Admlty), [2008] 2 CLC 953.

[13] [2010] UKSC 18, 2010 SCLR 379 (hereinafter "*Farstad* v *Enviroco*").

[14] See, eg, Chapter 13 of the first edition of this work; G Gordon, "Indemnification and Contribution: *Farstad Supply AS* v *Enviroco Ltd*" (2010) 14 Edin LR 102; T Hewitt, "Who is to Blame? Allocating Liability in Upstream Project Contract" (2008) 26 JENRL 177 at 182; T Daintith, G Willoughby and A Hill, *United Kingdom Oil and Gas Law* (3rd edn, looseleaf, 2000–date), para 1-845; D Sharp, *Offshore Oil and Gas Insurance* (1994) at p 108.

[15] See, eg, LOGIC, Supply *of Major Items of Plant and Equipment* (2nd edn), available online at: http://www.logic-oil.com/supply2.pdf (accessed 21 February 2011), cl 22.

[16] Discussed further in paras 14.66–14.70.

[17] See, eg, LOGIC, *Industry Mutual Hold Harmless: About*, available for download from: http://www.imhh.com/about.cfm (accessed 21 February 2011).

[18] LOGIC, Mutual Indemnity and Hold Harmless Deed, available for download from: http://www.imhh.com/deed/IMHH_Deed.pdf (accessed 21 February 2011).

[19] *Ibid*, cl 2

provision containing elements of indemnity and exclusion.[20] Whether it operated as an indemnity or an exclusion would depend upon whether the clause sought to determine who was to bear responsibility for "third party exposure" (in which case the clause would be an indemnity) or whether it resolved "direct exposure to the other contracting party" (in which case it would be an exclusion).[21] On the facts of the case in question, the owner had suffered damage to his own property. The case was therefore seen by the Supreme Court as one of "direct exposure"; hence the clause was, on this occasion, to be seen as an exclusion of liability clause.[22] Although the full import of this decision is not yet clear, the fact that indemnity and hold harmless clauses have now been held by the most authoritative court in the land to operate, at least sometimes, as an exclusion of liability means that there will be occasions when such clauses will have to comply with the provisions of the Unfair Contract Terms Act 1977. See further the discussion at para 14.26.

Mutual indemnity and mutual indemnity and hold harmless clauses

14.5 A mutual indemnity – sometimes also called a "reciprocal indemnity", a "cross-indemnity" or a "knock for knock" indemnity – is a contractual device where the parties with the one hand give and with the other hand take an indemnity in respect of a species of loss which, if the indemnity is to avoid circularity,[23] must not be identical to each other, but which are usually closely related. A mutual indemnity therefore differs from a simple indemnity, where one party has the *burden* of giving the indemnity (acts as indemnifier) and the other party has the *benefit* of being indemnified. In a mutual indemnity, each party is simultaneously both an *indemnifier* (in relation to one species of loss) and the *indemnified* (in relation to a different, but related, species of loss.) In the oil and gas context, it is usual for the

---

[20] In so holding, their Lordships laid considerable emphasis upon the fact that the parties to the contract had entitled their clause "Exceptions/Indemnities". This, thought Lord Clarke, (delivering a speech concurred in by Lord Phillips) was a feature of "particular importance", and strong evidence of the parties' intentions (*Farstad* v *Enviroco* per Lord Clarke at para 22; see also Lord Mance at para 56). However, their Lordships seem to have failed to notice that there were a number of indications of a contrary intention within the clause, including the obligation to exchange "mutual hold harmless indemnities" with other parties in certain circumstances. This wording might tend to suggest that the words "hold harmless" were intended only to describe a particular type of indemnity clause. Speculation is to an extent idle, but given the importance apparently attached to the title of the clause, one cannot help but wonder how their Lordships' decision would have differed had the parties followed the form of the LOGIC contracts and entitled their clause "Indemnities".

[21] *Farstad* v *Enviroco* per Lord Mance, para 59.

[22] *Ibid* Lord Clarke at para 29 and per Lord Mance at para 59.

[23] Circularity is discussed later in this paragraph.

parties to enter into not just mutual indemnity provisions but into mutual indemnity *and hold harmless* clauses, thus bringing into play the further conceptual issues described at para 14.4.

It is important to appreciate that, to be effective, a mutual **14.6** indemnity or mutual indemnity and hold harmless clause must not be drawn so as to provide that each party indemnifies (or indemnifies and holds harmless) the other against the occurrence of *exactly the same species of loss*. To illustrate the point by way of example, let us imagine that A and B enter into an arrangement where A grants B an indemnity against B's house burning down, and B also grants A an indemnity against B's house burning down. In such a situation, all the clause succeeds in achieving is a position where the losses arising if the house burns down is passed from one party to another *ad infinitum*. Such a clause (sometimes described as a "circular indemnity"[24]) is ineffectual[25] and leaves the risk it purports to allocate to be borne by the parties in the way provided for by the law at large.

Let us now consider an example where A indemnifies B in respect **14.7** of the losses incurred by B if B's house burns down, and B in turn indemnifies A against the losses that A suffers if A's house burns down. At first glance this may look similar to the example given immediately above. There is, however, one crucial difference. The species of loss in respect of which the indemnity is given, although conceptually related (they both pertain to the losses suffered when houses burn down) are not *exactly* the same: A agrees to accept the losses to *B's* property, and B agrees to accept the losses to *A's* property. Thus the parties have, on this occasion, avoided circularity and succeeded in reallocating the respective risk factors.

Indemnity and hold harmless provisions in context

Introduction to simple indemnity and hold harmless clauses in oil and gas contracts

Simple indemnity clauses are used in oil and gas contracts in at least **14.8** two ways. First, the petroleum industry sometimes just provides the commercial context for the kind of risk factor described at

---

[24] *Slessor* v *Vetco Gray*, unreported, 7 July 2006, Court of Session, Outer House, available for download from: http://www.scotcourts.gov.uk/opinions/2006CSOH104. html (accessed 1 February 2011). See the submissions of counsel summarised by Lord Glennie at para 6. On the facts, the court rejected the argument that the indemnity was circular.

[25] It is also commercially unrealistic: why on earth would B indemnify A against the loss of B's own house? However, the example is given because in practice one does, from time to time, encounter circular indemnities – almost invariably they arise by accident, when something has gone wrong in the drafting of the indemnity clause.

para 14.3. Oil and gas contracts therefore commonly contain a number of simple indemnity clauses of a type no different to those routinely found in commercial agreements. In addition, some, but no means all,[26] up- or midstream oil and gas contracts will also contain one or more simple indemnity and hold harmless clauses designed to allocate between the parties some of the risk factors specific to the petroleum industry. These clauses will frequently be supplemented by a provision stating that the indemnifier[27] will not just indemnify and hold harmless the indemnified party, but also *defend* claims taken against the indemnified party.[28] This has the effect of imposing upon the indemnifier the burden of conducting the defence of any litigation that may arise, but also of conferring upon the indemnifier the right to control the manner in which the defence is conducted. Many indemnifiers consider that the benefit of the right to control the conduct of the defence outweighs the burden of conducting it. Best practice is now thought to be not to rely solely upon the word "defend" but to include a conduct of claims clause expressly stipulating the way in which claims are to be handled. Such a clause is absent in the present draft of the LOGIC standard form contracts, but is commonly revised into contracts based upon the LOGIC standard forms.

14.9   Many examples could be given of occasions where one party will usually offer the other the benefit of a simple indemnity and hold harmless provision. As we have already seen at para 12.39, a joint operating agreement will commonly contain a clause by which the non-operators cumulatively and in accordance with their respective percentage interests indemnify and hold harmless the operator against all losses incurred by the joint venture, with the exception of those occasioned by the operator's wilful misconduct. The justification is that, as the operator acts gratuitously, it would be inequitable if it were to bear all or a disproportionate share of the joint venture's commercial risk. And in operator-to-contractor contracts which involve the creation

---

[26] See para 14.24.

[27] Although, as we have seen, the Supreme Court held in *Farstad* v *Enviroco* (discussed at para 14.4) that the words "hold harmless" add an additional element to an indemnity clause, meaning that indemnity and hold harmless clauses will in certain circumstances operate not merely as indemnities but also as exclusion clauses, for the sake of brevity and convenience the parties giving and receiving these clauses will be described as the indemnifier and the indemnified party throughout this chapter.

[28] See the observations by LP Rodger in the Inner House phase of *Caledonia North Sea Ltd* v *London Bridge Engineering Ltd* 2000 SLT 1123 at 1155. The standard contracts for the oil industry developed as part of the CRINE initiative and now maintained by LOGIC contain such a provision: see, eg, LOGIC, *General Conditions of Contract for Services (On- and off-shore)* (2nd edn, 2003), available for download from: http://www.logic-oil.com/contracts.cfm (accessed 1 February 2011) (hereinafter "LOGIC, *Services*") at cl 19.1: "The contractor shall ... Save, indemnify, *defend* and hold harmless ...". See also the discussion on the IMHH deed at para 14.56.

of, or direct intervention with, the well – for instance, contracts for the hire of a mobile drilling unit[29] or for the provision of well services[30] – the indemnity and hold harmless provisions are usually significantly more complex than those associated with other operator-to-contractor contracts. The operator will ordinarily indemnify and hold harmless the contractor against risks such as loss of or damage to the hole,[31] blowout, fire, the well becoming uncontrollable or damage to the reservoir, geological formation or underground strata, howsoever caused.

The courts have sometimes viewed indemnity clauses with suspicion, on the basis that when they are found in a contract, this is because a dominant party has imposed them upon a weaker one.[32] However, in UKCS operator-to-contractor agreements, unilateral indemnity and hold harmless clauses are most commonly granted by the *operator* to the *contractor*.[33] Such indemnities are not given because the operator is weak, but because it is strong. The losses that could accrue in the event that the well is lost or damaged are potentially very substantial; so large that it might not be economic, or perhaps even possible, for contractors to obtain insurance against these contingencies. However, the operator requires the well to be drilled if he is to produce from the discovery, and is (or traditionally has been – given the changing face of the UKCS, this proposition is no longer universally true) of a sufficient size to absorb the losses if they come to pass.[34] It is (or has been) therefore willing to accept them.   14.10

The author is, however, aware of at least one area where the industry's practice is less innocent. It is not unknown for oil and   14.11

---

[29] See, eg, LOGIC, *General Conditions of Contract for Mobile Drilling Rigs* (2002), available for download from: http://www.logic-oil.com/contracts.cfm (accessed 21 February 2011) (hereinafter "LOGIC, *Mobile Drilling Rigs*") at cl 18.

[30] See eg LOGIC, *General Conditions of Contract for Well Services* (2nd edn, 2002), available for download from: http://www.logic-oil.com/contracts.cfm (accessed 21 February 2011) (hereinafter "LOGIC, Well Services") at cl 19.

[31] However, these indemnities may differ somewhat in their precise content. Note, for instance, that in LOGIC, *Well Services*, cl 19.9(a) the operator offers a full indemnity in respect of loss of or damage to the hole, while in LOGIC, *Mobile Drilling Rigs*, cl 18.6(a) an indemnity is given subject to a (quite tightly confined) carve-out provision in respect of damage to hole caused by contractor's negligence. "Carve outs" (qualifications to indemnities) are discussed at paras 14.21–14.23.

[32] This belief informs US controls on indemnification which are discussed further at para 14.26. See also the discussion of the *Orbit Valve* case at para 14.35.

[33] Perhaps the major exception to this is in the case of offshore construction works where the contractor will commonly be asked to provide a one-sided indemnity to the operator in respect of the recovery, removal or marking of any wreck or debris associated with the work under the contract: see, eg, LOGIC, *General Conditions of Contract for Marine Construction* (2nd edn, 2004), available for download from: http://www.logic-oil.com/contracts.cfm (accessed 21 February 2011) at cl 22.2(5)(a).

[34] As the UKCS matures and a more diverse set of companies become operators, there will be a greater need for operators to carry insurance against such risks.

gas companies entering into contracts with employment agencies for the provision of workers to demand an indemnity from the agency against the risk that the workers make an employment tribunal claim against the company, and to seek to justify this on the basis that this is a standard oil industry indemnity clause. With respect, it is nothing of the kind. This has nothing to do with the sorts of physical or insurable risks which have thus far been under discussion; it is instead an attempt to secure an indemnity in relation to a commercial risk of a nature which it is inequitable to ask the agency to bear. Such use of indemnity clauses is to be deprecated.

Introduction to mutual indemnity and hold harmless provisions in oil and gas contracts

14.12 As has already been noted, the oil and gas industry is by no means alone in making use of indemnity clauses. However, the oil and gas industry utilises indemnity and hold harmless clauses in a more thoroughgoing way than most other industries. This is borne out by, for example, the amount of time invested by the court in *Caledonia North Sea Ltd* v *London Bridge Engineering Ltd* ("*London Bridge*")[35] in examining the particular features of the oil industry which give rise to what is still viewed as an unusual and rather counter-intuitive practice.[36]

14.13   There is a tendency to view mutual indemnity and hold harmless provisions as difficult clauses to draft and understand.[37] There is considerable justification for this. Even experienced lawyers or contract analysts entering the oil and gas industry for the first time may find it is not easy to draft a wholly satisfactory set of indemnity provisions,[38] as the failed attempts and "borderline successes" which litter the case reports readily attest.[39] All that said, many of the

---

[35] Rather confusingly, as a number of defenders settled the claims against them and dropped out of the case in the period between the Inner House appeal and the case's hearing in the House of Lords, the House of Lords phase of the case is reported as *Caledonia North Sea Ltd* v *British Telecommunications plc*. In the interests of consistency the case will be referred to as "*London Bridge*" throughout.

[36] In the Inner House of the Court of Session (*London Bridge*, 2000 SLT 1123) see, eg, section 2.5 of Lord Rodger's speech, from 1150, Lord Sutherland at 1174E–F and L, and Lord Gill at 1213F–H. In the House of Lords (*London Bridge*, orse *British Telecommunications plc* 2002 SC (HL) 117, [2002] 1 All ER (Comm) 321), see Lord Bingham at paras 7–9 and Lord Hoffmann at paras 81–82.

[37] See, eg, D Peng, "Mutual Indemnities in North Sea Contracts – Liability and Insurance Clauses" in D Peng (ed), *Insurance and Legal Issues in the Oil Industry* (1993) at p 156.

[38] The presence of industry-accepted styles such as the LOGIC contracts referred to at paras 14.8 and 14.9 and the IMHH Deed described at paras 14.50–14.64 makes the process less daunting than once it was, albeit that, as with all styles, the terms of these documents should never be adopted uncritically.

[39] See the cases and issues discussed throughout paras 14.35–14.47.

problems that arise with indemnification are essentially points of detail, most of which arise because of the complexity and hazardous nature of the operations and risks that the contract seeks to govern, but some of which as a result of the unnatural interpretation the courts have traditionally given to indemnity clauses.[40] These difficulties are generally susceptible to being resolved by careful thought and skilful drafting, although this can lead to lengthy and complex clauses.[41] However, following *Farstad v Enviroco*, the twin questions of what is the true legal nature of the clause and what consequences flow from its legal nature arise much more acutely than previously.

While there are certainly difficulties here, the commercial purpose   **14.14**
of an indemnity and hold harmless clause is quite simple. The parties are allocating (more properly, *re-allocating*[42]) between themselves the risk of the occurrence of a particular type of loss. As we have already seen, in the context of a simple indemnity and hold harmless clause, one party is agreeing that it is better placed then the other to bear the risk of a particular type of loss.[43] By contrast, in the case of a mutual indemnity and hold harmless clause, the parties are generally saying that neither of them should have sole responsibility for a particular species of risk – for instance, the risk that people engaged on the contract may be injured or killed – but that it is appropriate to divide between themselves the responsibility for that type of risk. The clause will therefore commence with the party identifying the aspect(s) of a given type of loss for which it is willing to take responsibility, and those in respect of which it is not. Each party then agrees to indemnify and hold harmless the other in respect of the element of the potential loss that it has accepted, and in return receives the benefit of an indemnity and hold harmless provision relative to the aspect of the potential loss accepted by the other party. So if A and B are respectively an oil company and a contractor who have entered into a contract, in a typical mutual hold-harmless indemnity provision pertaining to the risk that personal injury or death will befall one or another of the parties' personnel while engaged on the contract,[44] A

---

[40] Again, see the discussion at paras 14.35–14.47.

[41] See, eg, LOGIC, *Mobile Drilling Rigs*, cl 18.

[42] This exercise does not take place in a vacuum; the law has a pre-existing view on how, in the absence of agreement, such risks should be borne. See further the discussion at para 14.25.

[43] See paras 14.3 and 14.7–14.9.

[44] Such as may be found throughout the suite of LOGIC Standard Conditions: see, eg, LOGIC, General Term and Conditions of *Contract for Supply of Major Items of Plant and Equipment* (2nd edn, 2003), available for download from: http://www.logic-oil.com/contracts.cfm (accessed 21 February 2011) (hereinafter "LOGIC, *Supply of Major Items*"), cll 22.1(b) and 22.2(b). For a discussion on the potential impact, following *Farstad v Enviroco*, of the Unfair Contract Terms Act 1977 upon such clauses, see para 14.26.

will confirm that it accepts responsibility for any injuries or fatalities suffered by A's own personnel, however caused, and that it will indemnify and hold harmless B in respect of that category of loss. B agrees the converse: that it will accept responsibility for any injuries or fatalities suffered by B's own personnel, irrespective of how these were caused, and that it will indemnify and hold harmless A in respect of such loss.[45]

14.15   Mutual indemnity and hold harmless provisions will also commonly be agreed in relation to other categories of risk. An operator-to-contractor agreement will typically also contain such a clause in respect of loss of or damage to property, where A confirms that it accepts responsibility for loss of or damage to A's property, however caused, and that it will indemnify and hold harmless B in respect of that category of loss, and B agrees to accept responsibility for loss of or damage to B's property, howsoever caused, and indemnifies and holds harmless A relative to such losses.[46] Pollution risk will also sometimes be divided up along similar lines, with the contractor accepting certain kinds of pollution – commonly, that emanating from its own equipment – and the operator accepting other kinds – typically, all other instances;[47] however it is important to note that indemnities for pollution risk are more likely than those already discussed to be cut into by a qualification.[48] Consequential losses will also commonly be the subject of exclusions or indemnity provisions; see further the discussion at paras 14.66–14.50.

The rationale for a mutual indemnity and hold harmless regime in the oil and gas context

14.16   The rationale underlying simple indemnity and hold harmless provisions has already been given.[49] A number of factors have been advanced as the reason for the oil and gas industry's use of mutual indemnity and hold harmless clauses. In the leading work on UK offshore oil and gas insurance, the rationale for is presented thus:

> "If an individual is injured he will expect to have a right to sue any party who may have been guilty of negligence leading to the circumstances which caused the injury. This party may be another contractor, the Principal or his employer, or any combination of all three. The

---

[45] For a discussion of drafting issues relative to "personnel" and cognate phrases, see para 14.46.

[46] For an example of such sub-clause, see LOGIC, *Supply of Major Items*, cll 22.1(a) and 22.2(2). For a discussion of drafting issues concerning the definition of "property", see para 14.47.

[47] See LOGIC, *Mobile Drilling Rigs*, cll 18.3 and 18.4.

[48] See paras 14.21 and 14.22.

[49] See paras 14.7–14.9.

issue can become complicated by reason of contributory negligence. Determining liability and awarding costs can be a lengthy process in these circumstances, and this can only add to the anguish of the injured party, or the dependents of the deceased who may have been the sole breadwinner. The employer therefore accepts a responsibility to provide for his employees and will generally give the party with whom he is contracting a full indemnity in respect of any suit or action brought against that other party."[50]

Sharp's justification was accepted by several of the judges in *London Bridge*, the main piece of litigation to arise out of the Piper Alpha disaster.[51] However, it is only partially convincing. By definition, it can only serve to explain why the industry adopts such an approach in relation to personal injury; it cannot explain why the industry takes a virtually identical approach in relation to damage to property, or a broadly similar approach in relation to other matters such as pollution costs and consequential loss. It is certainly true that by and large the industry prefers swift and certain resolution to its disputes, and that it does not generally favour time-consuming and costly litigation.[52] But in so far as Sharp suggests that the *primary reason* for the existence of the mutual indemnity regime is the industry's desire to give an effectual remedy to, or diminish the anguish of, the injured party or his dependants, he would seem to overstate his position. It is unreal-

14.17

---

[50] D Sharp, *Offshore Oil and Gas Insurance* (1994) at p 108.

[51] In the House of Lords phase of the case, reported at 2002 SC (HL) 117, [2002] 1 All ER (Comm) 321, see the *dictum* of Lord Bingham at para 7 and that of Lord Hoffmann at para 82. In the earlier Inner House phase, reported at 2000 SLT 1123, see LP Rodger (who is rather more agnostic about Sharp's justification than his colleagues) at 1150L–1151B, Lord Sutherland at 1174F, Lord Coulsfield at 1202K and Lord Gill at 1213J–K.

[52] See, eg, Peng "Mutual Indemnities" at 157. Among the main reasons given for the practice are "that it permits the parties to assess and accept the risks more easily" and that "it avoids delays in claim settlement and it reduces the fighting of lawsuits". However, it is not immediately apparent to the present author that indemnification reduces disputes. Clauses are scrutinised carefully before claims are accepted and, if there is disagreement between the parties (or more particularly, between the parties' insurers) about the proper construction of the clause, litigation will follow which may prove to be time-consuming and costly: see, eg, *London Bridge*. The Piper Alpha disaster occurred on 6 July 1988. The proof began on 3 March 1993; in all, 391 days of evidence were heard. The case was not finally concluded until judgment was handed down in the House of Lords on 7 February 2002. See also the comments of Circuit Judge Brown in *Fontenot v Mesa Petroleum Co*, quoted by LP Rodger in *London Bridge* 2000 SLT 1123 at 1151C–F. It may be that in some cases the fact of indemnification brings a quicker resolution *to the claim of the injured party*: this seems to have occurred in both *London Bridge* and *Campbell v Conoco (UK) Ltd* [2003] 1 All ER (Comm) 35 at para 6. Even this, however, does not seem to be a universal truth: see the experience of the pursuer in *Slessor v Vetco Gray*. The pursuer suffered severe injuries in an accident in May 2003. Liability was in principle established on 23 March 2007 (see 2007 SLT 400) but even then a number of issues remained outstanding, among them the construction of the contractual indemnity clause, discussed further at paras 14.41–14.42.

istic to suggest that such altruistic concerns lie at the very heart of the industry's approach to risk allocation. These factors are more likely to be a fortunate side-effect of the practice than its *raison d'être*. The principal reasons for the mutual indemnification regime are far more likely to be business ones. This was recognised by Lord President Rodger in the Court of Session phase of *London Bridge* when he noted that the practice of indemnification was "fundamental to the economics of the North Sea operation".[53] Insurance (and the broader but related concept of risk management) is the economic driver that makes this so.[54] It may at first sight be surprising that something which seems to be an ancillary matter should be so fundamental. However, in a high-risk endeavour such as the offshore oil and gas industry, insurance premia are not marginal costs but major expenses.[55]

14.18 If the contractual arrangements associated with oil and gas operations were simple, the mere fact that insurance is expensive might not justify the effort of superimposing a risk allocation model upon that already provided by law. However, they are not. In *London Bridge*, Lord Bingham identified two key features which underpinned an understanding of the case. The first was the hazardous nature of oil and gas operations, which we have already discussed. The second was "the involvement of many contractors and sub-contractors".[56] Oil platforms are not staffed wholly, or even mainly, by the operator's personnel. At any given moment in time one can reasonably expect there to be representatives from upwards of 20 other companies on board.[57] If a large

---

[53] *London Bridge* 2000 SLT 1123 at 1150I.

[54] See T Daintith, G Willoughby and A Hill, *United Kingdom Oil and Gas Law* (3rd edn, looseleaf, 2000–date), para 1-845: "The client will, any event, normally carry insurance cover for his own employees and his own property and the cost of this insurance would not be reduced if the particular contractor was also required to be insured against the same risks. It is thus normal for the client and the contractor to assume full liability, and give each other mutual indemnities, for claims arising out of death of or injury to their own employees and for loss or damage to their own property ..., regardless of any negligence or default on the part of the other party or its employees, agents or sub-contractors."

[55] So great is the expense that some super majors commonly choose to self-insure (ie not to enter into contracts of insurance) where the law permits. See, eg, BP, *Annual Report and Accounts 2005* at 26, "INSURANCE: The group generally restricts its purchase of insurance to situations where this is required for legal or contractual reasons. This is because external insurance is not considered an economic means of financing losses for the group. Losses will therefore be borne as they arise rather than being spread over time through insurance premiums with attendant transaction costs." This choice may seem startling, but as insurers are commercial organisations who include a profit element in the price of their premia, if one is sufficiently asset-rich to be able to absorb serious one-off losses, one should find that, in the long term, it is more efficient not to insure than to do so. Naturally, however, this approach is too high-risk to be prudent for smaller companies.

[56] 2002 SC (HL) 117, [2002] 1 All ER (Comm) 321 per Lord Bingham of Cornhill at para 2.

[57] For instance, of the 165 people on the platform who lost their lives in the Piper Alpha disaster (167 people died in all; 2 were crew of the fast rescue ship *Westhaven*), 31 were

proportion of these companies were required to carry insurance against the fairly remote, but potentially catastrophic, risk that they might cause or contribute towards the destruction of the platform and/or widespread injury or loss of life among those on board,[58] then, always assuming that such insurance cover could be obtained, the cumulative cost of doing so would be very considerable. Nor would any additional sum of insurance be being bought for the additional expense: the policies would simply run in parallel, and in the event of a catastrophic event (assuming that the cause of the calamity could be identified, and was attributable to one contractor) only one policy would be claimed upon, and the remaining contractors' policies, and that of the operator, would prove to have been surplus to requirements. This would add considerably to the cost of operations without adding any value to them. Counter-intuitive as it may at first appear, on analysis it can be seen that there are sound economic and operational reasons for the practice of mutual indemnification.

Back-to-back indemnity and hold harmless provisions in oil and gas contracts

Although at any given time there may be somewhere between 20 and 50 contractors on a producing platform, only a handful of these parties will be in a *direct* contractual relationship with the operator. So for instance, in the production phase of a platform's life, the operator will ordinarily enter into a handful of lead contracts through which it will entrust important parts of the platform's functions to three or four contractors – typically a rig services manager, a well services supervisor, and a drilling company. Most of the other "contractors" represented on the platform will be in a direct contractual relationship not with the operator, but with either the layer of contractors just described, or with their subcontractors. Viewed from the operator's perspective, these parties will be subcontractors, sub-subcontractors,

14.19

---

employed by the operator. The remaining 134 were employed by 24 different contractors: see London Bridge 2002 SC (HL) 117, [2002] 1 All ER (Comm) 321 per Lord Bingham of Cornhill at para 2. See also LOGIC, *About Industry Mutual Hold Harmless*, available for download from: http://www.imhh.com/about.cfm (accessed 21 February 2011) (hereinafter "LOGIC, *About*"), under the heading "The Problem" – "On a production or drilling facility it is not unusual to have 25 to 50 contractors working alongside each other".

[58] Not all contractors would necessarily be in a position to cause catastrophic loss. It is hard to imagine, for example, that the catering contractor could cause the total loss of a platform. But a fire in the kitchen or major food poisoning incident on a platform might very well cause the installation to be shut down for a period of time, potentially causing significant loss of profit. For a further discussion on claims for loss of profit, see the discussion on consequential loss in paras 14.66–14.70.

and so on. Thus at any given time[59] there will be a number of chains of contractual relationships in place.[60]

14.20   The significance of the above to is that every link in the chain is a contract in which the parties have to agree how to allocate risk as between themselves. The full economic benefits[61] of instituting an indemnity and hold harmless regime do not accrue if only some of the parties are included in it; moreover, if some parties are part of the regime and others are not, there is a serious risk of misunderstandings as to who bears which risk, and of accompanying litigation and gaps in insurance cover.[62] The general practice is therefore for each of the contracts within the chain to contain so-called "back-to-back" provisions. The overall intent of such a set of provisions is generally that, when all the clauses are read together across the set of contracts, they should have the effect that, in respect of the risk element(s) with which the indemnity clauses deal, each party in the chain bears the loss or damage directly identified with it, and such loss only. However to achieve this result requires something of a leap of faith. To make the losses migrate to the appropriate point in the chain, a contracting party has to, in the anterior contract, assume responsibility not just for the losses identified with itself, but also for the losses of the parties below it on the chain. However, in the posterior contract, it will require to be indemnified and held harmless by its subcontractor in respect of all losses identified with the subcontractor, and any subcontractors lying down the chain of whatever level. Equally, in the posterior contract, the subcontractor will demand an indemnity and hold harmless clause from the contractor in respect not just of the contractor's losses, but also those of the parties lying above him in the chain. The contractor will give that in the knowledge that in the anterior contract, he should already have obtained an indemnity in respect of the losses identified with the parties above him in the chain. Thus if a set of back-to-back mutual hold harmless indemnities pertaining to personnel and property operate as the parties intended, the operator will ultimately carry the risk of injury to or death of its own personnel and loss of

---

[59] Although the example focuses on the case of a producing platform, the position is similar in other phases of the platform's life. When it is being constructed, overhauled or decommissioned the usual position is for the operator to contract with a limited number of lead contractors and for them to let out parcels of work to appropriate subcontractors.
[60] See Figure 14.1 for an illustration of one of these chains; see Figure 14.3, part of para 14.48, for an illustration of how these various chains fit together.
[61] Discussed at paras 14.16–14.18.
[62] *Farstad* v *Enviroco* demonstrates the dangers which can be posed by the interaction between the contractual risk allocation provisions and the statutory law of contribution: see G Gordon, "Indemnification, Exclusion and Contribution: *Farstad* in the Supreme Court" (2011) 15 EdinLR, forthcoming.

or damage to its own property, but not any like losses suffered by the lead contractor or its sub-contractor; the lead contractor will bear the risk of injury or death in respect of its own personnel and loss of or damage to its own property, but not any like losses suffered by the operator or the subcontractor; and likewise the subcontractor will accept risk in relation to its own property and personnel only. This is shown diagrammatically in Figure 14.1.

Qualified indemnity and hold harmless provisions
As has already been noted, when parties agree to a comprehensive **14.21** mutual indemnity and hold harmless regime they agree to bear the risk of loss not on the basis of who was at fault, but on the basis of who is best placed to insure against the loss or otherwise absorb it. Sometimes, however, the parties will deviate from this paradigm and one or more of their provisions will be made subject to qualifications or so-called "carve-outs". Qualifications are commonly encountered in the provisions pertaining to responsibility for injury to or death of third-party personnel, or damage to third-party property. Here, the parties often state that the indemnity and hold harmless provision will be offered only to the extent that the injury, death or damage was caused by the negligence or breach of duty of the indemnifying party.[63] At first sight this is a major deviation from the standard indemnity and hold harmless regime. It is, however, justifiable in the case of third-party liability, as unlike the situation where one takes responsibility for one's own people and property come what may, neither party has a close association with a true third party such as would justify a deviation from the law's default position on how risk should be allocated.

At the level of oil-company-to-oil-company contracts, it is **14.22** common for such mutual indemnity and hold harmless provisions as are granted to be qualified by the statement that they will not apply in the case of wilful misconduct or gross negligence. The objective of such a clause is to protect the company from acts of deliberate sabotage or conduct which falls well below the standard of care which would ordinarily be expected in such operations. Neither "wilful misconduct" nor "gross negligence" has a wholly settled meaning in English or Scots law; as a result it is prudent, when the terms are used, to define them in the agreement.[64] Moreover, some (particularly some US) companies have a corporate policy of not accepting indemnity and hold harmless provisions which

---

[63] See, eg, LOGIC, *Supply of Major Items*, cll 22.1(c) and 22.2(c).
[64] Among the matters to be dealt with in the definition is, eg, the issue of whose gross negligence or wilful misconduct is relevant to the clause: for instance, all personnel or senior management only? For a further discussion of what is meant by these terms see para 12.21.

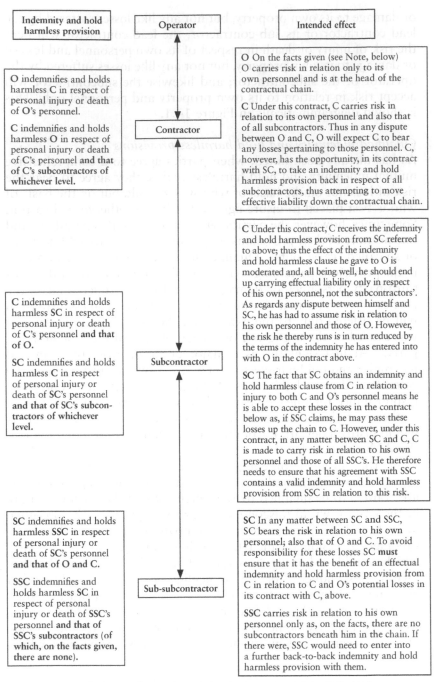

| Indemnity and hold harmless provision | Operator | Intended effect |

O indemnifies and holds harmless C in respect of personal injury or death of O's personnel.

C indemnifies and holds harmless O in respect of personal injury or death of C's personnel and that of C's subcontractors of whichever level.

Contractor

O On the facts given (see Note, below) O carries risk in relation only to its own personnel and is at the head of the contractual chain.

C Under this contract, C carries risk in relation to its own personnel and also that of all subcontractors. Thus in any dispute between O and C, O will expect C to bear any losses pertaining to those personnel. C, however, has the opportunity, in its contract with SC, to take an indemnity and hold harmless provision back in respect of all subcontractors, thus attempting to move effective liability down the contractual chain.

C indemnifies and holds harmless SC in respect of personal injury or death of C's personnel and that of O.

SC indemnifies and holds harmless C in respect of personal injury or death of SC's personnel and that of SC's subcontractors of whichever level.

Subcontractor

C Under this contract, C receives the indemnity and hold harmless provision from SC referred to above; thus the effect of the indemnity and hold harmless clause he gave to O is moderated and, all being well, he should end up carrying effectual liability only in respect of his own personnel, not the subcontractors'. As regards any dispute between himself and SC, he has had to assume risk in relation to his own personnel and those of O. However, the risk he thereby runs is in turn reduced by the terms of the indemnity he has entered into with O in the contract above.

SC The fact that SC obtains an indemnity and hold harmless clause from C in relation to injury to both C and O's personnel means he is able to accept these losses in the contract below as, if SSC claims, he may pass these losses up the chain to C. However, under this contract, in any matter between SC and C, C is made to carry risk in relation to his own personnel and those of all SSC's. He therefore needs to ensure that his agreement with SSC contains a valid indemnity and hold harmless provision from SSC in relation to this risk.

SC indemnifies and holds harmless SSC in respect of personal injury or death of SC's personnel and that of O and C.

SSC indemnifies and holds harmless SC in respect of personal injury or death of SSC's personnel and that of SSC's subcontractors (of which, on the facts given, there are none).

Sub-subcontractor

SC In any matter between SC and SSC, SC bears the risk in relation to his own personnel; also that of O and C. To avoid responsibility for these losses SC **must** ensure that it has the benefit of an effectual indemnity and hold harmless provision from C in relation to C and O's potential losses in its contract with C, above.

SSC carries risk in relation to his own personnel only as, on the facts, there are no subcontractors beneath him in the chain. If there were, SSC would need to enter into a further back-to-back indemnity and hold harmless provision with them.

Note: this is a simplified representation of one (rather short) contractual chain. With regard to any given producing platform, there will be more than one such chain: the operator is likely to have entered into direct contracts with at least a handful of parties. The relationship between the parties within this chain and those in others gives rise to further complications discussed at paras 14.48–14.49.

Figure 14.1 Simplified example of a mutual back-to-back indemnity and hold harmless provision relative to personal injury

operate in such a way as to permit a contractor to escape from the consequences of its gross negligence or wilful misconduct. Historically, some companies sought to exclude from the ambit of the indemnity and hold harmless provisions losses attributable to the "sole negligence"[65] of the other party or parties but this particular carve-out appears to be less common in current practice. Given the complexity of oil and gas operations and the inter-dependent way in which the various parties work, it is in practice quite rare for one party's actions to be the sole cause of an accident; and even when it is, the time, effort and money which may have to be expended in order to establish that fact may be very considerable.

Qualifying indemnity provisions is not without its benefits. One   **14.23** can readily understand why an operator would wish an obligation to re-drill to be "carved out" of the general indemnity and hold harmless provision which a drilling contractor will usually enjoy relative to loss of hole. However, any widespread practice of qualifying indemnity and hold harmless provisions has a number of drawbacks. It adds considerably to the complexity of and technical difficulty involved in drafting what are already rather awkward clauses. It also undercuts the economic benefits provided by the clause: the greater the number of exceptions carved out of the indemnity and hold harmless regime, the greater the risk the contractor is exposed to, and the more insurance cover it must purchase.[66] Deviating from standard practice can also lead parties into error concerning the precise forms of insurance cover which they require on this particular project. But ultimately the purpose of the risk allocation regime in any contract is to express the parties' intent, and the relative importance of these various factors, are matters for the parties to themselves determine.

Oil and gas contracts which reject the indemnity and hold harmless approach
As has already been noted, many up- and mid-stream contracts will   **14.24** contain indemnity and hold harmless provisions of the type described, albeit that they will differ in detail. There are, however, occasions where these provisions are not used at all, or where the risk allocation provisions differ so drastically from the standard approach as to be barely recognisable. This is relatively rare in operator-to-contractor contracts, or contractor-to-subcontractor ones, but will quite commonly be seen with some operator-to-operator contracts, particularly those which pertain to the use of or interference with existing items of infrastructure:

---

[65] The indemnity clauses litigated in the *London Bridge* case were in such terms: see the extracts from the relevant contracts reproduced at *London Bridge* 2000 SLT 1123 at 1126–1129.
[66] See paras 14.16–14.18.

for instance, tie-in agreements.[67] This is because the economic drivers that lead to the use of indemnity and hold harmless clauses in other parts of the industry are generally absent here. Where (in a JOA) operators are joining together mutually to develop an oil field, they share a common goal – to find hydrocarbon and make a profit by producing and selling it. Broadly speaking, their commercial interests will be aligned. And where operators, contractors and subcontractors are putting in place a suite of contracts to facilitate an oil or gas development, the operators' profit motive is again the economic driver. By contrast, where one operator approaches another seeking the use of infrastructure, the host operator will often have a producing field for which the infrastructure was built. The piece of infrastructure may very well be the only (or only commercially viable) means of getting oil and gas from the wellhead to the marketplace. In these circumstances, while it is not quite correct to say that the operator wishing to tie in is there on sufferance, because a tariff can be charged for the use of the infrastructure, it is true that the infrastructure owner's main commercial focus is likely to be the producing asset. The relatively small amount of money which the company stands to make by permitting the use of its facilities is dwarfed by the potential losses it will suffer if the accessing party compromises the infrastructure. In these circumstances, there is less in the way of a commercial imperative pushing the company towards accepting less than full compensation. However, one should not over-generalise: if, for example, the producing field is coming towards the end of its life and the value of the throughput tariff is comparatively large, then a stronger economic case can be made for allocating risk on the indemnity and hold harmless model – albeit that, even here, the indemnities may be subject to the sort of qualifications discussed at paras 14.21 and 14.22.

The oil and gas indemnity and hold harmless regime: a suite of provisions

14.25   As we have seen, the indemnity clause of an oil and gas contract will commonly consist of a range of different indemnities: some simple, some mutual, some qualified, some unqualified. These will typically be assembled one after the other, sub-clause by sub-clause,[68] and, if those drafting the indemnity clause have (a) been properly instructed

---

[67] R Palmer, "Tie-In Agreements" in M David (ed), *Oil and Gas Infrastructure and Midstream Agreements*, (1999) at 231 (hereinafter "Palmer, *Tie-In Agreements*") at 239f. Liability caps, discussed at paras 14.71–14.73, are sometimes, but not always, provided in such contracts: see para 7.23.

[68] Although this can appear laborious, the case law demonstrates that it can be dangerous to try to draft such clauses in too brief a form: see, eg, *Elf Enterprise Caledonia Ltd v Orbit Valve Co Europe* [1995] 1 All ER 174 (hereinafter "*Orbit Valve*"), discussed at para 14.34, and *Slessor v Vetco Gray*, discussed at para 14.39.

A (Operator)	B (contractor)
Accepts liability for:	*Accepts liability for:*
1. Injury to or loss of life of A's personnel [M] 2. Damage to A's property [M] 3. Pollution emanating from A's property [M] 4. Damage to third-party property and injury to or death of third-party employees **but** only if caused by the fault of A [M; Q] 5. Loss of hole (subject to B's requirement to re-drill if hole rendered useless as a result of B's fault) [M; Q] 6. Blowout, damage to reservoir, geological formation and underground strata etc [S]	1. Injury to or loss of life of B's personnel [M] 2. Damage to B's property [M] 3. Pollution emanating from B's property [M] 4. Damage to third-party property and injury to or death of third-party employees **but** only if caused by the fault of B [M; Q] 5. Liability to re-drill hole if requirement to do so arises as a result of B's fault [M; Q]
Receives indemnity and will be held harmless for	*Receives indemnity and will be held harmless for*
1. Injury to or loss of life of B's personnel [M] 2. Damage to B's property [M] 3. Pollution emanating from B's property [M] 4. Damage to third-party property and injury to or death of third-party employees caused by the fault of B [M; Q] 5. Cost of re-drilling hole if requirement to do so arises as a result of B's fault [M; Q]	1. Injury to or loss of life of A's personnel [M] 2. Damage to A's property [M] 3. Pollution emanating from A's property [M] 4. Damage to third-party property and injury to or death of third-party employees **but** only if caused by the fault of A [M; Q] 5. Loss of hole (subject to B's requirement to re-drill if hole rendered useless as a result of B's fault) [M; Q] 6. Blowout, damage to reservoir, geological formation and underground strata etc [S]

Key: M = Mutual indemnity; Q = qualified indemnity; S = simple indemnity

Figure 14.2 Hypothetical liabilities matrix based on a relatively simple set of operator–contractor indemnity and hold harmless provisions

on the precise risk factors thought likely to affect the works underlying the contract and (b) taken adequate care in drafting the clause, the indemnity provisions thus completed should succeed in mapping out the scope of the parties respective liabilities for the kind of physical risks which might assail the project.[69] Such a "map" may look something like that shown in Figure 14.2.

Selected further issues in indemnification law and practice in the UKCS

Statutory control of indemnity and hold harmless clauses
Unlike some other jurisdictions, for instance, several of the petroleum-producing states of the United States of America,[70] the United   **14.26**

---

[69] Always assuming, of course, that the manner in which the parties have allocated the risks is permitted by law: see further para 14.26.
[70] So-called anti-indemnity statutes have been enacted in Texas, Louisiana, New Mexico, Wyoming and Oregon: see P Gerald and H Williams, "Injuries to Third Parties Arising From Oil and Gas Operations: An Analytical Framework for Examining Indemnity and

Kingdom has imposed no specific statutory controls on the use of indemnity and hold harmless clauses in the oil and gas industry. So far as the general body of commercial law statutes is concerned, the Unfair Contract Terms Act 1977 as amended (hereinafter "UCTA") and the Unfair Terms in Consumer Contracts Regulations 1999 (SI 1999/2083) as amended (the "1999 Regulations") impose certain restrictions that might at first sight appear germane. However, the 1999 Regulations apply only to contracts with consumers[71] and can therefore be discounted. Turning now to UCTA, the limitations imposed upon the use of indemnity clauses apply only when the indemnifying party deals as a consumer.[72] This, together with the belief that indemnity and hold harmless clauses were mere indemnities, led the author to state in the first edition of this work that "there are therefore no statutory controls in force in the United Kingdom which impact upon the parties' ability to make use of indemnity clauses in commercial oil and gas contracts". Following *Farstad* v *Enviroco*, however, this claim can no longer be made. As indemnity and hold harmless clauses have now been held to operate as exclusions when they operate in the context of "direct exposure to the other contracting party"[73] (as opposed to third-party losses), then the restrictions imposed by UCTA relative to exclusion clauses also need to be considered. Of greatest concern to the oil and gas industry would be the rule contained in ss 2(1) and 16(1)(a) UCTA,[74] that any attempt to by a party to restrict its liability for death or personal injury resulting from negligence will be ineffectual. At first sight, this provision would seem to be triggered by an indemnity and hold harmless clause which pertains to losses associated with personal injury or death and which applies irrespective of negligence; and as Hewitt notes, "[t]he application of the section appears on its face to be strict and it does not appear to be possible for the parties to contract out of the Act".[75] However, Hewitt goes on to note that:

Additional Insured Issues", 15 J Nat Resources & Envtl L 21 at 28–31. For a detailed discussion of the position in Texas, see T Fox, "Return to Certainty in Risk Assessment, Management and Transfer: The Journey of the Texas Oilfield Anti-Indemnity Act" 2001 IELTR 18.

[71] 1999 Regulations, reg 4. "Consumer" is defined by reg 3(1) as "any natural person who, in contracts covered by these Regulations, is acting for purposes which are outside his trade, business or profession".

[72] 1977 Act, ss 4 (for Engllish law and that of Wales and Northern Ireland) and 18 (Scots law). A party deals as a consumer when he does not contract in the course of a business but the other party does: see s 12.

[73] *Farstad* v *Enviroco* per Lord Mance at para 59.

[74] Section 2(1) applies in English, Welsh and Northern Irish law and s 16(1)(a) in Scots law.

[75] T Hewitt, *Who is to Blame? Allocating Liability in Upstream Project Contracts* at p 205.

"indemnities concerning death and personal injury in the context of the oil and gas industry (even where they are caused by negligence) have been upheld, notably in *London Bridge*. This may be because the clauses concerned in London Bridge were not construed as exclusions of liability for death or injury but rather exclusions of liability for claims by third parties in respect of the same and were therefore not covered by the strict prohibition in section 2(1)".

Hewitt is, it is submitted, wrong to characterise the mutual hold harmless and indemnity clauses in *London Bridge* as clauses which involved an exclusion of liability. It is submitted that the clauses were, on their true construction, concerned not with extinguishing liability, but with its re-allocation.[76] He is, however, surely correct in conceptualising the *London Bridge* clauses as being essentially concerned with third-party claims. This would seem to mean that neither they (nor, it would seem, any other indemnity and hold harmless clause appertaining to liability for personal injury or death[77]) would, to use Lord Mance's *Farstad* v *Enviroco* formulation, seem to regulate "direct exposure to the other contracting party". Thus, in this context, indemnity and hold harmless clauses would seem to operate as indemnities, not exclusions. However, this will not be the case where the clause *does* seek to regulate direct exposure to the other contracting party. The classic example of such a situation will be where, as in *Farstad* v *Enviroco*, the claim pertains to property belonging to one of the parties. There the clause will be an exclusion, and UCTA (although not argued in *Farstad* v *Enviroco*) would appear to be relevant. However, the provisions engaged would not be the bright-line prohibition upon exclusion contained in s 2(1), but the (less draconian) reasonableness requirements contained elsewhere in the Act.[78] The party having the benefit of the indemnity and hold harmless clause has less to fear from these provisions than from ss 2(1) and 16(1)(a). Given the widespread use of indemnity and hold harmless clauses within the industry and the economic benefits of the practice, one would not expect such a clause to be struck down by the court other than in very unusual circumstances.[79]

---

[76] *Thompson* v *T Lohan (Plant Hire) Ltd* [1987] 1 WLR 649. See also Lord Mance's "direct exposure" formulation in *Farstad* v *Enviroco*, discussed later in this paragraph.

[77] A company, being an incorporeal corporation, can never itself suffer personal injury or death. Thus it would appear that, by definition, all deaths and personal injuries suffered as a result of the negligence of a company must be third-party losses for the purposes of Lord Mance's *Farstad* v *Enviroco* formulation.

[78] Ie ss 2(2) and 3 (in English, Welsh and Northern Irish law) and ss 16(1)(b) and 17 (in Scots law).

[79] See further the discussion of these provisions in the context of consequential loss at para 14.66.

The law's normal presumptions about the distribution of risk

14.27 The risk distribution exercise that the parties carry out by entering into an indemnity and hold harmless regime does not take place in isolation. It occurs against the background of the assumptions which, in the absence of specific agreement, the law of contract and tort/delict[80] makes about how certain risks are to be allocated. In contract law the broad expectation, under both Scots law and the law of England and Wales, is that, subject to considerations such as remoteness of damage and the need for the non-breaching party to take reasonable steps to mitigate its loss, the party in breach is obliged to make good the losses suffered by the non-breaching party.[81] If a loss occurs without either party breaching the contract then, viewed from the perspective of contract law, the loss will lie where it falls. In tort/delict, the breach of a statutory duty that causes a party loss may in some circumstances found an action in reparation.[82] And the founding principle of the tort/delict of negligence is that where a person owes another a duty of care and breaches that duty, causing a loss, he is under an obligation to make a payment of compensatory damages to make good that loss.[83] But if there is no breach of statutory or common law duty, neither party can sue and the loss lies where it falls. It can therefore be seen that the general law's default position is that liability follows breach of contract or breach of duty. Under this model, liability is wedded to fault. By contrast, as we have seen, carve-outs apart, the indemnity and hold harmless regime is predicated on the basis that liability should not flow along these lines, but that it should be accepted by the party best placed to insure against or otherwise absorb that particular type of loss. Thus the common law and the contractual regime that the industry creates to govern such matters are not closely aligned. The significance of this is that when the contractual regime fails for some reason – typically, because a clause is not sufficiently clearly drafted,

---

[80] The Anglo–American expression "tort" is not used in Scots law, which prefers "delict". However, at least in the field of the tort/delict of negligence, there is little to distinguish the laws of England and Scotland.

[81] For the position in England and Wales, see, eg, G Treitel, *The Law of Contract* (11th edn, 2003) (hereinafter "Treitel, *Contract*") at 926f. For the Scots position, see W McBryde, *The Law of Contract in Scotland* (3rd edn, 2007), Chapter 22.

[82] A Dugdale, M Jones *et al*, *Clerk and Lindsell on Torts* (19th edn, 2005) (hereinafter "*Clerk and Lindsell on Torts*") at paras 9.01–9.04; J Thomson, *Delictual Liabilty* (4th edn, 2009) (hereinafter "Thomson, *Delict*").

[83] See *Donoghue* v *Stevenson* [1932] AC 562; *Caparo Industries plc* v *Dickman* [1990] 2 AC 605. Reasons of public policy mean that the rule is modified for numerous classes of case, for instance, where what the parties seek to recover is pure economic loss or psychiatric injury, or where what is in issue is the liability of a public authority. For a comprehensive account of English tort law, see *Clerk and Lindsell on Torts*. For a concise but well-written account of the Scots law of delict, see Thomson, *Delict*.

but perhaps, post-*Farstad*, because it is deemed to be an exclusion clause and fails one of the tests set out in UCTA – and risk falls to be allocated under the general law, it will frequently be distributed in a way which is very different from that which the parties intended. This may very well mean that one or both of the parties will find themselves facing losses against which they are not insured. The stakes are therefore high when one is drafting an indemnity and hold harmless clause.

The position of third parties

While the law of both England and Scotland now permits the benefit   **14.28**
of a contract to be extended to a third party,[84] neither jurisdiction permits a contract to impose obligations upon someone who is not party to it. It is therefore not strictly correct to say, without saying more, that a well-drafted indemnity and hold harmless clause modifies or over-rides the law's conventional approach to risk allocation. It does so *only so far as the parties to the contract are concerned*. A stranger to the contract – usually described as a third party – who is injured or otherwise suffers a loss as a result in the course of the execution of the contract works will seek compensation through the time-honoured route of suing the person or persons whose negligence and/or breach of statutory duty caused his loss. Sometimes the person against whom the claim is directed will, by pure coincidence, happen to be the indemnifying party, in which case the indemnity and hold harmless clause will simply re-inforce the common law's approach. Where, however, the third party sues not the indemnifier, but the indemnified party, a claim will be made by the indemnified party under the indemnity and hold harmless clause. So, if the standard mutual indemnity and hold harmless provision is in place between companies A and B and C, one of company A's employees is injured by the negligence of one of contractor B's employees, he can be expected to sue B for negligence and/or breach of statutory duty.[85] B cannot defend C's claim on the basis that it has an indemnity, as that is irrelevant so far as C, a third party, is concerned. However, B can make a claim against A as a result of their contractual arrangements.

The fact that the third party is disinterested in the indemnity and   **14.29**
hold harmless clause has the potential to have serious implications

---

[84] In England, where the doctrine of privity of contract was traditionally very strong, this is as a result of the Contracts (Rights of Third Parties) Act 1999. In Scotland the common-law doctrine of *jus quaesitum tertio* has permitted third-party rights for centuries.

[85] Depending on the facts, he may in addition be able to raise a case directly against A in respect of A's breach of its non-delegable "duty to reasonable care to see that its employees are safe". See *Clerk and Lindsell on Torts* at 13.05.

for the parties, particularly in the event of insolvency. Unless it is fortified either by meaningful guarantees or by adequate levels of insurance, a right to be indemnified is only as strong as the financial covenant of the company providing it.

Interpreting indemnity and hold harmless clauses

The traditional approach to interpretation

14.30 **The general rules.** Although the precise formulation of the tests used in the jurisdictions traditionally differed, it is possible to say that both English and Scots law have traditionally taken an objective approach to the interpretation of contracts.[86] Although objective, neither jurisdiction has been wholly literal in approach:[87] both jurisdictions require the clause or phrase under discussion to be interpreted not in isolation but in the light of the written document as a whole.[88] Both have permitted evidence as to the objective factual background to be adduced with a view to allowing the court objectively to determine the aim or thrust of the agreement,[89] albeit there are differences between the two systems surrounding precisely when this is to be permitted.[90]

14.31 **Interpretation *contra proferentem*.** In addition to the generalities expressed above, both English and Scots law have traditionally deployed the *contra proferentem* rule to interpret exemption, limitation and indemnity clauses.[91] This means that "[a]mbiguous words in exemption clauses [will be] construed in the way least favourable to the party relying on them".[92] In the context of a simple indemnity, the party relying on the clause will be the one

---

[86] For the traditional position in England, see K Lewison, *The Interpretation of Contracts* (2nd edn, 1997) (hereinafter "Lewison, *Interpretation*") at para 1.05. For the position in Scotland, see Scottish Law Commission, Scot Law Com No 160, *Report on Interpretation in Private Law*, available for download from: http://www.scotlawcom.gov.uk/downloads/rep160.pdf (accessed 21 February 2011) (hereinafter "SLC, *Report on Interpretation*") at para 2.3.

[87] SLC, *Report on Interpretation*, para 2.1.

[88] See, eg, (in the law of England and Wales) *Re Jodrell* (1890) 44 Ch D 590; for a Scots example, see *Glen's Trs v Lancashire and Yorkshire Accident Insurance Co Ltd* (1906) 8 F 915.

[89] See Lewison, *Interpretation* at para 2.10

[90] In England, even before Lord Hoffmann's restatement (discussed at paras 14.32–14.33), there has been a general willingness to admit "matrix of fact" evidence: see Lewison, *Interpretation*, para 2.10. In Scotland, evidence as to surrounding circumstances is admissible only in the case of ambiguity, or if the contract was unintelligible without it: SLC, *Report on Interpretation*, para 2.3; see in particular the materials cited in fn 7 therein.

[91] For an excellent account of this area, see E Peel, "Whither *Contra Proferentem?*", in A Burrows and E Peel, *Contract Terms* (2007), pp 61–75.

[92] Treitel, *Contract*, p 221.

who stands to receive the benefit of it – ie, the indemnified party. But who is the *proferens* when the clause is mutual? The prevailing view appears to be that whichever party has the misfortune to have a claim directed towards it (and therefore requests indemnification under the contractual risk allocation provisions) is to be treated as the *proferens*.[93] This, however, reduces the question to a matter of happenstance. The arrangement is *mutual* – indemnity and hold harmless provisions travel in either direction – and had the facts been different the indemnity might have run in the opposite direction. It seems to be artificial, in such a situation, to contend that there is a *proferens* at all. This fact was recognised in the Scottish Outer House case of *Slessor v Vetco Gray*, where Lord Glennie stated:

> "I accept Mr Armstrong's submission that the *contra proferentem* approach, which in any event only applies in a case of ambiguity, has much less impact where the exemptions and indemnities are mutual or reciprocal. Both parties are, in a sense, the *proferens;* and it makes little sense to construe the clause against each one of them leaving the possibility of a hole in the middle."[94]

It is respectfully suggested that this approach is logical and takes cognisance of the realities of the parties' contractual arrangements. It therefore has much to commend it. However, on the balance of current authority it cannot be said to be the established view.

Towards contextualism: Lord Hoffmann's restatement. The tradi- **14.32**
tional approach referred to above requires now, at least in England, and possibly also in Scotland,[95] to be considered in the light of the *dictum* issued in *Investors Compensation Scheme Ltd v West Bromwich Building Society*[96] which has come to be known as "Lord Hoffmann's restatement". A comprehensive examination of the restatement is outside the scope of this chapter. However, putting the matter shortly, Lord Hoffmann suggested that two cases decided by the House of Lords in the 1970s[97] had effected a quiet

---

[93] *Orbit Valve* per Steyn LJ at 182g–h; *London Bridge*, (Inner House) 2000 SLT 1123 per LP Rodger at 1148C–L and per Lord Sutherland at 1174L. The House of Lords passed no concluded view upon the matter as their Lordships took the view that the clauses were clear and unambiguous: *London Bridge* (House of Lords) 2002 SC (HL) 117, [2002] 1 All ER (Comm) 321) per Lord Mackay of Clashfern at para 43.

[94] *Slessor v Vetco Gray* at para 12.

[95] The extent to which the restatement has been received into Scots law is presently unclear: see D Cabrelli, *Commercial Agreements in Scotland: Law and Practice* (2006) at paras 2.03–2.24 and McBryde, *Contract* (3rd edn), paras 8.25–8.27.

[96] *Investors Compensation Scheme Ltd v West Bromwich Building Society* (hereinafter "*Investors Compensation Scheme*") [1998] 1 WLR 896.

[97] Ie *Prenn v Simmonds* [1971] 1 WLR 1381 and *Reardon Smith Line Ltd v Hansen-Tangen* [1976] 1 WLR 989.

revolution: a shift away from formalism towards contextual interpretation. He considered the effect of these cases had been to discard
"[a]lmost all of the old intellectual baggage of 'legal' interpretation".[98]
In particular, Lord Hoffmann confirmed that contractual interpretation was still in a sense an objective exercise, in that it continued
to be a matter of ascertaining what a reasonable and objective
bystander would make of the parties' communings. However, he
added that such a bystander should be presumed to be aware of
at least most of[99] the background knowledge and circumstances
(otherwise the "matrix of fact") which comprised the setting in
which those communings took place. Moreover, as "the meaning
of the document is what the parties using those words against the
relevant background would reasonably have been understood to
mean", the bystander's knowledge of the background circumstances
might from time to time prompt him to conclude that the parties
must have used the wrong words. Such a conclusion would be
reached rarely as the courts would not readily accept that the parties
had made linguistic mistakes; however, when an appropriate case did
arise, the reasonable bystander should not attribute to the parties an
intention which they plainly could not have had.[100]

14.33 **The implications of Lord Hoffmann's restatement for drafting indemnity
and hold harmless clauses.** In spite of Lord Hoffmann's belief that his
dictum was not a radical departure, but merely a convenient synthesis
of what the law already said, the restatement has proven to be controversial. It has been both championed[101] and criticised.[102] The tension
between its adherents and its detractors has given rise to "a degree of
uncertainty in the law".[103] The place which it occupies in Scots law
continues to be uncertain. In these circumstances, the only prudent

---

[98] At first sight, this might appear to be a reference to formal legal rules such as *contra
proferentem*: see E McKendrick, *Contract Law: Cases, Text and Materials* (4th edn, 2010)
at 381; Peel, "Whither *Contra Proferentem?*", p 61. However, as McKendrick notes,
appearances can be deceptive: see further the discussion of *HIH Casualty & General
Insurance* at para 14.37.
[99] Previous negotiations and declarations of the parties' subjective intent continue to be
excluded from consideration.
[100] *Investors Compensation Scheme* [1998] 1 WLR 896 per Lord Hoffmann at 912–913.
[101] See, eg, A Kramer, "Common Sense Principles of Contractual Interpretation (And How
We've Been Using Them All Along)" (2003) 23 OJLS 173.
[102] *National Bank of Sharjah* v *Dellborg* [1993] Banking LR 109; *NLA Group Ltd* v
Bowers [1999] 1 Lloyd's Rep 109; *Partnership of MPV Ocean Quest* v *Finnings Ltd* 2000
SLT (Sh Ct) 157 at 161; McBryde, *Contract* (3rd edn), para 8.27, cited with approval in
the Inner House of the Court of Session in *Multi-Link Leisure Developments Ltd* v *North
Lanarkshire Council* [2009] CSIH 96, 2010 SC 302, opinion of the court at para 23. Note,
however, that the Supreme Court avoided any criticism of Lord Hoffmann's restatement:
Multi-Link Leisure Developments Ltd v *North Lanarkshire Council* [2010] UKSC 47.
[103] E McKendrick, *Contract Law: Cases, Text and Materials* (4th edn, 2010) at 381.

approach is for contractual draftsmen charged with the task of drafting indemnity and hold harmless clauses to disregard Lord Hoffmann's restatement, and to proceed instead on the basis that indemnity and hold harmless clauses will continue to be construed *contra proferentem*. Drafting in this manner should minimise the prospect of a dispute arising as to the true meaning of the clause. However, in the event that an indemnity clause is challenged on the ground that it does not satisfy one of the tests established by the traditional canons of interpretation, very careful consideration should be given to the assistance that might be provided by Lord Hoffmann's restatement and the recent case law influenced by it.[104] In addition, if the contract in question does not accurately express the intention of the parties, advice should be taken on the possibility of rectifying the deed.[105]

Some known problems of drafting and interpretation

Contra proferentem *and the problem of negligence and breach of statutory duty*

As has already been noted, when the parties to an oil and gas contract opt to include an indemnity and hold harmless regime in their contract, they are choosing to superimpose their own views on risk allocation upon the one provided by the common law. As we have seen, the common law generally expects liability to follow breach of contract or breach of duty. The courts have therefore considered it to be "a fundamental consideration in the construction of contracts of this kind that it is inherently improbable that one party to a contract should intend to absolve the other from the consequences of his own negligence",[106] and, have considered it to be, if anything, even less likely that one party would accept liability for another party's negligence.[107] While the courts stop short of saying that the parties cannot use the terms of their contracts to re-allocate risk in the way in which they see fit, they have traditionally invoked the *contra proferentem* rule to say that the parties must use clear language when they do.[108]

14.34

---

[104] The recent evolution of the rule of *contra proferentem* is further considered immediately below.

[105] For a general discussion on rectification of deeds, see (from the standpoint of English law) Lord Mackay of Clashfern (General Editor), *Halsbury's Laws of England* (4th edn, 2003 Reissue) (hereinafter "*Halsbury*"), vol 32, paras 52–69. For the position under Scots law, see J Murray and S Wolffe, "Judicial and Other Remedies", *The Laws of Scotland: Stair Memorial Encylcopaedia*, vol 13 (1992), paras 69–70.

[106] *Gillespie Bros & Co Ltd* v *Roy Bowles Transport Ltd* [1973] QB 400 per Buckley LJ at 419.

[107] *Smith* v *UMB Chrysler (Scotland) Ltd* 1978 SC (HL) 1 per Viscount Dilhorne at 7.

[108] See, eg, London Bridge (Inner House) 2000 SLT 1123 per LP Rodger at 1148K–L. See also *Orbit Valve* [1993] 4 All ER 165 (affirmed by the Court of Appeal: see [1995]1 All

Canada Steamship Lines Ltd v *The King*[109] is authority for the proposition that effect will be given to a term which expressly states that the indemnified party is to be relieved from the consequences of its own negligence.[110] However, the same case also provides that, if the clause does not expressly indemnify in respect of negligence or some synonym for it, it will operate to relieve the indemnified party from the consequences of its own negligence only if (i) the words used in the clause are "wide enough in their ordinary meaning to cover negligence" on the part of the indemnified party and (ii) no alternative ground of liability which is not either too remote or too fanciful to be in the parties' contemplation might exist.

14.35   This is not some abstruse point of theory for those engaged in drafting indemnity clauses. Unless there have been clear instructions that the indemnified party's own negligence is to be excluded from the ambit of the indemnity and hold harmless clause, a provision which is ineffectual against the indemnified party's own negligence is unlikely to be what a party to an oil and gas industry contract wanted. Worse, it is unlikely to match with the risks that the party has insured against. In *Orbit Valve*, a case determined by the English courts under English law, the employers of a man killed in the Piper Alpha disaster were sued by the operator, who sought reimbursement of the compensation which the operator had paid to settle a claim by the deceased's family. The operator, who accepted that the negligent actings of one of its employees had at least contributed towards the disaster, claimed that it was entitled to recover under the contractual indemnity and hold harmless clause. However, the contractor contended that the clause was ineffectual: the operator was seeking to be reimbursed for a loss incurred at least in part as a result of its own negligence; however, the clause did not expressly state that it would operate in these circumstances. Applying *Canada Steamship*, the Court of Appeal held that the clause contained words which were wide enough to have the effect of conferring an indemnity upon the indemnified party relative to the consequences of its own negligence. However, it refused to give effect to the clause on the basis that the second limb of the *Canada Steamship* test was not satisfied. The words were not necessarily

---

ER 174) per Hobhouse J at 173*f*: "The parties are always able, by the choice of appropriate language, to draft their contract so as to produce a different legal effect. The choice is theirs. In the present case, there would have been no problem in drafting the contract so as to produce the result for which the plaintiffs have contended; however, the contract was not so drafted and contains only generally working and is seriously lacking in clarity."
[109] *Canada Steamship Lines Ltd* v *The King* [1952] AC 192 (hereinafter "*Canada Steamship*").
[110] *Ibid* per Lord Morton of Shuna at 208.

directed towards the indemnified party's negligence, but could just as easily have been intended to exclude another head of claim, namely breach of statutory duty.[111] This head of claim was not either too remote or too fanciful to be in the parties' contemplation. The claim therefore failed.

In *London Bridge*, a Scots case which also arose out of the Piper   14.36
Alpha disaster, the operator sought to use indemnity and hold harmless provisions in order to recover from the various employers of personnel injured or killed in the disaster sums in respect of damages paid in order to settle the personal injury claims of the injured and the families of the deceased. After proof, it was held that the accident had occurred as a result of both the negligence of the operator and that of an employee of a specialist valve contractor.[112] The operator was again met with the argument that the clause did not provide it with a remedy as it required to be interpreted *contra proferentem*[113] and did not deal sufficiently clearly with the issue of negligence to satisfy the *Canada Steamship* requirements. This time, however, the indemnity clauses[114] were drafted differently to the clause in *Orbit Valve*. The clauses were rather inelegantly drafted and did not address the question of negligence as expressly as one might have desired. However, they did make express provision for how issues of *contributory* negligence were to be resolved.[115] This fact was sufficient to permit the court to conclude that the parties had intended that the mutual indemnity and hold harmless provision would take effect even in circumstances where one of the parties was seeking protection from consequences of its own negligence.[116] The claim for indemnity therefore succeeded.

Away from the oil and gas context, the House of Lords has   14.37
had an opportunity to consider the continued role for the rules in *Canada Steamship* following Lord Hoffmann's restatement. Its decision makes for interesting reading. *HIH Casualty & General Insurance Ltd v Chase Manhattan Bank*[117] *("HIH Casualty & General*

---

[111] *Orbit Valve* [1995] 1 All ER 174 per Steyn LJ at 181h–j.

[112] This finding was significant as the relevant clause contained a "sole-negligence" carve-out, and had liability not been at least partially the fault of another party, the pursuer's claim would have failed: *London Bridge* (Inner House) 2000 SLT 1123 per LP Rodger at 1131.

[113] See also the discussion at para 14.31.

[114] The case involved a multiplicity of parties; seven separate sets of indemnity provisions were under consideration.

[115] See the extracts from the relevant contracts reproduced at *London Bridge* 2000 SLT 1123 at 1126–1129.

[116] See *London Bridge* (House of Lords) 2002 SC (HL) 117, [2002] 1 All ER (Comm) 321 per Lord Mackay of Clashfern at paras 40–43.

[117] [2003] UKHL 6, [2003] 2 Lloyd's Rep 297. For an excellent summary, see E Peel, "Whither *Contra Proferentem*?" at pp 61–64.

Insurance") was concerned with the interpretation of an insurance policy designed to pay out to the insured (who were investors in films) in the event that the films in which they had invested did not make enough money to permit the repayment of the investor's loans. This rather specialised "high risk, high-premium"[118] insurance product was designed and marketed by a firm of brokers who also acted as the insured's agent when presenting the proposal to the insurers. The policy contained a "truth of statement" clause which, put shortly, provided that the insured (ie the investors) "would have no liability of any nature to the insurers for any information provided by any other parties", and in particular that any information either provided or not disclosed by the brokers would not be a ground by which the insurers could avoid or escape their liability to make payment under the policy. This clause was included in the policy in order to protect the insured against the risk of unwittingly becoming responsible for anything said or known by the many other players involved in the procurement of finance for any of the films in question.[119] In the event, there were substantial shortfalls in the films' revenue and the investors claimed under the policies. The insurers repudiated liability on the grounds of misrepresentation and non-disclosure, either fraudulent or negligent, on the part of the broker. The insurers contended that the wording of the "truth of statement" clause was not sufficiently specific to meet the terms of the *Canada Steamship* rules in that although the wording was sufficiently wide to extend to negligence or fraud, it could just as readily be intended to exclude other causes of action which it was not fanciful to imagine the parties to have had in contemplation, such as innocent misrepresentation or non-disclosure. The House of Lords agreed relative to fraud, holding, by majority, it to be "a thing apart",[120] a species of liability which "must be excluded in clear and unmistakeable terms on the face of the contract".[121] Importantly, however, the House of Lords unanimously rejected the insurers' argument relative to negligence. Although, as

---

[118] Lord Hoffmann at para 25. This paragraph contains an evocative description of the film investment industry which the author commends to the reader.

[119] A multiplicity of parties were involved, including the broker: see *HIH Casualty & General Insurance* per Lord Hoffmann at paras 26–33. The insured needed to be protected against the risk (not a fanciful one, given the manifold duties generally imposed by the law upon an insured, the contract being one of utmost good faith) of being deemed to have constructive knowledge of things known by persons deemed to be the insured's agent.

[120] *HIH Casualty & General Insurance* per Lord Bingham at para 15. His Lordship continued: "Parties entering into a commercial contract will no doubt recognise and accept the risk of errors and omissions in the preceding negotiations, even negligent errors and omissions. But each party will assume the honesty and good faith of the other; absent such an assumption they would not deal."

[121] *Ibid* per Lord Bingham at para 16.

Peel notes, "[t]here was no suggestion from their Lordships that [the possibility that the parties might have had in contemplation innocent misrepresentation or non-disclosure] was regarded as fanciful",[122] the so-called *Canada Steamship* "rules" were relegated to the status of helpful but non-determinative guidance[123] as opposed to a code. As Lord Bingham put it:

> "The passage does not provide a litmus test which, applied to the terms of the contract, yields a certain and predictable result. The courts' task of ascertaining what the particular parties intended, in their particular commercial context, remains."[124]

In turning to that task, the House of Lords had no hesitation in holding that the parties had used "comprehensive language, clearly chosen to give [the investor] an extended immunity".[125] It found "nothing commercially surprising in this interpretation"[126] as in a transaction of this kind "the possibility that [the broker] might make and fail to correct a representation which was later held to be both untrue and negligent would be very real".[127] Thus, while it would appear that *contra proferentem* has survived the purge of "[a]lmost all of the old intellectual baggage of 'legal' interpretation", it has not emerged unchanged from its brush with Lord Hoffmann's restatement. Fraud continues to be "a thing apart"; negligence, it would seem, is not. The strict and unyielding approach of *Orbit Valve* stands in stark contrast to the contextual and commercially aware decision in *HIH Casualty & General Insurance*.

14.38 The indemnity and hold harmless clauses presently in wide use within the industry make express reference to the parties' intention that the clauses will be effectual irrespective of negligence or breach of duty, whether statutory or otherwise.[128] It would be foolish for contractual

---

[122] E Peel, "Whither *Contra Proferentem?*" at 62.

[123] As Lord Hoffmann notes at paras 61–63, they had also been characterised as mere guidelines not to be mechanistically followed in *Smith v South Wales Switchgear Co Ltd* [1978] 1 WLR 165, *Hollier v Rambler Motors (AMC) Ltd* [1972] 2 QB 71 and *Ailsa Craig Fishing Co Ltd v Malvern Fishing Co Ltd* [1983] 1 WLR 964.

[124] *HIH Casualty & General Insurance* per Lord Bingham at 11.

[125] *Ibid* per Lord Bingham at 12

[126] *Ibid.* See also Lord Hoffmann at 67: "There is no inherent improbability in such an intention. As Rix LJ said, in a case like this the question of negligence can never be all that far from the contemplation of the parties."

[127] *HIH Casualty & General Insurance* per Lord Bingham at 13. See also Lord Hoffmann at 67: "And it seems to me that the commercial objective of the Truth of Statement clause would be substantially undermined if Chase's right to the policy monies depended upon an inquiry into whether Heaths had or had not taken reasonable care in checking the truth of representations or deciding which facts should be disclosed."

[128] See eg LOGIC, *Mobile Drilling Rigs* at cl 18.8; see also the discussion the IMHH Deed at para 14.51.

draftsmen deliberately to deviate from that practice. However, in the event that a clause is, upon examination following intimation of a claim, found to have been drafted in a way which is less explicit on this point than one might wish, Lord Hoffman's restatement, *London Bridge* and (most promisingly of all) *HIH Casualty & General Insurance* all suggest that the courts will be willing to take a somewhat more forgiving approach than was seen in *Orbit Valve*. More radically – and more speculatively – if Lord Glennie's *dictum* in *Slessor*[129] finds favour then the *contra proferentem* rule will be found to be wholly irrelevant in the case of *mutual* indemnity and hold harmless clauses.[130]

Words delimiting the circumstances in which the indemnity and hold harmless provision will take effect

14.39   Another subtle but important issue which arises in the drafting of an indemnity and hold harmless clause is the need to delimit the set of circumstances in which the indemnity is to take effect. The indemnity and hold harmless provision will not be being given generally, for all times and for all circumstances. Instead, it is given because it has been rendered necessary by the fact that one party intends to carry out work under a particular contract. Words need to be included in the clause which make this clear and state the circumstances in which the provision is to take effect. If this is not done, the provision is in danger of being either struck down as a result of its indeterminate scope, or of applying in circumstances not intended by the parties. However, and again, exercising prudence as a result of the possible continued application of the *contra proferentem* rule, draftsmen must give careful thought to the words they use. It is dangerous to draw too narrow a connection between the operation of the indemnity and the scope of work under the contract. This is so because there are a host of circumstances in which property may be lost or personnel injured or killed while they are on an operator's platform. Taking the example of an injury on an offshore platform, such an event may befall a worker as a result of an accident directly connected to the scope of work to be done under the contract. However, it may also occur as a result of an accident occurring while he was carrying out work, but for reasons wholly unconnected to it, or while he is on the platform but not engaged in this work.[131]

---

[129] See para 14.31.

[130] The rule would continue in operation in the case of simple indemnities.

[131] A worker may, for example, be at rest in the accommodation module when a fire breaks out, as happened to many of those killed or injured in the Piper Alpha disaster. Or the injury or illness may be the result of a more mundane accident. For instance, the employee may be injured falling from his bunk (as occurred in *Robb v Salamis M & I Ltd*, 2007 SLT 158, albeit no indemnification issue was litigated here), or may suffer food poisoning while having his supper in the canteen.

Smith v *South Wales Switchgear* is authority for the proposition   14.40
that if an indemnity is drawn so that it takes effect only if injuries
are suffered during the "execution of this Order" it will capture
only injuries occurring as a result of the doing of the contractual
work.[132] The dangers that this judgment poses to the party claiming
the indemnity are clear. In *Campbell* v *Conoco (UK) Ltd,*[133] it was
argued that a clause which provided that the sub-contractor would
indemnify and hold harmless the lead contractor[134] against all injuries
suffered by the subcontractor's employees "as a result of or arising
out of or in connection with the performance or non-performance
of the contract" did not take effect in circumstances where the
employee suffered injuries after being struck in the back by a blast
of compressed air discharged from equipment which had nothing to
do with the job he was doing, but which happened to be positioned
close to the area in which he was working. The subcontractors
contended that the indemnity would be triggered only if the injuries
were directly attributable to the performance of work under the
contract.[135] The Court of Appeal held that the wording of that
particular clause did not bear any such construction, and that
the phrase in question was wide enough to encompass at least a
situation where the injury occurred while the worker was engaged
in his work,[136] and may well have been wide enough to encompass
a situation where injury occurred while the worker was at rest.[137]
However, the court also observed that "each contract depends on
its own wording and context". Thus if they wish the clause to be
effective for the whole period when the worker covered is on the
platform, drafters of indemnity and hold harmless clauses must be
careful not to use words which tie the triggering of the clause too
closely to the performance of the contract or its works.[138]

---

[132] *Smith* v *South Wales Switchgear* [1978] 1 WLR 165 per Lord Keith at 178.

[133] *Campbell* v *Conoco (UK) Ltd* [2003] 1 All E R (Comm) 35 (hereinafter "*Campbell*").

[134] The terminology used throughout the case is rather confusing: because the case
concerns a subcontract which incorporated the terms of the lead contract *mutatis
mutandis,* the contract describes the parties as operator and contractor. However, in
context this is to be read respectively as contractor (Amec) and sub-contractor (Salamis):
Campbell at paras 6–7.

[135] *Ibid* at para 10.

[136] *Ibid* per Rix L J at paras 18–19.

[137] This point was left open as it was not necessary for the court to decide it: see *Campbell*
per Rix LJ at para 24. In *Orbit Valve,* similar wording was held not to limit the indemnity
only to occasions when the injured party was actively carrying out work under the
contract but to extend also to injuries occurring while the inujured party was on the
platform but at rest: *Orbit Valve* [1995] 1 All E R 174 at 186.

[138] The modern LOGIC standard contract wording, "arising from, relating to or in
connection with the performance of or non-performance of the CONTRACT", is a good
example of a broadly drawn formulation: see, eg, LOGIC, *Services,* para 19.2(b).

Multi-party issues

14.41 Sometimes, for instance, in a consortium or alliancing agreement, there will be more than two parties to the contract. This does nothing to alter the central concept of the indemnity and hold harmless clause. However, the addition of further parties does add a further layer of complexity to the drafting exercise. *Slessor v Vetco Gray* illustrates the difficulties that can be caused by attempting to provide for an unfamiliar situation. This case concerned the interpretation of an indemnity clause contained not in a standard services contract but within a multi-party consortium agreement. The clause was in the following terms: "The Parties hereto mutually and irrevocably undertake to release, defend and indemnify each other for damage to any property and/or injury to/or death of the personnel of the others, arising out of or in connection with the Work, howsoever caused."[139]

14.42 At first glance this may look very like a fairly standard mutual indemnity and hold harmless clause (albeit one in which the parties use the expression "release" rather than "hold harmless"). However, it differs from such a clause in one crucial respect. Ordinarily, A will indemnify B in respect of any injuries suffered by A's personnel. This clause was held to achieve something quite different: A here indemnifies B and C for any injury suffered by B and C's personnel while B gives a like indemnity to A and C in respect of injury or death to their personnel, and party C similarly indemnifies A and B. The court declined to interpret the clause *contra proferentem*, for the reasons which were given above,[140] and recognised that it would be unusual for the parties intentionally to draft a clause in these terms.[141] However, the court felt that the words used by the draftsman were clear and unambiguous, and that effect must be given to them.[142] This was a Scottish case and no attempt was made to persuade the court to apply Lord Hoffmann's restatement. Without knowing what matrix of fact evidence would have been available, it is idle to speculate on what the outcome would have been had the case been an English one,

---

[139] *Slessor v Vetco Gray* at para 3.

[140] See the discussion at para 14.31.

[141] *Slessor v Vetco Gray* per Lord Glennie at para 11. The court observed that the usual regime could easily have been put in place by substituting the contentious phrase with "their own personnel". A yet safer way of drafting the clause might have been to individually list out each party's responsibilities to the others. This can be cumbersome, particularly where multiple parties are concerned, but in such matters elegance is less important than clarity. Inverting the intentions of the parties, which seems to be what occurred in *Slessor*, may seem an extreme drafting error, but there is always a risk, when trying to draft indemnities in too concise a form, of inadvertently creating ambiguity, or of failing to consider which result would obtain under the clause in any given factual situation.

[142] *Slessor v Vetco Gray* at para 11.

or had the parties sought to persuade the judge that Lord Hoffmann's restatement is part of Scots law. However, given that the wording achieved the diametric opposite of one what would ordinarily expect an indemnity clause to be seeking to achieve, one cannot help but wonder if this may have been one of the occasions referred to by Lord Hoffmann, where "the language has gone wrong".

"Full and primary"
In *London Bridge*, one of the arguments advanced in the attempt   14.43
to defeat the operators' claim under the indemnity was that, as the operators' insurers had already settled the claims of the contractor's employees or their representatives, the operators had suffered no loss in respect of which they required to be indemnified. It was also argued that the operators' insurers could not claim under the indemnity either, on the basis that both the insurers and the contractual indemnifiers had offered primary indemnities, and the insurers were therefore not entitled to rights of subrogation, but only to contribution;[143] the argument ran that subrogation rights were enjoyed only by a secondary indemnifier who has paid "out of order", to allow it to recover from the primary indemnifier who has a stronger obligation to settle the claim. The contract was silent on this aspect of the nature of the indemnity. On the particular facts of *London Bridge*, it was held that the contractual indemnity was primary and the insurers were secondary indemnifiers entitled to their right of subrogation. Thus they could claim to be reimbursed in full. However it must be emphasised that this decision does not settle all such debates once and for all; for instance, the decision was based at least in part upon the fact that there was no contractual obligation upon the operators to insure.[144] How the court would have decided the matter if there had been such an obligation is therefore an open question. Best practice (which does not appear to have been followed in the LOGIC Standard contracts, but which is in evidence in the IMHH[145]) is therefore to expressly state that the indemnities are "full and primary".

Stray indemnities
Throughout this chapter, references have from time to time been   14.44
made to the "indemnity clause" or the "indemnity and hold harmless clause". However, an oil and gas contract will not necessarily have one "indemnity clause", or even one "set of indemnity provisions". For the reasons given at para 14.7, in addition to the main

---

[143] The Scots law of contribution is concerned with the respective liabilities of joint wrongdoers and is contained in s 3 of the Law Reform (Miscellaneous Provisions) (Scotland) Act 1940.
[144] *London Bridge* per Lord Hoffmann at para 97.
[145] See para 14.51.

indemnity and hold harmless provision, which may be labelled "indemnities",[146] or "indemnities and exceptions"[147] there may very well be one or more less obvious indemnities lurking elsewhere in the contract. These are sometimes described as "stray indemnities". The drafter or reviewer of the contract needs to give some thought as to how these indemnities are intended to fit together. Are *all* indemnities under the contract intended to be given "irrespective of negligence or breach of duty, whether statutory or otherwise", or just the ones in the main indemnity provision? Likewise, do the parties intend to extend the benefit of *all* indemnities to the relevant group(s)? The client's intentions should be checked before the contract is finalised.

Definitional issues

14.45 **Company groups.** In practice it is common for the parties to intend the effect of the indemnity clause to extend beyond the immediate parties so as to include their respective groups. Thus, in an operator-to-contractor contract, a contractor will commonly agree to indemnify and hold harmless the operator's group against loss of or damage to the contractor group's property, and the injury or death of the contractor group's personnel; likewise the operator[148] will usually agree to indemnify the contractor group against loss of or damage to the operator group's property, and the injury or death of the operator group's personnel. Typically, an operator group will be defined so as to include the operator itself, its co-ventures, its and their respective affiliates and its and their respective directors, officers and employees and personnel.[149] A contractor group will generally include the contractor, its subcontractors and its subcontractors' own subcontractors of whatever level, and its and their respective affiliates and its and their respective directors, officers and employees and personnel.[150] This is done in recognition of the fact that contractors and operators will commonly use other members of their groups to carry out the activities and operations envisaged by the contract and, if the benefits of the indemnity regime discussed at paras 14.16–14.18 are to accrue fully, it is necessary for the effect[151]

---

[146] As in the LOGIC contracts: see, eg, Well Services, cl 19.

[147] As in *Farstad* v *Enviroco*; see the contractual provisions reproduced as the Appendix to Lord Clarke's judgment.

[148] The operator is generally referred to, in such contracts, as the "company", and its group as the "company group". However, in the interests of keeping terminology consistent the term "operator" is used throughout this chapter.

[149] See, eg, LOGIC, *Services*, cl 1.2.

[150] See, eg, *ibid*, cl 1.6.

[151] The term "effect" is used because persons who are not party to a contract cannot be directly bound by it; the grouping provisions do not *directly* bind the non-signatory members of the group, but achieve their effect circuitously. If there is a contract between

of the indemnity provisions to extend to all parts of the group. It will usually be the intention of the parties to establish an indemnity regime on a grouped basis. However, parties need to be mindful in such cases not just to scrutinise the indemnity clause but also carefully to check the definition of "group" or whatever cognate expression is being used in the contractual documentation, and to ensure that the implications of accepting those indemnity provisions, read together with that definition, are what is truly intended.[152]

Employees and personnel. As we have seen, many indemnity clauses are concerned with dividing up responsibility for injuries, illnesses or fatalities sustained by people during the course of the project. The expectation will ordinarily be that each party takes responsibility for its own people. Great care needs to be taken in how this intention is expressed. In particular, it should not be expressed too specifically or narrowly, by using a word which has a technical legal meaning, such as "employee" or even "worker". Many people working on a platform will not be "employees" in the formal legal sense, but contractors. If the indemnity refers only to "employees" it is most unlikely to reflect the will of the parties. The current general practice is to frame the indemnity using a less technical term, such as "personnel", and then to define that term broadly.

14.46

Property. Similarly, many indemnity clauses will be concerned with apportioning responsibility for damage to property. Again, it is important for the parties – most particularly, contractors and any subcontractors entrusted with expensive pieces of equipment which they do not own – not to be lured into a false sense of security by observing that the contract contains a clause of this nature, but to give critical thought as to its precise terms, and the terms of any accompanying definition. Contractors will usually want "company property" to be given an expanded definition so that it encompasses not just items owned by the company but all items on the platform which the contractor might be called upon to use and/or which might reasonably be affected by the works carried out by the contractor. The operator will not necessarily own all the expensive or important items of property on the platform: some may be hired, or subject to

14.47

A and B, and a dispute arises between A and a company (B2) which is part of B's group, if A and B's contract states that neither will be liable for the relevant species of loss and provide each other with indemnities in respect of it, then, while B2 is still entitled to sue A if B2 suffers such a loss, A can claim an indemnity in respect of it from B.

[152] A second *Farstad* v *Enviroco* case arising from the same incident as the first but argued in the English courts and pertaining to the definition of "subsidiary" of a parent company group has at time of writing been argued in front of, but not decided by, the Supreme Court: see http://www.supremecourt.gov.uk/current-cases/CCCaseDetails/case_2010_0008.html (accessed 21 February 2011).

retention of title clauses, or may be the property of other contractors, for instance the drilling contractor.

The problem of multiple parties

Introduction to the problem

14.48   As we have already seen, at any given time there is likely to be a multiplicity of parties with personnel and/or property on a production platform.[153] We have already discussed the special difficulties caused by ensuring that all subcontractors within a given contractual chain have appropriate risk allocation terms in place. This, however, is only part of the picture, and the relatively easy part at that. Although the great majority of the undertakings with personnel on a platform at any given time are likely to be in a contractual relationship with *someone*, unless special measures have been put in place,[154] they will not *all* be in a contractual relationship with each other. They will all be involved in *a* contractual chain; however, they will not all be involved in *the same* contractual chain. Diagrammatically, the situation can be shown as in Figure 14.3.

If, for example, subcontractor D2 negligently causes an explosion which injures personnel from D, A, D1A and B2, then there will be a direct contractual link (and presumably an indemnity and hold harmless provision) between D2 and D. Moreover, it is likely that back-to-back provisions will exist which, issues such as insolvency and drafting errors apart, will have the effect of apportioning risk throughout D2's contractual chain: ie from A, through D and D2 down to D2A. However, there is no contractual connection, and therefore no contractual indemnity, between D2 and D1A, or between D2 and B2.

14.49   There are a number of ways in which to resolve this issue. One option available at least in theory is for the parties to simply take the view that such risk will be dealt with by the law at large.[155] This, however, means that all contractors on the platform are going to have to take out extensive insurance cover against the contingency that they cause injury to each other's personnel, or damage each other's property. For the reasons already given,[156] this solution would undercut much of the economic benefits of the indemnity regime; it is therefore unattractive. A system whereby the parties entering into individual mutual hold harmless agreements with all other contractors with whom they would otherwise have no contractual

---

[153] See paras 14.19–14.21.
[154] See para 14.49.
[155] Discussed at para 14.27.
[156] See paras 14.16–14.18.

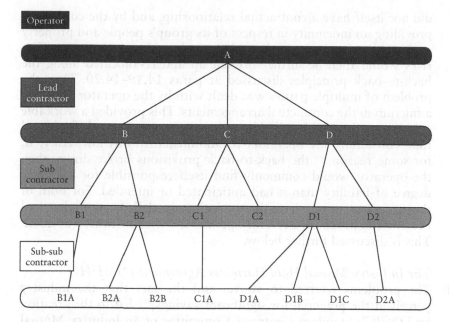

Figure 14.3 Simplified example of contractual relations on a production platform

link is also a possibility, but would require significant administrative effort, expense and co-ordination and would have the potential to go awry, leaving dangerous gaps in insurance cover if, for instance, a new contractor or subcontractor not previously known to operate on the platform was awarded a contract and information about this was not promptly disseminated among the contracting community on that platform. This potential solution is therefore again unattractive in practice. Until the early 2000s, the practice in the UKCS was generally that the operator and contractor would grant indemnities on a grouped basis, with the operator's group[157] defined so as to include "other contractors"[158] and the contractor's group defined so as to include its affiliates and all subcontractors of whatever level. The operator provided the contractor with an indemnity in respect of all claims relative to the people and property not just of the operator, but also of all contractors with whom the contractor

---

[157] See para 14.45.

[158] This term would be defined so as to include all contractors involved in operations other than the contractor's own subcontractors of whatever level. If one refers to Figure 14.3, if the operator (A) was contracting with contractor D on this model, A would define its Group so as to include all contractors of whatever level within the chain of contractual relationships flowing from its contracts with B and C.

did not itself have a contractual relationship, and by the contractor providing an indemnity in respect of its group's people and property not just to the operator, but also to the other contractors. The risks would then be further broken up and re-allocated along the back-to-back principles discussed at paras 14.19–14.20. Thus the problem of multiple parties was dealt with by the operator acting as a fulcrum in the contractual arrangements. This provided a workable solution to the problem.[159] However, the practice was difficult and time consuming for operators to administer. It was also risky: if, for some reason,[160] the back-to-back provisions broke down, then the operator would commonly find itself responsible for a greater degree of liability than it had anticipated or intended. For both of these reasons a more ambitious solution, modelled upon what had become the practice of certain operators,[161] was instituted in 2002. This is discussed further below.

The Industry Mutual Hold Harmless Agreement ("IMHH")

14.50   The problems referred to above, and the fact that the industry perceived the potential for significant savings,[162] led to the creation by LOGIC's Standard Contracts Committee of an Industry Mutual Hold Harmless sub-committee which, after extensive consultation, recommended the institution of a Mutual Hold Harmless Scheme and prepared a draft of the relevant Deed.[163] This scheme was initially effected by the Mutual Indemnity and Hold Harmless Deed

---

[159] This approach continues to be used in a number of jurisdictions, including Norway. The author is grateful to Prof Knut Kaasen of the Scandinavian Institute of Maritime Law, University of Oslo, for this information.

[160] Eg, drafting error such that the first level of indemnification worked but the back-to-back provision was ineffectual; or a failure to ensure that a back-to-back arrangement was entered into.

[161] Eg Shell.

[162] See LOGIC, *Benefits for Participants*, available for download from: http://www.imhh.com/benefits.cfm (accessed 21 February 2011): "It is believed that the industry as whole will make a significant financial saving from an effective implementation of the IMHH Scheme. It is impossible to put precise figures on this saving but industry discussions have suggested that a saving in legal fees of £17MM per annum may be possible. In addition to this there are the internal costs of all the parties involved in claims and counter claims which must be significant. The benefit across the industry could exceed £20MM per annum."

[163] LOGIC, *About*: see text under the heading, "Introduction". Note that although the word "indemnity" is not used by LOGIC in its introductory discussion of the Deed, as we shall see, the core risk allocation provision of the Deed is clearly a mutual hold harmless and indemnity clause.

(the "IMHH Deed")[164] which had been signed by 93 parties[165] when the scheme became effectual on 1 July 2002.[166] A significant number of other contractors have subsequently entered the scheme since by executing standard Deeds of Adherence.[167] At the time of writing, some 620 parties were shown as registered on the IMHH website.[168] The scheme is presently administered by LOGIC[169] (which is itself the beneficiary of extensive simple indemnity provisions relative to losses which might arise as a result of the manner in which it carries out its administrative function: see IMHH Deed, cll 4.2 and 4.3 read together with cl 6.1(ii)). LOGIC's primary functions are to act as the signatories' attorney in executing Deeds of Adherence with new parties, receive and intimate to the remaining parties any notices of withdrawal, ascertain and act upon the will of the signatories upon the occurrence of any of the events which allow signatories to vote on whether to terminate the scheme, and to maintain the IMHH website. The form of the Deed which is currently in force (the "2002 Deed") expires at the end of 31 December 2011. A replacement Deed (the "2012 Deed"[170]), which will enter into force immediately upon the expiry of the 2002 Deed, is already in existence and has to date been signed by some 220 parties. The terms of the 2002 Deed will be discussed immediately below. The core provisions of the 2012 Deed are virtually identical to those of its 2002 counterpart. However, the 2012 Deed differs in its scope, geographical extent, and in the powers enjoyed by its Administrator. These differences will be discussed at para 14.61.

The 2002 Deed's core indemnity provisions. The central purpose of   **14.51** the Deed is to provide an efficient and practical means of bringing into existence an effectual set[171] of hold harmless indemnities between parties who, save for the purposes of entering into an

---

[164] Although the Deed bringing the scheme into existence is clearly entitled the "Mutual Indemnity and Hold Harmless Deed", it is known throughout the industry as the "IMHH Deed". This chapter will follow the prevailing industry practice.

[165] Listed in Sch 1 to the IMHH Deed.

[166] IMHH Deed, cl 7.1, read together with the date of the Deed.

[167] A pro-forma Deed of Adherence is annexed to the IMHH Deed as Sch 2.

[168] See LOGIC, *List of Signatories*, available for download from: http://www.imhh.com/signatories.cfm (accessed 21 February 2011). This compares with some 320 at the time when the first edition of this book was published in 2007.

[169] IMHH Deed, cl 1.1, definition of "Administrator". The Administrator may be replaced when a majority of signatories believe it has carried out its duties incompetently: see IMHH Deed, cl 4.4.

[170] Both versions of the Deed are available for download from http://www.imhh.com/deed.cfm (accessed 21 February 2011).

[171] As we shall see, the Deed does not provide for a wholly comprehensive set of indemnities: matters such as pollution are not included. See para 14.52.

agreement about the allocation of physical risks, would have no commercial imperative to contract with each other. The IMHH Deed achieves this by providing that (subject to certain very significant exceptions which are discussed at para 14.59),

> "the Signatories shall be solely responsible for and shall defend, indemnify and hold harmless the other Signatories and the other members of their respective Groups against all Claims arising from, out of, or relating to the Services in connection with:
> (i) personal injury to or sickness, disease or death of Personnel of the Indemnifying Signatory or any other members of its Group; and
> (ii) loss of, recovery of, or damage to any Property of the Indemnifying Signatory or any other members of its Group; and
> (iii) Consequential Loss suffered by the Indemnifying Signatory or any other members of its Group".[172]

The "indemnities given pursuant to this Deed"[173] are expressed as being "full and primary" and to apply "irrespective of cause and notwithstanding the negligence or breach of duty (whether statutory or otherwise) of the Indemnified Party and shall apply irrespective of any claim in tort, under contract or otherwise at law".[174]

14.52　　Taking the main indemnity and hold harmless clause phrase by phrase, in connection with all claims arising from, out of, or relating to the services[175] that it covers,[176] it provides a full and primary[177] mutual indemnity and hold harmless regime drawn on a grouped basis,[178] operating irrespective of negligence or breach of duty, whether statutory or otherwise,[179] and covering (1) personal injury, sickness, disease or death of an expansively-drawn set of people defined as "Personnel"; and (2) loss of, recovery of, or damage to "Property" and (3) a class of loss defined as "Consequential Loss".[180] Thus the IMHH Deed provides indemnities and a hold harmless provisions in respect of many, but by no means all, of the areas where the industry commonly utilises mutual indemnity clauses.[181]

---

[172] IMHH Deed cl 2.1.
[173] Note that this term is habile to include not just the main cl 2.1 indemnity but also others that may exist throughout the Deed – eg the indemnities given to the Administrator by cl 4.2 and 4.3, discussed at para 14.50.
[174] IMHH Deed cl 2.2.
[175] As defined by IMHH Deed cl 1.1
[176] Note the important exceptions discussed at para 14.60.
[177] The importance of obtaining a "full and primary" indemnity is discussed at para 14.43.
[178] Grouped indemnities are discussed at para 14.45.
[179] See the discussion at paras 14.34–14.38.
[180] Note that each of these terms are given extended definitions: see the IMHH Deed, para 1.1.
[181] The Deed does not cover, for instance, pollution: this is because "[t] he prevailing consensus in the industry was that the scheme should apply to personal injury, property

The indemnity clause is supported by a clause providing for a waiver of rights of subrogation[182] and is a meticulously drafted clause which avoids the errors and ambiguities of many of the clauses which have been litigated in the past.[183] It is superior to the standard LOGIC indemnity and hold harmless provision in that it expressly states that the indemnity is "full and primary".

Other important provisions. The IMHH contains a number of other significant provisions which will be discussed briefly in turn.   14.53

Entry into force. As has already been noted, the IMHH Deed entered into force as between its original signatories on 1 July 2002.[184] The Deed becomes effective as between those parties from that date.[185] However, many parties have entered the IMHH scheme since it was instituted. Such parties do so by entering into a Deed of Adherence[186] between themselves and all the other current members of the scheme, who sign per the Administrator as attorney.[187] Such parties are known as "New Parties"[188] and become members of the scheme only from the date on which a Deed of Adherence signed by that Signatory has been dated by the Administrator".[189] The IMHH website displays the date when each party to the Deed became a member of the scheme.[190] The Deed expressly states that the cl 2 indemnities[191] do not apply and are not enforceable "in respect of any Claims arising out of events occurring prior to the date on which   14.54

---

damage and consequential losses only. Other areas of risk such as pollution were considered, but were ultimately discounted. One of the main reasons for having a mutual hold harmless arrangement in respect of a Signatory's own property, personnel and consequential loss is that the Signatory is best placed to assess the value at risk and, if required, make the appropriate insurance arrangements. Pollution risks are less quantifiable and hence would have created a complication to the IMHH provisions which was not widely welcomed". See LOGIC, *IMHH Frequently Asked Questions*, available for download from: http://www.imhh.com/faq.cfm (accessed 21 February 2011) (hereinafter "LOGIC, FAQ").

[182] IMHH Deed, cl 5. This clause is further discussed at para 14.57.
[183] Note, however, that as the IMHH Deed uses identical wording to the clause litigated in *Farstad v Enviroco*, there may now be occasions when its provisions will have to withstand a challenge under the terms of UCTA. See para 14.26.
[184] IMHH Deed, cl 7.1, read together with the date of the Deed.
[185] *Ibid*, cl 11.
[186] *Ibid*, cl 4.1; see also Sch 2 to the Deed for the prescribed for of the Deed of Adherence.
[187] IMHH Deed, cl 4.2.
[188] *Ibid*, cl 4.1.
[189] *Ibid*, cl 11.
[190] See http://www.imhh.com/signatories.cfm (accessed 21 February 2011). To view the dates, click on the hyperlink embedded within the name of each of the parties.
[191] Ie the core indemnity provisions discussed at paras 14.51–14.52.

that Signatory became a Signatory".[192] For original signatories, that relevant date is 1 July 2002; for new parties, the date of their Deed of Adherence.

14.55   *Order of precedence.* The Deed expressly provides that it "shall not take precedence over, amend, modify or apply to the terms of any agreement between Signatories entered into prior to, on or after this Deed becoming effective in relation to such Signatories".[193] It is worth emphasising that the Deed refers to "*any*" agreement. So where a particular incident involves a dispute between signatories to the Deed who are at the material time in a contractual relationship germane to the provision of Services as understood by the Deed,[194] the specific contract will take precedence over the general Deed. This is so even where the specific contract is silent – either by accident or design – on the question of risk allocation. Thus the IMHH Deed will not ride to the rescue if signatories to it are in a direct contractual relationship and omit to include indemnity provisions, or include provisions which are ineffectual. This is to provide signatories with the freedom to enter into different liability arrangements if they so wish.

14.56   *Extension of benefits to groups.* In common with many oil and gas indemnity clauses in the UKCS,[195] the indemnity and hold harmless provisions in the IMHH Deed are drawn so as to be for the benefit only of the Deed's immediate signatories but also to "the other members of their respective Groups".[196] The Deed defines "Group" broadly so as to include *inter alia* "the Signatory in question and its respective Affiliates, the Personnel of all of the foregoing and their Invitees",[197] and cl 6.1(i) utilises the provisions of the Contracts (Rights of Third Parties) Act 1999 to extend the benefits of the core, cl 2 indemnity provision, and also the waiver of subrogation clause, discussed immediately below, to all members of a Signatory's Group.[198]

14.57   *Waiver of rights of subrogation.* The IMHH Deed provides that the signatories thereto shall procure that their insurers shall waive their

---

[192] IMHH Deed, cl 2.3.

[193] *Ibid*, cl 11.

[194] See the definition in the IMHH Deed, cl 1.1

[195] Discussed at para 14.45.

[196] IMHH Deed, cl 2.1.

[197] For the full definition, see IMHH Deed, cl 1.1, "Group" read together with the other defined terms which themselves feature within that definition.

[198] The IMHH cl 6.1(ii) extends the benefit of the cl 4 indemnities referred to at para 14.50 to the Administrator who, although extensively mentioned throughout the Deed, is not a party to it.

rights of subrogation or any other rights they may have to proceed against the other signatories or members of those signatories' groups in relation to the matters covered by the Deed.[199] Signatories are entitled to require each other to exhibit evidence of the waiver.[200] The Deed also states that, in the event that the parties fail to procure the relevant waiver, the failing party's rights to enforce its rights and benefits under the IMHH Deed shall be suspended.[201]

Right to defend. As has already been noted, the obligation to **14.58** indemnify and hold harmless is separate and distinct from the right and obligation to defend a claim; however, it is relatively common within the UKCS for the indemnifier to accept (or demand) responsibility for conducting the defence of any claim made against the party it is indemnifying.[202] Under the IMHH Deed, the indemnifying signatory (ie the party who is, in the event of a claim, liable under the Deed to indemnify whosoever the claim is initially directed towards by the party suffering a loss) is entitled, but not obliged, to take over the conduct of the defence to any such claim.[203] Where this option is exercised the indemnifying signatory accepts certain obligations concerning the provision of information to,[204] and consulting with,[205] the indemnified signatory, and is in turn entitled to reasonable assistance from the indemnified signatory in the conduct of the defence.

Parties to the IMHH Deed enter into a contractual relationship **14.59** which radically re-allocates the legal liabilities they carry.[206] Where a company is a member of the IMHH scheme, other members of the scheme are likely to feel entitled to refrain from entering into mutual hold harmless indemnity contracts, and/or to purchase less insurance cover which they would otherwise have been likely to believe they required. It is therefore imperative that signatories to the Deed know with certainty which parties are members of the scheme at any given time. For this reason, the right to withdraw from the scheme is quite heavily regulated. Upon signature, the parties are locked in to membership of the scheme until 31 December 2011 subject only to

---

[199] IMHH Deed, cl 5.1.

[200] *Ibid*, cl 5.2

[201] *Ibid*, cl 5.3.

[202] See para 14.8.

[203] IMHH Deed, cl 3.2. Where it does not take up this option, the Indemnified Party assumes an obligation not to settle the case without the consent of the Indemnifying Signatory: IMHH Deed, cl 3.4.

[204] IMHH Deed, cl 3.2(ii).

[205] *Ibid*, cl 3.2(iii).

[206] For a general discussion on the effect that an indemnity clause has upon the normal system of risk allocation provided by the underlying law, see para 14.27.

potential escape points occurring on 1 April 2004, 2006, 2008 and 2010 where they may withdraw, but only in the event that they have provided the Administrator with 60 days' notice of this intention.[207] Such a withdrawal takes effect "from 00:01 hours on the date of such withdrawal"[208] and does not have retrospective effect.

14.60   *Exceptions.* A number of exceptions are carved out of the IMHH Deed's core indemnity and hold harmless provisions or introduced by way of the Deed's defined terms. Each of these has a very significant practical impact upon the Deed's scope. Each is discussed below.

- *Transportation by air excluded.* None of the cl 2 indemnities applies or is given in relation to "any Claims arising from, out of or relating to the transportation by air of any member of a Signatory's Group". Thus, transportation by air falls wholly outside the scope of the IMHH Scheme.
- *Limited application to certain defined services.* Clause 2.5 of the IMHH Deed provides that the cl 2.1(ii) and (iii) indemnities[209] do not apply and are not given in respect of any claims that arise from, out of, or relate to: (i) the carriage of goods by sea, (ii) the provision of emergency response and rescue vessels or services associated with them, or (iii) heavy lift services involving a heavy lift vessel.[210] Note, however, that unlike transportation by air, these services are not altogether excluded from the scope of the core indemnities; the cl 2.1(i) indemnity relative to personal injury, sickness, disease or death continues to apply.
- *Landward areas.* Despite the fact that, in practice, onshore works will quite commonly be the subject of indemnity provisions similar to those governing offshore,[211] the IMHH Deed applies only to services and/or supplies "carried out on or in the United Kingdom Continental Shelf and/or between the United Kingdom low water mark and the innermost boundary of the United Kingdom Continental Shelf".[212] Thus, services or supplies carried out on the landward side of the UK low water mark are excluded. This has the effect of excluding onshore

---

[207] IMHH Deed, cl 7.2. The Administrator is obliged by the same clause to notify all other parties in writing.

[208] *Ibid*, cl 7.2, read with the definition of "Signatory".

[209] Ie the indemnities given in respect of property and consequential loss discussed in greater detail at paras 14.51–14.52.

[210] Note that the IMHH Deed gives extended definitions to each of these terms: see cl 2.5, read with cl 1.1.

[211] LOGIC, *Services* is intended to be applied both on- and offshore. Note also that the pursuer in *Slessor* v *Vetco Gray* was working onshore when he was injured.

[212] IMHH Deed, cl 1.1, definition of "Services".

services, and will also have the effect of excluding any services or supplies carried out in the part of the territorial sea which lies on the landward side of the low water mark.[213] It was decided to so limit the effect of the IMHH Deed because:

"The general industry view was that extending the IMHH to cover onshore activities as well as offshore activities could have inadvertently led to the application of the IMHH in circumstances where it was not intended (e.g. motor vehicle accidents) and, as such, in order to avoid any ambiguity it was limited to offshore activities only."[214]

- *Operators.* Although operators played a substantial part in bring it into being, the IMHH Deed is designed for, and signed by, the contracting sector. It is not well suited to operator-to-operator situations[215] and, given that the operator sits at the top of the contractual pyramid, operators should already be in a direct or at least indirect contractual relationship with anyone who steps onto their platform for commercial purposes, and therefore in a position to negotiate whatever contractual risk allocation regime the parties to those contracts choose.[216]

The 2012 Deed. The 2012 Deed differs from its 2002 counterpart in three material respects.[217] First, the geographical extent of the 2012 Deed is broader; it applies not only to services provided on or in the United Kingdom Continental Shelf and/or between the United Kingdom low water mark and the innermost boundary of the United Kingdom Continental Shelf, but also to those carried out within Irish territorial waters and upon the Irish Continental Shelf.[218] Second, the limitations imposed upon the scope of the indemnity and hold harmless provisions by cl 2(5) of the 2002 Deed relative to the carriage of goods by sea, emergency response and rescue services and heavy lift services are not repeated in the 2012 Deed. Thus such services now fall to be treated in like manner to other services for the purposes of the 2012 Deed. Third, the administrator, LOGIC, is provided with a more explicit right to outsource the performance of its administrative duties than it previously enjoyed: cl 4.4 states that the administrator shall be "entitled to discharge any of its obligations and/or duties under this Deed by

14.61

---

[213] A surprisingly large area, although not one in which large amounts of oil and gas operations have been undertaken: see para 4.1.

[214] See LOGIC, *FAQ*.

[215] The possibility of an operator-to-operator IMHH Deed is discussed at para 14.65.

[216] See LOGIC, *FAQ*, under the heading "Can Operators sign?".

[217] It should be noted that, as at the time of writing, the 2012 Deed is not in force: the conflicting provisions of the 2002 Deed will govern the issues discussed in this paragraph until the 2002 Deed expires at the end of 2011.

[218] 2012 Deed, para 1.1, definition of "Services".

procuring that such obligations or duties are performed on its behalf by another person", to be known as the Service Provider. The service provider, like the administrator, may be replaced if the majority of the parties to the Deed so wish. The service provider does not, through the operation of the IMHH Deed itself, obtain a right to share in the simple indemnity and hold harmless provision granted to but one would presume that any person agreeing to act in that capacity would insist upon obtaining the benefit of a back-to-back indemnity from the administrator in any contract appointing them to the position.

14.62 **Commentary and conclusions on the IMHH Scheme.** Some brief concluding words on the scheme are offered below.

The contractual nature of the scheme

14.63 It is important to appreciate that the Deed (in either its 2002 or 2012 incarnation) is not a document in the nature of a piece of legislation. It does not impose rights and create obligations by virtue of the mere fact that it exists. It is a contractual solution to a problem; it is just not *the same* contractual solution that the oil and gas industry previously deployed. It is axiomatic, therefore, that it takes effect only between those parties who have executed it, or those who have entered into a Deed of Adherence. It needs to be emphasised that some very important oil and gas contractors are not adherents to the Deed, and are therefore outside the ambit of the scheme. In particular, very few drilling companies have signed the deed. It is understood that this is because the potential losses which may be suffered by drilling contractors, whose equipment is extremely valuable, and who will commonly have relatively large numbers of personnel on a rig or platform, is substantially larger than most contractors, and the drilling community have by and large yet to be persuaded of the value of the scheme. Other contractors will need to take appropriate steps to accommodate the risk caused by this refusal, either by seeking an indemnity from the operator, entering into a mutual hold harmless and indemnity arrangement directly with the driller, or simply by accepting the exposure and insuring accordingly. In addition, and as noted above, the Deed's order of precedence clause means that the Deed is rendered irrelevant if there is any direct contractual relationship bearing upon "Services" as understood by the Deed.

Potential dangers of the IMHH

14.64 The IMHH was launched with considerable fanfare and broad industry backing[219] and has quickly been accepted by the majority of

---

[219] It was launched under the auspices of LOGIC and with the support of UKOOA, IMCA, OCA and WSCA.

the contracting community in the UKCS. It provides a solution to a problem which has caused considerable difficulties and inefficiencies for some time. There is no reason to believe that in general terms the scheme has been, or will continue to be, anything other than a success. However, the IMHH initiative – or perhaps more properly, the initiative's application in practice – is not without its potential pitfalls. The Deed, while by no means long, is, of necessity, relatively complex. While many of the contractors who operate within the UKCS are large and sophisticated companies possessing the under-standing and resources to ensure that their personnel understand the full import of the scheme, this is not true of all contractors. It is least possible that, in spite of the efforts which have been made by LOGIC to promote an understanding of the Deed, not all signatories to the scheme are fully conversant with all its subtleties. Certainly in the early days of the IMHH Deed's implementation it is fair to say that the import of the Deed's precedence provisions was not univer-sally appreciated,[220] and some parties seemed to be unaware of the fact that the indemnities on the Deed did not cover true third-party visitors to a platform. Such misconceptions are alarming as, if the parties do not have a full comprehension of the way the IMHH Deed allocates risk, there is a danger of gaps in insurance cover. While one would hope that the Deed is now better understood, this should not be assumed: new contractors, some of whom work in the offshore field only semi-regularly, are signing up all the time. Moreover the natural turnover of staff within even the more established players means that ongoing training and education is essential. In addition, and rather perversely, as the Deed becomes more broadly accepted, there is the danger that familiarity may breed contempt. Procedures may become sloppy, and parties may simply assume that everyone working on a particular rig or platform with whom they are not in a contractual relationship is a subscriber to the IMHH Deed. As we have already seen, however, this is unlikely to be true of the driller, and may not be true of all other contractors. If the contractor is to minimise risk it is incumbent upon it to ascertain whose property and personnel is or will be on the platform at the material time and to check that those on board fall within the ambit of the IMHH scheme, or to obtain a binding contractual undertaking from the operator that (apart from true third parties), only subscribers to the IMHH will be permitted onto the platform. None of this is intended to attack the principles underlying the IMHH Deed, which

---

[220] Discussed at para 14.55. For a time, a number of parties held the belief that the IMHH Deed could rectify a defective indemnity in an existing contract.

the author considers to be sound, but simply to urge due care in the scheme's application.

Other potential developments: operator-to-operator hold harmless

14.65 At the time of publication of the previous edition of this book, Oil & Gas UK Ltd was promoting discussions on the possibility of establishing an operator-to-operator hold-harmless scheme.[221] It was noted that as operator-to-operator activities are by no means always undertaken on a mutual indemnity basis the prospects of an operator-to-operator scheme were perhaps rather remote, and so it has proved. At time of writing there seems to be no realistic prospect of such a Deed coming into existence in the near future.

LIABILITY FOR "CONSEQUENTIAL" LOSS

14.66 In addition to containing the indemnity and indemnity and hold harmless provisions described above, a wide variety of oil and gas contracts will also include clauses which exclude, limit[222] or put in place an indemnity and hold harmless regime[223] in respect of liability for so-called "consequential or indirect" losses.[224] Such provisions are commonplace in operator-to-contractor contracts[225] and are seen in some – but by no means all – oil-company-to-oil-company contracts.[226]

---

[221] Correspondence with UKOOA in February 2007, held on file.

[222] With reference to the discussion at para 14.24, in so far as these contracts "exclude" or "limit" such loss they are subject to the provisions of the Unfair Contract Terms Act 1977, but not the 1999 Regulations. However, the courts have repeatedly held that, while they will always consider full circumstances of the case (see, eg, *Motours Ltd* v *Eurobell (West Kent) Ltd* [2003] EWHC 614 (QB)), it will be only in unusual circumstances that they will hold a business–business exclusion of consequential loss clause unreasonable: see *Wessanen Foods Ltd* v *Jofson Ltd* [2006] EWHC 1325 (TCC); *Photo Production Ltd* v *Securicor Transport Ltd* [1980] AC 827.

[223] A carefully drafted mutual indemnity regime is thought necessary where the intention is to extend the effect of the consequential loss provisions to groups: if there is a contract between A and B, and a dispute arises between A and a company (B2) which is part of B's group, a simple exclusion or limitation of consequential loss will not be binding upon B2. However, if A and B state that neither will be liable for the other group's consequential losses and provide each other with indemnities and hold harmless provisions in respect of such loss, then, while B2 is still entitled to sue A if B2 suffers a consequential loss, A can claim an indemnity back from B.

[224] The precise terminology varies: sometimes "consequential loss" or "indirect loss" is used on its own. Sometimes "damages" is used instead of "loss". See the discussion in *London Bridge* (Inner House) 2000 SLT 1123 per LP Rodger at 1156D–E.

[225] They appear throughout the LOGIC standard contracts series. See, eg, LOGIC, *Supply of Major Items* at cl 24.

[226] See A Jennings, "FPSO Agreements" and J Izod, "Satellite Tie-back and Processing Agreements", both in M David (ed), *Oil and Gas Infrastructure and Midstream Agreements*, (1999), at 209f and 170 respectively.

Where such clauses are used, their purpose is to protect parties from the full consequences of causing certain types of loss, typically delays in or loss of production, loss of use, loss of profits, and business interruption. The quantum of such losses is generally difficult to anticipate in advance, and may be hard to quantify even retrospectively.[227] However, they tend to accrue on a daily basis and, if a particular field, facility or critical piece of infrastructure is "knocked out" for a sustained period of time, these losses can rise to extraordinary and alarming levels. As such, they are frequently either excessively expensive or simply impossible for a contractor to insure against, and the industry has by and large accepted that such losses should lie where they fall. Thus we can see that economic factors very similar to those that drive the indemnity regime underpin the exclusion or limitation of consequential losses.

What is "consequential loss"?

There is considerable uncertainty over what, if any, fixed meaning the term "consequential loss" conveys. For a time, the prevailing interpretation was that the expression had become something of a term of art, and that it denoted a reference to the category of losses encompassed by the second limb of the rule in *Hadley* v *Baxendale*.[228] On this analysis, if a contract excluded liability for consequential loss, the parties would still be able to recover the sort of damages envisaged by the first limb of *Hadley* v *Baxendale*, which is to say, losses "such as may be fairly and reasonably be considered ... [as] arising naturally, i.e. according to the usual course of things, according to the breach itself". However, the parties would not be entitled to recover in respect of the second limb, which is to say, for damages "such as may reasonably be supposed to be in the contemplation of the parties at the time they made the contract as the probable result of the breach".[229] This line of

14.67

---

[227] Note the difficulties which occurred in this regard in *BHP Petroleum Ltd* v *British Steel plc and Dalmine SpA* [2000] 2 Lloyd's Rep 277 (hereinafter "*BHP Petroleum*").

[228] (1854) 9 Ex 341. The line of reasoning sprang from the House of Lords' decision in *Czarnikow Ltd* v *Koufos (The Heron II)* [1969] 1 AC 350. For examples of cases which followed this approach, see, eg, *Croudace Construction Ltd* v *Cawoods Concrete Products Ltd* [1978] 2 Lloyd's Rep 55 and *British Sugar plc* v *NEI Power Products Ltd* (1997) 87 BLR 42.

[229] Note that if this line of reasoning continues to be good law (which is, for the reasons given below, doubted) then it would appear that the House of Lords' decision in *Transfield* v *Mercator* [2008] UKHL 48, [2008] 3 WLR 345 may have had the effect of at least somewhat narrowing the scope of what is meant by direct damages (and concomitantly, expanding the ambit of indirect or consequential damages). In *Transfield*, the House of Lords held that the definition of direct damages was less expansive than had been suggested in *Czarnikow Ltd* v *Koufos*, albeit the *ratio* of Transfield is far from clear: see G Gordon, "Hadley v Baxendale Revisited: Transfield Shipping Inc v Mercator Shipping Inc" (2009) 13 EdinLR 125.

reasoning was, however, disapproved of in *London Bridge*.[230] It would therefore seem to be of no application in the law of Scotland, and it is submitted that it is now of questionable authority in English law. In *London Bridge*, the court held that it was not appropriate to attach "a special, technical meaning" to the phrase "indirect or consequential loss" so that the phrase would be "interpreted as referring to losses which would be regarded as indirect or consequential under the rules in *Hadley* v *Baxendale* and subsequent cases".[231] Instead, while prior court decisions were certainly a relevant consideration, they were not to be thought of as determinative. The court's primary task was to interpret the words in the context in which they were used.[232] When such an approach was taken, the Court of Session held, and the House of Lords confirmed, that the disputed loss in *London Bridge*[233] did not fall to be considered as "indirect or consequential" but was a direct loss.

Commentary and conclusions on consequential loss

14.68   It is wholly understandable that the parties to oil and gas contracts should seek to exclude, place limits upon the recovery of, or seek indemnities in respect of, certain types of potentially exorbitant losses. It is, however, perhaps unfortunate that the term "consequential loss" was ever adopted as the vehicle for attempting to do so. Even when the term was thought to be a synonym for the losses envisaged by the second leg of the *Hadley* v *Baxendale* test, it created difficulties.[234] It is not always easy to ascertain whether a particular type of loss is going to fall within limb one of the test or limb two. There was a clear danger that the contractual draftsman would assume that the

---

[230] As we shall see, the detailed reasoning is contained in the Inner House phase of the case. However, this reasoning was expressly approved of by Lord Mackay of Clashfern in the House of Lords: 2002 SC (HL) 117, [2002] 1 All E.R. (Comm) 321 at para 69. Lord Mackay's judgment was in turn concurred in by all the other judges in the House.

[231] Lord Rodger at 1154.

[232] *London Bridge* (Inner House) 2000 SLT 1123 per LP Rodger at 1156.

[233] The circumstances were rather unusual. Because the operator had a material connection to Texas, they feared (with considerable justification) that if the damages claims of the persons injured and those of the families killed in the disaster were not settled on a generous basis, they might be sued in Texas, where the level of awards of damages were significantly higher than in Scotland. The claims of the injured parties and the families of the deceased were therefore settled on a "mid-Atlantic" basis, which is to say, at a level somewhere between traditional Scots awards and those which could be expected in the state of Texas. The defenders accepted that the element of the Scots element of the damages award was a direct loss, but that the "mid-Atlantic" augmentation was an indirect or consequential loss.

[234] As Treitel notes, "the application of this test gives rise to many problems". See Treitel, *Contract*, at p 965.

expression was a convenient shorthand for *all* of the types of potentially exorbitant or hard to insure losses that he wished to exclude.
However, it was not. Many of the most onerous losses which might
be suffered during oil and gas operations do not clearly fall under the
rubric of the *second* limb of *Hadley* v *Baxendale*, but may instead
be captured by the *first* limb of the test. This can be illustrated by
considering the factual circumstances described in *BHP Petroleum*. In
this case, a contract was entered into for the procurement of steel for
a gas reinjection pipeline. The purpose of the project was to improve
production from a producing oilfield. The steel was in due course
found not to conform to specification. It required to be replaced and
the gas reinjection programme was delayed. In such circumstances,
it is not just the cost of replacing the pipe that "[arises] naturally,
i.e. according to the usual course of things, according to the breach
itself". It is also plainly apparent that production from that oil field
will be delayed for a period of time while these works are carried
out. Production lost during that period of time would therefore
appear to be a direct loss, not a "consequential or indirect" one. So
a clause which – without saying more – excludes "consequential or
indirect" loss is unlikely to exclude the loss described. And while the
London Bridge approach is, it is submitted, a just and sensible one,
it does little to make the situation more straightforward. Although,
as with the contextual approach more generally, it may very well
make the outcome of any given litigation fairer, the uncertainty that
it engenders arguably increases the chances of litigation occurring in
the first place, and may very well make the scope of enquiries of any
litigation which does result more wide ranging.

Against this rather shifting background, the safest way in which to **14.69**
construct a clause excluding or limiting the type of losses which the
oil industry has tended to design as "consequential or indirect" is to
make the working presumption that those words will of themselves
convey very little reliable protection, and to define all essential
content into them. This means that the draftsman must give consideration to the types of uninsurable or potentially exorbitant losses
that might befall the project, and must list them out in the clause.
This is the approach taken by most of the contractual documents in
broad use in the industry just now. There is some disagreement on
whether the best practice is to define consequential loss by reference
to a closed list, or to state that consequential loss "includes but is not
limited to" the potential heads of loss items listed. Jennings favours
the former approach on the basis of clarity,[235] but the latter approach

---

[235] A Jennings, "FPSO Agreements" in M David (ed), *Oil and Gas Infrastructure and Midstream Agreements* (1999) at p 210.

is the one which is used more commonly throughout the industry's standardised contractual documentation. Thus the Industry Mutual Hold Harmless Deed defines consequential loss as:

> "(i) consequential loss under applicable law; and
> (ii) loss and/or deferral of production, loss of product, loss of use and loss of revenue, profit or anticipated profit (if any) whether direct or indirect to the extent that these are not included in (i), whether or not foreseeable at the date of execution of this Deed".[236]

14.70 Finally on this topic, where, as will frequently be the case, the contract contains both an indemnity regime and either an exclusion, limitation or an indemnity in respect of consequential loss, thought needs to be given to the interaction between these provisions. They may very well overlap. It will generally be intended that the consequential loss clause will take precedence over the indemnity provisions.[237] Whatever the parties intend, clear words should be used to express their wishes.

OVERALL LIMITATIONS OF LIABILITY

14.71 An overall limitation of liability[238] – sometimes described as a "liability cap" – is a clause that seeks to limit a party's liability not by reference to particular species of loss, but by reference to a total sum payable. In any given clause, the limit or cap may be expressed in one of a number of different ways: either as a fixed sum of money, or as a proportion (or multiple) of the sum payable for the job. However it is expressed, the level at which the cap is to be set is a commercial matter to be agreed between the parties; the maximum amount of readily available insurance will frequently be the determining factor in such discussions.

14.72 Liability caps are commonplace in oil and gas contracting practice.[239] Such clauses are less frequently written about, simpler to understand and less technically demanding to draft than either indemnity or consequential loss provisions.[240] However, they

---

[236] See the IMHH Deed, cl 1.

[237] See, eg, LOGIC, *Supply of Major Items*, at cl 24.

[238] A straightforward liability cap is of course a limitation clause and is therefore subject to a number of the controls imposed in UCTA, discussed at paras 14.26 and 14.66. For the reasons given at para 14.66, it is thought unlikely that the courts would decline to enforce a cap on liability in all but the most unusual circumstances. However, it is also possible to draft these clauses as indemnities: for reasons similar to those given in para 14.63, this is necessary if the intention is to extend the effect of the cap to groups.

[239] See, eg, LOGIC, *Supply of Major Items*, cl 35.

[240] This is not to say that such clauses create no difficulties. One sometimes encounters liability caps which are subject to exclusions – where this is so, proper risk management requires that the effect of the exclusion must be clearly understood before the clause is agreed to. In addition, the inter-relationship between the liability cap and the warranties provisions in the contract needs to be closely considered.

continue to be of very considerable practical importance, particularly in circumstances where the parties are not prepared to agree to a mutual hold-harmless indemnity and/or consequential loss regime.[241] In these cases, the liability cap is the only clause which stands between a party and the prospect of unlimited – and potentially exorbitant – liability. The importance of the clause is perhaps most clearly demonstrated in the context of applications for access to infrastructure, where owners' refusal in some cases to agree to the *bona fide* enquirer's request for a liability cap has jeopardised or even thwarted the whole commercial deal.[242]

A liability cap is in theory somewhat less important in cases where **14.73** the parties have agreed upon an indemnity regime and/or exclusion of liability for consequential loss. The combined effect of these clauses is, or should be, to shut out a large number of the heads of claim which may result in losses disproportionate to the gains that a party had in contemplation when commencing on the project. However even here a contractor should seek to obtain a liability cap, for two reasons. First, some oil and gas projects are so valuable that even the potential losses which are unequivocally direct may be more than a contractor can comfortably bear. And second, even if the losses which the contractor fears should, strictly speaking, be shut out by the indemnity and/or consequential loss clause, there is always a risk that those clauses might for some reason be susceptible to challenge. A liability cap therefore performs the valuable function of providing a second line of defence against indeterminate or disproportionate liability. Any embarrassment felt by asking for a second line of protection should be swiftly overcome by considering just how dreadful the consequences are likely to be if something has gone wrong with the drafting of the indemnity or consequential loss clause.

---

[241] As we have already seen, indemnities are not uniformly accepted in all oil and gas contracts: see para 14.24.
[242] See para 7.23.

CHAPTER 15

LAW AND TECHNOLOGY IN THE OILFIELD

Martin Ewan

THE IMPORTANCE OF INNOVATION

As has already been noted,[1] by most accepted measures, the UKCS **15.1** has passed the point of peak oil production and is in decline. The core areas of the UKCS – the southern, central and northern North Sea – are maturing; the area is well explored, large fields are found increasingly rarely and those prospects that remain are both smaller and more difficult economically to exploit. At the same time, in the remaining, less explored areas of the UKCS – specifically the North Atlantic Margin – water depth, metocean (meteorological and oceanographic) and geological conditions provide significant challenges to both exploration and development.

For a number of reasons, the UKCS is also a relatively expensive **15.2** place in which to operate. UKCS projects must compete for priority and project funding on a global basis and factors including government fiscal and regulatory policy, the harsh natural environment[2] and the highly complex facilities and skilled personnel required to operate offshore all contribute to a relatively high industrial cost base.

For the foregoing reasons, innovation focused on the twin **15.3** pressures of technical challenge and cost containment is necessary to drive the next generation of North Sea activity. Examples of such activity include developments in subsea technology and automated (usually unmanned) platforms to reduce costs;[3] the use of 4D seismic to identify precision-drilling opportunities

---

[1] See the discussion at Chapter 2.
[2] See para 8.1.
[3] By eliminating the need for a permanent presence on board, health and safety risk is also reduced.

to access small pockets of by-passed oil, thereby increasing recovery from and deferring the decommissioning liabilities of existing fields; and developing techniques for exploiting previously unrecoverable oil (for example, heavy oil and high pressure/ high temperature (HP/HT) fields). In the frontier province of the Atlantic Margin, the focus is on improved seismic imaging (many prospects lie below dense, basaltic sills) and on the adaptation of deep water operations developed for the Outer Shelf of the Gulf of Mexico and for West African and Brazilian waters to the more hostile conditions of the North Atlantic. For over 40 years, innovation has been at the heart of the development of the North Sea, and innovation, both in processes and technology, remains the dominant prerequisite to slowing the basin's rate of decline and ensuring its future.

THE COMMERCIAL CHALLENGE FOR INNOVATORS

15.4 It is axiomatic that innovation in any industry is challenging. Those engaged in technological innovation are by definition operating at the outer edge of their discipline and seeking to solve hitherto unresolved problems. But there are also significant commercial challenges which compound the technical ones. In sectors where innovation is demand led (ie driven by customer requirements rather than academic investigation), there may be multiple competing efforts, each seeking to solve the same practical technical problem. As a result, in the early stages of development, there may be a variety of technical solutions or basic product designs for the same task. Only one – or at best a few – of these will ultimately succeed in the commercial marketplace.

15.5   There is, therefore, a distinct "first-mover" advantage for technical innovators. The first viable product which achieves broad field acceptance tends to benefit from (a) network effects (whereby both the innovator's suppliers and customers build experience of the product and adopt congruent behaviours which make them reluctant to change to an alternative); (b) learning curve effects (the innovator's staff become the leaders in the field, and its solutions benefit from the lessons learned in earlier operations); and, potentially – although because of the comparative size of the oil and gas target customer market this is of less importance than for many consumer products – (c) economies of scale. If an innovative company misses the window of opportunity to become the dominant, or at least a significant, supplier, then, regardless of how technically superior its solution might be, it will be extremely hard to dislodge the incumbent to achieve commercial success.

In order to prove the viability of a product, the innovator **15.6**
must carry out field testing to an appropriate standard. With
this requirement in mind it is perhaps worth pausing to consider
the contracting structure of the upstream oil industry in the
UK, which over the past 20 years has developed a tiered nature.
Operators directly undertake relatively few operations; rather,
they contract the operations to what can best be described as
the oligopoly of "tier one" contractors that emerged from the
major consolidation of the service sector in the early 1990s.[4]
These tier one contractors each offer a broad – and generally
the entire – range of services needed for a particular function.
For example, the tier one contractors in the drilling and well
operations sector are each capable of providing all necessary
services and products required to drill a well, mostly from their
own internal resources. Only those products and services which
are infrequently required, or are so highly specialised as to be
uneconomic to develop internally, are purchased from second tier
suppliers.

Operators are therefore increasingly accustomed to the "one-stop **15.7**
shop" approach offered by the tier one contractors, with all the
service benefits of co-ordination and interoperability that that
implies. However, the side-effect of this structure is that these tier
one contractors can act as a gateway to the operators, filtering
customer requirements that might otherwise drive innovation and
passing to second tier suppliers only those they themselves are
unwilling or unable to deliver.

The practical difficulties faced by an innovative small company **15.8**
in gaining the field trial experience which is crucial to proving
a concept can be significant – even fatal. The author is aware of
technological innovations that have left the UK not because they
were not of value to UKCS operations, but because their developers were unable to gain the early field experience necessary to
commercialise the product. It is also notable that many innovative
start-ups choose to exit by way of trade sale to a first-tier contractor,
rather than to pursue development of a global presence themselves.
Of course, many of the tier one contractors are also hot-beds
of innovation; possessing both the financial resources to attack
big problems and the necessary access to both field testing and
markets.

---

[4] Research on R&D funding carried out by Cambridge Energy Research Associates in
2004 produced what is now regarded as the "classic" pattern of a drop in R&D funding
by E&P companies against a correlative increase by service companies, which they state
is still directionally true. See http://www.spe.org/jpt/2009/01/firm-provides-insights-on-rd-
trends-for-the-ep-sector/ (accessed 18 March 2011).

15.9   These challenges are, of course, commercial rather than legal, but the practising lawyer will recognise the importance of not only establishing and preserving the value of innovation through effective protection of intellectual property, but also obtaining appropriate contractual protection against the backdrop of these fundamental industry dynamics.

15.10   The importance of innovation has been recognised by the industry and one particular initiative seems to be producing positive results. The Industry Technology Facilitator (ITF) is a "not for profit" organisation owned by 21 major global operators and service companies.[5] Since its inception, it has been responsible for almost 140 projects (involving direct funding of around £40 million). The ITF's methodology is to establish the dominant technological needs from among its membership and then to advertise a "call for papers", seeking technical proposals for new technology from around the globe. Appropriate technology can then gain access to development funding through the ITF, be engaged in Joint Industry Projects and (crucially) obtain access to field trial opportunities.

15.11   The academic community has also moved to embrace the challenges and opportunities presented specifically by the subsea technology market, by creating the National Subsea Research Institute (NSRI), as a focus for subsea research, development and testing. NSRI was formed by a partnership between the University of Aberdeen, the University of Dundee and the Robert Gordon University, in collaboration with the industry body Subsea UK. It seeks to bring together the expertise, know-how and innovation of partner organisations (spanning academia, industry and the supply chain) in order to develop a national strategy designed to facilitate the delivery of a sustainable UK base in subsea technology.

THE LEGAL PROTECTION OF OILFIELD TECHNOLOGY: AN OVERVIEW OF INTELLECTUAL PROPERTY

15.12   The legal protection of technology is largely the province of intellectual property (IP) law. More specifically, it is the areas of patents, copyright and confidential information[6] which form the bedrock of

---

[5] Further information on ITF is available at http://www.oil-itf.com (accessed 13 March 2011).

[6] Although not strictly a species of "property" right, the area of confidential information has come to be accepted under the heading of IP law. For an academic analysis of the nature and results of the distinction, see W Cornish and D Llewelyn, *Intellectual Property: Patents, Copyright, Trade Marks and Allied Rights* (2007), paras 8.50 *et seq*.

law in this area.[7] For ease of reference, a note of the main features of each topic follows, together with examples of its application to the industry.

Patents

Patents are potentially the most commercially valuable species of   **15.13**
IP, as they provide a monopoly to the holder to exploit the relevant invention, process or use for a particular period of time (up to 20 years in the UK).[8] A patent holder has the right to stop others from making, using, importing, disposing of or offering for disposal the patented subject-matter.[9]

In order to obtain a granted patent, the Patent Office (now   **15.14**
operated as part of the Intellectual Property Office) must be satisfied that the subject-matter of the patent application: (a) is novel[10] (ie not copied or already existing in the public domain); (b) displays an inventive step[11] which is not an obvious development to someone skilled in the relevant art;[12] (c) has a practical/industrial use;[13] and (d) is not one of the statutorily excluded subjects.[14]

A patent holder (or applicant) has the option of exploiting the   **15.15**
patent itself (eg by manufacturing and selling the relevant product or utilising the relevant process); or of licensing the patent to a third party[15] (eg in return for payment of royalties); or of selling the patent. As an item of incorporeal moveable property, assignation/

---

[7] The focus of this chapter is technology developed for application in the oilfield, and therefore the law of trade marks and of designs, although significant branches of IP law in their own right, are excluded from consideration, as being of comparatively little practical relevance. The application of database rights, in terms of the Copyright and Rights in Databases Regulations 1997 (SI 1997/3032), is an area which has thus far made little obvious impact on the industry (despite the fact that it could be tremendously relevant, in terms of its application (for example) to seismic data). For this reason – and as it is largely analogous to copyright in its approach – a specific treatment of this area within this chapter was also deemed otiose.

[8] Patents Act 1977, s 25(1). An as-amended version of the Act can be downloaded from http://legislation.gov.uk/ukpga/1977/37/contents (accessed 18 March 2011).

[9] Patents Act 1977, s 60.

[10] *Ibid*, s 1(1)(a).

[11] *Ibid*, s 1(1)(b).

[12] *Ibid*, s 3.

[13] *Ibid*, s 1(1)(c).

[14] *Ibid*, s 1(1)(d).

[15] *Ibid*, ss 30(4) and 31(4). IP licensing is discussed below in more detail at paras 15.46ff.

assignment is the mechanism of disposal and a patent can also be offered in security.[16]

15.16   It is important to remember that, notwithstanding various international co-operative measures, a patent is fundamentally a national instrument, offering protection only in the jurisdiction of grant. The European patent system, which provides a mechanism by which a single patent application may be filed at the European Patent Office under the European Patent Convention to obtain patents in various signatory states, does not produce a "European" patent enforceable throughout the EU – but rather a set of national patents, each in the specific designated jurisdictions. Similarly, the "international patent system" established under the Patent Co-operation Treaty[17] allows a single application to provide initial protection in relevant states, but individual national applications must be made during the national/regional phase.[18]

15.17   The Patent Office does not maintain industry-specific statistics which would show the level of usage made by the oil industry of the patent system, but reported cases illustrate clearly that expensive and complex patent disputes are fought – particularly by and between oil service companies determined to protect their own patents and/or prevent a competitor from obtaining the state-backed monopoly which a patent constitutes. These can cover a wide variety of industry technologies, including heat-insulated pipe-in-pipe assemblies for use on seabed pipelines,[19] roller-cone drill bits[20] and offshore accommodation modules.[21]

Copyright

15.18   Although the terms "literary" and "artistic" works may not intuitively seem particularly relevant to the oil industry, it is through these headings that the main application of copyright law flows into the activities of the North Sea. Copyright will exist in almost any document, whether an instruction manual, a field report, a purchase specification – all of which tend to fall within the category of "literary work";[22] and almost any technical drawing, photograph,

---

[16] Patents Act 1977, ss 30(2) and 31(3).

[17] The Patent Co-operation Treaty of 19 June 1970. The Treaty is available for download in its as-amended form from http://www.wipo.int/pct/en/texts/articles/atoc.htm (accessed 18 March 2011).

[18] Part II of the Patents Act 1977 governs European and international patent applications.

[19] *ITP SA* v *Coflexip Stena Offshore Ltd* 2004 SLT 1285.

[20] *Halliburton Energy Services Inc* v *Smith International (North Sea) Ltd* [2006] RPC 2.

[21] *Consafe Engineering (UK) Ltd* v *Emtunga UK Ltd* [1999] RPC 154.

[22] Copyright, Designs and Patents Act 1988, s 3(1). An as-amended version of the Act

diagram or schematic – all of which tend to fall within the category of "artistic work".[23] Unlike some overseas jurisdictions, no formal registration process is required to create copyright in the UK – all that is needed is that the relevant work be recorded[24] in some semi-permanent form. This usually means being written down or electronically recorded.

The only major prerequisites to an item being protected by copyright are that it is: (a) original[25] (ie not copied from somewhere else) and (b) substantial enough to constitute a "work" (this latter prerequisite is qualitative, rather than quantitative, but case law[26] suggests that something more than a single word is required to be a "literary work").

15.19

Once a work has been created, a copyright holder has the right to authorise or prohibit any copying of it,[27] including issuing copies[28] or renting or lending the work to the public.[29] The copyright holder therefore has the option of exploiting the copyright itself (eg by reproducing the training materials and selling them with training services; or by reproducing technical manuals and selling them); or of licensing the copyright to third parties. Licensing to third parties can be either explicit or implied and is discussed below in more detail.[30]

15.20

The wealth of items in which copyright can subsist means that this is an area which frequently raises questions of infringement (often quite involuntary and innocent). For example, due to the mobility of employees and contractors in the industry, training manuals showing best practice often find their way from company to company. The author has seen situations where training materials produced by one company have been copied by another and incorporated into its training programme; and where materials produced by various links in the supply chain, such as manufacturing drawings or recommended maintenance procedure specifications prepared by original equipment manufacturers, have similarly been taken by individuals for use in subsequent jobs. In many cases, the individuals concerned have no idea that their actions may be breaching copyright and

15.21

---

can be downloaded from http://legislation.gov.uk/ukpga/1988/48/contents (accessed 18 March 2011).
[23] Copyright, Designs and Patents Act 1988, s 4.
[24] *Ibid*, s 3(2).
[25] *Ibid*, s 1(1).
[26] *Exxon Corporation and others* v *Exxon Life Insurance Consultants International Ltd* [1982] Ch 119.
[27] Copyright, Designs and Patents Act 1988, s 17(1).
[28] *Ibid*, s 18.
[29] *Ibid*, s 18A.
[30] See paras 15.46*ff*.

creating liabilities for them and/or their employer. There is often a tacit inclination to believe that the materials are able to be used without restriction, either due to them being in the public domain or due to the prevalence of the practice of copying. In any event, significant liabilities can arise as the result of this practice and companies which do not adequately address the education and actions of their workforce may face hefty damages claims and even potential criminal liability.[31]

15.22   The fact that a large number of skilled engineers in the industry are all drawing on a collective pool of ideas, experience and principles to meet their current challenges also illustrates one of the important – yet often fine – distinctions of copyright law. As a point of principle, the law will not protect someone's mere idea. It will only protect the specific expression of that idea in a tangible form (whether that tangible form might be a written document, a drawing or whatever). It is nevertheless extremely difficult to define exactly where the dividing line is between a work which the law ought to protect from illegitimate copying and the "common stock" of concepts (whether engineering, physical, geological, seismological or otherwise) which might incidentally be expressed in technical specifications or drawings and which should be capable of future application or development, without risk of infringement.

15.23   Overseas judgments have been quoted with approval to the effect that "the law does not prevent one [engineer] from following in the footsteps of a colleague; [but] it does prevent him from copying the plans of his colleague so as to enable him to follow in those footsteps; and it does prevent him from physically reproducing those footsteps and thereby following them".[32] Thus, it would be perfectly legitimate for an individual engineer to inspect drawings or a tool in operation and, having appreciated the principles by which it operates, to return to his own drawing board to design his own tool, provided that the new design does not reproduce a substantial part of the original. The dividing line is often unclear and, as ever, the individual facts and circumstances will play a defining role.

Copyright in software

15.24 Another facet of the breadth of copyright is that it is also the principal method by which the law has chosen to protect software.[33]

---

[31] The topic of IP Infringement, whether incurring civil or criminal liabilities, is outwith the scope of this chapter.

[32] *Jones* v *Tower Hamlets* [2001] RPC 23 at 418.

[33] The vexed question of whether and to what extent software might be patentable is

The significance of software to the oil industry (and indeed almost any modern industry[34]) does not require to be asserted. Software is ubiquitous, supporting not only almost every conceivable aspect of business, but also being embedded into the tools and equipment of the industry. It seems natural that copyright should afford protection to the expression of some concept in a programming language, but a computer program in any form is deemed to be a "literary work"[35] and therefore capable of protection in the same way, and subject to the same conditions, as any other.

15.25 In the case of an article or a book, the concept of "copying" (which is the key act restricted by copyright) connotes something along the lines of a photocopy. However, the statutory restriction is much broader and specifically refers to "storing the work in any medium by electronic means".[36] Thus, when a program is uploaded or run on a PC, it is being copied – even although there is no discrete "pirate" copy being produced in the way that one might otherwise tend to conceptualise copying. Unlike a book, however, the making of entire, "necessary", back-up copies is permitted by statute.[37] The concept of licensing[38] is used (either explicitly or impliedly) to permit the legitimate licensee to use the software in the normal course of the operations for which it was obtained from the licensor. Within a limited number of statutory constraints, the licensor may as a matter of contract set such limitations on the use of the licensed software as it feels commercially appropriate; typically by limiting the number of copies that can be installed, or the number of contemporaneous users, or the business locations at which the licensee is entitled to use the software.

15.26 The mobility of the workforce within the oil industry and the ease with which perfect digital copies of applications can be transported (eg on laptops or even memory sticks) gives rise to similar risks as have already been noted above in relation to the copying of training manuals, etc. Unlicensed duplication of software and its relative documentation or manuals is widely understood to be illegal and tends, once discovered, to be self-evident. In reality, the market for "bootleg" technical software, and particularly specialised software

---

outwith the scope of this book.
[34] As recognised by Recital (3) to the EU Directive on the legal protection of computer programs (2009/24/EC): "computer program technology can accordingly be considered as being of fundamental importance for the Community's industrial development".
[35] Copyright, Designs and Patents Act 1988, s 3(1)(b).
[36] *Ibid*, s 217(2).
[37] *Ibid*, s 50A.
[38] Licensing is discussed further at paras 15.46*ff.*

such as that used in geo-science and petroleum engineering, is small in comparison with, for example, an office application. The author is not aware of criminal sanctions ever having been applied in respect of the unauthorised distribution of oilfield applications. In any event, most licensors protect their products using either software- or hardware- ("dongle") based licence management software.

Confidential information

15.27 The third pillar of IP law highlighted, the law of confidentiality, is frequently the only route by which investment in intangible innovations, and particularly novel or improved processes, can be protected. For example, knowledge of optimal formulations of mud for drilling the formations encountered in a particular area may result from long (and costly) experience. With non-productive time reaching as much as 40 per cent[39] in some drilling operations, a track record of success can justify a premium price and a mud contractor would not wish such information to be shared with its competitors.

15.28 Such information is often called "know-how". Although this term is widely used to describe confidential commercial information, particularly that of a practical or technical nature, it has no statutory basis in UK law. In the United States the favoured term is "trade secret", where it is defined as comprising:[40]

> "... any formula, pattern, device or compilation of information which is used in one's business, and which gives him an opportunity to obtain an advantage over competitors who do not know or use it. It may be a formula for a chemical compound, a process of manufacturing, treating or preserving materials, a pattern for a machine or other device, or a list of customers. A substantial element of secrecy must exist, so that, except by the use of improper means, there would be difficulty in acquiring the information."

This succinct definition encapsulates the key commercial elements of know-how, namely information that is retained as secret, knowledge of which can give advantage.

15.29 In the United Kingdom, however, there is no such concise definition. The nearest thing to a statutory definition to be found in UK law is in the context of competition law, specifically in the Technology Transfer Block Exemption.[41] European law defines "know-how" as "a package of non-patented practical information,

---

[39] C Berry, "Drilling Failure Costs Quickly Add Up" (2009) 61(8) SPE *Journal of Petroleum Technology*.
[40] American Law Institute, *Restatement of Torts*, §757, comment b.
[41] Regulation 772/2004 on the application of Article 81(3) of the Treaty to categories of technology transfer agreements ([2004] OJ L123/11) (hereinafter the "Block Exemption").

resulting from experience and testing which is secret, substantial and identified".[42] "Secret" means that the information is "not generally known or easily accessible";[43] "substantial" means that the information is "significant and useful for the production of the contract products";[44] and "identified" means that the information is "described in a sufficiently comprehensive manner so as to make it possible to verify that it fulfils the criteria of secrecy and substantiality".[45]

In general, however, know-how is treated under the common law   15.30 of confidentiality. This has a number of implications. In contrast with patents, there is no recognised proprietorial right in the knowledge embodied in the know-how. Certainly the expression of such knowledge in writing or drawing may be protected by copyright but, unlike patents, the knowledge itself is neither owned nor protected. In consequence, there is no monopoly right of exploitation and any person independently developing similar know-how may use or disseminate it freely. That said, in circumstances where know-how is properly controlled and a duty of confidentiality can be established, the law of confidentiality can potentially come closer than copyright to protecting the essential idea, rather than the mere expression of it.

The substance of the law in both Scotland and England is the   15.31 same.[46] In order for the law to protect a piece of information as confidential information, that information in question must have "the necessary quality of confidence about it, namely, it must not be something which is public property and public knowledge"[47] and it must be disclosed "in circumstances importing an obligation of confidence".[48] The fact that a concept is relatively simple will not, of itself, prevent it from constituting protectable confidential information; the concept must, however, be sufficiently developed and be capable of identification with reasonable particularity.[49] Further, for a right of action to be established in relation to such a piece of confidential information, there must be "unauthorised use ... to the

---

[42] Block Exemption, Art 1(1)(i).
[43] *Ibid*, Art 1(1)(i)(i).
[44] *Ibid*, Art 1(1)(i)(ii).
[45] *Ibid*, Art 1(1)(i)(iii).
[46] *Lord Advocate* v *Scotsman Publications Ltd* 1989 SC (HL) 122, per Lord Keith at 164.
[47] *Saltman Engineering Co Ltd* v *Campbell Engineering Co Ltd* [1948] 65 RPC 203, per Greene M R at 215.
[48] *Coco* v *A N Clark (Engineers) Ltd* [1969] RPC 41, per Megarry J at 47.
[49] See the submissions made by Counsel in *Pine Energy Consultants Ltd* v *Talisman Energy (UK) Ltd* [2008] CSOH 10, per Lord Glennie at para 21. The case concerned the development of Talisman's Beatrice oilfield into an industrial deep water offshore wind farm.

detriment of the party communicating it".[50] It is clear, therefore, that know-how can only be protected for so long as it remains confidential and that, to the extent that it is disclosed, such disclosure must at least imply circumstances of confidentiality. Explicit agreement, such as by way of a confidentiality or non-disclosure agreement, is the most unambiguous way to establish the relationship of confidence (and certainly the most advisable), but the law will imply an obligation of confidence where the discloser and recipient are in a fiduciary relationship and in any other situation where the infamous "reasonable man" would realise that an obligation of confidence in the circumstances is equitable. There is extensive case law on the circumstances that import the obligation, particularly in the case of disclosure or use of know-how by employees, ex-employees and consultants.[51] In general the courts have proven willing to imply a term of strict confidentiality into contracts of employment and, albeit to a lesser degree, consultancy,[52] while in doing so attempting to balance the rights of individuals freely to exploit acquired knowledge and skill.[53]

15.32   Oil & Gas UK has recently published a model form of confidentiality agreement.[54] While the intention is clearly to reduce the administrative burden on companies seeking to agree relevant contractual terms, due to its relative youth (it was published in January 2009), the document has yet to achieve wide industry currency.

Ownership of intellectual property: employee versus contractor

15.33   Unless the company has a process in place for identifying and recording valuable know-how, it may reside exclusively inside the minds of the workforce. This means that the ex-employee is a particular risk point in relation to confidential information. Not only does he represent a more likely source of dissatisfaction with the business and therefore of information "leakage", but the protection of confidential information afforded to a business as an employer (in terms of the implied obligation of good faith in an employment relationship) is in practical terms stronger than that afforded to a business as an ex-employer (by reason of the law's reluctance to prejudice an ex-employee's legitimate right to utilise the general

---

[50] *Coco v A N Clark (Engineers) Ltd* [1969] RPC 41, per Megarry J at 47.
[51] See, eg, *Faccenda Chicken Ltd v Fowler* [1986] 1 All ER 617.
[52] *Vestergaard Frandsen A/S v Bestnet Europe Ltd* [2009] EWHC 657 (Ch).
[53] See, eg, the opinion of Cross J in *Printers & Finishers Ltd v Holloway* [1965] 1 WLR 1.
[54] Oil & Gas UK, *Industry Model Form: Confidentiality Agreement* (January 2009).

skills, knowledge and experience which someone in his position would have acquired, in order to earn a living).[55]

The general position is that the first owner of an IP right will **15.34** be the person who created it. However, if that person created the item in the course of employment, then the ownership will usually vest in the employer.[56] Due to the prevalence of non-employee contractors (ie persons working not under contracts of service, but contracts for the provision of services) in the industry, there is a key risk exposure for companies where they engage a contractor to create an item comprising IP. The author has seen countless cases where a contractor has been engaged to design or contribute to a tool, a piece of software or some other work, has been well paid for so doing, but has not been engaged on contractual terms which transfer the ownership of the IP to the company who engaged and paid him. In those circumstances, the contractor will retain any copyright which he created. Depending on the surrounding factual matrix, the law will usually imply a licence from the contractor to the company, but the scope of that licence may not include all the uses to which the company intends to put the IP (especially if it intends to develop it further) and it will have no right of ownership which it could otherwise sell to realise value. Companies which have engaged the services of a contractor are often horrified to find that the contractor is free to use the product of that work to compete with them.

Companies should therefore ensure that, where a contractor is **15.35** to be engaged and any IP is possibly going to be generated by him, the contract contains assignation/assignment provisions in favour of the commissioning company. In order to be effective an assignation/assignment of copyright requires to be in writing and signed by the assignor,[57] so, while a more limited licence of the relevant rights may be implied by the law, without such an express written contractual provision no ownership will pass.[58]

The position in relation to inventions has a small degree of added **15.36** complexity. In addition to the employer owning any rights in inventions created in the course of employment, the employer will also own the rights in inventions created in the course of a task outwith the course of employment if specifically assigned to the employee, or where the employee held a sufficiently senior position, so as to be assessed as having a "special obligation to further the interests of

---

[55] *Faccenda Chicken Ltd* v *Fowler* [1986] 1 All ER 617.
[56] Copyright, Designs and Patents Act 1988, ss 11(2) and 215(3).
[57] *Ibid*, s 90(3).
[58] Only design rights vest automatically in the commissioning party.

the employer's undertaking".[59] Further, any purported assignation/ assignment of rights in future inventions by an employee in favour of an employer is unenforceable. Such assignations/assignments of inventions therefore need to be agreed and documented on an individual case-by-case basis – and only once the relevant rights have been created.

15.37   Companies should also be aware that there is a non-excludable statutory right for an employee to obtain "compensation" where (a) he creates an invention which is successfully patented by the employer, (b) the patent is of outstanding benefit to the employer, and (c) it is just that such compensation payment be made.[60]

CONTRACTING STRUCTURES AND TRENDS

Collaborations[61]

15.38   When used in connection with technology development, the term "collaboration" is usually used to denote a structure where the contractual counter-parties are each contributing some material effort to the development of the technology in question. In situations where one party is contributing capital only (ie effectively paying for the other to develop technology), the relationship might more accurately be characterised as a "commissioned development" or "contract research" agreement. However, often for cosmetic reasons of the paying party, even this type of situation is designated as a "collaboration". The exact structure of a collaboration can vary from an intense and binding interaction between the counter-parties (such as a corporate joint venture) to a bare sub-contract relationship of relatively short duration. The defining feature is simply the co-operation (in some form) of the counter-parties towards a defined technical project goal.

15.39   A collaboration can be put in place in order to capitalise on the synergistic competences of the counter-parties (eg where experts in chemical polymers collaborate with drillers of heavy oil to use their combined expertise to develop an enhanced oil recovery process) or in order to compensate for a shortage of resources or skills of a party (eg where a university department's specialist and expensive

---

[59] Patents Act 1977, s 39(1)(b).

[60] *Ibid*, s 40.

[61] The interaction of two or more parties in a collaboration (or a licensing transaction) raises the possibility that there may be competition law implications for them in relation to their project and/or their joint commercialisation of the project outputs. For a discussion of competition law, see Chapter 11.

laboratory equipment and academic team are engaged to develop new seismic techniques).

There is currently no such thing as a model technical collaboration 15.40 agreement for the UKCS and they are therefore still quite bespoke creatures of contract. However, there are certain key features which should almost always be covered including:

- definition of the project aim and a detailed project scope;
- who has responsibility for carrying out which parts of the project scope;
- who has responsibility for paying for (and who will own) equipment or other tangible items required by the project scope;
- what happens if the project aim is not achieved (either for technical reasons or because the parties fall into dispute);
- how the resultant IP ("foreground IP" or "project IP") is to be owned and exploited by the parties;
- how the IP owned by each party at the start of the relationship (their respective "background IP") is to be documented and regulated, in order to enable effective exploitation of the foreground IP, without infringing or otherwise prejudicing the background IP; and
- what (if any) indemnity cover should be provided in relation to the background IP provided by each party.[62]

Of course, each of the key features above could be broken down into a multitude of sub-issues and complexities; and the relevant agreement should additionally make all usual "boilerplate" provisions for two parties interacting in a project, such as confidentiality obligations, dispute resolution provisions, etc.

Two issues typically relevant to collaborations (and which have 15.41 broader application when dealing with technology) are the topics of (a) joint ownership of IP; and (b) indemnities in respect of potential IP infringement.

Joint ownership

Intuitively, joint ownership is regarded by many collaborators as 15.42 being a fair outcome. However, many parties do not fully appreciate the restrictions and difficulties which may apply to co-owners. For example, a co-owner of copyright will not be entitled to exercise the jointly owned rights without the consent of the other co-owner(s).

---

[62] Discussed further at paras 15.44*ff*.

The precise rights and freedoms of co-owners vary as between the different species of IP rights, but generally:

- a co-owner will not have the right to assign its title to IP (or license the IP) to any third party, without the consent of the other co-owner(s); and
- a co-owner is unable to bring an action for infringement to prevent unlawful use of the IP without the other co-owner(s) being a party to the proceedings.

This can produce situations which are quite contrary to the commercial expectations of the parties. For example, consider a scenario where: (1) two companies collaborate to develop a patented product and agree that the rights in such patent will be owned by them jointly; (2) the parties are then unable to agree the terms upon which the IP should be licensed or assigned to a third party; and (3) one of the parties is a technical design specialist, while the other is a manufacturer. In that scenario, the party who has the ability to manufacture the products themselves may have the right (as co-owner) to do so; while the other co-owner who does not have such in-house capability is (factually) unable to self-produce and also (legally) unable to license to any third party.

15.43   If joint ownership is nevertheless desired, the contract could explicitly provide for wide rights of exploitation for each co-owner (effectively a cross-licence structure which broadens the natural implications of co-ownership at law). Alternatively, if a structure in keeping with the intuitive appeal of joint ownership is sought, it is generally preferable to provide for one party to own the IP, with the other receiving an irrevocable (royalty-free) licence, both subject to terms which explicitly set out the rights and obligations of the parties. In this situation, however, the issue of insolvency risk of the licensor should be considered.

Indemnities

15.44   In the commercial licensing of IP, it is relatively common for the licensee to seek an indemnity from the licensor in respect of any infringement of a third party's IP.[63] In a simple licensing transaction, the rationale is clearly illustrated. If Company A has a design for a tool, which it wishes to license to Company B to manufacture and sell within a particular geographical market, in return for a royalty on each product sold, then Company B (as licensee) will want a

---

[63] For a discussion on the appropriate contractual treatment of the risks of "alleged" (cf proven) infringement, see para 15.59.

certain level of contractual comfort that Company A has good title to the design rights and has not simply copied them from a third party. Otherwise, Company B could find itself on the receiving end of an infringement claim from the third party in respect of its manufacturing and sales activities. Indemnification is the common mechanism by which this objective is achieved.[64]

In the situation where Company A and Company B are collabo- **15.45** rating to develop a product and each is contributing respective background IP, the same principle arises. Before either counter-party invests significant time and effort incorporating that background IP into the foreground IP to be produced in terms of the collaboration, it will want some comfort that the outputs will be free from third-party challenge and available for the parties' exploitation without undue restriction. Reciprocal indemnities in respect of any third-party infringement claim are therefore usually negotiated in some form, although a practical view may be taken where the bulk of the IP is coming from one party, rather than the other or where sensible verification (due diligence) of the provenance of the relevant IP is possible. In collaborations which are not being carried out for payment or are otherwise not on a full commercial basis, there are sometimes no indemnities given and each party collaborates on an "as-is" basis. In that situation, thorough due diligence is even more key.

IP licensing

As noted at para 4.3, a licence is a permission authorising an activity **15.46** the conduct of which would otherwise be unlawful. In the context of IP licensing, it is essentially an undertaking by the holder of the relevant right (as licensor) not to pursue the licensee in respect of activities which would otherwise constitute infringement of the relevant IP right (provided, of course, that the remaining terms of the licence agreement are adhered to). Thus, a patent holder may license a party to manufacture its patented product in return for certain royalty payments. Without the licence, the actions of the licensee would infringe the patent and be actionable.

The nature and extent of licences can vary greatly. Most readers **15.47** will be familiar with software licences which provide a neat example of how licensing operates. In order to run a piece of software, a computer requires to copy the code. Thus, in the absence of the concept of a licence, running the software could theoretically infringe the copyright in the software. In the absence of a contractual

---

[64] The treatment of IP indemnities under the LOGIC regime is referred to at paras 15.58*ff*.

agreement, the law will often imply a licence as a matter of implied contract, but the terms of that implied licence may well not be extensive. In most circumstances – and certainly in any situation where valuable consideration is involved – it is prudent to put in place explicit contractual terms outlining the extent of the licence.

15.48 Typical issues when considering a licence of IP include the following:

- identification of the parties (individual companies or corporate groups);
- specification of the IP rights which are being licensed (present or future);
- specification of the scope of the licence (the permitted activities which are covered; the geographical region, etc);
- specification of the price or a mechanism for calculating the price (whether in lump sum or royalty form);
- the nature of the licence (eg revocable versus irrevocable; exclusive versus non-exclusive versus sole);
- termination/duration of the licence;
- provision for dealing with any claims of IP infringement by third parties or any claims alleging that the licensed IP infringes any third-party rights; and
- indemnities in respect of IP infringement.

LOGIC contracts

Introduction

15.49 Since their introduction as part of the CRINE[65] response to the market downturn of the mid-1990s, the standard form contracts[66] published by LOGIC (CRINE's successor, and now part of the industry forum, Oil & Gas UK) have been widely adopted and adapted in the UKCS. The purpose of this suite of documents is to reduce the cost of negotiating contracts for the supply of various goods and services by providing "a commonly known and understood foundation around which the [parties] can build their particular requirements".[67]

---

[65] "Cost Reduction in the New Era", part of the Oil & Gas Industry Task Force (OGITF) established in 1998 as an industry/Government initiative in recognition of the dramatic fall in oil prices, the maturing of the UKCS, and the urgent need to reduce the cost base of activity in the basin.
[66] Available for download from http://www.logic-oil.com/contracts2.cfm (accessed 30 April 2010).
[67] See, eg, LOGIC, *Guidance Notes for General Conditions of Contract for Well Services* (Edition 2, March 2001), available for download from http://www.logic-oil.com/well2.pdf (accessed 18 March 2011), p 1.

The approach to the management of IP adopted in the LOGIC **15.50** contracts is straightforward. These provisions may be divided into three parts: (a) ownership and retention of title to existing (background) IP; (b) title to and licensing of IP developed in the course of the contract; and (c) indemnification against infringement of third-party IP.[68] In line with LOGIC's objective of building a well-understood foundation, these provisions are essentially identical across the suite of contracts.

Background IP

Existing (background) IP is intended to be retained by the party **15.51** providing it. The scope of such IP is stated to extend to "any patent, copyright, proprietary right or confidential know how, trademark or process provided". Care is taken to restrict the scope of any implied licence for each party to use the other's background IP by stating that "[the other party shall not] have the right of use [of background IP], other than for the purposes of the CONTRACT,[69] whether directly or indirectly" and that "the intellectual property rights in such [background IP] shall remain with the party providing [it]". While this wording clearly extends to and provides a strong contractual basis for the protection of recognised forms of intellectual property (patents, copyright and trade marks), it is less clear whether it fully protects know-how and process, which, as we have mentioned, may underlie innovations that a party would wish to protect.

Confidentiality is addressed separately from patents and propri- **15.52** etary rights.[70] An obligation is placed on the contractor to mark confidential information clearly as such, although there are carve-outs for information relating to the contractor's pricing and trade secrets, which are deemed confidential. Practically, however, contractors would be advised to mark all information disclosed to their clients as confidential.

As noted above, the law of confidential information requires that **15.53** disclosure of know-how or trade secrets be controlled. However, rig site operations generally involve contact with numerous other contractors, some of which may well be competitors. The

---

[68] See, eg, LOGIC, *General Conditions for Construction* (Edition 2, October 2003), available for download from http://www.logic-oil.com/construct2.pdf (accessed 18 March 2011), cl 20: "Patents and Other Proprietary Rights".

[69] "CONTRACT" is defined (through Section I – Form of Agreement) as including the published general conditions (Section II(a)), any bespoke special conditions (Section II(b)) and a set of sections appropriate to the type of contract.

[70] See, eg, "Confidentiality", LOGIC, *General Conditions for the Supply of Major Plant and Equipment* (Edition 2, December 2005), available for download from http://www. logic-oil.com/supply2.pdf (accessed 18 March 2011), cl 25.

requirement to maintain confidentiality gives rise to clear practical difficulties and leakage of know-how – particularly know-how related to process optimisation – is almost inevitable. By way of example, the matching of drill bits and drilling parameters to maximise rate of penetration through a given formation while minimising the risk of vibration damage is valuable know-how for a directional drilling contractor, but impossible to keep "secret" from the drill crew, mud logging contractor and many others involved.

15.54   Legally, the difficulty lies in the fact that there is neither a contractual nexus between the various contractors working side by side at a rig site[71] nor a clear duty of care owed by one contractor to another in relation to the protection of confidence, under which a claim in tort/delict might be made. This issue is one which the law and current practice seem unable to tackle effectively. Maintaining the secrecy of certain operational information would be practically unworkable (as in the drilling example scenario above); while agreeing confidentiality agreements among all the contractors on a work site would also be prohibitively administratively burdensome. Industry practice therefore appears to accept this risk in principle.[72]

15.55   The LOGIC provisions permit the client to disclose confidential information to, and to authorise its use by, a wide group of associated companies[73] and third parties. While the latter right is subject to the consent of the contractor (not to be unreasonably withheld or delayed) and restricted "to the extent necessary for the execution and maintenance of the project in connection with which the WORK is to be performed", this arrangement tends to favour the client. There is no explicit obligation that any such disclosure be made under conditions of confidentiality; and, in respect of disclosures to affiliates, there is not even a requirement that the disclosure to such affiliate is necessary for the performance of the contract. While there are circumstances where it is perhaps appropriate for the proprietary

---

[71] Although they will each have a contract with the operator, the contractors will not have any contract with each other.

[72] The same problem existed previously in relation to mutual hold harmless obligations and has (to a large extent) been addressed by the Industry Mutual Hold Harmless Deed, discussed at paras 14.50–14.64 above, which seeks to implement reciprocal obligations among the contractors. Perhaps a similar solution will ultimately evolve in relation to confidentiality.

[73] Members of the COMPANY GROUP, which is widely defined and includes the client, its co-venturers under any joint operating, unitisation or similar agreement (eg a joint bidding or area of mutual interest agreement) relating to the operations in respect of which the contract is let, and its and their affiliated companies, which itself extends to the entire company group.

information of the contractor to be made available to others – for example, copyright engineering drawings may be needed to repair or maintain equipment, or an operator may require to explain some novel approach to its co-venturers in order to gain JOC (Joint Operating Committee) approval to its adoption – the LOGIC terms go beyond what is often required to protect the operator's interests. Contractors are well advised to consider carefully how such contract terms will impact on their specific activities.

Foreground IP

Foreground IP is addressed in a more satisfactory manner. **15.56** Developments leading to a potential patent or other registrable right made by either party which are enhancements of its existing IP or based wholly on that party's "data, equipment, processes, substances and the like" in its possession at the date of commencement of the contract vest in that party. Where developments are made jointly, any potential patents or other registrable right vests in the party or parties specified.[74]

Non-registrable foreground IP, and particularly copyright, **15.57** is addressed within the ambit of the provisions dealing with ownership. While following the same general pattern, these differ among the various LOGIC contracts, with those dealing with design and construction being (quite naturally) more extensive than the services contracts.[75] In general, however, copyright in documents prepared for the purposes of or within the scope of the work to be undertaken under the contract vests in the client on their creation.

Indemnities

The third aspect of the LOGIC IP provisions deals with indemnity **15.58** for infringement of "patent or proprietary or protected right" arising out of the performance of the contract. Mutual cross-indemnities are granted, with each party holding harmless and indemnifying the other against third-party claims for infringement arising from the use of IP that it has provided or, in the case of the client, instructions given.

Somewhat surprisingly, there is no right for the indemnitor to **15.59** take over, be enjoined in the defence of, or manage, any action for

---

[74] The party in question being designated in Appendix 1 to the Form of Agreement.
[75] Compare LOGIC, *General Conditions of Contract for Marine Construction* (Edition 2, October 2004), available for download from http://www.logic-oil.com/marine2.pdf (accessed 18 March 2011), cl 19 with LOGIC, *General Conditions of Contract for Well Services* (Edition 2, March 2001), available for download from http://www.logic-oil.com/well2.pdf (accessed 18 March 2011), cl 16.

alleged infringement. For example, a third-party patent holder of a down-hole tool could choose to pursue an infringement action against not only the contractor supplier of the allegedly infringing product, but also its user, which could be the operator's personnel and/or the personnel of another contractor on the rig site. Given the threat of disruption and the large losses (whether in terms of production or delayed operations) which could flow from this and the fact that, in terms of indemnities granted elsewhere in the LOGIC contracts in respect of consequential loss,[76] such losses would not be recoverable, an operator faced with the threat of infringement action might be tempted to choose to pay a settlement, knowing that it is fully indemnified by the supplier, even if the case for actual infringement were weak. In many cases, it has been the ongoing and largely reciprocal relationships between the contractor and operator community in the UKCS which have prevented such damaging short-term actions. However, as economic conditions harden and as further new entrants enter the basin, the accepted conventions may change. With that in mind, it is advisable to consider how the risk of "alleged" infringement should be handled. Options could include applying the indemnity only to "proven" infringements and/or including a "conduct of claims" provision, which allows the indemnitor an appropriate degree of control over the (alleged) infringement proceedings to protect their interest.

CONCLUSION

15.60 The UK's national interest in maximising domestic hydrocarbon recovery, which, in turn, feeds into issues of energy security and global competitive advantage,[77] is clear. Government and industry therefore need to work together to find efficient solutions which combat rising lifting costs and ageing infrastructure. These solutions are dependent on the technical expertise of our engineers and ensuring that their efforts are appropriately protected and efficiently exploited. Initiatives such as the ITF and NSRI are a start on that journey – but an enhanced commitment to collaborative working and investment (including sensible contractual risk allocation) among all levels of the supply chain community is what would really make the difference. With oil and gas contributing a greater amount of tax revenues to the UK Treasury than any other industry, it is no exaggeration to say that the individuals working on the technical

---

[76] See, eg, "Consequential Loss", LOGIC, *General Conditions for the Supply of Major Plant and Equipment* (Edition 2, December 2005), cl 24. Consequential loss is further discussed at paras 14.66–14.70 above.

[77] See Chapter 3; see also M Porter, *The Competitive Advantage of Nations* (1990).

and commercial aspects of the next generation of technologies in the North Sea will be serving their country in a vital way. Educating and engaging the engineers, commercial managers and lawyers of tomorrow in this phenomenal industry must be a priority.

CHAPTER 16

ACQUISITIONS AND DISPOSALS OF UPSTREAM OIL AND GAS INTERESTS

Norman Wisely

Notwithstanding recent global recession and continued oil and gas **16.1** price fluctuation, the continued trading of oil and gas assets remains of significant importance to oil companies and the UK Government alike.[1] This chapter will summarise and provide an overview of the legal process involved in the acquisition and disposal of upstream UK oil and gas licence interests, concentrating primarily on acquisitions and disposals by way of asset sale for a cash consideration. This chapter does not purport to deal with public takeovers, or deal with more complex forms of consideration in any great detail.

PORTFOLIO MANAGEMENT

There are many motivating factors behind oil companies' decisions **16.2** to invest in, or dispose of, existing oil and gas interests. Set out below are some of the most common reasons. In recent years, as the North Sea has developed into a mature basin, it has become ever more common for oil majors to rationalise their portfolios and divest of a number of non-core assets, non-operated assets or smaller percentage interest holdings.[2] Some entities may seek to divest of oil and gas assets because they are costly to operate or in order to avoid decommissioning costs, while others may be intent on leaving the UKCS to concentrate on other potentially more profitable jurisdictions. Some

---

[1] See generally Oil & Gas UK Ltd, *2008 Economic Report*, available for download from http://www.oilandgasuk.co.uk/cmsfiles/modules/publications/pdfs/EC009.pdf (accessed 14 March 2011) (hereinafter "*2008 Economic Report*").
[2] See generally "UKCS Players and Commercial Activity" in *2008 Economic Report*, p 36.

sellers may need cash to finance debts or may simply consider that the time is right to capitalise on a particular asset. The buyer may be a smaller organisation that is more suited to extracting value from assets in a mature basin than larger companies who may find it uneconomic due to larger associated overheads. Alternatively, a buyer may wish to acquire assets in a certain geographic "heartland" that it knows and understands well. A buyer may be seeking to gain a dominant vote in an existing JOA to which it is party or it may seek to acquire an oil and gas interest because it feels it can gain more value from an asset underused and underexplored by the seller. Moreover, a buyer may be motivated by reasons outwith the immediate prospectivity of the interest being acquired, for instance, buying in order to secure transportation rights or to acquire data relevant to another area. In addition, purchase of production acreage can finance exploration and purchase of exploration acreage can reduce tax exposure on production profits. Ultimately, for any sale and purchase to occur there needs to be a mutuality of interest between seller and buyer.

ACQUISITION STRUCTURES

16.3   Other than by way of being granted an oil and gas licence by the Government, there are essentially two distinct ways of acquiring an interest in oil and gas interests: either by purchase of the assets themselves, or by way of a share purchase of a company which directly or indirectly owns oil and gas interests, usually by way of a purchase of 100 per cent of such a company's shares.

Types of asset purchases

16.4   With an asset purchase the "asset" which the buyer seeks to acquire is the seller's interests in the relevant licence(s) and a multitude of rights and obligations under the associated field documents, including the agreements mentioned earlier in this book.[3] At completion of the transfer, the buyer will pay some form of consideration. There are many variations on asset purchases, the principal difference between which essentially relates to the consideration payable for the oil and gas interests in question. The main forms are discussed below.

Monetary consideration

16.5   In this arrangement, the buyer will pay the seller a monetary consideration at completion. Elements of monetary consideration may be deferred in some cases, for instance where an element of the

---

[3] See Chapter 12.

consideration is based on future production levels of the asset being acquired.

Farm-in

Here the consideration payable by the buyer is the performance of **16.6** a field obligation (usually drilling work), whether by way of actual performance of that obligation or reimbursement of the seller's costs of the operator performing such obligation. A farm-in might also entail an additional element whereby in the event of a drilling success the buyer will also fund the seller's share of costs of field development in return for an uplifted re-payment post first production either by way of a production royalty or net profit interest.[4]

Earn-in

This is often now used interchangeably with a "farm-in" as described **16.7** above but specifically refers to circumstances where the farm-in relates to a work obligation under the licence and where (typically) the Secretary of State is more reluctant to allow parties to "farm out" their interests, meaning that usually the interest may not be transferred until completion of all relevant work obligations.

Swap/exchange

An alternative structure is where some or all of the consideration **16.8** payable by the buyer is the transfer of another oil and gas interest(s) to the seller.

Advantages and disadvantages of asset purchase versus a corporate purchase

Much will depend on the specific facts and circumstances of any proposed transaction, but some typical reasons for choosing a share purchase over an asset purchase and vice versa are summarised below:

No pre-emption

Any pre-emption clauses in UK JOAs or other licence interest **16.9** documents are unlikely to prevent an acquisition of the relevant party's shares, the justification being that a JOA, for instance, should not prejudice a party's shareholders' ability to trade their shares. For

---

[4] This has been a business model adopted by some "non-cash rich" promote licensees in particular, in order to ensure that they can participate in any potential future field development. See paras 4.62–4.68.

this reason, a company purchase has the advantage of avoiding any pre-emption restrictions in the licensed interest documents.[5]

16.10   If the buyer is proposing to acquire all or part of the issued share capital of a private limited company owning oil and gas assets, it will rarely find pre-emption rights directly affecting the seller's shares in the target.[6] As a general rule, therefore, the assignment of shares in private oil companies is far freer of contractual restrictions than the assignment of their oil and gas assets.

Mechanical simplicity

16.11   A share sale is (certainly in theory) legally and mechanically simpler that an asset sale since all that is required legally to transfer title to shares is a stock transfer form and registration in the register of members of the target, as opposed to the suite of assignments, novations and consents required to transfer title to assets. In practice, however, this is not always the case, and share sales can be as complex as asset deals. In a share sale, in addition to the sale and purchase agreement, a suite of documentation is usually also required, including a tax indemnity, a disclosure letter and additional documentation attending to the corporate formalities (including board minutes, director resignations and similar).

Consents

16.12   Generally the governmental and third-party consents required on a share sale will be less extensive than those on an asset sale.[7]

Operatorship transfer

16.13   A corporate purchase will allow the buyer to take operatorship more easily than on an asset transfer. For instance, often the terms of the JOA will allow the existing co-venturers to appoint one of their number to be operator upon resignation of the existing operator. The JOA will provide for the seller to give notice of resignation such that the seller would need to resign pre-completion of the asset transfer in order to ensure that it does not remain as operator post-completion of the asset transfer (which may not be permitted under the terms of the JOA or even if permitted would be undesirable from the seller's perspective). The seller is thus resigning at a point when

---

[5] See further at paras 16.33*ff*.

[6] Provisions of companies legislation requiring all private companies to impose restrictions on transfer of shares were repealed in 1980. That said, however, if the target is a publicly listed company, although its shares may *prima facie* be freely transferred, hurdles will nevertheless be thrown up by (in the case of a UK company) the City Code on Takeovers and Mergers and the Listing Rules of the London Stock Exchange.

[7] See paras 16.28*ff*, for further details.

the buyer would not be a party to the JOA (assuming that it was not already involved in licence operations in the block in question) and could not be appointed operator, unless otherwise agreed by the other co-venturers.[8] If operatorship is important to the buyer and the co-venturers are likely to be resistant to it being appointed as operator, a share sale would allow the buyer to assume operatorship by stepping into the shoes of the existing operator in this respect.

Due diligence

Legal due diligence on a company purchase requires to be more extensive than for an asset purchase as the buyer would, in addition to the oil and gas assets, typically need to review all other relevant company records including those relating to employees, property and pensions. 16.14

Liabilities

Purchase of shares in a company has the disadvantage for the buyer that it would, on completion, assume all historic liabilities of the company, whether or not relating to the oil and gas assets, for instance in relation to pensions, tax, employees, the environment and any other operations carried out by the target. 16.15

Tax

Often, the reasons for electing to buy and sell assets by way of a corporate sale rather than an asset sale or vice versa relate to tax issues. For example, a share sale would allow the buyer to assume any Corporation Tax losses of the company being acquired (something not available on an asset sale) and would likely allow the seller to take advantage of the substantial shareholdings exemption to capital gains tax.[9] An asset purchase would allow the buyer to take the benefit of existing capital allowances in respect of the assets. 16.16

THE DUE DILIGENCE PROCESS

Seller due diligence

Where a seller decides to divest of oil and gas assets it will need to undertake certain due diligence on the legal agreements relevant to those assets. This should be done at an early stage in order to consider whether any counter-parties to such agreements could 16.17

---

[8] Note, however, that it may be possible to deal with such a provision, depending on the facts and circumstances, by acquiring the asset in tranches and thereby becoming party to the JOA pre-completion of the transfer of the second tranche.

[9] Taxation of Chargeable Gains Act 1992, s 7AC.

prevent disclosure of the agreements to prospective buyers or, more importantly, prevent disclosure of data and information held under such agreements to interested buyers and to establish whether any third parties otherwise have rights to block the deal or have preferential rights to purchase. Clearly any such rights can affect a seller's position as to whether it will sell the assets at all and/or as to how to structure any such sale.

Confidentiality

16.18   A seller will review relevant licensed interest documents to consider whether the agreements and any information and data held in connection with such agreements can be disclosed to potential buyers without the consent of the other parties thereto. If they cannot, and consent of the counter-parties to those agreements is required to such disclosure, this would give counter-parties early notice (often earlier than commercially intended) of the intended divestiture. While there will almost always be a confidentiality clause in oil and gas agreements preventing disclosure of data and information without consent, there is also often a "bona fide buyer" exception to this such that such information can be passed to a prospective buyer upon the seller in turn obtaining an undertaking of confidentiality from such intended assignee.[10]

Assignment

16.19   Similarly, a seller will want to check the assignment provisions in all affected agreements in order to check the counter-parties' rights with regard to assignment. Several common provisions can affect transferability of the affected agreements and these are considered below.[11] It may be that a right of pre-emption or difficulties surrounding assignment could encourage the seller instead to sell by way of a share sale. Additionally, the distinction between assignment (whereby the benefit of the agreement can be transferred) and novation (whereby the benefits and obligations of the seller are transferred) needs to be borne in mind, as, ultimately, in novating an agreement, the "consent" of all parties is required.[12]

---

[10] Note, however, that in some JOAs this refers to a bona fide buyer of the asset and not the shares of a company, meaning that specific consent may be required in respect of a share acquisition.

[11] See paras 16.32*ff.*

[12] A novation terminates the old contract and constitutes a new contract on the same terms and conditions but with different parties. Practice in the oil and gas industry is to proceed with any transfers by way of novation and it is often assumed that "assignment" means "novation" for the purposes of most assignment clauses and effect is given to the provisions of "assignment" clauses accordingly. However, a clause in a JOA that simply

The "data room"

If a sale is initiated by a seller, in order to maximise potential value, **16.20** many sellers now elect to dispose of their assets by way of an auction process whereby certain parties selected by the seller will be allowed access to a data room into which all relevant technical, financial, commercial and legal data and agreements are placed. This will often now consist of a "virtual" data room accessible on-line for a limited time-period. Invited potential buyers and their advisers will be invited to undertake a due diligence on such data and information and make a bid for the asset or company (usually together with a marked-up sale and purchase agreement). Not surprisingly, legal due diligence is only part of the overall due diligence process conducted by the buyer. Where shares are anticipated to be sold, any person offering to sell shares must be authorised under the UK financial services legislation.[13]

Buyer due diligence

The level of due diligence carried out by a buyer will vary from deal **16.21** to deal, depending on whether the buyer has prior knowledge of the asset. While some buyers will elect to carry out a full and detailed legal due diligence, others will carry out a more minimal legal due diligence and seek to rely on extensive warranties and indemnities in the sale and purchase agreement. The latter option, however, is not advisable, due to uncertainties surrounding recovery of loss and likely expenses involved, and the fact that the seller will seek to disclose all legal agreements and information it has provided to the buyer against the warranties it gives, meaning that a review of such legal agreements and information will be necessary in any event. It is worth noting that in this context it is in both parties' interests to keep accurate ongoing records of what has been disclosed to the buyer, to avoid later dispute.

Investigation of title

A seller's chain of title to the assets needs to be fully checked, given **16.22** that there is no conclusive legal register as to title to oil and gas assets. Essentially a buyer will seek to confirm that the seller is on the licence and has the percentage interest it claims to have under the JOA and will look for a valid chain of licence assignments and JOA novations from date of licence award which, in the case

---

provides for consent to assignment not to be unreasonably withheld would not in itself impose any obligation on a party to enter into a novation.

[13] Financial Services and Markets Act 2000, s 19(1).

of some more mature North Sea assets, can be a time-consuming business. If any defects are discovered, then, depending upon their nature, there can be a requirement to remedy defective title by way of correcting historical assignments and novations, and this too can be time consuming and lead to delay. The Department of Energy and Climate Change maintains a website that records the current parties to onshore and offshore licences and their percentage interests in the different areas thereunder,[14] but this is a record only and not conclusive, and should not be used as a substitute for due diligence on title. If the transfer is by way of a share sale, the seller's title to the shares being sold needs to be checked in addition to the above.

Encumbrances, charges, royalties and third-party rights

16.23 A buyer will typically check for any encumbrances, charges and third-party rights over the assets (and, where relevant, shares) being sold. A search carried out at the Companies Registry will assist in disclosing the existence of any charges in respect of UK companies and their assets and would allow the buyer to ascertain whether a deed of release or certificate of non-crystallisation of floating charge is required. Any overriding royalties over the seller's interest in a licence will affect the financial value of the interests and, therefore, a buyer will be particularly interested in these.

Existence of agreements and main commercial terms

16.24 Gaining a clear understanding of the main commercial terms of the various relevant agreements will be of utmost importance to the buyer. The level of commercial review undertaken varies from transaction to transaction and differs according to whether the asset is an older producing field or a newly awarded exploration licence. A buyer will require to ascertain that the seller has the necessary rights under the various agreements and that there are no unduly onerous commercial terms. For example, if a producing asset is being purchased, is the seller party to agreements that allow for the transportation of oil produced to shore and for the processing and lifting of such production? On what terms are such agreements and is there anything unduly burdensome that affects the value? What are the JOA voting rights and are they appropriate given the interest being purchased? Is there any evidence of breach of contract or licence obligations by the licensee or others within its group? Are there current or anticipated claims and litigation in connection with the asset? Are there contractual provisions (in addition to pre-emption

---

[14] DECC, *Licensing Data*, https://www.og.decc.gov.uk/information/licensing.htm (accessed 3 May 2010).

provisions) that would be breached by the acquisition, for example, provisions in agreements for the purchase of seismic data which require the data to be returned, or an additional payment to be made in respect thereof, if control of the purchasing company changes? Are there any contingent liabilities, such as outstanding guarantees and payment obligations falling due on the occurrence of certain specified events?

Assignment/change of control
It is vital that the buyer gains an understanding of the possible rights 16.25 of pre-emption or grounds for refusal of consent in relation to any asset transfers as, ultimately, if such provisions are ignored, a buyer could undertake a lot of preliminary work only to find that the deal is snatched away from it by one or more of the seller's co-venturers. On a share sale the buyer will need to check for any "change of control" clauses in the legal agreements that would affect its share purchase.[15]

Decommissioning
The buyer should be able to understand at an early juncture what 16.26 (if any) existing agreements are in place for final decommissioning of an oil and gas asset and what (if any) security it needs to provide to the co-venturers in respect thereof and when such security needs to be provided (bearing in mind that it may also have to provide security to the seller under the sale and purchase agreement). If there is provision in the existing agreements, and this involves entry into a trust deed or provision of a bank guarantee or letter of credit, this requires attention at an early stage to avoid delay to the transaction.[16]

General corporate
Irrespective of whether the acquisition is to be an asset sale or a 16.27 corporate sale, the buyer would, as with any purchase, need to check the corporate capacity of the seller and its ability and authority to dispose freely of the relevant assets or shares. If a share sale, a full corporate due diligence would need to be carried out, including review of all corporate constitutional documentation and all rights and liabilities otherwise affecting the target company. It is, however, not within the remit of this book to consider further such non-oil and gas due diligence.

---

[15] Even if no change of control provisions are to be found in the JOA or other field agreements, there can be change of control provisions in seismic licensing agreements whereby an additional licensing fee can be payable on change of control of the licensee.
[16] See paras 10.54–10.59.

APPROVALS AND CONSENTS

Asset sale

16.28   In an asset sale, under Model Cl 40(1),[17] Secretary of State approval is required for any transaction involving the assignment or other transfer of benefit under a licence.[18] In practice this is now actioned by electronically sending a standard application form to the Secretary of State. Ultimately, the Secretary of State looks at the financial and technical capability of a licensee in considering whether to allow such a transfer. Sometimes he will request a letter of support from the proposed assignee's parent company (where it has one). Given the current trend of smaller oil companies acquiring interests in the North Sea, financial capability is a matter of increasing concern for the Secretary of State. Typically, Secretary of State approval for a smaller less complex deal can take between 1 and 3 weeks, although if the buyer is new to the UKCS approval may take longer and the Secretary of State will have to verify the buyer fully and will require additional information as to corporate structure and health and safety capability among other things. Although the Secretary of State has powers to request copies of draft transaction documentation, in practice, this is not used.

16.29   If the sale involves the buyer assuming operatorship, a further Secretary of State consent is required under Model Cl 24(1). This is commonly dealt with in the same application form and the Secretary of State will look for similar criteria of financial and technical capability, although, generally speaking, more so.

The role of the Secretary of State

16.30   Typically, the purchase of oil and gas interests will, after the buyer has conducted due diligence and entered into a sale and purchase agreement with a seller, involve the following steps:

(a) the seller will apply for the Secretary of State's consent to a licence assignment;

(b) the Secretary of State will transmit its consent, which is conditional on confirmation of the deed, to (i) the form set out in

---

[17] For the purposes of this chapter, references to Model Clause are references are to those applicable to 25th and 26th Round production licences as set out in the Petroleum Licensing (Production) (Seaward Areas) Regulations 2008 (SI 2008/225). Model Clauses applicable to previous licences generally contain similar provisions.

[18] Note that the Open Permission (Operating Agreements) granted by the Secretary of State on 21 September 2010 makes provision for a waiver of any requirement for prior Secretary of State consent for transfers of percentage interests between existing licensees, provided no licence assignment is required.

the Master Deed,[19] or (ii) the older standard form of deed (deed of assignment);

(c) the buyer, seller and remaining participants create and execute their own deed of assignment or execution deed in Master Deed form;

(d) the buyer and seller inform the Secretary of State of execution and completion;

(e) the Secretary of State updates its records.

It is the execution and completion under (c) which perfects the buyer's legal title to the assets. Typically, many other agreements also require to be novated simultaneously to the buyer. The Secretary of State's records are created only from information passed to the Secretary of State by licensees.

Share sale

Although no governmental consent is strictly necessary to buy or sell assets by way of a share sale, attention needs to be given to Model Cl 41(3). This provides that the Secretary of State may revoke a licence if a licensee undergoes a change of control which is not followed by such further change of control as the Secretary of State requests and within such period of time as the Secretary of State specifies by written notice. "Control" is very widely defined.[20] As such, it is common practice in share transactions to obtain a letter of comfort from the Secretary of State prior to completion of such transaction that he will not seek to exercise such power to order a further change of control. Ultimately such "comfort" is no more than that and consists of a relatively standard form letter from the Secretary of State that it is not presently his intention to so exercise such power. This is not legally binding but is usually sufficient for the parties concerned. It should be noted that the Secretary of State may also revoke the licence under Model Cl 24(2) where he considers that the operator is no longer competent to exercise such function. As such, in the event of a change of control of the operator, similar prior assurance is sought from the Secretary of State that he will not exercise such power to revoke the licence.

16.31

---

[19] See para 16.37.

[20] This is defined with reference to s 416(2) and (4)–(6) of the Income and Corporation Taxes Act 1988. "Control" would, for example, include acquisition of a 33% interest in a licensee. "Change of control" is defined in Model Cl 41(4) as the acquisition of control by a person who did not previously have control and might even capture intra-group share reorganisations in addition to share acquisitions by third parties.

PRE-EMPTION AND RESTRICTIONS ON ASSIGNMENT AND CONSENTS AND APPROVALS

16.32 Pre-emption rights are of great importance in oil and gas deals and much attention is rightly focused upon them. A right of pre-emption (typically found in a JOA or JOAUOA) allows co-venturers to pre-empt any agreed deal with a third party and thereby acquire a proportionate part of the interest intended to be disposed of to a prospective buyer.[21]

Pre-emption, right of first refusal or right to negotiate

16.33 The language used in a "pre-emption" clause is important. Each clause needs to be looked at very carefully, but generally speaking tends to take one of the following forms:

- an obligation on a party to offer a deal that has been agreed with a prospective buyer to its co-venturers (a true right of pre-emption);
- a right of first refusal: the intent of such clauses is that a seller must offer its co-venturers the interest before agreeing the deal with a third-party prospective buyer – usually, it may not then sell to such third-party prospective buyer on lesser terms than those offered by any co-venturer;
- a lesser right on the part of a co-venturer to negotiate with a seller for a period of time, following which the seller may freely assign to a third party irrespective as to price obtained.

Often a pre-emption clause will catch a transfer of assets for cash but may not catch a swap or other variations, so such clauses need to be analysed carefully.

16.34 In practice, the seller and buyer will, at an early stage, need to consider whether the clause catches their proposed deal, and also the practical likelihood of a co-venturer pre-empting, in order then to ascertain whether they need to restructure the proposed deal in any way. If, for example, the proposed deal involves several assets, will the buyer go ahead and purchase the remainder if it is pre-empted on one particular asset?

16.35 In analysing pre-emption clauses, great care is needed to ascertain the "trigger point" of operation. This is of particular importance as sometimes the trigger point can be at an early stage, before the

---

[21] See para 12.12 for a discussion of pre-emption rights generally. See also Major, "A Practical Look at Pre-emption Provisions in Upstream Oil and Gas Contracts" [2005] IELTR 117.

intended buyer and seller have even agreed the deal in principle, for instance where the seller first considers or intends that it may wish to dispose of the asset.

Typically, pre-emption clauses cause more concern to the buyer **16.36** than to the seller as it will not want to waste time agreeing a deal only to be pre-empted. The seller may not care as it will receive the same consideration for the asset on the same terms.

Master Deed

The Government became concerned that pre-emption rights under **16.37** JOAs were discouraging new entrants' participation in the UKCS and encouraged the industry to adopt new pre-emption arrangements in order to give buyers increased confidence and clarity. Parties to a JOA that are also parties to the UKCS Master Deed[22] are subject to "New Pre-emption Arrangements" whereby existing pre-emption clauses in JOAs to which they are party are read and construed in accordance with the New Pre-emption Arrangements set out in the Master Deed. This does not apply to share sales or "swaps" (unless, in respect of swaps, there is already provision for conversion into a monetary amount within the JOA).

When informed of an assignment, irrespective of the pre-emption **16.38** provisions in the JOA, parties to a JOA will have an initial 7-day period in which to waive or reserve their rights of pre-emption if the seller wishes to serve a notice of its intention to transfer an interest under the JOA. Thereafter, if the parties to the JOA have reserved their rights, they will have a 30-day period (once a pre-emption notice has been given by the seller, post the signing of a sale and purchase agreement) in which to decide whether or not to pre-empt. This has facilitated the speeding-up of the deals process. It does not remove the risk that newer, smaller entrants will contract to buy into an asset, only to find themselves "pre-empted out" but, under the new pre-emption arrangements, if a buyer is particularly concerned, then the seller may serve a notice on co-venturers to test the water, even before a sale and purchase agreement has been signed. Co-venturers must reserve (or waive) their right to pre-empt within 7 days or, where a pre-emption notice is served after the agreement to sell has been reached, they must pre-empt within 30 days. This is certainly an improvement on some of the lengthy and complicated

---

[22] See the Master Deed website (www.masterdeed.com) for a summary of the UKCS Industry Master Deed.

JOA pre-emption arrangements with which buyers and sellers were formerly faced.[23]

16.39   It is worth noting that the Secretary of State will now not approve any new JOAs containing pre-emption provisions (in respect of licences granted after 1 July 2002) without justification being provided therefor.[24] As a result, most new JOAs do not contain pre-emption provisions.

The unmatchable deal

16.40   How, then, can a buyer and seller seek to avoid the deal being pre-empted by co-venturers? An example often given of how to avoid many pre-emption clauses is by offering a non-cash consideration that the co-venturers cannot match. For instance, in a swap/exchange, the co-venturers wishing to pre-empt will not be able to match the consideration offered by the buyer, being an interest in a specific piece of acreage that the co-venturers do not possess. Many JOA pre-emption clauses, however, require the seller to allocate a cash consideration value where non-cash consideration is envisaged. A co-venturer may then pre-empt by paying this cash equivalent sum. If there is no requirement to allocate a cash consideration, the argument is usually run that the unmatchable deal route around pre-emption has been well within the contemplation of JOA negotiators for years, and could be legislated for in the contract, therefore pre-emption is not applicable with respect to the proposed transfer.

The package deal

16.41   The other example is the "package deal" whereby the seller offers to sell an apparently indivisible package of assets which cannot be split. The argument here runs that the seller is only willing to dispose of a package of assets for a certain consideration and that a co-venturer cannot pre-empt as there is no separate ascertainable consideration for the pre-emptable interest. Ultimately, this route

---

[23] Issues can, however, arise pursuant to the Master Deed pre-emption arrangements centred around the interpretation and application of existing pre-emption and right of first refusal clauses in JOAs in connection with the requirement that such clauses are to be "read and construed" in accordance with the New Pre-emption Arrangements set out in the Master Deed. See cl 3(2) of the Master Deed.

[24] Additionally, the Open Permission (Operating Agreements) granted by the Secretary of State on 21 September 2010 allows automatic approval of new JOAs for licences granted after 1 July 2002 that do not contain pre-emption arrangements. Any new JOAs entered into in respect of licences granted up to 30 June 2002 may contain pre-emption clauses but only if the wording is equivalent to that set out in the Master Deed.

can lead to argument, depending on the precise wording of the JOA. The co-venturer may claim that it cannot be denied its rights in this manner and that a fair value must be apportioned to the relevant asset,[25] or may claim that it is entitled to pre-empt the whole package.

Affiliate route

As mentioned previously, share sales are not generally caught by **16.42** pre-emption rights in UK JOAs. A share sale of the company holding the asset may not always be attractive to the parties, for reasons mentioned previously, but the other way of typically avoiding pre-emption is the "affiliate route". Here, the seller will hive down the relevant interests into a newly incorporated affiliate and then sell that affiliate to a third party by way of a corporate sale. Most JOAs will allow the transfer of the asset to affiliates without triggering the pre-emption clause principally because companies require freedom to reorganise their groups for many different commercial and tax reasons and often this does not have an adverse effect on co-venturers.

However, there are some difficulties in a seller opting to take **16.43** the "affiliate route" to avoid pre-emption. Some JOAs will contain restrictions on this sort of avoidance technique. For instance, while transfers to affiliates may be permitted, it may be that if such affiliate ceases to be an affiliate of the transferor within a period of 2 years, the co-venturers may require the transaction to be unwound, such that their rights of pre-emption are not fettered.

Furthermore, the definition of "affiliate" in the relevant JOA will **16.44** be relevant. Often this definition will be linked to the Companies Acts definitions[26] which allow beneficial ownership to be taken into account when considering whether a company is an affiliate of another. There is therefore often an argument raised that if arrangements are already in place to on-sell that affiliate at the time of giving notice to co-venturers, it is not a true affiliate at all and that this transfer could itself be pre-empted. Clearly, the stronger the deal with a buyer at the time of hive-down, the greater likelihood of attack on this basis.

Although JOAs will allow transfer to affiliates, often there is **16.45** financial capability test whereby the co-venturers can refuse consent

---

[25] Indeed, often an allocation between different assets in a package will be required for allocation of capital allowances and will be set out in the sale and purchase agreement, leading to difficulties in the seller pursuing such an argument.

[26] Companies Act 2006, s 1159; and formerly in respect of agreements entered into prior to it coming into force, the Companies Act 1985, s 736 (as amended by the Companies Act 1989, s 144). The forthcoming Supreme Court decision in *Farstad Supply AS v Enviroco Ltd (No 2)* will be relevant to the definition of "affiliate".

to a transfer to a less financially capable affiliate. If the affiliate is a company with no other assets at the time of transfer, attack on these grounds is also possible.

16.46   Other arguments are also given as to why the affiliate route may be attacked. In particular, in the case of *Texas Eastern*[27] the courts implied certain terms into commercial agreements in order to prevent pre-emption avoidance techniques. However, it is submitted that such a result should be unlikely where there is a well-drafted JOA between commercial parties, since the courts would generally be reluctant to interfere and imply terms not set out in such agreement.

16.47   Finally, there could be challenge to a circumvention of the pre-emption provisions by way of the affiliate route or the unmatchable deal route on the grounds of appeal to fiduciary duties.[28]

16.48   An alternative would be to transfer out all other assets the seller wished to retain into another of its companies, leaving the existing interest owned by a company with nothing in it other than the interests. This may be more effective, as there is no transfer of relevant pre-emptable assets involved, but clearly involves the buyer taking on additional exposure in acquiring an older company with the associated liabilities and the seller taking on cost and administration, and the potential further legal and tax complications and associated delay in transferring assets into other group companies.

Financial capability/unreasonably withheld

16.49   Even if pre-emption has successfully been avoided or not exercised, or if there is no pre-emption clause at all, JOAs will make provision for the co-venturers to consent to any intended transfer. This often provides that the co-venturers can only withhold consent to any intended disposal of assets on grounds of lack of financial and technical capability of the buyer, or the JOA sometimes states more simply that consent may not be unreasonably withheld.[29] In both

---

[27] *Texas Eastern* v *EE Caledonia* (CA) (1989) unreported. Although the licence interests of the subsidiaries had been split so that it was not easy to see in what proportions the pre-empting parties should acquire the share capital of the Texas Eastern subsidiary, the Court of Appeal held that there was an underlying commitment to a reasonable solution and that the problem of the proportions in which the shares should be acquired could be likened to that of ascertaining the contract price under a contract for sale at a reasonable price. In short, it implied a term of reasonableness to fill the gaps in the mechanism and to give business efficacy to the contract.

[28] On fiduciary duties and joint ventures, see G Bean, *Fiduciary Obligations and Joint Ventures* (1995). See also P Roberts, "Fault Lines in the Joint Operating Agreement: Fiduciary Duties" [2008] IELR 218.

[29] This is an objective test. See *British Gas Trading* v *Eastern Electricity plc* [1996] EWCA Civ 1239 (18 December 1996).

cases this can provide co-venturers with the opportunity to extract guarantees from the buyer's parent or bank in return for consent, which can make any deal potentially more expensive for a buyer. It is more unusual in JOAs for there to be an absolute discretion on the part of co-venturers.

A typical JOA will prohibit the transfer of a licensed interest 16.50 unless the interest in question is an "undivided" interest under the licence and JOA. The idea behind this is to prevent a party from assigning rights without the corresponding obligations and also to prevent it transferring its interest in respect of one part of the licence area, while retaining its interest in respect of the remainder. If the latter is what is proposed, specific agreement will have to be reached for the purposes of splitting the JOA so that it will apply as two separate agreements to the two different areas. This does not prohibit the assignment of part (or a proportion) of the seller's total percentage interest in the licence and JOA, although some JOAs also provide that a party may not transfer part of its interest if the transfer would result in the assignor or the assignee holding less than a certain specified percentage interest.

SALE AND PURCHASE AGREEMENT

Following due diligence, the buyer and seller will negotiate the 16.51 acquisition agreement, setting out the terms of their sale and purchase. The aim of this section is not to give a detailed account of such agreements but rather to note specific points relevant to an oil and gas deal, given that the sale and purchase agreement itself is otherwise no different from a typical sale and purchase agreement for a corporate or business/asset sale and purchase. Here, the focus will primarily be upon a sale and purchase agreement in respect of assets for a monetary consideration.

The asset sale and purchase agreement

The assets
An important issue in any asset acquisition is identification of the 16.52 oil and gas assets that are being sold and purchased. As mentioned above, under an asset deal, the buyer is not buying any physical assets, but a series of interrelated rights and obligations in the licence(s) and various agreements. Typically, this will consist of an interest in the licence(s) in question and a working interest under the relevant JOA(s) and any associated agreements. If the asset is producing there will be rights under various field agreements, and potentially the buyer may also want (or may have to take) certain of the seller's rights under product sales agreements. In addition, the

buyer will want title to the data owned by the seller in respect of the assets and, where operatorship is being transferred, the buyer will need to take on the rights of and assets held by the seller in its capacity as operator.

Consideration

16.53   The asset sale and purchase agreement will state what consideration is payable for the asset and when it is payable. As discussed above, consideration can take various forms. In a straightforward "cash for asset" deal, the consideration will be payable at completion, although the seller may look for a deposit payable upon signing which might be retained in the event of a failure to complete the transaction due to the buyer's fault. Additionally, there may be circumstances where the buyer will request a retention and look to defer a portion of the consideration until, for example, the end of the warranty period, so as to protect its position if the asset acquired is not as warranted by the seller. Some of the consideration may also be deferred until the occurrence of a specified event such as the granting of field development consent or occurrence of certain levels of production. In addition, sometimes the seller itself (as part of sale of exploration acreage, for example) may require the grant of a production royalty or net profit interest so as to benefit in any future upside of the asset. Where the consideration is cash, this will typically be adjusted for various reasons.

16.54   There will be an "economic date", which is the date at which the buyer has valued the assets. The valuation of oil and gas interests is based on a net present value of projected after tax net cash flows from the interest at a specified date and will, therefore, assume that all costs and benefits from this date onwards would accrue to the buyer. Any convenient historic date for which accurate and up-to-date figures are available is used to set the economic date and for interests subject to Petroleum Revenue Tax (PRT) this will usually be 1 January or 1 July to coincide with the PRT return periods. The end of a PRT period is often used for PRT-paying assets, so as to avoid apportionment of that tax between seller and buyer for any chargeable period. Year end is often used (for both PRT and joint venture billing purposes).

16.55   The asset sale and purchase agreement will reflect the economic date such that the buyer upon completion will be treated as if it has beneficially owned the assets since the economic date (that is, the economic risk and benefit is the buyer's). As such, there will be a headline consideration which the buyer is willing to pay for the assets as at the economic date which is then adjusted whereby any receipts (for example, from petroleum sales) received by the seller in the period of time from the economic date to completion are treated as being the buyer's such that the headline consideration is adjusted downwards accordingly. Any expenditure incurred by the seller (for example, operating expenditure under the JOA) in relation to the interests in this period will similarly necessitate an upwards adjustment of the purchase price. Working capital in respect of the interests at the economic date is often also added to the consideration, since it is not accounted for in the valuation (which, as mentioned above, is based on future cash flow) – this is effectively the present position of the interests at the economic date, and would include oil and gas stock (in platform, pipeline and terminals), equipment stocks and spares, receivables and payables as at the economic date and the seller's liability for any historic "overlifting" or benefit of any historical "underlifting" of production (all as per the relevant operator's and corporate statements, as and when they are produced).

Notional interest is added to the various adjustments in order to put the seller and the buyer in the same position that they would have been in had completion occurred at the economic date and earned interest on monies received. Similarly, additional income and capital gains tax paid or saved by the seller as a result of the completion not occurring on the economic date will also be adjusted for. There will usually be a mechanism post-completion to allow these adjustments to be calculated accurately and agreed. There is also a broader type of tax adjustment which is common in asset sale agreements and which "tax effects" all payments and receipts taken into account in valuing such payment or receipt in the hands of the seller and/or the buyer (as the case may be). For example, if the seller receives payment for a cargo of oil lifted after the economic date, this revenue is for the buyer's account and the purchase price will be reduced accordingly; however, in calculating the amount of the reduction, it will not be the gross revenues which are deducted, but the actual value of the revenue. This will be its post-tax value. A percentage of the revenue will be lost in Corporation Tax (and perhaps also PRT) and since it is the seller that would bear the tax, it is in most cases, therefore, inappropriate for the gross amount to be deducted from the purchase price. **16.56**

The above adjustments to the purchase price are agreed to give the parties a "clean break" going forward, rather than continuing to account to each other in respect of pre- and post-economic date benefits and liabilities. However, to back this up there are usually also indemnities set out in the sale and purchase agreement which will be given in respect of pre- and post-economic date activities **16.57** to deal with the circumstance where a benefit or liability comes to light in the future but has been omitted from the adjustments calculations.

Conditions precedent

16.58   Since the various consents described above[30] need to be obtained before the buyer can acquire the interest, signing and completion under an asset sale and purchase agreement will not be simultaneous and, therefore, there will be a time gap (often referred to as the "interim period") between the signing of the sale and purchase agreement (or "exchange") and completion. Therefore, there are usually certain "conditions precedent" stated in the sale and purchase agreement which need to be satisfied before the parties are under an obligation to complete the deal. Typically these are:

- Secretary of State consents and approvals;
- waiver by co-venturers of their pre-emption rights. Note, however, that it is possible for the parties to agree that if pre-emption rights are successfully exercised the whole deal will not fall away and that the buyer is still bound to purchase the non-pre-empted part of the assets;
- third-party consents: these will include the execution by such third parties of necessary assignments and novations to transfer the rights and obligations under the relevant agreements from the seller to the buyer (or in the case of the Master Deed process, by the UKCS Administrator on their behalf).[31] Where executed by third parties, these agreements are in effect held in escrow by the buyer and seller until completion;
- there will probably be other items that the parties may add as conditions precedent, for example release of the seller from certain guarantees previously given to third parties.

The fewer conditions precedent, the greater certainty that the deal will complete. The seller will want to resist any conditions precedent around anything else not within its control so as to limit the possibility of the deal not completing, such as conditions precedent in connection with the obtaining of finance by the buyer or the buyer being satisfied with further due diligence, for example.

Interim period

16.59   As described above, there will be a period where the sale and purchase agreement has been signed but the assets will be owned by

---

[30] See paras 16.32*ff*.
[31] See paras. 16.74*ff* for details of the Master Deed execution process.

the seller. As such, the buyer will insist on certain provisions being set out in the sale and purchase agreement restricting what the seller may or may not do with the assets, since pending and subject to completion those assets are effectively being held in trust for it by the seller. A balance must be struck whereby the seller may continue to run the assets in a relatively unfettered manner (bearing in mind that if the conditions precedent are not satisfied the seller will remain the owner) but will be bound to supply certain information to the buyer and sufficient comfort that it will not do anything to affect adversely the value or existence of the assets. Typically this will involve provisions including the following:

- The buyer will want to ensure that the assets continue to be run in the ordinary course and in accordance with good and prudent UK oil and gas field practice.
- Restrictions will be imposed on the seller's ability to dispose of or otherwise encumber the assets and a positive obligation will be imposed to take necessary steps to protect the assets.
- The seller will, subject to any relevant co-venturer approvals, be required to make available material information and data to the buyer.
- The seller will not be permitted to make any material change to the assets, for instance by amending any relevant assets agreements without consultation with the buyer or approving onerous future work programmes without consultation.
- Although the buyer may want to exercise the seller's JOA voting rights in the interim period, this can lead to practical difficulties, as this may constitute a breach of Model Cl 40. It may also give rise to difficulties with co-venturers who may be unwilling to allow this (and may indeed also breach confidentiality provisions given to its co-venturers) and/or may give rise to fiduciary duty issues.[32] The seller will therefore usually allow only a right of consultation in relation to voting and will agree to take into account any representations made to it by the buyer.
- Often the seller may have to ensure that any existing insurance policies continue in force, although practice varies, since this can be contrary to the notion of risk passing to the buyer at signing.

In a share sale interim period, the buyer will require a longer list of **16.60** negative covenants from the seller relating to the way it will run the business pending completion. The buyer will not want the seller to

---

[32] See Bean, n 28 above.

do anything that would devalue the company, such as paying cash out to the seller group in dividends or entering into commitments which are outside the usual course of its business.

Warranties

16.61 As with any other transaction, the seller will be required to give certain warranties to the buyer as to the assets in order to provide a buyer with a remedy against the seller if these are untrue and as a result it has paid too much for the assets (the buyer will generally be able to recover the loss in value resulting from such warranty being untrue). Warranties also encourage the seller to make specific disclosures against them, highlighting at an early stage to the buyer any potential items of concern. There are some items for which typically the seller will assume risk, pursuant to the warranties, and others where the buyer will normally take the risk.

16.62 Warranties will vary from deal to deal but a typical example of the minimum warranties commonly sought is as follows:

- **Title:** clearly, this is most important to the buyer – that the seller has title to the assets it purports to dispose of and that these are not encumbered in any way.
- **Default, withdrawal, revocation, surrender:** the seller will warrant that it is not in default under the JOA, or has not elected otherwise to withdraw from or surrender its licence and that no other licensee has undertaken similar action, nor is there any circumstance whereby the licence may be revoked. Similarly, it might warrant that it has satisfied all accrued JOA obligations and has not committed to any expenditure not disclosed.
- **Sole risk/non-consent:** the seller would warrant that neither it nor its co-venturers has undertaken or elected not to undertake such operations (which might clearly have an effect on both the interests being purchased and the value thereof).
- **Information/agreements:** the seller would warrant that the information and agreements provided to the buyer are accurate and complete and that there are no other agreements or information relevant to the interests.
- **Litigation:** the seller will warrant to the buyer that it is not involved in any litigation which may affect the interest and that it is not aware of any litigation pending.
- **Assignment/change of control:** the seller will often be asked to give a specific warranty that assignment provisions have been disclosed and that there are no other restrictions on its ability to transfer the interests to the buyer.
- **Miscellaneous:** various other warranties will be given depending on the matters of importance to the buyer (and the

bargaining power of the buyer). For instance, it is not unusual to see warranties that the seller has plugged and abandoned all relevant non-producing wells in accordance with prudent oil and gas field practice, that it has not received any notices regarding compliance with environmental or health and safety legislation, warranties as to completeness of financial information and data, warranties as to available capital allowances and other tax matters, and any other specific matters the buyer wishes to cover. In addition, standard warranties regarding corporate capacity and authority to enter the transaction are usually given by both the buyer and the seller.

From a seller's perspective, it will want to exclude any potential **16.63** warranties relating to reserves and reservoir performance and also generally anything relating to the physical condition of equipment utilised in joint operations, since these are often potentially large and often unquantifiable and uncertain exposures which the seller will be unwilling to take risk on.

Much negotiation will be spent on agreeing appropriate caps, time **16.64** limits and other restrictions on warranty claims and the disclosure letter (where the seller will usually try to disclose all documentation available in the data room), as for any other non-oil and gas asset deal. As for any transaction, bargaining power usually dictates the final position on warranties.

The warranties schedule of a share sale agreement will contain **16.65** a section of statements, similar to the above, relating to the target company's oil and gas interests. But there will also be warranties relating to all other aspects of the company being acquired: for example, its real property, employees, pension schemes, accounts, tax affairs, intellectual property, corporate activities since the valuation date, other property, debt position, and so on.

Indemnities and decommissioning

As for any other corporate or asset deal, indemnities may be set out **16.66** in the sale and purchase agreement to cover any particular areas of concern for the buyer such that the buyer will have greater comfort that it can fully recover its loss than under a warranty. For instance, where a particular matter is disclosed in connection with a warranty requested by the buyer (for instance, the existence of litigation), the buyer may wish to add a specific indemnity to the sale and purchase agreement to cater for this in order to allow for full recovery of any loss.

In addition, the seller will typically expect the buyer to indemnify **16.67** it in respect of any decommissioning or environmental liability so as to effect, in so far as possible, a "clean break" from the interests. Such matters are of importance to the seller as liability can potentially be attributed to it many years after selling the relevant interests.[33] This can be the case even in a corporate sale.[34]

16.68   Decommissioning liability is a particular concern for sellers. The Secretary of State is typically reluctant to allow a formal release of a seller from s 29 notices[35] where the incoming buyer is less financially capable. Even where the Secretary of State releases a seller, post-completion of a transfer of interests to the buyer, he may still, under s 34 of the Petroleum Act 1998, require the seller (or an associated company) to prepare an abandonment programme and fulfil its abandonment obligations. As such, many sellers (and their affiliates) face potential exposure to decommissioning liabilities post-exit from the relevant asset. Given the size of potential liability, most sellers are simply not willing to accept an indemnity from the buyer in respect of this risk, given that an indemnity is only as good as the future financial capability of the party providing it, and will instead often seek specific security in respect of this potential liability from the buyer: a parent company guarantee or, more typically, the provision of an annual renewable letter of credit. This can cause difficulties for the buyer as it may (depending on the JOA and any field decommissioning security agreement in place) also be required to post security to its new co-venturers in respect of future decommissioning costs. As such, the buyer could potentially have to post security twice in respect of one liability.[36]

COMPLETION

16.69   With an asset purchase, the closing documents necessary to transfer legal title in the assets to the buyer will include a licence assignment and almost certainly one or more JOA (or bidding agreement) novations. There may also be novations for UOAs, transportation,

---

[33] See paras 10.54–10.57.

[34] As the provisions of the Petroleum Act 1998, s 29 could give rise to liability in respect of decommissioning on the part of (previous) "affiliates" for failure to comply with that section.

[35] See paras 10.39–10.47 for a discussion of notices issued under s 29 of the Petroleum Act 1998.

[36] One solution is for the buyer and the seller to endeavour to wind the JOA co-venturers, the seller and any other historic asset owners that may require or be entitled to security into one decommissioning security agreement whereby security can be posted for the benefit of all beneficiaries. See, for example, J Aldersey-Williams, "The Decommissioning Cost Provision Deed: Facilitating Asset Transfers on the UKCS" [2008] IELR 169.

processing, petroleum sales agreements and all other project contracts and, in some cases, a working interest assignment.[37]

The novation will release the assignor from its liabilities under **16.70** the relevant JOA and other agreements and substitute the assignee therefor, as if the assignee has always been party. The allocation of such liability between the assignor and assignee will, however, be governed by the sale and purchase agreement. For the co-venturers, on and from the execution of the novation, they can look to the assignee in respect of all obligations and liabilities.

Stamp duty is no longer payable on transfers of oil and gas assets, **16.71** although if any transfer involves an interest in UK land, it is potentially subject to stamp duty land tax. For example, asset transfers involving "interests" in onshore pipelines and terminals and onshore oil and gas licence transfers may potentially be subject to stamp duty land tax, although the position as regards onshore licences is not altogether clear.[38] Formerly, it was common to execute a stamp duty agreement, where the sale and purchase agreement and/or the working interest assignment was to be executed and held outside the UK for the purposes of avoiding paying the *ad valorem* duty on the conveyance or transfer on sale. Note that stamp duty is payable in respect of share transfers, currently at a rate of 0.5 per cent of the consideration.[39]

There is a prescribed form Deed of Licence Assignment[40] and **16.72** deviation from this model may only be actioned with the consent of the Secretary of State. The JOA and any other agreements should be novated at the same time as any transfer to ensure the assignee steps into the shoes of the assignor in respect of the assigned interest and the rights and responsibilities attached to it. The transferee will covenant with the continuing co-venturers that it will undertake the obligations in respect of the transferred interest, and the continuing co-venturers will accept such substitution and will release the transferor from its obligations.

As mentioned previously, these documents will be negotiated and **16.73** signed by the counter-parties in the interim period under the sale

---

[37] The working interest assignment is the conveyance of the beneficial interest in the relevant asset underset out in the sale and purchase agreement. This was historically used for stamp duty purposes as the stampable document. The common view is that this is no longer strictly required given standard wording in the licence assignment and novations, but it can be useful in some circumstances to evidence completion of the transfer of the interest, particularly where there is no need for any novation of a JOA.

[38] See H Jones, S Greaves and J Phelan, "Oil and Gas Licences – QED? Stamp Duty Land Tax Issues in Transfers of UK Oil and Gas Licences" [2006] IELTR 125 for a discussion.

[39] Stamp Act 1891, s 55.

[40] A copy of which can be found on the DECC website: https://www.org.decc.gov.uk/upstream/licensing/licguide/App4.doc (visited 14 March 2011).

and purchase agreement such that the buyer and seller can execute at completion and "complete" the deal.

The Master Deed

16.74 In addition, to the "New Pre-emption Arrangements" described above, the Master Deed[41] also introduced "New Transfer Arrangements". Under these arrangements, a seller can elect to use a standard execution deed form for licence assignments and novations of the JOA and any other agreements that require to be novated to the seller in an asset deal.[42] The UKCS Administrator is appointed as attorney to execute execution deeds on behalf of the counter-parties to the various agreements that are "Contracting Parties".[43] A seller will issue "Notices of Transfer" to such counter-parties together with the draft execution deed and a form of "Consent to Transfer". These counter-parties will each return a "Consent to Transfer" duly signed by them authorising the UKCS Administrator to execute the execution deed on their behalf.

16.75 These "New Transfer Arrangements" have a twin benefit in that the standardisation of the "execution deed" ensures that asset transfers are not delayed through prolonged negotiation of the novation agreement(s). Gone (to a large extent) are the days of quibbling over the small print in the novation agreements and dealing with conflicting drafting requests from co-venturers. Second, the fact that Consents to Transfer require only one signature avoids any associated delays with having licence assignments (and sometimes novations) signed as deeds often necessitating execution by directors/secretaries of the counter-party and/or use of a company seal, and associated delay that goes with that.

16.76 In a UKCS acquisition/divestment, it is entirely the decision of the seller whether to use the "New Transfer Arrangements". Indeed, often a seller may elect not to use the Master Deed transfer process and instead revert to the "traditional" assignment and novation process where, for example, there are very few other counter-parties to the relevant agreements, meaning that use of the Master Deed process (and therefore having the Administrator sign on behalf of only one other counter-party for example) would only serve to add an additional layer of administration and expense to a given deal.

---

[41] See para 16.37.
[42] There is now a short form version of the standard execution deed which incorporates the standard wording set out in the Master Deed by reference. This is commonly used.
[43] That is, parties to the Master Deed.

Finally, once Notices of Transfer have been sent, and Consents **16.77** to Transfer received, the seller will issue all documentation to the UKCS Administrator to execute on behalf of all relevant Contracting Parties. The seller will then receive and hold the originals and the seller and buyer, can, with certainty, confirm their completion date, knowing that it cannot be delayed by a slow, or deliberately awkward, third party.

CONCLUSION

The scale of the assets involved in acquisitions and disposals of **16.78** upstream oil and gas interests and the scale of the potential liabilities mean that these are complex transactions. It is accordingly vital that the buyer and seller and their respective professional advisers give due attention at an early stage to the preparation and structure of any sale or acquisition in order to minimise cost and delay at a later stage.

CHAPTER 17

ASPECTS OF LAND LAW RELATIVE
TO THE TRANSPORTATION OF OIL
AND GAS IN SCOTLAND

Roderick Paisley

Oil and gas companies have a product that requires physical trans-   **17.1**
portation from source to customer to enable it to be exploited to any
extent. From the wellhead to the filling station, oil companies require
rights to enable this transportation. At the various stages of the
journey the rights are of different natures, largely because of changes
in the state of the substance to be transported and alterations in the
nature of the legal rights held by other parties. Final distribution
of oil to filling stations almost invariably involves the use of the
public right of highway in that the oil is transported in tankers
passing along public roads. Final distribution of gas frequently
involves pipelines laid in public roads by means of statutory right.[1]
However, up to the stage of refining, petroleum in its various forms
is kept off the public roads and the large pipelines used are not laid
under public roads: instead, they are laid on routes that pass across
the countryside. This chapter will look at the nature of the rights
required by the oil and gas companies to convey their product along
pipelines passing through land in private ownership. This situation
occurs throughout those parts of the world where private ownership
of land is recognised. Specialities and local variants as to land rights
may exist in various jurisdictions but the general pattern is broadly

---

[1] An express statutory right is granted to gas transporters to break open streets in terms of
the Gas Act 1986, Sch 4, para 1 (as applied to Scotland by para 7). It is a highly surprising
omission from the Gas Act 1986 that it provides expressly for the breaking open of streets
to install gas pipes but makes no express provision for the subsequent use thereof. The
existence of the right for subsequent use is undoubted but its nature is obscure.

the same. In Scotland and England, where the petroleum originates below the North Sea, the part of the transportation process which involves oil and its derivatives traversing land in private ownership is the geographic part of the journey between the point at which oil comes on shore to the point at which it reaches the refinery. As private ownership in land may begin at the outer edges of the territorial sea,[2] it is possible for oil pipelines to encounter private property some 12 miles before they reach dry land.[3]

17.2   As a postscript to this introduction, one should note that a study of Scots law has particular advantages for oil and gas lawyers. As a "mixed" jurisdiction, Scotland stands between the Civilian and Common law traditions. The mixture of traditions has facilitated the development of sophisticated solutions to difficult legal problems in the oil and gas industry.[4] Albeit by no means perfect, Scots law has much to offer lawyers from other jurisdictions wishing to develop their land law rules to facilitate the use of pipelines for the petroleum industry. Consequently, in this chapter the primary illustrations and authority for the legal propositions under discussion will be drawn from Scots law, with the similarities to, and differences between, certain other legal systems being highlighted when appropriate.

NO SEPARATE CODE OF OIL AND GAS LAW

17.3   Despite the existence of textbooks on the topic, "oil and gas law" is not a hermetically sealed division of civil law to which only special rules apply. Broadly speaking,[5] oil and gas companies have no greater right to enter the lands of third parties to transport their products than any other commercial enterprise possessing limited compulsory purchase powers. In the main,[6] a landowner has a right to preclude uninvited access to his lands as a trespass. While his property right subsists and remains unencumbered by derivative rights, he can prevent others building on his land even if it can be shown that such building would be in the national interest.

---

[2] Eg *Lord Advocate* v *Wemyss* (1896) 24 R 216, (1899) 2 F (HL) 1.

[3] Territorial Sea Act 1987, s 1 applies to the territorial sea adjacent to the United Kingdom of Great Britain and Northern Ireland.

[4] The mixture is not consistent in every field of land law. While it may be argued that the law of commercial leases and fixtures has been influenced by English law, the law of ownership and servitudes remains principally Civilian.

[5] For limited exceptions, see orders and agreements relating to the storage and transport of gas: Gas Act 1965, ss 4–5, 12 and 13.

[6] The most general exception – the public right of access across open land created by the Land Reform (Scotland) Act 2003 – permits only passage and has no application to oil and gas transport.

This is why oil and gas lawyers require an understanding of land law. To enable the laying of a pipeline and the passage of materials through that pipeline the oil and gas companies must obtain a right from the landowner. In certain circumstances,[7] where the landowner refuses to grant the right, it may be obtained under statutory compulsion, a process that usually requires a demonstration that the right conforms to the stated statutory purpose and is necessary. The process of compulsory acquisition usually involves the payment of compensation to the landowner. Many compulsory purchase statutes do not include a power to acquire new rights and, as such, are unsuitable for use in the creation of new pipeline systems.[8] Whatever the case, the right sought by an oil and gas company must be one known to the general law. For example, in Scotland, the right must be a right of ownership, a lease or a servitude. These rights are the "products" that the Scottish legal system makes available for parties who wish to deal in land within the jurisdiction: oil and gas companies cannot simply decide to use another right with which they are familiar in another state. This limited choice is known by land lawyers as the *numerus clausus* principle: the principle of the "closed list". What it means in practice is that the right used by an oil and gas company to transport oil in Scotland is not a right of a nature unique to oil and gas companies. Put another way, oil and gas companies must abide by the local land law in all the particular legal systems in which they operate.

In addition to this, many oil and gas lawyers are familiar with the negotiation of contracts but the right required by the oil and gas company to transport their product is much more than a mere contract. A contract simply imposes a personal obligation on the parties who enter into the agreement. Except in unusual circumstances,[9] it will not bind a person who purchases land from the original landowner who entered into the contract, even if the contract in express terms purports to bind such a party.[10] Furthermore, a contract is vulnerable to the insolvency of the

17.4

---

[7] For a general overview of the law, see J Rowan Robinson, *Compulsory Purchase and Compensation* (2nd edn, 2003). For detail as to oil and gas, see the statutory provisions noted at n 20 below.

[8] *Sovmots Investments Ltd* v *Secretary of State for the Environment* [1979] AC 144.

[9] A company can always expressly agree to be bound by the contract originally entered into by another company. This is known as "novation". It is sometimes encountered when a purchaser decides to renew the security and maintenance contracts held respectively by a security company or a tradesman in respect of newly purchased premises.

[10] *H J Banks and Co Ltd* v *Shell Chemicals UK Ltd*, Lord Clarke, 8 September 2005, CA11/05 [2005] CSOH 123, available on Court of Session website and noted at 2005 GWD 29–557.

contracting party. A contract therefore carries the risk for an oil company that the personal right created in it is only as strong as the party with whom the oil company has contracted. Except where the contracting party has a covenant equivalent to that of the Government, such a state of affairs is inadequate for most oil companies as they may invest vast sums in developing extensive pipelines and distribution networks which will in all likelihood be expected to be in existence for a considerable period of time. Instead of a mere contract, the right required by an oil and gas company to sustain a major pipeline requires to be a "real right". This is a right that is enforceable not only against the granter, but also against his successors and against the rest of the world even though these parties were not signatories of any agreement. Furthermore, these real rights are needed in respect of every part of the pipeline because the chain of rights is only as strong as the weakest link. It is clear therefore that every major pipeline development involves considerable work for oil and gas lawyers who specialise in land law. It is on their work that the subsequent uninterrupted and efficient working of the pipeline will rely. The responsibility is great.

17.5   A final footnote is required for those who deal with trans-border pipelines. The fact that a real right has been obtained will not protect the pipeline from the instability of a state. A real right is enforceable against the world because it is a right recognised by a particular legal system. If that legal system collapses, or the relevant legal rules are altered by a new regime so that the pipeline is expropriated, then no real right will serve to protect the interests of the oil and gas company.[11] Those lawyers who practise in the United Kingdom may legitimately expect this last comment to have little immediate relevance to pipelines crossing the border between the stable democratic nations of Scotland or England. However, oil and gas transport is part of an international industry and the very same lawyers may find they have to advise on pipelines in less stable parts of the world.

---

[11] Cf *Burmah Oil Co (Burma Trading) Ltd* v *Lord Advocate* 1964 SC (HL) 117, where Scottish companies pursued a successful common-law claim for compensation against the Crown for the lawful destruction of oil installations in Burma (including oil wells and pipelines) by British forces to prevent them falling into the hands of the advancing Japanese army. The claim could be brought only because the Scottish legal system and the United Kingdom as a state both remained intact after the Second World War. In any event, these particular rights to receive compensation were extinguished by the War Damage Act 1965.

REAL RIGHTS

Oil and gas lawyers cannot simply dream up a new real right to   **17.6**
suit their own purpose. To install a pipeline across land in private
ownership they must choose from the limited number of real rights
recognised by the relevant legal system. In Scotland, as in many other
legal systems, the three most suitable real rights are: (a) ownership;
(b) lease; and (c) praedial[12] servitude. Of all of these, the primary
real right employed for pipelines is a praedial servitude and these
are generally known by the abbreviated term "servitudes" because,
as a general rule, no other form of servitude is known to the law
of Scotland.[13] In Common law jurisdictions such as England, India,
most other jurisdictions within the British Commonwealth and
many American states, the equivalents of praedial servitudes are
"easements". Why servitudes are the most suitable of the three real
rights on offer will be explored below as the limitations of the other
rights are outlined. It should be noted, however, that the right of
servitude is not one which is completely suited to oil and gas transportation and some of the more important limitations are also noted
below.

An oil and gas company will wish to obtain rights from each and   **17.7**
every proprietor who owns land along the route of the pipeline. This
in itself involves a massive effort of co-ordination and expertise as
property lawyers seek to ensure that there is no gap left between
the geographic areas covered by the rights granted. Parties such as
tenants or security holders who are entitled to derivative real rights
affecting the land in question will require to consent to the grant of
the servitude,[14] otherwise they will not be bound by the grant of the
servitude.[15] Frequently, however, landowners who envisage that they
might wish to grant a pipeline servitude at some time in the future
will reserve an express power to do so when they grant a lease or
security over land. In this way the problem of obtaining the consent
of a tenant or creditor is elided. There is no requirement in Scots
law[16] that a real right of the same nature is used for every patch of

---

[12] The term "praedial" denotes a link to a plot of land known as the "dominant tenement" or "benefited property".

[13] Historically, a real right known as a proper liferent was regarded as a form of personal servitude but this classification has been abandoned almost completely.

[14] *Viz* the principle recognised in *Buchan* v *Sir William Cockburn* (1739) Elch "Clause" 2; M 6528. For application to servitudes, see: Cusine and Paisley, *Servitudes and Rights of Way* (1998), para 5.20.

[15] This general principle is found across jurisdictions, eg the South African position noted in C G van der Merwe and M J de Waal, *The Law of Things and Servitudes* (1993) at para 269.

[16] Cusine and Paisley, *Servitudes and Rights of Way*, para 17.39. English law is to similar effect: *Todrick* v *Western National Omnibus Co* [1934] Ch 561. See also *Moody* v *Steggles* (1879) 12 Ch 261 at 267, per Fry J.

land all the way along the length of the same pipeline.[17] It is possible that most of the pipeline could be supported by servitudes, smaller areas by leasehold rights and some remaining areas by rights of ownership. However, for the sake of consistency it is best for an oil or gas company to seek to establish the pipeline by a chain of similar, if not identical, real rights all the way along the pipeline.

17.8   The rights that an oil or gas company has in land are primarily aimed at enabling it to carry out its business. A subsidiary, albeit only marginally less important, function of the property rights is to enable the oil and gas company to raise finance by using the property and rights as security. Invariably finance is raised from banks and other financiers by offering the funder a security over the rights in land,[18] various forms of securitisation[19] or by pledging the shares of the company to the bank. For this reason the rights require to be "institutionally acceptable", meaning that the terms of the rights are what a bank would accept and can pass on to a purchaser if the bank is forced to call up the loan and sell the assets of the debtor company or even sell the entire debtor company as a going concern. Albeit the major oil companies have some of the best covenants in the world, it is not unknown for minor players in the oil and gas market to fail.

17.9   One final point requires noting at this juncture. In any state with a history of oil and gas exploration and transport it will inevitably be the case that the legislature will have enacted a limited number of statutes specially to deal with pipelines and the oil and gas industry in general. That is certainly the case in the United Kingdom.[20] Oil and gas lawyers are also familiar with a relatively large body of detailed regulation specially enacted for their industry. Albeit parts of the legislation enable compulsory acquisition of real rights[21] and

---

[17] This requirement appears to exist in certain legal systems such as Sri Lanka, following (and perhaps misunderstanding) an old rule of Roman Dutch law: Voet, *Pandects*, 8,4,19. See, eg, *Cornelis v Fernando* (1962) 65 NLR 93; G L Peiris, *The Law of Property in Sri Lanka*, vol 3: "Servitudes and Partition" (2nd edn, 2004), pp 3–5.

[18] The forms of security available in Scotland are a standard security (a fixed security) and a floating charge (a security that can affect the assets and undertaking of the company as it exists from time to time).

[19] These may involve complex legal structures.

[20] Eg Gas Act 1965; Offshore Petroleum Development (Scotland) Act 1975; Gas Act 1986; Petroleum Act 1987; Gas Act 1995; Petroleum Act 1998; Utilities Act 2000, Pt V.

[21] Eg Offshore Petroleum Development (Scotland) Act 1975; Petroleum Act 1998, s 7 (ancillary rights); Petroleum Act 1987, s 27 (compulsory acquisition of rights); Gas Act 1965, ss 12–13 (the right to store gas underground and related rights and compulsory purchase of rights as respects well, boreholes and shafts in storage area and protective area). Other legal systems provide similar compulsory powers, eg Louisiana: *Exxon Pipeline Co v LeBlanc*, 763 So 2d 128 (La App 1 Cir 2000) (expropriation of pipeline servitude).

regulate the passage of oil and gas through pipelines,[22] none of the statutes in Scotland creates a generally applicable right for oil companies to transport oil and gas in pipelines through the land of other parties. It is all the more the case that landowners are not simply obliged to accept that a pipeline can be laid across their property just because it is in the national interest or profitable for oil and gas companies.

OWNERSHIP

Ownership is a real right frequently used by oil and gas companies **17.10** for structures such as refineries, offices and transport yards. It is also used for smaller areas situated along the length of pipelines, such as sites of monitoring equipment. The benefit is that a right of property confers a right of exclusive occupation on the owner. It remains a theoretical possibility that an oil and gas company might wish to own the entirety of the strips of land in which a pipeline is laid. This is the approach that was almost universally adopted by the constructors of railway lines in the 19th century, as the tracks were usually laid on a strip of ground owned by the railway network. The benefit of this approach is that an oil company will have a greater control over the pipeline and, after acquisition, can largely deal with it as it wishes. After laying the pipeline in its own ground, the oil company will retain the ownership in the structure of the pipeline even if it is regarded as a fixture and accedes to the ground.

There are, however, drawbacks to this approach of seeking **17.11** ownership of a strip of ground. First, it is relatively costly. Ownership of land is always more expensive than the obtaining of a limited right. Second, many landowners do not wish to sell such a right as thereby they lose all rights in the land and their estates on either side are separated by a long, narrow strip. Third, ownership itself attracts certain liabilities which can sometimes be avoided by the use of a more limited right. For example, where a statute imposes liability on the "occupier" of a piece of land,[23] an owner will almost invariably fall within that definition but the holder of a lesser real right, such as a servitude, may not. Much will depend on the nature of the possession attendant upon the exercise of the relevant derivative real right. Fourth, ownership is perpetual and the oil company will be left with ownership of a strip of land long after the pipeline has

---

[22] Eg Petroleum Act 1998, Pt III.
[23] Eg Occupiers' Liability (Scotland) Act 1960 applied to a servitude of way in *Cooper v Strathclyde RC*, July 1993, IH, unreported but noted briefly at 1993 GWD 31–2013, available on LEXIS. For England and Wales, see: Occupiers' Liability Act 1984.

ceased to be used, unless it can dispose of the ownership to others. As the remnants of the closed local railway lines demonstrate, such unusually shaped properties are not particularly attractive even to the adjacent landowners. Ownership cannot be lost by abandonment in Scotland.

LEASEHOLD RIGHTS

17.12 Oil companies frequently make use of leases in relation to premises for offices and other business facilities. This makes business sense in that there is usually no initial capital outlay for the premises and, instead, an annual return is paid to the landlord in the form of rent. Unlike a property right which is perpetual, the lease will have a finite term.[24] It is possible for facilities, such as pumping stations or refineries, located along the route, or at the end of pipelines, to be held on leasehold tenure. The benefit is that the tenant is entitled to exclusive possession. He can exclude everyone – even the landlord[25] – from entering the subjects during the period of the lease. Of course, the lease may make some specific exceptions to this and permit to the landlord rights of entry for the purposes of inspection and survey to enable the landlord to check that the terms of the lease are being complied with. If the reservations are so extensive as to derogate materially from the right afforded to the tenant it is possible to argue that no real right has been granted to the tenant.[26] It is relatively rare, albeit not unknown, for a major oil and gas pipeline to be held by a lease, but leases are relatively common for small pipelines.[27] A benefit of a lease is that it can be held wholly separately from any other land (and in that respect it is akin to a personal servitude): unlike a praedial servitude, there is no necessary requirement that the holder of the right is the owner of any other plot of land. The land subject to a lease remains owned by the landlord. Consequently, any fixture placed in the ground will become owned by the landlord[28] albeit subject to the lease which probably will contain a right of removal on the part of the tenant.

---

[24] Since 9 June 2000 the maximum duration for a lease in Scotland is 175 years: Abolition of Feudal Tenure etc (Scotland) Act 2000, s 67. The 175-year maximum does not apply to leases existing prior to that date.

[25] Rankine, *The Law of Leases in Scotland* (1916), Chapter X.

[26] *TCS Holdings Ltd v Ashtead Plant Hire Co Ltd* 2003 SLT 177; *South Lanarkshire Council v Taylor* 2005 1 SC 182.

[27] See, eg, Lease between The Provost, Magistrates and Councillors of the Burgh of Falkirk and The Scottish Gas Board dated 28 September and 12 October 1970 and recorded GRS (Stirling) (Book 2276) (Folio 103) on 4 September 1972. The right to lay pipes is contained in Clause (Fourth) on page second.

[28] *Shetland Islands Council v BP Petroleum Development Ltd* 1990 SLT 82.

Commercial leases comprise a specialist area and only a very brief **17.13** overview in the context of the oil and gas industry is offered here.[29] Unlike many jurisdictions such as England and Wales, in Scotland there is a general absence of landlord and tenant legislation in the commercial sphere. Consequently, the terms of a lease in Scotland assume great importance. A well-drafted lease should contain provisions permitting the landlord to control the use of the leased land to some extent. In addition, there will be detailed provisions in terms of which the tenant insures the buildings if these were originally provided by the landlord. The tenant will be obliged to comply with all relevant statutory requirements and to indemnify the landlord for damage to land caused by the activity of the tenant.[30] These provisions are important in situations where pollution could be caused to the underlying or adjacent land because of an oil or gas leak. As the lease will inevitably come to an end at some time, the lease should contain detailed provisions as to the final removal of the pipeline structure and land restoration. During the period of the lease the landlord is free to transfer his property right to others albeit that, in some cases, the tenant will seek a right of pre-emption enabling the tenant to acquire his landlord's interest on such occasion at a price determined by a formula set out in the lease. Unless suitably drafted, the effect of such a pre-emption may link the price payable to the covenant of the tenant and the oil company potentially may end up paying more if it is a successful company. By contrast, the transfer of the tenant's interest in the lease is likely to be limited by a provision conferring on the landlord some power of approval, perhaps even an absolute veto, as to the proposed assignee. Clearly a landlord will not wish a lease of a major oil installation to be transferred to a company with little expertise in the oil and gas industry or a company with a substantially lesser covenant than its existing tenant. A lease requires a continuing return to a landlord in a form of rent and it is common in long leases to find a mechanism in the lease enabling periodic rent review. This enables the passing rent to be reviewed from time to time to prevent it from being devalued by the effects of inflation.

SERVITUDES

The primary real right for supporting oil and gas pipelines is **17.14** a servitude of pipeline. Albeit there was little authority for the

---

[29] For Scotland: M J Ross and D J McKichan, *Drafting and Negotiating Commercial Leases in Scotland* (2nd edn, 1993). For England: *Halsbury's Laws of England: Landlord and Tenant*, Reissue, vols 27(1)–(3) (4th edn, 2006).
[30] Cf the issues of indemnities discussed at para 17.24.

existence of these servitude rights at common law,[31] there has been recent retrospective legislation confirming that they always have been recognised by Scots law.[32] A servitude of pipeline, when suitably and appropriately drafted, enables not only a pipeline to be laid in land owned by someone else but also oil and gas to be transported through that pipe for commercial purposes.[33] Most existing deeds, however, are not sufficiently extensively drafted for the use thereof to be altered to transmit other products such as carbon dioxide unless this is ancillary to oil and gas transportation. Clearly, a wholesale alteration of the use of an oil or gas pipeline to facilitate an entirely different industry by the transport of waste gases is likely to be outwith the terms of most existing deeds of servitude. When appropriately drafted, a deed of servitude will comprise a vast array of provisions additional to the basic right of oil and gas transportation. This additional material includes provisions relating to (a) rights to repair, maintain, renew and upgrade the pipeline; (b) rights of access for installation, repair, removal and all other necessary purposes, including a right to take all necessary equipment and personnel along the designated routes of access; (c) patrolling,[34] surveying and inspection rights, including, perhaps, rights of overflight with helicopters or fixed-wing aircraft (to enable ease of inspection and security checks); (d) a right to preclude building or invasive activity such as the growing of trees or the parking of vehicles on the surface of the land immediately above and beside the pipeline; (e) obligations on the oil company to keep the pipeline in a good state of repair conform to all relevant regulations; (f) indemnities relating to potential pollution and damage to adjacent land; (g) rights of general access to various points along the length of the pipeline from the nearest public road and specific rights of access over adjacent ground to carry out emergency repairs;[35] (h) rights to install markers, safety equipment and other necessary equipment at various points along the pipeline; (i) provisions precluding the removal of vertical or lateral support for the pipeline; (j) arbitration or other dispute resolution provisions to ease the swift resolution

---

[31] *Viz Labinski Ltd* v *BP Oil Development Ltd*, 24 January 2003, IH, and 18 December 2001, OH, both available on Scottish Courts website. See also *Assessor for Strathclyde Region* v *BP Refinery Grangemouth Ltd* 1983 SC 18.

[32] Title Conditions (Scotland) Act 2003, s 77.

[33] In all cases the terms of the deed should be consulted to ascertain that there are no special limitations or restrictions, eg limitations on pressure, chemical composition or temperature of contents.

[34] Eg the Texas cases *Gulf Pipe Line Co* v *Thomason* (1927, Tex Civ App) 299 SW 532 and *Gulf Pipe Line Co* v *Kaderli* (1927, Tex Civ App) 299 SW 534.

[35] Eg the Canadian case: *Alliance Pipeline Ltd* v *Seibert* [2003] 25 Alta LR (4th) 365, Alberta Court of Queen's Bench, Topolniski J.

of disputes without recourse to the courts;[36] (k) provisions enabling any works to be carried out not only by the oil and gas company but also by authorised contractors and agents; and (l) provisions for the abandonment of the pipeline. The whole aim of these additional rights is to ensure that the oil and gas company can comply with any obligations imposed on it by general regulation, safety concerns and licensing requirements while providing an appropriate measure of protection for the landowner. No matter how extensive the drafting, there is considerable difficulty in providing for increased regulatory burdens. The general rule is that the servitude may not become more onerous for the servient proprietor as a consequence of these increased regulations unless, of course, the deed envisages that this may occur.

There is no statutory form for such a deed but a form of servitude **17.15** deed has evolved from years of use and has become well established throughout the oil and gas industry. Albeit a deed of servitude used in Scotland will have certain aspects relevant only to the peculi-arities of Scottish land law, the basic terms reflect what is required anywhere else in the world and the terms would be readily capable of understanding by an oil and gas lawyer practising in other juris-dictions. Each jurisdiction, however, will have its own registration requirements in terms of which the deed may require to be registered in a public register. In Scotland that register is the Land Register of Scotland or, in some cases, the older Sasine Register but the Scottish provisions for pipeline servitudes are relatively lax. Indeed, regis-tration for such servitudes is permissive and not mandatory.[37]

Benefits of deeds of servitudes

The benefits of such a deed of servitude are many. First, servitudes **17.16** confer on oil and gas companies a real right to transport their products across the lands of others. It is a right enforceable against the rest of the world including successors of the original granter.[38] Consequently, the oil and gas companies do not need to purchase the underlying land. They acquire only such rights as they require and no more.

Second, the landowner, typically a farmer, retains ownership **17.17** of the ground. Albeit restrained from some of the more invasive

---

[36] See generally Chapter 18.
[37] Title Conditions (Scotland) Act 2003, s 75(3)(b). For England: *Halsbury's Laws of England: Equitable Interests in Land: Restrictive Covenants*, Reissue, vol 16(2) (4th edn, 2003), para 613ff.
[38] Cusine and Paisley, *Servitudes and Rights of Way*, para 1.62.

building or farming activities by express[39] or implied[40] terms of the servitude, he is still able to cultivate the surface to some extent.[41] He can pass over to his land on either side of the pipeline without having to retain access rights to do so. Agricultural production is not unduly hampered. Claims for compensation for disruption are thus minimised.

17.18   Third, when the use of the pipeline comes to an end, the oil and gas company can remove the pipe or abandon it if the servitude deed so allows. Provided the terms of the servitude deed permit this, the right of servitude, albeit potentially perpetual, may be abandoned whenever the pipeline ceases its economic lifetime. Alternatively, there may be provision to install a replacement pipeline. In still other cases there may be provision to divert the pipeline to a different use. This, however, appears to be rare in practice.

17.19   Fourth, the deed provides a focus for the rights and responsibilities of the two persons who have an interest in the land in question. Broadly speaking, the deed should make provision for all foreseeable events and seek to set out a means for resolution of disputes. The aim is to avoid litigation and the public airing of disputes. If it is intended that more than one party will have servitude rights in respect of the pipeline, it is prudent to provide for the regulation of the relationship between those parties.

17.20   Fifth, it is inevitable that a deed of servitude cannot foresee everything. In such a case where there is no provision within the deed, the general law of servitudes will apply.[42] The parties

---

[39] Eg the Canadian case *Canadian Western Natural Gas Co v Empire Trucking Parts (1985) Ltd* [1998] 61 Alta LR (3rd) 1, Alberta Court of Queen's Bench, Moshansky J: oil and gas pipeline servitude prohibiting erection of structures held to include cars and vehicles placed on surface in addition to a wall, fence or means of storing trucks. They were therefore to be removed as interfering with access to pipeline.

[40] *Central RC v Ferns* 1979 SC 136 (loading of soil and material on top of pipeline); *Hamilton-Gray v Sherwood*, Sheriff Court, 27 August 2002, K Reid and G Gretton, *Conveyancing* 2002, p 6, noted in (2002) 59 *Greens Property Law Bulletin* 7 (building of wall on top of pipeline); Louisiana: *El Paso Field Service, Inc v Stephen Minvielle*, 867 So 2d 120 (La App 3d Cir, 2004) (owner of servient tenement interdicted from engaging in crawfish operations in a pond over the route of a servitude of underground gas pipeline); Missouri: *Southern Star Central Gas Pipeline, Inc v Murray* 190 SW 3d 423 Mo App SD, 2006 (court ordered removal of trees that hindered helicopter inspection and potentially could cause root damage to pipeline but court refused to order removal of a mobile home within 5 feet of the pipeline).

[41] Eg Ohio: *Besser v Buckeye Pipe Line Co* (1937) 57 Ohio App 341, 13 NE 2d 927; *Industrial Gas Co v Jones* (1939) 62 Ohio App 553, 24 NE 2d 830, Missouri: *Bahler v Shell Pipe Line Corp* (1940, DC Mo) 34 F Supp 10.

[42] For Scotland: Cusine and Paisley, *Servitudes and Rights of Way*; Louisiana: A N Yiannopoulos, *Louisiana Civil Law Treatise*, vol. 4: "Predial Servitudes" (3rd edn, 2004); England: C Sara, *Boundaries and Easements* (3rd edn, 2002); Gale, *Easements* (16th

therefore have the comfort of knowing that there is no absolute "black hole" in the legal arrangements they have set up and reference can be made to the general principles of servitudes to supply an answer to their queries. In Scotland there is also a recognition that the provision in any deed of servitude may be overtaken by events and become unreasonable in the light of new circumstances. In such a case the landowner and any other against whom the servitude is enforceable[43] is permitted by statute to apply to the Lands Tribunal for Scotland to seek variation or discharge of the servitude.[44] Under current legislation, such a variation or discharge of a servitude will be permitted if it is "reasonable" to grant the application.[45] In theory such statutory provisions may be used to require the re-routing of a pipeline.[46] However, given the probable disruption of transport and production consequent upon such an operation and the attendant costs, it appears to be unlikely that such an application would succeed as regards a large pipeline except in very special situations. In any event, such applications for variation are usually used as part of the process to obtain a negotiated settlement.

Limitations of servitudes

Servitudes are a class of rights developed originally in Roman times.[47] **17.21**
English easements have been developed largely from Roman notions to the extent that it is true to say that easements are derived from servitudes and not servitudes from easements.[48] The fact that servitudes are still used today is testament to the stability and flexibility of the basic structure of Scottish land law based on these Civilian foundations. However, the historical origins are still reflected in some

---

edn, 1997); South Africa: C G van der Merwe and M J de Waal, *The Law of Things and Servitudes*; Australia: A Bradbrook and M Neave, *Easements and Restrictive Covenants in Australia* (2nd edn, 2000).

[43] This excludes the person benefited by the servitude. Consequently, that person cannot apply to have the servitude re-routed or extended. A possible way forward in such a case is for the deed to have been drafted with express powers to effect a re-routing or extension.

[44] Title Conditions (Scotland) Act 2003, Pt 9.

[45] *Ibid*, s 98.

[46] All the reported cases relate to re-routing of servitudes of access but the principles applicable are identical. See, eg, *George Wimpey East Scotland Ltd v Fleming* 2006 SLT (Lands Tr) 2. See Reid and Gretton, *Conveyancing 2005*, pp 7–8 and 102.

[47] *Digest*, Book 8; *Las Siete Partidas*, 3, 31 and 3, 32; translated by Samuel Parsons Scott (ed Robert I Burns, SJ), *Las Siete Partidas*: vol 3, *Medieval Law: Lawyers And Their Work* (2001), pp 855–876; Voet, *Pandects*, 8, 1, 1–8, 6, 14; Rudolf Elvers, *Die Römische Servitutenlehre* (1856).

[48] C Sara, *Boundaries and Easements*, p 214, para 11.11; W W Buckland and A D McNair, *Roman Law and Common Law: A Comparison in Outline* (2nd edn, 1952), p 142.

characteristics of servitudes that, as yet, have not been sufficiently well adapted to modern social or economic conditions. It would be fair to say that there are certain limitations inherent in the concept of servitude that are not ideally suited to the oil and gas industry.

Exclusion of the owner

17.22 The right of servitude held by the benefited proprietor co-exists with the property right of the burdened proprietor. A basic principle of the law of servitudes is that the two rights simultaneously affect the same thing and the owner of the burdened property is excluded only to the extent that the proper exercise of the servitude requires.[49] A further basic principle is that no servitude can be inconsistent with the underlying property right of the burdened proprietor.[50] Albeit there is some obscurity in the application of this principle to particular cases, a major factor is the degree to which the burdened proprietor is physically excluded from the use of the burdened property: the greater the degree of exclusion, the greater chance that the purported servitude will be regarded as inconsistent with the servient tenement. For this reason the device of servitude cannot be used by oil companies to construct and exclusively occupy refineries, offices or other large buildings and complexes on the servient tenement.[51] Similarly, any attempt to create a servitude of storage for the purposes of installation of large-scale oil or gas tanks would probably be unacceptable.[52] However, the application of this principle to servitudes of pipeline is uncertain even though the practical and intended effect of the construction and operation of a gas and oil pipeline is that the burdened proprietor will be physically excluded from the area within the pipeline.[53]

---

[49] Erskine, *Inst* 2, 9, 34; Bell, *Prin*, s 987; *Rattray* v *Tayport Patent Slip Co* (1868) 5 SLR 219, per Lord Deas at 219.

[50] The common law rule was established in *Dyce* v *Hay* (1852) 1 Macq 305 and is repeated for expressly created servitudes in Title Conditions (Scotland) Act 2003, s 76(2).

[51] This would be inconsistent with the underlying right of property and thus repugnant with ownership: *Wright* v *Logan* (1829) 8 S 247 at 249 in the sheriff's note; *Pickard* v *Somers* (1932) 48 Sh Ct Rep 237 at 240, per the Dean of Guild; Title Conditions (Scotland) Act 2003, s 76(2). For a similar principle in England: Luther, "Easements and Exclusive Possession" (1996) 16 *Legal Studies* 51–62.

[52] Cusine and Paisley, *Servitudes and Rights of Way*, para 3.16; *Moncrieff* v *Jamieson* 2004 SCLR 135, Lerwick Sheriff Court (Sheriff Colin Scott Mackenzie), 2005 SLT 225. Cf the more favourable position of Common law jurisdictions as developed by a Scottish judge by reference to Scottish authority: *Attorney-General of Southern Nigeria* v *John Holt & Co Ltd* [1915] AC 599 (PC (S Nigeria)), per Lord Shaw of Dunfermline at 617, citing *Dyce* v *Hay* (1852) 1 Macq 305, per Lord St Leonards LC.

[53] Viz a case in which the House of Lords considered that this matter was so fundamental that it construed a deed of servitude as conveying a property right: *Glasgow Corporation* v *McEwan* (1899) 2 F (HL) 25.

Admittedly, total exclusion of the burdened proprietor is recognised in the context of other servitudes such as those relating to inundation and dam,[54] septic tank[55] and, to a smaller physical extent, water and drainage pipes. There is clearly an acceptance of total exclusion of the burdened proprietor in these traditionally accepted servitudes and it remains to be seen if this will be extended to servitudes relative to oil and gas pipelines. Safety and security concerns alone would indicate that such an extension is desirable as it would be wholly unsafe if the oil and gas company could not exclude the landowner from accessing or using the pipeline. The lack of any challenge to oil and gas pipeline servitudes on this basis suggests that it has been so extended at least in practice if not by the courts. The cynic might simply suggest that the point has never occurred to anyone.

Dominant tenement – basic principles

A praedial servitude cannot exist in its own right. It must exist together with and for the benefit of another piece of land known as the "dominant tenement" or the "benefited property".[56] The owner of that land is entitled to use the servitude but only for the purpose of benefiting that particular land.[57] The same rule applies

17.23

---

[54] A right of storage in the form of a servitude is recognised as regards the storage of water for power generation and it seems a small step from that to permit the storage of gas or oil for power generation. For servitudes of water storage for power generation, see *Gairlton v Stevenson* (1677) M 12769; *Carlile v Douglas* (1731) M 14524; *Bruce v Dalrymple* (1731) Elch Serv No 2; 5 Brown's Supp 220, commented on in Ersk, *Inst* 2, 9, 4, note; *Gray v Maxwell* (1762) M 12800; *Christie v Wemyss* (1842) 5 D 242; *Scottish Highland Distillery Co v Reid* (1877) 4 R 1118; *Williams' Trs v Macandrew and Jenkins* 1960 SLT 246. See also the similar position in South African law: *Fourie v Marandellas Town Council* 1972 *Rhodesian Law Reports* 164.

[55] See, eg, *McLellan v Hunter* 1987 GWD 21–799; *Todd v Scoular* 1988 GWD 24–1041; *Clark v Craig*, unreported, Stonehaven Sheriff Court, 12 February 1993, case ref A149/91, noted in Cusine and Paisley, *Servitudes and Rights of Way*, paras 1.41, 1.71 and 3.50; *Buchan v Hunter* in Paisley and Cusine, *Unreported Property Cases* (1993), p 311. This mirrors development in other mixed jurisdictions such as Québec: *Gustave Rochon c Suzanne Charron*, 2 May 2002, Cour Du Québec, QCCQ 705-22-003035-001, available at canlii. For Common law jurisdictions: *Wong Kwok-chiang and Others v Longo Construction Ltd and Another* (1987) *Hong Kong Law Reports* 345; *Callan v McAvinue*, unreported, Irish High Court, Pringle J, 11 May 1973, noted in Bland, *The Law of Easements and Profits à Prendre* (1997), para 5-22; *Lackey v Joule*, App, 577 SW 2d 114. See also *Professor McDonald's Conveyancing* Opinions (ed C Waelde) (1998), Opinion 22, pp 94–97.

[56] *Lord Blantyre v Waterworks Commissioners of Dumbarton* (1886) 15 R (HL) 56 at 57, per LC Halsbury.

[57] *Irvine Knitters Ltd v North Ayrshire Co-operative Society Ltd* 1978 SC 109; *Scott v Bogle*, 6 July 1809, FC.

in Common law systems such as England[58] and Canada[59] and in mixed jurisdictions such as South Africa.[60] In a number of jurisdictions throughout the world[61] there has been modest relaxation of the rule but, typically, the relaxation is granted on an equitable basis to remedy problems arising from an existing state of affairs. No lawyer advising in relation to the laying or use of a major pipeline should confidently rely on such a relaxation being granted in advance. The effect of the rule limiting use to a particular dominant tenement is most easily illustrated by reference to a servitude of access. The owner of a plot of land benefited by a servitude of access may use the access servitude to take access to the benefited property. He cannot use the access servitude to gain access to any other property even if the other property is adjacent to the benefited property. For pipelines, this means that a servitude of pipeline held by an oil and gas company cannot exist in its own right. It must benefit other land owned by that same oil and gas company. The pumping station and refineries at each end of the pipeline are obvious candidates for the role of these benefited properties. In addition, certain deeds are drafted so that small areas of ground located along the route of the pipelines and used for safety equipment linked to the pipeline are also owned by the oil and gas companies and these are also designated as benefited properties. In addition, at least in so far as Scots law is concerned, the servitude must benefit the right of ownership in the dominant tenement. In contrast to English law,[62] Scots law does not recognise that a servitude may be constituted in favour of a leasehold right alone.[63] However, a servitude of pipeline created in favour of the property right in a benefited property may be exercised by the tenant in that benefited property provided the terms of the relevant lease include the right to the pipeline.

---

[58] *Skull* v *Glenister* (1864) 16 CB (NS) 81; *Peacock* v *Custins* [2001] 2 All ER 827, [2001] 13 EG 152, CA; *Macepark (Wittlebury) Ltd* v *Sargeant* [2003] 2 P & CR 12 (Gabriel Moss, QC, Deputy High Court Judge).

[59] *Friedman* v *Murray* [1952] OWN 295, [1952] 3 DLR 159 (HC), affirmed [1953] OWN 486; [1953] 3 DLR 313 (CA); *Liscombe* v *Maughan* (1928) 62 OLR 328, [1928] 3 DLR 397 (CA).

[60] Voet, *Pandects*, 8, 4, 13; *Berdur Properties (Pty) Ltd* v *76 Commercial Road (Pty) Ltd* 1998 (4) SA 62 (D).

[61] Eg Germany: BGB § 1019, V Zivilsenat Urt V 5 Oktober 1965 1 SJ (Kl) w K (Bekl) V ZR 73/63. Entscheidungen des Bundesgerichtshof in Zivilsachen, 44, 171; Washington: *Brown* v *Voss* 105 Wash 2d 366, 715 P 2d 514 (1986); Samuels, *Stories Out of School: Teaching the Case of Brown v Voss* (1995) 16 *Cardozo Law Review* 1445.

[62] Eg *Macepark (Wittlebury) Ltd* v *Sargeant* [2003] 2 P & CR 12 (Gabriel Moss, QC, Deputy High Court Judge).

[63] *Safeway Food Stores Ltd* v *Wellington Motor Co (Ayr) Ltd* 1976 SLT 53; Cusine and Paisley, *Servitudes and Rights of Way*, para 2.12.

Application of the basic principles

These general principles relative to the existence of a dominant **17.24** tenement can cause some surprises when applied to oil and gas pipelines. First, an oil and gas company that owns no land clearly does not own a dominant tenement and, by definition, cannot hold a servitude of pipeline. The oil and gas company itself cannot constitute the dominant tenement just because it is a company that owns some property such as moveable property or leases.[64] Moveable property – such as oil or gas itself – cannot be the dominant tenement in a servitude. As already mentioned, it is not sufficient for the oil and gas company to hold a lease of a refinery or other premises and purport to constitute the servitude in favour of that lease. Instead, the oil and gas company must ensure that the landlord of the leased premises is entitled to the servitude and that the lease in favour of the oil and gas company includes the right to enjoy the pipeline. Of course, this immediately exposes the landlord as dominant proprietor to all the counter obligations in the servitude deed (known as "servitude conditions"[65]) – such as the obligations relating to repair, maintenance and the indemnities relating to pollution. A lawyer acting for the landlord will wish to ensure that the lease to the oil and gas company will make provision to off-set the liabilities, as it is unlikely that the burdened proprietor in the deed of servitude will accept that these obligations are enforceable only against the party operating the pipeline. The lawyer acting for the landlord will also be acutely aware that the value of these indemnities is measured by the covenant of the oil company. This will cause the landlord to be particularly careful about the assignation provisions in any lease, as he will not wish a satisfactory tenant to be replaced by one with a substantially lesser covenant. If the tenant company in question becomes insolvent then the indemnities may turn out to be worthless and the landlord will be stuck with the liabilities to the servient proprietor in the pipeline servitude.

Second, the deed of servitude requires to identify the benefited **17.25** property to enable it to be distinguished from all other land. The very best a land lawyer can hope for is for the deed to contain a plan identifying exactly the location and extent of the dominant tenement. However, many deeds fall short of this ideal. Many deeds contain a written description of the property and some even contain a very general description of the property benefited. What

---

[64] Cf the approach of English law which is scarcely justifiable on principle: *Re Salvin's Indenture* [1938] 2 All ER 498; H W Wilkinson, *Pipes, Mains, Cables and Sewers* (6th edn, 1995), pp 5 and 21.

[65] Cusine and Paisley, *Servitudes and Rights of Way*, Chapters 13 and 14.

is the minimum standard that is acceptable? In this regard, Scots law is rather lax and admits the possibility that extrinsic evidence may be used to identify the benefited property where the deed itself lacks the relevant information.[66] This means that a general and rather unspecific phrase used in a deed of servitude may be explained by evidence showing that in fact a certain property is benefited by the servitude and was intended to be so benefited when the servitude of pipeline was created. Many deeds of servitude identify the dominant tenement as "the assets and undertaking" of the relevant oil and gas company. This is indeed rather vague but it appears to be acceptable to interpret this language by showing that as at the date of the grant of the relevant servitude this "undertaking" did indeed include the property right in a plot of land owned by the oil and gas company and actually benefited by the pipeline. It should be made clear, however, that even such a general phrase probably cannot be used to claim that the benefited property includes land acquired by the oil and gas company after the deed of servitude was entered into.[67]

17.26   Third, once a plot of land is created as the dominant tenement in a particular servitude of pipeline it will remain so until the servitude is discharged or limited in a manner that excludes the particular plot of land. The oil and gas company cannot transfer the benefit of the servitude to another plot of land without acquiring a fresh grant of servitude. It cannot expand the lands benefited by the servitude without acquiring a fresh grant of servitude in suitably expansive terms. All of this tends to limit the usefulness of servitudes of pipeline where the network of pipelines is growing and new installations are being created. Furthermore, an oil or gas company owning a benefited tenement will find that if it transfers that tenement to another company the benefit of the servitude will automatically transfer with the ownership of the land. This may be precisely the opposite of what the oil company intends. However, the basic characteristic of a servitude as an inseverable pertinent of the benefited property means that the benefit of the servitude of pipeline cannot be retained separately from that land. Clearly the flexibility of servitudes may not be so great as to accommodate all the land transactions that an oil and gas company may wish to carry out.

---

[66] Eg *Lean* v *Hunter* 1950 SLT (Notes) 32.

[67] There is slight authority in favour of the possibility in Scotland. See Cusine and Paisley, *Servitudes and Rights of Way*, para 2.43, discussing *North British Railway* v *Park Yard Co Ltd* (1898) 25 R (HL) 47. The position in English law appears to be more strict and more principled: *London & Blenheim Estates Ltd* v *Ladbroke Retail Parks Ltd* [1993] 4 All ER 157; *Voice* v *Bell* [1993] EGCS 128, (1993) 68 P & CR 441.

Fourth, any servitude requires that a dominant tenement is **17.27** identified in respect of that right but also that the servitude actually is for the benefit of the dominant property. This is known by land lawyers as the *utilitas* or praedial utility of the servitude.[68] It is accepted in Scotland that this requirement is sufficiently flexible to include a business run on the dominant tenement. The benefited property must be sufficiently close to the pipeline for such utility to be demonstrated. This aspect of utility is known as the requirement of vicinity.[69] However, with a very long pipeline the existence of such utility and vicinity is at least questionable.[70] In many cases the pipeline appears to exist in its own right with no manifest utility to any plots of land, even if they are located at both ends of the pipeline. Certainly, in some particular cases the notion of utility is reversed from what is required for servitudes. For example, where small plots of land are retained along the route of the pipeline and these plots of land contain pumping stations or other safety equipment linked to the pipeline, it would seem that the plots of land are there to serve the pipeline and not *vice versa*. This point also holds good in England and other Common law jurisdictions. In those legal systems, an easement must "accommodate" a dominant tenement.[71] This is effectively a formulation similar, if not functionally identical, to the Civilian requirement of *utilitas*.[72]

Fifth, the benefited proprietor can communicate the use of the **17.28** pipeline only to parties having a legitimate link with the relevant dominant tenement.[73] This means that an oil and gas company cannot permit a third party to use the pipeline where that third party has no link whatsoever with the benefited property.[74] Where a right to use a servitude is dressed up to comply with this rule by adding therein a right to use the relevant dominant tenement, the whole right may be struck down as a sham if there is no substance to the right to use the dominant tenement.[75] This rule potentially has major implications for any system of pipelines where the operator seeks, or is obliged to accept, transportation of oil and gas belonging to third

---

[68] *Digest*, 8, 1, 8; Voet, *Pandects*, 8, 1, 1–2; Cusine and Paisley, *Servitudes and Rights of Way*, para 2.49.

[69] Erskine, *Inst*, 2, 9, 33.

[70] Cf the more optimistic view expressed in Cusine and Paisley, *Servitudes and Rights of Way*, para 12.176.

[71] *Re Ellenborough Park* [1956] 1 Ch 131 at 163, per Evershed MR; *Huckvale v Aegean Hotels Ltd* (1989) 58 P & CR 163 at 168, per Nourse LJ.

[72] C Seebo, *Servitus und Easement: Die Rezeption des römischen Servitutenrechts in England* (2005), pp 127–151.

[73] Cusine and Paisley, *Servitudes and Rights of Way*, para 1.57.

[74] *Murray v Mags of Peebles*, 8 Dec 1808, FC; *Stewart v Stewart* (1788) Hume 731.

[75] Viz the Canadian case *Jengle v Keetch* (1992) 89 DLR (4th) 15.

parties who have no rights other than the ownership of the oil and gas itself.[76]

17.29   Sixth, the servitude of pipeline cannot itself form the dominant tenement for servitudes of access over adjacent fields along the length of the pipeline even if these rights of access are required to take access to parts of the pipeline from the nearest public road. This follows from the basic point, noted above,[77] that a servitude is a pertinent of a right of ownership: a mere servitude cannot form the dominant tenement for another servitude. In such cases it seems preferable to create these access rights by means of separate leases from the adjacent landowner: it will be remembered that a lease requires no benefited tenement and the user clause of such a lease may restrict its use to one of access for the purpose of the pipeline.

17.30   Seventh, the operator of the pipeline may wish to create some negative restraints on the burdened landowner to prevent him from building on land immediately above and adjacent to the site of the pipeline. In some cases these negative restraints may legitimately be argued to be inherent in the positive servitude to convey oil and gas along the pipeline. For example, it is easy to imply the negative restraint not to build on top of the pipeline with structures of such a weight that they will crush the pipeline or render access to it more costly. However, this line of reasoning is more difficult to sustain where the strip on either side of the pipeline is very wide and the activity on the strip does not amount to any obstruction to the conveyance of the oil and gas. Certainly, in both England[78] and Scotland, such negative restraints will not be implied just because a sterilised zone on either side of the pipeline is required in terms of applicable regulation. In such cases the negative restraint may require to be set up by other legal devices known as real burdens in Scots law.[79] The equivalent device in Common law jurisdictions is the restrictive covenant. In Scotland the registration requirements for real burdens are more exacting than those for pipeline servitudes.[80]

---

[76] *Viz* the definition of "owner" in Petroleum Act 1998, s 27 and the acquisition of rights to use controlled petroleum pipelines in Petroleum Act 1998, s 17F. See also Gas Act 1995, s 19 (acquisition of rights to use pipeline systems). See further Chapter 7.

[77] See text at n 56 above.

[78] *Hayns* v *Secretary of State for the Environment* (1978) 36 P & CR 317 (sight lines required in terms of modern planning requirements not to be implied within an easement of road).

[79] See Title Conditions (Scotland) Act 2003.

[80] See the double registration requirements for real burdens in Title Conditions (Scotland) Act 2003, Pt 1 and the exemption of pipeline servitudes from double registration in Title Conditions (Scotland) Act 2003, s 75(3)(b).

The concept of personal servitude

One method of avoiding the drawbacks in servitudes as presently **17.31** known to the law of Scotland would be to develop the device of "personal" servitude. The equivalent in Common law jurisdictions is the easement "in gross".[81] Despite the use of the word "personal", this form of servitude is a real right. The significant difference from traditional "praedial" servitudes is that such a right can be held, exercised and transferred without reference to a dominant tenement. As yet, such a device has not generally been recognised in Scots law[82] albeit that there are a number of devices known as statutory wayleaves that bear some resemblance to personal servitudes.[83] The severance of a servitude from any dominant tenement will serve to elide the limitations outlined above which arise directly from this requirement of praedial servitudes. However, the further requirement that a servitude should not be inconsistent with the underlying property right will presumably apply to personal servitudes also. Clarification is needed to confirm the legitimacy of the exclusive possession necessarily attendant upon oil and gas pipelines. In addition, it may be prudent to vary the law of fixtures to preclude accession to the underlying land and to enable ownership of the pipeline structure to rest with the oil company.

CONCLUSION

The above discussion will show that land law issues have an impact **17.32** on the business of oil and gas lawyers to a degree which is far greater than expected by many in that industry. The potential effect of the rules of land law is far reaching and cannot be ignored. Oil and gas companies should always employ specialist lawyers to deal with land law issues. Furthermore, those lawyers who work for oil and gas companies in relation to other matters such as safety compliance, contracts negotiation or licensing should always have regard to the underlying land law rights and the ability of the oil and gas companies to comply with obligations placed upon them.

---

[81] This is not recognised in all Common law jurisdictions: Sturley, "Easements in Gross" (1980) 96 LQR 556; Sturley, "The Land Obligation: An English Proposal for Reform" (1982) 55 S Calif L Rev 1417.

[82] R R M Paisley, "Personal Real Burdens" (2005) Jurl Rev 377–422.

[83] See, eg, orders and agreements relating to the storage and transport of gas: (Gas Act 1965, ss 4–5, 12 and 13); necessary wayleaves for electricity supply (Electricity Act 1989, Sch 4, para 6(6)(a) and (b); and rights acquired by agreement or court order for telecommunications (Telecommunications Act 1984, Sch 2, paras 2–6).

CHAPTER 18

DISPUTE MANAGEMENT AND RESOLUTION

Margaret Ross

Industry culture

Dispute resolution processes are used imaginatively in the oil and gas industry and close attention is paid to the choice of process appropriate to the dispute. This is influenced by a number of factors: need, preference and, above all, commercial intuition. There is a need for processes that are fast, effective, and cause minimum disruption to working processes and relationships. The preference is for processes which are both private and flexible. They require to be capable of crossing both international boundaries and business cultures. While, traditionally, there has been a limited pool of industry players, they have operated within a global marketplace. These factors combined to create an incentive to avoid making future enemies out of the present dispute, and drew into the range of choices the dispute resolution experiences and preferences of many nationalities and professions. As the industry has matured and expanded over time, slightly more willingness to use adversarial methods has become evident, driven less by regard for long-term relationships and more by desire for court-ordered enforceable remedies and perceived speed of return.

18.1

The dynamism of the industry had drawn parties and their advisers to possible choices in a spectrum of dispute resolution mechanisms more swiftly than had been the case in other industries where cultures can be more adversarial, and ongoing relationships less vital. These choices might be described as "exit points" from the dispute. The industry found routes away from the dispute with an eye to prospective dealings and opportunities.[1] In other

18.2

---

[1] This topic features heavily in specialist repositories of material available on subscription only, namely Oil, Gas & Energy Law (OGEL), accessible at www.

commercial contexts dispute resolution choices have often been less imaginative, and more closely tied to traditional retrospective adjudicative processes of litigation and arbitration. However, there is some evidence of change across the corporate context.[2] The predominance of in-house counsel and specialist external counsel has helped to ensure that in commerce more broadly the processes selected are driven by the client's commercial imperatives rather than norms of civil litigators.[3] However, lawyers in European Member States continue to report much more familiarity with litigation than mediation.[4]

Dispute resolution spectrum of choice

18.3   This chapter will examine the methods of dispute resolution that have been found to be of particular use in the oil and gas industry; the specific benefits and detractions of these; examples of their usage as exit points or levers in a spectrum from informal and unilateral action to litigation; and some qualitative commentary on them influenced by interviews with industry players.[5]

---

gasandoil.com/ogel, and Transnational Dispute Management (TDM), accessible at www. transnational-dispute-management-com.

[2] Queen Mary University London and Price Waterhouse Coopers, *International Arbitration: Corporate attitudes and practices 2006*, available at http://www.pwc.co.uk/eng/publications/International_arbitration.html (accessed 21 March 2011) (hereinafter "QMU & PWC, *Corporate Attributes 2006*") (accessed 21 March 2011), notes that many contracts now disclose sophisticated stepped dispute resolution processes, akin to those found in many oil and gas contracts. www.adr.org – the website of the American Arbitration Association – includes articles and access to specialist energy sector dispute resolution processes; www.mediate.com has material on consensual dispute resolution systems generally, including system design. See also P Roberts, *Gas Sales and Gas Transportation Agreements: Principles and Practice* (2004), Chapter 35, "Dispute Resolution".

[3] Explored in the *Report of the Business Experts and Law Forum (BELF)*, Scottish Government, November 2008, particularly Chapter 3, available at www.scotland.gov. uk/Publications/2008/10/30105800/11 and in *Dispute Resolution in London and the UK 2010*, a report of TheCityUK (a commercial membership organisation), available at www.thecityuk.com. B Clark and C Dawson, "ADR and Scottish Commercial Litigators: A study of Attitudes and Experience", 2007 CJQ, 26(Apr) 228–249 at 247 notes the phenomenon of commercial clients driving lawyers' advice, referring to studies in the USA identifying that corporate lawyers are "tools" or "conduits" of their clients.

[4] ADR Center (funded by EU and in association with European Association of Craft, Small and Medium-Sized Enterprises and European Company Lawyers Association), *The Cost of Non ADR – Surveying and Showing the Actual Costs of Intra-Community Commercial Litigation*, June 2010, available at www.adrcenter.com/jamsinternational/civil-justice/Survey_Data_Report.pdf (accessed 21 March 2011); part of the Lawyers and ADR EU project.

[5] The author has carried out questionnaire surveys and structured interviews with lawyers and managers in a range of oil industry players operating in the North Sea (although most also have experience of business in other parts of the world). The broad outcomes of these are reflected in this chapter.

The spectrum of dispute resolution processes referred to above is   **18.4**
divided for the purposes of this chapter into six sections, although
there is overlap between them.[6]

1. unilateral action;
2. collaboration and negotiation;
3. assisted collaborative non-binding processes;
4. expert determination;
5. arbitration and litigation;
6. implementation and enforcement processes.

The parties may use a combination of these, consecutively or
contemporaneously.

In general it is advisable to anticipate disputes in advance and   **18.5**
provide for them by way of escalating or stepped dispute resolution
clauses.[7] However, there is merit in coming back to the issue of
choice at times when disputes arise or are ongoing, or even when
they have been played out in a process which has not been able
to deal with all of the underlying aspects in a way which will
make most commercial sense for the future. The immediacy and
commercial cost of dispute in the oil and gas industry mean that
time spent on unsuitable processes is wasted. Time spent between
lawyer and client merely to understand and articulate the dispute in
a court or arbitration for the benefit of a third-party decision-maker
may be expensive and unproductive. There is the risk that parties
from outside the industry or those who are new to it will not understand the commercial imperative to reach an outcome in the dispute,
quite apart from lawyers and judges having to try to understand the
technical aspects of the dispute. If lawyers are unfamiliar with the
industry but accustomed to the normative delays of civil litigation,
they might err towards adjudicative processes which put off the evil
day of settlement, payment or enforcement.

Dispute anticipation and management

This chapter also considers the topic of dispute management through   **18.6**
anticipation and avoidance. Increasingly, processes that have been

---

[6] For a thorough general description of dispute resolution processes and the factors that
influence choice, see H Brown and A Marriott, *ADR Principles and Practice* (2nd edn,
1999).

[7] On stepped dispute resolution provisions, see P O'Neill, "International Arbitral
Jurisdiction: When taking control goes out of control", *Dispute Resolution Journal*, May/
Jul 2003; 58, 2, 68–77 and 85. Such a clause existed in the contract disputed in *Thames
Valley Power Ltd* v *Total Gas & Power Ltd* [2006] Lloyd's Rep 441 but was not activated
because no "real" dispute existed.

used in the resolution of disputes when they arise are recognised
for their potential in managing situations in which disputes may be
predictable, and building consensus in advance of activity so that
opportunities for dispute are minimised. Consensus-building and
risk management processes which engage potentially affected parties
in the "stakeholder" range are now commonplace in the industry.
This can shift the timeline for considering disputes to the develop-
mental end of business activities, particularly when environmental
risks have to be managed.

UNILATERAL ACTION

Complaints to companies, regulators

18.7　The oil and gas industry is heavily regulated, and some disputes
may have as their first port of call the complaints procedures
of a particular company or regulator or industry ombudsmen.
For example, DECC procedures are subject to oversight by the
Parliamentary Commissioner for Administration;[8] activities within
a particular country may be subject to oversight by state commissioners within that country, and activities funded by the International
Finance Corporation of the World Bank will be subject to review by
that body's Compliance Advisor Ombudsman.

18.8　　Rarely will such processes exclude other dispute resolution choices
completely, since the jurisdiction of the regulator or ombudsman will
be limited. However, an application to court for a remedy on that
specific point within the remit of the regulator might be challenged
on jurisdiction or prematurity grounds. Usually the processes will
exist in parallel, and unless both parties agree not to use such process
they may require to do so. Indeed even if the parties are agreed to
proceed in a different way towards resolution, or reach resolution on
particular terms, it may be essential to bow to the regulator's powers,
procedures and standards in what those settlement terms are, or in
how they are reached. So for example, if a regulator has the responsibility to consult third parties before agreeing to the amendment of
a term of licence, it will not be sufficient for the parties to come to
amicable agreement of a dispute over terms without having regard
to the requirements of the regulatory regime and its determining
processes.

---

[8] For further information, see http://www.ombudsman.org.uk (accessed 21 March 2011).

Avoidance

In any problem within the industry that might develop into dispute, **18.9** some parties choose, even without discussion, that the way of dealing with the matter is to ignore it as a dispute. Discussions with industry players suggested that this can happen to a significant degree. It is often the case that a situation which could give rise to a lawful claim or contractual breach is, on economic or business relationship terms, simply ignored. The parties proceed as if it had not occurred, or treat it as if it had occurred due to the unilateral failure of one of them who volunteers to rectify the situation. Repeated occurrence of a similar problem might attract a different reaction (dependent on scale and value), and if a choice of alternative supplier exists the decision might be simply to choose not to deal with that person or company again rather than to identify this as a dispute and attempt to resolve it.

Dominant parties

A dominant party may choose to trigger termination options or break **18.10** the contract in order to walk away from the contractual situation as soon as possible, in the expectation that the other, perhaps less powerful, party will be unable or unwilling to resist this by litigation or other dispute resolution process. The *force majeure* clause has been used by parties keen to break the contract not just because of the unexpected event, but because of other points of dispute.[9]

Missed opportunities?

While it is undoubtedly the case that unilateral avoidance occurs in **18.11** all justiciable situations,[10] it is reported as occurring very frequently in this industry. The reasons given for it are comparative economic strength at the time of the disputable event and desire for future business harmony. There is a tendency to "put things down to experience" and to avoid letting others know that something has gone wrong. No doubt in some situations a party is wise in the wish to keep quiet on the reasons for unilateral action, but, commercial sensitivities apart, it might be productive in others to share the fact that this decision has been taken and the reasoning behind that decision.

---

[9] See, eg, *Thames Valley Power Ltd v Total Gas & Power Ltd* [2006] Lloyd's Rep 441.
[10] Noted to be widespread in studies funded by the Nuffield Foundation: H Genn (with S Beinart), *Paths to Justice* (1999) and H Genn and A Paterson, *Paths to Justice Scotland* (2001).

18.12   Viewed objectively, and for good governance, both parties can learn more from discussing the situation and sharing their reasons for avoidance decisions than from internalising them. Even when discussion does occur, it may not be recorded in a way to influence decisions in future cases or inform the actions of subsequent decision-makers. Sharing the reasoning may be perceived as a sign of weakness or of a bullying tactic, depending upon which side you are on, and some parties feel that they simply have to "get to know" the dispute tactics of the other players over time. New entrants to the sector either fall into the same approach or follow more traditional legal avenues of seeking to enforce rights and responsibilities. In an industry known for its pragmatic and tailored solutions to technical and other issues, engaging in more open discussion about attitudes to disputes might be a valuable exercise, preferably at the time of forming the business relationship rather than waiting for a dispute to arise.

COLLABORATION AND NEGOTIATION

Collaboration to build consensus

18.13 Increasingly, commercial enterprises within a risk management culture are thinking ahead to the potential for dispute and embarking on consensus-building methods to reduce risk as part of the process of planning and implementing business activities. This has been evident in the oil and gas industry. Anticipating the environmental impact of activities, whether exploration, production or decommissioning, has led to predictive discussions with neighbouring proprietors, regulatory agencies and environmental campaigners. The example of the multi-party negotiation facilitated by the Environment Council around the proposed decommissioning of the Brent Spar is a high-profile example of this process operating to effect an imaginative solution to address environmental concerns in advance.[11] It is not possible to prevent all disputes in this way, and adversarial methods might be necessary to deal with actual or anticipated dispute[12] but there is evidence that predictive consensus building can achieve reduced costs and improved outcomes for both the industry and its neighbours. Neighbours (whether individuals, groups or agencies) who might be affected by commercial activity are now often treated

---

[11] Given as an example in L Boulle and M Nesic, *Mediation: Principles, Process and Practice* (1st edn, reprint 2005) at p 334. For a fuller discussion of the Brent Spar case, see Chapter 10 above.

[12] For example, to interdict anticipated delictual wrong by environmental campaigners as in *Allseas UK Ltd v Greenpeace* 2001 SC 844.

as "stakeholders" and that recognition and respect in itself helps to provide a foundation for consensual management of disputes once the commercial activities are ongoing.

Evidence from the USA suggests that potentially disruptive or polluting activities can be approached very positively by this *advance* collaboration with stakeholders, and indeed with insurers who offer policies to cover the stakeholders collectively for clean-up costs or mitigation of environmental impact.[13] Clearly this is preferable to "after the event" damage management, as in the aftermath of the Deepwater Horizon explosion in the Gulf of Mexico. In the USA and the UK, the liberalisation of energy supply markets prompted collaborative activity between industry players and regulators to standardise information for consumers, contractual terms and dispute resolution processes, thus pre-empting and managing disputes to avoid escalation to adversarial processes.[14] Even prior to the paradigm of Deepwater Horizon and BP, the impact of adverse events such as high-profile disputes played out in public had begun to be measured in terms of "reputation equity", with direct impact on share prices being measured.[15] This adds pressure upon companies to create effective processes and to allocate appropriate people to problem management and communication in order to minimise the economic impact of bad publicity from adverse events and the processing of the claims arising.   **18.14**

These dispute management examples focus on adverse dispute impact *for the company* arising from disputes, but a survey conducted in 2003 among Chief Executive Officers across a range of large commercial bodies revealed significant evidence (67 per cent of respondents) to the effect that commercial disputes generate *personal* stresses for CEOs including sleeplessness and relationship problems.[16] No doubt such impact is often felt but under-reported in the business context. Disputes clearly can have a corrosive impact upon work performance and personal reputation. The evidence points clearly to the wisdom of time and money spent on creative and effective dispute management and avoidance measures.   **18.15**

---

[13] For further explanation and discussion of Insured Fixed Price Clean-ups, see M Hill, "A tale of two sites: How insured fixed-price cleanups expedite protections, reduce costs, and help EPA, the SEC and the public" American Bar Association Science and Technology Committee Newsletter, Vol 3, No 2, 17.

[14] Information is available from Ofgem (www.ofgem.gov.uk) and the Centre for Advanced Energy Markets (www.caem.org).

[15] Measurement of impacts of reputation changing events upon share value has been carried out for various large insurers and commercial entities by Oxford Metrica (www.oxfordmetrica.com). The impact of the Deepwater Horizon explosion for BP's commercial value has been much publicised in 2010.

[16] BDO Stoy Hayward Commercial Disputes Survey 2003.

Collaborative deal-building

18.16 Deal-building has traditionally been handled by negotiation between parties' employees or managers, assisted by lawyers as appropriate. There is evidence that mediation is being used in some deals to broker the most productive deal for both sides.[17] This might be useful in situations where preliminary consideration of the issues suggests that there might be significant stumbling blocks in direct negotiation either because of the nature of the commercial activity, or the personalities of the participants in it. Mediation can assist in identifying underlying issues that a party may not wish to divulge in direct negotiation, but which can be divulged to a mediator so that they be addressed productively through the mediator within the negotiation process. Collaborative negotiation techniques have also been used to produce dedicated approaches to disputes anticipated from changing energy markets.[18] They have also been pivotal in the creation of standard form contracts for the industry in the UK[19] and in alliancing and partnering arrangements.[20]

Negotiation practices

18.17 Industry players report that negotiation is the principal means of resolving disputes. Because much of the discussion about ADR worldwide has compared it to litigation or other adjudicated processes, the fact that negotiation is the most widely used process is often overlooked. Negotiation at operational or manager level is likely to be used first, and to be most productive, in that those closest to the operation or supply which is the subject of the contract are the most knowledgeable as to the issues that give rise to dispute and the means of resolving those issues. Many contracts in the oil and gas industry provide for dispute negotiation by managers, with provision for escalation to negotiation by the senior representatives of the

---

[17] L Boulle and M Nesic in *Mediation: Principles, Process and Practice* (1st edn reprint 2005) give examples at p 298, and cite M Hager and R Pritchard, "Hither the Deal Mediators" (1999) 10(10) *ICCLR* 291 and R Buckley "The applicability of mediation skills to the creation of contracts" (1992) *Australian Dispute Resolution Journal* 227.

[18] For example the National Association of Regulatory Utility Commissioners in the USA (NARUC) funded by the US Department of Energy, worked with the Center for the Advancement of Energy Markets (CAEM) to develop and review uniform business terms to deal with the changing energy markets.

[19] LOGIC (Leading Oil and Gas Industry Competitiveness) standard form contracts (previously CRINE) are accessible at www.logic-oil.com.

[20] A Ledger, "An Agenda for Collaborative Working Arrangements: The Role of Partnering and Alliancing in the UK", *Dispute Resolution Journal*, May/Jul 2003; 58, 2, pp 38–45; K Kaasen, "Offshore Project Alliancing: The Aim, the Constraints and the Contracts", Scandinavian Institute of Maritime Law, *Yearbook 1997*, s 141.

company.[21] If the matter is referred to lawyers it is usually for advice at first, so that managers can continue to negotiate on commercial or technical levels. However, lawyers do become involved in negotiating certain disputes to resolution or to a point at which other dispute resolution processes can be chosen. In most instances, lawyers alone will not have the technical industry expertise to conduct negotiations without the parties or appropriate managers present, unless the matter at issue falls within a neat point of law, and negotiating parameters can be set in advance. Hence it can be said that the model of negotiation within the industry is client centred.

The professionalisation of a client-centred approach to dispute resolution is often associated with the influence of blue chip companies in the USA in the 1980s. Their insistence on practical solutions rather than the expense and delay of litigation drove their lawyers (both in-house and external) to engage in a range of consensual dispute resolution processes. In the same decade the Harvard Negotiation Project analysed and articulated negotiation as a skill, and advocated the principled or problem-solving approach. This focuses on the benefits for negotiation in identifying underlying interests of the parties, exploring options for mutual gain, seeking objective criteria against which to measure what is being offered, and thinking in advance of the negotiation about what is the best alternative to a negotiated agreement or "BATNA": for example, is there another supplier, a prior offer, or a remedy in litigation which would be preferable to a final offer in the negotiation?[22] **18.18**

Negotiation as a specialism

Training and skills

The role of negotiation is recognised widely, yet training in negotiation techniques has been patchy in its usage in legal practice. It is often assumed that lawyers will be good negotiators without any attention to the skills or training underlying that assumption. Negotiation training is more evident in management education and in-house skills development. In the international context the importance of negotiation of global transactions has been recog- **18.19**

---

[21] See, for instance, LOGIC, *General Conditions of Contract, Construction* (2nd edn, 2003), cl 37.1. All LOGIC standard contracts are available via http://www.logic-oil.com/contracts2.cfm (accessed 21 March 2011).

[22] The books emerging from the project have become best-sellers, particularly R Fisher and W Ury (2nd edn with B Patton), *Getting to Yes* (2nd edn, 1991), R Fisher and W Ury *Getting Past No* (Bantam, New York, 1993) and W Ury, *The Power of a Positive No* (2007). See also the project website http://www.pon.harvard.edu (accessed 21 March 2011).

nised for some decades. An Association of International Petroleum Negotiators (AIPN)[23] has existed since 1981, and provides research reports, training events and style documents. Industry-specific texts are few,[24] but general texts on negotiation styles and strategies help in developing one's own approach and understanding the approaches of other negotiators.[25]

18.20   Increasingly, management education and legal education includes negotiation, and scope for experimentation with different techniques in the "safe" context of role-play. Individuals engaged in dispute resolution in the industry also comment that individuals' approaches to negotiation and dispute resolution are affected by their own experience of using or being drawn into different styles and methods in the workplace, and that cultural or national factors do appear to make a difference.[26] So, fear of corruption in the judicial system in some countries makes players there very interested in negotiation or mediation.[27] In others, such as Holland, Denmark and the Nordic countries, a "pragmatic approach" to dispute resolution is notable in systems and in daily life.[28] In the USA, where ADR processes have been operating for some decades, negotiation takes place with the knowledge that many choices exist for consensual resolution, but there may still be a tendency to file a suit just to secure jurisdiction and discovery.

Lawyers and negotiation

18.21   Lawyers will be most closely connected to the legal parameters around the dispute and therefore most likely to negotiate in that shadow. Managers and technical specialists report that lawyers can over-legalise the dispute and its resolution, rather than have a sense

---

[23] www.aipn.org (accessed 21 March 2011).

[24] For example L Mosburg, *Advanced Concepts of Oil and Gas Contract Negotiation and Deal Structure* (1984); S Sayer, "Negotiating and Structuring International Joint Venture Agreements": http://www.dundee.ac.uk/cepmlp/journal/html/vol5/article5-1.html.

[25] R Fisher and W Ury, (2nd edn with B Patton), *Getting to Yes* (2nd edn, 1991; 1st edn, 1981), R Fisher and W Ury, *Getting Past No* (1993) and W Ury, *The Power of a Positive No* (2007). See also the project website www.pon.harvard.edu/hnp. Other sources include S Covey, *The 7 Habits of Highly Effective People* (revd edn, 1999), S Le Poole, *Never take No for an Answer* (2nd edn, 1991), B Scott, *The Skills of Negotiating* (1981) and L Sweeney, "Addressing some negotiating difficulties", 1996 (41) JLSS 349.

[26] For an interesting comment on cultural issues, see B Marsh, "The Development of Mediation in Central and Eastern Europe" in C Newmark and A Monaghan (eds), *Butterworths Mediators on Mediation* (2005).

[27] *Ibid*, para 21.21. The fear is expressed by those in business within the country rather than those outside it.

[28] G De Palo and S Carmeli, "Mediation in Continental Europe: A meandering path toward efficient regulation" at paras 19.29–19.36 in C Newmark and A Monaghan (eds), *Butterworths Mediators on Mediation* (2005).

of what is needed to make the solution work in practice. Essentially, lawyers are advisers and partners rather than leaders in the negotiation process in the industry. They can advise on the strength of the party's case in the substantive law of contract, the options available in procedural law before the courts and in arbitration (including matters of private or public international if the contract involves parties in different countries or state parties); the terms of the contract in so far as they define the parties' choice in dispute resolution processes; and the impact of other legal factors such as public law effects of licensing, environmental regulation, or international convention. Success of negotiation at all stages of the dispute is affected by the awareness of those engaged in the negotiation of the next stages open to the parties if negotiation fails, and their understanding of the approaches to settlement of those senior in the dispute management process. In a study of choices in international arbitration published in 2010, lawyer interviewees noted the difficulties in getting involved in dispute process negotiation at an early enough stage and to sufficient degree, noting that they were called in late, after the commercial terms had been agreed.[29]

Some players report differences in culture between companies, **18.22** where those with a UK origin use the lawyers as advisers only, but negotiation is conducted by the "businessmen" in the company, while in companies with US origins lawyers are expected to be part of a business team, taking part in business decisions as partners rather than specialist advisers. While it may be a generalisation to link these differences to the country of origin of a company, the scope for differences in lawyer role is apparent nevertheless.[30]

Negotiating in teams
Given the technical nature of disputes that may arise in the oil **18.23** and gas industries, some negotiations require to be carried out by a team of people who can, collectively, bring the necessary expertise (for example technical, legal, financial) to the dispute and its resolution. If such negotiations are to be effective, it is key to the process to nominate a leader for the process at the outset, who has the power to agree upon an outcome if the members of the team are not agreed. This is equally (if not more) important when that negotiating team enters into a process where the negotiation

---

[29] Queen Mary, University of London with White & Case, *2010 International Arbitration Survey: Choices in International Arbitration*, available at www.arbitrationonline. org/research/2010 (hereinafter "QMU and White & Case, *International Arbitration Surveryor*") (accessed 21 March 2011), p 11.
[30] These roles are explored in the context of mediation in B Clark, "Mediation and Scottish Lawyers: Past, Present and Future" (2009) 13 *Edin LR* 252–277.

is assisted by a third party (mediator or conciliator). It is no doubt the case that those involved in a negotiating team will have to carry out some negotiation between them, but someone has to have the ultimate power to settle. If no-one in the team has the power to settle the matter, then the negotiation is in difficulty from the start, since at very best the team can agree to take the matter back to the decision-maker for the final say. This is undermining of the negotiating team, and risks the other side (particularly if it has a settlement mandate) losing patience. The negotiating team should have parameters and authority for settlement agreed in advance, or access on the day to those who can authorise the settlement terms.

Timing of negotiation of dispute resolution options

18.24   As is clear from other chapters,[31] much effort goes into negotiating contracts that are in terms which are particular to the industry context and are reflective of parties' needs and business imperatives. Within that process of negotiation falls the negotiation of dispute resolution clauses, and most contracts will provide in some form for processes to be used in the event of dispute. Those clauses may be silent on the matter of negotiation, making the assumption that negotiation will always be attempted and that resort to the clause will be necessary only if negotiation fails. However, clauses requiring a tier of negotiation by senior managers are common in the industry, providing for this as a pre-requisite to other consensual ADR processes or to litigation. In the LOGIC standard form contract for services, three levels of negotiation are provided for and parties are expected to attempt these before proceeding to other dispute resolution process.[32] In the LOGIC short form of purchase and sale agreement the condensed form is that "the parties shall meet as soon a possible in good faith with each other to try to resolve the matter in an amicable way".[33]

18.25   At the time of contract formation the parties are intent upon working together and thinking positively, and dispute resolution processes can be tailored to fit with other approaches in the contract, or series of linked contracts. On the other hand, parties at that stage are often very anxious to have the contract completed; have their minds on the operational and production clauses rather than those

---

[31] See, in particular, Chapters 12, 13 and 14 above.
[32] For example, LOGIC General Conditions of Contract for Services On and Off Shore (October 2003), Chapter 30; General Conditions of Contract for Design, Chapter 33. All LOGIC standard contracts available via http://www.logic-oil.com/contracts2.cfm.
[33] LOGIC Purchase Order Terms and Conditions Short Form (December 2005), para D8.

directed to potential problems; have future successes in mind rather than failures; and are unable or unwilling to imagine what issues, conflicts or disputes may arise. They may call the lawyers in only to tie up small print, and too late to give much attention to dispute resolution processes.[34] They are also unable to predict with certainty market factors which may make aspects of the current contract more or less attractive in the future, and which may prompt one or other party to break some aspect of the contract in the future. A tendency to use preferred styles of contract may lead to other parties feeling that they have no power to suggest change, or that the compromise that arises from trading off clauses leads to unsatisfactory situations for both parties.

ASSISTED COLLABORATIVE NON-BINDING PROCESSES

Introduction

Escalating dispute resolution processes may provide for a step beyond negotiation but before the stage at which it is passed to a third-party adjudicator (such as an arbitrator, or expert or court) for determination and imposition of an outcome. This stage in the spectrum is consensual, in that the parties have agreed to attempt it and are not bound to reach an outcome. If they do, it is enforceable only as a contractual obligation, not as if a court order. Settlement is dependent on their agreement but, unlike consensus-building in the form of negotiation, a third party is engaged to facilitate, and, possibly, to provide advisory evaluation. These processes are often collectively called Alternative Dispute Resolution or ADR although some feel that the "alternative" description is not particularly helpful.[35] The third party is most commonly a mediator, or a conciliator, although the terms are often used indiscriminately and interchangeably,[36] but could alternatively be a neutral evaluator.[37]

18.26

---

[34] QMU and White & Case, *International Arbitration Survey*, p 11.

[35] CEDR, the main provider of dispute resolution training and services in England and Wales, refers now to EDR (effective dispute resolution) and Core Solutions, who operate a similar service in Scotland refer to management of differences. However, in the LOGIC short form of purchase and sale agreement the dispute resolution clause (D8) provides, following reference to meeting to resolve the matter: "If no agreement is reached the parties may attempt to settle the dispute by a form of Alternative Dispute Resolution to be agreed between the parties."

[36] Conciliation is more commonly associated with relationship mediation, including an element of evaluation and conciliator steerage towards a particular settlement.

[37] For a discussion on neutral evaluation, see para 18.46.

Consensual ADR and mediation

18.27 Contracts in the oil and gas industry may provide for dispute resolution mechanisms to be attempted and this can include mediation, or when disputes arise parties may consider entering into ADR governed by a standalone agreement. Consensual dispute resolution is recognised as a process which may be selected in preference to adjudicative processes, so in England the Arbitration Act 1996 allows for a dispute resolution clause in a contract to be observed before any party can insist on arbitration under the contract.[38] Mediation may be the subject of bespoke contractual agreement by the parties (either when entering into the original contract or by separate contract when the dispute arises) or parties can take advantage of model clauses that are widely available via mediation providers when that provider is selected.[39]

Mediation process

18.28 The term "mediation" refers to placing a person in the middle of the dispute. The key features of mediation are that the person is neutral and impartial and has no power to impose any outcome on the parties. By a process of listening and questioning in joint and private meetings with parties, the mediator assists them to explore the nature of the dispute, its causes and effects and then to look to the future potential solutions which address underlying interests and needs. The mediator looks for mutual ground between the parties which is often entirely outside the parties' expectations, and helps them to build consensus on that.[40] The process has a recognised capability to expand options for settlement. It certainly extends beyond those traditional remedies available within litigation and arbitration, but also beyond the scope of direct negotiation, whether lawyer aided or not. This is because confidential information can be disclosed by parties to the mediator and managed by the mediator for more productive and enduring settlement terms.[41] Mediation is of particular value in disputes with multiple parties or involving linked contracts,[42] both of which are common in the oil and gas industry.

---

[38] Arbitration Act 1996, s 12.

[39] See, eg, www.cedr.com; www.uncitral.org; www.core-solutions.com; and www.adrgroup.co.uk (all accessed 21 March 2011).

[40] For exploration of the process, see H Brown and A Marriott, *ADR Principles and Practice*, (2nd edn, 1999); M Noone, *Mediation* (1996); L Boulle and M Nesic, *Mediation: Principles, Process and Practice* (1st edn reprint 2005); S Roberts and M Palmer, *ADR and the Primary Forms of Decision Making* (2nd edn, 2005).

[41] For a detailed consideration of mediation processes and practices, see L Boulle and M Nesic, *Mediation: Principles, Process and Practice* (1st edn reprint, 2005).

[42] See D Richbell, "Mediating Multi-party Disputes" in C Newmark and A Monaghan

Role and skills of the mediator

Given the neutrality and non-adjudicative nature of the media- **18.29** tor's role, there is in theory no reason for the mediator to have expert knowledge or skill in anything other than the mediation process. Indeed, since one of the mediator's functions is to explore motives and possibilities, it is important that nothing should be left to assumption by the mediator. At the very least, mediators with dedicated and rigorous training in the process and reasonable volume of experience as sole or joint mediator would be sought. Industry disputes would usually involve legal representation in preparation for and participation in the mediation. Increasingly, mediator involvement in the preparation *before* mediation is found to make the mediation process most effective, and lawyers who are trained or knowledgeable in or about mediation can play a very productive role in that preparation.[43]

Nonetheless, in oil and gas disputes it is recognised that benefit **18.30** may arise from the mediator having specialist knowledge of the industry or of a technical process used within it. Awareness of its culture and familiarity with its terminology are also valued. Industry players note that time can be wasted in the mediation context itself in dealing with questions from the mediator that are essentially for the education of the mediator, when those questions would not arise if the mediator had industry knowledge or relevant technical expertise. Settlement expectations may be skewed if a mediator explores a general possibility which, in industry terms, is in fact a blind alley. Engineers, architects, accountants and quantity surveyors are, with lawyers, among the ranks of those trained mediators available commercially to provide mediation services. Biographical data is available from commercial agencies and mediator websites to assist in choice, although personal recommendation is the most influential factor.

Lawyers and mediation

Views are mixed on whether lawyers make appropriate mediators, **18.31** even when trained in mediation,[44] but the fact is that many lawyers

---

(eds), *Butterworths Mediators on Mediation* (2005), pp 229–238.

[43] The Law Society of Scotland now recognises lawyers who advise in mediation, as well as mediation practitioners, for specialist accreditation in mediation: "Mediation lawyers can apply" (2010) 55(11) *JLSS* 34.

[44] B Clark and C Dawson, "ADR and Scottish Commercial Litigators: A study of Attitudes and Experience", 2007 *CJQ* 26(Apr) 228–249 at 240 note the concerns raised by writers that lawyers as trained advisers and partisan litigators are not suited to the consensual nature of mediation, but this survey of commercial lawyers came out in broad support of lawyers as mediators, although that support was slightly lower among those with experience of representing clients in mediation.

do act as mediators. It is accepted that lawyers have a very important part to play in advising clients in commercial mediation.[45] There are specialist texts and training courses on this topic.[46] It is important for the lawyer to have awareness of the mediation process so that appropriate advice and support can be given to clients in choosing and dealing with the process. Many report lack of familiarity with processes outside litigation, simply due to comparative volumes of experience.[47] They may feel that they cannot advise the client as to its risks and benefits. Some clients report that they have led the lawyer to mediation, because of personal experience of it or having it recommended by others in the industry. Evidence suggests that companies look for specialist legal advice before embarking on high-value arbitration, and it is to be expected that the same may be needed for mediation.

Methods of mediation

18.32 Mediation method has been characterised into three main types: facilitative, evaluative and transformative. Agreement to use a particular method lies with the parties. The facilitative method involves the mediator shunning any comment on the strength or weakness of any party's side of the dispute, although by reality testing, role-reversal or questioning about objective criteria the mediator can guide parties into a rigorous evaluation of their own side. Most mediators are trained in that method, and adopt it, particularly in the earlier exploratory phases of the mediation. However, parties may prefer a mediator to express a view about the case. Some lawyers hope that the mediator will come to a view that accords with the lawyer's evaluation and thereby assist in persuading the client of weaknesses that were not accepted on the lawyer's word alone. Mediators and parties also note that as time passes in the mediation, the scoping of the dispute has been done, and the end of the day or allotted time approaches, some evaluation by the mediator may at that stage be permitted, even when the process chosen originally was facilitative. Of course mediators may well form a personal view on aspects of the case, but training includes techniques to suppress any uninvited influence or assumption arising from the mediator's own view.

---

[45] Lawyers' relationship with mediation is explored from a number of angles in B Clark, "Mediation and Scottish Lawyers: Past, Present and Future" (2009) 13 *Edin LR* 252.

[46] M Stone, *Representing Clients in Mediation* (1998).

[47] ADR Center (funded by EU and in association with European Association of Craft, Small and Medium-Sized Enterprises and European Company Lawyers Association, *The Cost of Non ADR – Surveying and Showing the Actual Costs of Intra-Community Commercial Litigation*, June 2010, available at www.adrcenter.com/civiljustice/cms; part of the Lawyers and ADR EU project.

An alternative is the purposive selection of an evaluative method, **18.33** and this is more common within specialist industries than outside them. If the mediator has industry knowledge, there is value in applying that knowledge to weigh the strengths and weaknesses of a party's side and share that in private with each party (but not with the other party unless confidentiality is waived). Transformative mediation method concentrates on getting below the current problem to identify and work on conflicting issues of personality and problem-solving so that not only can the disputants be empowered to work on resolving the present problem themselves, but they will be equipped to approach disputes more effectively in the future. The transformative method[48] is the least embedded in commercial contexts, but increasingly mediators report that facilitative or evaluation mediation draws upon transformative techniques.

Institutional direction towards ADR

Civil procedures in the UK

Some courts here in the UK may by procedural rules be encouraged **18.34** to manage or expedite the progress of the case[49] or expect the parties to consider ADR and explain its non-use. In England, following the Woolf reforms on Access to Justice,[50] the Civil Procedure Rules 1998 have required the court to encourage the parties to use a form of ADR if the court considers that appropriate, and to facilitate the use of such procedure.[51] Indeed the Rules' latest revision stresses that litigation should be the last resort. A Practice Direction on Pre-action Conduct expects parties to attempt ADR,[52] and to exchange information and attempt settlement before the case is even filed. A party can seek a stay of proceedings for ADR to take place.[53] The CPR allow the court to allocate costs taking into account efforts made to attempt to resolve the dispute,[54] and taking account of compliance

---

[48] As articulated by R Baruch Bush and J Folger in *The Promise of Mediation: Responding to Conflict through Empowerment and Recognition* (revd edn, 2005; 1st edn, 1994).

[49] As in options hearing procedure in the sheriff courts in Scotland under the Ordinary Cause Rules 1993, as amended, r 9.13.

[50] Lord Woolf, Interim Report to the Lord Chancellor on the Civil Justice System in England and Wales, June 1995; Final Report: *Access to Justice*, July 1996. See also N Andrews, *English Civil Procedure*, (2003), paras 23.12–23.28.

[51] Civil Procedure Rules 1998 (CPR), r 1.4.(2)(e) and Pt 36.

[52] CPR Practice Direction on Pre-Action Conduct, available at http://www.justice.gov.uk/ civil/procrules_fin/contents/practice_directions/pd_pre-action_conduct.htm (accessed 21 March 2011).

[53] CPR, r 26.4(1).

[54] *Ibid*, r 44.5(a).

or non-compliance with the pre-action protocol.[55] Courts have taken account of *inter alia* whether the refusing party had a reasonable belief that it would win on the merits at trial, previous settlement attempts, risk of delaying trial by attempting ADR and whether mediation had a reasonable prospect of success.[56] If the court has recommended ADR then cost sanctions will more readily be applied to a party who refuses. If ADR has been suggested by one party and refused by another, then in the event of the refuser being successful, the onus would be on the losing party to make the case that it was unreasonable for the winner to have refused; however, it is competent for that to be argued.[57] This approach to ADR and the allocation of costs was supported by Lord Justice Jackson in his report on the review of costs of civil litigation in England and Wales. However, he recommends that judges become more aware of the ADR options that have been open to parties.[58]

18.35 In Scotland, there is no equivalent pre-action protocol in civil cases generally.[59] In the review of civil courts led by Lord Gill, reporting in September 2009,[60] more use of pre-action protocols and case management was proposed among a suite of reforms. Scottish Government responses to the report in advance of legislative change are supportive of those aspects of the report and indicate a stronger will to link ADR to the court process than had been indicated in the Gill Report itself.[61] Parties who select the Commercial Cause procedure may find the judge or sheriff asking whether ADR has been attempted, continuing the case for it to be attempted or using techniques which may sound similar to some of the processes here discussed as alternatives.[62]

---

[55] Practice Direction on Pre-Action Conduct, Pt 8.

[56] *Halsey v Milton Keynes General NHS Trust* [2004] 1 WLR 3002; *R (ex parte Cowl)* v *Plymouth City Council* [2002] 1 WLR 903; *Dunnett v Railtrack plc* [2002] 1 WLR 2434; *Hurst v Leeming* [2003] 1 Lloyd's Rep 279. On the difficulties of timing, see *Nigel Witham Ltd v Smith (No 2)* [2008] EWHC 12 (TCC) per Coulson J. For the impact of timing more generally, see L Blomgren Bingham *et al*, "Dispute Resolution and the Vanishing Trial: Comparing Federal Government Litigation and ADR Outcomes" (2008–2009) 24 *Ohio St J on Disp Resol* 225.

[57] *Halsey v Milton Keynes General NHS Trust* [2004] 1 WLR 3002.

[58] Lord Justice Jackson, *Review of Civil Litigation Costs: Final Report*, Chapter 36, Ministry of Justice, December 2009, available via www.judiciary.gov.uk.

[59] A voluntary protocol was introduced for personal injury cases only in 2006.

[60] Lord Gill, *Report of the Scottish Civil Courts Review* (Scottish Government, Edinburgh), September 2009, available at www.scotcourts.gov.uk/civilcourtsreview.

[61] *Scottish Government Response to the Report and Recommendations of the Scottish Civil Courts Review* (Scottish Government, Edinburgh, November 2010), available at www.scotland.gov.uk/Publications/2010/11/09114610/0.

[62] Sheriff Court Ordinary Cause Rules, Chapter 40; Rules of the Court of Session, Chapter 47.

Other jurisdictions
In the settlement conference used at a fairly early stage in civil   18.36
litigation in the Netherlands, the judge will give a strong steer on the
merits of the claim, and court-ordered mediation has now been built
into the court process across the Netherlands ordered prior to or at
the settlement conference stage, particularly if it appears that the
litigation process will not in itself be able to determine all aspects of
the dispute between the parties.[63] Many US states and federal courts
(including appeal courts) have court-annexed or court-ordered ADR
programmes that have, on evaluation, proved to be very effective.[64]
If jurisdictional choices exist, selection of the court should take into
account whether that court will interpose a particular process of
dispute resolution.

In many countries, for example in Norway and parts of the   18.37
USA, statutes in certain situations require mediation before parties
are permitted to resort to adjudication in the domestic courts.[65] A
European Union Directive promotes the use of ADR in civil and
commercial disputes and provides in particular for confidentiality,
and for time limitation rules for litigation in Member States to be
stayed to allow for the use of ADR.[66] The EU has, in its Civil Justice
programme, funded a number of research activities which have
produced information on use of information in Member States, and
the cost of not using ADR in cross-state disputes.[67]

Processes insisted upon in particular types of dispute
Choice may be influenced by factors specific to the nature of the   18.38
dispute within the oil and gas context. Hence, employment disputes
within the industry governed by employment law in England or
Scotland are expected to be the subject of formalised complaints and
dispute resolution processes before the matter goes to an employment

---

[63] See M Pel, *Referral to Mediation* (2008).
[64] See L Blomgren Bingham *et al*, "Dispute Resolution and the Vanishing Trial: Comparing Federal Government Litigation and ADR Outcomes" (2008–2009) 24 *Ohio St J on Disp Resol* 225.
[65] For the situation in different parts of the world, see N Alexander (ed), *Global Trends in Mediation* (2nd edn, 2006); C Newmark and A Monaghan (eds), *Butterworths Mediators on Mediation* (2005), and Pryles (ed), *Dispute Resolution in Asia* (2nd edn, 2002).
[66] Directive 2008/52/EC of the European Parliament and of the Council of 21 May 2008 on certain aspects of mediation in civil and commercial matters. See also European Communities, Green Paper on alternative dispute resolution in civil and commercial law, COM(2002) 196 Brussels, 2002; Council of Europe, Alternatives to Litigation between Administrative Authorities and Private Parties, Rec (2001) 9, (2002).
[67] The research was led by the ADR Center; see further n 4 above.

tribunal.[68] Mediation is encouraged, and judicial mediation may be undertaken, with the parties' consent, after the case enters the tribunal system.[69] In other countries the law regulating a type of business also may dictate dispute resolution process. So in many European countries mediation is required for employment disputes, but also, for example, in Italy and Sweden for telecommunications disputes, and in Australia and the UK for certain tax disputes.[70]

Disputes with states or state organisations

18.39   Within the oil and gas industries the potential for state parties to contracts and hence to disputes brings an interface with public international law in the form of international treaties concerning trade with state parties. The World Trade Organization (WTO) dispute settlement processes[71] are for disputes in which one state party feels that the other is "violating an agreement or a commitment that it is has made in the WTO".[72] The Energy Charter Treaty which provides "a legal framework for international energy cooperation" has as signatories some countries which are not yet members of the WTO but which aim to collaborate effectively in the worldwide energy industry. That treaty provides for consensual dispute resolution at source, by reference to national courts or tribunals, in accordance with contractually chosen dispute resolution processes, or by reference to international arbitration or conciliation.[73] The International Centre for Settlement of Investment Disputes (ICSID), a centre of the World Bank,[74] offers conciliation and arbitration

---

[68] Employment Act 2008, Pt 1. This followed the recommendations of M Gibbons, *A review of employment dispute resolution in Great Britain* (2007), available for download from http://www.dti.gov.uk/files/file38516.pdf (the "Gibbons Report").

[69] Employment Tribunals Act 1996, s 7(3AA), inserted by the Employment Act 2008, s 4.

[70] A number of useful texts have collated information about the use of, and state approaches to, mediation in different countries. See, eg, N Alexander (ed), *Global Trends in Mediation* (2nd edn, 2006); C Newmark and A Monaghan (eds), *Butterworths Mediators on Mediation* (2005); Pryles (ed), *Dispute Resolution in Asia* (2nd edn, 2002); G De Palo and M Trevor (eds), *Arbitration and Mediation in the Southern Mediterranean Countries* (2007), www.adrcenter.com/international/cms for a repository of information on use of mediation and lawyers in mediation in EU Member States.

[71] WTO General Agreement on Trade in Services (GATS), Art XXIII, available at www.wto.org/english/docs_e/legal_e/26_gats.pdf.

[72] The WTO website at http://www.wto.org/english/tratop_e/dispu_e/dispu_e/htm/ gives more details on the Dispute Settlement Understanding and contains details of disputes referred. Most of the disputes referred relate to commodities other than oil and gas, although some relate to anti-dumping and to gasoline specification by the USA. See also Valenstein and Hembrey, "The WTO Gasoline Dispute: A Case Study in WTO Dispute Resolution", 1996 14(8) *OGLTR* 332.

[73] Energy Charter Treaty, Pt V, Art 26, available at www.encharter.org.

[74] Established under the Convention on the Settlement of Investment Disputes between States and Nationals of Other States in 1966. See www.worldbank.org/icsid.

processes for disputes involving states and nationals of other states,[75] and is accessible for disputes referred under the dispute resolution provisions of the Energy Charter Treaty. An investor may choose to refer to the ICSID arbitration process regardless of what may have been agreed contractually.[76] However, parties are wise to have provided for non-ICSID arbitration as an alternative if the dispute is held not to fall within the jurisdiction of the ICSID process.[77] A detailed examination of these is beyond the scope of this text, but many specialist texts are available.[78]

Concerns about ADR

Power imbalances

Power imbalances may exist between the parties. These can influence   18.40
the management of the dispute in many ways, including the selection and implementation of choices of dispute resolution process. The small company designing and manufacturing a particular component or engineering process may seem to be the weaker player in a dispute with an international operating company, and on many levels, such as access to specialist advice, financial security, and industry domination, that may be so. On the other hand, in operational terms, that company's knowhow may be essential to the productivity and viability of a high-value project and in the dispute "power" is not placed quite as clearly as it might appear. Unlike the blunter instrument of litigation, mediation of the dispute has the scope to elicit the finer details of power balance (particularly in private meetings) and those can be acknowledged and used to move the dispute towards a commercially viable resolution.[79] Mediation training focuses on fair and impartial handling of power imbalances

---

[75] ICSID publishes numbers and details of cases registered for dispute resolution, most of which are for arbitration, and a number of oil and gas disputes have been registered. Most cases appear to take a number of years from registration to conclusion.

[76] G Turner, "Investment protection through arbitration: the dispute resolution provisions of the Energy Charter Treaty", 1998 1 (5) *Int Arbitration Law Review* 166.

[77] J Bowman and A T Martin, "Negotiating and Drafting Dispute Resolution Provisions for International Petroleum Contracts" (2007) 5(4) *OGEL Intelligence*.

[78] Eg A Stone Sweet, "Investor–State Arbitration: Proportionality's New Frontier" (2010) 4(1) *Law and Ethics of Human Rights* 47; P Pinsolle, "The Dispute Resolution Provisions of the Energy Charter Treaty" (2007) 10(3) *Int Arbitration Law Review* 82; N Palmeter, *Dispute Resolution in the World Trade Organisation: Practice and Procedure* (2nd edn, 2004); C Carmody, *Remedies and the WTO Agreement* (2005); M Sornarajah, *The Settlement of Foreign Investment Disputes* (2000).

[79] On this point, see G Chornenki, "Mediating Commercial Disputes: Exchanging 'Power Over' for 'Power With' in J MacFarlane (ed), *Rethinking Disputes: The Mediation Alternative* (1997).

and, in reality, power within the mediation may be placed differently from what may appear in advance.

18.41   In the industry there is perceived power imbalance at the point of selection of dispute resolution in the contracting process. One party may have a policy not to mediate or a standard form dispute resolution clause which the smaller player must take or leave, and within which processes are determined by the larger player. Dispute resolution and arbitration clauses are sometimes the subject of trade-off in contractual negotiation, and some companies with hindsight regret concessions made.[80] The only counter to this is to be very clear on what the processes are and what will be the implications of, for example, conceding on the seat of arbitration in exchange for an extra tier of ADR.

18.42   The conversation about a process can be had again when a dispute arises and this allows parties, or more probably their advisers, to think again then about where "power" lies. They may step back then, perhaps with more time to focus on dispute resolution than there had been at the time of initial contracting, and consider what are the interests of the respective parties *at the point of dispute* and how might these be managed most effectively in a dispute resolution process.

Non-binding nature

18.43   Mediation produces outcomes by agreement only. It is not possible to impose an outcome. Unlike court or arbitration, any agreed outcome will become contractually binding, but not more enforceable than any other contract. If mediation takes place alongside a litigation or arbitration process its outcomes may be incorporated into a court order which would be enforceable, but the court order will only be able to address matters which would have been within the decision power of the court, and collateral matters (which often form part of a mediated settlement) may have to be omitted from the court order and left to contractual terms.

Disclosure and confidentiality

18.44   Mediation agreements usually provide for confidentiality of communings in the mediation, and that nothing in the mediation will be recoverable in court proceedings. The application of "without prejudice" rules and negotiation privilege has been the subject of review in the courts in England.[81] From these a degree of confidence in the privileged nature of mediation discussions emerges, including

---

[80] QMU & PWC, *Corporate Attitudes 2006*, para 4.3.3.
[81] *Aird v Prime Meridian Ltd* [2006] EWCA Civ 1866 (Court of Appeal); *Reed Executive plc v Reed Business Information Ltd* [2004] 1 WLR 3026.

that mediated negotiations in essence carry the same protection as direct negotiations, and clarification that a clause in a mediation agreement which purports to protect communications and settlement made "in the mediation" can include open offers taken from the mediation without agreement but which then become agreed by direct negotiation between the parties.[82] If outright admissions are made in the context of negotiation or mediation they may not fall within the "without prejudice" privilege.[83] An important decision of the UK Supreme Court clarifies that "objective facts" that come out during the settlement discussions (in this case what was meant by a technical process term) can be admitted in court to assist in interpretation of the settlement agreement.[84] However, when the parties at the case management stage of litigation agreed that the mediator be called as a witness on the question of whether settlement was influenced by economic duress, the court has held that there is no remaining contractual duty of confidentiality or privilege to be invoked by the mediator if the interests of justice require disclosure.[85]

Parties sometimes fear that to discuss the dispute in mediation **18.45** will reveal commercially sensitive information which they could withhold in litigation, and unscrupulous disputants may use the mediation simply to fish for information without any intention of coming to agreement. However, in most procedural regimes in the UK, continental Europe and the USA the parties are expected to disclose relevant material to the court in so far as it is not privileged. Even in Scotland, where secrecy of preparation has survived for longer than in many other countries, it is expected that expert reports will be exchanged and parties can use procedural steps to flush out the evidence that is likely to be led by the other side.

---

[82] *Brown v Rice, Patel and the ADR Group* [2007] WL 763674.

[83] As in *Daks Simpson Group plc v Kuiper* 1994 SLT 689.

[84] *Oceanbulk Shipping and Trading SA v TMT Asia Ltd* (also known as *TMT Asia Ltd v Oceanbulk Shipping and Trading SA*) [2010] UKSC 44.

[85] *Farm Assist Ltd (in liquidation) v Secretary of State for the Environment, Food and Rural Affairs (No 2)* [2009] EWHC 1102 (TCC). Ramsey J at para 44, after reviewing case law and academic commentaries, concludes in general terms: "(1) Confidentiality. The proceedings are confidential both as between the parties and as between the parties and the mediator. As a result even if the parties agree that matters can be referred to outside the mediation, the mediator can enforce the confidentiality provision. The court will generally uphold that confidentiality but where it is necessary in the interests of justice for evidence to be given of confidential matters, the Courts will order or permit that evidence to be given or produced. (2) Without Prejudice Privilege: The proceedings are covered by without prejudice privilege. This is a privilege which exists as between the parties and is not a privilege of the mediator. The parties can waive that privilege. (3) Other Privileges: If another privilege attaches to documents which are produced by a party and shown to a mediator, that party retains that privilege and it is not waived by disclosure to the mediator or by waiver of the without prejudice privilege."

If parties withhold information from the courts or from an ADR neutral the resolution is less likely to be satisfactory to either party. Mediators note that they can tell quite early in the mediation if one party is attempting to use the process in this way, and the mediator will react to that by attempting to overcome this, or by ending the mediation. The benefit of disclosing information to an ADR neutral is that a conversation can be held with that neutral around what, if any, of that information will be disclosed to the other party, and discussion of this even with the neutral alone means that the information can in some way influence the resolution rather than be kept out of the picture. Some industry players, particularly service companies, note that contracts contain very demanding audit provisions, making it difficult to conceal the true reasons behind points of conflict.

Early neutral evaluation

18.46   Parties may, if they agree (or have provided for it in the underlying contract), put the dispute before a neutral person who will evaluate its merits and offer a view to both parties.[86] It is entirely up to the parties to decide what to place before the neutral and what power to give the neutral to investigate beyond that, such as looking for objective data against which to measure the strengths and weaknesses of the parties' positions in the dispute. The evaluation is not binding on the parties (unless they choose to adopt it and determine the dispute in accordance with the evaluation). The purpose of the evaluation is to assist the parties in deciding where to go with the dispute, and it can be all that is needed to prompt focused and realistic negotiations. Because of its evaluative and non-binding nature it would be possible for the neutral to proceed to act as a mediator (having got to know the dispute as neutral evaluator), but parties choosing to go forward in that way probably could not expect the neutral in a mediator role to shake off the evaluative mantle. If a purely facilitative mediation was sought after using the evaluation as a starting point, another person should be sought to mediate.

Mini-trial or executive tribunal

18.47   In this model of ADR a neutral is appointed who sits with senior representatives of the two (or more) disputing parties. They hear submissions (sometimes supported by an agreed and limited volume

---

[86] For a standalone agreement to secure an early neutral evaluation, see www.cedr.com/library/documents/ene_agreement.pdf (accessed 21 March 2011).

of oral evidence) after which the neutral assists the two representatives to negotiate an outcome in light of what has been presented. If they do not come to an agreement (with the mediation assistance of the neutral) they may empower the neutral to offer an evaluation which will influence future ADR choices, or they may allow the neutral to mediate in accordance with usual mediation practices, or the neutral could be asked to arbitrate. The advantage of this process is that it puts senior executives in the position of listening to the case as adjudicators and negotiators, with the additional input of a neutral applying facilitative techniques. However, the facilitative non-binding nature of the process allows the neutral to be used thereafter for evaluative or determinative purposes. This process holds considerable potential for the oil and gas industry, as an option within stepped dispute resolution or on an ad hoc basis.[87] In Australia and Hong Kong the same process is often termed Senior Executive Appraisal Mediation (SEAM) where it is used widely in construction disputes.

Med-arb

Disputants may agree upon med-arb, whereby a dispute on which the parties have failed to reach agreement is turned over to the original mediator for arbitration. The benefit is the saving in time and cost through using the same person in both roles. However, the mediator will have heard the parties' accounts in mediation and is not able fully to ignore this when acting as arbitrator. Parties may be less open with the mediator in private session if it is known that ultimately the mediator may act as arbitrator.   18.48

Expert determination

Nature of the process
There is widespread use of expert determination in the oil and gas industry within the spectrum of available processes. Expert determination clauses appear routinely in contracts within the industry and they are used in many technical commercial disputes.[88] It is   18.49

---

[87] There is an executive tribunal agreement in www.cedr.com/library/documents/executive_tribunal.pdf. More information about it is available via the extensive resource of the American Arbitration Association (www.adr.org) where it is called "mini trial".
[88] A sample standalone expert determination agreement is available at www.cedr.com/library/documents/expert_determination.pdf. For discussion of expert accountability, see R King, "The Accountability of Experts in Unitisation Determination: Amoco (UK) Exploration Co v Amerada Hess" 1994 12(6) *OGLTR* 185. For activation of the clause,

a determinative, expert and reliable process, without many of the disadvantages and costs associated with formal arbitration discussed below. The process has developed its own characteristics as a result of it being a negotiated process defined by the parties. In a recent attempt by a party to define an expert determination as an arbitration, the Inner House of the Court of Session has acknowledged it is entirely separate in nature from arbitration, noting that, although expert determination may have arisen from practice in England,

> "expert determination, understood as an alternative to arbitration, has taken root in Scottish legal practice, as a consequence of its attractiveness to the commercial community as a relatively quick and informal means of resolving matters of disagreement or potential disagreement. It is now a well recognised means of resolving disputes in almost any area of commercial life, and owes its success to the fact that it generally works well and is found to be commercially useful. The difference between the role of an expert and that of an arbiter has become well understood in general terms, although the boundary between them can sometimes, in particular circumstances, be difficult to draw".[89]

In the case before the court, this interpretation was assisted by the extent to which parties had excluded the use of arbitration in some parts of their agreements. Stating in the contract that the matter is referred to the expert "as an expert and not an arbitrator" help to make the distinction clear. The role of the expert, although possessed of the power to make a decision that binds the parties, is not a judicial one.[90] As has been noted in England, the clause gives the expert the power to make a decision contrary to that which a court would have made on the same facts.[91]

Scope

18.50 The parties may determine procedures which the expert should follow, but need not do so, in which case the expert will determine a procedure appropriate to understanding and determining the dispute in a manner which is neutral, impartial and transparent. This

---

see *Thames Valley Power Ltd* v *Total Gas & Power Ltd* [2006] 1 Lloyd's Rep 441 and for the interpretation of such a clause, see *Veba Oil Supply And Trading GMBH* v *Petrotrade Inc* [2001] 2 Lloyd's Rep 731.

[89] *MacDonald Estates plc* v *National Car Parks Ltd* 2010 SLT 36, per Lord Reed at para [22].

[90] *Holland House Property Investments Ltd* v *Crabbe* 2008 SLT 777, followed in *MacDonald Estates plc* v *National Car Parks Ltd* 2010 SLT 36.

[91] Said by Hoffmann LJ (as he then was) in *Director General of Telecommunications* v *Mercury Communications Ltd*, CA, unreported at that level of decision.

could include gathering information independently of the parties, particularly of a technical and objective nature. It is not essential that the expert seeks submissions from both parties if the parties do not specify it[92] (a feature one would expect of most adjudicative processes). Clearly it is essential that an expert chosen is not only neutral of the parties and expert in the technical subject-matter of the dispute, but will conduct the process in a fair and open manner. The parties must specify the extent of the expert's substantive (as compared to procedural) power, for example what the expert should determine,[93] and whether or not to award interest.

Statutory adjudication

A statutory adjudication process under the Housing Grants, **18.51** Construction and Regeneration Act 1996, Pt II applies to "construction operations",[94] defined broadly to include external and internal construction on or under land, but oil and gas activities are fairly clearly excluded. Part II of the Act provides for an adjudicative process which can be triggered by either party (but does not apply in disputes with domestic proprietors), in which an independent adjudicator (usually skilled in construction and trained in adjudication methods) determines the particular dispute for the specific and interim purpose of keeping the construction contract moving. The ruling of the adjudicator is binding only until the dispute can be the subject of agreement of the parties, or of final determination in arbitration or litigation.

Those engaged in the oil and gas industries have important **18.52** exemption from the compulsory statutory process by virtue of s 105(2) of the 1996 Act. Drilling for or extraction of oil or natural gas are *not* construction operations within the meaning of the Act,[95] nor are assembly, installation or demolition of plant or machinery or access construction on a site where the primary activity is the production, transmission, processing or bulk storage (other than warehousing) of oil or gas.[96] Any attempt to rely upon statutory adjudication in a dispute within the oil and gas industry can be resisted on this basis. The Act does empower the Secretary of State

---

[92] Confirmed in *MacDonald Estates plc* v *National Car Parks Ltd* 2010 SC 250.
[93] A point of dispute in *Thames Valley Power Ltd* v *Total Gas & Power Ltd* [2006] Lloyd's Rep 441 and in *Veba Oil Supply And Trading GMBH* v *Petrotrade Inc* [2001] 2 Lloyd's Rep 731.
[94] Defined in s 105.
[95] s 105(2)(a).
[96] s 105(2)(c).

by order to amend these definitions, but no such amendment has been effected by the time of writing.[97]

18.53   The statutory requirement applies to construction in the England, Wales or Scotland whether or not the contract between the parties is governed by laws of England or Scotland.[98] The process has generated much litigation in itself, particularly around the scope of the adjudicator's powers, and claims of exceeding powers have been used frequently by parties unhappy with adjudication decisions. Although the adjudication outcome is interim, the commercial effect has been to drive parties to settle under its influence. It is a form of dispute resolution which combines features of early neutral evaluation (discussed above) and expert determination (discussed below). Its difficulties in terms of scale of challenge in court are no doubt due to it being imposed by law as a process which one party can choose regardless of the views of the other's wish, so the other is prompted to challenge its outcomes in process terms if unhappy with them.

ADJUDICATIVE PROCESSES

Arbitration

General

18.54 It is not surprising to find arbitration clauses in some oil and gas industry contracts,[99] particularly when the contract involves cross-border activity. Arbitration has long been a preferred method of dispute adjudication in standard form construction, engineering and related contracts in the UK. In most jurisdictions worldwide it is a recognised mode of adjudication in international trade as an alternative to the risks of submitting complex disputes to determination by generalist judges in national courts. An arbitration clause[100]

---

[97] s 105(3), but this must be subject to affirmative resolution of both Houses of Parliament (s 105(4)). In Scotland this would be a reserved matter, so there would have to be acquiescence to any amendment by way of Sewel Motion, or separate legislative activity by the Scottish Parliament (none known at the date of writing).

[98] s 104(6) and (7).

[99] Bentham, "Arbitration and Litigation in the Oil Industry", 1986/87 5(2) OGLTR 35. UK petroleum production licences provide that some (but by no means all) of the potential disputes which might arise between the state and the licensee are to be arbitrated. Arbitration is not provided for in the LOGIC standard form contracts agreed by the UK Oil and Gas industry task force, see www.logic-oil.com and www.pilottaskforce.co.uk. These are permissive as to the parties' freedom to choose ADR after escalated levels of negotiations have failed, but assume litigation as the process of adjudication.

[100] Most jurisdictions require arbitration agreements to be in writing, eg, Arbitration Act 1996, s 5. On arbitration in Scotland pre-2010, see Lord Hope of Craighead, "Arbitration", *Stair Memorial Encyclopaedia Reissue* (1998) and in England and Wales,

is respected in usurping the jurisdiction of courts[101] and allows for decision-makers to be involved for their specialist technical knowledge, as well as allowing the interests of disputing parties to be balanced in selection of arbitral panels. It draws upon consensus in choice of method combined with the certainty of a determined outcome, appealable usually only on the ground of arbitrator misconduct or exceeding jurisdiction. Parties retain the power, on agreement, to withdraw the dispute from arbitration prior to the issue of a final award. Court jurisdiction is retained where necessary for preservative and directive orders needed to support the arbitration. The binding choice of arbitration relies entirely upon the effectiveness of the contract by which it is created. Lack of clarity in the contract will leave scope for one party to argue that the arbitration clause does not apply. The courts in the UK are robust in their protection of the arbitration choice against litigation raised by one party in face of an arbitration clause.[102]

Process
Since arbitration withdraws the dispute from the system of civil process in national courts, a substitute procedural system must be set up for the arbitration. In many countries a domestic arbitration statute will regulate matters in the absence of a chosen set of procedures. In the UK the Arbitration Act 1996 applies in England and Wales. In Scotland the law is now to be found in the Arbitration (Scotland) Act 2010 which provides a system that is intended for use in both domestic and international arbitrations. In theory parties may write their own arbitration processes from scratch, but few would be interested in doing so, and rules have tended to be the subject of national[103] or international collaboration. Many parties agree to the arbitral rules of the United Nations Commission

18.55

M Mustill and S Boyd, *Commercial Arbitration* (2nd edn, 1989 and companion volume 2002).
[101] Re arbitration in Scotland *Hamlyn & Co v Talisker Distillery* (1894) 21 R (HL) 21 at 25 and Arbitration (Scotland) Act 2010, ss 1 and 10; re an arbitration with its seat in England and Wales, Arbitration Act 1996, s 1.
[102] As in *Midgulf International Ltd v Groupe Chimique Tunisien* [2010] EWCA 66 (Civ).
[103] A Scottish Arbitration Code was a collaborative project of Scottish Branch of the Chartered Institute and the Scottish Council for International Arbitration and endorsed by the Lord President, in 1999. A revised 2007 version may be downloaded from: http://www.ciarb.org/scotland/downloads/scottish_arbitration_code_2007.pdf (accessed 21 March 2011). See F Davidson, "Some thoughts on the Scottish Arbitration Code 2007" (2008) 74 *Arbitration* 348. For arbitrations set up after May 2010 it is likely to be overtaken by the Scottish Arbitration Rules set out in Sch 1 to the Arbitration (Scotland) Act 2010.

on International Trade Law (UNCITRAL),[104] or submit to rules and services of arbitration institutions such as the International Chamber of Commerce, International Court of Arbitration (ICC); the London Court of International Arbitration (LCIA); or the American Arbitration Association/the International Court of Dispute Resolution (AAA/ICDR). Recent research indicates that 68 per cent of commercial respondents have a dispute resolution policy, and that in opting for arbitration parties are drawn first to the control of language and confidentiality that is available in arbitration, and then to choice of law followed by choice of rules.[105]

18.56   It would be folly to allow the choice of arbitration which the parties have made to be undermined by failure to specify an agreed procedure, and industry players would be very unhappy with accepting default procedures from the seat of the arbitration. To rely on default procedures of the arbitral seat assumes both that the chosen seat has a domestic arbitration law, and that it is suitable for the determination of the dispute.

18.57   Parties may select any rules of procedure, and these need not be consistent with the rules of the seat, but if it is intended to enforce an arbitral award in another country, national courts may, on the application of a party but not of its own accord, refuse to recognise or enforce a foreign award if it has been arrived at by a process or by application of law which is not conform to the law or procedure of the seat.[106] A survey of corporate users of arbitration published in 2006 suggested that the impact of the seat of arbitration is not well understood, and the location (which could by choice be different from the seat but often is not) is chosen simply for convenience and perceived neutrality.[107] A further survey published in 2010 shows that the legal infrastructure of a particular location, and linkage with the law governing the contract are additional factors in choice of seat.[108]

---

[104] Prior to the enactment of the Arbitration (Scotland) Act 2010, international arbitrations with their seat in Scotland were, in the absence of specified procedure, conducted according to UNCITRAL rules (Law Reform Miscellaneous Provisions (Scotland) Act 1990, s 66 and Sch 7). The 2010 Act creates Scottish rules that mirror the UNCITRAL rules with some optional additions. The UNCITRAL Model Law on International Commercial Arbitration 1985 and UNCITRAL Model Law on International Commercial Conciliation 2002 are both available via www.uncitral.org/uncitral/en/uncitral_texts.html.

[105] QMU and White & Case, *International Arbitration Survey*, p 4.

[106] New York Convention, Art V, para 1.

[107] QMU and PWC, *Corporate Attitudes 2006*.

[108] QMU and White & Case, *International Arbitration Survey*, p 17.

Scotland as a centre of choice for international dispute resolution

Until 2010 Scotland had limited statutory involvement in **18.58** arbitration, apart from some peripheral provisions and adoption of the UNCITRAL rules for an international arbitration with its seat in Scotland. However, the revamp of a Scottish Arbitration Code in 2007 and a change of Government came together with commercial interest in a dispute resolution culture[109] to culminate in the Arbitration (Scotland) Act 2010. This Act does not adopt the UNCITRAL rules, but restates them within a set of mandatory and default (opt-out) rules underpinned by statements of founding principles to which regard must be had when construing the Act, namely:

> "(a) that the object of arbitration is to resolve disputes fairly, impartially and without unnecessary delay or expense,
> (b) that parties should be free to agree how to resolve disputes subject only to such safeguards as are necessary in the public interest,
> (c) that the court should not intervene in an arbitration except as provided for by this Act."[110]

The Act came into force in May 2010 and it is too early to evaluate its impact. It is being promoted internationally[111] for its merits and with a view to Scotland becoming a neutral arbitral seat of choice. The interface with the courts, other than in cases of challenge to the award on the widely recognised grounds of irregularity or misconduct, is dictated by the parties in the form of default (rather than mandatory) rules. One can allow for a point of law to be referred to the Outer House of the Court of Session,[112] or appeal on error of law,[113] but neither will apply if the parties choose to keep those matters from the court.

The founding principles highlight to the arbitrator and the **18.59** court that the party choice, speed and fairness must be kept to the forefront, and success of the new regime will to some extent depend upon the strength of support for this from the arbitrators and judges when faced with party or lawyer delay and initiation of court procedures in face of an arbitration clause. Work is being done to secure

---

[109] *Report of the Business Experts and Law Forum (BELF)*, Scottish Government, November 2008, particularly Chapter 3, available at http://www.scotland.gov.uk/Publications/2008/10/30105800/11.
[110] Arbitration (Scotland) Act 2010, s 1.
[111] H Dundas, "The Arbitration (Scotland) Act 2010; Converting Vision into Reality" (2010) 76 *Arbitration* 2.
[112] Arbitration (Scotland) Act 2010, Sch 1 (Scottish Arbitration Rules), r 41.
[113] Scottish Arbitration Rules, r 69.

a procedural interface with the court that will satisfy the founding principles of avoiding unnecessary delay and expense.[114]

The reach of the arbitration clause

18.60 As noted above, activity in the oil and gas sector often involves a series of contracts that are linked to a central activity. Yet within each contractual relationship scope exists for choice of dispute resolution process. It may be the case that there is not a match between contracts in choice of arbitration. The arbitration clause in one contract may specify that it applies to all claims "arising out of or relating to" the agreement between the parties. This may bring in to the legitimate scope of the arbitration other agreements or contractual relationships that do not themselves provide for arbitration. The reach of the phrase "arising out of" may limit the arbitration to the fulfilment of the agreement in which the clause is contained, but "relating to" was found to have a broader reach in *Norscot Rig Management PVT Ltd* v *Essar Oilfields Services*[115] and led to the court supporting the arbitrator's decision to include in his remit a dispute in relation to set-off arising from a separate contract without an arbitration clause.

Arbitration as an alternative to litigation

18.61 Arbitration has been associated with speed and efficiency as compared with litigation, but experiences of arbitration seem often to involve delay, expense, procedural complexity, and legal challenges to jurisdiction or competence of proceedings. Nevertheless the advantages are widely believed to outweigh disadvantages and if weighed against the prospect of litigating an international dispute in a remote national court the choice is clear. Some commercial users of arbitration still fear interference by national courts, but the risk of interference is more easily managed than affording jurisdiction to such courts by default.

18.62 Results of surveys concerning corporate attitudes and practices in International Arbitration published in 2006[116] and 2010[117] reveal substantial reliance on arbitration in commercial contracts with an international dimension (at the adjudication end of a sophisticated spectrum of choices), and a likelihood of continued use and growth,

---

[114] Minutes of Court of Session Rules Council, October 2010.

[115] [2010] EWHC 195 (Comm).

[116] QMU and PWC, *Corporate Attitudes 2006*.

[117] QMU and White & Case, *International Arbitration Survey*. 13% of respondents were from this sector.

reflecting the growth in international trade.[118] Respondents have called for a larger pool of arbitrators and more regional institutional arbitration centres,[119] as most[120] use institutional arbitration rather than ad hoc procedures.[121] More evidence also now exists about preferred and less-preferred rules, institutions and seats for international commercial arbitration.[122]

While privacy is often claimed as an advantage of arbitration,[123]   **18.63** publication of progress and outcomes of arbitrations conducted under some of the international arbitration providers does occur. This could act as an aid to choice of process and provider, or as a disincentive to use a provider which will publish such material. Corporate disputants report seeking legal advice from specialist arbitration counsel rather than using their own in-house or external counsel for large international disputes.[124] Some counsel report being called in only at a late stage in the dispute to discuss the arbitration choices.[125]

Litigation

Sometimes it will be necessary to have a decision from the court   **18.64** on a point of law, or a protective or injunctive remedy, so litigation will be unavoidable, at least for the aspect of the dispute for which the order is necessary.[126] Decisions then remain as to whether there is economic or other imperative for having the court deal with the other aspects. The important thing is not to assume that because one aspect must be litigated it follows that all aspects must be, and always to keep open the thought processes about which dispute resolution process will be best suited to the dispute or aspects of it at a particular point in time.

---

[118] Of those who responded 65% use arbitration, and 95% of the total respondents said they would use it in the future, anticipating greater international activity in commerce.

[119] QMU and PWC, *Corporate Attitudes 2006*, section 12.2.

[120] 76%.

[121] QMU and PWC, *Corporate Attitudes 2006*, section 5.1.

[122] QMU and White & Case, *International Arbitration Survey*.

[123] And was cited as a key reason for choice of the process in the 2010 survey.

[124] *International Arbitration: Corporate attitudes and practices 2006*, section 9. The survey also notes some confusion on the part of corporate disputants between the legal concept of the seat of arbitration (which means that the procedural laws of the courts of the seat can be engaged to support the arbitration) and the actual locus of the arbitrating body (which may be selected for geographical convenience or perceived neutrality from the parties): see section 6.

[125] QMU and White & Case, *International Arbitration Survey*.

[126] For example a party to arbitration may seek a court order for security for costs to be lodged by the other party, as in *Regia Autonoma de Electricitate Renel* v *Gulf Petroleum International Ltd* [1996] 1 Lloyd's Rep 67.

18.65   Once a case is in court, lawyers and the courts may assume that the parties have expressly or implicitly opted for litigation over other dispute resolution processes. That may be founded on an incorrect assumption that a party embarking on litigation for the first time knows exactly what the court can and cannot do in relation to the dispute. Any assumption that the parties get more polarised and less open to mediated settlement as the case lasts longer in the court are not supported by evidence from the US Federal Courts. Here it was found that the time between court referral to mediation and settlement remained much the same regardless of the stage of the case at which it was referred to mediation. If referred early the parties and the court were spared the cost of further procedure, but if referred even at a late stage in the case it would settle within a similar period of time.[127]

18.66   The contractual or consensual backdrop to most dispute resolution processes allows the tailoring of process to dispute, and ensures that disputes need not be made to fit the "one size fits all" model of litigation or statutory adjudication. Litigation in general is beyond the scope of this chapter, but some special procedures bear mention.[128]

Commercial court procedures

18.67   In the UK commercial court procedures provide a fast-track and commercially aware procedure for dealing with commercial cases. Parties opt into the procedure when the case is commenced. Specific judges are designated for commercial court cases. Because the rules for general civil actions promote dispute resolution processes and case management, the main difference in the commercial court is the shortened procedure and the specialist judge.[129] In the Scottish courts the rules do not yet provide for case management or dispute resolution in civil cases generally, but there is provision in commercial actions in addition to reduced timescales and specialist judges. Commercial action procedure in the Court of Session[130] requires the commercial judge to ensure speedy determination of the action.[131] In the similar

---

[127] L Blomgren Bingham *et al*, "Dispute Resolution and the Vanishing Trial: Comparing Federal Government Litigation and ADR Outcomes" (2008–2009) 24 *Ohio St J on Disp Resol* 225.

[128] For a reflective and predictive account of the problems of litigation in the industry, see J Wallace, *Litigating an International Oil Dispute* (1980–81) 2 *NYLSch J Int'l & Comp L* 253.

[129] CPR, Pt 58 and Practice Direction, Commercial Court.

[130] Rules of the Court of Session, Ch 47 and Practice Note 6 of 2004.

[131] RCS, r 47.11(1)(e).

but not identical procedure in the sheriff court[132] the commercial judge is enjoined to make orders for the speedy resolution of the action (including the use of alternative dispute resolution).[133] In the sheriff court hearings may be conducted by telephone, or e-mail, and early evaluation of its use in Glasgow suggests that the procedure is effective and popular.[134] However, there is no evidence of judges or sheriffs moving the parties towards dispute resolution processes once they have raised a commercial action. Also, the Inner House has disapproved the sheriffs' use of problem-solving and dispute- (rather than litigation-) focused approaches in a commercial case as contrary to adversarial norms.[135]

Summary trial; special case
In the Court of Session parties may opt for summary trial procedure. **18.68** They may nominate a particular judge of the outer house to deal with an issue of fact or law in dispute between them and forgo a right of appeal.[136] If an authoritative ruling is required purely on a point of law, a special case may be filed for decision by the Inner House.[137]

Construction and Arbitration List of the Civil Court
In England and Wales a Construction and Arbitration List of the **18.69** Civil Court operates under a designated judge.[138] Parties opt into the procedure, but cases may be transferred out of it on order of the judge. It is designated for engineering, construction and arbitration cases but other appropriate cases can be admitted to it. The procedures are similar to those of the commercial court, but particular attention is paid to the exchange and discussion of expert reports. The relevant Practice Direction also provides that: "At the summons for directions the court shall be informed whether any and if so what attempts have been made to resolve the dispute or any part of it by mediation. This requirement does not entail disclosing the details of any mediation, only the fact of it having taken place."

---

[132] Ordinary Cause Rules, Ch 40.
[133] *Ibid*, r 40.12(3)(m).
[134] E Samuel, *Commercial Procedure in Glasgow Sheriff Court* (2005).
[135] *Jackson v Hughes Dowdall* 2008 SC 637. For a commentary on the case, see M Ross, "Commercial actions and Jackson v Hughes Dowdall" 2009 13(2) *Edin LR*.
[136] RCS, Ch 77.
[137] Court of Session Act 1988, s 27; RCS, Ch 78.
[138] Practice Direction 6.1.

IMPLEMENTATION AND ENFORCEMENT

18.70 Parties may simply implement outcomes of adjudicated processes or proceed to appeal by any means available. Indeed, many cases settle before arbitration or litigation gets to evidential stages. There is considerable anecdotal evidence that parties will implement negotiated outcomes more readily than those imposed by an arbitrator or a court. If the outcome is not implemented, or there is delay, appeal or resistance, parties require to be as attentive to the range of options available at this stage as they do when embarking on choice of process for dispute management.

Dispute resolution processes after adjudication

18.71 The consensual nature of dispute resolution processes allows for their adoption (if the parties agree) at any stage including after there has been litigation or arbitration on a particular dispute. If the parties are unhappy with the outcome of litigation or arbitration, or realise that it does not of itself address the dispute, the option of another process remains. Clearly this is difficult if the "winning" party in the litigation is happy with the outcome in total and proceeds to enforce the decree or award. However, if, as is often the case, the outcome of litigation merely makes clearer (or not) the application of laws to the averred facts of the dispute, the underlying problem, or a form of it now altered by the experience of the adjudicative process and/ or its outcome, may remain. As is discussed above, the industry has embraced processes such as early neutral evaluation or expert determination which seek to avoid ill-fitting and binding litigated remedies. However, when there has been litigation, much remains to be considered in terms of whether dispute resolution processes can improve the fit of the outcome to the parties' commercial situation.

18.72 In most states in the USA and in many other countries mediation schemes operate within the appeal court. In England mediation is offered in the Court of Appeal, and may be recommended by the judge in appropriate cases under the general authority of the Civil Procedure Rules, although not provided for expressly in the relevant appeal rules

18.73

Global acknowledgement of arbitration awards

Many countries are parties to the New York Convention on the recognition and enforcement of international arbitral awards,[139] with new members joining recently. For example, in 2006 UAE and Gabon became signatories and the total in 2010 stood at 144, including most oil- and gas-producing countries.[140] The interpretation of grounds for refusing to recognise or enforce an award may vary from country to country[141] and will directly affect the outcomes for disputants and their decision to attempt to enforce.[142] It must be noted that some countries will not recognise or enforce awards if they provide for the accumulation of interest as distinct from the award of a specified sum of money.[143]

18.74

CONCLUSION AND FUTURE SCOPE

This chapter notes that the oil and gas industry can and does make productive use of a range of dispute resolution processes. Although, a decade ago, the industry was ahead of others in its choices, the dispute resolution landscape worldwide and in the UK has moved to a wider range of options and there is much greater access to evidence of what influences choice. This increased experience and awareness of options, changes in substantive and procedural laws, and expansion of markets globally sits uncomfortably alongside global financial constraints. Business efficiency should drive parties further towards a choice of process that uses least time and expense, but in a situation where a party is unable to implement the contract due to financial constraints, a speedy solution may not be desirable and simply add pressure to fulfil.

18.75

Contracts in the industry that allow for periodic renegotiation enable both parties to respond to changing circumstances, but put

---

[139] United Nations Convention on the Recognition and Enforcement of Foreign Arbitral Awards (New York, 10 June 1958).

[140] Details of signatories are available on www.newyorkconvention.org/new-york-convention-countries/contracting-states.

[141] For example there is a perception that the power of a court of its own accord to refuse recognition or enforcement on grounds of public policy (New York Convention, Art V, para 2(b)) may be used by courts, whether or not argued by a party, to favour disputants with greatest connection with that country, and disfavour those from countries with diverging political norms. A body of case law from different countries is kept on the Convention website: www.newyorkconvention.org/ new-york-convention-countries/court-decisions.

[142] Queen Mary, University of London and PriceWaterhouseCoopers LLP, *International Arbitration: Corporate Attitudes and Practice 2008*, available at www.arbitrationonline.org/research/2008.

[143] This is a particular issue in some Islamic countries.

even greater emphasis on the need for skilled and well-informed negotiators. The industry runs a slight risk of being tied to well-known dispute resolution processes based on historical and personal experience and self-assessment of bargaining power, and may not yet take maximum benefit to be had from open discussion over the choices available and the flexibility with which they may be combined. The industry has much to offer by way of collective experience in dispute resolution. It has much to gain by exploiting further potential for imaginative resolutions that are effective and productive for the disputants, the industry and wider environmental and financial domains in which it functions.

INDEX

Location references are to paragraph numbers. References to footnotes have the paragraph number followed by "*n*", eg "4.17*n*". Authors are indexed if they are mentioned in the main text.

AA (appropriate assessment), 9.34
AAA/ICDR (American Arbitration Association/International Court of Dispute Resolution), 18.55
AAPL Form 610, 12.2, 12.34
abandonment *see* decommissioning
abandonment programme
  see also decommissioning
  approved, 10.39–10.47
  date for submission, 10.39
  duty to secure the carrying out, 10.43
  financial security, 10.45
  notice to carry out, 10.45, 10.46
  requirement when selling, 16.68
  revised, 10.42
  section 29 notice *see* section 29 notice
abuse of dominance, 11.17–11.18
access to infrastructure
  ageing, 7.2
  application for access, 7.5
  automatic referral notice, 7.35, 7.36
  bona fide enquiry, 7.25
  competition, 7.40, 7.55, 11.49
  conflict of interest issues, 7.27
  controlled petroleum pipelines, 7.10*n*
  determination by Secretary of State, 7.39, 7.53
  dispute resolution process, 7.10
  DTI/DECC Guidance on disputes, 7.1, 7.17, 7.41–7.55
  Energy Act 2008 powers, 7.8–7.16
  framework for negotiations, 7.35
  further specific information, 7.24
  gas infrastructure, 7.26
  generally, 1.10
  high-level capacity information, 7.23
  information provision, 7.22–7.25
  Infrastructure Code of Practice, 7.17–7.40
  knock for knock, 7.34
  lack of transparency, 7.17

  liabilities and indemnities, 7.30, 7.32–7.34
  non-discriminatory access, 7.28
  notice determining third-party rights, 7.4
  Petroleum Act 1998, 7.4, 7.16
  pipelines, former emphasis on, 7.7
  prior legal obligations, 7.52
  publication of key commercial terms, 7.26
  reasonable available capacity, 7.50
  reasonable provision, 7.28
  Rules and Procedures Governing Access, 7.17
  section 17F notification, 7.4, 7.16
  separation of services, 7.29
  tariffs, 7.31
  third-party access, 7.9, 7.10, 7.16
  tie-in/modification phase, 7.33
  timely negotiation, 7.35
  transnational infrastructure, 7.54
  transportation and processing phase, 7.34
  unbundling of services, 7.29
Access to Justice Report 1996, 18.34
access to land, 17.3
acquisition agreement *see* asset sale and purchase agreement
acquisition structures, 16.3
acquisitions and disposals of interests, 1.20
acreage
  announcement of available, 4.19
  application, 4.20
  recycling of discarded, 4.49
  relinquishment, 2.4
acreage rentals, 4.57
acreage selection
  environmental issues, 4.24–4.27
  Habitats Directive, 4.24, 4.25
  Strategic Environmental Assessment Directive, 4.24, 4.26–4.27
active Fallow A class, 5.26
adjudication, statutory, 18.51–18.53
ADR (alternative dispute resolution)
  see also arbitration; dispute resolution; mediation
  civil procedures in UK, 18.34–18.35